IBPS

Institute of Banking Personnel Selection

Common Recruitment Process

Bank Clerk

Recruitment Exam 2019

Phase–I

20
Practice Papers

Includes
Solved Papers 2017 & 2018

CL MEDIA (P) LTD.

Edition : 2019

© PUBLISHER

ISBN : **978-93-89573-04-6**

Typeset by : *CL Media DTP Unit*

Administrative and Production Offices

Published by : **CL Media (P) Ltd.**

A-45, Mohan Cooperative Industrial Area, Near Mohan Estate Metro Station, New Delhi - 110044

Marketed by : **G.K. Publications (P) Ltd.**

A-45, Mohan Cooperative Industrial Area, Near Mohan Estate Metro Station, New Delhi - 110044

For product information :

Visit ***www.gkpublications.com*** or email to ***gkp@gkpublications.com***

CONTENTS

ABOUT THE EXAMINATION

Phase-I : Preliminary Examination: Preliminary Examination consisting of Objective Tests of 100 marks will be conducted online. This test would be of 1 hour duration consisting of 3 Sections as follows.

Part	Subject	No. of Questions	Maximum Marks	Duration
I	English Language	30	30	
II	Numerical Ability	35	35	1 hour
III	Reasoning Ability	35	35	
	Total	**100**	**100**	

REASONING ABILITY

Directions (Q. 1 to 5): Study the given information carefully and answer the given questions:

Seven persons A, B, C, D, E, F and G are watching movies on different days of the week (starting on Monday and ending on Sunday) not necessarily in the same order. B is going to watch movie on Tuesday. F is going to watch movie on adjacent day of B. There are three days gap between the days on which F and A are going to watch movie. G is going to watch movie just after D. There are as many persons are watching movie between A and G, same as between D and C. C is watching movie before D but not just before.

1. Who among the following is going to watch movie on Wednesday?

   (a) B   (b) C

   (c) F   (d) E

   (e) None of these

2. Who among the following person is going to watch movie just after A?

   (a) C   (b) D

   (c) F   (d) G

   (e) None of these

3. If F and G interchange their days of watching movie, then on which day G is watching movie?

   (a) Monday   (b) Wednesday

   (c) Friday   (d) Saturday

   (e) None of these

4. C is watching movie on which day?

   (a) Friday   (b) Saturday

   (c) Wednesday   (d) Thursday

   (e) Tuesday

5. How many persons are watching movie between B and A?

   (a) Two   (b) Three

   (c) One   (d) Four

   (e) None of these

Directions (Q. 6 to 8): Study the following information carefully and answer the questions given below:

There are six persons who all are of different height. A is taller than C and D but shorter than E. The one who is third shortest is 102cm in height. B is taller than A. E is not the tallest. The one who is second tallest is 119cm in height. Neither A nor C is the third shortest person among all. C is not the shortest among all. F is taller than D.

6. Who among the following is the second tallest?

   (a) F   (b) E

   (c) A   (d) C

   (e) None of these

7. What will be the possible height of A?

   (a) 120 cm   (b) 100 cm

   (c) 112 cm   (d) 101 cm

   (e) None of these

8. Who among the following is third shortest?

   (a) A   (b) C

   (c) B   (d) F

   (e) None of these

Direction (Q. 9 to 13): Study the following information carefully and answer the given questions.

Twelve persons are sitting in two parallel rows at equal distance facing each other. Q, R, S, T, U and V are sitting in Row 1 facing south. B, C, D, E, F and G are sitting in Row 2 facing north (but not necessarily in the same order). G sits third to the right of B and one of them sits at the end of the row. Q sits at the right end of the row. Three persons sit between Q and T. F sits to the immediate left of G. Two persons sit between F and C. C who faces R sits to the immediate right of E. S faces D. U sits to the immediate left of S.

9. Which of the following pair sits at the extreme ends of the Row 2?

   (a) B & E   (b) G & E

   (c) B & C   (d) G & C

   (e) None of these

10. Who sits second to the left of the person facing V?

   (a) B   (b) D

   (c) F   (d) C

   (e) G

11. What is the position of U with respect to R?

    (a) Third to the left

    (b) Second to the left

    (c) Second to the right

    (d) Third to the right

    (e) None of these

12. Who is facing F?

    (a) T (b) U

    (c) Q (d) S

    (e) None of these

13. If the positions of all persons sitting in Row 2 are arranged as per the English alphabetical order from left to right, then who among the following faces D?

    (a) Q (b) R

    (c) S (d) T

    (e) None of these

Directions (Q. 14 to 16): In each of the following questions some statements are given and these statements are followed by two conclusions numbered (I) and (II). You have to take the given statements to be true even if they seem to be at variance from commonly known facts. Read the conclusions and then decide which of the given conclusions logically follows from the given statements, disregarding commonly known facts.

Give answer:

(a) If only (I) conclusion follows.

(b) If only (II) conclusion follows.

(c) If either (I) or (II) follows.

(d) If neither (I) nor (II) follows.

(e) If both (I) and (II) follow.

14. **Statements:** All DSLR are Lenses.

    Some Camera are DSLR.

    Conclusions: I. All camera is lenses.

    II. Some lenses are camera.

15. **Statements:** All Label are Packets.

    All Mobiles are Cables.

    Some Mobiles are packets.

    Conclusions: I. Some Label is mobile.

    II. Some Cables are Label.

16. **Statements:** Some Book are Pen.

    Some Pens are Pencil.

    Conclusions: I. No Book is pencil.

    II. All Pencils are Book.

Directions (Q. 17 to 21): Study the following information to answer the given questions

Eight students A, B, C, D, E, F, G and H are sitting around a square table in such a way four of them sit at four corners while four sit in the middle of each of the four sides. The one who sit at the corners face the centre and others facing outside.

A who faces the centre sits third to the left of F. E who faces the centre is not an immediate neighbour of F. Only one person sits between F and G. D sits second to right of B. B faces the centre. C is not an immediate neighbour of A.

17. Which one does not belong to that group out of five ?

    (a) B (b) C

    (c) E (d) D

    (e) A

18. Which will come in the place of ?

    BCE EHA AGD ?

    (a) DFB (b) DGA

    (c) DCG (d) DCF

    (e) None of these

19. What is the position of G with respect to C ?

    (a) Third to the right

    (b) Second to the left

    (c) Second to the right

    (d) Fourth to the right

    (e) None of these

20. Who sits third to the left of B ?

    (a) H (b) A

    (c) G (d) F

    (e) None of these

21. Which is true from the given arrangement?

    (a) G faces the centre (b) B faces outside

    (c) H faces inside (d) A face the centre

    (e) None of these

22. How many pairs of letter are there in the word 'DECLARING' (both backward and forward), each of which has as many letters between them as in the word as there are in the English alphabet?

    (a) One (b) three

    (c) Four (d) Five

    (e) None of these

Directions (Q. 23 to 25): Study the following information carefully and answer the questions given below:

Point C is 15m in the east of point F. Point A is 10m west of point B which is 15m north of point H. Point D is 15 west of point E. Point B is 15 m south of point C. Point E is 5m east of point H. Point G is 15m north of point A.

23. In which direction and at what distance is point G from point C?

    (a) 10m east   (b) 5m, east

    (c) 10m, west   (d) 5m, west

    (e) None of these

24. Point D is in which direction with respect to point A?

    (a) South   (b) North

    (c) North East   (d) West

    (e) None of these

25. Point F is in which direction with respect to point E?

    (a) North East   (b) South West

    (c) South East   (d) North West

    (e) None of these

Directions (Q. 26 to 30): Following questions are based on the five words given below, Study the following words and answer the following questions.

TAP   NOT   MAT   PQR   STB

(The new words formed after performing the mentioned operations may not necessarily be a meaningful English word.)

26. If the given words are arranged in the order as they appear in a dictionary from right to left, which of the following will be second from the left end?

    (a) MAT   (b) NOT

    (c) STB   (d) TAP

    (e) None of these

27. How many letters are there in the English alphabetical series between the third letter of the word which is second from the left end and the second letter of the word which is third from the right end?

    (a) 20   (b) 19

    (c) 18   (d) 17

    (e) None of these

28. If in each of the word given, the second alphabet is replaced by its following alphabet and third alphabet is replaced by its preceding alphabet as per the English alphabetical order, then how many words thus formed will be without any vowels?

    (a) None   (b) One

    (c) Two   (d) Three

    (e) Four

29. If the positions of the first and the third alphabet in each of the words given are interchanged, then how many meaningful word will be formed?

    (a) Two   (b) One

    (c) Four   (d) Three

    (e) None

30. If in each of the given words, every consonant is changed to its previous letter and every vowel is changed to its next letter according to the English alphabetical series, then in how many words, thus formed, at least one vowels will appear?

    (a) None   (b) One

    (c) Two   (d) Three

    (e) None of these

Directions (Q. 31 to 35): Study the following information carefully and answer the questions given below:

There are seven persons i.e. A, B, C, D, E, F and G. They all belongs to the different cities i.e. Kolkata, Mumbai, Chennai, Pune, Lucknow, Ahmadabad and Delhi but not necessarily in the same order. D belongs to Pune. Neither A nor F belongs to Kolkata. B belongs to Ahmedabad. C does not belong to Kolkata and Lucknow. G belongs to Mumbai. A does not belongs to Lucknow and Chennai.

31. Who among the following belongs to Kolkata?

    (a) A   (b) D

    (c) F   (d) G

    (e) None of these

32. Which of the following statement is true?

    (a) A belongs to Chennai

    (b) G belongs to Delhi

    (c) E belongs to Kolkata

    (d) F belongs to Pune

    (e) None of these

33. F belongs to which of the following City?

    (a) Chennai   (b) Mumbai

    (c) Delhi   (d) Lucknow

    (e) None of these

34. Which of the following combination is true?

    (a) A-Delhi   (b) D-Pune

    (c) E-Kolkata   (d) All are correct

    (c) All are incorrect

35. A belongs to which of the following city?

    (a) Delhi   (b) Mumbai

    (c) Kolkata   (d) Chennai

    (e) None of these

NUMERICAL ABILITY

Directions (Q. 36 to 40): What will come in the place of question (?) mark in the following number series.

36. 200, 193, 179, 158, ?, 95
    - (a) 135
    - (b) 133
    - (c) 132
    - (d) 130
    - (e) 128

37. 3, 43, 81, 115, 143, ?
    - (a) 163
    - (b) 172
    - (c) 166
    - (d) 160
    - (e) 168

38. 1, 6, 25, 76, 153, ?
    - (a) 152
    - (b) 154
    - (c) 153
    - (d) 155
    - (e) 156

39. 50, 54, 45, 61, 36, ?
    - (a) 66
    - (b) 72
    - (c) 75
    - (d) 80
    - (e) 84

40. 9, 45, 180, 540, ?, 1080
    - (a) 720
    - (b) 900
    - (c) 1080
    - (d) 1200
    - (e) 960

41. If the sum of upstream and downstream speed is 36 km/hr and the speed of the current is 3km/hr. Then find time taken to cover 52.5 km in downward?
    - (a) 2 hr
    - (b) 2.5 hr
    - (c) 3 hr
    - (d) 3.5 hr
    - (e) 4 hr

42. A sum becomes 1.6 times of itself in five years at simple rate of interest. Find rate of interest per annum?
    - (a) 10%
    - (b) 12.5%
    - (c) 15%
    - (d) 12%
    - (e) 8.5%

Directions (Q. 43 to 52): Calculate the exact value of the 'x' in the given following questions.

43. $x^2 + (9^2 + 34) \div 5 = 39$
    - (a) 5
    - (b) 4
    - (c) 8
    - (d) 6
    - (e) 9

44. $6 \times 16 \times 5 \div 3 - x^2 = 96$
    - (a) 6
    - (b) 7
    - (c) 8
    - (d) 9
    - (e) 5

45. $\sqrt{124 + x + 169} = 18$
    - (a) 27
    - (b) 28
    - (c) 29
    - (d) 30
    - (e) 31

46. $28^2 - x^3 = 7^3 + 225$
    - (a) 6
    - (b) 8
    - (c) 4
    - (d) 7
    - (e) 5

47. $298 - 13^2 - 2^3 = x \times 11$
    - (a) 51
    - (b) 41
    - (c) 21
    - (d) 11
    - (e) 31

48. $\sqrt[3]{729} + 3\frac{3}{5} \div x = \sqrt{16 \times 9}$
    - (a) 1
    - (b) 1.4
    - (c) 1.2
    - (d) 1.6
    - (e) 2

49. $x\% \text{ of } 300 + \sqrt{256} = 243 \div 3 + 7$
    - (a) 18
    - (b) 24
    - (c) 16
    - (d) 28
    - (e) 32

50. $x \times 3 \div 8 = \sqrt[3]{512} \times \sqrt{12^2}$
    - (a) 256
    - (b) 512
    - (c) 64
    - (d) 128
    - (e) 320

51. $136 \div 2^2 \times x = 17\% \text{ of } 500 \div 10$
    - (a) 1
    - (b) 0.5
    - (c) 0.25
    - (d) 0.125
    - (e) 1.25

52. $1836 \div x \div 9 = 12$
    - (a) 9
    - (b) 11
    - (c) 13
    - (d) 15
    - (e) 17

53. Ratio of present ages of two persons A and B is 3:2 and after four years ratio of their age (B : A) become 7:10. Then find the present age of B?
    - (a) 20 years
    - (b) 18 years
    - (c) 24 years
    - (d) 36 years
    - (e) 30 years

54. The difference between Circumference of circle A and diameter is 90 cm . If Radius of Circle B is 7 cm less than circle A then find area of Circle B?
    - (a) 556 cm²
    - (b) 616 cm²
    - (c) 588 cm²
    - (d) 532 cm²
    - (e) 630 cm²

55. There are 40 children in a class in which boys are 4 more than the girls. Average weight of all the students is 42.5 kg and the average weight of all the girls is 48 kg then find the average weight of all the boys.

(a) 39.5 kg   (b) 38 kg

(c) 40.5 kg   (d) 36.75 kg

(e) 40.25 kg

Directions (Q. 56 to 60): In each question two equations numbered (I) and (II) are given. Student should solve both the equations and mark appropriate answer.

(a) If x = y or no relation can be established

(b) If x > y

(c) If x < y

(d) If x > = y

(e) If x < = y

56. I. $8x^2 + 6x + 1 = 0$

   II. $3y^2 + 7y + 2 = 0$

57. I. $x^2 = 196$

   II. $y^2 - 26y + 169 = 0$

58. I. $9x^2 - 12x + 4 = 0$

   II. $8y^2 - 9y + 1 = 0$

59. I. $x^2 - 15x + 56 = 0$

   II. $y = \sqrt[3]{512}$

60. I. $3x^2 + 10x + 8 = 0$

   II. $2y^2 + 3y + 1 = 0$

61. A man invested 15% of his monthly income in LIC and remaining gave to his mother. Mother spend 10 % of it in household expenses and she had left with Rs 30,600 then find the salary of man?

(a) Rs 37,500   (b) Rs 36,000

(c) Rs 38,000   (d) Rs 42,000

(e) Rs 40,000

62. If 7 marks are awarded to right answer and 4 marks are penalty for wrong answer. Then Prabhat's score was 263. If he attempted 58 questions then find number of correctly attempted questions?

(a) 45   (b) 42

(c) 48   (d) 40

(e) 50

63. In a city, 68% of population is literate in which ratio of male to female is 11:6. And ratio of illiterate male to female is 3: 1. Find the ratio of literate female to illiterate female in that city.

(a) 3:2   (b) 2:1

(c) 3:1   (d) 4:1

(e) 5:2

64. Ratio of length to breadth of a rectangle is 4:3. If the area of that rectangle is 108 cm2 and breadth of this rectangle is equal to the side of a square then find the area of that square.

(a) 49 cm^2 (b) 100 cm^2

(c) 64 cm^2 (d) 81 cm^2

(e) 121 cm^2

65. A is 1.5 times as efficient as that of B and C takes half time as compared to that of A. If A and B takes $22\frac{2}{5}$ days to complete half of the work then find the time taken by A and C together to complete the whole work?

(a) $2\frac{1}{3}$ days   (b) $3\frac{1}{3}$ days

(c) $1\frac{1}{3}$ days   (d) $1\frac{2}{3}$ days

(e) $2\frac{2}{3}$ days

Directions (Q. 66 to 70): Given below table shows the number of cakes of five different types sold by a shopkeeper on four different days. Study the data and answer the questions that follow: Days/Type of Cake

Days/Type of Cake	A	B	C	D	E
Saturday	25	28	35	50	38
Sunday	35	65	48	42	47
Monday	38	60	40	24	29
Tuesday	46	54	55	44	30

66. What is the ratio of no. of cakes of type B sold by the shopkeeper on Saturday and Monday together to the no. of cakes of type E sold by him on the same days?

(a) 72:53   (b) 88:67

(c) 98:73   (d) 92:71

(e) 90:67

67. What is average no. of cakes of type C sold by shopkeeper on Saturday, Sunday and Tuesday?

(a) 38   (b) 40

(c) 42   (d) 44

(e) 46

68. The no. of cakes of type D and E sold together on Tuesday is what percent of the no. of cakes of type A & B sold together on Sunday?

(a) 72%   (b) 75%

(c) 74%   (d) 78%

(e) 80%

69. What is the difference between the total no. of cakes of all the given types sold by shopkeeper on Monday and the total no. of cakes of all the given types sold by shopkeeper on Tuesday?

   (a) 38   (b) 44

   (c) 42   (d) 40

   (e) 45

70. If the no. of cakes of type F sold by the shopkeeper in given four days is 25% more than the no. of cakes sold of type D in all the given days, then find the no. of cakes sold of type F in all the given days.

   (a) 164   (b) 160

   (c) 180   (d) 200

   (e) 240

ENGLISH LANGUAGE

Directions (Q. 71 to 76): Read the following passage and answer the questions that follow it. Some words are highlighted to help you answer some of the questions.

Conversations about the role of flexible working have shifted. It's no longer enough for companies to offer employees the option to either work from home or the office. Employees want to work from anywhere. Companies that want to attract and retain top talent, and ensure teams are highly productive, need to adapt their culture and technology to accommodate this shift in attitudes. And this is where the IT department can solidify its role as a valued contributor to the success of a company, by implementing technologies that enable secure and remote collaboration.

According to a recently commissioned Polycom survey, 24,000 respondents across 12 countries indicate that nearly two-thirds of today's global workforce take advantage of the anywhere working model. This is a significant shift since May of 2012 when only 14% of employees benefited from remote working. The survey results also provide insights into some of the concerns among companies in moving forward with the anywhere working model. Two significant concerns are a lack of trust and the perception that employees are not working as hard when they are not in the office. Also, among the 45-60-year-old age group, 59% worry that working anywhere will cause them to work longer hours. The fear of being always connected to work and overworking is a significant deterrent for this age group.

A good first step for companies to overcome the trust and perception concern is to ensure workers are measured by output and not by the hours they have worked, commonly referred to as 'presenteeism.' Countries like Brazil lead the pack here with 80% of employees adopting the anywhere working model, and 64% respondents use video to communicate several times a day. When respondents were asked how their companies could improve trust and perceptions with the anywhere working model, the most popular recommendations were to: Equip workers with

technology that is easy to use and which connects them to their colleagues; Ensure the same policies are applied to everyone in the business, regardless of seniority or their situation; and Provide guidelines on how to manage working from anywhere.

91% of those surveyed agreed that technology is a key factor in improving relationships and **fostering** better teamwork. This suggests that investing in the right technologies, in particular video collaboration, to get the most out of individuals and teams can help solve the lack of trust and perception concerns. And this is where the IT department can become a difference maker as they can implement technologies, such as video conferencing, to ensure colleagues can seamlessly collaborate wherever they are.

71. What is the shift in attitude of employees as discussed in the passage?

   (I) They want to work in office.

   (II) They want to work from home.

   (III) They want to work from anywhere.

   (a) Only (I)   (b) Both (II) & (III)

   (c) Only (III)   (d) Only (II)

   (e) None of (I), (II) & (III)

72. How could companies accommodate the recent shift in attitudes of employees as discussed in the passage?

   (a) By offering work from home option to employees

   (b) By enabling secure and remote collaboration

   (c) By increasing the salaries of employees

   (d) Options (a) & (b)

   (e) None of the above

73. Which of the followings mention(s) the concern of the companies to accommodate the latest preference of employees for working styles?

   (a) Lack of trust for employees;

   (b) Perception that employees will not work hard anywhere apart from office;

   (c) Working anywhere would make employees to work longer hours;

   (d) Options (b) & (c)

   (e) Options (a) & (b)

74. How could companies overcome their concerns for the latest preferences of employees for style of working?

   (a) By not offering work from home model

   (b) By measuring employees for the output, they generate and not by the hours they have worked

   (c) By offering work from anywhere model

   (d) By allowing only those who are interested to work from anywhere.

   (e) None of the above

75. Which of the following opinions as expressed in the survey about solving the trust and perception concerns of the companies in accommodating the latest preference of employees for style of work has received more than 91%?

(a) Investing in technology

(b) Providing guidelines on how to manage working from anywhere

(c) Ensuring the same policies are applied to everyone regardless of seniority

(d) Options (a) & (c)

(e) None of the above

76. Which of the following options has a meaning which is SIMILAR to the word 'fostering'?

(a) asserting   (b) focusing

(c) collaborating   (d) encouraging

(e) admitting

Directions (Q. 77 to 81): Rearrange the following five sentences (A), (B), (C), (D) and (E) in the proper sequence to form a meaningful paragraph and then answer the questions given below.

(A) Crucially, this loss of sheen is reflected in the account books of the sport's controversial administrator, among the richest in the world.

(B) The total income that was distributed by BCCI among players is reduced because of lower income from media rights.

(C) Television viewership for the game has dropped 40% to a weekly 61 gross rating points (GRPs).

(D) A Board of Control for Cricket in India official said, however, that this was because India wasn't playing enough at home.

(E) Cricket seems to be losing its crowd-pulling power.

77. Which of the followings is the FOURTH sentence of the final sequence?

(a) A   (b) D

(c) E   (d) B

(e) C

78. Which of the followings is the FIRST sentence of the final sequence?

(a) E   (b) C

(c) D   (d) A

(e) B

79. Which of the followings is the SECOND sentence of the final sequence?

(a) E   (b) A

(c) C   (d) D

(e) B

80. Which of the followings is the THIRD sentence of the final sequence?

(a) E   (b) A

(c) D   (d) C

(e) B

81. Which of the followings is the FIFTH sentence of the final sequence?

(a) C   (b) A

(c) E   (d) D

(e) B

Directions (Q. 82 to 85): In the following questions, a sentence is given consisting four highlighted words. Choose the option reflecting the word which is either misspelt or grammatically incorrect. If all the highlighted words are correct, choose option (e) i.e. "no error" as your answer choice.

82. **Making** the **request** for a non-smoking room seemed **resonable** for everyone since the woman was **allergic** to smoke.

(a) Making   (b) Request

(c) Resonable   (d) Allergic

(e) No error

83. When we are **involved** in large-scale projects, we must make **judgemants** on an **individual basis** about whether they are good or bad.

(a) involved   (b) judgemants

(c) individual   (d) basis

(e) No error

84. Several **expriments** were tried, to **determine** positively **whether** or not she had any **perception** of sound.

(a) expriments   (b) determine

(c) whether   (d) perception

(e) No error

85. When the man gave the **terrific** persuasive speech at the **conference**, the observers **applaud** with gusto by **putting** their hands together.

(a) terrific   (b) conference

(c) applaud   (d) putting

(e) No error

Directions (Q. 86 to 90): In the following questions two columns are given containing three sentences/phrases each. In first column, sentences/phrases are A, B and C and in the second column the sentences/phrases are D, E and F. A sentence/phrase from the first column may or may not connect with another sentence/phrase from the second column to make a grammatically and contextually correct sentence. Each question has five options which display the sequence(s) in which the sentences/phrases can be joined to form a grammatically and contextually correct sentence. Choose the correct combination of parts that make a meaningful sentence.

86.

COLUMN I	COLUMN II
(A) There is emerging International recognition	(D) and create societies where all can live with hope and dignity.
(B) It can serve as the driving force to restore hope	(E) our work makes us feel productive and empowered.
(C) The earnest Determination distilled in these words is the spirit we all need	(F) that women's participation is key to effective climate action.

(a) C-F, A-D and A-E   (b) B-E
(c) A-F   (d) A-D and C-E
(e) A-F and B-E

87.

COLUMN I	COLUMN II
(A) Over time, there are changes that take place	(D) where they house an array of species.
(B) In the case of primary succession,	(E) that ecological communities move from possessing very little species diversity
(C) In other cases, a pre-existing group of species is replaced by a new group of species,	(F) in the composition of speci

(a) C-E, A-D and A-F   (b) B-D
(c) A-F   (d) B-E and C-D
(e) B-D

88.

Column I	Column II
(A) The increase in MSP for rabi crops comes	(D) The government said in a release.
(B) There are notified crops	(E) Just ahead of the RBI monetary policy announcement.
(C) For big companies, there are instances	(F) Of even the infrastructure getting damaged.

(a) C-F   (b) C-E and B-F
(c) A-E   (d) C-F and A-E
(e) B-F, B-E and A-D

89.

Column I	Column II
(A) India will be the third largest aviation	(D) market globally a year sooner.
(B) The biggest contribution in	(E) as the world's largest aviation
(C) Firstly, we are seeing an/a	(F) restrictive protectionist measures

(a) C-D, A-F and B-D   (b) B-F
(c) A-D   (d) C-E and B-D
(e) B-E

90.

COLUMN I	COLUMN II
(A) Researchers are only beginning to understand the power	(D) cannot be borne by science alone.
(B) As our understanding grows, we will have the potential	(E) to edit out genes that cause fatal diseases.
(C) The burden of gene editing	(F) would not be passed down the family tree.

(a) A-D, B-E and B-D   (b) B-E and C-D
(c) A-F   (d) B-F and C-E
(e) C-E

Directions (Q. 91 to 95): Given below are sentences consisting a blank in each. Identify the most suitable alternative among the five given that fits into the blank to make the sentence logical and meaningful.

91. In _________________ to picking up milk from the grocery store, we also need to get some bread, because my cousin ate all of it this past week.

(a) further   (b) addition
(c) computation   (d) aftermath
(e) besides

92. He _________________ on things being done in the most efficient way and he usually does them that way himself.

(a) requesting   (b) conserves
(c) urge   (d) insists
(e) discourages

93. If the quality of your product meets with our customer's approval, we will place _____________ orders.

(a) interrupted   (b) reduced
(c) regular   (d) choice
(e) conditional

94. Tom seems to be unwilling to believe that Mary was the one who _________________ his credit cards.
    - (a) stole
    - (b) run
    - (c) accept
    - (d) delivery
    - (e) checking

95. The Circular will guide the regional investment _________________ and budgeting processes for FY 2020 Budget.
    - (a) programming
    - (b) scheduled
    - (c) arrange
    - (d) planned
    - (e) records

Direction (Q. 96 to 100): The following questions consist of a sentence with a highlighted phrase which may or may not be grammatically or contextually correct. Choose the most suitable option that will replace the incorrect highlighted phrase to form a grammatically correct and meaningful sentence. If the given highlighted phrase is correct, choose option (e) i.e. "no replacement required" as your answer choice.

96. India has suffered from terrorism. So has Pakistan. And **it turns out**, now the first world too is not immune.
    - (a) turning out to
    - (b) it turns to
    - (c) it turned out to be
    - (d) it turning out
    - (e) No replacement required

97. The advocate declared in the court that his client **has prepared to** surrender.
    - (a) Was prepared to
    - (b) Has been preparing for
    - (c) Was prepared at
    - (d) Has prepared for
    - (e) No correction required

98. Any step that the Prime Minister takes to remove violence in the country **will be appreciate**.
    - (a) will appreciated
    - (b) will have appreciated
    - (c) was appreciating
    - (d) will be appreciated
    - (e) were appreciating

99. If this is freedom of speech, then it **must been curtailed** immediately.
    - (a) have being curtailing
    - (b) must be curtailed
    - (c) must have been curtailed
    - (d) have been curtailed
    - (e) No correction required

100. When the police started asking questions, the suspect **clammed up**.
    - (a) camped down
    - (b) clamped up
    - (c) clam out
    - (d) clamed off
    - (e) No Correction Required

ANSWERS

1. (d)	**2.** (b)	**3.** (a)	**4.** (d)	**5.** (a)	**6.** (b)	**7.** (c)	**8.** (d)	**9.** (c)	**10.** (b)
11. (d)	**12.** (b)	**13.** (e)	**14.** (b)	**15.** (d)	**16.** (d)	**17.** (b)	**18.** (a)	**19.** (d)	**20.** (a)
21. (d)	**22.** (d)	**23.** (c)	**24.** (a)	**25.** (d)	**26.** (c)	**27.** (c)	**28.** (d)	**29.** (d)	**30.** (d)
31. (e)	**32.** (c)	**33.** (d)	**34.** (d)	**35.** (a)	**36.** (d)	**37.** (a)	**38.** (b)	**39.** (b)	**40.** (c)
41. (b)	**42.** (d	**43.** (b)	**44.** (c)	**45.** (e)	**46.** (a)	**47.** (d)	**48.** (c)	**49.** (b)	**50.** (a)
51. (c)	**52.** (e)	**53.** (c)	**54.** (b)	**55.** (b)	**56.** (a)	**57.** (a)	**58.** (a)	**59.** (e)	**60.** (c)
61. (e)	**62.** (a)	**63.** (c)	**64.** (d)	**65.** (e)	**66.** (b)	**67.** (e)	**68.** (c)	**69.** (a)	**70.** (d)
71. (c)	**72.** (b)	**73.** (e)	**74.** (b)	**75.** (a)	**76.** (d)	**77.** (d)	**78.** (a)	**79.** (c)	**80.** (b)
81. (d)	**82.** (c)	**83.** (b)	**84.** (a)	**85.** (e)	**86.** (c)	**87.** (c)	**88.** (d)	**89.** (c)	**90.** (b)
91. (b)	**92.** (d)	**93.** (c)	**94.** (a)	**95.** (a)	**96.** (e)	**97.** (a)	**98.** (d)	**99.** (b)	**100.** (e)

EXPLANATIONS

For questions (1 to 5):

Days	Persons
Mon	F
Tue	B
Wed	E
Thu	C
Fri	A
Sat	D
Sun	G

For questions (6 to 8):

B > E > A > F > C > D

For questions (9 to 13):

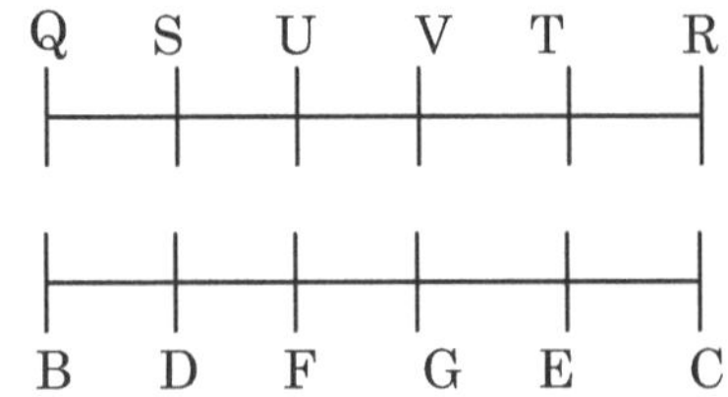

14. 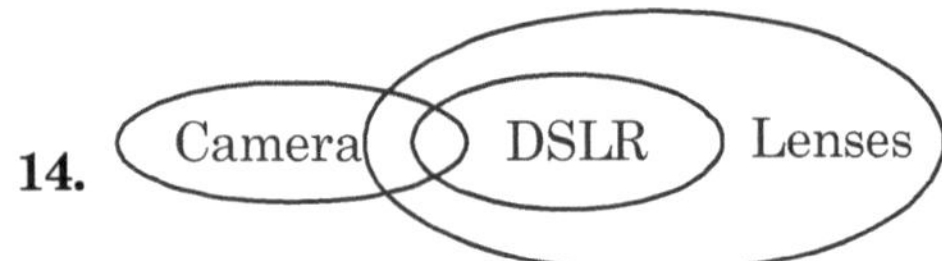

15. 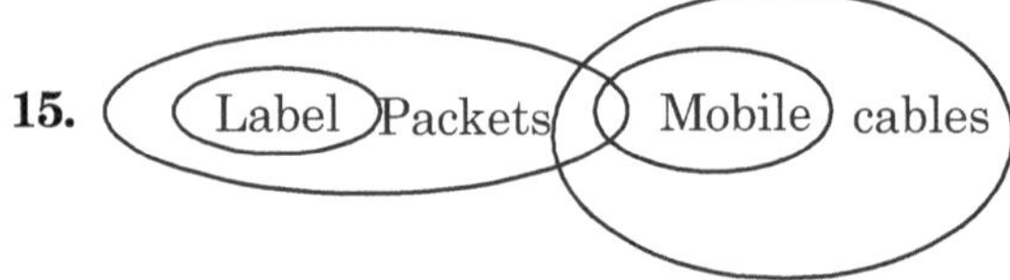

16. 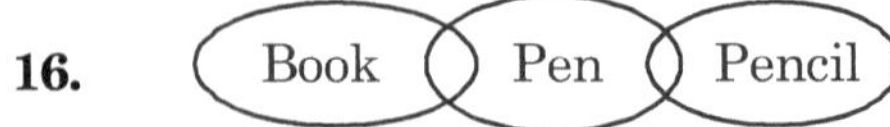

For questions (17 to 21):

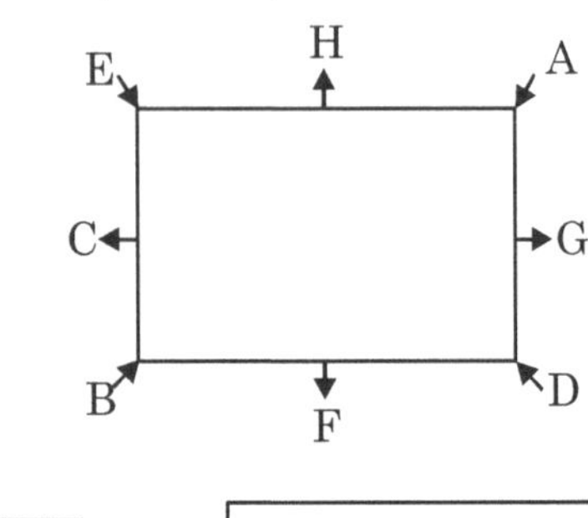

22. 

For questions (23 to 25):

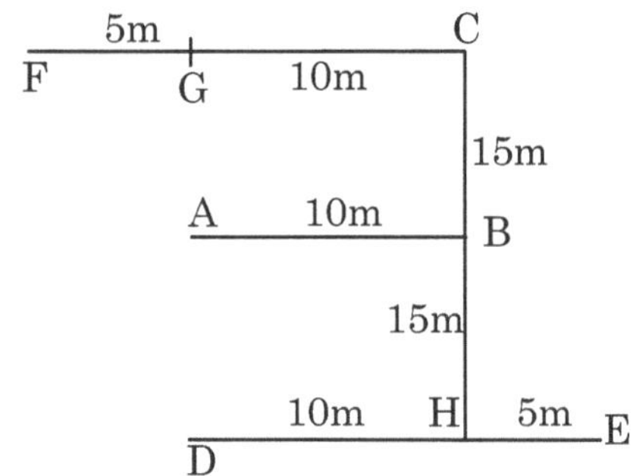

26. TAP NOT MAT PQR STB
TAP STB PQR NOT MAT

27. TAP NOT MAT PQR STB

Hence, there are 18 letters between A and T.

28. TAP NOT MAT PQR STB
TBO NPS MBS PRQ SUA

29. TAP NOT MAT PQR STB
PAT TON TAM RQP BTS

30. TAP NOT MAT PQR STB
SBO MPS LBS OPQ RSA

For questions (31 to 35):

Persons	City
A	Delhi
B	Ahmedabad
C	Chennai
D	Pune
E	Kolkata
F	Lucknow
G	Mumbai

36. 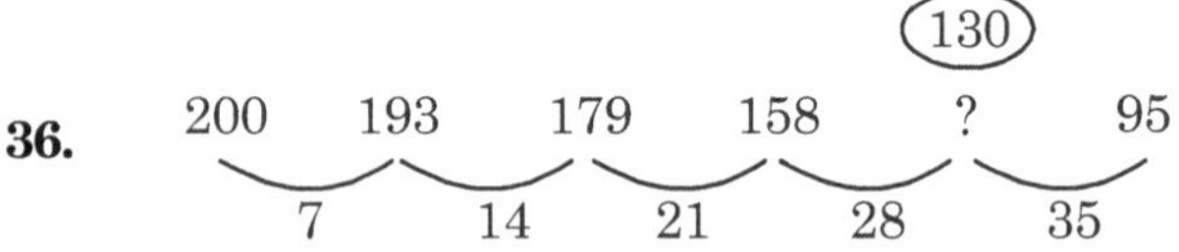

37. 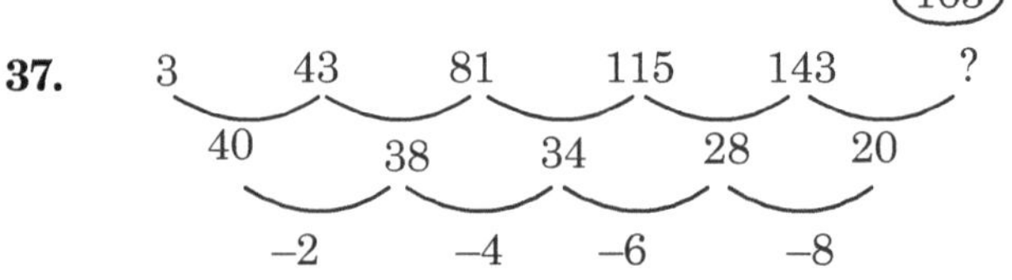

38. 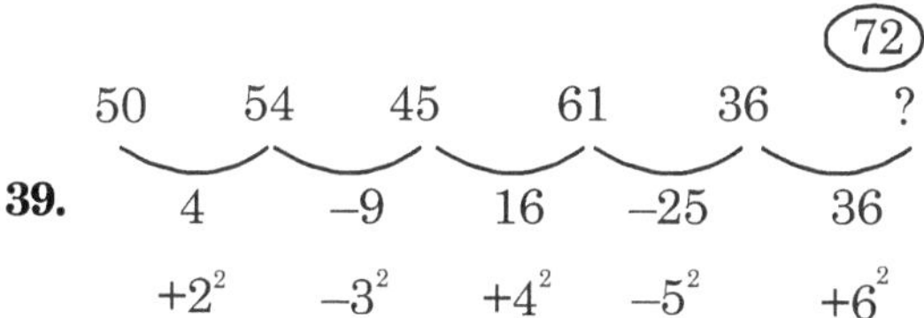

39. 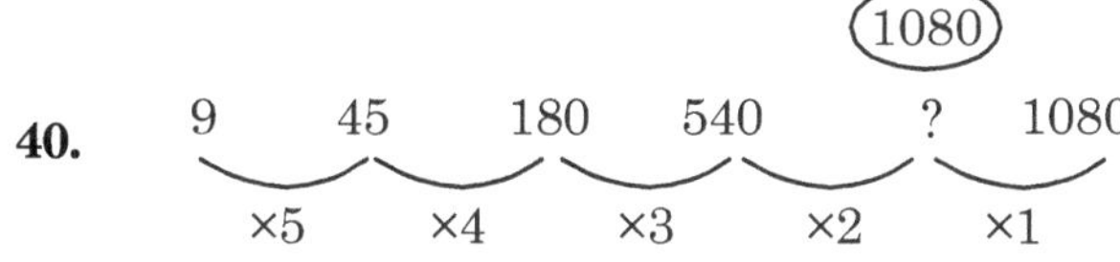

40.

$$\begin{matrix} 9 & 45 & 180 & 540 & ? & 1080 \\ \end{matrix}$$
$$\times 5 \quad \times 4 \quad \times 3 \quad \times 2 \quad \times 1$$

(1080)

41. Let the speed of boat in still water be x km/hr

ATQ

$x + 3 + x - 3 = 36$

$x = 18$

Required time = $\dfrac{52.5}{21} = 2.5 \ hr$

42. Let that sum be Rs 'p' and rate of interest be 'r'% per annum

Amount = Rs 1.6p

SI = Rs 0.6p

ATQ

$0.6p = \dfrac{p \times r \times 5}{100}$

$r = 12\%$

43. $x^2 + (81 + 34) \div 5 = 39$

$x^2 + \dfrac{115}{5} = 39$

$x^2 = 39 - 23 = 16$

$x = 4$

44. $\dfrac{6 \times 16 \times 5}{3} - x^2 = 96$

$160 - 96 = x^2$

$64 = x^2$

$8 = x$

45. $\sqrt{293 + x} = 18$

Or, $293 + x = 324$

Or, $x = 324 - 293 = 31$

46. $784 - x^2 = 343 + 225$

$x^3 = 784 - 568 = 216$

$x = 6$

47. $298 - 169 - 8 = x \times 11$

$121 = x \times 11$

$x = 11$

48. $9 + \dfrac{18}{5x} = 12 \Rightarrow \dfrac{18}{5x} = 3$

$\Rightarrow x = 1.2$

49. $x \times 3 + 16 = 81 + 7$

$\Rightarrow 3x = 72$

$\Rightarrow x = 24$

50. $\Rightarrow \dfrac{3x}{8} = 8 \times 12$

$\Rightarrow 3x = 64 \times 12$

$\Rightarrow x = 256$

51. $\Rightarrow \dfrac{136}{4} \times x = \dfrac{85}{10} \Rightarrow x = \dfrac{85 \times 4}{10 \times 36} = \dfrac{1}{4} = 0.25$

52. $\Rightarrow \dfrac{1836}{9x} = 12$

$\Rightarrow x = \dfrac{1836}{12 \times 9}$

$\Rightarrow x = 17$

53. Let the present age of A and B be 3x and 2x years respectively

ATQ

$\dfrac{3x + 4}{2x + 4} = \dfrac{10}{7}$

$x = 12$

Present age of B = 24 yr

54. Let radius of circle A be r cm

ATQ

$2\pi r - 2r = 90$

$r = 21$ cm

Radius of circle B = 14 cm

Area of circle B = 616 cm^2

55. Let the number of girls be x

Then, boys = x+ 4

ATQ

x + 4 + x=40

x =18

total weight of all students = 40× 42.5 = 1700kg

total weight of girls = 18 × 48 = 864 kg

weight of all boys = 1700 − 864 = 836 kg

average weight of all boys = $\dfrac{836}{22}$ = 38 kg

56. I. $8x^2 + 6x +1= 0$

$\Rightarrow 8x^2 + 4x + 2x +1= 0$

$\Rightarrow (4x +1)(2x +1)= 0$

$x = -\dfrac{1}{4}, -\dfrac{1}{2}$

II. $3y^2 + 7y + 2=0$

$\Rightarrow y = -2, -\dfrac{1}{3}$

No relation

57. I. $x^2 = 196$

x = −14, 14

II. $y^2 − 26y +169 = 0$

$\Rightarrow y = 13$

No relation

58. I. $9x^2 −12x + 4 = 0$

$\Rightarrow 9x^2 − 6x − 6x + 4 = 0$

$x = \dfrac{2}{3}, \dfrac{2}{3}$

II. $8y^2 − 9y + 1 = 0$

$\Rightarrow y = 1, \dfrac{1}{8}$

No relation

59. I. $x^2 − 15x + 56 = 0$

x = 8, 7

II. $y = \sqrt[3]{512}$

$\Rightarrow y = 8$

y ≥ x

60. I. $3x^2 +10x + 8 = 0$

$x = -2, -\dfrac{4}{3}$

II. $2y^2 + 3y + 1= 0$

$\Rightarrow y = -1, -\dfrac{1}{2}$

y > x

61. Let the salary of man be Rs x

Amount given to mother= 0.85x

ATQ

0.85x × 0.90 = 30,600

x = Rs. 40,000

62. Let number of correct questions be x

Then, incorrect question = (58 − x)

ATQ

x × 7 − (58 − x) × 4 = 263

x = 45

63. Let the total population of that city be 100x

Then literate population = 68x

Literate male = 68x × $\dfrac{11}{17}$ = 44x

Literate female = 24x

Illiterate population = 32x

Illiterate female = 32x × $\dfrac{1}{4}$ = 8x

Required ratio = $\dfrac{24x}{8x} = 3 : 1$

64. Let the length and breadth of that rectangle be 4x and 3x cm respectively

ATQ

4x × 3x = 108

x = 3 cm

Breadth = 9 cm

Area of square = 81 cm²

65. Let the efficiency of A and B be 3x and 2x unit/ day respectively

Efficiency of C = 6x units/day

Total work = $\dfrac{12}{5} × 2 × 5x = 24x$ units

Required time = $\dfrac{24x}{9} = 2\dfrac{2}{3}$ days

66. Required ratio = $\dfrac{28+60}{38+29} = \dfrac{88}{67}$

67. Required average = $\dfrac{35+48+55}{3} = \dfrac{138}{3} = 46$

68. Required percentage

$$= \dfrac{(44+30)}{(35+65)} \times 100 = \dfrac{74}{100} \times 100 = 74\%$$

69. Total cakes sold on Monday = 38 + 60 + 40 + 24 + 29 = 191

Total cakes sold on Tuesday = 46 + 54 + 55 + 44 + 30 = 229

Difference = 229 – 191 = 38

70. No. of cakes of type F

$$= \dfrac{125}{100} \times (50 + 42 + 24 + 44)$$

$$= \dfrac{5}{4} \times 160 = 200$$

71. The answer to the question can be derived from the third and fourth sentences of the first paragraph which is *'Employees want to work from anywhere. Companies that want to attract and retain top talent, and ensure teams are highly productive, need to adapt their culture and technology to accommodate this shift in attitudes'*.

Hence, the statement (III) or option (c) is the correct answer.

72. The recent shift in attitudes of employees is that they want to work from anywhere. Companies can accommodate this shift in attitude by enabling secure and remote collaboration so that work from anywhere could be enabled. The answer can also be inferred from the first paragraph, especially the last sentence of the first paragraph.

Hence, option (b) is the correct answer.

73. The latest preference of employees for working styles is to *work from anywhere*. The answer to the question can be derived from the last third sentence of the second paragraph: 'The survey results also provide insights into some of the concerns among companies in moving forward with the anywhere working model. *Two significant concerns are a lack of trust and the perception that employees are not working as hard when they are not in the office'*.

Hence, option (e) is the correct answer.

74. The latest preference of employees for style of working, as discussed in the passage, is *working from anywhere*. The companies can overcome their concerns for the *working from anywhere* model through, as mentioned in the first sentence of the third paragraph, 'presenteeism'. Meaning that the workers are measured by output and not by the hours they have worked.

Hence, option (b) is the correct answer.

75. The answer to the question can be derived from the first sentence of the fourth paragraph *'91% of those surveyed agreed that technology is a key factor in improving relationships and fostering better teamwork'*. From the highlighted sentence, it could be inferred that the 91% of those surveyed agreed that investing in technology would solve the lack of trust and perception concerns.

Hence, option (a) is the correct answer.

76. fostering [foster, verb] means *'encourage the development of (something, especially something desirable)*;

asserting [assert, verb] means *'state a fact or belief confidently and forcefully'*;

focusing [focus, verb] means *'adapt to the prevailing level of light and become able to see clearly'*;

collaborating [collaborate, verb] means *'work jointly on an activity or project'*;

encouraging [encourage, verb] means *'give support, confidence, or hope to (someone)'*;

admitting [admit, verb] means *'confess to be true or to be the case'*;

From above, it could be understood that the word *'encourage'* has the meaning which is SIMILAR to the meaning of the work *'foster'*.

Hence, option (d) is the correct answer.

77. The final sequence we get is ECABD.

Sentence B is the FOURTH sentence of the final sequence.

The option (d) is the correct answer.

The sentence (E) introduces the theme of the paragraph which is discussing dying of cricket in India. So, the sentence (E) should be the first sentence of the paragraph.

Though, both sentences (A) and (B) take the information presented in the sentence (C) forward, it is more coherent for the sentence (A) to follow the sentence (C). And it is more coherent for the sentence (B) to follow the sentence (A). The sentence (D) is an appropriate concluding sentence as it provides the reason for the downfall of the cricket.

So, the final sequence we get is ECABD and the option (d) is the correct answer.

78. The final sequence we get is ECABD. Sentence E is the FIRST sentence of the final sequence. The option (a) is the correct answer. The sentence (E) introduces the theme of the paragraph which is discussing dying of cricket in India. So, the sentence (E) should be the first sentence of the paragraph. Though, both sentences (A) and (B) take the information presented in the sentence (C) forward, it is more coherent for the sentence (A) to follow the sentence (C). And it is more coherent for the sentence (B) to follow the sentence (A). The sentence (D) is an appropriate concluding sentence as it provides the reason for the downfall of the cricket.

So, the final sequence we get is ECABD and the option (a) is the correct answer.

79. The final sequence we get is ECABD.

Sentence C is the SECOND sentence of the final sequence.

The option (c) is the correct answer.

The sentence (E) introduces the theme of the paragraph which is discussing dying of cricket in India. So, the sentence (E) should be the first sentence of the paragraph.

Though, both sentences (A) and (B) take the information presented in the sentence (C) forward, it is more coherent for the sentence (A) to follow the sentence (C). And it is more coherent for the sentence (B) to follow the sentence (A). The sentence (D) is an appropriate concluding sentence as it provides the reason for the downfall of the cricket.

So, the final sequence we get is ECABD and the option (c) is the correct answer.

80. The final sequence we get is ECABD.

Sentence A is the THIRD sentence of the final sequence.

The option (b) is the correct answer.

The sentence (E) introduces the theme of the paragraph which is discussing dying of cricket in India. So, the sentence (E) should be the first sentence of the paragraph.

Though, both sentences (A) and (B) take the information presented in the sentence (C) forward, it is more coherent for the sentence (A) to follow the sentence (C). And it is more coherent for the sentence (B) to follow the sentence (A). The sentence (D) is an appropriate concluding sentence as it provides the reason for the downfall of the cricket.

So, the final sequence we get is ECABD and the option (b) is the correct answer.

81. The final sequence we get is ECABD.

Sentence D is the FIFTH sentence of the final sequence.

The option (d) is the correct answer.

The sentence (E) introduces the theme of the paragraph which is discussing dying of cricket in India. So, the sentence (E) should be the first sentence of the paragraph.

Though, both sentences (A) and (B) take the information presented in the sentence (C) forward, it is more coherent for the sentence (A) to follow the sentence (C). And it is more coherent for the sentence (B) to follow the sentence (A). The sentence (D) is an appropriate concluding sentence as it provides the reason for the downfall of the cricket.

So, the final sequence we get is ECABD and the option (d) is the correct answer.

82. Among the highlighted words the misspelt word is "resonable". However, the precise spelling of the word is "REASONABLE" and it means having sound judgment; fair and sensible. All the other words have been spelt correctly and are in appropriate grammatical syntax. Hence, option (c) is the most suitable answer choice.

83. Among the highlighted words the misspelt word is "judgemants". However, the precise spelling of the word is "JUDGMENTS" and it means the ability to make considered decisions or come to sensible conclusions. All the other words have been spelt correctly and are in appropriate grammatical syntax. Hence, option (b) is the most suitable answer choice.

84. Among the highlighted words the misspelt word is "expriments". However, the precise spelling of the word is "EXPERIMENTS" and it means perform a scientific procedure, especially in a laboratory, to determine something. All the other words have been spelt correctly and are in appropriate grammatical syntax. Hence, option (a) is the most suitable answer choice.

85. All the highlighted words of the sentence are grammatically correct and contextually meaningful with precise spellings. Since there is no error option (e) becomes the most suitable answer choice.

86. Combination A-F forms grammatically viable and contextually meaningful sentence as the relevant phrases are of similar context and in appropriate grammatical syntax. The sentence thus formed is, "There is emerging international recognition that women's participation is key to effective climate action".

87. Combination A-F forms grammatically viable and contextually meaningful sentence as the relevant phrases are of similar context and in appropriate grammatical syntax. The sentence thus formed is, "Over time, there are changes that take place in the composition of species that constitute an ecological community."

88. For big companies, there are instances of even the infrastructure getting damaged, Sentence (C) and (F) makes proper combination as a sentence. The increase in MSP for rabi crops comes just ahead of the RBI monetary policy announcement, (A) and (E) makes the perfect match as in sentence.

89. Only sentence (A) and (D) makes a perfect match as a sentence, India will be the third largest aviation market globally a year sooner.

90. Combination B-E and C-D successfully form grammatically viable and contextually meaningful sentence as the relevant phrases are of similar context and in appropriate grammatical syntax.

91. The most appropriate word to fill the blank is "addition" as "in addition to" is phrase which is used for saying that something extra exists or is happening together with the thing that you are talking about. All the other words fail to form a comprehensive sentence. Hence, option (b) is the most suitable answer choice.

Computation means the action of mathematical calculation.

Aftermath means the consequences or after-effects of a significant unpleasant event.

92. The most appropriate word to fill the blank is "insists". "insists" is a verb which means persist in (doing something). Some of the other words however may seem contextually meaningful yet they are grammatically incorrect. Hence, option (d) is the most suitable answer choice.

Conserves means protect (something, especially something of environmental or cultural importance) from harm or destruction.

Urge means try earnestly or persistently to persuade (someone) to do something.

93. The most appropriate word to fill the blank is "regular". "regular" means recurring at uniform intervals. Since the sentence is describing about the matching of quality of the product with the customer's need, the next part of the sentence should complement the earlier part. Therefore all the other words become contextually incorrect. Hence, option (c) is the most appropriate answer choice.

Interrupted means stop the continuous progress of (an activity or process).

Reduced means make smaller or less in amount, degree, or size.

Conditional means subject to one or more conditions or requirements being met

94. The most appropriate word to fill the blank is "stole". "Stole" means take (another person's property) without permission or legal right and without intending to return it. All the other words are grammatically and contextually correct.

95. The most appropriate word to fill the blank is "programming" as it means the process of scheduling something. All the other words become contextually incorrect. Hence, option (c) is the most appropriate answer choice.

Schedule means a plan for carrying out a process or procedure, giving lists of intended events and times.

Arrange means put (things) in a neat, attractive, or required order.

96. The sentence is grammatically correct.

97. 'Has prepared to' will not be used, instead 'was prepared to' will be used because the given sentence is in indirect narration in which reporting verb 'declared' is in past tense and because of which reported speech will also be in past tense.

98. Instead of *'appreciate'* in the highlighted part, *'appreciated'* would be used. In passive voice, *'to be [is / are / am / was / were / be / / being / been] + V3* form is always used.

Hence, the option (d) is the correct answer.

99. Curtail means reduce in extent or quantity; impose a restriction on.

100. Clam up means to refuse to speak.

ENGLISH LANGUAGE

Directions (Q. 1 to 5): Read the following passage and answer the questions based on the passage.

Late in "A Suitable Boy," Vikram Seth's fictional panorama of early 1950s India, the difficult but decent politician Mahesh Kapoor receives advice from an underling: "We should think above divisions, splits, cliques! ... This is India ... the country where faction was invented before the zero. If even the heart is divided into four parts can you expect us Indians to divide ourselves into less than 400?"

This statement, equal parts plea and diagnosis, only begins to describe the challenge confronting modern-day India. As Muhammad Ali Jinnah, the Indian leader of the Muslim League, said ruefully in a 1940 speech, seven years before he founded Pakistan: "The Hindus and Muslims belong to two different religious philosophies, social customs and literature. They neither intermarry, nor inter-dine together, and indeed they belong to two different civilizations." To say that India is driven by myriad factions and castes and, more fundamentally, divided between two religions is to describe a particularly vicious curse.

One of the achievements of Ramachandra Guha's deeply felt new history is that the author remains acutely aware of both the truths and falsehoods contained in Jinnah's remark. A visitor to the world's second most populous country can, without much effort, witness nasty and sectarian politicking in New Delhi or Mumbai. And the consequences - vicious religious rioting, scars on both India's landscape and her people - are all too visible. Yet Hindus and Muslims do dine in one another's homes, and they play on the same cricket teams. Guha's central aim is to register these discordant notes, and for the most part he succeeds admirably.

"India After Gandhi" begins with the British, who after years of resisting Indian self-government on the grounds that the country was both too mature ("much too old to learn that business," Kipling remarked) and too young ("they are still infants," one colonialist said), abruptly quit the subcontinent in 1947. Gandhi was murdered less than six months later by a Hindu extremist, and millions were uprooted during the partition of India and Pakistan, many of them killed in religious violence. The new Indian state faced the dual challenges of integrating its remaining Muslim population and appeasing its Hindu majority.

Much of what was accomplished in the next 15 years was due to the popularity and will of India's first Prime Minister, Jawaharlal Nehru. Despite enormous obstacles within his own Congress Party, Nehru set out to ensure more rights for women and the downtrodden. Guha expertly traces Nehru's leadership in the writing of India's Constitution, where legislators overcame potentially fatal disagreements over issues like what language the document would appear in. The finished product, which Guha refers to as a liberal, humanist credo, not only protected numerous basic rights but also provided reservations for "untouchables."

Some scholars, Sunil Khilnani among them, have argued that by identifying caste as an organizing principle in Indian society, Nehru and his allies inadvertently laid the groundwork for a more **schismatic** political culture, greater discrimination against Muslims and eventually, the success of the Hindu right. Guha, who is perceptive about both the hardships faced by Muslims over the past 60 years and the caste-based conflicts that endure to this day, disappointingly declines to address these charges. Rather, he implies that Nehru did the best he could under the circumstances to prevent further split. His success with the Constitution, as well as his support for bills that raised the status of Hindu women and altered unfair property laws, are just some of the ways in which he had a positive impact on India's young democracy. Guha paints a convincing portrait of Nehru's good political sense (if never really giving us much insight into his personality).

1. What is Ramachandra Guha's aim while he mentions Muhammad Ali Jinnah's statement?

   (1) To register the validity of Muhammad Ali Jinnah's statements.

   (2) To bring out the contradictory notions about Hindus and Muslims that they are stuck in a vicious cycle.

   (3) To portray Nehru's good political sense and efforts towards the formation of our Constitution.

   (4) o show that India is divided between two opposite religions- Hindu and Muslim.

   (5) To discuss the economic problems of India.

2. Why does the author mention "A Suitable Boy" in the beginning of the passage?

(1) To catch the attention of the reader.

(2) To show India's fictional panorama.

(3) To show the challenges of modern day India.

(4) To make one learn that one should think above divisions.

(5) To emphasise Indian writings in English.

3. The author would most agree to which of the following?

(1) The British considered India mature enough to handle two different religious philosophies.

(2) Nehru failed in writing the Indian constitution.

(3) India, during its independence, never faced challenges of appeasing its Hindu majority.

(4) The accomplishment of India after its independence was mainly because of Nehru.

(5) India can never become a superpower.

4. The passage could be an extract from:

(1) An article on famous Indian authors

(2) A book review of Ramchandra Guha's book.

(3) A newspaper article about Hindu and Muslim.

(4) A scholarly article.

(5) A school magazine

5. What does the word "Schismatic" mean according to the paragraph?

(1) Heterodox　　　(2) Orthodox

(3) Mainstream　　(4) Conformist

(5) Conventional

Directions (Q. 6 to 10): Each question below has two blanks, each blank indicating that something has been omitted. Choose the set of words for each blank which best fits the meaning of the sentence as a whole.

6. Of Krishna and Lakhsman, the ______ works the ______.

(1) last, sturdier　　(2) first, miser

(3) latest, most　　(4) later, more

(5) latter, harder

7. On ______ at the foot of the hill, he ______ his whistle.

(1) looking, strummed

(2) driving, flew

(3) climbing, beat

(4) arriving, blew

(5) coming, blown

8. When Caesar ______ Brutus among the assassins, he ______ his face with his gown.

(1) saw, covered

(2) has seen, covers

(3) was seen, was covered

(4) have seen, covered

(5) see, covers

9. Virat Kohli is a ______ player than Rohit Sharma and therefore, he must ______ his place in the team.

(1) superb, get　　　(2) tactful, positions

(3) better, take　　　(4) fast, secure

(5) best, replace

10. They tried to ______ the policeman, but he was too ______ for them.

(1) charged, cool　　(2) fool, favourite

(3) bribes, smart　　(4) bribed, foolish

(5) bribe, clever

Directions (Q. 11 to 15): Read each sentence to find out whether there is any grammatical error or idiomatic error in it. The error, if any, will be in one part of the sentence. The letter of that part is the answer. If there is no error, the answer is (5). (Ignore errors of punctuation, if any.)

11. Hostility between the (1)/ two groups have (2)/increased in the (3)/ past few months. (4)No error (5)

12. Her class is very special (1)/ because it has children (2)/ with many different (3)/ abilities and skills. (4) No error (5)

13. Many peoples were (1)/ brought to safety (2)/ by the army helicopters (3)/ from the flood hit area. (4) No error (5)

14. It is difficult to (1)/ understand the problems (2)/ that the physically challenged people (3)/ encounters in their daily life. (4)No error (5)

15. I had gone only a little way (1)/ down the street (2)/ when I realised that (3)/ I had not lock the door. (4) No error (5)

Directions (Q. 16 to 20): Rearrange the following sentences A, B, C, D, E and F in proper sequence to form a meaningful paragraph and then answer the questions given below them.

A. The farmer called his neighbours and asked them to help him put mud into the well but the mule thought that he was calling the neighbours to help him get out of the well.

B. A farmer wanted to get rid of his old mule and buy a new one but the mule always came back wherever the farmer left him.

C. He walked away from his cruel master and never returned.

D. One day the mule fell into a well and the farmer thought, "Why not bury it there so that I don't have to worry about getting rid of it?"

E. The mule started shaking off all the mud that fell on him and kept climbing on the heap of mud as it fell into the well; soon he was on top of the mud he and he easily got out of the well.

F. When they started putting mud in the well the mule realized his master's plan and started thinking of ways to save himself.

16. Which of the following should be the **FIFTH** sentence in the rearrangement?

   (1) D   (2) B
   (3) A   (4) F
   (5) E

17. Which of the following should the **FOURTH** sentence in the rearrangement?

   (1) A   (2) F
   (3) B   (4) C
   (5) D

18. Which of the following should be the **LAST (SIXTH)** sentence in the rearrangement?

   (1) B   (2) E
   (3) C   (4) A
   (5) D

19. Which of the following should be the **FIRST** sentence in the rearrangement?

   (1) D   (2) A
   (3) C   (4) B
   (5) F

20. Which of the following should be the **SECOND** sentence in the rearrangement?

   (1) B   (2) F
   (3) E   (4) D
   (5) A

Directions (21 to 25): Which of the phrases (1), (2), (3) and (4) given below each statement should replace the phrase printed in bold in the sentence to make it grammatically correct? If the sentence is correct as it is given and 'No correction is required', mark (5) as the answer.

21. Many **students waits anxiously** at the college gate to know their results.

   (1) student waited anxiously
   (2) students waiting anxiously
   (3) students waited anxiously
   (4) students waited anxious
   (5) No correction required

22. Through a fortuitous circumstance Rakhi met her childhood friend on the bus in which **she was travelling**.

   (1) she was travelled
   (2) she did travel
   (3) she has travelling
   (4) she were travelling
   (5) No correction required

23. The opposition party has alleged that the prices of essential commodities have been soaring like never **before on the last** three decades.

   (1) before on the next
   (2) before in the last
   (3) before at the last
   (4) previously in the next
   (5) No correction required

24. The salaries and the perks of the employees in this institution **are not in according** with the rest of the industry.

   (1) are not in accordance
   (2) is not in accordance
   (3) are not according
   (4) is not on accordance
   (5) No correction required

25. The soldiers deployed in the town **were instructed to exercising** restraint and handle the situation peacefully.

   (1) was instructed to exercising
   (2) were instructed for exercise
   (3) were instructed to exercise
   (4) was instructing to exercising
   (5) No Correction required

Directions (Q. 26 to 30): In the following passage there are blanks, each of which has been numbered. These numbers are printed below the passage and against each, five words are suggested, one of which fits the blank appropriately. Find out the appropriate word in each case.

Clement Atlee became the Prime Minister of England after the Second World War. Winston Churchill, who had successfully __(26)__ England and the allies to victory over Hitler was now rejected by the English people at the hustings. Labour Party was swept to power and Atlee became the Prime Minister. One of his memorable tasks was that he was __(27)__ in granting India its freedom. Atlee was born in a well-to-do family but he always had concern for the poor and the downtrodden. He is known for keeping __(28)__ and cooperation among his cabinet colleagues. Not that there were no differences of opinion among his cabinet members, but Atlee, by his __(29)__ nature and positive approach, always managed to keep them together and had control over them. Besides being sympathetic to the cause of India, and granting India freedom, he __(30)__ many a constructive activity for his country too, like nationalization of some industries, and starting National Health Scheme.

26. (1) marginalised   (2) led
   (3) isolated   (4) established
   (5) conquered

27. (1) reluctant   (2) particular
   (3) interested   (4) instrumental
   (5) eager

28. (1) faith   (2) conflict
   (3) assistance   (4) conviction
   (5) harmony

29. (1) aggressive   (2) docile
   (3) withdrawing   (4) gentle
   (5) stubborn

30. (1) observed   (2) did
   (3) demonstrated   (4) imitated
   (5) bypassed

NUMERICAL ABILITY

Directions for questions 31 to 35: What will come in place of question mark (?) in the following questions?

31. 37.5% of $300 - \dfrac{1}{12}$ of $543 = ?\%$ of 538

   (1) 8.33   (2) 12.5
   (3) 18   (4) 21
   (5) 17.5

32. $\sqrt{\dfrac{4761 \times 1296 \times 3125}{3375 \times 1728 \times 529}} = ?$

   (1) 2.5   (2) 1.25
   (3) 1.5   (4) 2.25
   (5) None of these

33. $15\dfrac{3}{5} - 17\dfrac{1}{3} \times 2\dfrac{5}{13} + 12\dfrac{1}{2} = -?$

   (1) $-\dfrac{397}{15}$ (2) $-\dfrac{397}{30}$
   (3) $-\dfrac{83}{6}$ (4) 22
   (5) None of these

34. $4567 - 2789 + 6 \times 167 = ? \times 139$

   (1) 15   (2) 18
   (3) 20   (4) 22
   (5) 19

35. $4^{12.25} \times 8^{16.5} \div 16^{18.25} = \sqrt[8]{?}$

   (1) 128   (2) 256
   (3) 64   (4) 512
   (5) 32

36. Amit distributed 300 apples, 225 mangoes and 270 bananas among his friends such that each friend got same number of fruits and of only one type. Find the possible number of his friends among the given options.

   (1) 53   (2) 54
   (3) 56   (4) 55
   (5) 48

37. If 375% of a number is 1762.5, then what will 65% of that number?

   (1) 305.5   (2) 315.5
   (3) 295.5   (4) 285.5
   (5) 325.5

38. A trader buys 40 mirrors for Rs.6,000 and wants to sell them by making a profit of Rs.45 per mirror. What would be his overall gain percent if he sells 80% of the mirrors and the rest gets destroyed?

   (1) 0.04%   (2) 0.4%
   (3) 0.025%   (4) 0.25%
   (5) 4%

39. Mamta invested a certain amount at the rate of 8% p.a. for 5 years and obtained a simple interest of Rs. 31,400. Had she invested the same amount at the same rate of interest for 2 years, how much compound interest would she have obtained at the end of 2 years?

   (1) Rs. 18,276.24   (2) Rs. 14,226.24
   (3) Rs. 19,096.44   (4) Rs. 12,266.44
   (5) Rs. 13,062.4

40. Ratio of the number of students in three classes of a school is 14 : 17 : 18. There is a proposal to increase these seats by 40%, 50% and 75% respectively. What will be the ratio of increased seats?

   (1) 5 : 7 : 9   (2) 3 : 5 : 7
   (3) 147 : 175 : 285   (4) 196 : 255 : 315
   (5) None of these

Directions for questions 41 to 45: The shoe manufacturing company BADIDAS was established on 1st January 2012. It manufactures only two types of shoes i.e. sports and formal. Assume that all the shoes manufactured by BADIDAS are sold in the same year.

Year	Number of pair of formal shoes manufactured by BADIDAS	Average Selling Price per pair
2012	200	500
2013	170	600
2014	130	700
2015	80	800

Year	Number of pair of sports shoes manufactured by BADIDAS	Average Selling Price per pair
2012	100	900
2013	120	850
2014	150	750
2015	190	600

41. What was the revenue of BADIDAS in the year 2015?
    - (1) Rs. 1,87,000
    - (2) Rs. 1,78,000
    - (3) Rs. 1,14,000
    - (4) Rs. 64,000
    - (5) Cannot be determined

42. In BADIDAS, for which year is the profit as the percentage of revenue maximum for sports shoes?
    - (1) 2012
    - (2) 2013
    - (3) 2014
    - (4) 2015
    - (5) Cannot be determined

43. What is the percentage profit earned by BADIDAS in 2013 if the cost price for each pair of shoes of both types is Rs. 500?
    - (1) 30.8%
    - (2) 50.1%
    - (3) 35.2%
    - (4) 45.7%
    - (5) 40.7%

44. As compared to the previous year, which year experienced the maximum rise in revenue from sports shoes?
    - (1) 2013
    - (2) 2014
    - (3) 2015
    - (4) Both 2013 and 2014
    - (5) Both 2013 and 2015

45. In which year was the drop in the number of pairs of shoes manufactured as a percentage of that of the previous year the maximum?
    - (1) 2013
    - (2) 2014
    - (3) 2015
    - (4) 2013, 2014 and 2015
    - (5) None of these

46. Find the ratio in which tea costing Rs. 185 per kg is to be mixed with tea costing Rs. 145 per kg so that the mixed tea when sold, for Rs. 204 per kg, gives a profit of 20%.
    - (1) 2 : 3
    - (2) 3 : 2
    - (3) 5 : 3
    - (4) 3 : 5
    - (5) None of these

47. Pintu, Sintu and Mintu rent a pasture. Pintu puts 9 cows for 6 months, Mintu puts 11 cows for 8 months and Sintu puts 12 cows for 4 months for grazing. If the rent of the pasture is Rs. 285, how much must Mintu pay as his share of rent?
    - (1) Rs. 81
    - (2) Rs. 72
    - (3) Rs. 132
    - (4) Rs. 144
    - (5) None of these

48. If the average marks of three batches of 45, 60 and 45 students respectively is 45, 50 and 60, then find the average marks of all the students.
    - (1) 48.75
    - (2) 50.4
    - (3) 51.5
    - (4) 52.25
    - (5) 49.84

49. Present ages of Amit and Ajay are in the ratio of 4 : 5 respectively. After four years, the ratio of their ages will become 9 : 11 respectively. What is the difference in their present ages?
    - (1) 6 years
    - (2) 7 years
    - (3) 8 years
    - (4) 9 years
    - (5) 10 years

50. A and B can do a piece of work in 36 days, B and C can do it in 30 days while C and A in 45 days. They all work together for 20 days and then B and C quit it. How many more days will A take to finish the work?
    - (1) 20 days
    - (2) 15 days
    - (3) 18 days
    - (4) 10 days
    - (5) 21 days

Directions for questions 51 to 55: What will come in place of question mark (?) in the following number series?

51. 6, 12, 30, 56, 132, ?
    - (1) 172
    - (2) 152
    - (3) 182
    - (4) 162
    - (5) 142

52. 2131, 2240, 1413, 1441, 1424, ?
    - (1) 4440
    - (2) 4132
    - (3) 2141
    - (4) 4032
    - (5) 3141

53. 5, 11, 19, 29, 41, ?

(1) 52   (2) 45

(3) 54   (4) 49

(5) 55

54. 2385, 2470, 2565, 2670, ?

(1) 2935   (2) 2785

(3) 2885   (4) 2930

(5) 2940

55. 86, 101, 120, 135, 154, ?

(1) 169   (2) 171

(3) 157   (4) 159

(5) 162

56. The percentage profit earned by selling an article for Rs. 1,920 is equal to the percentage loss incurred by selling the same article for Rs. 1,280. At what price should the article be sold to make 40% profit?

(1) Rs. 1,860   (2) Rs. 1,960

(3) Rs. 2,110   (4) Rs. 1,680

(5) None of these

57. Abhishek completes a journey in 22 hours. He travels first half of the journey at the rate of 15 km/hr and second half at the rate of 18 km/hr. Find the total distance travelled by him.

(1) 90 km   (2) 180 km

(3) 360 km   (4) 270 km

(5) None of these

58. Excluding stoppages, the speed of a train is 75 km/hr and including stoppages, it is 45 km/hr. For how many minutes does the train stop per hour?

(1) 0.24 hrs   (2) 0.36 hrs

(3) 0.4 hrs   (4) 0.25 hrs

(5) None of these

59. Triangles ABC and PQR are similar to each other such that AB = x cm, BC = (x + 14) cm and CA = (y + 11) cm, PQ = 15 cm, QR = (x + 26) cm and PR = 39 cm. Find the area of the larger of the two triangles.

(1) 135 cm^2 (2) 270 cm^2

(3) 240 cm^2 (4) 145 cm^2

(5) None of these

60. If the diagonal of a square is increased by 2 cm then its area is increased by 22 cm^2. Find the length of the side of the initial square.

(1) 8 cm   (2) 10 cm

(3) 6 cm   (4) 5 cm

(5) None of these

Directions for questions 61 to 65: What will come in place of question mark (?) in the following questions?

61. $91 \div 13 \times 36 - 203 = ?^2$

(1) 49   (2) 45

(3) 48   (4) 7

(5) None of these

62. $(5\sqrt{7} - 4\sqrt{2})^2 = ? - \sqrt{22400} + 7$

(1) 200   (2) 202

(3) 204   (4) 207

(5) None of these

63. $\dfrac{208}{17} \times \dfrac{187}{169} \div \dfrac{16}{91} = ?$

(1) 66   (2) 77

(3) 64   (4) 75

(5) None of these

64. $(11.99)^2 - (6.01)^2 + (5.99)^3 = ?$

(1) 324   (2) 284

(3) 328   (4) 295

(5) 285

65. 2153 × 15 + 3265 − 28758 = ?

(1) 6802   (2) 6572

(3) 5288   (4) 6402

(5) 6285

REASONING ABILITY

66. P's son Q is married to R whose sister S is married to T who is the brother of Q. How S is related to P?

(1) Daughter   (2) Daughter-in-law

(3) Cousin   (4) Neice

(5) None of these

67. Pointing towards a man, a lady said, "His mother is the only daughter of my mother". How is the lady related to the man?

(1) Aunty   (2) Mother

(3) Sister   (4) Cousin

(5) None of these

68. Pintu ranked 19th from the top and 37th from the bottom among those who passed an examination. Seventeen boys did not participate in the examination and eleven failed in it. How many students were there in the class?

(1) 82   (2) 83

(3) 84   (4) 81

(5) None of these

69. A, B, C, D and E are five friends such that E is taller than D while C is taller than A. If E is shorter than A and B is not the tallest, then who is the tallest?

(1) A   (2) B

(3) C   (4) D

(5) E

70. If in a certain code language, COULD is written as BQRPY, then how will SCOLDING be written in that code?

(1) RELPYOGO   (2) RELQYOHO

(3) REMPYOGN   (4) RELIYOPO

(5) None of these

71. If in a certain code language, CID is written as 788, BAT is written as 4240 and CAT is written as 6240 then what would be the code for DAM?

(1) 2826   (2) 8226

(3) 826   (4) 846

(5) 246

72. How many pairs of letters are there in the word 'POTENENTIAL' which have as many letters between them as are in the english alphabet in both forward and reverse directions?

(1) One   (2) Three

(3) Five   (4) Four

(5) None of these

73. N, O, P, Q, R and S are sitting in a row facing North. R is to the immediate right of Q. Q is fourth to the right of S. O is the neighbour of P and N. Person who is third to the left of P is at one of ends. Who is sitting at the left end of the row?

(1) O   (2) P

(3) Q   (4) N

(5) None of these

74. Each of the odd digits of the number '32154628976' is decreased by 1 and each of the even digits is increased by 1 and then rearranged in ascending order. Find the digit that will come at the middle position.

(1) 3   (2) 4

(3) 5   (4) 6

(5) 7

75. Each of the vowels in the word 'CONVENTIONAL' is replaced by the letter that comes at the third position after it in the English alphabet, and each of the consonants is replaced by the letter immediately preceding it and then rearranged in the order of English alphabet. Find the letter that will come at the seventh position.

(1) L   (2) M

(3) U   (4) R

(5) S

Directions for questions 76 to 80: Read the following information carefully and answer the questions based on it.

M, N, O, P, Q, R, S and T are sitting around a circular table and facing the center. Each of them is related to M as brother, brother-in-law, sister, sister-in-law, mother, father and wife. It is also known that:

  (i) M is not an immediate neighbour of his sister.

 (ii) M's sister-in-law and sister sit opposite to each other.

(iii) T, the male member, isn't the blood relative of M.

(iv) R sits third to right of N.

 (v) Neither R nor T, who sits second to left of M, is the wife of M.

(vi) Q, the father sits third to right of his son-in-law.

(vii) P sits third to the right of his/her mother S.

76. Who are the female members in the family?

(1) T, R, P and S   (2) O, R, P and T

(3) O, T, N and P   (4) O, R, N and S

(5) None of these

77. Who is sitting third to the right of O?

(1) T   (2) P

(3) S   (4) Q

(5) None of these

78. How is O related to P?

(1) Sister   (2) Wife

(3) Brother   (4) Sister-in-law

(5) None of these

79. Who is sitting diagonally opposite to P?

(1) Father   (2) Sister

(3) Mother   (4) Brother

(5) None of these

80. What is the position of M with respect to N?

(1) Second to the right

(2) Third to the right

(3) Third to the left

(4) Fourth to the left

(5) None of these

Directions for questions 81 to 85: Read the following information carefully and answer the questions based on it.

A, B, C, D, E, F, G, H, I and J are five married couples who sit in two parallel rows such that each member faces another. It is also known that:

  (i) C is facing H at one of the extreme ends of the row. One person is sitting between B and C.

 (ii) H is facing south and his wife G is sitting at the left end of the row. A is facing south.

(iii) B is sitting opposite to J and to the right of J's husband, F. A is not sitting next to his wife.

(iv) A, F, I, H and B are the male members of the group.

(v) I is married to D and the two are not sitting in the same row.

(vi) Two persons are sitting between D and E, who is facing G. H and G are not in the same row.

81. Who is facing D?

(1) Her husband   (2) Husband of G

(3) F   (4) J

(5) G

82. How many persons are sitting between A and H?

(1) One   (2) Two

(3) Three   (4) Four

(5) None

83. How many male members face north?

(1) One   (2) Two

(3) Three   (4) Four

(5) Five

84. Four of the five options are alike in a certain way and thus form a group. Find the one that does not belong to that group.

(1) G   (2) H

(3) E   (4) C

(5) B

85. Which of the following statements is incorrect?

(1) E is sitting second to the right of J

(2) H is sitting to the left of D

(3) F is facing A

(4) C, E, G and H are sitting at the extreme ends

(5) None of these

Directions for questions 86 to 90: Answer the questions on the basis of the information given below.

In a certain code language 'he dances well' is written as '@ $!'; 'boy sings very well' is written as '& $ ^ #'; 'he sings like us' is written as '% & ! *'; and 'very dances like us' is written as '# @ % *'.

86. Which of the following may represent 'us dances well'?

(1) * @ $ (2) * % $

(3) & @ $ (4) * % #

(5) & @ !

87. What is the code for 'like'?

(1) !   (2) @

(3) $ (4) %

(5) Cannot be determined

88. What is the code for 'very'?

(1) %   (2) ^

(3) *   (4) #

(5) None of these

89. What is the code for 'he'?

(1) !   (2) @

(3) #   (4) $

(5) *

90. What does the code '*' stand for?

(1) us   (2) sings

(3) like   (4) boy

(5) Either 'like' or 'us'

Directions for questions 91 to 95: Read the following information carefully and answer the questions based on it.

Ankush, Amol, Manish, Rajat, Ketan and Pal decided to have lunch together. Each one had different choice for food out of Punjabi, Sea-food and Chinese which are non-vegetarian and Italian, Russian and South Indian which are vegetarian, not necessarily in the same order.

Exactly three people eat non-vegetarian. Ketan loves Italian food. Amol doesn't like Chinese and Sea food because both of them are non-vegetarian foods. Pal doesn't like Punjabi and Sea food; Rajat eats Russian. Each person had only one type of food.

91. Who had the Chinese food?

(1) Rajat   (2) Ankush

(3) Pal   (4) Manish

(5) Amol

92. Who among the following had Sea food?

(1) Manish   (2) Ankush

(3) Ketan   (4) Either (1) or (2)

(5) None of these

93. Which of the following foods could Ankush have had?

(1) Punjabi   (2) Chinese

(3) Italian   (4) Russian

(5) South Indian

94. Who among the following had South Indian food?

(1) Manish   (2) Ankush

(3) Ketan   (4) Pal

(5) Amol

95. Who among the following could have ordered Punjabi food?

(1) Pal   (2) Ankush

(3) Ketan   (4) Manish

(5) Cannot be determined

Directions for questions 96 to 100: Answer each of the following questions independently.

In the following questions the symbols (*, #, =, @, $) are used with the following meanings:

A * B means A is neither less than nor equal to B

A # B means A is not less than B

A = B means A is neither less nor greater than B.

A @ B means A is neither greater than nor equal to B.

A $ B means A is not greater than B.

Now in each of the following questions assuming the given statements to be true, find which of the four conclusions I, II, III and IV given below them is/are definitely true and give your answer accordingly.

96. **Statements :** P @ S, M = T, T $ Z, S * M

    Conclusions :   I. Z * M

                      II. M = Z

                      III. S * T

                      IV. M @ P

    (1) Only I is true

    (2) Only I and III are true

    (3) Either IV or II are true

    (4) Only III is true

    (5) Only III and either I or II are true

97. **Statements:** A # P, P @ S, P = K, M @ S

    Conclusions: I. S * K

                      II. A @ S

                      III. M * S

                      IV. S # A

    (1) Only I is true

    (2) Only II is true

    (3) Only I and III is true

    (4) Only II and IV is true

    (5) All I, II, III and IV are true

98. **Statements:** R $ P, P * Q, R # M, Q @ S

    Conclusions: I. P * M

                      II. Q * R

                      III. M @ S

                      IV. P = M

    (1) Only I is true

    (2) Only II is true

    (3) Either I or IV is true

    (4) None is true

    (5) Only III is true

99. **Statements:** L @ C, C * Z, Z # F $ K

    Conclusions: I. L # K

                      II. F $ C

                      III. L @ K

                      IV. C * F

    (1) Only IV is true

    (2) Only III is true

    (3) Only II is true

    (4) None is true

    (5) Either I or III and IV is true

100. **Statements:** Z @ B, N # S, B @ N, S $ W

    Conclusions: I. B = Z

                      II. S $ B

                      III. N # Z

                      IV. S @ B

    (1) Only I is true   (2) Only II is true

    (3) Only III is true   (4) Only IV is true

    (5) None is true

ANSWERS

1. (2)	**2.** (3)	**3.** (4)	**4.** (2)	**5.** (1)	**6.** (5)	**7.** (4)	**8.** (1)	**9.** (3)	**10.** (5)
11. (2)	**12.** (3)	**13.** (1)	**14.** (4)	**15.** (4)	**16.** (5)	**17.** (2)	**18.** (3)	**19.** (4)	**20.** (4)
21. (3)	**22.** (5)	**23.** (2)	**24.** (1)	**25.** (3)	**26.** (2)	**27.** (4)	**28.** (5)	**29.** (4)	**30.** (2)
31. (2)	**32.** (3)	**33.** (5)	**34.** (3)	**35.** (2)	**36.** (1)	**37.** (1)	**38.** (5)	**39.** (5)	**40.** (4)
41. (2)	**42.** (5)	**43.** (5)	**44.** (1)	**45.** (3)	**46.** (3)	**47.** (2)	**48.** (5)	**49.** (3)	**50.** (1)
51. (3)	**52.** (1)	**53.** (5)	**54.** (2)	**55.** (1)	**56.** (5)	**57.** (3)	**58.** (3)	**59.** (2)	**60.** (5)
61. (5)	**62.** (1)	**63.** (2)	**64.** (1)	**65.** (1)	**66.** (2)	**67.** (2)	**68.** (2)	**69.** (3)	**70.** (1)
71. (2)	**72.** (3)	**73.** (5)	**74.** (3)	**75.** (2)	**76.** (4)	**77.** (1)	**78.** (1)	**79.** (1)	**80.** (4)
81. (1)	**82.** (2)	**83.** (3)	**84.** (4)	**85.** (5)	**86.** (1)	**87.** (5)	**88.** (4)	**89.** (1)	**90.** (5)
91. (3)	**92.** (4)	**93.** (1)	**94.** (5)	**95.** (5)	**96.** (5)	**97.** (1)	**98.** (3)	**99.** (1)	**100.** (5)

EXPLANATIONS

1. Even a man of Jinnah's calibre had rigid ideas about Hindus and Muslims. See paragraph 3 last sentence.

2. The extract from 'A Suitable Boy' leads to the second paragraph defining the challenge confronting modern-day India which is furthermore defined in the entire passage. Thus, making option (3) as the correct answer.

3. Refer to the fifth paragraph for the answer.

4. See paragraph 3, sentence 1.

5. Split into many divisions.

6. "Latter" is the correct usage because it denotes the position of the subject in the sentence.

7. Simple past tense should be used for the second blank.

8. Only option (1) is correct in terms of subject-verb agreement.

9. The first blank should be in the comparative degree of the verb.

10. The first blank should be in the infinitive form.

11. Replace 'have' with 'has.'

12. Delete 'many'.

13. Replace 'peoples' with 'people'.

14. Replace 'encounters' with 'encounter.'

15. Replace 'lock' with 'locked.'

16. The correct sequence of the sentences should be BDAFEC.

21. The verb should be in the past tense.

22. The sentence is grammatically correct.

23. 'In' is the correct preposition.

24. 'Accordance' is the correct form.

25. 'Exercise' should be in the infinitive form.

26. 'Led' is the most appropriate word in the context of the sentence.

27. 'Instrumental' refers to being pivotal in something.

28. 'Harmony' and 'Cooperation' are synonyms.

29. Nature of an individual can best be 'gentle'.

30. Activities can be done.

31. $112.5 - 45.25 = ? \times \dfrac{538}{100}$

$\Rightarrow ? = 12.5$

32. $\sqrt{\dfrac{4761 \times 1296 \times 3125}{3375 \times 1728 \times 529}}$

$= \sqrt{\dfrac{(69 \times 69) \times (36 \times 36) \times (25 \times 25 \times 5)}{(15 \times 15 \times 15) \times (12 \times 12 \times 12) \times (23 \times 23)}}$

$= 2.5.$

33. $15\dfrac{3}{5} - 17\dfrac{1}{3} \times 2\dfrac{5}{13} \div 12\dfrac{1}{2}$

$= \dfrac{78}{5} - \dfrac{52}{3} \times \dfrac{31}{13} \div \dfrac{25}{2} = -\dfrac{83}{6}$

$\Rightarrow ? = \dfrac{83}{6}.$

34. $4567 - 2789 + 6 \times 167 = ? \times 139$

$\Rightarrow 2780 = ? \times 139$

$\Rightarrow ? = 20$

35. $4^{12.25} \times 8^{16.5} \div 16^{18.25} = \sqrt[8]{?}$

$\Rightarrow 2^{24.5} \times 2^{49.5} \div 2^{73} = \sqrt[8]{?}$

$\Rightarrow 2 = \sqrt[8]{?}$

$\Rightarrow ? = 256$

36. Maximum number of fruits that each of the friends can get according to the given condition.

= HCF of 300, 225 and 270 = 15

Thus, the possible number would be 20 + 15 + 18 = 53.

37. $3.75 \times x = 1762.5$ or $x = 470$

$\Rightarrow 0.65 \times x = 0.65 \times 470 = 305.5.$

38. Revenue received = 32 × (150 + 45) = Rs. 6240

$\Rightarrow$ Required percent = $\dfrac{6240 - 6000}{6000} \times 100 = 4\%$

39. Let the principal be Rs. x

$\Rightarrow x \times 0.4 = 31400$ or $x = $ Rs. 78500

Required CI = 78500 × 1.08 × 1.08 − 78500 = Rs. 13,062.40

40. Let the required initial numbers be 140, 170 and 180 so that we can get the increased numbers in integers.

$\Rightarrow$ After increase the ratio becomes: 196 : 255 : 315

41. Revenue in 2015 = 80 × 800 + 190 × 600 = Rs. 1,78,000.

42. Actual profit is not known so we cannot determine it.

43. Profit = 17000 + 42000 = 59000

Profit percentage = $\dfrac{59000}{145000} \times 100 \approx 40.7\%.$

44. Maximum rise in revenue occurred in 2013.

Year	Number of sports shoes manufactured by BADIDAS (X)	Average Selling Price per pair(y)	Net Revenue = x × y	Rise in revenue from previous year
2012	100	900	90000	–
2013	120	850	102000	12000
2014	150	750	112500	10500
2015	190	600	114000	1500

45. Since absolute decrement is same, percentage drop would be maximum for 2015.

Year	Number of pairs manufactured
2012	300
2013	290
2014	280
2015	270

46. Required price without profit = Rs. 170

Applying alligation we get the required ratio as,

(170 − 145) : (180 − 170) = 25 : 15 = 5 : 3.

47. Ratio of their rents = 9 × 6 : 11 × 8 : 12 × 4 = 27 : 44 : 24

$\Rightarrow$ Required amount = $\dfrac{285}{27 + 44 + 24} \times 24 = $ Rs. 72

48. Required average

$= \dfrac{45 \times 45 + 60 \times 50 + 45 \times 60}{45 + 50 + 60} = 49.84$

49. 4x + 4 : 5x + 4 = 9 : 11

Hence, required difference or x = 8 years.

50. Let the total work be 180 units i.e. LCM of 36, 30 and 45.

Work done in 1 day by A and B, B and C and C and A will be 5 units, 6 units and 4 units respectively.

$\Rightarrow$ Work done by A, B and C together in 1 day will be 7.5 units

Thus, in 20 days they will complete 7.5 × 20 = 150 units

Hence, A will complete the remaining 30 units in 20 days.

51. 2 × (2 + 1), 3 × (3 + 1), 5 × (5 + 1), 7 × (7 + 1), 11 × (11 + 1),

? = 13 × (13 + 1) = 182.

52. 2131 = 2 + 1 + 3 + 1 = 7

2240 = 2 + 2 + 4 + 0 = 8

1413 = 1 + 4 + 1 + 3 = 9

1441 = 1 + 4 + 4 + 1 = 10

1424 = 1 + 4 + 2 + 4 = 11

Thus, ? = 4440 = 4 + 4 + 4 + 0 = 12

53. $2^2 + 1, 3^2 + 2, 4^2 + 3, 5^2 + 4, 6^2 + 5$ and $? = 7^2 + 6 = 55$

54. 2385 + 85 = 2470

2470 + 95 = 2565

2565 + 105 = 2670

? = 2670 + 115 = 2785

55. 86 + 15 = 101

101 + 19 = 120

120 + 15 = 135

135 + 19 = 154

? = 154 + 15 = 169

56. CP = $\dfrac{1920 - 1280}{2}$ = Rs. 1,600

Hence, required amount = 1600 × 1.4 = Rs. 2,240.

57. Let the required distance be 2x

$\dfrac{x}{15} + \dfrac{x}{18} = 22$

$\Rightarrow$ x = 180 km $\Rightarrow$ 2x = 360 km.

58. Distance travelled in 1 hr = 75 km so at this speed he would have travelled 45 km in 36 minutes.

Hence, required time = 24 min = 0.4 hrs.

59.

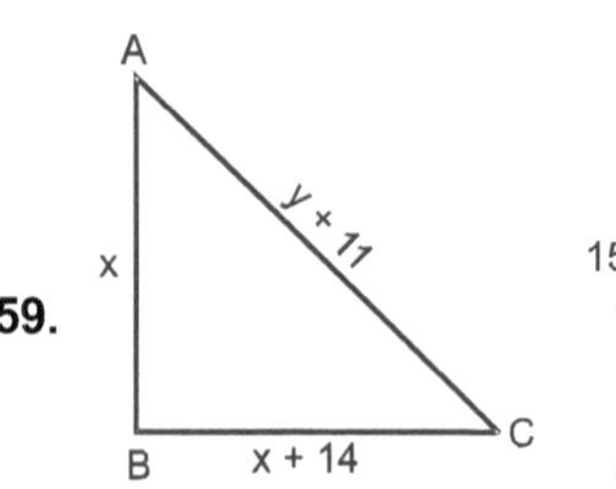

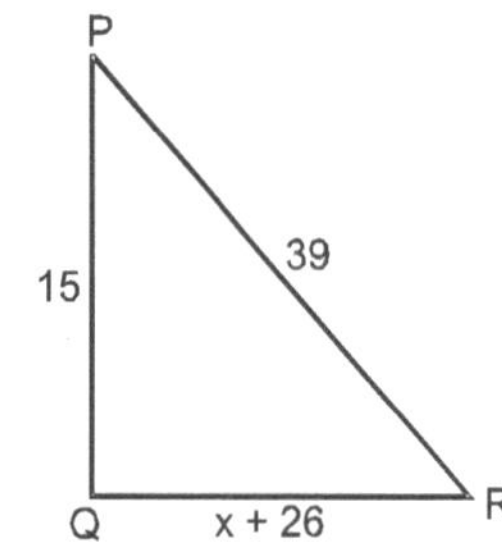

$\dfrac{x}{x+14} = \dfrac{15}{x+26}$

$\Rightarrow x^2 + 26x = 15x + 210$

$\Rightarrow x^2 + 11x = 210$

Thus, x = 10, – 21 (Negative value will be ruled out)

Again, $\dfrac{x}{15} = \dfrac{y+11}{39}$ or $\dfrac{10}{15} = \dfrac{y+11}{39}$

$\Rightarrow$ y = 15 which gives both the traingles as right angled.

Hence, required area = 0.5 × 15 × (10 + 26)

= 270 cm².

60. Let the side of the initial square be of x cm and the diagonal be $x\sqrt{2}$ cm.

Area of the square = $x^2 = \dfrac{x\sqrt{2} \times x\sqrt{2}}{2}$

$\Rightarrow \dfrac{(x\sqrt{2}+2) \times (x\sqrt{2}+2)}{2} = x^2 + 22$

$\Rightarrow$ x = $5\sqrt{2}$ cm.

61. 7 × 36 – 203 = 49

$\Rightarrow$? = 7, – 7

62. $(5\sqrt{7} - 4\sqrt{2})^2 = ? - \sqrt{22400} + 7$

$\Rightarrow 175 + 32 - 40\sqrt{14} = ? - 40\sqrt{14} + 7$

$\Rightarrow$? = 200

63. $\dfrac{208}{17} \times \dfrac{187}{169} \div \dfrac{16}{91}$

= 11 × 7 = 77

64. $(11.99)^2 - (6.01)^2 + (5.99)^3$

= 144 – 36 + 216 = 324

65. 2153 × 15 + 3265 – 28758 = 6802

66. S is the wife of T who is the son of P.

Hence, S would be daughter-in-law of P.

67. Lady will be the mother of the man.

68. Required number = (19 + 37 – 1) + 17 + 11 = 83

69. Required arrangement is given below:

C > A > E > D; B

Irrespective of B's height, C would remain the tallest.

70. C (– 1) = B

O (+ 2) = Q

U (– 3) = R

L (+ 4) = P

D (– 5) = Y

Similarly, the code for SCOLDING will be RELPYOGO.

71. CID = 3 9 4; thus 788 = 2 × 394

BAT = 2 1 20; thus 4240 = 2 × 2120

CAT = 3 1 20; thus 6240 = 2 × 3120

Similarly, DAM = 4 1 13; thus answer = 2 × 4113

= 8226.

72. Required pairs are: PO, EA and LT.

73. Required arrangement is given below:

S – N – O – P – Q – R

74. Given number : 32154628976

Changed number : 23045739867

Final number : 02334567789

Hence, the required digit would be 5.

75. Given word : CONVENTIONAL

Changed word : BRMUHMSLRMDK

Final word : BDHKLMMMRRSU

Hence, the required letter would be M.

For questions 76 to 80:

Required arrangement is given below:

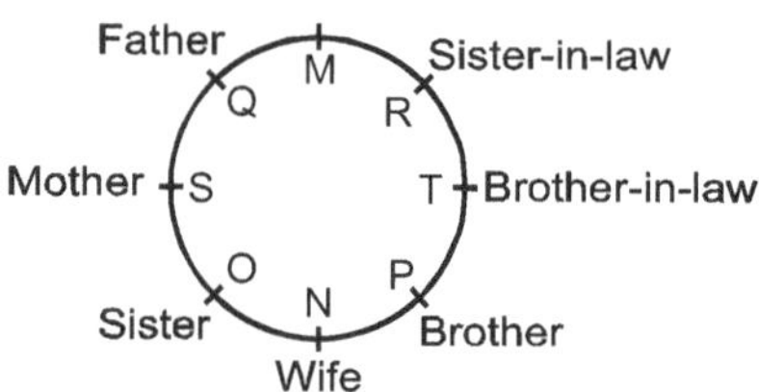

For questions 81 to 85: Required arrangement and married couples are given below:

	E	A	J	D	H	
South	G	F	B	I	C	North

Husbands	Wifes
A	C
F	J
I	D
H	G
B	E

For questions 86 to 90:

He	Dances	Well	Boy	Sings	Very	Like	Us
!	@	$	^	&	#	% or *	* or %

For questions 91 to 95:

Ankush	Amol	Manish	Rajat	Kuti	Pal
Punjabi/Seafood	South Indian	Seafood/Punjabi	Russian	Italian	Chinese
Non-veg	Veg	Non-veg	Veg	Veg	Non-veg

For questions 96 to 100:

96. **Statements :** P @ S, M = T, T $ Z, S * M

    $\Rightarrow$ P < S > M = T $\leq$ Z

    Conclusions:

    I.   Z * M $\Rightarrow$ Z > M May or may not be true

    II. M = Z $\Rightarrow$ M = Z May or may not be true

    III. S * T $\Rightarrow$ S > T   True

    IV. M @ P $\Rightarrow$ M < T Not true

97. **Statements:** A # P, P @ S, P = K, M @ S

    $\Rightarrow$ A $\geq$ P = K < S > M

    Conclusions:

    I.   S * K $\Rightarrow$ S > K True

    II. A @ S $\Rightarrow$ A < S Not true

    III. M * S $\Rightarrow$ M > S Not true

    IV. S # A $\Rightarrow$ S $\geq$ A Not true

98. **Statements:** R $ P, P * Q, R # M, Q @ S

    $\Rightarrow$ M $\leq$ R $\leq$ P > Q < S

    Conclusions:

    I.   P * M $\Rightarrow$ P > M Either I or IV is true

    II. Q * R $\Rightarrow$ Q > R Not true

    III. M @ S $\Rightarrow$ M < S Not true

    IV. P = M $\Rightarrow$ P = M Either I or IV is true

99. **Statements:** L @ C, C * Z, Z # F $ K

    $\Rightarrow$ L < C > Z $\geq$ F $\leq$ K

    Conclusions:

    I.   L # K $\Rightarrow$ L $\geq$ K Not true

    II. F $ C $\Rightarrow$ F $\leq$ C Not true

    III. L @ K $\Rightarrow$ L < K Not true

    IV. C * F $\Rightarrow$ C > F   True

100. **Statements:** Z @ B, N # S, B @ N, S $ W

    $\Rightarrow$ Z < B < N $\geq$ S $\leq$ W

    Conclusions:

    I.   B = Z $\Rightarrow$ B = Z Not true

    II. S $ B $\Rightarrow$ S $\leq$ B Not true

    III. N # Z $\Rightarrow$ N $\geq$ Z Not true

    IV. S @ B $\Rightarrow$ S < B Not true

ENGLISH LANGUAGE

Directions (Q. 1 to 10): The questions in this section are based on a single passage. The questions are to be answered on the basis of what is stated or implied in the passage. Kindly note that more than one of the choices may conceivably answer some of the questions. However, you are to choose the most appropriate answer, that is, the response that most accurately and completely answers the question.

Traditional knowledge has been used for centuries by indigenous local communities to manage natural resources under local laws, customs, and traditions. Many traditional societies all over the world revere and worship nature and consider certain plants and animals sacred. The sacred **groves** in the Western Ghats are small patches of ancient forest dedicated to local animistic deities. These groves are a rich source of fruit bearing trees and small water bodies and act as habitat for several birds and reptiles. Resource extraction in the groves is limited by a variety of rules to placate the deity. This has resulted in the development of relict patches of climax forest. Cultural and biological diversity is even today relevant as a tool for nature conservation that is foremost for sacred grove conservation in Maharashtra.

The Western Ghats of India are one of the 34 globally important biodiversity hot spots. In 2006 the Western Ghats were proposed as a protected "World Heritage Site" and this has now been accepted by UNESCO. Mulshi District nested in the Ghats is a key site for conservation action. In Maharashtra the "sacred groves" in the Ghats which are locally called "Devrai" are key hot spots of biological diversity. The Devrai word came from two local words; that is, Dev means 'God' and 'Rai' means forest. So it means god's forest is Devrai. Such forest patches are considered a sacred forest by locals so they are called sacred groves. The groves thus act as key benchmarks of less disturbed vegetation in a **mosaic** of other traditional and modern forms of land use. The groves play a role in maintenance of the local ecological balance, conservation of watersheds, and preservation of bio-resources. Sustainable use of resources and use of management principles for different landscape elements are frequently linked to culturally distinct sentiments.

In the villages in which groves are protected, regionally relevant folk knowledge supports traditional conservation practices. Local people have evolved their own traditional rules and management based on ancient practices which led to conservation and maintenance of the groves as relatively intact patches of forests as a by-product of their religious sentiments. During the last two decades farmers have sold large pieces of land to speculators for urbanization. This is due to the enormous rise in the price of land. This change has triggered several socioeconomic and cultural aspects in the region with a consequent loss of protective sentiments for the sacred groves.

This study has been carried out in and around the sacred groves of Mulshi region in Maharashtra. The research data has been collected through transects walks and discussions with local people. Seven detailed expert interviews with local priests and ninety-three semi-structured interviews were carried out with elders and local village folk, to understand the local relevant institutional management used for protecting their sacred groves. Semi-structured interviews are the ones that have a flexible and fluid structure, unlike structured interviews that have a prepared sequence of questions to be asked in the same way of all interviewees. The semi-structured interviews can modify or deflect from topic as per the requirement of study. During the interviews mostly the locals diverted from the topic but the given information was also useful. So in such case the formal interviews sessions were avoided and we had supple interview session with the locals.

The fifteen sacred groves studied are linked to tribal deities and often occur in inaccessible areas at higher elevations near the crest line of the Ghats at a considerable distance from the villages. Among the fifteen sacred groves, ten are dedicated to female deities and five to male deities. The female deities of the groves are unshaped stones painted with red color (sindhur) and the male deities are often roughly sculpted black stone figures. The names of the animistic deities are frequently related to the ferocious tigers or tigresses that once roamed these forests which had to be **appeased**.

Each village is located around their sacred grove. So that villagers can access the grove for worship and resource extraction. The tribal communities Dhangar and Mahadeo Koli and the agro-pastoral community Maratha worship the deities and look after the groves. They are forest dependent communities and Marathas carry out agricultural practices. Dhangar and Mahadeo Koli survive by extracting forest resources and sometimes also work on agricultural field of Marathas, such as on their agricultural field, and take care of their cattle.

Transect walks were made with local stakeholders to study the utilization of resources from the groves which are commonly collected by local communities for consumptive and productive uses from within and outside the grove. The knowledge of the resources that can be collected from the groves and those that are considered taboo is spread from one person to another without any written rules. The groves vary from one to eight hectares in size but are occasionally much larger. The forest patches contain a rich **repository** of plant species, massive old trees, covered with lianas and climbers. They are frequently associated with an emergent stream and have better soil as compared to adjacent areas.

The groves have not been measured or demarcated by the Forest Department, Revenue Administration, or by the local Panchayats (local government). This makes the boundary rather flexible and denoted only by the change in vegetation. There was no evidence to show that the groves were maintained for their biodiversity conservation potential or for protecting their natural resource for the future. The preservation of groves is a result of strong ancient beliefs that any damage to the grove would anger the deity who would take revenge on the intruder who desecrates its integrity. In Mulshi most groves cannot be entered by local women. Incidentally women are the main resource collectors in this region and this norm may act as an additional protection against overexploitation of resources within the groves.

Levels of sustainability have been considered in terms of the different local consumptive and productive uses of resources and ecological services provided by the grove. There has been a perceptible loss of protective sentiments and religious perceptions of local people towards the preservation of these groves during the last couple of decades. New strategies for their management must thus attempt to drive unsustainable practices towards sustainable levels through local specific management by enhancing local community initiatives if the groves are to be conserved in the future.

Need for conservation of sacred groves: Most authorities in the past and others emphasized that extraction of resources from the grove was strictly prohibited. This is not so today in the groves of the Mulshi District where development in the form of land use change is increasing rapidly over the last decade. These groves are important today as they are potential banks of genetic diversity that must be preserved. In the local context the sacred groves have ecological values, economic concerns, societal functions and use of traditional sacred rituals, and customs for management. The long term economic value of sacred groves is difficult to assess as it will only become overt when new uses are found for its rare and **endemic** species of flora and fauna. Conservation of sacred groves however acts as a contributor to maintenance of local and regional biodiversity and maintenance of the comprehensive health of a landscape and preservation of the sociocultural integrity of local communities.

Policy and institutional aspects of resource management in the sacred groves: In the sacred groves resource use is controlled by local institutional arrangements that have protected the groves through many generations. These norms are known not only to the presiding priests, but also to most of the villagers of all the different local communities in each village. This includes complete protection in one grove and partial protection in twelve groves. Two of the groves have been completely destroyed due to construction of a dam. For example, complete protection is observed in the Kalkai sacred grove where nothing can be taken or used. In the Bhiravwadi and Wadwathar groves "toddy" (liquor) is tapped. In the Kanguram sacred grove medicinal plants such as "ringni" is used to cure dental problems. From the eight groves fruits such as Mangifera indica and Artocarpus heterophyllus are collected. The seasonal collection of flowers from the grove includes over extraction of Curcuma elata, a flower used for rituals at the Ganesh festival. These flowers are extensively collected in eight groves from August to October. In six of the groves grazing cattle is permitted. In nine groves dead fallen branches of the trees can be used as fuel wood.

1. Which of the following statements is correct according to the passage?

    (1) Local people have developed their own traditional rules and management techniques which have their origins in the ancient age.

    (2) The Western Ghats is the most important biodiversity hot spot in India.

    (3) Sustainable resources are always linked to cultural sentiments.

    (4) The study that the author mentioned in the fourth paragraph resulted in more than a dozen detailed interviews with priests.

    (5) The information collected from the locals in the interviews was hardly useful.

2. What can be the most likely profession of the author?

    (1) An author   (2) A politician

    (3) A tourist   (4) A critic

    (5) An environmentalist

3. Which of the following options can be a possible title for the passage?

    (1) The close relationship between the bio-diversity of Mulshi district and the local people.

    (2) The rich bio-diversity of the Western Ghats.

    (3) The poverty of Mulshi.

    (4) The cultural heritage of the Marathas.

    (5) Policies pertaining to resource management.

4. According to the author, why are the groves so religiously maintained?

    (1) The local people maintained the groves because of their conservation potential.

    (2) The locals wanted to preserve the groves for future generations.

    (3) The locals considered the groves to be religious and hence, sacred.

    (4) The local people are often threatened by the forest department if they cut down trees.

    (5) The groves help in earning valuable foreign revenue and so, they are maintained.

5. According to the author, why is each village located around a sacred grove?

    (1) Villagers often sell the logs to dealers.

    (2) Villagers often use the groves for recreational purposes.

    (3) The groves act as a natural defence against natural catastrophes.

    (4) The groves make the surrounding areas cool even in summer.

    (5) Villagers can use the grove for religious sites.

Directions (Q. 6 to 8): Which of the following options would come closest to the word printed in bold as used in the passage?

6. Grove

    (1) River   (2) Hill

    (3) Terrain   (4) Topography

    (5) Forest

7. Repository

    (1) Archive   (2) Management

    (3) Organisation   (4) Gardening tool

    (5) Forms

8. Mosaic

    (1) A form of tile   (2) Building material

    (3) Motley   (4) Homogeneity

    (5) Native

Directions (Q. 9 and 10): Which of the following options would come opposite to the word printed in bold as used in the passage?

9. Endemic

    (1) Parochial   (2) Patriarchal

    (3) Local   (4) Regional

    (5) Global

10. Appease

    (1) Mitigate   (2) Placate

    (3) Aggravate   (4) Mollify

    (5) Soothe

Directions (Q. 11 to 15): Each question below has two blanks, each blank indicating that something has been omitted. Choose the set of words for each blank which best fits the meaning of the sentence as a whole.

11. Forest department officials said that when the elephants were made to _____ from their trucks, they went straight to the spot where they had been _____ during the camp.

    (1) jump, killed   (2) alight, tied

    (3) enter, hurt   (4) step, played

    (5) exit, enjoyed

12. Excise officials seized pouches of whisky _____ a bus travelling _____ Maharashtra.

    (1) from, to   (2) in, for

    (3) for, towards   (4) inside, on

    (5) through, till

13. Organisations _____ for the victims _____ the inhuman and unjust attitude of the government.

    (1) fighting, applauded   (2) lobbying, supported

    (3) working, condemned (4) stand, opposed

    (5) trying, spoke

14. A collision between two buses _____ six people dead, _____ the driver of one of the buses.

    (1) made, also   (2) left, including

    (3) caused, combined   (4) resulted, except

    (5) got, surpassing

15. The court _____ revenue authorities and PCB officials to _____ teams and visit pharma units.

    (1) directed, form

    (2) announced, arrange

    (3) commanded, display

    (4) ruled, make

    (5) told, carve

Directions (Q. 16 to 20): Rearrange the following six sentences (A), (B), (C), (D), (E) and (F) in the proper sequence to form a meaningful paragraph then answer the questions given below 'them'.

(A) The wise man told them to cut down the tree and divide the fruits between themselves

(B) Ram and Shyam were the best of friends.

(C) Ram was very hurt, "He would let Shyam take ownership of the tree rather than cut it down."

(D) One day, they had a dispute among themselves regarding the mango tree.

(E) On hearing this, the wise man declared Ram the rightful owner of the mango tree.

(F) They went to the wise man in the village to solve their problem.

16. Which of the following should be the **SIXTH (LAST)** sentence after the rearrangement?

(1) A   (2) E

(3) F   (4) C

(5) None of these

17. Which of the following should be the **FIFTH** sentence after the rearrangement?

(1) A   (2) E

(3) F   (4) C

(5) None of these

18. Which of the following should be the **FIRST** sentence after the rearrangement?

(1) B   (2) E

(3) C   (4) F

(5) A

19. Which of the following should be the **SECOND** sentence after the rearrangement?

(1) F   (2) B

(3) D   (4) E

(5) C

20. Which of the following should be the **FOURTH** sentence after the rearrangement?

(1) A   (2) B

(3) E   (4) C

(5) D

Directions (Q. 21 to 25): Read each sentence to find out whether there is any grammatical error or idiomatic error in it. The error, if any, will be in one part of the sentence. The number of that part is the answer. If there is no error, the answer is (5). (Ignore errors of punctuation, if any.)

21. Either of the two persons (1)/ who applied for (2)/ the job (3)/ are going to be hired. (4)/ No error (5)

22. Her ability (1)/ for writing essays (2)/ will be put to test (3)/ in the competition. (4)/ No error (5)

23. I prefer basketball (1)/ compared to (2)/ football as the latter (3)/ is too rough. (4)/ No error (5)

24. I am expecting (1)/ a friend of my mine (2)/ to drop into my house (3)/ tomorrow. (4)/ No error (5)

25. There are (1)/ some people in my class (2)/ who's parents (3)/ are very strict. (4)/ No error (5)

Directions (Q. 26 to 30): Given below is a passage with five blanks numbered 26 to 30. Options for the blanks are given against corresponding numbers below the passage. Fill up the blanks with the most appropriate word from the options given.

Only public universities have the potential to be truly world-class institutions. Institutions and programmes of national ___26___ have already been identified by the Government.

But these institutions have not been ___27___ or consistently supported. The top institutions require sustained funding from public sources. Academic salaries must be high enough to attract excellent scientists and scholars. Fellowships and other grants should be available for bright students. An academic culture that is based on merit-based norms and competition for advancement and research funds is a necessary component, as is a ___28___ mix of autonomy to do creative research and accountability to ___29___ productivity. World class universities require world class professors and students - and a culture to sustain and ___30___ them.

26. (1) prominence   (2) level

     (3) standards   (4) symbol

     (5) level

27. (1) primarily   (2) compulsorily

     (3) precisely   (4) adequately

     (5) sufficient

28. (1) fundamental   (2) judicious

     (3) relevant   (4) nominal

     (5) reverent

29. (1) ensure   (2) disable

     (3) contribute   (4) arrange

     (5) ensue

30. (1) decode   (2) stimulate

     (3) provoke   (4) demote

     (5) demotivate

NUMERICAL ABILITY

31. A motorboat in still water travels at a speed of 36 kmph. It goes 56 km upstream in 1 hour 45 minutes. The time taken by it to cover the same distance down the stream will be

(1) 2 hours 25 minutes   (2) 3 hours

(3) 1 hour 24 minutes   (4) 2 hours 21 minutes

(5) 2 hours

32. A can do a piece of work in 25 days and B can do the same work in 35 days. A started the work and after working for 10 days, he went on a leave for 7 days. B started working on the work in absence of A. A joined B after his leave and they working together completed the rest of the work. How long (in days) did the two work together?

(1) $5\dfrac{1}{6}$ (2) $5\dfrac{1}{2}$

(3) $5\dfrac{5}{6}$ (4) $6\dfrac{1}{6}$

(5) None of these

33. The area of a square is one-fifth the area of a rectangle. The area of the rectangle is 1620 sq.cm. and the length of the rectangle is 54 cm. What is the difference between the side of the square and the breadth of the rectangle?

(1) 12 cm   (2) 24 cm

(3) 25 cm   (4) 15 cm

(5) None of these

34. Tickets numbered from 0 to 99 are mixed up together and then a ticket is drawn at random. The probability that the ticket has a number that is a multiple of 8 or 9, is

(1) $\dfrac{22}{99}$ (2) $\dfrac{23}{99}$

(3) $\dfrac{23}{100}$ (4) $\dfrac{21}{100}$

(5) None of these

35. P, Q and R invested Rs. 45,000, Rs. 70,000 and Rs.90,000 respectively to start a business. At the end of two years, they earned a profit of Rs.1,64,000 What will be Q's share in the profit?

(1) Rs. 56,000   (2) Rs.36,000

(3) Rs. 72,000   (4) Rs. 64,000

(5) None of these

Directions (Q. 36 to 40): Answer the questions on the basis of the information given below.

The table given below shows the number of athletes (in hundreds) who participated in a sports event from five different cities during the period 2009 to 2014.

Year \ Cities	I		J		K		L		M	
	Male	Female	Male	Female	Male	Female	Male	Female	Male	Female
2009	4.4	3.3	6.3	4.2	4.5	3.1	5.6	4.1	4.7	2.1
2010	6.6	4.2	8.4	6.2	6.9	3.3	8.4	6.3	7.8	5.2
2011	4.6	1.8	7.4	4.8	4.8	2.8	9.3	7.3	8.7	6.5
2012	9.6	4.9	11.4	8.4	6.6	4.2	12.6	9.4	8.9	5.8
2013	11.8	6.4	10.6	5.2	7.9	6.3	14.4	10.2	11.8	9.2
2014	8.2	5.2	6.4	7.2	10.8	6.9	15.6	12.1	13.6	9.8

36. In which of the following years was the total number of participants (athletes) the second highest from city K?

(1) 2009   (2) 2010

(3) 2011   (4) 2012

(5) None of these

37. What was the average number of female athletes who participated from city J during the period 2009 to 2014?

(1) 1200   (2) 400

(3) 600   (4) 1800

(5) 3600

38. What was the approximate percentage decrease in the number of male athletes who participated from city K in the year 2011 as compared to the previous year?

(1) 21   (2) 30

(3) 35   (4) 39

(5) 25

39. The number of female athletes who participated from city M in the year 2013 was approximately what percentage of the total number of athletes who participated from city J in the year 2012?

(1) 40   (2) 46

(3) 50   (4) 56

(5) 60

40. In which of the following cities is the difference between the number of male and female participants second highest in the year 2010?

(1) I   (2) J

(3) K   (4) L

(5) M

41. Rs. 500 was invested at 12% per annum simple interest and a certain sum of money invested at 10% per annum simple interest. If the sum of the interests on both the sums after 4 yeras is Rs. 480, the latter sum of money is:

(1) Rs. 450   (2) Rs. 750

(3) Rs. 600   (4) Rs. 550

(5) Rs. 400

42. If the length and the breadth of a rectangle are increased by 10% and 15% respectively, then what is the percentage increase in the perimeter of the rectangle?

(1) 25%   (2) 26.5%

(3) 27.5%   (4) 26%

(5) Cannot be determined

43. The sum of the age of a father and his son is 100 years now. 5 years ago their age were in the ratio of 2 : 1. The ratio of the age of father and son after 10 years will be

(1) 5 : 3   (2) 4 : 3

(3) 10 : 7   (4) 3 : 5

(5) 2 : 3

44. There are two containers of equal capacity. The ratio of milk to water in the first container is 3 : 1, in the second container 5 : 2. If they are mixed up, the ratio of milk to water in the mixture will be

    (1) 28 : 41   (2) 41 : 28

    (3) 15 : 41   (4) 41 : 15

    (5) None of these

45. A man buys a certain number of oranges at 20 for Rs. 60 and an equal number at 30 for Rs. 60. He mixes them and sells them at 25 for Rs. 60. What is gain or loss percent?

    (1) Gain of 4%

    (2) Loss of 4%

    (3) Neither gain nor loss

    (4) Loss of 5%

    (5) None of these

Directions (Q. 46 to 50): In each of the following questions, complete the given series.

46. 117, 235, 706, 2825, ?

    (1) 14126   (2) 11301

    (3) 14726   (4) 12506

    (5) 10257

47. 1, 9, 35, 91, ?

    (1) 197   (2) 164

    (3) 171   (4) 189

    (5) 176

48. 29, 45, 70, 106, ?

    (1) 132   (2) 121

    (3) 148   (4) 176

    (5) 155

49. 3375, 4096, 4913, 5832, ?

    (1) 6344   (2) 8271

    (3) 6859   (4) 9261

    (5) None of these

50. 128, 384, 1536, 7680, ?

    (1) 46080   (2) 42350

    (3) 48710   (4) 32400

    (5) 40600

Directions (Q. 51 to 55): In each of the following questions two questions are given. You have to solve both the questions and find out values of x and y and give answers.

    (1) if x > y

    (2) if x < y

    (3) if x ≥ y

    (4) if x ≤ y

    (5) if x = y or relationship cannot be established

51. I. $x^2 + 13x + 40 = 0$

     II. $y^2 + 7y + 10 = 0$

52. I. $8x + 13y = 62$

     II. $13x - 17y + 128 = 0$

53. I. $2x^2 + 5x - 33 = 0$

     II. $y^2 - y - 6 = 0$

54. I. $42x - 17y = -67$

     II. $7x + 12y = -26$

55. I. $3x - 2y = 10$

     II. $5x - 6y = 6$

Directions (Q. 56 to 60): What approximate value should come in place of the question mark (?) in the following questions ? (You are not expected to calculate the exact value.)

56. $2\dfrac{3}{10} \times 4\dfrac{6}{7} \times 7\dfrac{1}{2} = ?$

    (1) 68   (2) 72

    (3) 93   (4) 84

    (5) 101

57. 12.564 × 22.009 × 17.932 = ?

    (1) 4901   (2) 4895

    (3) 4800   (4) 4959

    (5) 4350

58. 16.978 + 27.007 + 36.984 − 12.969 − 9.003 = ?

    (1) 72   (2) 42

    (3) 60   (4) 51

    (5) 65

59. 18% of 609 + 27.5% of 450 = ?

    (1) 220   (2) 233

    (3) 267   (4) 248

    (5) 274

60. 3942 ÷ 64 ÷ 3 = ?

    (1) 29   (2) 32

    (3) 21   (4) 17

    (5) 11

Directions (Q. 61 to 65): Answer the following questions based on the given information.

There are two charts given below. The bar-graph depicts the export and production of coffee (in million kg) during the period of 2009 to 2014. The line chart depicts the per capita availability of coffee (in gm) during the given period

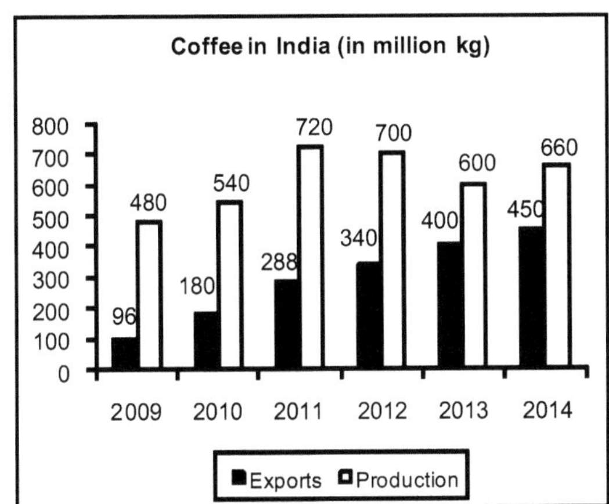

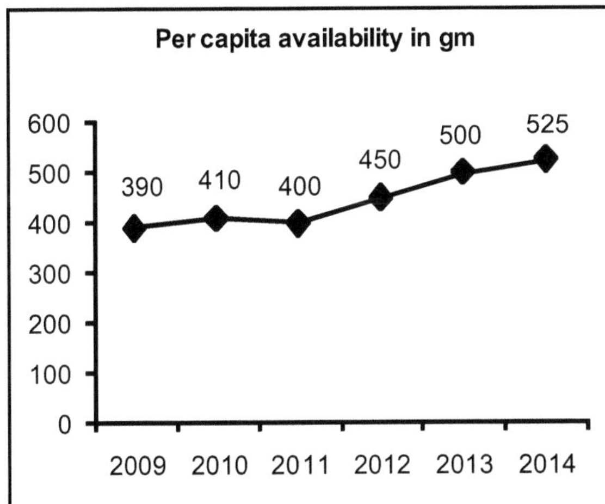

61. Which year shows the minimum percentage of export with respect to production?

(1) 2012   (2) 2010

(3) 2014   (4) 2009

(5) 2011

62. The percentage increase or decrease in population from year 2011 to year 2013 was?

(1) 56.48%   (2) 36.42%

(3) 62.96%   (4) 69.32%

(5) 47.92%

63. For how many years, the coffee production was more than the average coffee production over the given period?

(1) 1   (2) 2

(3) 3   (4) 4

(5) None of these

64. Which year had the maximum percentage growth in per capita availability of coffee as compared to the previous year?

(1) 2013   (2) 2014

(3) 2010   (4) 2012

(5) Cannot be determined

65. If population of India in a year K is represented as Pop (K) which three set of years X, Y and Z satisfy the equation Pop (X) = Pop (Y) + Pop (Z)?

(1) 2010, 2013, 2014

(2) 2012, 2013, 2014

(3) 2011, 2012, 2013

(4) 2009, 2012, 2014

(5) 2009, 2010, 2011

REASONING ABILITY

66. A starts from his house at 9.00 am. After taking his bike, he turns right from his house and starts moving along a straight road. After covering 80 m, he turns left and continues for another 20 m. Realizing that he is low on petrol, he turns right and goes to nearest petrol pump which is 20 m away. He then turns left and rides for another 5 m after which he reaches his friends house. What is the shortest distance from his house to the friend's house?

(1) 125 m   (2) 105 m

(3) 103 m   (4) 107 m

(5) 122 m

67. A man starts from his house towards west. After walking a distance of 30 m he turned towards right and walked 20 m. He then turned left and after moving a distance of 10 m, turned to his left again and walked 40 m. He now turned to the left and walks 5 m. Finally he turns to his left. In which direction is he walking now?

(1) Towards north   (2) Towards south

(3) Towards east   (4) Towards west

(5) Cannot be determined

Directions (Q. 68 to 70): Answer the following questions based on the given information.

Bajaj family has 9 members A, B, C, D, E, F, G, H and I. There are three generations in the family.

  i. F has three children in which two are married.

  ii. G is C's daughter-in-law and has two children.

  iii. E who is I's uncle is unmarried.

  iv. D is the grandson of F.

68. If B is the sister-in-law of E, then how is H related to F?

(1) Son in law   (2) Mother

(3) Son   (4) Father

(5) None of these

69. What is the number of males in the family?

(1) 3   (2) 4

(3) 5   (4) 6

(5) Cannot be determined

70. If there are 3 sons and 2 daughters in the family, then how is I related to C?

    (1) Grandson   (2) Granddaughter

    (3) Grandmother   (4) Grandfather

    (5) Niece

Directions (Q. 71 to 75): Answer the questions on the basis of the information given below.

Puja, Neelu, Rajan, Sonia, Tanu and Manvi are six students of a school, one each studies in class I-VI. Each of them has a favourite colour from red, black, blue, yellow, pink and green, not necessarily in the same order.

Neelu likes black and does not study in class IV or V. The one who studies in Class IV does not like green. Puja studies in Class II. Manvi likes blue and does not study in Class IV. The one who likes yellow studies in class VI. Sonia likes pink and studies in Class I. Rajan does not study in Class VI.

71. In which class does the person who likes red colour study?

    (1) V   (2) III

    (3) IV   (4) Data inadequate

    (5) None of these

72. Which colour does Rajan like?

    (1) Black   (2) Yellow

    (3) Green   (4) Blue

    (5) None of these

73. Which colour does Puja like?

    (1) Green   (2) Yellow

    (3) Red   (4) Data inadequate

    (5) None of these

74. Which of the following combinations is correct?

    (1) Puja-II-Yellow

    (2) Neelu-III- Green

    (3) Sonia-I- Black

    (4) Tanu-V- Yellow

    (5) None of these

75. In which class does Manvi study?

    (1) IV   (2) III

    (3) II   (4) V

    (5) None of these

Directions (Q. 76 to 80) : Answer the following questions based on the given information.

In a certain code, 'he is waiting there' is written as la pa ro ta', 'there is the train' is written as 'zo ro ji la', 'waiting at the station' is written as 'ma ta fu ji' and 'is this a station' is written as 'fu bi ro vi'

76. What is the code for 'he'?

    (1) la   (2) pa

    (3) ro   (4) ta

    (5) Either la or zo

77. What does 'la' stand for?

    (1) is   (2) train

    (3) waiting   (4) the

    (5) there

78. Which of the following represents 'the train station'?

    (1) zo la ma   (2) fu ji ta

    (3) fu ji zo   (4) ro zo fu

    (5) Cannot be determined

79. What is the code for 'at'?

    (1) ma   (2) ji

    (3) fu   (4) ta

    (5) Cannot be determined

80. Which of the following may represent 'guard is waiting'?

    (1) ro ta zo   (2) ta ki ro

    (3) fu zo ki   (4) ta ro ji

    (5) la ma ro

Directions (Q. 81 to 85): Answer the questions on the basis of the information given below.

Ten people are sitting in two parallel rows containing five people each, in such a way that there is an equal distance between adjacent persons. In row 1, Pranav, Qureshi, Romi, Sahil and Tarun are seated and all of them are facing south. In row 2, Akhil, Bala, Chirag, Dolly and Ekta are seated and all of them are facing north. Therefore, in the given seating arrangement, each member seated in a row faces another member of the other row.

Dolly sits third to the left of Akhil. Pranav faces immediate neighbour of Dolly. Romi sits second to the right of Pranav. Only one person sits between Qureshi and Sahil. Bala and Ekta are immediate neighbours. Ekta does not face Pranav and Qureshi.

81. How many persons are seated between Qureshi and Tarun?

    (1) None   (2) One

    (3) Two   (4) Three

    (5) Cannot be determined

82. Four of the following five are alike in a certain way and thus form a group. Which is the one that does not belong to that group?

    (1) Romi   (2) Sahil

    (3) Chirag   (4) Tarun

    (5) Akhil

83. Who amongst the following are sitting exactly in the middle of the rows?

(1) Pranav, Ekta   (2) Sahil, Dolly

(3) Sahil, Akhil   (4) Akhil, Romi

(5) Pranav, Bala

84. Which of the following is true regarding Bala?

(1) Akhil and Chirag are immediate neighbours of Bala.

(2) Bala sits at one of the extreme ends of the line.

(3) Qureshi faces Bala.

(4) Tarun is an immediate neighbour of the person facing Bala.

(5) Dolly sits to the immediate left of Bala.

85. Four of the following five are alike in a certain way and thus form a group. Which is the one that does not belong to that group?

(1) Tarun - Ekta

(2) Qureshi - Chirag

(3) Sahil - Bala

(4) Romi - Akhil

(5) Pranav - Dolly

Directions (Q. 86 to 90): Answer the questions on the basis of the information given below.

Eight friends I, J, K, L, M, N, P and R are sitting in a circle, but not necessarily in the same order. Four of them are facing outside and four of them are facing the centre.

M faces outside. Both the immediate neighbours of M face the centre. R sits second to the right of M. J sits third to the left of M.

L faces the centre. Both the immediate neighbours of L face outside.

P sits second to the left of I. J sits third to the right of R.

N is an immediate neighbour of L. K is an immediate neighbour of P.

L is not an immediate neighbour of J.

86. Who amongst the following sits to the immediate right of R?

(1) I   (2) L

(3) K   (4) P

(5) None of these

87. Who amongst the following sits third to the right of I?

(1) L   (2) M

(3) N   (4) I

(5) None of these

88. Four of the following five are alike in a certain way, based on the information given above and so form a group. Which is the one that does not belong to that group?

(1) RI   (2) NR

(3) PK   (4) LI

(5) IM

89. If all the people are made to sit in an alphabetical order, in clockwise direction, starting from I. the position of whom amongst the following remains the same (excluding I)?

(1) M   (2) N

(3) K   (4) P

(5) None of these

90. How many people are seated between I and K (counting clockwise from I)?

(1) Two

(2) Four

(3) None

(4) One

(5) Three

Directions (Q. 91 to 95): In the following questions, the symbols @ ,$,%,# and & are used with the following meaning as illustrated below.

'M @ N' means 'M is not smaller than N'.

'M $ N' means 'M is not greater than N'.

'M # N' means 'M is neither smaller nor equal to N'.

'M % N' means 'M is neither greater nor equal to N'.

'M & N' means 'M is neither greater nor smaller than N'.

Now, in each of the following questions, assuming the given statements to be true, find which of the four conclusions I, II, III and IV given below then is/are definitely true and give your answer accordingly.

91. Statements:

R $ S, S % T, T & M, M @ X

Conclusions:

I. S @ M

II. R $ T

III. S % M

IV. T & X

(1) Only I is true

(2) Only III is true

(3) Only II and III are true

(4) Only I and IV are true

(5) None of these

92. Statements:
K @ L, L # N, N & W, W $ Q

Conclusions:
I. K & Q
II. K # N
III. N % Q
IV. N @ Q

(1) Only I, II and III are true
(2) Only II is true
(3) Only II and III are true
(4) Only III is true
(5) None of these

93. Statements:
A # B, B # D, D @ F, F & R

Conclusions:
I. A # R
II. B & R
III. B @ F
IV. D % A

(1) Only I and IV are true
(2) Only I is true
(3) Only III and II are true
(4) Only IV is true
(5) None of these

94. Statements:
E $ F, F % G, G @ D, D & K

Conclusions:
I. G @ K
II. D & F
III. E & G
IV. F # K

(1) Only II is true   (2) Only I and III are true
(3) Only II and IV are true   (4) Only I is true
(5) None of these

95. Statements:
P $ W, W & F, F % O, O @ D

Conclusions:
I. O & D
II. P % O
III. W & O
IV. P @ D

(1) Only I is true   (2) Only II, III and IV are true
(3) Only III is true   (4) Only IV is true
(5) None of these

Directions (Q. 96-100): In each question below are given two statements numbered I and II. You have to take the two given statements as true even if they seem to be at variance with commonly known facts. Read all the conclusions and then decide which of the given conclusions logically follow from the given statements, disregarding commonly known facts.

96. Statements:
All hotels are Chinese food.

All cities are hotels.

Some cities are expensive.

Conclusions:
I. All cities are Chinese food.
II. All Chinese food is expensive.

(1) Only I follows   (2) Only II follows
(3) Both I and II follow   (4) Either I or II follows
(5) Neither I nor II follows

97. Statements:
Some Parkers are pens.

Reynolds is a pen.

Some Reynolds are pencil.

Conclusions:
I. No Reynolds is a Parker.
II. Some Parkers may be Reynolds.

(1) Only I follows   (2) Only II follows
(3) Both I and II follow   (4) Either I or II follows
(5) Neither I nor II follows

98. Statements:
Some painters are artists.

All artists stay in London.

Some painters stay in Cuba.

Conclusions:
I. Some painters, who are not artists, stay in London.
II. All painters, who are artists, stay in Cuba.

(1) Only I follows   (2) Only II follows
(3) Both I and II follow   (4) Either I or II follows
(5) Neither I nor II follows

99. Statements:
All movies are entertaining.

Titanic is entertaining.

Some crap are movies.

Conclusions:
I. Titanic is a movie.   II. Titanic is not crap.

(1) Only I follows   (2) Only II follows
(3) Both I and II follow   (4) Either I or II follows
(5) Neither I nor II follows

100. Statements:
Some houses are homes.

No house is beautiful.

All beautiful are pretty.

Conclusions:
I. Some homes are beautiful.
II. Some pretty are beautiful.

(1) Only I follows
(2) Only II follows
(3) Both I and II follow
(4) Either I or II follows
(5) Neither I nor II follows

ANSWERS

1. (1)	**2.** (5)	**3.** (1)	**4.** (3)	**5.** (5)	**6.** (5)	**7.** (1)	**8.** (3)	**9.** (5)	**10.** (3)
11. (2)	**12.** (1)	**13.** (3)	**14.** (2)	**15.** (1)	**16.** (2)	**17.** 4	**18.** 1	**19.** 3	**20.** (1)
21. (4)	**22.** (2)	**23.** (2)	**24.** (3)	**25.** (3)	**26.** (1)	**27.** (4)	**28.** (2)	**29.** (1)	**30.** (2)
31. (3)	**32.** (3)	**33.** 1	**34.** (5)	**35.** (1)	**36.** (5)	**37.** (3)	**38.** (2)	**39.** (2)	**40.** (5)
41. (3)	**42.** (5)	**43.** (1)	**44.** (4)	**45.** (2)	**46.** (1)	**47.** (4)	**48.** (5)	**49.** (3)	**50.** (1)
51. (4)	**52.** (2)	**53.** (4)	**54.** (2)	**55.** (1)	**56.** (4)	**57.** (4)	**58.** (3)	**59.** (2)	**60.** (3)
61. (4)	**62.** (3)	**63.** (3)	**64.** (4)	**65.** (2)	**66.** (3)	**67.** (1)	**68.** (3)	**69.** (5)	**70.** (2)
71. (3)	**72.** (5)	**73.** (1)	**74.** (5)	**75.** (4)	**76.** (2)	**77.** (5)	**78.** (3)	**79.** (1)	**80.** (2)
81. (3)	**82.** (2)	**83.** (5)	**84.** (5)	**85.** (4)	**86.** (4)	**87.** (3)	**88.** (3)	**89.** (2)	**90.** (1)
91. (2)	**92.** (2)	**93.** (1)	**94.** (4)	**95.** (5)	**96.** (1)	**97.** (3)	**98.** (5)	**99.** (5)	**100.** (2)

EXPLANATIONS

1. (1) Refer to the second sentence of the third paragraph where the author mentions the evolution of traditional rules and management practices by local people. The other options are not true in the light of the passage. Options (2) and (3) can be ruled out in the context of the second and third paragraphs.

2. (5) The author is certainly an environmentalist. He is concerned about the biological diversity of Mulshi district in the Western Ghats.

3. (1) The passage talks about the close relationship that the people of Mulshi share with the sacred groves in the villages. The other options are narrow in scope.

4. (3) Refer to the eighth paragraph for the answer. The author clearly mentions the reason why the locals preserve the groves.

5. (5) Refer to the second sentence of the sixth paragraph where the author mentions the reason why each village is located around a sacred grove.

6. (5) 'Grove' refers to a forest.

7. (1) 'Repository' refers to a storehouse or an archive.

8. (3) 'Mosaic' refers to a mixed set of people or objects. 'Heterogeneous', 'motley' can be synonyms.

9. (5) 'Endemic stands for 'regional' or 'local'. Hence, 'global' is the opposite word.

10. (3) 'Appease' means to pacify or soothe. Hence, 'aggravate' can be an antonym.

11. (2) Only 'alight' and 'tied' makes sense in the context of the sentence.

12. (1) 'From' and 'to' indicates the origin and destination of the bus.

13. (3) 'Working' and 'condemned' makes sense in the context of the sentence.

14. (2) 'Left' and 'including' makes sense.

15. (1) 'Directed' and 'form' makes sense.

16. (2) The correct sequence of sentences should be BDFACE.

21. (4) Either of the two persons means one of the two and hence, it talks about a singular subject. So, the verb should also be singular.

22. (2) One has the ability 'to do something' and not 'for doing something'.

23. (2) 'Prefer to' shows preference and 'compared' is redundant in the given context.

24. (3) The phrase to be used is 'drop in' which means to *pay a brief visit*. 'Drop into' means *to let someone or something fall into something*.

25. (3) 'Who's' is a contraction of who is while 'whose' is the possessive form of who or which.

26. (1) The preceding line suggests that the institutions and programmes that have been identified by the government must be of national prominence, i.e. they are important on a national level. The other options do not logically fit in the sentence.

27. (4) The sentence suggests that even though the given institutions are of national prominence, they have not received enough or consistent support. Hence, 'adequately' logically fits in the sentence.

28. (2) The sentence talks of a mix of autonomy and accountability which should be 'judicious' in nature to be productive. The other options do not justify the importance of the mix in ensuring productivity.

29. (1) Option (1) logically fits into the sentence. Productivity has to be 'ensured' and not 'disabled'. 'To contribute' to something is the correct usage of this word and hence, is negated. 'Arrange' does not logically fit into the context of the passage and hence, is negated.

30. (2) Option (1) does not logically fit into the sentence because 'decode' refers to deciphering something. Option (3) is inappropriate as the students do not need to be provoked but need to be stimulated, i.e. to make a person active or excited. Option (4) is negated because of the negative connotation of the word. 'Sustain' suggests that the blank will take a positive word. So, option (5) is also negated, making option (2) the answer.

31. (3) Speed of the motorboat upstream

$$= \frac{56}{1+\frac{3}{4}} \text{ km/hours } = \frac{56 \times 4}{7} = 32 \text{ kmph}$$

Let the speed of the current be x kmph

$\therefore \quad 36 - x = 32$

$\Rightarrow \qquad x = 36 - 32 = 4 \text{ kmph}$

Speed of motor boat downsteam = 36 + 4 = 40 kmph

$\therefore$ Time taken to cover 56 km at 40 kmph

$$= \frac{56}{40} = \frac{7}{5} \text{ hours or 1 hour 24 minutes.}$$

32. (3) Work done by A in one day $= \dfrac{1}{25}$

Work done by A in 10 days $= \dfrac{10}{25} = \dfrac{2}{5}$

Work done by B in one day $= \dfrac{1}{35}$

Work done by B in 7 days $= \dfrac{7}{35} = \dfrac{1}{5}$

Total work done by the time A joins again $= \dfrac{3}{5}$

Work left $= 1 - \dfrac{3}{5} = \dfrac{2}{5}$

Work done by both A and B in one day

$$= \frac{1}{25} + \frac{1}{35} = \frac{12}{175}$$

Let the number of days required be x.

$$x\left(\frac{12}{175}\right) = \frac{2}{5}$$

$$\Rightarrow x = \frac{35}{6} = 5\frac{5}{6}.$$

33. (1) Area of the rectangle = 1620 = length × breadth

$\Rightarrow$ Breadth = 30 cm

Area of the square $= \dfrac{1}{5} \times 1620 = 324$

$\Rightarrow$ Side of the square = 18 cm

Required difference = 30 -18 = 12 cm

34. (5) Total tickets = 100

The numbers of multiples of 8 or 9 = (8, 9, 16, 18, 24, 27, 32, 36, 40, 45, 48, 54, 56, 63, 64, 72, 80, 81, 88, 90, 96 and 99) = 22

$$\therefore \text{ Required probability} = \frac{22}{100} = \frac{11}{50}$$

35. (1) The investment was made in the ratio = 45000 : 70000 : 90000 = 9 : 14 : 18

Share of Q in the profit $= \dfrac{14}{41} \times 164000 = ₹56,000$

36. (5) Number of participants (athletes) from city K

In the year 2010 $\Rightarrow$ (6.9 + 3.3) × 100 = 1020

In the year 2012 $\Rightarrow$ (6.6 + 4.2) × 100 = 1080

In the year 2013 $\Rightarrow$ (7.9 + 6.3) × 100 = 1420

In the year 2014 $\Rightarrow$ (10.8 + 6.9) × 100 = 1770

37. (3) Required average number of female athletes

$$= \frac{4.2 + 6.2 + 4.8 + 8.4 + 5.2 + 7.2}{6} \times 100$$

$$= \frac{36 \times 100}{6} = 600$$

38. (2) Required percentage decrease

$$= \left(\frac{6.9 - 4.8}{6.9} \times 100\right) \approx 30$$

39. (2) Required percentage

$$= \frac{9.2}{11.4 + 8.4} \times 100 = \frac{9.2 \times 100}{19.8} \approx 46\%.$$

40. (5) Difference between the number of male and female participants:

City I : (6.6 − 4.2) × 100 = 240

City J : (8.4 − 6.2) × 100 = 220

City K : (6.9 − 3.3) × 100 = 360

City L : (8.4 − 6.3) × 100 = 210

City M : (7.8 − 5.2) × 100 = 260

41. (3) Simple interest gained from Rs. 500

$$= \frac{500 \times 12 \times 4}{100} = \text{Rs.240}$$

Let the other principal be x.

S.I. gained = Rs. (480 − 240) = Rs. 240

$$\therefore \quad \frac{x \times 10 \times 4}{100} = 240$$

$$\Rightarrow \quad x = \frac{240 \times 100}{40} = \text{Rs. } 600.$$

42. (5) Let the length and the breadth of the rectangle be L and B respectively.

Original perimeter = 2(L + B)

New perimeter = 2(1.1L + 1.15B)

As we don't know the respective values of L and B. Thus, the answer to the question cannot be determined.

43. (1) 5 years ago, let the age of father = 2x years

Then, age of son = x years

$\therefore$ 2x + 5 + x + 5 = 100

$\Rightarrow$ 3x = 100 − 10 = 90

$$\Rightarrow \quad x = \frac{90}{3} = 30$$

$\therefore$ Father's present age

= 2x + 5 = 60 + 5 = 65 years

Son's present age = x + 5

= 30 + 5 = 35 years

After 10 years,

$$\text{ratio} = \frac{65 + 10}{35 + 10} = \frac{75}{45} = \frac{5}{3} = 5 : 3.$$

44. (4) Let capacity of each container = x litre

In first container,

$$\text{Milk} = \frac{3x}{4} \text{litres,}$$

$$\text{Water} = \frac{x}{4} \text{litres}$$

In second container,

$$\text{Milk} = \frac{5x}{7} \text{litres,}$$

$$\text{Water} = \frac{2x}{7} \text{litres}$$

On mixing both

$$\text{Quantity of milk} = \frac{3x}{4} + \frac{5x}{7} = \frac{41x}{28}$$

$$\text{Quantity of water} \ \frac{7x + 8x}{28} \text{litres} = \frac{15x}{28} \text{litres}$$

$$\therefore \text{Required ratio} = \frac{41x}{28} : \frac{15x}{28} = 41 : 15.$$

45. (2) Let the man buy 60 oranges (LCM of 20 and 30) of each kind. CP of the 60 oranges of the first kind

$$= \frac{60}{20} \times 60 = \text{Rs. } 180.$$

CP of oranges of second kind $\frac{60}{30} \times 60 = \text{Rs. } 120$

Total CP of 120 oranges

= (180 + 120) = Rs. 300

$$\text{Their SP} = \frac{60}{25} \times 120 = \text{Rs. } 288$$

Loss = Rs. (300 − 288) = Rs.12

$$\therefore \text{Loss percent} = \frac{12}{300} \times 100 = 4\%.$$

46. (1) The series follows as:

117 × 2 + 1 = 235

235 × 3 + 1 = 706

706 × 4 + 1 = 2825

2825 × 5 + 1 = 14126

Hence, the term replacing (?) will be 14126.

47. (4) The series follows as:

$1^3 = 1$

$1^3 + 2^3 = 9$

$2^3 + 3^3 = 35$

$3^3 + 4^3 = 91$

$4^3 + 5^3 = 189$

Hence, the term replacing (?) will be 189.

48. (5) The series follows as the difference between the consecutive terms is increasing as a square of the consecutive natural numbers starting from 4. i.e.

29 + 16 = 45

45 + 25 = 70

70 + 36 = 106

106 + 49 = 155

Hence, the term replacing (?) will be 106 + 49 = 155.

49. (3) The series follows as the cube of the natural numbers 15, 16, 17, 18 and 19. Hence, the next number satisfying the given condition will be $19^3 = 6859.$

50. (1) The series follows as:

128 × 3 = 384

384 × 4 = 1536

1536 × 5 = 7680

7680 × 6 = 46080

Hence, the term replacing (?) will be 46080.

51. (4) I. $x^2 + 13x + 40 = 0$

$\therefore \qquad x = -8, -5$

II. $y^2 + 7y + 10 = 0$

∴ $y = -5, -2$

This gives , $y \geq x$

52. (2) $8x + 13y = 62$

$13x - 17y + 128 = 0$

This gives , $x = -2$ and $y = 6$

∴ $y > x$

53. (4) I. $2x^2 + 5x - 33 = 0$

∴ $x = 3, \dfrac{-11}{2}$

II. $y^2 - y - 6 = 0$

∴ $y = 3, -2$

This gives, $y \geq x$

54. (2) $42x - 17y = -67$

$7x + 12y = -26$

This gives , $x = -2$ and $y = -1$

∴ $y > x$

55. (1) $3x - 2y = 10$

$5x - 6y = 6$

This gives , $x = 6$ and $y = 5$

∴ $x > y$

56. (4) $? = \dfrac{23}{10} \times \dfrac{34}{7} \times \dfrac{15}{2} \approx 84$

57. (4) $? = 12.564 \times 22.009 \times 17.932$

$\approx 13 \times 22 \times 18 \approx 4959$

58. (3) $? = 16.978 + 27.007 + 36.984 - 12.969 - 9.003$

$\approx 17 + 27 + 37 - 13 - 9$

≈ 60

59. (2) $? = \dfrac{18}{100} \times 609 + \dfrac{27.5}{100} \times 450$

$= 109.62 + 123.75$

$= 233.37$

≈ 233

60. (3) $? = 3942 \div 64 \div 3$

$\approx 61.5 \div 3$

≈ 21

61. (4) Percentage of export with respect to production is given by $\left(\dfrac{\text{Export}}{\text{Production}} \right) \times 100$

which is minimum for the year 2009.

Short cut: It is clearly evident from the graph that export as a percentage of production is minimum in the year 2009.

62. (3) Population in year 2011 = $\dfrac{(720 - 288)}{0.4} = 1080$ million

Population in year 2013 = $\dfrac{(600 - 400)}{0.5} = 400$ million

Percentage decrease = $\left(\dfrac{(1080 - 400)}{1080} \right) \times 100$

$= 62.96 \%$

63. (3) Average coffee production = $\dfrac{3700}{6}$

$= 616.67$ million kg.

The production is greater than average in 3 years viz. 2011, 2012 and 2014.

64. (4) Percentage growth in year 2010 = $\dfrac{410}{390} = 1.051$

Percentage growth in year 2012 = $\dfrac{450}{400} = 1.125$

Percentage growth in year 2013 = $\dfrac{500}{450} = 1.11$

Percentage growth in year 2014 = $\dfrac{525}{500} = 1.05$

Thus, the maximum percentage growth was registered in the year 2012.

65. (2) Population in year 2009 = $\dfrac{(480 - 96)}{0.390} = 984.6$ million

Population in year 2010 = $\dfrac{(540 - 180)}{0.410} = 878$ million

Population in year 2011 = 1080 million

Population in year 2012 = $\dfrac{(700 - 340)}{0.450} = 800$ million

Population in year 2013 = 400 million

Population in year 2014 = $\dfrac{(660 - 450)}{0.525} = 400$ million

Thus, we can see that the given satisfies for years 2012, 2013 and 2014.

66. (3)

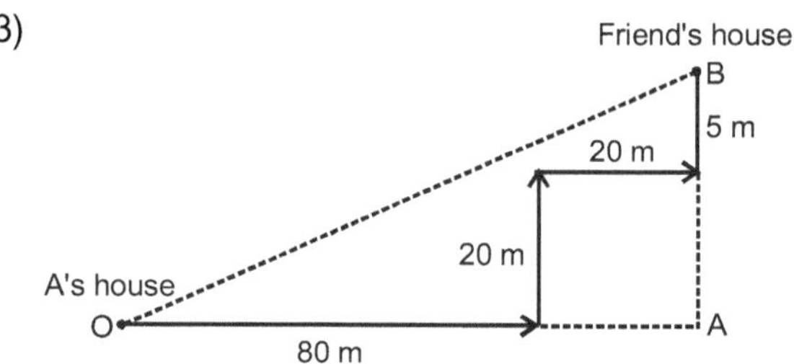

OA = 80 + 20 = 100 m

AB = 20 + 5 = 25 m

∴ Shortest distance (OB) = $\sqrt{100^2 + 25^2}$

≈ 103 m (approx)

67. (1)

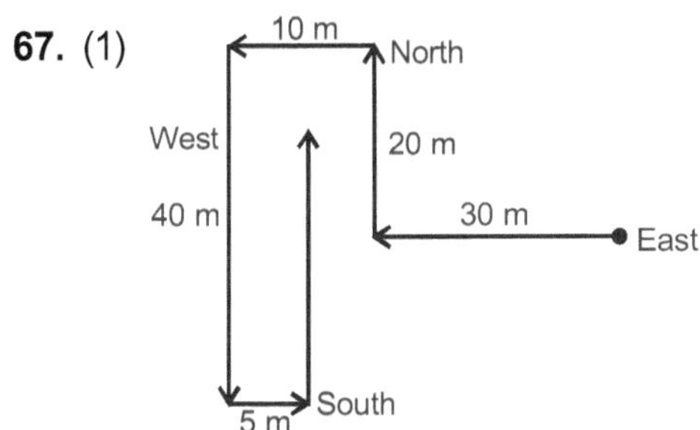

Finally he is walking towards north.

For questions 68 to 70: The family tree is given below:

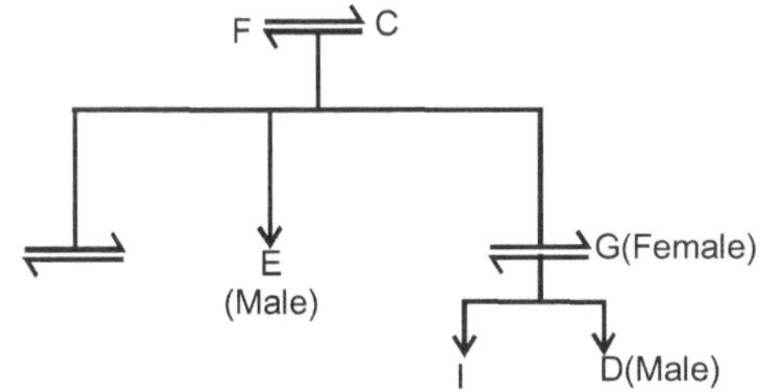

68. (3) If B is the sister-in-law of E, then A and H both are the brothers of E. Hence, H is the son of F.

69. (5) The gender of I is not clear. Hence, number of males in the family will be either 5 or 6.

70. (2) E and D are sons and G is daughter-in-law in the family. Therefore, one of the among A, B and H will be a son in the family. Therefore, 'I' will be a daughter in the family. Hence, 'I' is the granddaughter of C.

For questions 71 to 75:

Student	Colour	Class
Puja	Green	II
Neelu	Black	III
Rajan	Red	IV
Sonia	Pink	I
Tanu	Yellow	VI
Manvi	Blue	V

For questions 76 to 80:

From the given statements the codes for the following words can be determined as:

he	is	waiting	there	the	train	at	station	a	this
pa	ro	ta	la	ji	zo	ma	fu	bi/vi	vi/bi

For questions 81-85:

Row 1: Romi Qureshi Pranav Sahil Tarun ↓ South facing

Row 2: Chirag Dolly Bala Ekta Akhil ↑ North facing

81. (3) Pranav and Sahil are seated between Qureshi and Tarun

82. (2) All others are sitting at the ends.

83. (5) Pranav and Bala are sitting exactly between the rows.

84. (5) Dolly sits on the immediate left of Bala .

85. (4) In all others, the second is the neighbor of the one facing the first .

For questions 86 to 90:

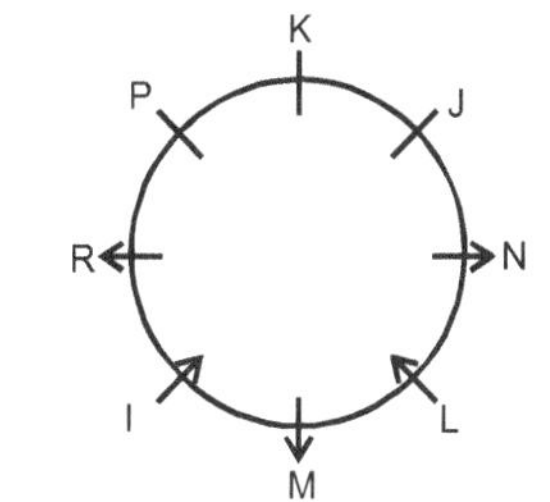

89. (2)

91. (2) Statements:

R \$ S, S % T, T & M, M @ X $\Rightarrow$ R $\leq$ S < T = M $\geq$ X

Conclusions:

I.   S @ M $\Rightarrow$ S $\geq$ M does not follow

II. R \$ T $\Rightarrow$ R $\leq$ T does not follow

III. S % M $\Rightarrow$ S < M follows

IV. T & X $\Rightarrow$ T = X does not follow

92. (2) Statements:

K @ L, L # N, N & W, W \$ Q $\Rightarrow$ K $\geq$ L > N = W $\leq$ Q

Conclusions:

I.   K & Q $\Rightarrow$ K = Q does not follow

II. K # N $\Rightarrow$ K > N follows

III. N % Q $\Rightarrow$ N < Q does not follow

IV. N @ Q $\Rightarrow$ N $\geq$ Q does not follow

93. (1) Statements:

A # B, B # D, D @ F, F & R $\Rightarrow$ A > B > D $\geq$ F = R

Conclusions:

I.   A # R $\Rightarrow$ A > R follows

II. B & R $\Rightarrow$ B = R does not follow

III. B @ F $\Rightarrow$ B $\geq$ F does not follow

IV. D % A $\Rightarrow$ D < A follows

94. (4) Statements:

E $ F, F % G, G @ D, D & K $\Rightarrow$ E $\leq$ F < G $\geq$ D = K

Conclusions:

I.   G @ K $\Rightarrow$ G $\geq$ K follows

II. D & F $\Rightarrow$ D = F does not follow

III. E & G $\Rightarrow$ E = G does not follow

IV. F # K $\Rightarrow$ F > K does not follow

95. (5) Statements:

P $ W, W & F, F % O, O @ D $\Rightarrow$ P $\leq$ W = F < O $\geq$ D

Conclusions:

I.   O & D $\Rightarrow$ O = D does not follow

II. P % O $\Rightarrow$ P < O follows

III. W & O $\Rightarrow$ W = O does not follow

IV. P @ D $\Rightarrow$ P $\geq$ D does not follow

96. (1)

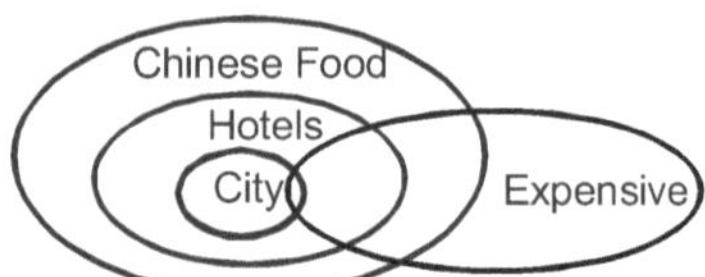

97. (3) 1.

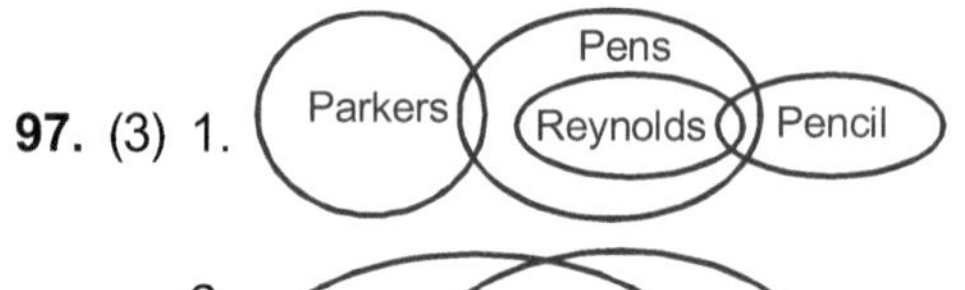

2.

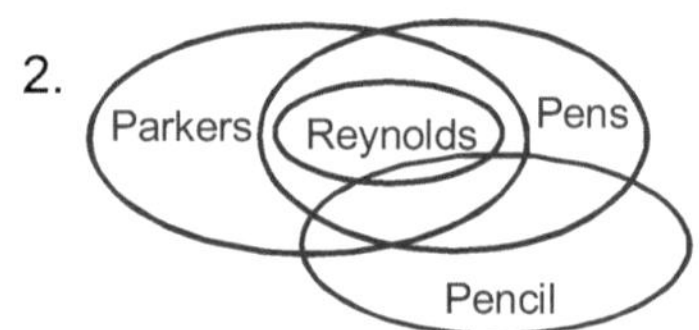

98. (5)

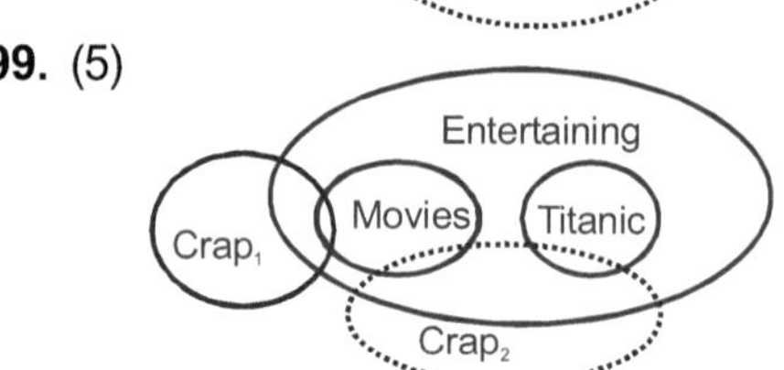

99. (5)

100. (2)

PRACTICE PAPER – 2

ENGLISH LANGUAGE

Directions (Q. 1 to 5): Read each sentence to find out whether there is any grammatical error in it. The error, if any, will be in one part of the sentence. The number of that part will be the answer. If there is no error, mark (5) as the answer. (Ignore errors of punctuation, if any.)

1. In emerging economies, (1) / the private credit market (2) / remains highly segmented and thus (3) / weaken power of monetary policy.(4) / No error (5)

2. The recent election campaign (1) / has been one of (2) / the most noisiest campaigns (3) / in the last decade.(4) / No error (5)

3. Wholesome strategic planning (1) / was the focus as (2) / the firm manage through a difficult period (3) / a couple of years ago.(4) / No error (5)

4. In spite of the best governmental efforts,(1) / emission of greenhouse gases (2) / and noxious chemicals (3) / remain a cause of worry.(4) / No error

5. The rate of metabolism of (1) / a body is comparatively lowest when (2) / it is at rest and is (3) / thus optimum for examination.(4) / No error (5)

Directions (Q. 6 to 10): In the following passage there are blanks, each of which has been numbered. These numbers are printed below the passage and against each, five words/phrases are suggested, one of which fits the blank appropriately. Find out the appropriate word/phrase in each case.

Rural healthcare in India is __6__ by a huge gap between supply and demand. Currently, rural healthcare needs are met either by limited government facilities and private nursing homes, which have not been able to keep pace with increasing demand, __7__ by a number of quacks who practise medicine in rural areas. The quality of infrastructure is usually poor and people end up having to go to nearby large cities if they need high-quality care.

Rural India deserves better, since the ability to pay has gone up over the last few years, driven by growth in income and penetration of government healthcare programmes. Increasing demand, __8__ with the failure of existing infrastructure to scale, has resulted in rural healthcare being a large under-served market. Absence of a viable business model __9__ conversion of the huge rural expenditure on health into an economic activity that generates incomes and serves the poor. It is this __10__ that entrepreneurs are looking to plug.

6. (1) performed   (2) displayed
   (3) furthered   (4) characterised
   (5) made

7. (1) also   (2) nor
   (3) but   (4) or
   (5) and

8. (1) couple   (2) combined
   (3) mention in   (4) engaged
   (5) resulting

9. (1) to   (2) makes
   (3) so   (4) ceasing
   (5) prevents

10. (1) gap   (2) truth
    (3) progress   (4) catastrophes
    (5) divides

Directions (Q. 11 to 15): Fill in the blank by choosing the most appropriate option.

11. Can you ___ me a good example which ___ be illustrative?
    (1) answer, question
    (2) provide, will
    (3) exemplify, substantiate
    (4) request, doubt
    (5) resist, has

12. He met ___ an accident ____ the highway.
    (1) in, above   (2) from, to
    (3) with, on   (4) will, until
    (5) No preposition required.

13. He had ____ very bad accident ___ days back.
    (1) a, some   (2) an, many
    (3) the, much   (4) in, below
    (5) no article

14. He went to a university in London that ____ quite famous ___ Europe.
    (1) is, in
    (2) are, at
    (3) were, up
    (4) had, on
    (5) will, above

15. There ____ various modern sports centers in Gujarat which are excellent ____ infrastructure.

 (1) is, at   (2) are, in

 (3) was, were   (4) has been, have been

 (5) would, could

Directions (Q. 16 to 25): Read the given passage carefully and answer the questions following it.

The deciding factor in any business's ability to exploit its product innovations commercially is the relationship between its marketing and R&D departments. In spite of this, however, many innovations still fail because of a fundamental misunderstanding of what marketing is.

Success for any product or service depends on identifying a target market and testing its commercial viability with that target market to strike the right balance between product or service quality and the price consumers are willing to pay.

However, while many large, successful businesses have systems in place to ensure research and development is market-led, their scale can make them slow to respond to market changes. While smaller businesses may be more flexible, limited resources often mean smaller marketing departments are more sales-focused, concentrating on what happens once a product has been made, rather than feeding into the product development process.

"Marketing is not just about advertising and communications once a new product has been developed, it's about getting under the skin of consumers, identifying target markets and formulating the best market positioning for a new product," says David Nicholls, global client director of international marketing consultancy Added Value. "Yet all too often R&D and marketing departments fail to work closely together. The result is that marketing is a fundamental missing link whose absence profoundly limits a company's ability to deliver commercially successful product innovation." he adds.

A marketing department's involvement in product development should begin right at the start of the process. Only in this way can a team know that the product they are developing will be relevant to a specific target market, and packaged and presented accordingly.

"Unless you continually market or test a product innovation throughout its development, the risk is it will no longer be relevant to the market by the time of its launch." Says Manlio Minale, a consultant at brand consultancy Wolff Olins. "And unless you keep testing it once its in the market, as big a danger is the risk that a products' rivals will quickly catch up."

Staying ahead of the competition has been an important issue for Marina, a business built on its development of the Marina wind-up radio which now produces a diverse range of self-sufficient power products. "While the best way we can protect our market position is by ensuring we continue to make the best self-generating energy products on the market, it is also important for us to continually update and innovate our product's quality and functionality so as people copy us we stay one step ahead, which is where marketing insight truly comes into its own," says Rory Stone, Marina's executive chairman. Achieving this, however, has taken time.

When a business is engineering-led there is a tendency to focus only on producing the best product. "But you can't create a Rolls-Royce in a market where you'll only ever be able to command a Ford Mondea price." Mr Stone points out. "You've got to learn how to compromise without undermining your product's quality and integrity. It's about knowing what your market wants, and what your market will bear."

Getting the right culture within an organisation - not only to foster innovation but channel it effectively to maximise its commercial return - is a significant challenge for many businesses. Engineers focusing on product development don't naturally think about the consumer when they're doing what they do, which is why feeding the consumer insight and even retailer's opinions into the product development process where feasible is really important.

Another obstacle can be a company's internal structure and the impact this may have on corporate culture. "Marketers must force themselves into the product development process, and to do this they need the support of a chief executive who thinks this is important, too." Mr. Stone says. "Commercially successful innovation depends on vision, a desire to be radical, to challenge and to break the mould that must come from the top down within an organisation." Mr Nicholls at Added Value believes.

He says, "Every consumer need is already satisfied by at least 20 products, That's why innovation must be driven by marketing rather than product design". Consumer insight is not just a by-word for market research, however, "it's not about data and reports, it is about understanding your consumer and putting that understanding at the heart of everything your business does." Mr Nicholls adds.

"As Markets become saturated and more products find it harder to differentiate themselves from their rivals by functionality alone, customer service is becoming an increasingly important differentiator between products. As a result, how consumers experience products and services is becoming an increasingly important part of marketing especially for innovations." says Mr Minale at Wolff Olins. "I-pod isn't just a great product innovation; Apple is creating a whole economy around it with the development of related services such as itunes." he explains. "Apple is working to reinvent the music market by creating its own world, something it has in common with all successful product innovators. The best product and service innovations use consumer insight to change the way we think about doing things."

Without doubt successfully bringing product innovations to market is getting tougher as products grow more similar and consumer needs decline. Not so long ago a business could ask itself: "What consumer need can this new product satisfy". In today's climate, however, few , if anyone, can afford to think like that anymore.

16. The fact that innovations fail shows:

(1) organisations' lack of business acumen.

(2) an inability to exploit innovative products.

(3) that marketing is misunderstood by businesses.

(4) there is a weak relationship between marketing and research.

(5) the common people are often misled by innovations.

17. Which of the following is NOT true of smaller businesses with respect to the demands of the market?

(1) Smaller businesses mean smaller marketing departments.

(2) Smaller businesses are more flexible.

(3) Smaller marketing departments have limited resources.

(4) The product development process is the most important part of a business.

(5) Smaller businesses often do not pay taxes.

18. Which of the following is NOT a point made by David Nicholls in the passage while discussing marketing?

(1) R&D and marketing departments fail to work closely together.

(2) Marketing calls for identifying target markets.

(3) Marketing is all about advertising and communications.

(4) Marketing means formulating the best market positioning for a new product.

(5) Marketing is best developed in Latin American countries.

19. The author envisages which of the following roles for the marketing department with respect to product development?

(1) An active R&D role which brings the marketing and the research departments closer.

(2) A role commencing at the inception of product development.

(3) A keen interest in packaging should help in the marketing process.

(4) A role which looks after the positioning of the product is desirable.

(5) Marketing department is essential to gain a foothold in the share market.

20. Which of the following is NOT true of Marina's business model?

(1) It produces a diverse range of self-sufficient power products.

(2) It makes the best self-generating energy products on the market.

(3) It continually updates and innovates their product's quality and functionality.

(4) It keeps building its brand image to plug the gaps in marketing.

(5) It collects donations from foreign investors.

21. According to the passage, which of the following could be the greatest challenge in an engineering–led business?

(1) producing the best product

(2) knowing what the market wants

(3) knowing where your market stands

(4) learning to compromise

(5) catering to the poor

22. Which one of the following is NOT a challenge for businesses?]

(1) Getting the right culture within an organisation

(2) Overcoming the rigidity of a company's internal structure

(3) To foster innovation in the businesses

(4) Keeping marketers out of the product development process'

(5) Tap the market of under developed countries.

23. The passage quotes Mr Nicholls to drive home which of the following insights?

(1) Every consumer need is already taken care of.

(2) Innovation must be driven by marketing.

(3) A belief in the importance of consumer insight.

(4) Product design should not be considered.

(5) Product design can be tampered with.

24. How can a business differentiate itself in a saturated market?

(1) Product differentiation

(2) Area of functionality

(3) Customer services experience

(4) Innovative products

(5) Efficient sales

25. Which of the following is NOT reflected in the example of Apple's i-pod?

   (1) It is a great product innovation.

   (2) It has succeeded in creating an entire economy around it.

   (3) It has reinvented the music market.

   (4) It has created effective marketing campaigns.

   (5) It is unpopular in Australia.

Directions (Q. 26 to 30): In this section, each passage consists of six sentences. The first and the sixth sentences are given in the beginning. The middle four sentences in each passage have been removed and jumbled up. These are labeled M, N, O and P. You are required to find out the proper sequence of the four sentences and mark accordingly on the Answer Sheet.

26. S1: Research efforts have been focused on the impacts of new technology on human health.

   M. The mobile phone industry is one of the fastest growing industries.

   N. These devices are connecting people in convenient ways.

   O. One of the leading new factors is the technology of cell phones.

   P. Today, most people have portable phones in their home, and/or cell phones.

   S6: But the health effects of mobile phones are becoming the focus of research.

   (1) PONM   (2) OMPN

   (3) NOPM   (4) MNOP

   (5) MPNO

27. S1: Since early history and the ancient civilization of man, women have played a secondary role.

   M. They want to stand on their own two feet.

   N. Many women today want and desire careers and a place in this world.

   O. It is clear that women in all careers are striving to gain equality in the work force today.

   P. A women's role in society was that of raising children, and duties surrounding the household.

   S6: There are many issues that surround women and their workplace.

   (1) NOPM   (2) OPMN

   (3) PNMO   (4) PMNO

   (5) MNOP

28. 1. When Weiner was traveling in India, he visited a factory where he saw small frail children sitting on damp floors.

   P. The answer he got was that they were weaving carpets there.

Q. Weiner was shocked at the plight of the child workers.

R. At once he decided to study the problems of child labour in India.

S. Out of curiosity he asked, "What are you all doing there?"

6. Recently Weiner has published his book on 'Child Labour in India' and it is winning him acclaim all over the world.

(1) SPQR   (2) PRQS

(3) QSPR   (4) PQSR

(5) SRQP

29. 1. The dodo, the great ponderous waddling pigeon, the size of a goose, once inhabited the island of Mauritius.

P. The dodo surveyed these new arrivals with an air of innocent interest.

Q. But, as well as losing the power of flight, it seemed to have lost the power of recognizing an enemy when it saw one, for it was apparently an extremely sane and confiding creature.

R. Then man discovered the dodo's paradise in about 1507, and with him came his evil familiars; dogs, cats, pigs, rats and goats.

S. Secure in its island home, this bird had lost the power of flight since there were no enemies to fly from; it nested on the ground in complete safety.

6. Then the slaughter began and by 1681, the fat, ungainly and harmless pigeon was extinct - as dead as the dodo.

(1) SQRP   (2) RQPS

(3) RSPQ   (4) SRQP

(5) RPQS

30. 1. Over the centuries the face of the earth has become crowded with monuments and memorials.

P. Films, pictures and even miniature models can be made of the relics for posterity interested in knowing about them.

Q. Some people however would contend that antiquity should be preserved for future generations.

R. If they were all to be preserved, we will have very little space for other, more useful things.

S. Personally, I do not agree with their contention.

6. We must have more space for building new things and developing open countryside.

(1) RSQP   (2) RPSQ

(3) SRPQ   (4) SRQP

(5) RQSP

NUMERICAL ABILITY

Directions (Q. 31 to 35): Answer the questions on the basis of the information given below.

The table given below shows the number of candidates appeared in the examination and percentage of students passed from various institutes over the years

Institute	P		Q		R		S		T		U	
Year	App.	%Pass	App.	%Pass	App.	%Pass	App.	%Pass	App.	%Pass	App.	%Pass
2008	450	60	540	40	300	65	640	50	600	45	680	60
2009	520	50	430	70	350	60	620	40	580	70	560	70
2010	430	60	490	70	380	50	580	50	680	70	700	66
2011	400	65	600	75	450	70	600	75	720	60	780	70
2012	480	50	570	50	400	75	700	65	700	48	560	50
2013	550	40	450	60	500	68	750	60	450	50	650	60
2014	500	58	470	60	470	60	720	70	560	60	720	50

31. What is the total number of students passed from all institutes together in year 2013?

(1) 1895   (2) 1985

(3) 1295   (4) 1465

(5) None of these

32. Approximately, what is the overall percentage of students passed from institute R for all the years?

(1) 60   (2) 70

(3) 75   (4) 55

(5) 65

33. What is the ratio between the number of students passed from institute U in 2010 and the number of students passed from institute Q in 2012 respectively?

(1) 95 : 154   (2) 154 : 95

(3) 94 : 155   (4) 155 : 94

(5) None of these

34. What is the ratio between the number of students appeared from institute P for all the years and that from institute S respectively?

(1) 463 : 353   (2) 353 : 463

(3) 461 : 333   (4) 333 : 461

(5) None of these

35. What is the overall percentage of students passed from the all institutes together in 2011 (rounded off to nearest integer)?

(1) 68   (2) 70

(3) 69   (4) 71

(5) None of these

36. A 476 metre long moving train crosses a pole in 14 seconds. The length of a platform is equal to the distance covered by the train in 20 seconds. A man crosses the same platform in 7 minutes and 5 seconds. What is the speed of the man in metre/ second?

(1) 1.8   (2) 1.4

(3) 1.6   (4) 2

(5) 1.2

37. A particular job can be completed by a team of 10 men in 12 days. The same job can be completed by a team of 10 women in 6 days. How many days are needed to complete the job if the two teams work together?

(1) 4   (2) 6

(3) 9   (4) 18

(5) None of these

38. The circumference of a circle is twice the perimeter of a rectangle. The area of the circle is 5544 cm^2. What is the area of the rectangle if the length of the rectangle is 40 cm?

(1) 1120 cm^2 (2) 1020 cm^2

(3) 1140 cm^2 (4) 1040 cm^2

(5) None of these

39. In how many ways the letters of the word SACRED can be arranged so that vowels come together?

(1) 240   (2) 120

(3) 320   (4) 720

(5) None of these

40. Rs. 33,630 are divided among A, B and C in such a manner that the ratio of the amount of A to that of B is 3 : 7 and the ratio of the amount of B to that of C is 6 : 5. The amount of money received by B is

(1) Rs. 14,868   (2) Rs. 16,257

(3) Rs. 13,290   (4) Rs. 12,390

(5) Rs. 15,270

Directions (Q. 41 to 45): In the following questions two equations numbered I and II are given. You have to solve both the equations and give answer if

(1) $x > y$

(2) $x \geq y$

(3) $x < y$

(4) $x \leq y$

(5) $x = y$ or the relationship cannot be established

41. I. $x^2 - 10x + 21 = 0$

    II. $y^2 - 16y + 63 = 0$

42. I. $x^2 - (16)^2 = (23)^2 - 56$

    II. $y^{1/3} - 55 + 376 = (18)^2$

43. I. $\dfrac{12}{\sqrt{x}} + \dfrac{8}{\sqrt{x}} = \sqrt{x}$

    II. $y - \dfrac{(18)^{\frac{9}{2}}}{\sqrt{y}} = 0$

44. I. $\sqrt{36x} + \sqrt{64} = 0$

    II. $\sqrt{81y} + (4)^2 = 0$

45. I. $\dfrac{25}{\sqrt{x}} + \dfrac{9}{\sqrt{x}} = 17\sqrt{x}$

    II. $\dfrac{\sqrt{y}}{3} + \dfrac{5\sqrt{y}}{6} = \dfrac{3}{\sqrt{y}}$

46. The simple interest accrued on a certain principal is Rs. 35,672 in seven years at the rate of 8% p.a. What would be the compound interest accrued on that principal at the rate of 2% p.a. in 2 years?

(1) Rs. 2,573.48   (2) Rs. 2,564.86

(3) Rs. 2,753.86   (4) Rs. 2,654.48

(5) None of these

47. In a class there are 60 students, out of whom 15 percent are girls. Each girl's monthly fee is Rs. 250 and each boy's monthly fee is 34 percent more than a girl. What is the total monthly fees of girls and boys together?

(1) Rs. 19,335

(2) Rs. 18,435

(3) Rs. 19,345

(4) Rs. 19,435

(5) None of these

48. Rita's present age is four times her daughter's present age and two-thirds of her mother's present age. The total of the present ages of all of them is 154 years. What is the difference between Rita's and her mother's present age?

(1) 28 years

(2) 34 years

(3) 32 years

(4) Cannot be determined

(5) None of these

49. Two vessels, A and B of capacity 20 litre and 24 litre contains solution of rum and water in the ratio of 5 : 3 and 1 : 5 respectively. If the total volume of both the vessels is transferred to another vessel, then what will be the final ratio between the rum and water in the new vessel?

(1) 11 : 8   (2) 7 : 5

(3) 3 : 5   (4) 2 : 3

(5) 6 : 5

50. Reeyaz sells two laptops for Rs. 17,550. He gains 15% on one and losses 20% on another. If the cost price of both the laptops was same, then what was the combined cost price of laptops?

(1) Rs.18,000

(2) Rs.16,000

(3) Rs.21,000

(4) Rs.18,500

(5) Rs.16,640

Directions (Q. 51 to 55): In each of the following questions, find the wrong number in the series.

51. 21, 26, 33, 42, 57, 74

(1) 74   (2) 42

(3) 26   (4) 33

(5) 57

52. 80, 150, 180, 392, 576, 810

(1) 810   (2) 392

(3) 576   (4) 180

(5) 80

53. 48, 56, 71, 106, 183, 326

(1) 326   (2) 71

(3) 48   (4) 106

(5) 56

54. 1, 2, 66, 102, 794, 1523, 2523

(1) 1523   (2) 794

(3) 2   (4) 66

(5) 102

55. 41, 43, 83, 127, 211, 338, 549

(1) 83   (2) 338

(3) 211   (4) 549

(5) 127

Directions (Q. 56 to 60): Answer the questions on the basis of the information given below.

The bar graph given below shows the percentage of students passing in various standards in a school.

Maximum marks for each subject of every class is same.

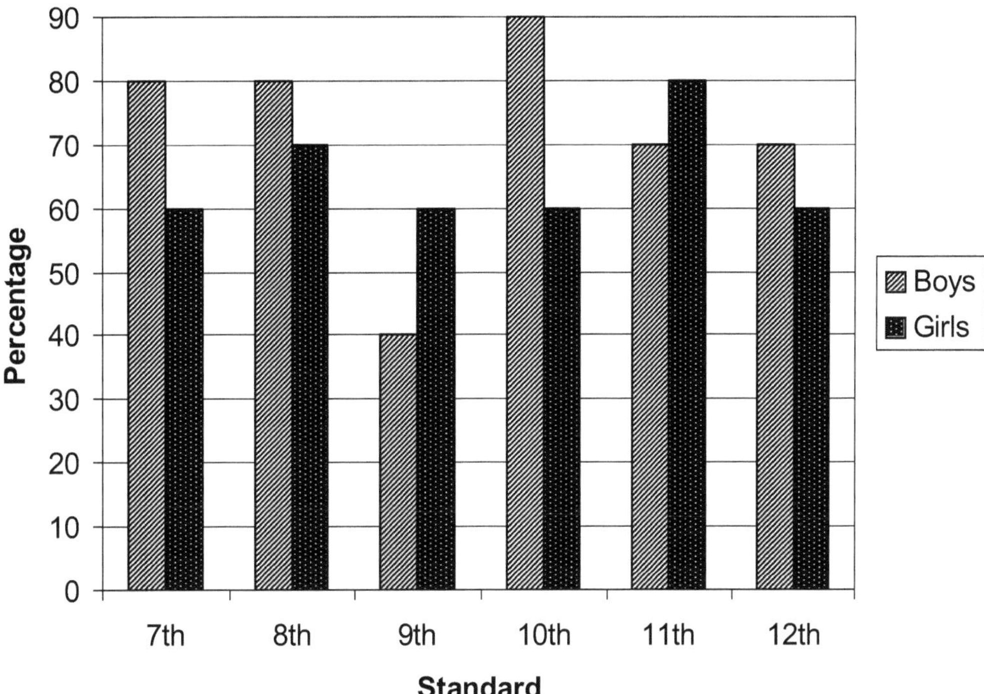

56. If the number of boys and girls passing in standard 7th are the same, then what is the ratio between the number of boys and number of girls in standard 7th?

(1) 4 : 3 (2) 3 : 4

(3) 3 : 8 (4) 8 : 3

(5) 5 : 8

57. In 9th standard, 44% of the total students passed. If total number of boys in 9th standard is 200. What is the total number of girls in 9th standard?

(1) 50 (2) 65

(3) 80 (4) 100

(5) 90

58. If the total number of boys and girls in each standard is 150 and 120 respectively, then what is overall pass percentage of the school?

(1) 39% (2) 59%

(3) 49% (4) 69%

(5) 52%

59. If the ratio between the number of boys and the number of girls in standard 11th is 4 : 1, then what is the ratio between number of boys passed and number of girls passed in standard 11th?

(1) 5 : 11 (2) 7 : 2

(3) 11 : 5 (4) 11 : 2

(5) 2 : 11

60. Assuming the data of question 58, if the over-all average marks of boys is 50% and that of girls is 60%, then what is average marks of the students in the school?

(1) 54.44%

(2) 64.44%

(3) 47.85%

(4) 58.32%

(5) Non of these

Directions (Q. 61 to 65): What approximate value should come in place of the question mark (?) in the following questions? (You are not expected to calculate the exact value)

61. $54.35 \times 39.87 \div 13.35 = ?$

(1) 174 (2) 156

(3) 162 (4) 168

(5) 152

62. $\sqrt{3219} \times \sqrt{4178} = ?$

(1) 3953 (2) 3528

(3) 3498 (4) 3667

(5) 3591

63. $(749 - 325 - 124) \div (1254 - 1100) = ?$

(1) 2 (2) 4

(3) 6 (4) 8

(5) 12

64. $(47)^2 \div 3.25 \times 2.5 = ?$

(1) 1624   (2) 1535

(3) 1687   (4) 1593

(5) 1699

65. 115% of 624 + $\dfrac{2}{7}$ of 419 =?

(1) 887   (2) 837

(3) 765   (4) 756

(5) 787

REASONING ABILITY

Directions (Q. 66 to 70): Answer the questions on the basis of the information given below.

Nine people, P, Q, R, S, T, M, N, O and J stay in a building, but not necessarily in the same order. The building has nine floors and only one person stays on one floor. All of them own one car each, and each car is of a different colour, i.e. blue, grey, white, black, yellow, green, red, orange and pink, but not necessarily in the same order. The ground floor is numbered 1, the floor above it is numbered 2, and so on, and the topmost floor is numbered 9.

O owns a black-coloured car and stays on an even-numbered floor. P stays on any even-numbered floor below the floor on which O stays. The one who owns an orange-coloured car stays on the fourth floor. T stays on the second floor and owns a white-coloured car. The one who owns a pink-coloured car stays on the third floor. P does not own a green-coloured car. There are two floors between the floors on which the people owning the red and the black-coloured cars stay. R owns a grey-coloured car. There are three floors between the floors on which R and N stay. S stays on a floor immediately above J's floor. There is one floor between the floors on which M and N stay. M does not own the pink- coloured car. The one who owns the blue car stays on the topmost floor. M does not stay on the ground floor.

66. Who amongst the following owns the green-coloured car?

(1) S   (2) J

(3) N   (4) M

(5) None of these

67. Who amongst the following stays on the topmost floor?

(1) M   (2) N

(3) S   (4) R

(5) None of these

68. P owns a car of which of the following colours?

(1) Orange   (2) Pink

(3) Yellow   (4) Blue

(5) None of these

69. Who stays on the floor which is exactly between the floor on which O stays and the floor on which P stays?

(1) Q   (2) N

(3) R   (4) M

(5) None of these

70. How many floors are there between the floor on which J stays and the floor on which R stays?

(1) One   (2) Two

(3) None   (4) Three

(5) More than three

71. Amit travelled 15 km Eastward, then turned left and travelled 5 km, then turned left and travelled 15 km. How far was Amit from the starting point?

(1) 30 km   (2) 35 km

(3) 15 km   (4) 5 km

(5) 10 km

72. A man walks 6 km towards the north, then turns towards his left and walks for 4 km. He again turns left and walks for 6 km. At this point he turns to his right and walks for 6 km. How many km and in what direction is he from the starting point?

(1) 10 km and West   (2) 6 km and South

(3) 4 km and South   (4) 8 km and West

(5) 5 km and North

73. Arun said, "This girl is the wife of the grandson of my mother". Who is Arun to the girl?

(1) Grandfather   (2) Husband

(3) Father-in-law   (4) Father

(5) Brother

74. Maya said, "My mother is the sister of Ranjeet's brother". What is Ranjeet's relation with Maya?

(1) Cousin   (2) Maternal uncle

(3) Uncle   (4) Brother-in-Law

(5) Brother

75. Introducing Asha to guests, Bhaskar said, "Her father is the only son of my father". How is Asha related to Bhaskar?

(1) Cousin   (2) Granddaughter

(3) Mother   (4) Daughter

(5) Sister

Directions (Q. 76 to 80): Answer the following questions based on the given information.

In a certain code, 'more money in market' is written as 'zo li aa to' 'share in market profit' is written as 'vo to je li' 'making more profit now' is written as 'su je zo ka' 'now the market gains' is written as 'do li yo su'

76. Which of the following does 'vo' stand for?

    (1) profit   (2) in

    (3) share   (4) market

    (5) in or profit

77. What is the code for 'making'?

    (1) ka   (2) su

    (3) je   (4) zo

    (5) Cannot be determined

78. Which of the following is the code for 'gain'?

    (1) su   (2) li

    (3) yo   (4) do

    (5) yo or do

79. Which of the following can be the code for 'the more you share'?

    (1) do yo zo vo   (2) vo wi zo do

    (3) vo zo wi bu   (4) yo je vo wi

    (5) su vo zo do

80. 'to ka li aa' is a code for which of the following?

    (1) share more in market

    (2) now share more gains

    (3) the gains in market

    (4) the gains in profit

    (5) making money in market

Directions (Q. 81 to 85): Answer the questions on the basis of the information given below.

Arun, Bhupendra, Dhiman, Manoj, Priyank, Rashul, Tanmay, Varun and Wasim are sitting around a circle facing the centre. Dhiman is third to the left of Arun, who is second to the left of Wasim. Bhupendra is second to the right of Wasim and fourth to the left of Manoj. Varun is fourth to the right of Rashul, who is not an immediate neighbour of Arun. Tanmay is fourth to the left of Priyank.

81. Who is on the immediate left of Dhiman?

    (1) Priyank   (2) Varun

    (3) Bhupendra   (4) Manoj

    (5) Data inadequate

82. Who is second to the right of Rashul?

    (1) Bhupendra   (2) Priyank

    (3) Dhiman   (4) Data inadequate

    (5) None of these

83. Who is third to the right of Tanmay?

    (1) Rashul

    (2) Priyank

    (3) Varun

    (4) Bhupendra

    (5) None of these

84. In which of the following combinations is the first person sitting in between the second and the third persons?

    (1) Dhiman, Varun, Manoj

    (2) Bhupendra, Priyank, Dhiman

    (3) Wasim, Rashul, Bhupendra

    (4) Tanmay, Arun, Wasim

    (5) Arun, Manoj, Wasim

85. Four of the following five are alike in a certain way based on the above seating arrangement and so form a group. Which is the one that does not belong to that group?

    (1) Manoj, Dhiman   (2) Rashul, Priyank

    (3) Arun, Varun   (4) Rashul, Tanmay

    (5) Dhiman, Bhupendra

Directions (Q. 86 to 90): In each of the following questions the symbols &, #, @, % and $ are used with following meaning as illustrated below:

A&B means 'A is not less than B'

A#B means 'A is neither less than nor equal to B'

A@B means 'A is neither less than nor greater than B'

A%B means 'A is not greater than B'

A$B means 'A is neither greater than nor equal to B'

Based on the statements given in each of the questions below, find out which of the conclusion follows.

Mark the answer as:

 (1) if only conclusion I follows.

 (2) if only conclusion II follows.

 (3) if both conclusions follow.

 (4) if either conclusion I or conclusion II follows.

 (5) if neither conclusion I nor conclusion II follows.

86. **Statement:**

    E@F, C&E, D$C

    Conclusion:

    I. C# F

    II. D@E

87. **Statement:**

    Y#Z, V@Z, U$V

    Conclusion:

    I. Y# V

    II. U$Z

88. **Statement:**

    N%Q, M&P, Q@P

    Conclusion:

    I. P@N

    II. N$Q

89. Statement:

R$T, S#X, T%X

Conclusion:

I.   S&T

II. X#R

90. Statement:

H&K, G%L, H#G

Conclusion:

I.   G$H

II. K&G

Directions (Q. 91 to 95) : Answer the following questions based on the given information.

Eight members Pranav, Qureen, Reshma, Sidharth, Tarun, Vishal, Hemant and Lalit are sitting in two rows with equal number of members in each row. Members of one row are facing North and those in the other row are facing South. Each member in one row is sitting exactly opposite to a member in the other row. Pranav sits in row facing North, to the immediate right of Hemant, who is sitting exactly opposite to Reshma. Lalit is sitting to the immediate right of Reshma and Sidharth is sitting exactly opposite to Tarun, who is sitting immediately right of Pranav. Vishal does not sit at any of the ends of any row.

91. Which of the following members sit exactly opposite to each other?

    (1) Vishal-Qureen   (2) Lalit-Vishal

    (3) Vishal-Hemant   (4) Vishal-Pranav

    (5) None of these

92. Which of the following members sit at ends of the same row?

    (1) Tarun-Hemant

    (2) Sidharth-Reshma

    (3) Lalit-Qureen

    (4) Lalit-Tarun

    (5) None of these

93. Who sits to the immediate right of Qureen?

    (1) Hemant   (2) Lalit

    (3) Vishal   (4) Reshma

    (5) None of these

94. Who sits opposite to Pranav ?

    (1) Lalit

    (2) Qureen

    (3) Vishal

    (4) Either (1) or (3)

    (5) Cannot be determined

95. Who sits to the immediate right of Vishal?

    (1) Tarun

    (2) Sidharth

    (3) Reshma

    (4) Lalit

    (5) None of these

Directions (Q. 96 to 100): In each of the questions, below are given four statements followed by four conclusions numbered I, II, III and IV. You have to take the given statements to be true even if they seem to be at variance from commonly known facts. Read all the conclusions and then decide which of the given conclusions logically follows from the given statements disregarding commonly known facts.

96. Statements:

All silver are metals.

All metals are steel.

Some steel are stones.

All stones are stands.

Conclusions:

I.   Some stands are metals

II. Some stones are silver.

III. Some stands are steel.

IV. Some stones are steel.

    (1) Only III and IV follow

    (2) Only I follows

    (3) Only II follows

    (4) Only III follows

    (5) None of these

97. Statements:

All chairs are tables.

All tables are songs.

Some songs are rhythms.

Some rhythms are pillows.

Conclusions:

I.   Some tables are chairs

II. All tables are rhythms

III. All chairs are songs..

IV. Some pillows are songs.

    (1) Only I and III follow

    (2) Only I and IV follows

    (3) Only I follows

    (4) Only II follows

    (5) None follows

98. Statements:

Some mobiles are pens.

Some pens are covers.

Some covers are plates.

All plates are papers

Conclusions:

I.   All mobiles are covers.

II. Some pens are papers.

III. All plates are pens.

IV. Some papers are mobiles.

(1) Only I follows

(2) Only II follow

(3) Only I and IV follows

(4) Only II and IV follow

(5) None follows

99. Statements:

All shoes are tables.

Some tables are lanes.

All caps are lanes

Some lanes are rows.

Conclusions:

I.   Some tables are rows

II. Some tables are shoes

III. Some rows are caps

IV. Some lanes are shoes.

(1) Only I and II follow

(2) Only II follows

(3) Only IIII follows

(4) Only either I or IV follows

(5) None of these

100. Statements:

All brands are bottles.

All bottles are machines.

All machines are files.

All files are roots.

Conclusions:

I.   Some files are machines.

II. Some brands are roots.

III. Some machines are roots.

IV. All brands are files.

(1) None follows

(2) Only I follows

(3) Only V follows

(4) Only II and III follow

(5) All follow

ANSWERS

1. (4)	**2.** (3)	**3.** (3)	**4.** (4)	**5.** (2)	**6.** (4)	**7.** (4)	**8.** (2)	**9.** (5)	**10.** (1)
11. (2)	**12.** (3)	**13.** (1)	**14.** (1)	**15.** (2)	**16.** (3)	**17.** (4)	**18.** (3)	**19.** (2)	**20.** (4)
21. (2)	**22.** (4)	**23.** (2)	**24.** (3)	**25.** (4)	**26.** (2)	**27.** (3)	**28.** (1)	**29.** (1)	**30.** (5)
31. (1)	**32.** (5)	**33.** (2)	**34.** (4)	**35.** (3)	**36.** (3)	**37.** (1)	**38.** (4)	**39.** (1)	**40.** (1)
41. (4)	**42.** (4)	**43.** (3)	**44.** (1)	**45.** (3)	**46.** (1)	**47.** (1)	**48.** (1)	**49.** (3)	**50.** (1)
51. (2)	**52.** (4)	**53.** (3)	**54.** (5)	**55.** (1)	**56.** (2)	**57.** (1)	**58.** (4)	**59.** (2)	**60.** (1)
61. (4)	**62.** (5)	**63.** (1)	**64.** (5)	**65.** (2)	**66.** (4)	**67.** (5)	**68.** (3)	**69.** (4)	**70.** (1)
71. (4)	**72.** (1)	**73.** (3)	**74.** (2)	**75.** (4)	**76.** (3)	**77.** (1)	**78.** (5)	**79.** (2)	**80.** (5)
81. (1)	**82.** (2)	**83.** (4)	**84.** (4)	**85.** (2)	**86.** (5)	**87.** (3)	**88.** (4)	**89.** (2)	**90.** (1)
91. (4)	**92.** (5)	**93.** (1)	**94.** (3)	**95.** (3)	**96.** (1)	**97.** (1)	**98.** (5)	**99.** (2)	**100.** (5)

EXPLANATIONS

1. (4) The subject is 'private credit market', which is singular. So, 'weaken' will be replaced by 'weakens'.

2. (3) 'Most' in part (c) is redundant.

3. (3) Use 'managed' in place of 'manage'. The sentence shows past time.

4. (4) The subject is 'emission'. So, 'remain' will be replaced by 'remains'.

5. (2) With 'comparatively', we use 'lower'.

6. (4) A huge gap between supply and demand is a feature or characteristic of rural healthcare in India.

7. (4) The sentence uses 'either…or'.

8. (2) Both, increasing demand and failure of existing infrastructure to scale have resulted in the mentioned effect. Option (1) is wrong because the blank should be filled by a word, which signifies coexistence of the factors, using past tense.

9. (5) The sentence talks of a hindrance or shortcoming.

10. (1) The passage talks of a 'gap' that needs to be plugged.

11. (2) 'Provide' means to give which is appropriate in the given context. 'Will' is the correct word.

12. (3) To meet with an accident is to be involved in an accident. The other prepositions are not suitable for the given expression. 'On' is the right preposition for the second blank.

13. (1) The sentence refers to a single accident and accident is a countable noun. 'Some' is the right word for the second blank.

14. (1) The university (singular noun) is being described in the sentence. 'In' is the right preposition for the second blank.

15. (2) As the subject is plural, a plural verb (are) should be used. 'In' is the right preposition for the second blank.

16. (3) Refer to the line, "…many innovations still fail because of a fundamental misunderstanding of what marketing is."

17. (4) Options (1), (2) and (3) are supported by the third paragraph of the passage.

18. (3) Refer to the fourth paragraph of the passage. The passage states that David Nicholls feels that there is more to marketing than advertising and communications.

19. (2) Refer to the first line of the fifth paragraph.

20. (4) All options, except option (4), are supported by the seventh paragraph of the passage.

21. (2) Refer to the eighth paragraph. It states that a engineering-led business focuses only on producing the best product and tends to overlook what the market wants.

22. (4) Options (1), (2) and (3) are supported by the ninth and the the tenth paragraphs. Option (4) is not a challenge; instead, the passage says that "marketers must force …development process."

23. (2) Options (1) and (3) are mentioned in the passage but the conclusion mentioned in the eleventh paragraph, is stated in option (2). Option (4) is not supported by the passage.

24. (3) The eleventh paragraph supports option (3). The passage states that a business cannot be differentiated in a saturated market using the methods mentioned in options (1) and (2). Option (4) is not mentioned in the passage.

25. (4) The penultimate paragraph supports options (1), (2) and (3).

26. (2) S1 suggests that the passage is related to technology and its effects on human health. Sentence O should be the next line because it gives an example of new technology, i.e. cell phones. Only option (2) has sentence O as the first line. Sentence M goes on to describe the mobile phone industry as the fastest growing industry. Sentence P talks of the situation today in the context of the mobile phone industry. Sentence N talks of 'these devices' which are mentioned in sentence P. This makes PN a mandatory pair.

27. (3) Sentence P definitely has to be the first line because it explains the woman's role that has been introduced in sentence S1. So, we can negate options (1) and (2). Sentence N provides a contradiction by talking of what women of today want in comparison to what their earlier role was. Sentence M further states what women want. So, PNM is a mandatory sequence, which is present only in option (3).

28. (1) Statement S is in continuation to the idea introduced in the first statement given. Statement P provides the answer to the question that Weiner asked the children. Statement Q logically follows statement P because he was shocked after he got the reply from the child workers.

29. (1) Statement S talks of dodo losing the power of flight and statement Q talks of the other power that dodo seemed to have lost in addition to the power of flight. So, SQ is a mandatory pair. Statement P talks of 'these new arrivals' which are mentioned in statement R. So, RP also becomes a mandatory pair.

30. (5) Statement R is the first line amongst the jumbled sentences because 'they' refers to the monuments and memorials mentioned in statement 1. Statement Q would follow because it provides justification for statement R. Statement S is a contradiction of statement Q and hence, should follow statement Q.

31. (1) $\left(\dfrac{40}{100} \times 550\right) + \left(\dfrac{60}{100} \times 450\right) + \left(\dfrac{68}{100} \times 500\right) +$

$\left(\dfrac{60}{100} \times 750\right) + \left(\dfrac{50}{100} \times 450\right) + \left(\dfrac{60}{100} \times 650\right)$

$= 1895$

32. (5) $\dfrac{\text{Total pass}}{\text{Total appearing}} \times 100 = \dfrac{1832}{2850} \times 100$

$= 64.28\% \approx 65\%$

33. (2) Pass in 2010 from U : Pass in 2012 from Q

$= \left(\dfrac{66}{100} \times 700\right) : \left(\dfrac{50}{100} \times 570\right)$

$= 462 : 285 = 154 : 95$

34. (4) $3330 : 4610 = 333 : 461$

35. (3) $\dfrac{2453}{3550} \times 100 = 69.09\% \approx 69\%$

36. (3) Speed of train $= \dfrac{476}{14} = 34\,\text{m/s}$

Length of platform = 34 × 20 = 680 metre.

($\because$ 7 minutes 5 seconds = 7 × 60 + 5 = 425 seconds)

Speed of man $= \dfrac{680}{425} = 1.6\,\text{m/s}$.

37. (1) According to question,

10 men's one day's work $= \dfrac{1}{12}$

$\therefore$ 1 man's one day's work

$= \dfrac{1}{12 \times 10} = \dfrac{1}{120}$

Similarly,

1 woman one day's work

$= \dfrac{1}{6 \times 10} = \dfrac{1}{60}$

$\therefore$ (1 man + 1 woman)'s one day's work

$= \dfrac{1}{120} + \dfrac{1}{60}$

$= \dfrac{1+2}{120} = \dfrac{3}{120} = \dfrac{1}{40}$

(10 men + 10 women)'s one day's work

$= \dfrac{10}{40} = \dfrac{1}{4}$

Therefore, both the teams together can finish the whole work in 4 days.

38. (4) Area of circle = πr^2 = 5544

$\Rightarrow r^2 = \dfrac{5544 \times 7}{22} = 1764$

$\Rightarrow r = 42$.

Circumference of circle = 2 × perimeter of rectangle

$\Rightarrow 2 \times \dfrac{22}{7} \times 42 = 2 \times$ perimeter of rectangle

$\Rightarrow$ Perimeter of rectangle = 132 cm

$\Rightarrow 2(l + b) = 132$

$\therefore l + b = 66$

$\therefore b = 66 - 40 = 26$

Area of rectangle = 40 × 26 = 1040 cm².

39. (1) The word SACRED consists of 4 consonants (SCRD) and two vowels (AE). On keeping vowels together we get SCRD(AE).

$\therefore$ Number of arrangements

$= 5! \times 2!$

$= 5 \times 4 \times 3 \times 2 \times 1 \times 1 \times 2$

$= 240$

40. (1) A : B = 3 : 7

B : C = 6 : 5

A : B : C = 3 × 6 : 7 × 6 : 7 × 5

$= 18 : 42 : 35$

Sum of the ratios

$= 18 + 42 + 35 = 95$

$\therefore$ B's share $= \dfrac{42}{95} \times 33630 = $ Rs. 14,868.

41. (4) **I.** $x^2 - 10x + 21 = 0$

$\Rightarrow x^2 - 7x - 3x + 21 = 0$

$\Rightarrow (x - 3)(x - 7) = 0$

$\Rightarrow x = 3, 7$

II. $y^2 - 16y + 63 = 0$

$\Rightarrow y^2 - 7y - 9y + 63 = 0$

$\Rightarrow (y - 9)(y - 7) = 0$

$\Rightarrow y = 9, 7$

$\therefore\ x \le y$

42. (4) I. $x^2 - (16)^2 = (23)^2 - 56$

$\Rightarrow x^2 - 256 = 529 - 56$

$\Rightarrow x = \sqrt{729} = \pm 27$

II. $y^{1/3} - 55 + 376 = (18)^2$

$\Rightarrow y^{1/3} = 324 + 55 - 376$

$\Rightarrow y = (3)^3 = 27$

$\therefore\ y \ge x$

43. (3) I. $\dfrac{12}{\sqrt{x}} + \dfrac{8}{\sqrt{x}} = \sqrt{x}$

$\qquad x = 20$

II. $y - \dfrac{(18)^{9/2}}{\sqrt{y}} = 0$

$\Rightarrow y^{3/2} - (18)^{9/2} = 0$

$\Rightarrow (y^3)^{1/2} = (18^9)^{1/2}$

$\Rightarrow y^3 = 18^9$

$\Rightarrow y = (18)^3$

$\therefore\ x < y$

44. (1) I. $\sqrt{36}\,x + \sqrt{64} = 0$

$\Rightarrow 6x + 8 = 0$

$\Rightarrow x = -\dfrac{4}{3}$

II. $\sqrt{81}\,y + (4)^2 = 0$

$\Rightarrow 9y + 16 = 0$

$\Rightarrow y = -\dfrac{16}{9}$

$\therefore\ x > y$

45. (3) I. $\dfrac{25}{\sqrt{x}} + \dfrac{9}{\sqrt{x}} = 17\sqrt{x}$

$\Rightarrow 34 = 17x$

$\Rightarrow x = 2$

II. $\dfrac{\sqrt{y}}{3} + \dfrac{5\sqrt{y}}{6} = \dfrac{3}{\sqrt{y}}$

$\Rightarrow \dfrac{6\sqrt{y} + 15\sqrt{y}}{18} = \dfrac{3}{\sqrt{y}}$

$\Rightarrow \dfrac{21\sqrt{y}}{18} = \dfrac{3}{\sqrt{y}}$

$\Rightarrow y = \dfrac{3 \times 18}{21} = \dfrac{18}{7}$

$\therefore\ x < y$

46. (1) Principal $= \dfrac{35672 \times 100}{7 \times 8} = 63700$

$CI = 63700\left(1 + \dfrac{2}{100}\right)^2 - 63700$

$\qquad = $ Rs. 2,573.48.

Quicker Method:

Rate $= 2 + 2 \times \dfrac{2 \times 2}{100} = 4.04$

$CI = \dfrac{4.04 \times 63700}{100} = $ Rs. 2,573.48

47. (1) Number of girls $= 60 \times \dfrac{15}{100} = 9$

Total monthly fee of girls = 250 × 9 = Rs. 2,250

Number of boys = 60 − 9 = 51

Monthly fee of one boy $= 250 \times \dfrac{134}{100} = $ Rs. 335

Total monthly fees of boys = 51 × 335 = Rs. 17,085

$\therefore$ Sum = 17085 + 2250 = Rs. 19,335.

48. (1) Let Rita's present age be x years.

Her daughter's age = x/4 years

Her mother's age = 3/2 x years

Now, total sum of ages of Rita, her daughter and her mother = 154

$\Rightarrow x + \dfrac{x}{4} + \dfrac{3}{2}x = 154$

$\Rightarrow \dfrac{4x + x + 6x}{4} = 154$

$\Rightarrow 11x = 154 \times 4$

$\Rightarrow x = 56$ years.

Rita's mother's age $= \dfrac{3}{2} \times 56 = 84$ years

$\therefore$ Difference = 84 − 56 = 28 years.

49. (3) Quantity of rum in vessel A $= \dfrac{5}{8} \times 20 = 12.5$ L

Quantity of water in vessel A = 20 − 12.5 = 7.5 L

Quantity of rum in vessel B $= \dfrac{1}{6} \times 24 = 4$ L

Quantity of water in vessel B = 24 − 4 = 20 L

Quantity of rum in new vessel = 12.5 + 4

$\qquad\qquad\qquad = 16.5$ L

Quantity of water in new vessel = 7.5 + 20

$$= 27.5 \text{ L}$$

Required ratio = 16.5 : 27.5 = 3 : 5

50. (1) Let us assume that the selling price of the laptops be Rs. x and Rs. (17,550 – x) respectively.

$$\Rightarrow \frac{x}{1.15} = \frac{17,550 - x}{0.8}$$

$$\Rightarrow 0.8x = 1.15 \times 17,550 - 1.15x$$

$$\Rightarrow 1.95x = 1.15 \times 17,550$$

$$\Rightarrow x = \text{Rs}.10,350$$

$$\text{CP of the laptop} = \frac{10,350}{1.15} = \text{Rs}.9,000$$

$$\text{CP of the laptop} = \frac{17,550 - 10,350}{0.8}$$

$$= \frac{7200}{0.8} = \text{Rs}.9,000$$

Total cost price = Rs.9,000 + Rs.9,000

$$= \text{Rs}.18,000$$

51. (2)

$$21, \ 26, \ 33, \ \boxed{42}, \ 57, \ 74$$
$$5 \quad 7 \quad 9 \quad 15 \quad 17$$

The differences would form an appropriate series with prime numbers.

$$21, \ 26, \ 33, \ \boxed{44}, \ 57, \ 74$$
$$5 \quad 7 \quad 11 \quad 13 \quad 17$$

Hence, the wrong number in the series is 42, which should be replaced with 44.

52. (4)

$$80 \ , \ 150 \ , \ \boxed{180} \ , \ 392 \ , \ 576 \ , \ 810$$
$$4^3 + 4^2 \ \ 5^3 + 5^2 \ \ \boxed{6^3 - 6^2} \ \ 7^3 + 7^2 \ \ 8^3 + 8^2 \ \ 9^3 + 9^2$$

Each of the numbers follows $(n^3 + n^2)$ pattern, except 180 which follows $n^3 - n^2$ pattern. Hence, 180 is the wrong number which should be replaced with $6^3 + 6^2 = 252$.

53. (3)

$$\boxed{48}, \quad 56, \quad 71, \quad 106 \ , \quad 183, \quad 326$$
$$+(2\times3) \ +(3\times5) \ +(5\times7) \ +(7\times11) \ +(11\times13)$$

The differences are multiples of two consecutive primes. The other numbers follow the pattern, except 48, which should be replaced with 50, so that

$$50 + (2 \times 3) = 56.$$

54. (5)

$$1, \quad 2, \quad 66, \quad \boxed{102}, 794, \quad 1523, \quad 2523$$
$$1 \quad 64 \quad 36 \qquad 729 \quad 1000$$
$$(1)^3 \ (4)^3 \ (6)^2 \ (?) \quad (9)^3 \quad (10)^3$$

The differences between the consecutive numbers indicate pattern of cubes of non-prime numbers. Hence, the wrong number is 102, which should be replaced with 282 to make the series appropriate as shown below.

$$1, \quad 2, \quad 66, \quad \boxed{282}, \ 794, \ 1523, \ 2523$$
$$1 \quad 64 \quad 216 \quad 512 \quad 729 \quad 1000$$
$$(1)^3 \ (4)^3 \ (6)^3 \ (8)^3 \ (9)^3 \ (10)^3$$

55. (1)

$$41, \quad 43, \quad \boxed{83}, \quad 127, \qquad 211, \qquad 338, \qquad 549,$$
$$43 + 84 \quad 84 + 127 \quad 127 + 211 \quad 211 + 338$$

If we observe 4th term onwards, the pattern of the series indicates an .... addition series. Hence, 83 should be replaced with 84, as shown below, to make the series appropriate.

56. (2) In standard 7th, let there be x boys and y girls.

Number of boys passing = 0.8 x

Number of girls passing = 0.6 y

$$0.8 \ x = 0.6y$$

or, $$\frac{x}{y} = \frac{3}{4} \Rightarrow x : y = 3 : 4$$

57. (1) Let the total number of girls in 9th standard = x

Total number of boys passed = 200 × 0.4 = 80

Total number of girls passed = x × 0.6 = 0.6x

$$\therefore \ \text{Passed percentage of students} = \frac{80 + 0.6x}{200 + x}$$

$$\Rightarrow \frac{44}{100} = \frac{80 + 0.6x}{200 + x}$$

$$\Rightarrow 8800 + 44x = 8000 + 60x$$

$$\rightarrow 16x = 800$$

$$\Rightarrow x = 50.$$

58. (4) There are 6 classes in all, total number of students

$$= 6 \times (150 + 120) = 1620$$

Overall pass percentage

$$= \frac{[150 \ (0.8 + 0.8 + 0.4 + 0.9 + 0.7 + 0.7] + 120 \ (0.6 + 0.7 + 0.6 + 0.6 + 0.8 + 0.6)]}{1620} \times 100$$

$$= \frac{645 + 468}{1620} \times 100 = \frac{1113}{1620} \times 100$$

$$= 69\% \text{(approx.)}$$

59. (2) Let there be 400 boys and 100 girls in standard 11th

Number of boys passed = 0.7 × 400 = 280

Number of girls passed = 0.8 × 100 = 80

Required ratio = 280 : 80 = 7 : 2.

60. (1) Required average of marks

$$\frac{50 \times 150 + 120 \times 60}{150 + 120} = \frac{14700}{270} = 54.44\%$$

61. (4) 54.35 × 39.87 ÷ 13.35

$$\approx 54 \times 40 \div 13$$

$$\approx 168$$

62. (5) $? = \sqrt{3219} \times \sqrt{4178}$

$$\approx 56 \times 64 \approx 3591$$

63. (1) ? = (749 – 325 – 124) ÷ (1254 – 1100)

$$= 300 \div 154$$

$$\approx 2$$

64. (5) $? = \dfrac{47 \times 47}{3.25} \times 2.5 \approx 1699$

65. (2) $? = \dfrac{115}{100} \times 624 + \dfrac{2}{7} \times 419$

$$\approx 717 + 120$$

$$\approx 837$$

For questions 66 to 70:

Person	Floor	Colour of car
P	6	Yellow
Q	9	Blue
R	1	Grey
S	4	Orange
T	2	White
M	7	Green
N	5	Red
O	8	Black
J	3	Pink

71. (4)

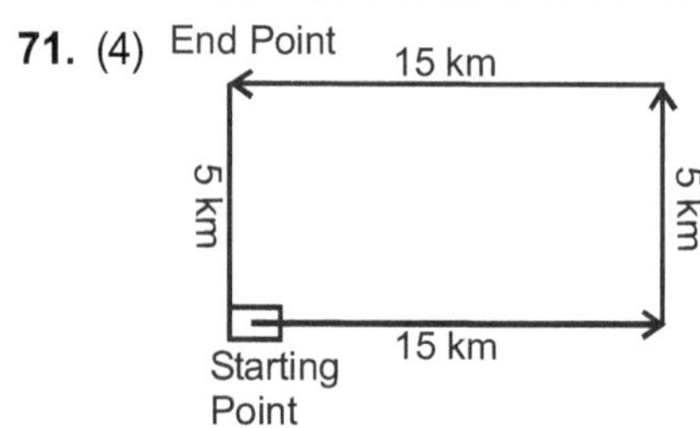

Amit is 5 km away from the starting opint.

72. (1)

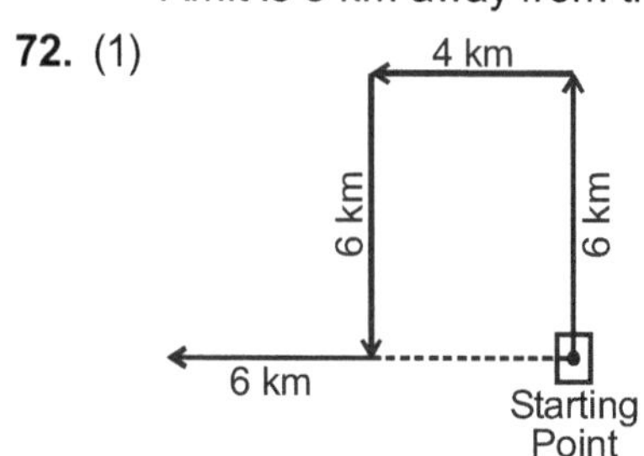

It is clear from the diagram that the man is 10 km towards west from the starting point.

73. (3) Grandson of Arun's mother means either son or nephew of Arun. Therefore, Arun is the father-in-law of that girl.

74. (2) Maya's mother is the sister of Ranjeet. So, Ranjeet is the maternal uncle of Maya.

75. (4) Only son of Bhaskar's father means Bhaskar himself. Therefore, Asha is the daughter of Bhaskar.

For questions 76 to 80: The codes for the following words can be determined from the statements given as :

more	money	in	market	share	profit	making	now	the	gains
zo	aa	to	li	vo	je	ka	su	yo/do	do/yo

For questions 81 to 85:

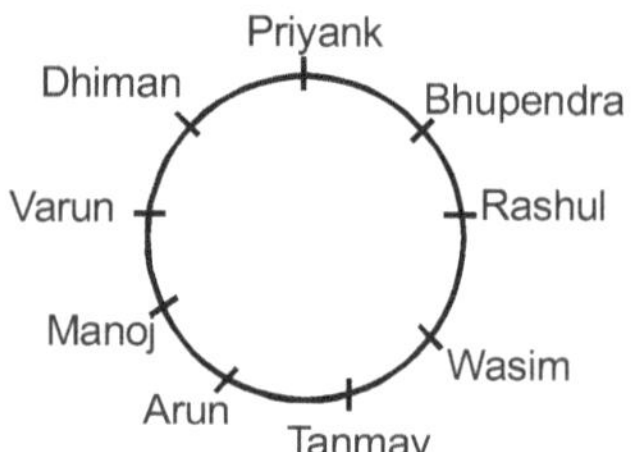

81. (1) 82. 2   83. 4 84. 4

85. (2) In all pairs except Rashul, Priyank, the second person is sitting on the left of the first person.

86. (5) E@F, C&E, D$C

$$\Rightarrow E = F, C \geq E, D < C$$

$$\Rightarrow C \geq E = F, C > D$$

Conclusion I: C#F $\Rightarrow$ C > F may or may not follow.

Conclusion II: D@E $\Rightarrow$ D = E does not follow.

Hence, neither conclusion I nor conclusion II follows.

87. (3) Y#Z, V@Z, U$V

$$\Rightarrow Y > Z, V = Z, U < V$$

$$\Rightarrow Y > Z = V > U$$

Conclusion I: Y#V $\Rightarrow$ Y > V follows.

Conclusion II: U$Z $\Rightarrow$ U < Z follows.

Hence, both conclusions follow.

88. (4) N%Q, M&P, Q@P

$$\Rightarrow N \leq Q, M \geq P, Q = P$$

$$\Rightarrow M \geq P = Q \geq N$$

Conclusion I: P@N $\Rightarrow$ P = N may or may not follow.

Conclusion II: N$Q $\Rightarrow$ N < Q may or may not follow.

Hence, either conclusion I or conclusion II follows.

89. (2) R$T , S#X, T%X

$\Rightarrow$ R < T, S > X, T $\leq$ X

$\Rightarrow$ S > X $\geq$ T > R

Conclusion I: S&T $\Rightarrow$ S $\geq$ T does not follow.

Conclusion II: X#R $\Rightarrow$ X > R follows.

Hence, only conclusion II follows.

90. (1) H&K, G%L, H#G

$\Rightarrow$ H $\geq$ K, G $\leq$ L, H > G

Conclusion I: G$H $\Rightarrow$ G < H follows.

Conclusion II: K&G $\Rightarrow$ K $\geq$ G does not follow.

Hence, only conclusion I follows.

For questions 91 to 95:

All the given information can be represented as:

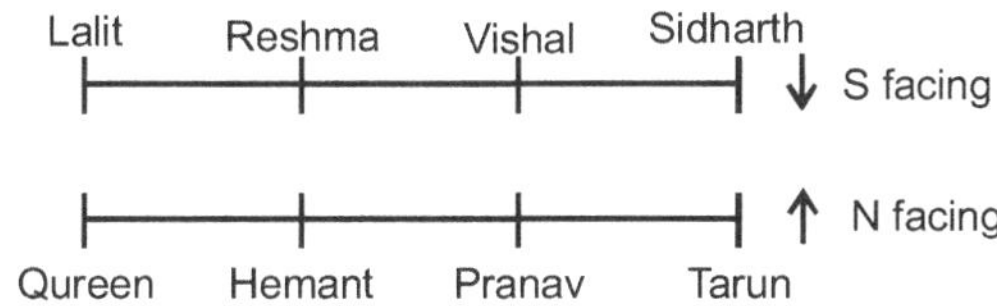

96. (1) 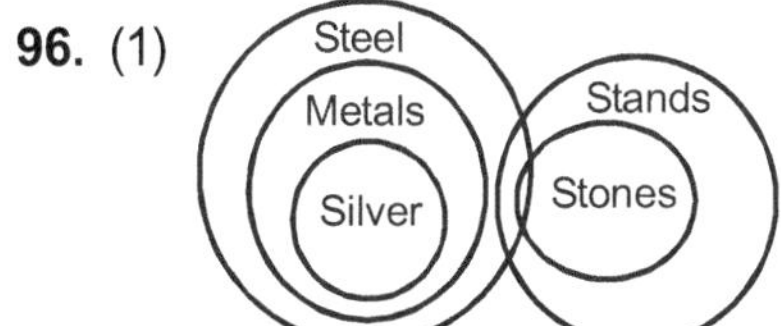

97. (1) 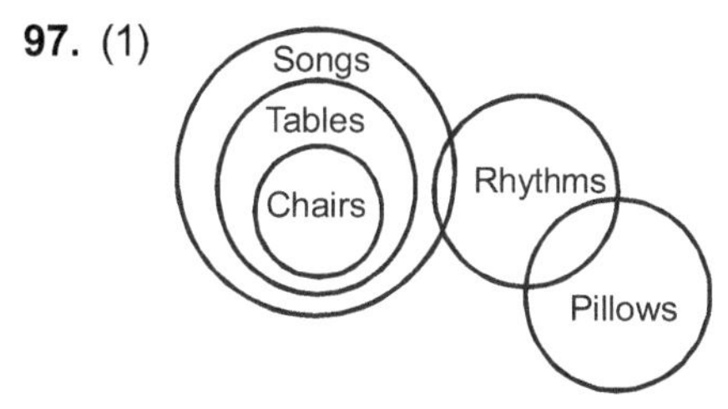

98. (5) 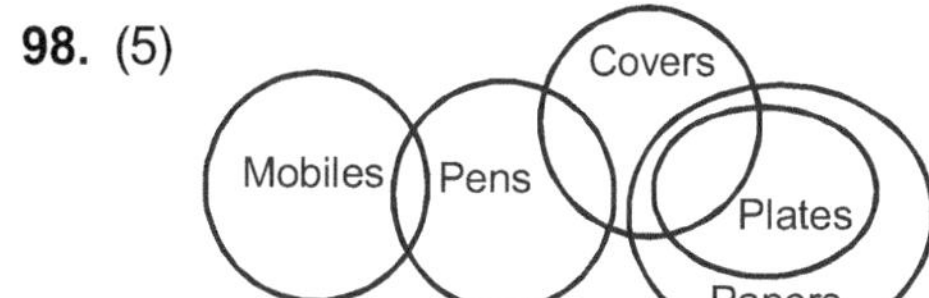

99. (2) 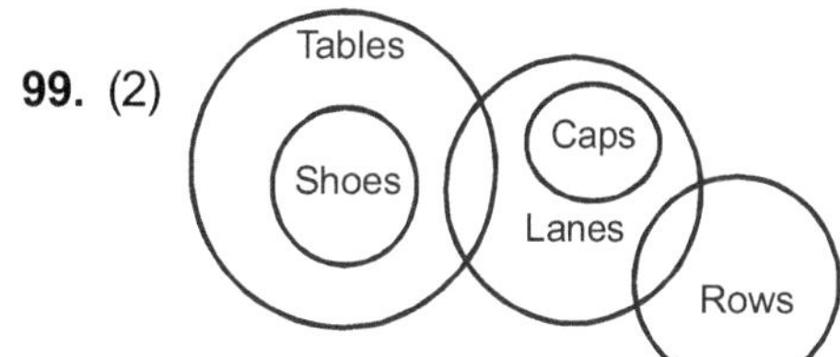

100. (5) 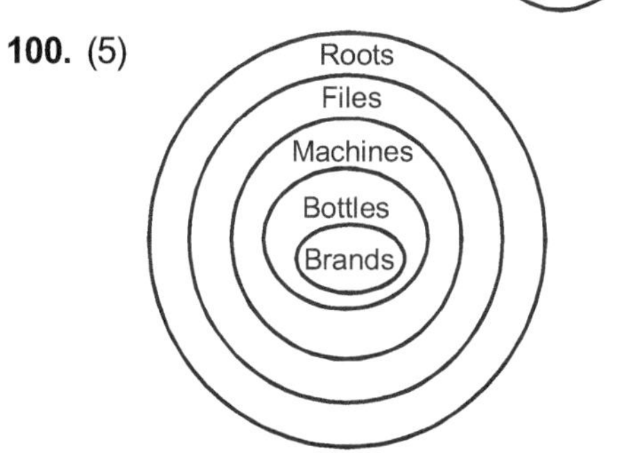

PRACTICE PAPER – 3

Directions (Q. 1 to 5): Fill in the blanks by choosing the most appropriate options.

1. Yesterday ____ European came ____ my office.
   - (1) a, to
   - (2) an, to
   - (3) the, in
   - (4) a, on
   - (5) an, above

2. At the eleventh hour, he retired _____ the contest, leaving the field open _____ his opponent.
   - (1) until, to
   - (2) from, to
   - (3) beyond, from
   - (4) till, to
   - (5) till, for

3. He impressed _____ them that sorcery was vital _____ their success.
   - (1) to, from
   - (2) on, with
   - (3) in, above
   - (4) to, from
   - (5) upon, for

4. This ticket will entitle you _____ a free seat _____ the concert.
   - (1) from, to
   - (2) to, above
   - (3) to, at
   - (4) into, for
   - (5) in, on

5. We are accountable _____ God _____ our actions.
   - (1) on, for
   - (2) before, to make
   - (3) to, for
   - (4) to, from
   - (5) for, from

Directions (Q. 6 to 10): Read each sentence to find out whether there is any grammatical error or idiomatic error in it. The error, if any, will be in one part of the sentence. The number of that part is the answer. If there is 'No error', the answer is (5). (Ignore errors of punctuation, if any).

6. The transit system's underground (1) / tunnels and stations will (2) / be constructed (3) / next heritage structures (4). / No error (5)

7. Residents have been planting (1) / the ornamental trees outside (2) / their homes and in lawns to (3) / add beauty and give their place a grand look (4). / No error (5)

8. A diamond jeweller's peon (1) / tipped off a gang (2) / about the gold (3) / in his employer's vault (4). / No error (5)

9. He said that the performance of the Indian team (1) / was satisfactory at the international meet (2) / and that they learnt a lot from (3) / watching top seeded players through action at the grand slam (4). / No error (5)

10. Watching the exponential (1) / talent of world tennis (2) / was the best things (3) / to happen to him. (4) / No error (5)

Directions (Q. 11 to 15): In the following passage there are blanks, each of which has been numbered. These numbers are printed below the passage and against each, five words are suggested, one of which fits the blank appropriate. Find out the appropriate word in each case.

One of the good things that happened to me __(11)__ in Patliputra, was the friendship of the farmer's daughter. This nine year old girl __(12)__ became very fond of me and her parents promised her that she could keep me forever as her toy. She was very good at needlecraft and __(13)__ clothes for her doll. In fact, on my first night there and during the rest of my stay in the farmer's house, I slept in her doll's cradle. That first night, they put the cradle on __(14)__ of a shelf far away from the danger of rats. As I slowly got to learn their language, I was able to talk to the girl and let her know my needs and she was able to make me __(15)__ comfortable. She made me seven shirts and was my teacher of the language. When I pointed to anything, she would call it by name, and soon I was able to talk easily with her.

11. (1) waiting
    - (2) truly
    - (3) till
    - (4) still
    - (5) while

12. (1) soon
    - (2) had
    - (3) was
    - (4) has
    - (5) forever

13. (1) tore
    - (2) tearing
    - (3) making
    - (4) wore
    - (5) make

14. (1) bottom
    - (2) top
    - (3) coating
    - (4) height
    - (5) wide

15. (1) every
    - (2) thorough
    - (3) total
    - (4) high
    - (5) more

Directions (Q. 16 to 20): Rearrange the following six sentences (A) , (B) , (C) , (D) , (E) and (F) in the proper sequence to form, a meaningful paragraph; then answer the questions given below thenm.

(A) The emperor was impressed with me and rewarded me suitably

(B) He then asked me to make it shorter without erasing its ends.

(C) One fine day the king decided to test my intelligence.

(D) By doing so, I could make the line shorter without erasing the ends.

(E) After thinking over it for some time, I drew longer lines on both the ends of the line that the emperor had drawn.

(F) He drew a line on the floor with the help of a chalk.

16. Which of the following should be the **FOURTH** sentence after rearrangement?

  (1) (B)   (2) (C)

  (3) (D)   (4) (E)

  (5) (F)

17. Which of the following should be the **THIRD** sentence after rearrangement?

  (1) (A)   (2) (B)

  (3) (C)   (4) (D)

  (5) (E)

18. Which of the following should be the **FIRST** sentence after rearrangement?

  (1) (A)   (2) (B)

  (3) (C)   (4) (D)

  (5) (E)

19. Which of the following should be the **LAST (SIXTH)** sentence after rearrangement?

  (1) (A)   (2) (B)

  (3) (C)   (4) (D)

  (5) (E)

20. Which of the following should be the **SECOND** sentence after rearrangement?

  (1) (B)   (2) (C)

  (3) (D) (4) (E)

  (5) (F)

Directions (Q. 21 to 30): Read the following passage carefully and answer the questions given below it. Certain words have been printed in bold to help you locate them while answering some of the questions.

The elimination of war, violence, and armed conflict has been a political and humanitarian objective of the global community. Yet that objective remains unachieved. War-related health threats are a rising concern as the number of people forced to flee their homes due to violent conflict has currently exceeded 51 million, the highest levels since the Second World War. This includes both internally displaced persons and refugees. Half of these are children. The United Nations High Commissioner for Refugees, António Guterres, has pointed out that humanitarian efforts cannot **quell** this magnitude of human suffering: "We are seeing here the immense costs of not ending wars, of failing to resolve or prevent conflict." Right to life in peace is an essential condition for the realization of the right to health. As such, the path toward international recognition of the right to life in peace is worthy of the attention and support of health professionals. First, we discuss the draft Declaration on the Right to Life in Peace that is currently being advanced within the UN Human Rights Council (HRC). We then refer briefly to the approach proposed by the Chairperson-Rapporteur of the Open-Ended Working Group on the right to life in peace in pursuit of the necessary consensus among different stakeholders on this topic. Next, we analyze the notion of violence as a public health problem, focusing on collective violence in particular. Barriers to realization of the right to health in a context of direct, structural, and cultural violence will be addressed. We discuss the relationship between the rights to life, health, and peace and analyze human dignity as a foundational core of these rights. Finally, we address the role health professionals play in the promotion of peace, including the need for cultural transformation. The HRC has been working on the "Promotion of the Right to Peace" since 2008. This proposed declaration has been inspired by previous resolutions on this issue approved by the UN General Assembly and the former UN Commission on Human Rights, particularly the General Assembly Resolutions on the "Declaration on the Preparation of Societies for Life in Peace" in 1978 and the "Declaration on the Right of Peoples to Peace" in 1984. In 2010, the HRC adopted a resolution asking the HRC Advisory Committee to prepare a draft declaration on the right of peoples to peace, in consultation with relevant stakeholders.

In 2012, the HRC established an Open-Ended Working Group (OEWG) "with the mandate of progressively negotiating a draft UN Declaration on the Right to Peace, on the basis of the draft submitted by the Advisory Committee, and without prejudging relevant past, present and future views and proposals." The OEWG is composed of representatives from States, civil society organizations, and other stakeholders. During its first session, the OEWG concluded that the existence of a right to peace was recognized by some governmental delegations and other stakeholders, who argued that some soft-law instruments already acknowledge this right. However, other stakeholders insisted that a right to peace does not exist under international law. From their perspective, peace is not a stand-alone human right, but the consequence of the full realization of all human rights. In June 2013, the HRC adopted a resolution asking the Chairperson-Rapporteur of the OEWG to prepare a new text on the right to peace and to present it prior to the second session of the working group for further discussion. The revised text was to be based on the OEWG's first session along with informal intersessional consultations. Following this, extensive consultations took place with stakeholder representatives worldwide, culminating in a new approach and draft Declaration.

The new approach is based on the relationship between the right to life and human rights, peace, and development, the notion of human dignity, the role of women in building peace, and the importance of prevention of armed conflicts in accordance with the UN Charter and other UN resolutions and international law. The Declaration not only recalls the linkage between the right to life and peace, but it also **explicates** and strengthens the right to life in connection to peace, human rights, and development. The approach was also inspired by the values and principles contained in the World Health Organization (WHO) Constitution and further elaborated in the international health legal system. It promotes the use of existing rights already consolidated in international law. The second session of the OEWG in 2014 had broad dialogue among relevant stakeholders including representatives of governments, regional groups, and civil society. The Chairperson Rapporteur proposed to further refine the declaration text through input from that meeting, along with additional stakeholder consultations, and the HRC later passed a resolution to this effect with the goal of finalizing the Declaration in 2015.The WHO was **incepted** with the spirit of promoting the health of all peoples and recognizes in the Preamble of its Constitution that health and peace are interrelated notions, stating that, "the health of all peoples is fundamental to the **attainment** of peace and security and is dependent upon the fullest co-operation of individuals and States." Violence has devastating consequences on human health, affecting both combatants and civilians. While some of the morbidity and mortality relates to the direct effects of violence, much of the civilian health impact is due to indirect consequences such as displacement and limited access to food, clean water, and health care. Even after a conflict has resolved, the affected population frequently suffers **repercussions** of physical and mental trauma.

Health care services are often constrained by disrupted infrastructure. Moreover, the spending on military operations may deplete funding for provision of health services. It is important to note that there are many other forms of violence that impact human health. These include abuse of children, intimate partner violence, sexual violence, elder abuse, self-directed violence, and youth violence. Indeed, homicide is the third-largest cause of death among young people aged 15-24 in the US. In addition to the direct effects of violence, exposure to violence during childhood is linked with chronic illness, such as asthma, and poorer health later in life.

21. Which of the following statement/s is/are true in the context of the passage?

    A. The Open Ended Working Group comprises only of representatives of states and civil society organisations.

    B. Armed conflicts have not been totally eliminated.

    C. Number of people forced to flee their homes because of wars has exceeded half a billion.

    (1) Only A   (2) Only (A) and (B)

    (3) Only (B) and (C)   (4) Only (B)

    (5) All (A), (B) and (C)

22. Which of the following is/are true in the light of the passage?

    A. The proposal pertaining to the "Promotion of the Right to Peace" by the UN Human Rights Council was the first of its kind resolutions drafted by the UN.

    B. War violence has catastrophic consequences on human health, affecting both soldiers and civilians.

    C. Homicide is the largest cause of death among young people aged 15-24 in the US.

    (1) Only (A)   (2) Only (A) and (B)

    (3) Only (B) and (C)   (4) Only (B)

    (5) All (A), (B) and (C)

23. What according to the author indirectly affects civilian health?

    (1) Restricted access to food, clean water and proper medical attention.

    (2) Excessive increase in the price of food items.

    (3) Lack of proper governance.

    (4) The negative influence of cultural violence.

    (5) High rate of taxes imposed by governments during war times.

24. Which of the following is possibly the most appropriate title for the passage?

    (1) The Right to Life in Peace: An Essential Condition for Realising the Right to Health

    (2) War and its Profound Negative Influence on Humanity

    (3) Role of UN in Promoting Public Health

    (4) The Problem of Refugees in Today's World

    (5) Hurdles Faced by Health Care Services

25. Which of the following depicts an indirect outcome of displacement?

    (1) Lack of proper education opportunities

    (2) Absence of strong cultural codes of conduct

    (3) Gender based violence is one of the effects

    (4) Child labour is often the result of a war ravaged country

    (5) Civilian health problems are indirect results of displacement.

Directions (Q. 26 to 28): Choose the word/group of words which is most similar to the word given in bold as used in the passage.

26. Repercussion

    (1) Influence   (2) Assent

    (3) Consent   (4) Consequence

    (5) Cause

27. Incepted

    (1) Constituted   (2) Arrested

    (3) Spirited   (4) Promoted

    (5) Related

28. Attainment

    (1) Failure   (2) Provocation

    (3) Drafting   (4) Elementary

    (5) Fulfilment

Directions (Q. 29 and 30): Choose the word/group of words which is most opposite in meaning to the word given in bold as used in the passage.

29. Explicate

    (1) Analyse   (2) Develop

    (3) Obfuscate   (4) Clarify

    (5) Demystify

30. Quell

    (1) Suppress   (2) Quash

    (3) Annihilate   (4) Incite

    (5) Extinguish

NUMERICAL ABILITY

31. The distance between Kanpur-Central and Mumbai is 750 km. Two trains simultaneously leave from Kanpur-Central and Mumbai. After they met, the train traveling towards Mumbai reached there after 9 hours, while train traveling towards Kanpur–Central reaches there after 4 hours. What is the speed of the train running towards Mumbai? (Assume that the speeds of both the trains remains constant)

    (1) 50 km/hr   (2) 75 km/hr

    (3) 60 km/hr   (4) 40 km/hr

    (5) 54 km/hr

32. A contractor employs 4 men, 6 women and 8 children to complete a certain job for Rs. 910. If their individual earnings are in the ratio of 4 : 2 : 3, then what is the sum of total money earned by women and children?

    (1) Rs.630   (2) Rs.700

    (3) Rs. 490   (4) Rs.570

    (5) None of these

33. The breadth of a rectangular hall is three-fourth of its length. If the area of the floor is 768 m^2, then the difference between the length and breadth of the hall is:

    (1) 8 metres   (2) 12 metres

    (3) 24 metres   (4) 32 metres

    (5) 16 metres

34. In how many different ways can the letters of the word 'BANKING' be arranged so that the vowels always come together?

    (1) 120   (2) 240

    (3) 360   (4) 540

    (5) 720

35. A sum of Rs. 221 is divided among X, Y and Z such that X gets Rs. 52 more than Y. Y gets Rs. 26 more than Z. The ratio of the shares of X, Y and Z respectively is :

    (1) 9 : 5 : 3   (2) 9 : 3 : 5

    (3) 5 : 9 : 3   (4) 10 : 6 : 5

    (5) None of these

36. Gaurav deposits an amount of Rs.7,200 in two parts on SI. He deposits one part at 8% per annum for 3 years and another part at 6% per annum for 2 years. If he receives Rs.1,200 as interest from both the amounts, then what were the amounts?

    (1) Rs.2,400, Rs.4,800

    (2) Rs.2,800, Rs. 4,400

    (3) Rs.4,200, Rs.3,000

    (4) Rs.5,600, Rs.1,600

    (5) None of these

37. In an exam 1100 boys and 900 girls appeared. If 50% of the boys and 40% of the girls passed the exam, then what is the percentage of failed candidates?

    (1) 45%

    (2) 45.5%

    (3) 54.5%

    (4) 59.2%

    (5) 48.5%

38. In 2005, I was one more than eleven times as old as my son. In 2014, I was seven more than three times as old as him. The age of my son in 2005 was?

   (1) 4 years   (2) 3 years

   (3) 8 years   (4) 5 years

   (5) None of these

39. A beaker contains milk and water in the ratio 5 : 3. If a person removes 6 L of this mixture and replaces it with pure water, the ratio of milk to water becomes 1 : 1 the amount of milk present in beaker initially is

   (1) 18.75 L   (2) 16.25 L

   (3) 20 L   (4) 18 L

   (5) 21 L

40. A dealer allows his customer a discount of 25% and still gains 25%. If the cost price of radio is Rs. 1,440, then it's marked price is

   (1) Rs. 2,500   (2) Rs. 2,440

   (3) Rs. 2,400   (4) Rs. 2,020

   (5) None of these

Directions (Q. 41 to 45) : Answer the following questions based on the given information.

The table given below shows the number of bottles of different types of cold-drinks consumed at the cafeteria's of different colleges in a year. Each cold-drink bottle of any type measures 300 ml.

College Name	Limca	Pepsi	Coke	Thumbs-up	Sprite
P	877	546	211	244	655
Q	234	454	545	215	534
R	451	321	452	254	574
S	248	654	328	214	353
T	874	545	565	540	653
U	324	564	144	685	257

41. Among the given type of cold-drinks, which type was consumed maximum by all the colleges put together in the given year?

   (1) Coke   (2) Pepsi

   (3) Limca   (4) Sprite

   (5) Thumbs-up

42. By what percentage was the total number of Pepsi bottles consumed more or less than the number of Limca bottles consumed in that year?

   (1) 3.02%

   (2) 1.76%

   (3) 4.53%

   (4) 102.46%

   (5) None of these

43. If each 300 ml bottle of any type costs Rs. 9.50, then what is the maximum amount spent on cold-drink by any college in that year?

   (1) Rs. 30,181.50   (2) Rs. 33,563.50

   (3) Rs. 28,994   (4) Rs. 31,546

   (5) None of these

44. What is the ratio between the number of bottles consumed in College R and College Q in that year?

   (1) 1.30 : 1   (2) 1.76 : 1

   (3) 0.53 : 1   (4) 1.03 : 1

   (5) 0.63 : 1

45. What is the difference between the quantity (in litres) of Limca to the quantity of Thumbs-up consumed by all the colleges in that year?

   (1) 302 L   (2) 276 L

   (3) 257 L   (4) 354 L

   (5) 198 L

Directions (Q. 46 to 50): In each of the following questions two questions are given. You have to solve both the questions and find out values of x and y and give answer.

(1) if $x > y$

(2) if $x < y$

(3) if $x \geq y$

(4) if $x \leq y$

(5) if $x = y$ or relationship cannot be established

46. I. $3x + 2y = 301$

   II. $7x - 5y = 74$

47. I. $6x + 7y = 52$

   II. $14x + 4y = 35$

48. I. $x^2 = 64$

   II. $2y^2 + 25y + 72 = 0$

49. I. $7x + 3y = 26$

   II. $2x + 17y = -41$

50. I. $3x + 8y = -2$

   II. $4x + 18y = 1$

Directions (Q. 51 to 55): In each of the following questions, find the odd man out.

51. 45,   72,   104,   132,   187,   240

   (1) 72   (2) 132

   (3) 240   (4) 187

   (5) 104

52. 78,   343,   658,   1060,   1550,   2138

   (1) 658   (2) 1550

   (3) 78   (4) 1060

   (5) 343

53. 36, 232, 440, 663, 804, 1166

   (1) 804   (2) 440

   (3) 663   (4) 1166

   (5) 232

54. 76, 98, 156, 257, 401, 601

   (1) 156   (2) 257

   (3) 76   (4) 401

   (5) 98

55. 17, 31, 77, 175, 345, 507

   (1) 175   (2) 77

   (3) 31   (4) 507

   (5) 345

Directions (Q. 56 to 60): Answer the following questions based on the given information.

There are 7200 students in a Medical Institute. The ratio of boys to girls is 7 : 5 respectively. All the students are enrolled in six different courses. B.Sc. (Nursing), B. Pharma, B.A.M.S., B.M.L.T., B.D.S. and M.B.B.S. 22 percent of the total numbers of students are in B.D.S. 16 percent of the girls are in B. Pharma. 18 percent of the boys are in B.A.M.S. Girls in M.B.B.S are 30 percent of the girls in B. Pharma. 15 percent of the boys are in B. Sc. Nursing. Boys in B. Pharma are 50 percent of the girls in the same. 15 percent of the girls are in B.M.L.T. The ratio of boys to girls in the M.B.B.S. is 3 : 1 respectively. 24 percent of the total number of students are in B. Sc. Nursing. The ratio of boys to girls in the B.M.L.T. is 12 : 5 respectively.

56. What is the total number of students enrolled in B.A.M.S. ?

   (1) 1062   (2) 1530

   (3) 1728   (4) 1584

   (5) None of these

57. What is the total number of boys enrolled in BDS?

   (1) 1080   (2) 1530

   (3) 756   (4) 1062

   (5) None of these

58. What is the total number of girls enrolled in BAMS and BDS together?

   (1) 972   (2) 666

   (3) 828   (4) 786

   (5) None of these

59. What is the respective ratio between the number of boys enrolled in B.Sc. (Nursing) to that enrolled in BMLT?

   (1) 2 : 9   (2) 7 : 12

   (3) 4 : 7   (4) 11 : 17

   (5) None of these

60. Total number of students enrolled in BMLT forms approximately what percent of the total number of students in the institute?

   (1) 21.25%

   (2) 22%

   (3) 15%

   (4) 14.75%

   (5) None of these

Directions (Q. 61 to 65): What approximate value will come in place of the question mark (?) in the following questions? (You are not expected to calculate the exact value.)

61. $5687.285 + 4872.35 \div 12 = ?$

   (1) 5995   (2) 5905

   (3) 6025   (4) 6095

   (5) 6295

62. $(35.95)^2 - (24.001)^2 = ?$

   (1) 680   (2) 700

   (3) 720   (4) 740

   (5) 730

63. $367.85 \div 22.95 \times 14.99 = ?$

   (1) 280   (2) 240

   (3) 260   (4) 220

   (5) 290

64. 75% of $430 - ? = 64\%$ of 249

   (1) 140   (2) 175

   (3) 220   (4) 165

   (5) 207

65. $(24.99)^2 + (31.05)^2 = (?)^2$

   (1) 45   (2) 36

   (3) 32   (4) 30

   (5) 40

REASONING ABILITY

66. Raghav starts walking towards South. After walking 10 m he turns towards his left and walks for 40 m. After that he again turns to his left and walks for 80 m. Finally, he turns towards his right and walks for 30 m before stopping. What is the minimum distance between his starting point and the end point?

   (1) $70\sqrt{2}$ m

   (2) $65\sqrt{2}$ m

   (3) 70 m

   (4) 140 m

   (5) None of these

67. Rohan walked 20 m towards East, took a right turn and walked 10 m. He then took a right turn and walked 9 m, again took a right turn to walk 5 m and again took a left turn and walked 12 m and finally took a right turn and walked 6 m. How far and in which direction is he from his starting point?

(1) $2\sqrt{2}$ m, South   (2) $2\sqrt{2}$ m, North

(3) $\sqrt{2}$ m, South-east   (4) $\sqrt{2}$ m, North-west

(5) None of these

68. If **A + B** means "A is the sister of B", **A × B** means "A is the wife of B", **A ÷ B** means "A is the father of B" and **A − B** means "A is the brother of B", then which of following expresses the relationship that "T is the daughter of P"?

(1) P × Q ÷ R + S − T   (2) P × Q ÷ R − T + S

(3) P × Q ÷ R + T − S   (4) P × Q ÷ R + S + T

(5) None of these

69. If A*B means A is father of B, A^B means A is mother of B, A@B means A is sister of B, then how is P related to Q in P^L*M@Q?

(1) Grandmother   (2) Granddaughter

(3) Nephew   (4) Data inadequate

(5) None of these

70. In a new year party, pointing to Gopi a woman said, "He is the father of my mother's son's only sister's son". How is Gopi related to woman?

(1) Brother-in-law   (2) Husband

(3) Wife   (4) Brother

(5) Son

Directions (Q.71-75): Study the following information to answer the given questions:

Out of five friends – Aman, Boman, Chaman, Dhaman and Eraman – two are businessmen while the other three belong to three different professions among Doctor, Engineer and Lawyer. A Cloth Merchant and a Lawyer stay in the same city Mumbai while the other three stay in three different cities – Delhi, Chennai and Kolkata. Two of these five friends are Hindu while the remaining three belong to three different communities – Muslim, Christian and Sikh.

It is also known that:

(i) One of the businessmen runs a Factory while the other is a Cloth Merchant.

(ii) Boman is a Sikh.

(iii) Dhaman is a Hindu.

(iv) Eraman runs a Factory and he does not live in Mumbai.

(v) Aman lives in Kolkata while Boman lives in Delhi.

(vi) Engineer is a Hindu.

(vii) Cloth Merchant is a Christian.

71. What is the occupation of Chaman?

(1) Lawyer   (2) Cloth Merchant

(3) Engineer   (4) Runs a Factory

(5) Doctor

72. Which of the following pairs stays in Mumbai?

(1) a Hindu and a Doctor

(2) a Sikh and a Lawyer

(3) Dhaman and an Engineer

(4) Chaman and a Lawyer

(5) None of these

73. Who is a Doctor?

(1) Chaman   (2) a Hindu

(3) Boman   (4) Eraman

(5) None of these

74. What is the occupation of Dhaman?

(1) Lawyer   (2) Doctor

(3) Engineer   (4) Runs a Factory

(5) Cloth Merchant

75. Who stays in Kolkata?

(1) a Sikh   (2) a Hindu

(3) a Christian   (4) a Muslim

(5) Cannot be determined

Directions (Q. 76-80): Answer the questions on the basis of the information given below.

In a certain code language.

(i) "simple game no rules" is written as "ro sa bi ka".

(ii) "no game played now" is written as "ka za bi te".

(iii) "why no rules given" is written as "ro fo ce ka".

(iv) "now we were given" is written as "ge te fo li".

76. What is the code for "now"?

(1) fo   (2) te

(3) ge   (4) ka

(5) li

77. What is the code for "game"?

(1) za   (2) sa

(3) ro   (4) bi

(5) ka

78. Which of the following is coded as 'ce'?

(1) why   (2) no

(3) rules   (4) given

(5) Cannot be determined

79. What is the code for "rules"?

    (1) fo   (2) sa

    (3) ro   (4) ka

    (5) bi

80. Which of the following is coded as 'fo' ?

    (1) why   (2) given

    (3) we   (4) rules

    (5) were

Directions (Q. 81-85): Study the given information carefully and answer the questions that follow.

Seven persons – A, B, C, D, E, F and G – of different ages – are standing in a row facing North.

It is also known that:

(i) The oldest person has as many persons to his left as to his right.

(ii) The youngest person is standing at the extreme left end of the row. The second youngest person is standing at the extreme right end of the row.

(iii) F is younger than C, who is standing immediately to the left of E.

(iv) There are exactly two persons between D and G, but E is not one of them.

(v) A is younger than G, who is not the oldest.

(vi) Neither D nor G is the youngest. E is not the second youngest.

(vii) F is older than E, but younger than B.

81. Who is the oldest person of the group?

    (1) C   (2) D

    (3) B   (4) F

    (5) None of these

82. How many persons are standing between C and G?

    (1) 3   (2) 2

    (3) 5   (4) 4

    (5) None of these

83. Who are the immediate neighbours of E?

    (1) F and B   (2) F and D

    (3) C and D   (4) A and C

    (5) None of these

84. How many different standing arrangement(s) can be formed?

    (1) 2   (2) 3

    (3) 1   (4) 4

    (5) None of these

85. Who is standing immediately to the left of D?

    (1) E   (2) C

    (3) B   (4) F

    (5) None of these

Directions (Q. 86-90): In the following questions, the symbols %, @, #, $ and & are used with the following meaning as illustrated below:

'P%Q' means 'P is neither smaller than nor equal to Q'.

'P@Q' means 'P is neither greater than nor equal to Q'.

'P#Q' means 'P is not greater than Q'.

'P$Q' means 'P is not smaller than Q'.

'P&Q' means 'P is neither smaller than nor greater than Q'.

Now in each of the following questions, assuming the given statements to be true, find which of the four conclusions I, II, III and IV given below them is/are definitely true and give your answer accordingly.

86. Statements : A%B, B$D, D&F, F@H

    Conclusions : I.   B%F

                    II.   D@A

                    III. H%D

                    IV. H#B

    (1) Only I   (2) Only II

    (3) Both II & III   (4) I, II & III

    (5) All I, II, III & IV

87. Statements : R&S, S#T, T%U, U$V

    Conclusions : I.   T&R

                    II.   U%S

                    III. V@T

                    IV. R#U

    (1) Only II   (2) Only I

    (3) Only IV   (4) Only III

    (5) None of these

88. Statements : K@L, L$M, M#N, N&J

    Conclusions : I.   J$M

                    II.   L&M

                    III. N#L

                    IV. L%K

    (1) Both I & IV   (2) Only I

    (3) Only IV   (4) I, II & IV

    (5) I, III & IV

89. Statements : C#E, G%E, R$G, R@W

    Conclusions : I.   R%E

                    II.   G&C

                    III. C@W

                    IV. R$E

    (1) Both I & II   (2) Both I & III

    (3) Both II & III   (4) I, II & III

    (5) I, III & IV

90. Statements : X$Y, Y%W, W&K, K@Z

    Conclusions : I. Z@W

               II. X%K

               III. Y&Z

               IV. Y@X

   (1) Only IV   (2) Both I & II

   (3) Both II & IV   (4) Both II & III

   (5) None of these

Directions (Q. 91-95) : Study the information and answer the questions given below :

Eight people-E, F, G, H, J, K, L and M are sitting around a circular table facing the centre. Each of them is of a different profession - Chartered Accountant, Columnist, Doctor, Engineer, Financial Analyst, Lawyer, Professor and Scientist but not necessarily in the same order. F is sitting second to the left of K. The Scientist is an immediate neighbour of K. There are only three people between the Scientist and E. Only one person sits between the Engineer and E. The Columnist is to the immediate right of the Engineer. M is second to the right of K. H is the Scientist. G and J are immediate neighbours of each other. Neither G nor J is an Engineer. The Financial Analyst is to the immediate left of F. The Lawyer is second to the right of the Columnist. The Professor is an immediate neighbour of the Engineer. G is second to the right of the Chartered Accountant.

91. Who is sitting second to the right of E?

   (1) The Lawyer   (2) G

   (3) The Engineer   (4) F

   (5) K

92. Who amongst the following is the Professor?

   (1) F   (2) L

   (3) M   (4) K

   (5) J

93. Four of the following five are alike in a certain way based on the given arrangement and hence form a group. Which of the following does not belong to that group?

   (1) Chartered Accountant - H

   (2) M - Doctor

   (3) J - Lawyer

   (4) Financial Analyst - L

   (5) Lawyer - K

94. What is the position of L with respect to the Scientist?

   (1) Third to the left

   (2) Second to the right

   (3) Second to the left

   (4) Third to the right

   (5) Immediate right

95. Which of the following statements is true according to the given arrangement?

   (1) The Lawyer is second to the left of the Doctor

   (2) E is an immediate neighbour of the Financial Analyst

   (3) H sits exactly between F and the Financial Analyst

   (4) Only four people sit between the Columinst and F

   (5) All of the given statements are true

Directions (Q. 96-100): In each of the questions below, statements are given followed by four conclusions numbered I, II, III and IV. You have to take the given statements to be true, even if they seem to be at a variance with commonly known facts. Read all the conclusions and then decide which of the given conclusions logically follows from the given statements, disregarding commonly known facts.

96. Statements:

   a. All beaks are trees.

   b. All trees are flowers.

   c. All flowers are fruits.

   Conclusions:

   I.   All fruits are beaks.

   II. All trees are fruits.

   III. Some fruits are flowers.

   IV. Some flowers are beaks.

   Select:

   (1) All follow

   (2) Only II, III and IV follow

   (3) Only III and IV follow

   (4) Only II and III follow

   (5) None of these

97. Statements:

   a. Some trains are radios.

   b. Some radios are rackets.

   c. All rings are rackets.

   Conclusions:

   I.   Some trains are rings.

   II. Some trains are rackets.

   III. No racket is train.

   IV. All rackets are rings.

   Select:

   (1) None follows

   (2) Both II and III follow

   (3) Only either II or III follows

   (4) Only either I or III follows

   (5) Only either I or IV follows

98. Statements:

    a. Some routes are rivers.

    b. All rivers are mountains.

    c. Some roads are mountains.

Conclusions:

    I. Some mountains are routes.

    II. Some roads are routes.

    III. Some roads are rivers.

    IV. Some mountains are roads.

Select:

(1) None follows

(2) Only I and II follow

(3) Only III and IV follow

(4) Only I and IV follow

(5) All follow

99. Statements:

    a. No toys are bugles.

    b. All bugles are windows.

    c. Some tigers are toys.

Conclusions:

    I. Some tigers are bugles

    II. Some windows are tigers.

    III. All toys are tigers.

    IV. Some windows are toys.

Select:

(1) None follows

(2) Only I and II follow

(3) Only III and IV follow

(4) Only I and III follow

(5) All follow

100. Statements:

    a. No horse is a groom.

    b. All corrupts are grooms.

    c. All grooms are teachers.

Conclusions:

    I. No horse is a teacher.

    II. All corrupts are teachers.

    III. Some teachers are not horses.

    IV. No corrupt is a horse.

Select:

(1) Only II, III and IV follow

(2) Only either I or IV follows

(3) Only either I or IV and III follow

(4) None follows

(5) All follow

ANSWERS

1. (1)	**2.** (2)	**3.** (5)	**4.** (3)	**5.** (3)	**6.** (4)	**7.** (5)	**8.** (5)	**9.** (4)	**10.** (3)
11. (5)	**12.** (1)	**13.** (3)	**14.** (2)	**15.** (5)	**16.** (4)	**17.** (2)	**18.** (3)	**19.** (1)	**20.** (5)
21. (3)	**22.** (4)	**23.** (1)	**24.** (1)	**25.** (5)	**26.** (4)	**27.** (1)	**28.** (5)	**29.** (3)	**30.** (4)
31. (1)	**32.** (1)	**33.** (1)	**34.** (5)	**35.** (1)	**36.** (2)	**37.** (3)	**38.** (2)	**39.** (1)	**40.** (3)
41. (2)	**42.** (5)	**43.** (1)	**44.** (4)	**45.** (3)	**46.** (2)	**47.** (2)	**48.** (3)	**49.** (1)	**50.** (2)
51. (2)	**52.** (5)	**53.** (1)	**54.** (2)	**55.** (4)	**56.** (1)	**57.** (4)	**58.** (3)	**59.** (2)	**60.** (1)
61. (4)	**62.** (3)	**63.** (2)	**64.** (4)	**65.** (5)	**66.** (1)	**67.** (4)	**68.** (2)	**69.** (1)	**70.** (2)
71. (2)	**72.** (4)	**73.** (3)	**74.** (1)	**75.** (2)	**76.** (2)	**77.** (4)	**78.** (1)	**79.** (3)	**80.** (2)
81. (2)	**82.** (4)	**83.** (3)	**84.** (1)	**85.** (1)	**86.** (3)	**87.** (4)	**88.** (1)	**89.** (2)	**90.** (5)
91. (2)	**92.** (4)	**93.** (3)	**94.** (2)	**95.** (1)	**96.** (2)	**97.** (3)	**98.** (4)	**99.** (1)	**100.** (1)

EXPLANATIONS

1. (1) The article should be 'a' and 'to' is the correct preposition.

2. (2) 'From' and 'to' are the correct prepositions.

3. (5) 'Upon' and 'For' are the correct prepositions.

4. (3) 'to, 'at' are the correct prepositions here.

5. (3) 'To' and 'For' are the correct prepositions.

6. (4) Replace " next" with "near"

7. (5) The sentence is grammatically correct.

8. (5) The sentence is grammatically correct.

9. (4) Replace "through" with "in"

10. (3) Replace "things" with "thing"

11. (5) 'While' refers to duration of stay.

12. (1) 'Soon' is the correct word in the context of the sentence.

13. (3) 'Making' clothes conveys sense.

14. (2) 'Top' is the correct word for the blank.

15. (5) 'More' is the correct word.

16. (4) The correct sequence of the sentences should be CFBEDA

21. (3) Refer to the first paragraph. Statements B and C are correct. Statement A is incorrect because according to the second paragraph, the Open Ended Working Group or OEWG also has other stakeholders apart from state representatives and civil society organisations.

22. (4) In the light of the third paragraph, we come to know that violence has devastating consequences on human health, affecting both combatants and civilians. Statement A is wrong because according to the first paragraph, the "Promotion of the Right to Peace" by the UN Human Rights Council was inspired by earlier resolutions approved by the UN General Assembly. Statement C is incorrect because according to the last paragraph, homicide is the third largest and not the largest cause of death among young people in the said age group.

23. (1) Refer to the second last sentence of the third paragraph for the answer. The other options can be ruled out in the context of the passage.

24. (1) Option (1) is the most appropriate title because it covers all the aspects of the passage. The other options are too narrow in scope.

25. (5) Refer to the third paragraph where the author states that civilian health problems are indirect effects of displacement. The other options can be ruled out.

26. (4) In the context of the passage, 'Repercussion' means 'consequence'.

27. (1) 'Constituted' is the correct definition of 'incepted' in the context of the passage.

28. (5) 'Fulfilment' is a synonym of 'attainment'.

29. (3) 'Obfuscate' is the antonym of 'explicate'. 'Obfuscate' means 'to confuse'. The other options are synonyms of 'explicate'.

30. (4) The correct antonym of 'quell' is 'incite'. The other options are synonyms of 'quell'.

31. (1) Let the speed of train running towards Mumbai and train running towards Kanpur–Central be V_M and V_K respectively.

$$\frac{V_K}{V_M} = \sqrt{\left(\frac{T_M}{T_K}\right)}$$

$$\Rightarrow \frac{V_K}{V_M} = \frac{3}{2}$$

Also, assume that at the time they meet the train running towards Mumbai covers x km.

Kanpur Central |——— x ———✶✶——— 750 – x ———| Mumbai

$$\frac{\dfrac{x}{V_K}}{\dfrac{750-x}{V_M}} = \frac{4}{9}$$

$$\Rightarrow \frac{x}{(750-x)} = \frac{2}{3}$$

$$\Rightarrow x = 300 \text{ km}$$

Now, the train running towards Mumbai covers the remaining distance i.e, 750 – 300 = 450 km in 9 hours. Thus, the speed of the train running towards Mumbai = $\dfrac{450}{9}$ = 50 km/hr

32. (1) Share of men, women and children in assigned money = 4 × 4 : 6 × 2 : 8 × 3 = 16 : 12 : 24 = 4 : 3 : 6

Sum of the part earned by women and children

$$-\frac{9}{13} \times 910 = \text{Rs.}630.$$

33. (1) Let the length of rectangular hall = x-metre

$$\therefore \quad \text{Breadth} = \left(\frac{3}{4} \times x\right) \text{metre}$$

Area of rectangular hall = Length × Breadth

$$= x \times \frac{3}{4}x \text{ sq. m.} = \frac{3}{4}x^2 \text{ m}^2$$

∴ According to question,

$$\frac{3}{4}x^2 = 768$$

$$\Rightarrow x^2 = \frac{768 \times 4}{3}$$

$$\Rightarrow x = \sqrt{\frac{768 \times 4}{3}} = 32 \text{ m}$$

∴ Length = 32 m and Breadth = 24m

∴ Required difference = 32 – 24 = 8 m.

34. (5) Vowels in BANKING = A and I

Required number of ways = $\dfrac{6!2!}{2!} = 720$ ways

35. (1)
$$x = y + 52$$
$$z = y - 26$$
∴ $\quad x + y + z = 221$
$$\Rightarrow y + 52 + y + y - 26 = 221$$
$$\Rightarrow \quad\quad 3y = 221 - 26 = 195$$
$$\Rightarrow \quad\quad y = \frac{195}{3} = 65$$
∴ $\quad\quad\quad x = 65 + 52 = 117$
∴ $\quad\quad\quad z = 65 - 26 = 39$
∴ $\quad x : y : z = 117 : 65 : 39$
$$= 9 : 5 : 3.$$

36. (2) Let the two parts be Rs. x and Rs.(7,200 – x) respectively.

$$x \times 3 \times \frac{8}{100} + (7,200 - x) \times 6 \times \frac{2}{100} = 1,200$$

$$\Rightarrow 24x + 7,200 \times 12 - 12x = 1,200 \times 100$$

$$\Rightarrow 12x = 1,20,000 - 86,400 = 33,600$$

$$\Rightarrow x = 2,800$$

Thus, the two parts are Rs.2,800 and Rs.4,400 respectively.

37. (3) Total number of boys that failed

$$= 1100 \times (1 - 0.50) = 550$$

Total number of girls that failed

$$= 900 \times (1 - 0.40) = 540$$

Total number of failed candidates

$$= 550 + 540 = 1090$$

Required percentage value

$$= \frac{1090}{2000} \times 100 = 54.5\%$$

38. (2) Let the age of son in 2005 be x years.

Age of father in 2005 = 11x + 1.

In 2014, 11x + 1 + 9 = 3 (x + 9) + 7

$$\Rightarrow 11x - 3x = 24$$

$$\Rightarrow x = 3 \text{ years}$$

39. (1) Let x be the initial amount of the mixture

∴ Amount of milk in it = $\dfrac{5}{8}x$ and water = $\dfrac{3}{8}x$

In 6 litre of mixture,

Milk $= 6 \times \dfrac{5}{8} = \dfrac{15}{4}$ litre and water $= 6 \times \dfrac{3}{8} = \dfrac{9}{4}$ litre

∴ $\dfrac{5}{8}x - \dfrac{15}{4} = \dfrac{3}{8}x - \dfrac{9}{4} + 6$

$$\Rightarrow 2x = 60 \Rightarrow x = 30 \text{ litre}$$

∴ Initial amount of milk $= 30 \times \dfrac{5}{8} = 18.75$ litre

40. (3) Cost price of the radio = Rs. 1,440

As we know, $\dfrac{CP}{MP} = \dfrac{100 - d\%}{100 + p\%}$, where d is the discount percent and p is the profit percent.

$$\Rightarrow \frac{1440}{MP} = \frac{100 - 25}{100 + 25}$$

$$\Rightarrow \frac{1440}{MP} = \frac{75}{125}$$

$$\Rightarrow MP = \text{Rs. } 2,400$$

41. (2) Number of Limca bottles consumed by all colleges = 3008

Number of Pepsi bottles consumed by all the colleges = 3084

Number of Coke bottles consumed by all the colleges = 2245

Number of Thumbs-up bottles consumed by all the colleges = 2152

Number of Sprite bottles consumed by all the colleges = 3026

It is clearly evident from the given table that maximum consumed cold-drink was Pepsi.

42. (5) Number of Pepsi bottles sold = 3084.

Number of Limca bottles sold = 3008.

Required percentage

$$= \frac{3084 - 3008}{3084} \times 100 \approx 2.46\%.$$

43. (1) Number of bottles consumed by college P = 2533

Number of bottles consumed by college Q = 1982

Number of bottles consumed by college R = 2052

Number of bottles consumed by college S = 1797

Number of bottles consumed by college T = 3177

Number of bottles consumed by college U = 1974

It is clearly evident that College T has consumed the maximum number of bottles. Thus, maximum amount is spent by College T.

Amount spent = 3177 × 9.50 = Rs. 30,181.50.

44. (4) Number of bottles consumed in college R = 2052

Number of bottles consumed in college Q = 1982

Required ratio = 2052 : 1982 ≈ 1.03:1.

45. (3) Quantity of Limca consumed = 3008 × 0.3 L

Quantity of Thumbs-up consumed = 2152 × 0.3 L

Required difference = (3008 − 2152) × 0.3 = 256.80 L.

46. (2) I. 3x + 2y = 301

II. 7x − 5y = 74

Solving I and II, we get

x = 57   and y = 65

∴ y > x

47. (2) I. 6x + 7y = 52

II. 14x + 4y = 35

Solving I and II, we get

$$x = \frac{1}{2} \text{ and } y = 7$$

∴ y > x

48. (3) I. $x^2 = 64$

∴ x = ±8

II. $2y^2 + 25y + 72 = 0$

∴ y = −8, −4.5

x ≥ y

49. (1) I. 7x + 3y = 26

II. 2x + 17y = −41

Solving I and II, we get

x = 5   and y = −3

∴ y < x

50. (2) I. 3x + 8y = −2

II. 4x + 18y = 1

Solving I and II, we get

$$x = -2 \text{ and } y = \frac{1}{2}$$

∴ y > x

51. (2) 45   72   104   **132**(142)   187   240

27   32   38   45   53

5   6   7   8

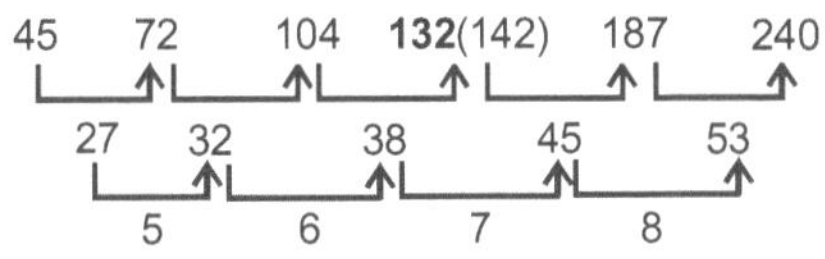

Hence, 132 is the wrong term.

52. (5) 78   **343**(334)   658   1060   1550   2138

256   324   402   490   588

68   78   88   98

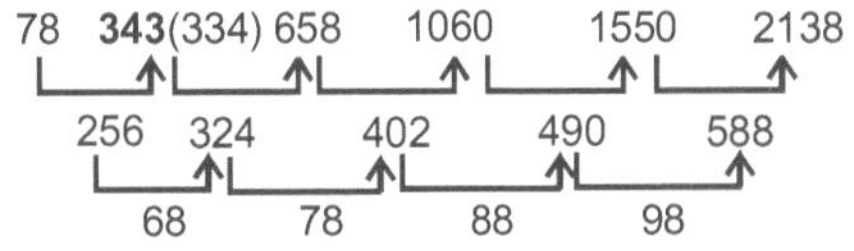

Hence, 343 is the wrong term.

53. (1) 36   232   440   663   **804**(904)   1166

196   208   223   241   262

12   15   18   21

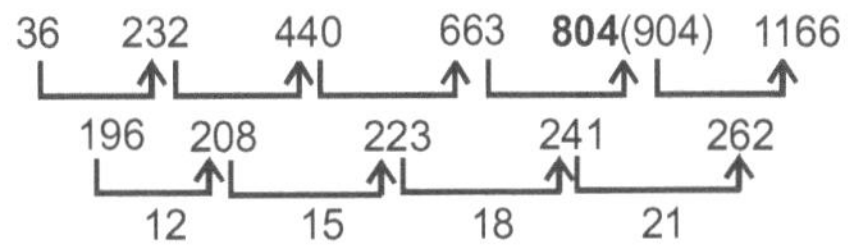

Hence, 804 is the wrong term.

54. (2) 76   98   156   **257**(255)   401   601

22   58   99   146   200

36   41   47   54

5   6   7

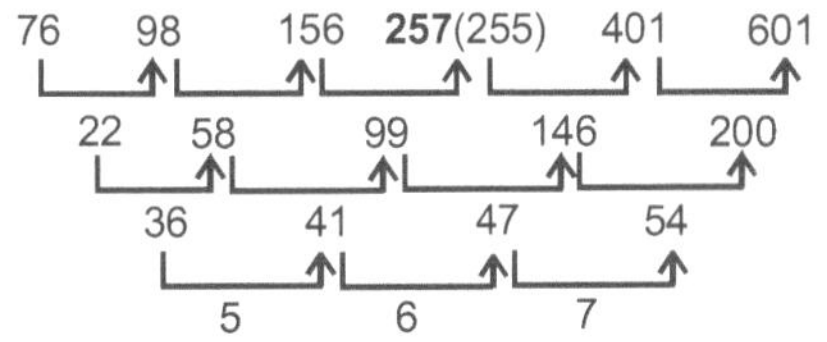

Hence, 257 is the wrong term.

55. (4) 17   31   77   175   345   **507**(607)

14   46   98   170   262

32   52   72   92

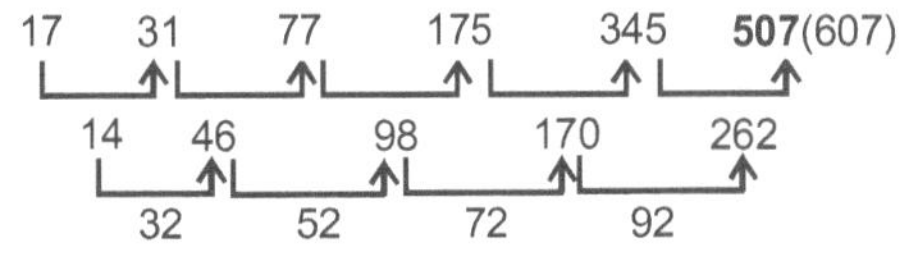

Hence, 507 is the wrong term.

For questions 56 to 60:

All of the given information can be tabulated as:

	B.Sc	B.Pharma	BAMS	BMLT	BDS	MBBS	Total
Boys	630	240	756	1080	1062	432	4200
Girls	1098	480	306	450	522	144	3000
Total	1728	720	1062	1530	1584	576	7200

56. (1) Total number of students enrolled in BAMS = 1062.

57. (4) Total number of boys enrolled in BDS = 1062.

58. (3) Total number of girls enrolled in BAMS and BDS = 306 + 522 = 828.

59. (2) Required ratio = $\dfrac{630}{1080} = \dfrac{7}{12}$ i.e. 7 :12.

60. (1) Total number of students enrolled in BMLT = 1530.

Total number of students in the institute = 7200.

∴ Required percentage

$$-\frac{1530}{7200} \times 100 = 21.25\%.$$

61. (4) $? = 5687.285 + 4872.35 \div 12$

$$\approx 5687 + 4872 \div 12$$

$$= 5687 + 406$$

$$= 6093 \approx 6095$$

62. (3) $? = (35.95)^2 - (24.001)^2$

$$\approx 36^2 - 24^2$$
$$= (36 - 24)(36 + 24)$$
$$= 12 \times 60$$
$$= 720$$

63. (2) $? = 367.85 \div 22.95 \times 14.99$

$$\approx 368 \div 23 \times 15$$
$$= 16 \times 15 = 240$$

64. (4) 75% of 430 – ? = 64% of 249

$$? = \frac{75}{100} \times 430 - \frac{64}{100} \times 249$$
$$= 322.5 - 159.36 = 163.14 \approx 165$$

65. (5) $(?)^2 = (24.99)^2 + (31.05)^2$

$$\approx (25)^2 + (31)^2$$
$$= 625 + 961 = 1586$$
$$? = 39.8 \approx 40$$

66. (1)

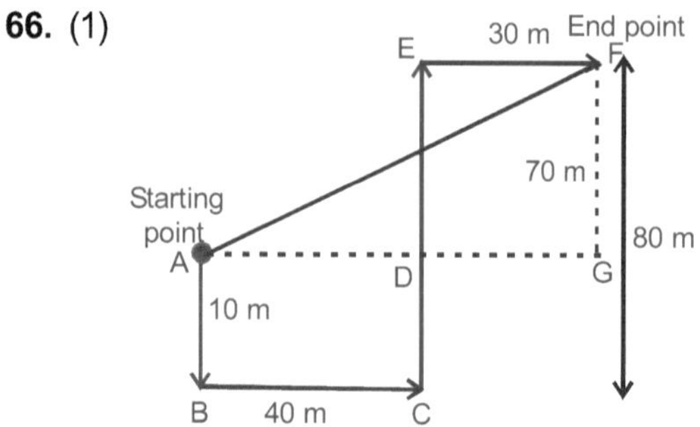

Minimum distance between the starting point and end point

$$= AF = \sqrt{AG^2 + FG^2}$$
$$= \sqrt{(40 + 30)^2 + 70^2} = 70\sqrt{2} \text{ m.}$$

67. (4)

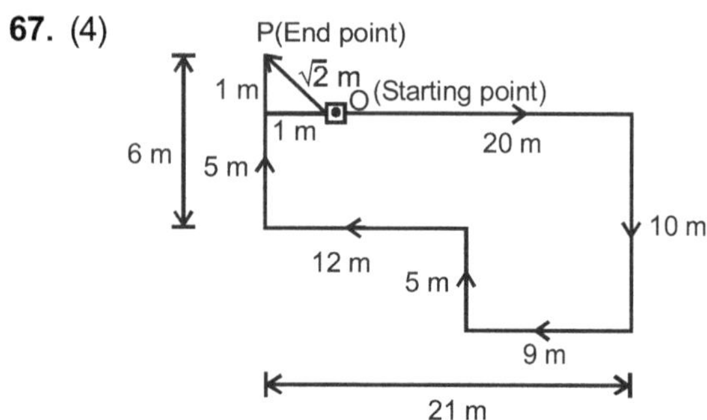

Hence, required distance,

$$OP = \sqrt{1^2 + 1^2} = \sqrt{2} \text{ m, North-west.}$$

68. (2) P × Q ÷ R – T + S

$\Rightarrow$ P is the wife of Q who is the father of R who is the brother of T who is the sister of S.

69. (1)

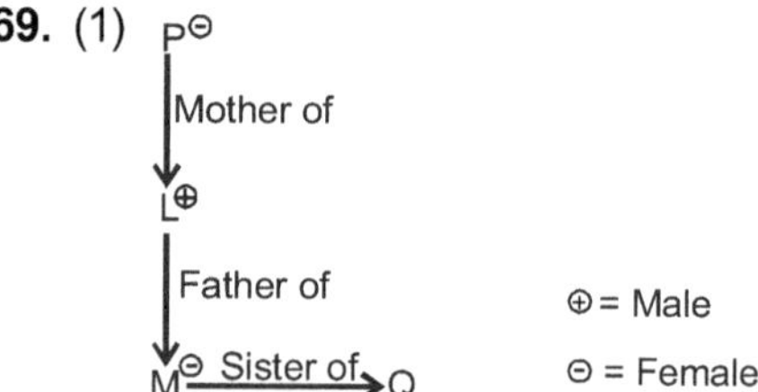

Hence, P is the Grandmother of Q.

70. (2) My mother's son's only sister is the woman. Gopi is the father of the woman's son. Hence, Gopi is the husband of woman.

For questions 71 to 75 : The given information can be shown as:

Friend	Aman	Boman	Chaman	Dhaman	Eraman
Occupation	Engineer	Doctor	Cloth Merchant	Lawyer	Runs a Factory
City	Kolkata	Delhi	Mumbai	Mumbai	Chennai
Community	Hindu	Sikh	Christian	Hindu	Muslim

For questions 76 to 80:

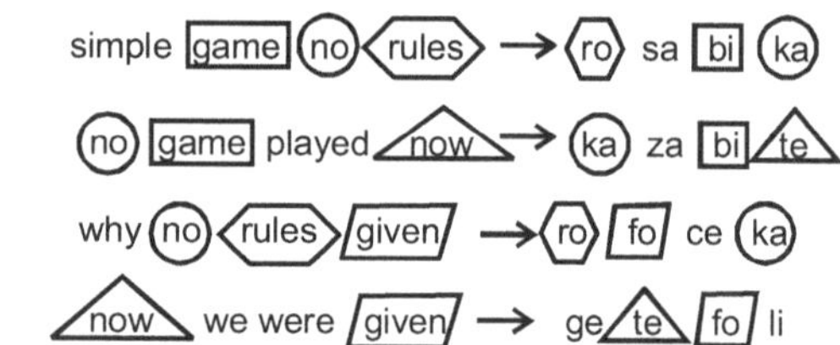

76. (2) now $\Rightarrow$ te

77. (4) game $\Rightarrow$ bi

78. (1) ce $\Rightarrow$ why

79. (3) rules $\Rightarrow$ ro

80. (2) fo $\Rightarrow$ given

For questions 81 to 85: Given information can be shown as below:

The given information can be shown as below:

A	C	E	D	F	B	G	↑North
Y_7	Y_2/Y_3	Y_5	Y_1	Y_4	Y_3/Y_2	Y_6	

or

A	C	E	D	B	F	G
Y_7	Y_2/Y_3	Y_5	Y_1	Y_3/Y_2	Y_4	Y_6

where Y_1 to Y_7 are ages of oldest to youngest persons in that order.

86. (3) **Statements:**

A%B, B$D, D&F, F@H $\Rightarrow$ A > B, B $\geq$ D, D = F, F < H $\Rightarrow$ A > B $\geq$ D = F; H > F = D.

Conclusions:

I. B%F $\Rightarrow$ B > F may or may not be true.

II. D@A $\Rightarrow$ D < A is true.

III. H%D ⇒ H > D is true.

IV. H#B ⇒ H ≤ B may or may not be true.

Hence, both statements II and III are true.

87. (4) Statements:

R&S, S#T, T%U, U$V ⇒ R = S, S ≤ T, T > U, U ≥ V

⇒ T ≥ S = R; T > U ≥ V.

Conclusions:

I. T&R ⇒ T = R may or may not be true.

II. U%S ⇒ U > S is not true.

III. V@T ⇒ V < T is true.

IV. R#U ⇒ R ≤ U is not true.

Hence, only statement III is true.

88. (1) Statements:

K@L, L$M, M#N, N&J ⇒ K < L, L ≥ M, M ≤ N, N = J ⇒ J = N ≥ M; L ≥ M; L > K.

Conclusions:

I. J$M ⇒ J ≥ M is true.

II. L&M ⇒ L = M may or may not be true.

III. N#L ⇒ N ≤ L is not true.

IV. L%K ⇒ L > K is true.

Hence, both statements I & IV are true.

89. (2) Statements:

C#E, G%E, R$G, R@W ⇒ C ≤ E, G > E, R ≥ G, R < W ⇒ W > R ≥ G > E ≥ C.

Conclusions:

I. R%E ⇒ R > E is true.

II. G&C ⇒ G = C is not true.

III. C@W ⇒ C < W is true.

IV. R$E ⇒ R ≥ E is not true.

Hence, both statements I & III are true.

90. (5) Statements:

X$Y, Y%W, W&K, K@Z ⇒ X ≥ Y, Y > W, W = K, K < Z ⇒ X ≥ Y > W = K; Z > K = W.

Conclusions:

I. Z@W ⇒ Z < W is not true.

II. X%K ⇒ X > K is true.

III. Y&Z ⇒ Y = Z may or may not be true.

IV. Y@X ⇒ Y < X may or may not be true.

Hence, only statement II is true.

For (Q. 91-95) : According to the given information the following sitting arrangement is follows

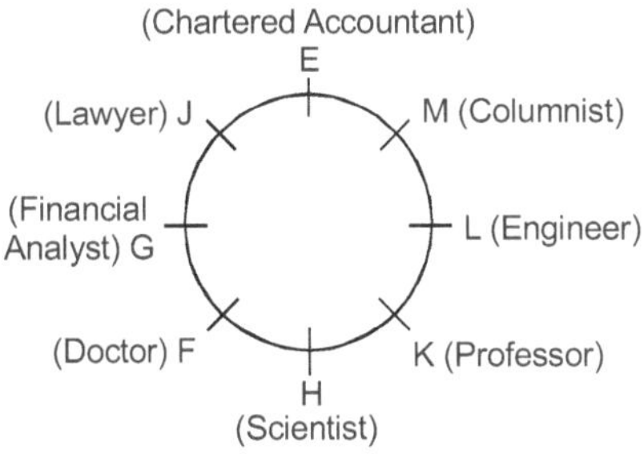

91. (2) G is sitting second to the right of E.

92. (4) K is the professor.

93. (3) J is lawyer and rest of the people do not match with their respective profession.

94. (2) L is second to the right of scientist.

95. (1) According to given arrangement, the lawyer is second to the left of doctor is true.

96. (2)

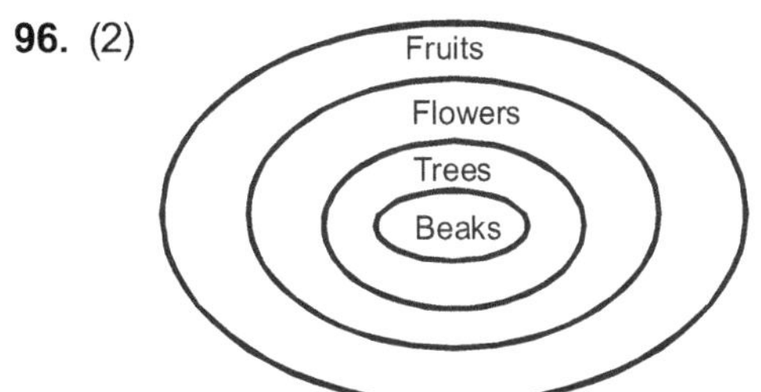

97. (3)

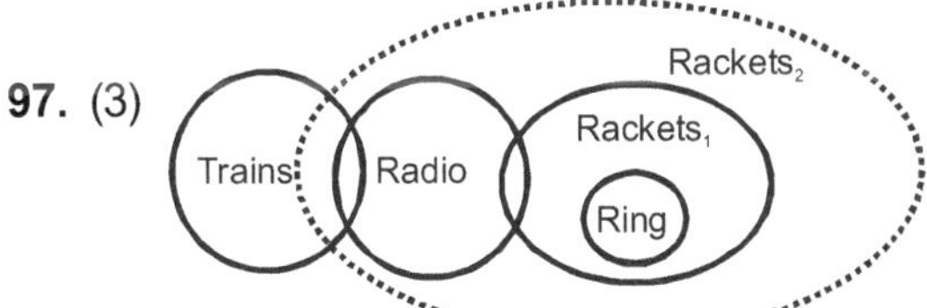

98. (4)

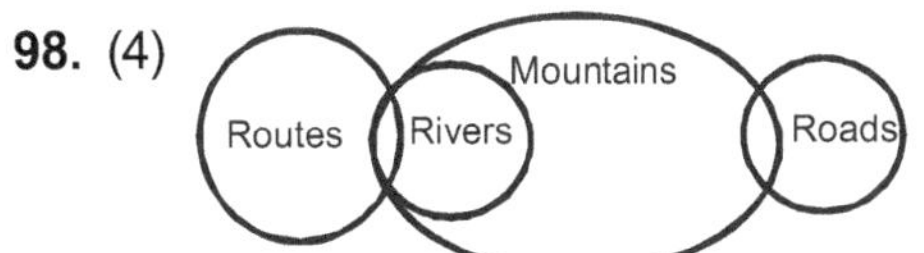

99. (1)

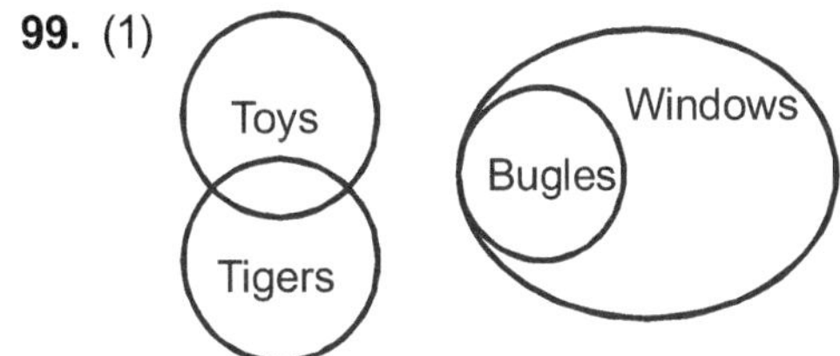

100. (1)

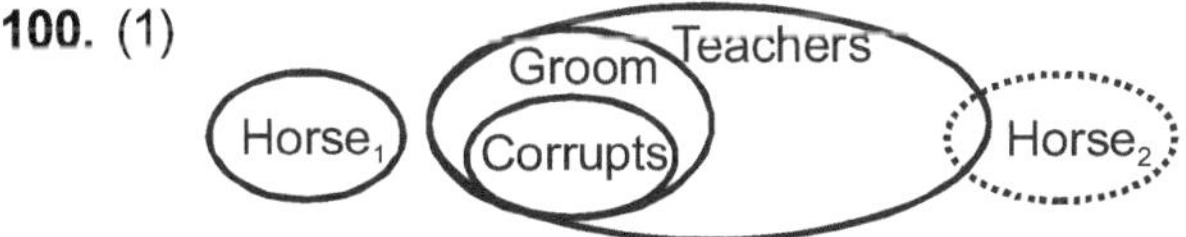

PRACTICE PAPER – 4

Directions (Q. 1 to 5) Which of the phrases given below each of the sentences should replace the phrase printed in bold in the sentence to make it grammatically correct?

1. The Indian cricket team **ruler of the roost** when it comes to matches in the sub-continent.
   - (1) rules the roost
   - (2) rulers of the rooster
   - (3) rule the rooster
   - (4) rake the roost
   - (5) rises the roost

2. Never **shy towards** doing something responsible in the office. It will help you in the long run.
   - (1) shied towards
   - (2) shy near from
   - (3) flies towards
   - (4) shy across
   - (5) shy away from

3. Please **size up** the situation before you go ahead to solve it.
   - (1) sized up
   - (2) size down
   - (3) sized down
   - (4) size in
   - (5) No changes required.

4. The memories of my first job gradually **faded apart**.
   - (1) faded away
   - (2) fading into
   - (3) faded on
   - (4) fades with
   - (5) fades through.

5. He always **runs around with** the same bunch of friends.
   - (1) ran away with
   - (2) run into
   - (3) run towards
   - (4) ran after
   - (5) No change required

Directions (Q. 6 to 10) Each question below has two blanks, indicating that something has been omitted. Find out which option can be used to fill up the blank in the sentence in the same sequence to make it meaningfully complete.

6. Aamir Khan's "Satyamev Jayate", the reality show _______ on Star TV, has failed to _______ the response it was expected to, given the program gradually lost viewers along the season.
   - (1) showed, collected
   - (2) displayed, garnered
   - (3) broadcast, garner
   - (4) communicated, pick
   - (5) displayed, promoted

7. The "Sky city" is a new project coming up in Tokyo in which the best civil engineers in the world will _____ to _____ the tallest, most advanced and secure building in the world.
   - (1) try, made
   - (2) expect, bring
   - (3) expect, destroyed
   - (4) hope, create
   - (5) pry, create

8. The British _____ a crucial role in the way India is _____ today.
   - (1) employed, stand
   - (2) played, shaped
   - (3) predict, employ
   - (4) did, perplex
   - (5) had, shape

9. Life in space has been an issue _____ by countless scientists over many years, but till this day no one has a _____ answer.
   - (1) debate, definition
   - (2) debated, definitive
   - (3) probation, proper
   - (4) promoted, shallow
   - (5) impede, definitive

10. The cold war _____ when the USSR segregated in 1991, and consequently lost the _____ to the USA.
    - (1) brims, world
    - (2) start, trial
    - (3) ended, edge
    - (4) edge, ended
    - (5) explode, edge

Directions (Q. 11 to 15) : In the following passage, there are blanks, each of which has been numbered.

These numbers are given below the passage and against each, five words are suggested, one of which fits the blanks appropriately. Find out the appropriate word in each case.

With the U.S. military tied down on two fronts and the rest of the world growing __(11)__ to American power, the challenges for Rice are as daunting as they have been for any Secretary of State in the past three decades. After six years of tussling with others on Bush's national-security team, Rice has seen off her rivals and __(12)__ as the principal spokesperson for Bush's foreign policy. Her reward has been to inherit responsibility for selling a failed policy in Iraq and framing a legacy for Bush at a time when few in the world are in the mood to help her. "Bush is severely __(13)__ and has very little credibility or support at home or abroad," says Leslie Gelb, former president of the Council of Foreign Relations. "That is also true for his Secretary of State. So they are basically flailing around."

That's a grim assessment, since the __(14)__ to international order are bigger today than at any other time since the end of the cold war. The most immediate source of instability emanates from Iraq, where the country's civil war risks __(15)__ a region wide conflict.

11. (1) resistant   (2) subservient
    (3) immune   (4) cordial
    (5) indifference

12. (1) renamed   (2) emerged
    (2) appointed   (4) entrusted
    (5) visited

13. (1) intensified   (2) master-minded
    (3) weakened   (4) projected
    (5) supported

14. (1) admirations   (2) threats
    (3) pleasantries   (4) demands
    (5) accolades

15. (1) defusing   (2) demolishing
    (3) terminating   (4) igniting
    (5) extinguishing

Directions (Q.16 to 25): Read the following passage carefully and answer the questions that follow.

After decades of declining numbers, bankruptcies and privatization, Israel's kibbutz movement is undergoing a remarkable revival, with rising numbers wanting to join the unique form of collective living.

The population of about 143,000 is the highest in its 102-year history, after growth of 20% between 2005 and 2010, according to the official Kibbutz Movement. More people are now joining kibbutzim than leaving – a reversal of the crisis years – and the **influx** of working-age adults and young children is helping to redress the balance of an ageing population.

Most kibbutzim have implemented reforms to become commercially viable and **stem** decline. Liberalization – including permitting differential incomes and home ownership – has increased their attractiveness to newcomers reluctant to commit to pure **communal** principles.

Only about 60 of Israel's 275 kibbutzim still operate a completely collective model, in which all members are paid the same regardless of their allotted job. Most of the rest have introduced wage differentials for people employed by the kibbutz – but, more importantly, many members now work outside the kibbutz and contribute a proportion of their salaries to the collective.

Other measures have included selling kibbutz businesses, charging for meals and services, and recruiting agricultural laborers from Southeast Asia. The changes, necessary for survival, have been painful,

particularly for a generation of kibbutz **pioneers** wedded to a socialist-Zionist dream.

Increasing numbers of families are attracted to kibbutz living by the quality of education, environment, space and security. But, according to AmikamOsem, a member of Kibbutz Afikim near the Sea of Galilee for 50 years after marrying a kibbutznik, the most important reason was a sense of community. "This is the principle of kibbutz life – mutual help and responsibility for each other." A kibbutz, he said, was like an orchestra with people playing different parts "but together we create something meaningful."

In the last two years, Afikim's membership has increased from 500 to 600, and there is now a waiting list of people wanting to join. Many are the children of members, wishing to raise their own families in a co-operative environment. Others have never previously lived on a kibbutz.

Afikim operates a progressive taxation system: the more you earn, the more you pay into the collective fund. There is a "safety net" minimum income for all, and the kibbutz subsidizes healthcare, education, social needs and care for the elderly. The kibbutz owns and runs several successful businesses, plus dairy and fish farms, and grows dates, bananas, avocados and olives on its land. The heavily subsidized dining room – the heart of the kibbutz – is open every day for lunch, and twice a week in the evenings.

Before being accepted as members with full voting rights, candidates rent homes on the kibbutz. Most members now own their own homes, which can be bequeathed to their children or sold back to the collective. Occasionally a candidate family decides that kibbutz life is not for them; sometimes the kibbutz admissions committee rejects candidates as unsuitable. Those with criminal records, a history of financial mismanagement or **unsocial** behavior are not invited to join.

"Here in the kibbutz, we're not neighbours – we're partners," says Osem. "The kibbutz movement is in a process of change in which there are many different directions. But the thing that unites all kibbutzim is mutual responsibility."

16. Which of the following is the author most likely to agree with?

    (1) After its remarkable revival, the kibbutz movement is shaping up to be what its founders had planned.

    (2) The revival of the kibbutz way of life has been driven by the increasing commercial viability of the kibbutz settlements.

    (3) Change, even when for the better, is necessarily painful.

    (4) The kibbutz experience proves that collective living is a defunct model.

    (5) The kibbutz still has more leavers than adopters.

17. To whom does the phrase '**pioneers wedded to a Socialist-Zionist dream**', in context of the passage, refer?

(1) The political supporters of the Kibbutz movement

(2) The initial members dedicated to the founding principles of the kibbutz movement

(3) Members of the generation born and brought up on the kibbutz settlements

(4) The generation of the latest entrants into the kibbutz way of life

(5) The people who left the kibbutz movement

18. Which of the following can be inferred from the passage?

(1) Most kibbutz have introduced wage differentials and there is thus the possibility of earning a higher income within the kibbutz than outside.

(2) Members have access to better quality education, healthcare and social security.

(3) In their struggle for survival, the kibbutz settlements are now no different from commercial farming establishments.

(4) It is now possible for members to live on the kibbutz and also be part of the outside world.

(5) None of these.

19. Which of the following can be inferred as the strongest proof of the revival of the kibbutz movement in Israel?

(1) Whereas earlier kibbutz living was only for the homeless and refugees, increasingly families are being drawn to the kibbutz way of life.

(2) Kibbutz members who work outside the settlements are now contributing a portion of their salaries to the collective.

(3) Innovative and modern practices, such as the progressive tax system, have been adopted by some settlements.

(4) The number of new people joining the kibbutz settlements is now higher than those leaving.

(5) None of these.

20. Which of the following, if true, weakens the author's assertion that Israel's kibbutz movement is undergoing a remarkable revival?

(1) Youngsters are taking to the kibbutz way of life as a sign of rebellion against the established norm.

(2) It is only the city elites who are opting for a kibbutz way of life as a sort of vacation activity.

(3) The data collected is only for those kibbutz settlements that are doing well and does not consider those that have failed.

(4) Only new immigrants into Israel adopt the kibbutz model of living as a first step towards integration into Israeli society.

(5) Kibbutizm has grown by only ten percent in the last year.

Directions (Q.21 to 23): Choose the word that is most similar in meaning to the word given in bold as used in the passage.

21. Influx

(1) Intervention   (2) Inflow

(3) Inception   (4) Invention

(5) Inhibition

22. Communal

(1) Common   (2) Trival

(3) Private   (4) Pushed

(5) Renovated

23. Stem

(1) Branch   (2) Base

(3) Allow   (4) Invite

(5) Arrest

Directions (Q.24 and 25): Choose the word that is the farthest in meaning to the word given in bold as used in the passage.

24. Unsocial

(1) Aloof   (2) Recluse

(3) Extrovert   (4) Unfriendly

(5) Withdrawn

25. Pioneers

(1) Leaders   (2) Initiators

(3) Pathfinders   (4) Trailblazers

(5) Followers

Directions (Q. 26 to 30) Rearrange the following sentences (A), (B), (C), (D), (E) and (F) to make a meaningful paragraph and then answer the questions which follow.

(A) At least two "piles" of rock the size of continents are crashing together as they shift at the bottom of Earth's mantle, 2,900 km beneath the Pacific Ocean, researchers say.

(B) This "super volcano", seismologists believe, is due to erupt in 200 million years' time.

(C) "What we may be detecting is the start of one of these large eruptive events that — if it ever happens — could cause very massive destruction on Earth," said the seismologist Michael Thorne.

(D) Life on Earth could be facing threat from a catastrophic "super volcano".

(E) However, disaster is not imminent. "This is the type of mechanism that may generate massive plume eruptions," he sums up.

(F) He is the study's principal author and an assistant professor of geology and geophysics at the University of Utah.

26. Which of the following should be the LAST of the rearrangement?

(1) A   (2) B
(3) C   (4) D
(5) E

27. Which of the following should the THIRD of the rearrangement?

(1) A   (2) B
(3) C   (4) D
(5) E

28. Which of the following should the FOURTH of the rearrangement?

(1) A   (2) B
(3) C   (4) D
(5) E

29. Which of the following should the FIRST of the rearrangement?

(1) A   (2) B
(3) C   (4) D
(5) E

30. Which of the following should the SECOND of the rearrangement?

(1) A   (2) B
(3) C   (4) D
(5) E

NUMERICAL ABILITY

Directions (Q. 31 to 35): In each of the following questions two equations are given. You have to solve both the equations and find out values of x and y and give answer.

(a) if $x > y$
(b) if $x < y$
(c) if $x \geq y$
(d) if $x \leq y$
(e) if $x = y$ or relationship cannot be established

31. I. $x^2 - 9x - 136 = 0$
     II. $y^2 + 2.5y - 1.5 = 0$

32. I. $4x - 7y = 2$
     II. $x + y = 6$

33. I. $2x + 4y = 4$
     II. $3x - y = 0.75$

34. I. $x^{\frac{1}{2}} = 5$
     II. $y^{\frac{1}{3}} = 3$

35. I. $x^2 + 6x - 7 = 0$
     II. $y^2 + 10y + 9 = 0$

Directions (Q. 36 to 40) : In each of the following questions, what should come in place of question (?) mark?

36. $60^2 - 54^2 = 57 \times ?$

(1) 6   (2) 9
(3) 12   (4) 114
(5) 24

37. $1605 - \dfrac{841}{29} \times 58 - 29 = ?$

(1) 107   (2) -105
(3) -206 (4) -96
(5) None of these

38. 18% of $4.88 - 15\%$ of $2.56 = ? + 0.1502$

(1) 0.2442   (2) 0.3422
(3) 0.2422   (4) 0.3442
(5) 1.3442

39. 8 of $(24 + 14) \div ? - 37 \times 4 = 4$

(1) 6   (2) 2
(3) 3   (4) 4
(5) None of these

40. $\dfrac{\frac{1}{3} \text{ of } \frac{1}{4} \div \frac{1}{5}}{\frac{1}{4} \div \frac{1}{3} \text{ of } \frac{1}{5}} = ?$

(1) $\dfrac{1}{9}$ (2) $\dfrac{25}{12}$
(3) 9   (4) $\dfrac{12}{25}$
(5) 1

41. An aeroplane can travel at 320 km/hr in still air. The wind is blowing at a constant speed of 40 km/hr. The total time for a journey against the wind is 135 min. What will be the time in minutes for the return journey with the wind ? (Ignore take off and landing time of the aeroplane)

(1) 94.5   (2) 105
(3) 125   (4) 120
(5) None of these

42. A and B can complete a job in 12 days and B and C can complete it in 16 days. A worked for 5 days and B for 7 days, and then C finished the rest of the work in 13 days. In how many days can C complete the work alone?

(1) 16 days   (2) 30 days

(3) 36 days   (4) 24 days

(5) 20 days

43. The circumference of a circular playground is 308 metre. There is 7 metre wide path around the ground. The area of the path is

(1) 2,130 sq. metre   (2) 2,410 sq. metre

(3) 2,510 sq. metre   (4) 2,310 sq. metre

(5) None of these

44. What is the probability that when 2 dice and 4 coins are thrown simultaneously, there is a sum of 9 on the dice and at least 2 heads on the coins?

(1) $\dfrac{11}{144}$ (2) $\dfrac{8}{144}$

(3) $\dfrac{11}{132}$ (4) $\dfrac{11}{169}$

(5) None of these

45. Rs. 9,700 has been divided among X, Y and Z such that if their shares are reduced by Rs. 30, Rs. 20 and Rs. 50, the balance are in the ratio of 3 : 4 : 5. What is Y's share?

(1) Rs. 3,180   (2) Rs. 3,220

(3) Rs. 3,253.33   (4) Rs. 3,200

(5) Rs. 2,420

Directions (Q. 46 to 50): Answer the following questions based on the given information.

There are two graphs given below. The table shows the population of five cities. The bar chart shows the gender ratio for each of the given city. Assume that these are the only cities in the state.

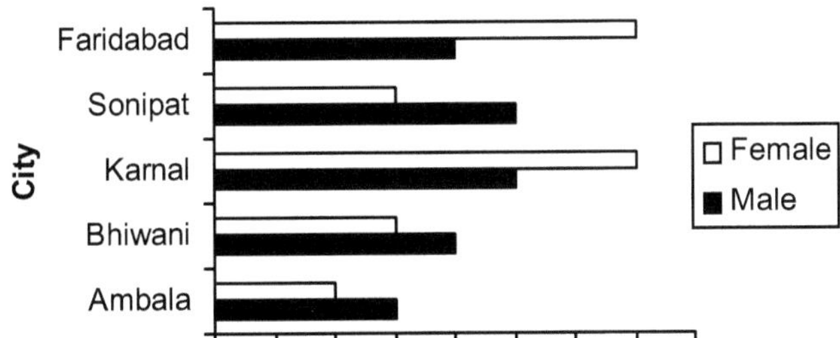

City	Population
Ambala	25535
Bhiwani	21910
Karnal	20736
Sonipat	21496
Faridabad	27742

46. What is the total number of females in the state?

(1) 48967   (2) 59364

(3) 57415   (4) 52309

(5) None of these

47. What is the difference between the total number of males from city Bhiwani and Sonipat together to the total number of females from city Ambala and Faridabad together?

(1) 1913   (2) 1980

(3) 2096   (4) 1845

(5) None of these

48. Total number of females in the state is by what percentage more or less than the total number of males in the state?

(1) 4.31%

(2) 2.98%

(3) 3.096%

(4) 4.50%

(5) 5.02%

49. The given state contains 25% of the total population of the country it belongs. Further, if another state contains 20% of the total population of the country it belongs, then what is the total population of that another state?

(1) 94627   (2) 85670

(3) 93935   (4) 87891

(5) 96542

50. Total number of females from city Karnal is what percent of the total number of males from city Faridabad?

(1) 121.33%   (2) 144.45%

(3) 109.4%   (4) 120%

(5) 118%

Directions (Q. 51 to 55) : In each of the following questions, complete the given series.

51. 14, 18, 24, 34, 48, 70, ?

(1) 94   (2) 96

(3) 98   (4) 92

(5) None of these

52. 16, 19, 25, 34, 46, 61, ?

(1) 75   (2) 77

(3) 79   (4) 81

(5) None of these

53. 3, 9, 19, 33, 51, 73, ?

(1) 100   (2) 98

(3) 89   (4) 101

(5) None of these

54. 2040, 1016, 504, 248, 120, 56, ?

(1) 28   (2) 26

(3) 18   (4) 34

(5) None of these

55. 6, 20, 42, 72, 110, 156, ?

(1) 240   (2) 210

(3) 182   (4) 225

(5) None of these

56. A father left a will of Rs. 85,000 to be divided between his two sons aged 10 years and 12 years such that they may get equal amount when each attains the age of 18 years. If the money is invested at 10% p.a. simple interest, then find how much the son of age 10 years gets at the time of the will.

(1) Rs. 30,000   (2) Rs. 40,000

(3) Rs. 45,000   (4) Rs. 48,000

(5) None of these

57. The price of sugar is increased by 20%. As a result, a family decreases its consumption by 25%. The expenditure of the family on sugar will decrease by

(1) 5%

(2) 25%

(3) 20%

(4) 10%

(5) None o f these

58. The average salary of 100 employees in an office is Rs. 16,000 per month. The management decided to raise salary of every employee by 5% but stopped the transport allowance of Rs. 800 per month which was paid earlier to every employee. What will be the new average monthly salary? (Assume transport allowance is not included in the salary)

(1) Rs. 16,000

(2) Rs. 16,500

(3) Rs. 16,800

(4) Rs. 15,200

(5) None of these

59. Two quantities of rice are mixed in the ratio 2 : 3 and sold at Rs. 22 per kilogram, resulting in a profit of 10%. If the cost of the smaller quantity be Rs. 14 per kilogram, what is the cost per kilogram of the larger quantity?

(1) Rs. 28

(2) Rs. 25

(3) Rs. 24

(4) Rs. 20

(5) None of these

60. A trader quotes Rs. 45 for an article whose cost price is Rs. 30. The customer pays him a fifty-rupee note. The trader does not have the change to give back Rs. 5 to the customer. He thus goes to a neighbouring shop to get change for Rs. 50. The customer collects his balance Rs. 5. The next day the neighbouring shop owner realizes that the fifty-rupee note was fake and demanded Rs. 50 back from the trader. What is the total loss to the trader?

(1) Rs. 95   (2) Rs. 100

(3) Rs. 55   (4) Rs. 85

(5) Rs. 35

Directions (Q. 61 to 65): Answer the questions on the basis of the information given below.

Monthly Bill (in rupees) of landline phone, electricity, laundry and mobile phone paid by three different people in five different months.

| Month | Monthly Bills | | | | | | | | | | | |
| | Landline Phone | | | Electricity | | | Laundry | | | Mobile Phone | | |
	Ravi	Dev	Manu	Ravi	Dev	Manu	Ravi	Dev	Manu	Ravi	Dev	Manu
March	234	190	113	145	245	315	93	323	65	144	234	345
April	124	234	321	270	220	135	151	134	35	164	221	325
May	156	432	211	86	150	98	232	442	132	143	532	332
June	87	123	124	124	150	116	213	324	184	245	134	125
July	221	104	156	235	103	131	143	532	143	324	432	543

61. What is the total amount of bill paid by Dev in the month of June for all the four commodities?

(1) Rs.608   (2) Rs.763

(3) Rs.731   (4) Rs.683

(5) None of these

62. What is the average electricity bill paid by Manu over all the five months together?

(1) Rs.183   (2) Rs.149

(3) Rs.159   (4) Rs.178

(5) None of these

63. What is the difference between the mobile phone bill paid by Ravi in the month of May and the laundry bill paid by Dev in the month of March?

(1) Rs.185   (2) Rs.176

(3) Rs.190   (4) Rs.167

(5) None of these

64. In which months respectively did Manu pay the second highest mobile phone bill and the lowest electricity bill?

(1) April and June

(2) April and May

(3) March and June

(4) March and May

(5) April and June

65. What is the respective ratio between the electricity bill paid by Manu in the month of April and the mobile phone bill paid by Ravi in the month of June?

(1) 27 : 49   (2) 27 : 65

(3) 34 : 49   (4) 65 : 27

(5) 49 : 27

REASONING ABILITY

Directions (Q. 66 to 70) : Answer the following questions based on the given information.

Five automobile companies decided to display their products in an Auto Expo show. The companies were Maruti, Hyundai, Skoda, Volkswagen and Mahindra. Each company displayed their products on a different day. Further, a representative was appointed to provide the information about each product. The representatives were Sumit, Harpreet, Pritam, Sonam and Raina. The dates were 15 Mar, 16 Mar, 18 Mar, 20 Mar and 21 Mar. Further information is given as:

(i) Pritam was the representative of Volkswagen.

(ii) Harpreet represented his stall on 16th March

(iii) Hyundai and Maruti were displayed on the consecutive days.

(iv) Sumit represented his stall three days before Pritam represented his stall.

(v) Sonam represented her stall on 15th March.

(vi) It was taken care of that the initials of any company and their representative weren't same.

66. Who was the representative of Maruti?

(1) Harpreet

(2) Raina

(3) Sonam

(4) Either Harpreet or Raina

(5) Cannot be determined

67. On which date does Skoda display its products?

(1) 21 March   (2) 16 March

(3) 20 March   (4) Either (2) or (3)

(5) None of these

68. Who represented the products on 21st March?

(1) Sumit   (2) Harpreet

(3) Sonam   (4) Pritam

(5) Raina

69. Which of the given pairs of combination is definitely correct?

(1) Sumit – Hyundai

(2) Hyundai – 15th March

(3) Pritam – 20th March

(4) Skoda - 21st March

(5) Sonam – Mahindra

70. How many days after Hyundai were the products of Mahindra displayed?

(1) One   (2) Two

(3) Three   (4) Either (2) or (3)

(5) Cannot be determined

71. A rat runs 20 m towards East and turns to right, runs 10 m and turns to right, runs 9 m and again turns to left, runs 5 m and then turns to left, runs 12 m and finally turns to left and runs 6 m. Now which direction is the rat facing?

(1) East   (2) North

(3) West   (4) South

(5) North-West

72. Vijayan started walking towards South. After walking 15 m, he turned to the left and walked 15 m. He again turned to his left and walked 15 m. How far is he form his original position and in which direction?

(1) 15 m, North   (2) 15 m, South

(3) 30 m, East   (4) 15 m, West

(5) None of these

73. Pointing to a man in a photograph, a woman said, "His brother's father is the only child of my grandfather". How is the woman related to that man in the photograph?

(1) Mother   (2) Sister

(3) Aunt   (4) Daughter

(5) Grandmother

74. Introducing a girl, Amrish said, "This girl is the wife of the grandson of my mother, who has only one son". How is Amrish related to that girl?

(1) Father   (2) Father-in-law

(3) Grandfather   (4) Husband

(5) Brother

75. Pointing to a man in a photograph, Ronika said, "His mother's only daughter is my mother". How is Ronika related to that man?

(1) Nephew   (2) Sister

(3) Niece   (4) Wife

(5) Granddaughter

Directions (Q. 76 to 80) : In each of the following questions, the symbols &, @, #, $ and % are used as follows.

M&N implies that N is greater than or equal to M.

M@N implies that M is equal to N.

M#N implies that M is greater than or equal to N.

M$N implies that M is greater than N.

M%N implies that N is greater than M.

Now in each of the following questions assuming that the given statements to be true, find which of the four conclusions I, II, III and IV given below them is/are definitely true and give your answer accordingly.

76. Statements: T@Q, P&S, R$S, Q#R

Conclusions:

I. P%T

II. R&P

III. T$R

IV. P@Q

(1) Only I   (2) Only III

(3) Both I and III   (4) Both I and IV

(5) I, II and III

77. Statements: A&B, B@C, P$D, D#C

Conclusions:

I. A@D

II. B$A

III. P&C

IV. A%P

(1) Only II   (2) Only IV

(3) I, II and IV   (4) Both II and III

(5) Both II and IV

78. Statements: A&B, C$D, A@X, B#C

Conclusions:

I. X%B

II. B@C

III. A$D

IV. C#X

(1) Only I

(2) Only II

(3) Both I and II

(4) II, III and IV

(5) None of the given statements is true.

79. Statements: M$N, N@P, P%Q, R#M

Conclusions:

I. R$M

II. P%M

III. N%Q

IV. Q@R

(1) Only II   (2) Only III

(3) Both II and III   (4) I, II and III

(5) None of these

80. Statements: F#H, H%J, J&K, K@Y

Conclusions:

I. H%Y

II. F$J

III. J&Y

IV. K#H

(1) Only I   (2) Only III

(3) I, II and III   (4) Both I and III

(5) I, III and IV

Directions (Q. 81 to 85) : Answer the questions on the basis of the information given below.

Seven persons - I, J, K, M, N,O and P - are sitting in a circle at equidistance but not necessarily in the same order. Some of them are facing towards the centre and some are facing outside the centre. O is facing outside. J sits second to the right of O. N is sitting second to the left of P. P is not an immediate neighbour of J or O. N is not an immediate neighbour of J. The immediate neighbour of K faces towards the centre. K and P face the same direction. I is sitting second to the right of N. The immediate neighbour of M faces outside. I and M face the same direction as that of J.

81. Who amongst the following are not facing the centre?

   (1) K, N, O and J   (2) I, M, N and P

   (3) J, M, I, O and N   (4) P, K, O and N

   (5) None of these

82. Which of the following is J's position with respect to N?

   (1) Third to the right

   (2) Fourth to the right

   (3) Third to the left

   (4) Second to the left

   (5) Fifth to the left

83. Which of the following is K's position with respect to M?

   (1) Third to the left

   (2) Third to the right

   (3) Fourth to the left

   (4) Second to the right

   (5) None of these

84. Who among the following is sitting exactly between M and K?

   (1) N   (2) P

   (3) O   (4) I

   (5) J

85. Which of the following is P's position with respect to J?

   (1) Third to the right   (2) Fourth to the left

   (3) Fourth to the right (4) Third to the left

   (5) Fifth to the left

Directions (Q. 86 to 90): Answer the questions on the basis of the information given below.

In a certain code, 'a friend of mine' is written as '4916', 'mine lots of metal' is written as '3109' and 'a piece of metal' is written as '7163'.

86. What is the code for 'piece'?

   (1) 3   (2) 6

   (3) 1   (4) 7

   (5) Cannot be determined

87. What does '9' stand for?

   (1) of   (2) mine

   (3) friend   (4) lots

   (5) metal

88. Which of the following may represent 'a pleasure of mine'?

   (1) 6309   (2) 5216

   (3) 9216   (4) 3694

   (5) 5041

89. What does '0' stand for?

   (1) mine   (2) metal

   (3) of   (4) lots

   (5) a

90. The code '873' could mean

   (1) a metal piece

   (2) metal for friend

   (3) piece of advice

   (4) friend of mine

   (5) large metal piece

Directions (Q. 91 to 95): Answer the following questions based on the given information.

Poonam, Charu, Reena, Savita, Tarun, Vaishali, Anshika and Yogita are seated in a straight line facing North. Poonam sits fourth to the left of Vaishali. Vaishali sits either sixth from the left end of the line or fourth from the right end of the line. Savita sits second to right of Reena. Reena is not an immediate neighbour of Vaishali. Tarun and Charu are immediate neighbours of each other but neither Tarun nor Charu sits at extreme ends of the line. Only one person sits between Tarun and Anshika. Anshika does not sit at the extreme end of the line.

91. What is the position of Charu with respect to Poonam?

   (1) Fifth to the right

   (2) Immediate neighbour

   (3) Second to right

   (4) Third to left

   (5) None of these

92. Which of the following represents persons seated at the two extreme ends of the line?

   (1) Poonam-Vaishal

   (2) Yogita-Savita

   (3) Vaishali-Yogita

   (4) Yogita-Poonam

   (5) Reena-Yogita

93. How many persons are seated between Reena and Tarun?

   (1) One   (2) Two

   (3) Three   (4) Four

   (5) None

94. If Poonam is related to Charu and Savita is related to Tarun in a certain way, which of the following would Vaishali be related to?

   (1) Yogita   (2) Poonam

   (3) Reena   (4) Savita

   (5) Anshika

95. Who amongst the following sits exactly in the middle of the persons who sit second from the left and the person who sits fifth from the right?

(1) Vaishali

(2) Charu

(3) Tarun

(4) Savita

(5) Poonam

Directions (Q. 96 to 100) : In each question below are three statements followed by two conclusions numbered I and II. You have to take the three given statements to be true even if they seem to be at variance from commonly known facts and then decide which of the given conclusions logically follows from the three statements disregarding commonly known facts. Give answer

(1) if only conclusion I follows.

(2) if only conclusion II follows..

(3) if either conclusion I or II follows.

(4) if neither conclusion I nor II follows.

(5) if both conclusions I and II follow.

96. Statements:

All bulbs are tubes.

Some tubes are knives.

All knives are frames.

Conclusions:

I.   Some frames are tubes.

II. Some knives are bulbs.

97. Statements:

Some tents are houses.

All houses are buildings.

Some buildings are huts.

Conclusions:

I.   Some huts are houses.

II. Some buildings are tents.

98. Statements:

Some beads are chairs.

All chairs are desks.

All desks are tables.

Conclusions:

I.   Some tables are beads.

II. Some desks are beads.

99. Statements:

All mangoes are apples.

All apples are bananas.

Some bananas are grapes.

Conclusions:

I.   Some grapes are mangoes.

II. Some bananas are mangoes.

100. Statements:

All books are pens.

Some pens are papers.Some papers are crystals.

Conclusions:

I.   Some crystals are pens,

II. Some papers are books,

ANSWERS

1. (1)	**2.** (5)	**3.** (5)	**4.** (1)	**5.** (5)	**6.** (3)	**7.** (4)	**8.** (2)	**9.** (2)	**10.** (3)
11. (1)	**12.** (2)	**13.** (3)	**14.** (2)	**15.** (4)	**16.** (2)	**17.** (2)	**18.** (4)	**19.** (4)	**20.** (3)
21. (2)	**22.** (1)	**23.** (5)	**24.** (3)	**25.** (5)	**26.** (5)	**27.** (1)	**28.** (3)	**29.** (4)	**30.** (2)
31. (5)	**32.** (1)	**33.** (2)	**34.** (2)	**35.** (5)	**36.** (3)	**37.** (5)	**38.** (4)	**39.** (2)	**40.** (1)
41. (2)	**42.** (4)	**43.** (4)	**44.** (1)	**45.** (2)	**46.** (3)	**47.** (1)	**48.** (1)	**49.** (3)	**50.** (4)
51. (2)	**52.** (3)	**53.** (5)	**54.** (5)	**55.** (2)	**56.** (2)	**57.** (4)	**58.** (3)	**59.** (3)	**60.** (5)
61. (3)	**62.** (3)	**63.** (5)	**64.** (4)	**65.** (1)	**66.** (1)	**67.** (3)	**68.** (4)	**69.** (2)	**70.** (3)
71. (2)	**72.** (5)	**73.** (2)	**74.** (2)	**75.** (3)	**76.** (1)	**77.** (2)	**78.** (5)	**79.** (3)	**80.** (4)
81. (3)	**82.** (1)	**83.** (4)	**84.** (2)	**85.** (5)	**86.** (4)	**87.** (2)	**88.** (3)	**89.** (4)	**90.** (5)
91. (3)	**92.** (5)	**93.** (3)	**94.** (1)	**95.** (4)	**96.** (1)	**97.** (2)	**98.** (5)	**99.** (2)	**100.** (4)

EXPLANATIONS

1. (1) The correct idiom is "rules the roost".

2. (5) The correct phrase is "shy away from".

3. (5) The given phrase is correct.

4. (1) "Faded away" is the correct phrase.

5. (5) The given idiom is correct.

6. (3) First, look at the second blank. "Collected","garnered" and "promoted" are not the correct forms of usage here. Hence, we can eliminate options (1),(2) and (5). For the first blank, TV shows are "broadcast", and not "communicated". Hence, the correct answer is option (3).

7. (4) Options (1) and (3) are incorrect because the second blank cannot be filled with a word in past tense. And going by the idea of the sentence, create is the most suitable word for the second blank. "Pry" is incorrect for the first blank as the word means to enquire too inquisitively into a person's private affairs. Thus, the correct answer is option (4).

8. (2) The correct phrase is 'played a crucial role'. The second blank will take a word that is in the past tense. So, only "shaped" fits in the blank.

9. (2) The first blank will take a word that is in the past tense. So, only options (2) and (4) fitin the first blank appropriately.The second blank will only take "definitive". "Shallow answer" is incorrect in the given context.

10. (3) Since we are talking about the past, only option (3) fits the blank appropriately.

11. (1) The passage talks about the challenges. So, the blank will take 'resistant', which means opposed to something.

12. (2) 'Seen of rivals' means defeated rivals. The only option that logically and grammatically fits in the blank is 'emerged'.

13. (3) 'Very little credibility' suggests that the blank will take 'weakened'.

14. (2) The passage talks about challenges. So, the blank will take 'threat'.

15. (4) The sentence talks about a risk. So, 'igniting' fits in the blank perfectly.

16. (2) Option (1) is incorrect since the passage does not say anything about what the founders of the kibbutz movement had envisioned for it. Option (3) is a general statement. The author states that change is necessary for survival. But, this change does not always have to be painful. Option (4) is clearly contrary to the kibbutz experience as described in the passage. Option (5) is incorrect as evidence contrary to this is provided in the first paragraph. Option (2) is the correct answer as it is clearly stated in the passage that 'most kibbutzim have implemented reforms to become commercially viable and stem decline'.

17. (2) A 'pioneer' is a person who is among the first to explore or settle a new country or area. Going by this meaning, option (2) is the correct answer since it mentions the 'initial members' of the kibbutz movement who were dedicated to the cause and principles of kibbutzim.

18. (4) Options (1), (2) and (3) cannot be inferred from the passage. While it is mentioned that wage differentials have been introduced within several kibbutz settlements, there is no comparison stating that because of the wage differentials, the members can earn more than what they can earn outside. The passage does state that families have been attracted to the kibbutz way of life by the quality of education, healthcare and social security offered by the settlements, but it does not imply that the quality offered in kibbutz is 'better' than anything found outside. While the kibbutz have undergone commercial revival, the essence of kibbutzim continues to be mutual responsibility. Only option (4) can be inferred from the passage as it is mentioned that 'many members now work outside the kibbutz', while continuing to be a part of the community. Thus, option (4) is the correct answer.

19. (4) Revival of the kibbutz movement can be best illustrated by showing that the kibbutz way of life is becoming more popular. The best proof for this would be an increase in the membership of the collectives. Option (4) describes a situation wherein there will be an increase in the membership of the collectives and is, therefore, the correct answer.

20. (3) Options (1), (2), (4) and (5) all give reasons that are indicative of a revival, however, partial, of the kibbutz movement. Option (3) is the only one that gives evidence of a bias in the data collected towards those kibbutz settlements that are doing well, and is the correct answer.

21. (2) 'Influx' is the same as 'inflow'. Intervention means to intercept something, 'inception' means beginning, 'invention' means to create something new and 'inhibition' means hindrance.

22. (1) 'Communal' means to something common to the community. Hence, the correct answer is (1).

23. (5) 'Stem' means to stop or to arrest something. Thus, the answer is option (5).

24. (3) While options (1), (2), (4) and (5) mean something very similar to 'unsocial', an 'extrovert' is someone who is very outgoing and very social. Hence, the correct answer is option (3).

25. (5) A 'pioneer' is someone who leads or initiates. Thus, 'followers' is the word farthest in meaning from the given word.

For questions 26 to 30:

The correct sequence is DBACFE. DB is a mandatory pair. 'This 'super volcano'' refers to the 'super volcano' mentioned in D. A gives a general opinion of researchers and precedes C which gives the view of a specific researcher, Michael Thorne. CF is a mandatory pair since F gives the details of the researcher mentioned in C. E ends the passage by quoting what Michael Thorne said. 'However' is the key word here.

31. (5) I. $x^2 - 9x - 136 = 0$

II. $y^2 + 2.5y - 1.5 = 0$

From I, we get $x = 17, -8$

From II, we get $y = 0.5, -3$

∴ Relationship cannot be established.

32. (1) I. $4x - 7y = 2$

II. $x + y = 6$

Solving I and II, we get

$x = 4$ and $y = 2$

∴ $x > y$

33. (2) I. $2x + 4y = 4$

II. $3x - y = 0.75$

Solving I and II, we get

$x = 0.5$ and $y = 0.75$

∴ $y > x$

34. (2) I. $x^{\frac{1}{2}} = 5$

II. $y^{\frac{1}{3}} = 3$

$x = 25$ and $y = 27$

∴ $y > x$

35. (5) I. $x^2 + 6x - 7 = 0$

II. $y^2 + 10y + 9 = 0$

From I, we get $x = 1, -7$

From II, we get $y = -1, -9$

∴ Relationship cannot be established.

36. (3) $60^2 - 54^2 = 57 \times ?$

$\Rightarrow (60 + 54)(60 - 54) = ? \times 57$

$\Rightarrow 114 \times 6 = ? \times 57$

$\Rightarrow 12 \times 57 = ? \times 57$

$\Rightarrow (?) = 12.$

37. (5) $? = 1605 - \dfrac{841}{29} \times 58 - 29$

$= 1605 - 29 \times 58 - 29$

$= 1605 - 29(58 + 1)$

$= 1605 - 29 \times 59$

$= 1605 - 1711$

$= -106.$

38. (4) 18% of $4.88 - 15\%$ of $2.56 = ? + 0.1502$

$\Rightarrow 0.18 \times 4.88 - 0.15 \times 2.56 = ? + 0.1502$

$\Rightarrow 0.8784 - 0.384 = ? + 0.1502$

$\Rightarrow 0.4944 = ? + 0.1502$

$\Rightarrow (?) = 0.4944 - 0.1502$

$\Rightarrow (?) = 0.3442.$

39. (2) 8 of $(24 + 14) \div ? - 37 \times 4 = 4$

$\Rightarrow$ 8 of $38 \div ? - 37 \times 4 = 4$

$\Rightarrow 304 \div ? - 37 \times 4 = 4$

$\Rightarrow \dfrac{304}{?} - 37 \times 4 = 4$

$\Rightarrow \dfrac{304}{?} - 148 = 4$

$\Rightarrow \dfrac{304}{?} = 152$

$\Rightarrow (?) = \dfrac{304}{152} = 2.$

40. (1) $\dfrac{\dfrac{1}{3} \text{ of } \dfrac{1}{4} \div \dfrac{1}{5}}{\dfrac{1}{4} \div \dfrac{1}{3} \text{ of } \dfrac{1}{5}}$

$= \dfrac{\dfrac{1}{12} \div \dfrac{1}{5}}{\dfrac{1}{4} \div \dfrac{1}{15}} = \dfrac{\dfrac{5}{12}}{\dfrac{15}{4}}$

$= \dfrac{5}{12} \times \dfrac{4}{15} = \dfrac{1}{9}.$

41. (2) Speed of aeroplane against the wind

$= (320 - 40) = 280$ km/hr.

∴ Distance travelled in 135 min or 2.25 hours

$= 2.25 \times 280 = 630$ km.

Speed of the aeroplane with the wind

$= (320 + 40) = 360$ km/hr.

∴ Time taken to cover 630 km with the wind

$= \dfrac{630}{360} \times 60 = 105$ min.

42. (4) Let whole work be 48 units i.e. LCM of (12, 16).

Work done by (A + B) in 1 day = $\dfrac{48}{12}$ = 4 units

Work done by (B + C) in 1 day = $\dfrac{48}{16}$ = 3 units

Work done by (A + B) in 5 days = 4 × 5 = 20 units

Work done by (B + C) in 2 days = 3 × 2 = 6 units

Work remaining = 48 − 26 = 22 units

C finishes remaining work in 11 days.

∴ Units of work done by C in 1 day = $\dfrac{22}{11}$ = 2

∴ Number of days required by C to complete

the whole work = $\dfrac{48}{2}$ = 24 days

43. (4) $2\pi r_1 = 308$ where r_1 = radius of circular playground

$\Rightarrow 2 \times \dfrac{22}{7} \times r_1 = 308$

$\Rightarrow r_1 = \dfrac{308 \times 7}{2 \times 22} = 49$ metre

∴ Area of the path $= \pi\left(r_2^2 - r_1^2\right)$

$= \dfrac{22}{7}\left(56^2 - 49^2\right)$

$= \dfrac{22}{7}\,(56 + 49)(56 - 49)$

$= 22 \times 105 = 2{,}310$ sq.m.

44. (1) Sum of '9' can be achieved in 4 ways i.e. (6, 3), (3, 6), (5, 4) and (4, 5).

Probability of a sum of 9 on the dice = $\dfrac{4}{36} = \dfrac{1}{9}$

Probability of at least 2 coins showing on head

$= {}^4C_2\left(\dfrac{1}{2}\right)^4 + {}^4C_3\left(\dfrac{1}{2}\right)^4 + {}^4C_4\left(\dfrac{1}{2}\right)^4 = \dfrac{11}{16}$

Hence, the required probability = $\dfrac{11 \times 1}{16 \times 9} = \dfrac{11}{144}$

45. (2) X's share = 3x + 30

Y's share = 4x + 20

Z's share = 5x + 50

Sum – Rs. 9,700

12x + 100 = 9700,

$\Rightarrow$ 12x = 9600

$\Rightarrow$ x = 800

$\Rightarrow$ Y's share = 4x + 20 = 3200 + 20 = Rs. 3,220.

For questions 46 to 50:

City	Male	Female
Ambala	15321	10214
Bhiwani	12520	9390
Karnal	8640	12096
Sonipat	13435	8061
Faridabad	10088	17654

46. (3) Total number of females in city Ambala

$= \dfrac{2}{5} \times 25535 = 10214$

Total number of females in city Bhiwani

$= \dfrac{3}{7} \times 21910 = 9390$

Total number of females in city Karnal

$= \dfrac{7}{12} \times 20736 = 12096$

Total number of females in city Sonipat

$= \dfrac{3}{8} \times 21496 = 8061$

Total number of females in city Faridabad

$= \dfrac{7}{11} \times 27742 = 17654$

Total number of females in the state

$= 10214 + 9390 + 12096 + 8061 + 17654$

$= 57415.$

47. (1) Number of males in city Bhiwani = 12520

Number of males in city Sonipat = 13435

Total number of males from the two cities

$= 12520 + 13435 = 25955$

Number of females in city Ambala = 10214

Number of females in city Faridabad = 17654

Total number of females from the two cities

$= 10214 + 17654 = 27868$

Required difference = 27868 − 25955 = 1913.

48. (1) Total number of males in the state

$= 15321 + 12520 + 8640 + 13435 + 10088$

$= 60004.$

Total number of females in the state

$= 10214 + 9390 + 12096 + 8061 + 17654$

$= 57415.$

Required percentage

$= \dfrac{60004 - 57415}{60004} \times 100 \approx 4.31\%.$

49. (3) Population of the country

$= \dfrac{117419}{0.25} = 469676.$

Population of another state

= 469676 × 0.20 = 93935.

50. (4) Number of females from city Karnal = 12096.

Number of males from city Faridabad = 10088.

Required percentage

$$= \frac{12096}{10088} \times 100 \approx 119.90\%.$$

51. (2)

| 14 | 18 | 24 | 34 | 48 | 70 | ? **(96)** |

+2×2 +3×2 +5×2 +7×2 +11×2 +13×2

52. (3)

| 16 | 19 | 25 | 34 | 46 | 61 | ? **(79)** |

+3 +6 +9 +12 +15 +18

53. (5)

| 3 | 9 | 19 | 33 | 51 | 73 | ? **(99)** |

$2(1)^2+1$ $2(2)^2+1$ $2(3)^2+1$ $2(4)^2+1$ $2(5)^2+1$ $2(6)^2+1$ $2(7)^2+1$

54. (5)

| 2040 | 1016 | 504 | 248 | 120 | 56 | ?(24) |

÷2–4 ÷2–4 ÷2–4 ÷2–4 ÷2–4 ÷2–4

55. (2)

| 6 | 20 | 42 | 72 | 110 | 156 | ?(210) |

3^2-3 5^2-5 7^2-7 9^2-9 11^2-11 13^2-13 15^2-15

56. (2) Let A_{10} and A_{12} be amount of 10 years and 12 years old son resepectively and P_{10} and P_{12} be the sum of 10 years old and 12 years old son resepectively, then

$$A_{10} = A_{12}$$

$$\Rightarrow P_{10} + \frac{P_{10} \times 10(18-10)}{100} = P_{12} + \frac{P_{12} \times 10(18-12)}{100}$$

$$\Rightarrow P_{10}[100 + 10(18-10)] = P_{12}[100 + 10(18-12)]$$

$$\Rightarrow \frac{P_{10}}{P_{12}} = \frac{160}{180} = \frac{8}{9}$$

$$\therefore \frac{8}{17} \times 85000 = \text{Rs. } 40,000$$

57. (4) Let the original consumption be 100 units and original price be Rs. 100 per unit

Original expenditure = (100 × 100) = Rs. 10,000

New expenditure = (120 × 75) = Rs. 9,000

Decrease in expenditure

$$= \frac{1000}{10000} \times 100\% = 10\%.$$

58. (3) Increase in salary = 5% of 16000 = Rs. 800

Hence, new monthly salary = Rs. 16,800.

59. (3) Let the quantity of rice be 2x and 3x kilograms.

Profit = 10%, SP = Rs. 22.

CP of 2x kg = Rs. 14 per kilogram.

Let CP of 3x kg = Rs. y per kilogram.

Total CP = Rs. (28x + 3xy)

Total SP = 22 × 5x = Rs. 110x.

$$SP = CP \frac{(100 + \text{Gain percentage})}{100}$$

$$110x = (28x + 3xy) \times \frac{110}{100}$$

$$\Rightarrow \quad 100 = 28 + 3y$$

$$\Rightarrow \quad y = \frac{72}{3} = \text{Rs. } 24.$$

60. (5) Total loss:

Cost price of the article = Rs. 30.

Balance to the customer = Rs. 5.

Total = Rs. 35.

61. (3) Total amount of bill paid by Dev in month of June for all four commodities

$$= (123 + 150 + 324 + 134) = \text{Rs.}731$$

62. (3) Average electricity bill paid by Manu over all the five months together

$$= \frac{315 + 135 + 98 + 116 + 131}{5}$$

$$= \frac{795}{5} = \text{Rs.}159$$

63. (5) Mobile phone bill paid by Ravi in month of May = Rs.143

and Laundry bill paid by Dev in month of March = Rs.323

Their difference = (323 – 143) = Rs.180.

64. (4) In the month of March, Manu paid second highest mobile phone bill of Rs.345 and in the month of May, Manu paid lowest electric bill of Rs.98.

65. (1) Electricity bill paid by Manu in the month of April = Rs.135 and mobile phone bill paid by Ravi in the month of June = Rs.245

$\therefore$ Respective ratio = 135 : 245 = 27 : 49.

For questions 66 to 70: All the given information can be tabulated as:

Representative	Company	Date
Sumit	Mahindra	18-Mar
Harpreet	Maruti	16-Mar
Pritam	Volkswagen	21-Mar
Sonam	Hyundai	15-Mar
Raina	Skoda	20-Mar

71. (2) The rat is facing in the North direction

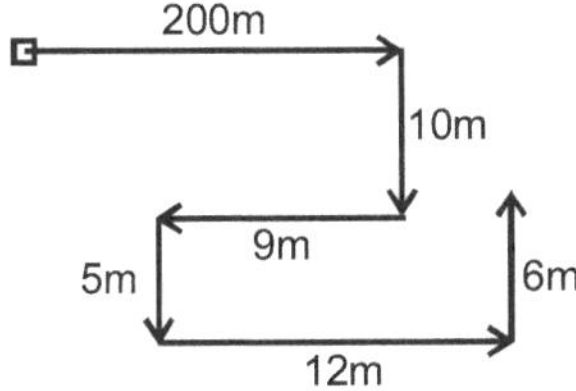

72. (5) He is 15m away in the East direction.

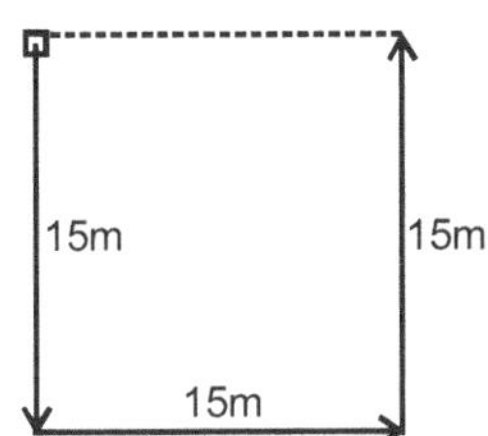

73. (2) Only child of the woman's grandfather will be her father. The man in the photograph will be her brother. So, she is the man's sister.

74. (2) Grandson of Amrish's mother is his son. He is the father-in-law of his son's wife.

75. (3) That man's mother is the grandmother of Ronika. So, that man is the maternal uncle of Ronika.

76. (1) After applying the changes, we get

$T = Q, S \geq P, R > S, Q \geq R$

$\Rightarrow T = Q \geq R > S \geq P$.

Now,

I. $P\%T \Rightarrow P < T$ is true.

II. $R\&P \Rightarrow R \leq P$ is not true.

III. $T\$R \Rightarrow T > R$ may or may not be true.

IV. $P@Q \Rightarrow P = Q$ is not true.

Thus, only statement I is true.

77. (2) After applying the changes, we get

$A \leq B, B = C, P > D, D \geq C$

$\Rightarrow A \leq B = C \leq D < P$

Now,

I. $A@D \Rightarrow A = D$ is not true

II. $B\$A \Rightarrow B > A$ may or may not be true.

III. $P\&C \Rightarrow P \leq C$ is not true.

IV. $A\%P \Rightarrow A < P$ is true.

Thus, only statement IV is true.

78. (5) After applying the changes, we get

$A \leq B, C > D, A = X, B \geq C$

$\Rightarrow X = A \leq B$ and $B \geq C > D$

Now,

I. $X \% B \Rightarrow X < B$ may or may not be true

II. $B@C \Rightarrow B = C$ may or may not be true

III. $A\$D \Rightarrow A > D$ is not true

IV. $C\#X \Rightarrow C \geq X$ is not true

Thus, none of the given statements is true.

79. (3) After applying the changes, we get

$M > N, N = P, P < Q, R \geq M$

$R \geq M > N = P; Q > P = N$.

Now,

I. $R\$M \Rightarrow R > M$ may or may not be true.

II. $P\%M \Rightarrow P < M$ is true.

III. $N\%Q \Rightarrow N < Q$ is true.

IV. $Q@R \Rightarrow Q = R$ is not true.

Thus, statements II and III are true.

80. (4) After applying the changes, we get

$F \geq H, H < J, J \leq K, K = Y$

$\Rightarrow Y = K \geq J > H; F \geq H$.

I. $H\%Y \Rightarrow H < Y$ is true.

II. $F\$J \Rightarrow F > J$ is not true.

III. $J\&Y \Rightarrow J \leq Y$ is true.

IV. $K\#H \Rightarrow K \geq H$ is not true.

Thus, statements I and III are true.

(81-85) :

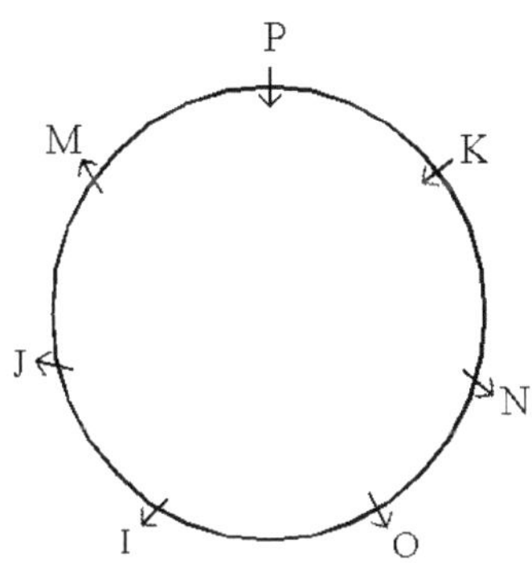

81. (3) P and K face the centre while N, O, I, J and M face outward.

82. (1) J is third to right of N. J is fourth to left of N.

83. (4) K is second to the right & fifth to the left of M

84. (2) P is sitting exactly between M and K.

85. (5) P is second to the right & fifth to the left of J.

For questions 86 to 90: The codes for the following words can be determined as:

Word	a	friend	of	mine	lots	metal	piece
Code	6	4	1	9	0	3	7

For questions 91 to 95:

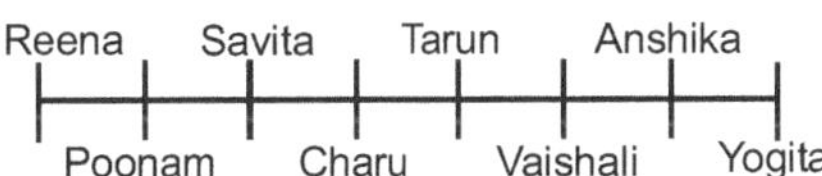

96. (1)

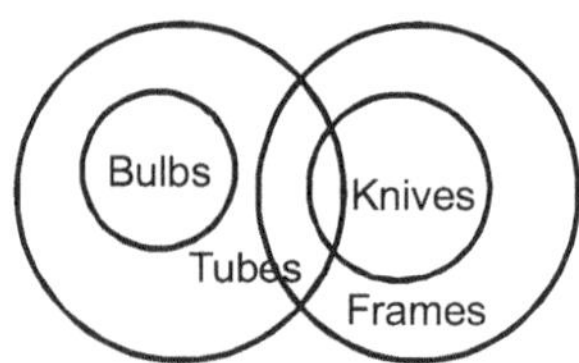

97. (2)

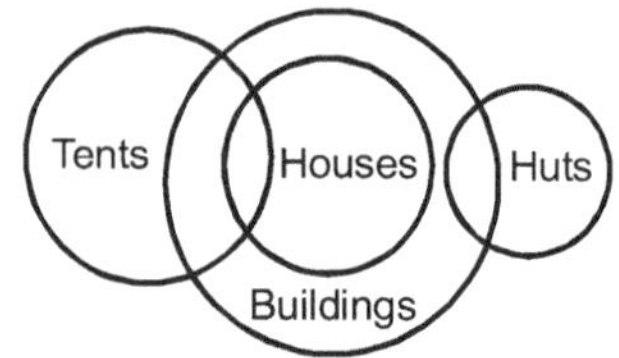

98. (5)

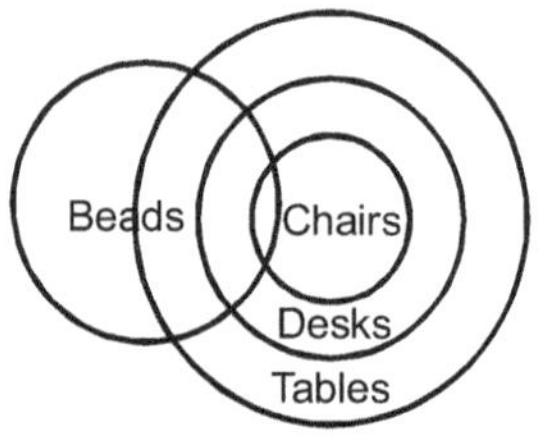

99. (2)

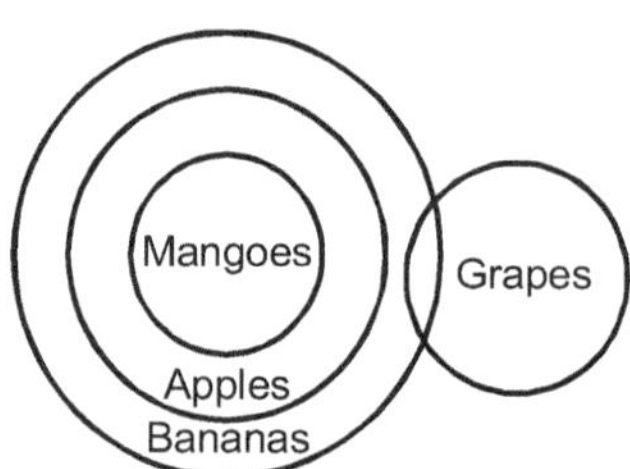

100. (4)

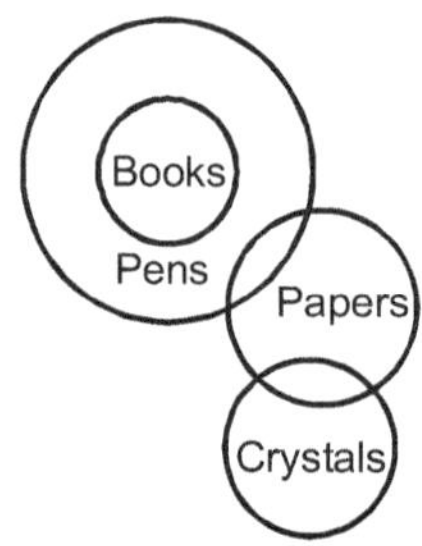

PRACTICE PAPER – 5

Directions (Q. 1 to 5): Fill in the blanks by choosing the most appropriate options.

1. He conversed ______ us on subjects ____ varied interest.
   - (1) with, of
   - (2) in, on
   - (3) of, among
   - (4) among, on
   - (5) between, on

2. He was born ______ humble parents _______ Madurai.
   - (1) of, at
   - (2) to, in
   - (3) from, in
   - (4) from, till
   - (5) among, at

3. Contrary ______ our high expectations, Samar failed ___ the exam.
   - (1) in, on
   - (2) of, in
   - (3) against, in
   - (4) to, on
   - (5) to, in

4. The burglar was taken to the ______ police station which is ______ to the school building.
   - (1) nearer, closer
   - (2) nearest, next
   - (3) closer, far
   - (4) far, further
   - (5) farthest, farther

5. I prefer the ____ proposition ____ the former.
   - (1) more later, than
   - (2) next, then
   - (3) latest, over
   - (4) later, from
   - (5) latter, to

Directions (Q. 6 to 10): Read each sentence to find out whether there is any grammatical error or idiomatic error in it. The error, if any, will be in one part of the sentence. The number of that part is the answer. If there is, no error, the answer is (5). Ignore errors of punctuation, if any.

6. The buzz at the party was (1)/ that a famous (2)/ film-star and politician, would (3)/ probable drop by for a while. (4)/ No error (5)

7. The Opposition disrupted proceedings (1)/ in both Houses of Parliament (2)/ for the second consecutive day (3)/ above the plight of farmers in the country. (4)/ No error (5)

8. In response to the growing crisis (1)/ the agency is urgently asking for (2)/more contributions to make up for (3)/ its sharp decline in purchasing power. (4)/ No error (5)

9. The tennis player easy through (1)/ the opening set before her opponent (2)/ rallied to take the final two sets (3)/ for the biggest victory of her young career. (4)/No error (5)

10. Aggression in some teenage boys (1)/ may be linkage to overly (2)/ large glands in their brains (3)/ a new study has found. (4)/No error (5)

Directions (Q. 11 to 15): In the following passage there are blanks, each of which has been numbered. These numbers are given below the passage and against each, five words are suggested, one of which fits the blank appropriately. Find out the appropriate word in each case.

Once upon a time, there lived a sparrow on a banyan tree. She laid her eggs in the nest. One afternoon, a wild elephant came under the tree and in a fit of rage, broke a branch of the tree on which the nest was __11__. Unfortunately, all the eggs of the sparrow broke after falling down though the sparrow was saved. The sparrow was full of grief and began weeping for her eggs.

A woodpecker, a close friend of the sparrow, heard her crying and asked her, "Why are you crying, my friend?" The sparrow said, "The __12__ elephant has, killed my offspring. If you are a true friend of mine, suggest a way to kill him." The woodpecker consoled her and told her that he knew a fly and she would definitely help them kill the elephant.

Both of them went to seek the help of the fly. The woodpacker said, "A wild elephant has crushed my friend's eggs. We need your help in killing him." The fly replied, "One of my friends is a frog. Let us go to him and take his help too." They went to the frog and __13__ the whole incident. The frog said, "What can an elephant do before a united crowd like us? Do what I tell you. Dear Fly, you go to the elephant and hum a sweet tune into his eyes. When he closes his eyes in delight, the woodkeeper will poke his eyes. This way, he will become blind. When he gets thirsty, he will __14__ for water. I will go to a marshy land and begin croaking there, Assuming that there is water, the elephant will come there. He will drown in the marshy area and __15__."

The next day in the noon, all of them played out the plan and the elephant was killed, as he drowned into a marshy area after being blinded by the woodpecker, when he closed his eyes in response to the music. Thus, the smartness of all the animals, enabled the sparrow, in taking her revenge on the elephant.

11. (1) broken   (2) found
     (3) born   (4) built
     (5) grown

12. (1) poor   (2) harmless
     (3) effective   (4) attacking
     (5) wicked

13. (1) mention   (2) narrated
     (3) said   (4) informed
     (5) revived

14. (1) drink   (2) demand
     (3) need   (4) want
     (5) search

15. (1) kill   (2) realise
     (3) hurt   (4) die
     (5) fall

Directions (Q. 16 to 25): The questions in this section are based on a single passage. The questions are to be answered on the basis of what is stated or implied in the passage. Kindly note that more than one of the choices may conceivably answer some of the questions. However, you are to choose the most appropriate answer, that is, the response that most accurately and completely answers the question.

The transformer is an essential component of modern electric power systems. Simply put, it can convert electricity with a low current and a high voltage into electricity with a high current and low voltage (and vice versa) with almost no loss of energy. The conversion is important because electric power is transmitted most efficiently at high voltages but is best generated and used at low voltages. Were it not for transformers, the distance separating generators from consumers would have to be minimized, many households and industries would require their own power stations, and electricity would be a much less practical form of energy.

In addition to its role in electric power systems, the transformer is an integral component of many things that run on electricity. Desk lamps, battery chargers, toy trains and television sets all rely on transformers to cut or boost voltage.

In all its multiplicity of applications, the transformer can range from tiny assemblies the size of a pea to behemoths weighing 500 tons or more. The principles that govern the functioning of electrical transformers are the same regardless of form or application.

The English physicist Michael Faraday discovered the basic action of the transformer during his pioneering investigations of electricity in 1831. Some fifty years later, the advent of a practical transformer, containing all the essential elements of the modern instrument, revolutionized the infant electric lighting industry. By the turn of the century, alternating-current power systems had been universally adopted and the transformer had assumed a key role in electrical transmission and distribution.

Yet, the transformer's tale does not end in 1900. Today's transformers can handle 500 times the power and 15 times the voltage of their turn-of-the-century ancestors; the weight per unit of power has dropped by a factor of ten and efficiency typically exceeds 99 per cent. These advances reflect the marriage of theoretical inquiry and engineering, that first **elucidated** and then exploited the phenomena governing transformer action. The Danish physicist Hans Christian Oersted, who had shown in 1820 that an electric current flowing through a conducting material creates a magnetic field around the conductor, inspired Faraday's investigations. At the time, Oersted's discovery was considered remarkable, since electricity and magnetism were thought to be separate and unrelated forces. If an electric current could generate a magnetic field, it seemed likely that a magnetic field could give rise to an electric current.

In 1831, Faraday demonstrated that in order for a magnetic field to induce a current in a conductor, the field must be changing. Faraday caused the strength of the field to **fluctuate** by making and breaking the electric circuit generating the field; the same effect can be achieved with a current whose direction alternates in time. This fascinating interaction of electricity and magnetism came to be known as electromagnetic induction.

16. The passage suggests that advances in the efficiency of the transformer are

     (1) based solely on Faraday's discovery of electromagnetic induction.

     (2) due to a combination of engineering and theoretical curiosity.

     (3) continuing to occur at an ever accelerated pace.

     (4) most likely at a peak that cannot be surpassed.

     (5) based on a technology borrowed from the U.S.

17. According to the passage, Oersted's discovery regarding the production of a magnetic field is considered remarkable because

     (1) the transformer had not yet been universally adopted.

     (2) Faraday had already demonstrated that this was impossible.

     (3) scientists believed that there was no relationship between electricity and magnetism.

     (4) it contradicted the established principles of electromagnetism.

     (5) It had the potential to be developed into nuclear power.

18. Which of the following is NOT true of transformers today as compared to the first transformers?

   (1) They comprise the same basic components.

   (2) They are lighter in weight.

   (3) They are many times more powerful.

   (4) They operate at a much lower voltage.

   (5) Today's transformers are structurally similar.

19. Which of the following statements is best supported by the passage?

   (1) Faraday was the first to show how an electric current could induce a magnetic field.

   (2) Oersted was the first to utilize transformers in a practical application, by using them to power electric lights.

   (3) Faraday invented the first practical transformer.

   (4) Faraday demonstrated that when a magnetic field is changing, it can produce an electric current in a conducting material.

   (5) Faraday's transformer was based on Einstein's Theory of Relativity.

20. According to the passage, electricity would be a much less practical form of energy if there were no transformers because

   (1) generating electricity would become much more expensive.

   (2) there would be no dependable source of electric power.

   (3) generators would have to be built close to consumers.

   (4) industries and households will have to be supplied with the same power.

   (5) generating electricity would require large swathes of land.

21. What is the meaning of the word 'elucidated'?

   (1) clarified   (2) crystallized

   (3) obfuscated   (4) illuminated

   (5) solidified

22. What is the antonym of the word 'fluctuate'?

   (1) sway   (2) vary

   (3) vacillate   (4) stable

   (5) unstable

23. According to the passage, which of the following is correct?

   (1) The transformer was invented by Michael Faraday in the year 1831.

   (2) Transformers operate on alternating-current power systems.

   (3) Hans Christian Oersted, the Danish physicist, postulated that electric current creates magnetic field and vice versa.

   (4) The governing principle of a transformer is a function of its size.

   (5) Transformer was first built by Japanese.

24. The author is being _____ in the passage.

   (1) comparative   (2) evaluative

   (3) admiring   (4) informative

   (5) ambiguous

25. With reference to the passage, which of the following statements is not correct?

   (1) Electromagnetic induction was first demonstrated by Hans Christian Oersted.

   (2) The principle of electromagnetic induction states that a changing magnetic field in a conductor induces electric current.

   (3) Electromagnetic effect can also be established with the help of alternating current.

   (4) For changing the strength of the magnetic field, Faraday alternately made and broke the electric circuit generating the field.

   (5) Oersted first demostrated that an electric current can create a magnetic field.

Directions (Q. 26 to 30): Rearrange the following six sentences (A) , (B) (C) , (D) , (E) and (F) in the proper sequence to form a meaningful paragraph, then answer the questions given below them.

(A) She eased out something from her waist folds.

(B) Maganlal welcomed a customer early in the day.

(C) Once visible, Maganlal realized it was a pair of gold bangles.

(D) The woman carefully counted the money and then left.

(E) He took the bangles and placed some money in the women's palm.

(F) This customer was a peasant woman wearing a discoloured sari and old anklets.

26. Which of the following should be the **FIRST** sentence after rearrangement?

   (1) A   (2) B

   (3) C   (4) D

   (5) E

27. Which of the following should be the **SECOND** sentence after rearrangement?

   (1) B   (2) C

   (3) D   (4) E

   (5) F

28. Which of the following should be the **THIRD** sentence after rearrangement?

    (1) A   (2) B

    (3) C   (4) D

    (5) E

29. Which of the following should be the **FOURTH** sentence after rearrangement?

    (1) B   (2) C

    (3) D   (4) E

    (5) F

30. Which of the following should be the **LAST (SIXTH)** sentence after rearrangement?

    (1) B   (2) C

    (3) D   (4) E

    (5) F

NUMERICAL ABILITY

Directions (Q. 31 to 35): What approximate vale should come in place of question mark (?) in the following questions?

31. 23.999 × 9.004 × 16.997 = ?

    (1) 3200   (2) 4100

    (3) 2700   (4) 3700

    (5) 4500

32. $5\dfrac{7}{9} \times 8\dfrac{4}{5} \times 9\dfrac{2}{3} = ?$

    (1) 490   (2) 590

    (3) 540   (4) 460

    (5) 520

33. 5940 ÷ 28 ÷ 6 = ?

    (1) 40   (2) 35

    (3) 46   (4) 52

    (5) 27

34. 15.5% of 850 + 24.8% of 650 = ?

    (1) 295   (2) 330

    (3) 270   (4) 375

    (5) 520

35. $\sqrt[2]{2230} = ?$

    (1) 54   (2) 59

    (3) 41   (4) 37

    (5) 47

Directions (Q. 36 to 40): In each of the following questions two equations are given. You have to solve both the equations and find out values of x and y and give answer.

    (1) if x > y

    (2) if x < y

    (3) if x ≥ y

    (4) if x ≤ y

    (5) if x = y or relationship cannot be established

36. I. $x^2 + 3x - 10 = 0$

    II. $y^2 + y - 12 = 0$

37. I. $5x^2 + 2x - 3 = 0$

    II. $8y^2 - 11y + 3 = 0$

38. I. $12x - 7y = 41$

    II. $5x + 3y = 94$

39. I. $2x^2 + x - 1 = 0$

    II. $6y^2 - 13y + 5 = 0$

40. I. $10x^2 - x - 24 = 0$

    II. $y^2 - 2y = 0$

41. Govind is travelling from his house to Noida by his bike at 10 km/hr and will reach there at 2 p.m. However, he will reach there at 12 noon, if he travels at 15 km/hr. At what speed must he travel to reach Noida at 4 p.m.?

    (1) 5 km/hr   (2) 6 km/hr

    (3) 7.5 km/hr   (4) 8 km/hr

    (5) None of these

42. A tap can fill a tank in 3 hours. But, due to a leak it took 210 minutes to fill the tank. The leak can drain all the water of the tank in

    (1) 42 hrs   (2) 21 hrs

    (3) 18 hrs   (4) 36 hrs

    (5) None of these

43. The dimensions of a room are 20 m × 15 m × 14 m. What is the cost of painting the four walls of the room at Rs. 15 per square metre if there is one door of dimensions 8 m × 5 m.

    (1) Rs. 12,780

    (2) Rs. 14,110

    (3) Rs. 13,575

    (4) Rs. 11,400

    (5) None of these

44. Box 1 consists of 3 red and 4 black balls. Box 2 consists of 3 black and 6 white balls. One ball is picked randomly from each of the two boxes. What is the probability that both of these balls are colored black?

    (1) $\dfrac{2}{21}$ (2) $\dfrac{3}{7}$

    (3) $\dfrac{2}{7}$ (4) $\dfrac{3}{14}$

    (5) $\dfrac{4}{21}$

45. Two number are in the ratio 2 : 5. If 14 and 10 are subtracted from the first and the second number respectively, the new numbers are in the ratio 1 : 5. Find the difference of the two numbers.

(1) 24   (2) 27

(3) 30   (4) 33

(5) None of these

Directions (Q. 46 to 50): Find the next term in the given series.

46. 3, 7, 13, 21, 31, ___

(1) 41   (2) 42

(3) 43   (4) 45

(5) 47

47. 0, 2, 24, 252, ___

(1) 1020   (2) 2120

(3) 3120   (4) 3430

(5) 5250

48. 0, 6, 24, 60, ___

(1) 80   (2) 120

(3) 180   (4) 240

(5) 320

49. 3, 3, 8, 15, 15, 35, 24, 63, ___

(1) 35   (2) 99

(3) 44   (4) 108

(5) 78

50. 2, 18, 84, 260, ___

(1) 360   (2) 630

(3) 420   (4) 340

(5) 525

Directions (Q. 51 to 55): Answer the following questions based on the given information.

The table given below shows the number of students passed and failed in five classes of a school over the given years.

	VI		VII		VIII		IX		X	
	P	**F**	**P**	**F**	**P**	**F**	**P**	**F**	**P**	**F**
2009	56	4	74	5	66	9	65	3	48	2
2010	78	7	77	11	65	8	72	6	92	17
2011	45	9	67	16	58	6	74	6	84	8
2012	66	8	64	13	92	13	81	10	76	8
2013	87	12	48	3	88	9	76	8	65	5
2014	90	10	55	7	52	4	90	11	58	3

51. What is the respective ratio of the total number of passed students to the total number of failed students for the year 2014?

(1) 23 : 2   (2) 64 : 13

(3) 13 : 23   (4) 7 : 64

(5) None of these

52. What is the number of appeared students for all the classes together in the year 2013?

(1) 431   (2) 335

(3) 401   (4) 380

(5) None of these

53. What is the total percentage of passed students of class X during the given period? (Round off upto the second decimal place)

(1) 93.47   (2) 90.77

(3) 87.57   (4) 84.67

(5) None of these

54. Which of the following classes has the maximum number of passed students over the given years?

(1) VI   (2) VII

(3) VIII   (4) IX

(5) X

55. What is the average of the number of appeared students for class VII for the given years?

(1) 74   (2) 78

(3) 76   (4) 72

(5) None of these

56. A sum of Rs. 1,200 amounts to Rs. 1,380 in 3 years at simple interest. If the interest rate is increased by 3 percentage points, then it would amount to how much?

(1) Rs. 1,390   (2) Rs. 1,400

(3) Rs. 1,428   (4) Rs. 1,448

(5) Rs. 1,488

57. The population of a village is 5500. If the number of males increases by 11% and the number of females increases by 21%, then the population becomes 6300. Find the original number of females in the town.

(1) 2150

(2) 3000

(3) 2000

(4) 3500

(5) None of these

58. The average age of 24 students and the principal is 15 years. When the principal's age is excluded, the average age decreases by 1 year. What is the age of the principal?

(1) 38 years

(2) 40 years

(3) 39 years

(4) Data inadequate

(5) 41 years

59. A mixture of 729 ml contains milk and water in the ratio 7 : 2. How much more water should be added to get a new mixture containing milk and water in the ratio 7 : 3?

(1) 68 ml   (2) 71 ml

(3) 89 ml   (4) 95 ml

(5) 81 ml

60. A trader buys 78 kg of wheat for Rs. 492. He sells 40% of this at a loss of 20%. What should be the percentage mark up on the remaining so as to gain an overall 25%?

(1) 55%   (2) 60%

(3) 28%   (4) 45%

(5) None of these

Directions (Q. 61 to 65): Study the following pie-chart and answer the given questions.

Percentagewise distribution of employees in six different professions

Total number of employees = 26800

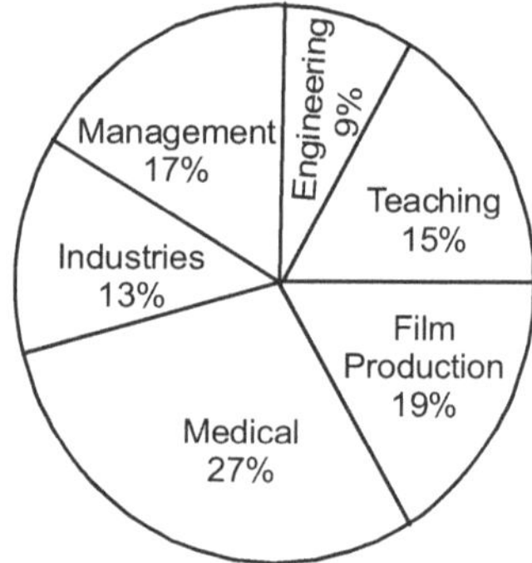

61. What is the difference between the total number of employees in teaching and medical profession together and the number of employees in management profession?

(1) 6770   (2) 7700

(3) 6700   (4) 7770

(5) 6000

62. In management profession three-fourth of the number of employees are female. What is the number of male employees in management profession?

(1) 1239   (2) 1143

(3) 1156   (4) 1139

(5) None of these

63. 25% of employees from film production profession went on a strike. What is the number of employees from film production who did not participate in the strike?

(1) 3271   (2) 3819

(3) 3948   (4) 1273

(5) None of these

64. What is the total number of employees in engineering profession and industries together?

(1) 5698   (2) 5884

(3) 5687   (4) 5890

(5) None of these

65. In teaching profession if three-fifth of the teachers are not permanent, what is the number of permanent teachers in the teaching profession?

(1) 1608   (2) 1640

(3) 1764   (4) 1704

(5) None of these

REASONING ABILITY

Directions (Q. 66 to 70): Answer the questions on the basis of the information given below.

Four friends – Arpit, Ashu, Kangkana and Nidhi – are to appear for four exams – Bank - PO, EPFO, CAT and FCI – not necessarily in that order. The centers for the exams are in four different colleges – BU, AU, DU and PU – which are situated in four different cities – P, Q, R and S – not necessarily in that order. It is also known that:

(i) Ashu's examination center is DU.

(ii) The college assigned to FCI is AU, which is situated in Q.

(iii) The friend, whose exam center is BU, is to visit S to take his/her exam.

(iv) Kangkana has applied for Bank-PO. Arpit is to visit R to take his exam.

66. Which is the correct 'city - center' combination for Kangkana?

(1) S - AU   (2) S - BU

(3) Q - BU   (4) Q - AU

(5) R - DU

67. In which city is Ashu's exam centre located?

(1) S   (2) P

(3) Q   (4) R

(5) Cannot be determined

68. Nidhi's exam center is

(1) BU   (2) DU

(3) AU   (4) PU

(5) Cannot be determined

69. Which of the following can be a correct combination of 'exam - city' for Arpit?

(1) EPFO - S

(2) FCI - R

(3) CAT - R

(4) EPFO - R

(5) Either (3) or (4)

70. Which of the following statements is definitely true?

(1) CAT is to be written by Ashu.

(2) Centre for EPFO is located in R.

(3) Exam center of Arpit is PU.

(4) FCI is to be written by Arpit.

(5) None is true.

71. Ajit goes 7 km towards west and takes a turn towards north and covers 5 km. Now he turns towards east and covers 2 km. Now he turns again and covers 9 km toward south. How far is he from the starting point?

(1) $\sqrt{65}$ km   (2) $\sqrt{56}$ km

(3) $\sqrt{12}$ km   (4) $\sqrt{41}$ km

(5) $\sqrt{39}$ km

72. A man rides his bike from point N towards north and goes 20 km straight then he takes a 45° turn to his right and goes $20\sqrt{2}$ km. Then he takes a 135° turn to his right and goes 60 km. He takes another 135° turn to his right and goes $20\sqrt{2}$ km and reaches the starting point. The area inscribed by the path of the rider is:

(1) 400 km²   (2) 440 km²

(3) 800 km²   (4) 840 km²

(5) 880 km²

Directions (Q. 73 and 74): Study the following information carefully and answer the questions given below:

(i) 'P × Q' means 'P is brother of Q'.

(ii) 'P – Q' means 'P is sister of Q'.

(iii) 'P ÷ Q' means 'P is father of Q'.

(iv) 'P + Q' means 'P is mother of Q'.

73. Which of the following means 'D is nephew of R'?

(1) D × M ÷ R   (2) R – M ÷ D

(3) R – M ÷ D × T   (4) R × M + D

(5) None of these

74. Which of the following means 'M is maternal uncle of T'?

(1) M × R + T   (2) M × R ÷ T

(3) T × J – N ÷ M   (4) M – R + T

(5) None of these

75. Pointing to a gentleman, Deepak said, "His only brother is the father of my daughter's father." How is the gentleman related to Deepak?

(1) Father   (2) Grandfather

(3) Brother   (4) Brother-in-law

(5) Uncle

Directions (Q.76 to 80): In the following questions, the symbol @, \$, δ, % and * are used with the following meaning as illustrated below

'P \$ Q' mean 'P is either greater than or equal to Q'.

'P * Q' means "P is neither greater than nor smaller than Q'.

'P @ Q' means 'P is neither smaller than nor equal to Q'

P % Q' means P is either smaller than or equal to Q'.

P δ Q' means 'P is neither greater than nor equal to Q'.

Now in each of the following questions assuming the given statements to be true, find which of conclusions I and II given below them is/are definitely true and give your answer accordingly.

Give answer (1) if only Conclusion I is true.

Give answer (2) if only Conclusion II is true.

Give answer (3) if either Conclusion I or II is true.

Give answer (4) if neither Conclusion I nor II is true.

Give answer (5) if both Conclusions I and II are true.

76. Statements:

H \$ J, J*T, T δ K

Conclusions:

I. T * H

II. T δ H

77. Statements:

Z % N, N @ D, D δ K

Conclusions:

I. K @ N

II. Z δ D

78. Statements:

W δ K, K%M, M\$H

Conclusions:

I. H * K

II. W δ M

79. Statements:

M * R, R%N, N\$B

Conclusions:

I. B δ R

II. N \$ M

80. Statements:

D % T, T δ K, K * W

Conclusions:

I. W @ T

II. K @ D

Directions (Q.81-85): Study the following information to answer the given questions:

Eight members – L, N, P, R, T, V, X and Y – are sitting at a square table such that exactly two members are sitting on each side of the table and all are facing the center. Each member is sitting exactly opposite to a member. R is sitting to the immediate left of X who is exactly opposite P. T is sitting two places right of Y who is right of P. L is the second to the right of R.

81. Who is sitting opposite to R?

(1) N   (2) Y

(3) V   (4) T

(5) None of these

82. Who is sitting second to the right of L?

(1) T   (2) R

(3) N   (4) P

(5) None of these

83. If V is sitting immediate right of L, then who is sitting immediate left of T?

(1) N   (2) R

(3) L   (4) X

(5) None of these

84. In which of the following pairs of members are sitting on the same side of the table?

(1) LV   (2) TN

(3) PT   (4) LT

(5) None of these

85. In which of the following pairs of members has the second member (starting from left) sitting left of the first member?

(1) LX   (2) PY

(3) RX   (4) TR

(5) None of these

Directions (Q.86-90): Answer the questions on the basis of the information given below.

In a certain code "little flower school" is coded as "pa li ka", "beautiful flower garden" is coded as "gu li bi" , "beautiful little girl" is coded as "bi pa sa" and "school reopens tomorrow" is coded as "ha ru ka".

86. What does the code "sa" stand for?

(1) reopens   (2) garden

(3) girl   (4) little

(5) school

87. What does "ha ru" represent?

(1) reopens tomorrow

(2) beautiful garden

(3) little girl

(4) tomorrow school

(5) school garden

88. What is the code for "flower garden"?

(1) li sa   (2) gu li

(3) bi pa   (4) gu ru

(5) pa gu

89. How can "tomorrow shop reopens" be coded?

(1) "ha li ru"

(2) "ru bi sa"

(3) "ha ru so"

(4) "ha pa ka"

(5) "ha ru gu"

90. What is the code for "tomorrow"?

(1) ha   (2) gu

(3) pa   (4) li

(5) Cannot be determined

Directions (Q.91-95): Study the following information to answer the questions:

Six persons – Sameer, Manish, Keshav, Ramesh, Harish and Deepak – went for a picnic along with their wives Shalini, Monika, Kareena, Ritika, Heena and Divya (not necessarily in the same order). Exactly two couples travelled in one car. Also, husband's name cannot start with the same alphabet as that of his wife's name. It is also given that:

(a) Keshav is not married to Shalini and Ramesh is not married to Divya.

(b) Manish is married to Kareena and Harish is married to Monika.

(c) Manish and Heena traveled in the same car.

(d) Ramesh and Divya traveled in the same car.

(e) Sameer and Monika traveled in the same car.

91. Manish and Heena traveled with whom in the same car?

(1) Deepak and Kareena

(2) Ramesh and Divya

(3) Harish and Ritika

(4) Sameer and Monika

(5) Keshav and Shalini

92. Which of the following is the correct combination of a husband-wife couple?

(1) Sameer and Divya

(2) Ramesh and Shalini

(3) Keshav and Ritika

(4) Keshav and Heena

(5) Sameer and Heena

93. Which of the following persons traveled in the same car?

    (1) Deepak and Sameer

    (2) Ramesh and Heena

    (3) Deepak and Manish

    (4) Sameer and Divya

    (5) Harish and Manish

94. Who is the husband of Ritika?

    (1) Deepak   (2) Manish

    (3) Keshav   (4) Sameer

    (5) None of these

95. Who is the female companion of Shalini in the car?

    (1) Kareena   (2) Monika

    (3) Divya   (4) Ritika

    (5) None of these

Directions (Q. 96 to 100): In each of the questions below, two statements are followed by four conclusions numbered I, II, III and IV are given. You have to take the given statements to be true even if they seem to be at variance with commonly known facts. Read all the conclusions and then decide which of the given conclusion(s) logically follow/follows from the given statements disregarding commonly known facts.

96. **Statements:** All cats are tigers. Some tigers are lions.

    Conclusions:

    I.   All cats are lions.

    II. All lions are cats.

    III. Some lions are cats.

    IV. Some cats are lions.

    (1) None follow

    (2) All follow

    (3) Only I and III follow

    (4) Only III and IV follow

    (5) Only I follows

97. **Statements:** All cups are plates. All plates are tables.

    Conclusions:

    I.   All cups are tables.

    II. All tables are cups.

    III. Some tables are cups.

    IV. No tables are plates.

    (1) All follow

    (2) Only I, III and IV follow

    (3) Only II, III and IV follow

    (4) Only I and III follow

    (5) Only I, II and IV follow

98. **Statements:** Some parrots are monkeys. Some monkeys are jackals.

    Conclusions:

    I.   Some parrots are jackals.

    II. Some jackals are parrots.

    III. Some jackals are monkeys.

    IV. Some monkeys are parrots.

    (1) All follow

    (2) Only I and III follow

    (3) Only III and IV follow

    (4) None follow

    (5) Only III follows

99. **Statements:** Some dogs are doors. All doors are chairs.

    Conclusions:

    I.   Some dogs are chairs.

    II. Some chairs are dogs.

    III. All chairs are doors.

    IV. No door is a dog.

    (1) None follow

    (2) All follow

    (3) Only I ,II and IV follow

    (4) Only I, III and IV follow

    (5) Only I and II follow

100. **Statements:** Man is a van. Van is a vehicle.

    Conclusions:

    I.   Some vans are men.

    II. Some vehicles are men.

    III. Man is a vehicle.

    IV. Some vehicles are not men.

    (1) All follow

    (2) Only II, III and IV follow

    (3) Only I, II and IV follow

    (4) Only I, II and III follow

    (5) None follow

ANSWERS

1. (1)	**2.** (2)	**3.** (5)	**4.** (2)	**5.** (5)	**6.** (4)	**7.** (4)	**8.** (5)	**9.** (1)	**10.** (2)
11. (4)	**12.** (5)	**13.** (2)	**14.** (5)	**15.** (4)	**16.** (2)	**17.** (3)	**18.** (4)	**19.** (4)	**20.** (3)
21. (1)	**22.** (4)	**23.** (2)	**24.** (4)	**25.** (1)	**26.** (2)	**27.** (5)	**28.** (1)	**29.** (2)	**30.** (3)
31. (4)	**32.** (1)	**33.** (2)	**34.** (1)	**35.** (5)	**36.** (5)	**37.** (5)	**38.** (2)	**39.** (4)	**40.** (5)
41. (3)	**42.** (2)	**43.** (5)	**44.** (5)	**45.** (5)	**46.** (3)	**47.** (3)	**48.** (2)	**49.** (1)	**50.** (2)
51. (5)	**52.** (3)	**53.** (2)	**54.** (4)	**55.** (5)	**56.** (5)	**57.** (5)	**58.** (3)	**59.** (5)	**60.** (1)
61. (3)	**62.** (4)	**63.** (2)	**64.** (5)	**65.** (1)	**66.** (2)	**67.** (2)	**68.** (3)	**69.** (5)	**70.** (3)
71. (4)	**72.** (3)	**73.** (3)	**74.** (1)	**75.** (5)	**76.** (3)	**77.** (4)	**78.** (2)	**79.** (2)	**80.** (5)
81. (2)	**82.** (4)	**83.** (1)	**84.** (5)	**85.** (1)	**86.** (3)	**87.** (1)	**88.** (2)	**89.** (3)	**90.** (5)
91. (1)	**92.** (2)	**93.** (3)	**94.** (4)	**95.** (3)	**96.** (1)	**97.** (4)	**98.** (3)	**99.** (5)	**100.** (4)

EXPLANATIONS

1. (1) 'With and 'of' are the correct prepositions.

2. (2) 'To' and 'in' are the right words for the blanks.

3. (5) 'To' and 'in' are the correct words. Contrary should be followed by 'to'.

4. (2) 'Nearest' and 'next' are the correct words for the first and second blanks respectively.

5. (5) Since 'former' is mentioned, 'latter' will be the correct option. 'Prefer' is always followed by the preposition 'to'.

6. (4) Replace 'probable' with 'probably'.

7. (4) Replace 'above' with 'regarding'.

8. (5) The sentence is grammatically correct.

9. (1) 'Easy' is used in a wrong way. The correct word should have been 'eased'.

10. (2) Replace 'linkage' with 'linked.'

11. (4) A nest is 'built' and not 'grown'.

12. (5) The sparrow wishes to kill the elephant. So, we can infer that the sparrow thinks of the elephant as 'wicked'.

13. (2) They recited the incident to the frog. So, 'narrated' fits in the meaning of the sentence.

14. (5) One will 'search' for water when thirsty.

15. (4) One trapped in marshy land, unless rescued, drowns and dies.

16. (2) Paragraph 5 lists several advances in the transformer. The list is followed by the statement that the 'advances reflect the marriage of theoretical inquiry and engineering that first elucidated and then exploited the phenomena governing transformer action.

17. (3) The answer to this question is directly stated in the passage. 'At the time, Oersted's discovery was considered remarkable, since electricity and magnetism were thought to be separate and unrelated forces'. Option (3) is a paraphrase of this sentence.

18. (4) The passage confirms that option (4) is not true. Transformers today are said to be able to 'handle…..15 times the voltage' (paragraph 5) of earlier transformers. Option (1) can be found in paragraph 3 which states that the first practical transformer contained all the essential elements of the modern instrument. Options (2) and (3) both have been mentioned in the discussion of the improvements in the transformer over the years (paragraph 5).

19. (4) The answer to this question can be found in the first sentence of the last paragraph. 'Faraday demonstrated that for a magnetic field to induce a current in a conductor the field must be changing'. (B) and (C) are not true statements. Only (A) is left, and it is also a misstatement; it is true about Oersted, not about Faraday.

20. (3) 'Were it not for transformers, the distance separating generators from consumers would have to be minimized. In other words, without transformers, generators would need to be built near consumers. Options (1), (2) and (4) are speculative and are not supported by the passage.

21. (1) 'Elucidate' means to make something clear by explaining it.

22. (4) 'Fluctuate' refers to rising and falling irregularly, that is, being unstable.

23. (2) Refer to the last line of the fourth paragraph; alternating-current power systems had been universally adopted by the turn of the century... From this statement, it can be clearly inferred that transformers operate on alternating-current power systems, making option (2) the correct answer. Option (1 is incorrect because Michael Faraday discovered, not invented, the basic action of the transformer. Option (3) is also incorrect because although Hans Christian showed that electric current creates a magnetic field, the passage is silent about whether he showed that a magnetic field also produces electric current. Option (4) is negated because it is mentioned in the last line of the second paragraph of the passage that the governing principles of all electrical transformers are the same, irrespective of their form or size.

24. (4) Option (4) is the correct answer because the author is giving information about a transformer, its basic operating principle, its advantages, its utility, etc. Option (1) can be negated because the author is not comparing anything in the passage. Option (2) is incorrect because the author is not evaluating a transformer or its application for that matter. Option (3) is also ruled out because the author is simply stating some facts about transformers, not stating any opinion.

25. (1) Option (1) is the correct answer because it is mentioned in the passage that Michael Faraday demonstrated the relation between electric current and magnetic field, which later came to be known as electromagnetic induction. Options (2), (3) and (4) are clearly mentioned in the passage.

26. (2) The correct sequence should be BFACED

31. (4)
$$? = 23.999 \times 9.004 \times 16.997$$
$$\approx 24 \times 9 \times 17$$
$$= 3672 \approx 3700$$

32. (1)
$$? = 5\frac{7}{9} \times 8\frac{4}{5} \times 9\frac{2}{3}$$
$$= \frac{52}{9} \times \frac{44}{5} \times \frac{29}{3} \approx 490.$$

33. (2)
$$? = 5940 \div 28 \div 6$$
$$= 35.35 \approx 35$$

34. (1)
$$? = \frac{15.5}{100} \times 850 + \frac{24.8}{100} \times 650$$
$$= 131.75 + 161.2$$
$$= 292.95 \approx 295$$

35. (5) $? = \sqrt[2]{2230} \approx 47.$

36. (5) I. $x^2 + 3x - 10 = 0$
II. $y^2 + y - 12 = 0$
Solving this, we get
$$x = -5, 2 \text{ and } y = 3, -4$$
∴ Relationship cannot be established.

37. (5) I. $5x^2 + 2x - 3 = 0$
II. $8y^2 - 11y + 3 = 0$
Solving this, we get
$$x = -1, \frac{3}{5} \text{ and } y = 1, \frac{3}{8}$$
∴ Relationship cannot be established.

38. (2) I. $12x - 7y = 41$
II. $5x + 3y = 94$
Solving this, we get
$$x = -13 \text{ and } y = 53$$
∴ $y > x$

39. (4) I. $2x^2 + x - 1 = 0$
II. $6y^2 - 13y + 5 = 0$
Solving this, we get
$$x = -1, \frac{1}{2} \text{ and } y = \frac{1}{2}, \frac{5}{3}$$
∴ $y \geq x$

40. (5) I. $10x^2 - x - 24 = 0$
II. $y^2 - 2y = 0$
Solving this, we get
$$x = \frac{8}{5}, -\frac{3}{2} \text{ and } y = 2, 0$$

41. (3) Let the required distance be x km.
$$\Rightarrow \frac{x}{10} - \frac{x}{15} = 2 \text{ or } x = 60 \text{ km}$$
Thus at 10 km/hr it takes him 6 hrs.
So to reach at 4 pm he has to travel for 8 hrs.
Hence, required speed = 60/8 = 7.5 km/hr.

42. (2) Work done by leak in 1 hr = $\frac{1}{3} - \frac{2}{7} = \frac{1}{21}$
Hence, the required time = 21 hrs.

43. (5) Required area to be painted
$$= 14 \times (20 + 15) \times 2 - 8 \times 5$$
$$= 940$$
Hence, required cost = 940 × 15 = Rs. 14100.

44. (5) Probability of picking a black ball from Box 1
$$= \frac{4}{3+4} = \frac{4}{7}$$

Probability of picking a black ball from Box 2

$$= \frac{3}{3+6} = \frac{1}{3}$$

∴　Probability of both the above events happening together $= \frac{4}{7} \times \frac{1}{3} = \frac{4}{21}$.

45. (5) Let the two numbers be 2x and 5x respectively.

$$\Rightarrow (2x - 14) : (5x - 10) = 1 : 5$$

Hence, x = 12 and required difference = 3x = 36.

46. (3) The series is moving as $(1)^2 + 2$, $(2)^2 + 3$, $(3)^2 + 4$,… Hence, answer is $(6)^2 + 7 = 43$

47. (3) The series is moving as $(1)^1 - 1$, $(2)^2 - 2$, $(3)^3 - 3$,… Hence, answer is $(5)^5 - 5 = 3120$

48. (2) The series is moving as $(1)^3 - 1$, $(2)^3 - 2$, $(3)^3 - 3$,… Hence, answer is $(5)^3 - 5 = 120$

49. (1) The series is an alternate series with the following segments:

$$3 + 5 = 8$$
$$8 + 7 = 15$$
$$15 + 9 = 24$$

Similarly,

$$3 + 12 = 15$$
$$15 + 20 = 35$$
$$35 + 28 = 63$$

Hence, answer will lie in the first series which

$$= 24 + 11 = 35.$$

50. (2) The series is moving as $(1)^4 + 1$, $(2)^4 + 2$, $(3)^4 + 3$,… Hence, answer is $(5)^4 + 5 = 630$

51. (5) The total number of passed students for the year 2014

$$= 90 + 55 + 52 + 90 + 58 = 345.$$

The total number of failed students for the year 2014

$$= 10 + 7 + 4 + 11 + 3 = 35.$$

Required ratio = 345 : 35 i.e. 69 : 7.

52. (3) The total number of appeared students in the year 2013

$$= 87 + 12 + 48 + 3 + 88 + 9 + 76 + 8 + 65 + 5$$
$$= 401.$$

53. (2) The total number of passed students of class X

$$= 48 + 92 + 84 + 76 + 65 + 58 = 423.$$

The total number of appeared students of class X

$$= 423 + (2 + 17 + 8 + 8 + 5 + 3) = 466.$$

Required percentage $= \dfrac{423}{466} \times 100 \approx 90.77\%$.

54. (4) The total number of passed students of class VI

$$= 422.$$

The total number of passed students of class VII = 385.

The total number of passed students of class VIII = 421.

The total number of passed students of class IX = 458.

The total number of passed students of class X = 423.

Hence, IX class has the maximum number of passed students.

55. (5) The average number of appeared students of class

$$\text{VII} = \frac{385 + (5 + 11 + 16 + 13 + 3 + 7)}{6}$$

$$= \frac{440}{6} \approx 73.33.$$

56. (5)　　$\text{S.I.} = (1,380 - 1,200) = \text{Rs. } 180,$

$$P = \text{Rs. } 1,200,$$
$$T = 3 \text{ years}$$

$$\therefore \ R = \left(\frac{100 \times 180}{1200 \times 3} \right) = 5\%$$

New rate $= (5 + 3) = 8\%$

New S.I. $= \dfrac{1200 \times 8 \times 3}{100} = \text{Rs. } 288$

∴　New amount = (1200 + 288) = Rs. 1,488.

57. (5) Let the number of males and females be x and y respectively.

According to the given condition,

$$x + y = 5500 \qquad\qquad …(i)$$

and 1.11x + 1.21y = 6300

$$\Rightarrow \ 111x + 121y = 630000 \qquad …(ii)$$

By solving equations (i) and (ii), we get

$$y = 1950.$$

Hence, the population of female in the village = 1950.

58. (3) Average age of 24 students and the principal

$$= 15 \text{ years.}$$

Total age of 24 students and the principal

$$= 15 \times 25 = 375 \text{ years.}$$

New average age of 24 students

$$= 15 - 1 = 14 \text{ years}$$

Total age of 24 students = 14 × 24 = 336 years

∴　Age of the principal = 375 – 336 = 39 years.

59. (5) The amount of milk $= \dfrac{7}{9} \times 729 = 567$ ml and the amount of water will be = (729 – 567) = 162 ml

Let 'x' ml of water is added to the mixture.

So, $\dfrac{567}{162+x} = \dfrac{7}{3} \Rightarrow x = 81$ ml

60. (1) CP per kilogram $= \dfrac{492}{78} = $ Rs. 6.30

For an overall gain of 25%, the SP of 78 kg

$$= 492 \times \dfrac{492}{78} = \text{Rs. } 615$$

By selling 40%, i.e. 31.2 kg at a loss of 20%.

$$SP_1 = 31.2 \times \left(\dfrac{492}{78}\right) \times \dfrac{80}{100}$$

$$= \text{Rs. } 157.44$$

Now the remaining i.e. $(78 - 31.2) = 46.8$ kg wheat is to be sold for $(615 - 157.44)$ i.e. Rs. 457.56.

$$SP_2 = \dfrac{457.56}{46.8} = \text{Rs. } 9.77 \text{ per kilogram}$$

$$\text{Mark-up} = \dfrac{9.77 - 6.3}{6.3} = 55\%.$$

61. (3) Total number of employees (in percent) in teaching and medical proffession $= [15 + 27]\%$ $= 42\%$ and Total number of employees (in percent) in management $= 17\%$

Difference in % $= (42 - 17)\% = 25\%$

$$\therefore \quad 25\% \text{ of } 26800 = \dfrac{25}{100} \times 26800 = 6700$$

Hence, required difference = 6700.

62. (4) In management proffession three-forth of employees are female i.e., $\left[\dfrac{3}{4} \times 100\right]\% = 75\%$

$\therefore$ In management proffession 25% of employees are male

Now total number of employees in management

$$\text{profession} = \dfrac{26800 \times 17}{100} = 4556$$

$\therefore$ Number of male employee in management

$$\text{profession} = \dfrac{4556 \times 25}{100} = 1139.$$

63. (2) According to questions, 25% of employees from film production proffession went on strike

$\therefore$ 75 % of employee of film production have not participated in strike

Now total employee of film production

$$= \dfrac{26800 \times 19}{100} = 5092$$

$\therefore$ Number of employees from film production who have not participated in strike

$$= \dfrac{5092 \times 75}{100} = 3819.$$

64. (5) Number of employee (in percent) of engineering profession = 9%

and number of employee (in percent) of industries proffesion = 13%

$\therefore$ Total percent $= (13 + 9)\% = 22\%$

$$\therefore \quad 22\% \text{ of } 26800 = \dfrac{26800 \times 22}{100} = 5896.$$

65. (1) According to question, three-fifth of teacher are not permanent i.e. $\left(\dfrac{3}{5} \times 100\right)\% = 60\%$

$\therefore$ Percent of permanent teacher = 40%

Number of teacher in teaching profession

$$= \dfrac{26800 \times 15}{100} = 4020$$

$\therefore$ Number of permanent teachers in teaching

$$\text{profession} = \dfrac{4020 \times 40}{100} = 1608.$$

For questions 66 to 70:

The information can be summarized as shown in the table given below.

Name	Kangkana	Nidhi	Ashu	Arpit
Exam Name	Bank-PO	FCI	EPFO/CAT	CAT/EPFO
Centre Name	BU	AU	DU	PU
Venue of Centre	S	Q	P	R

71. (4)

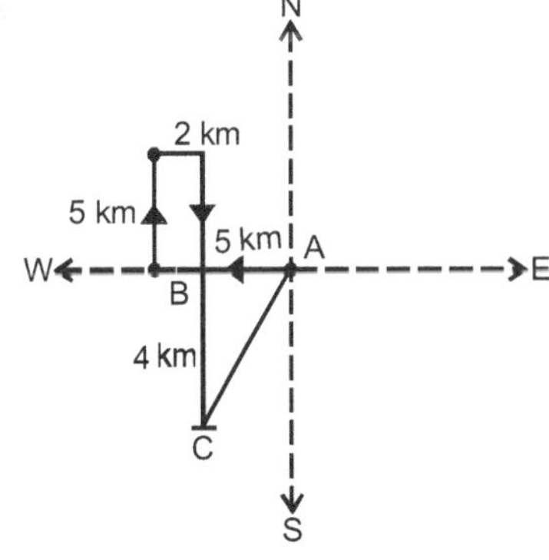

$$AB = 7 - 2 = 5 \text{ km},$$
$$BC = 9 - 5 = 4 \text{ km}$$
$$AC = \sqrt{5^2 + 4^2} = \sqrt{41} \text{ km}$$

72. (3)

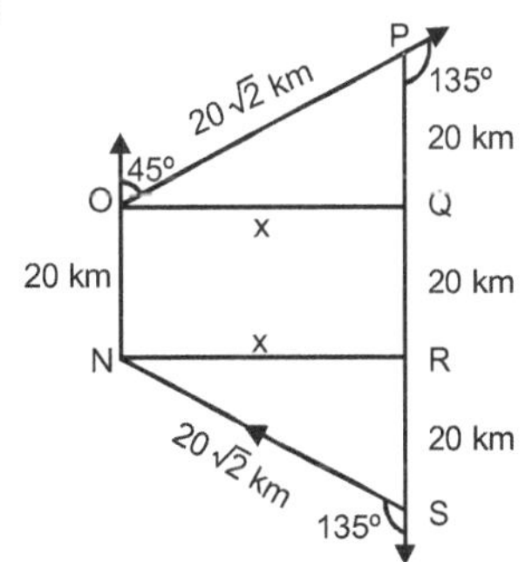

$$\frac{20}{X} = \tan 45^\circ$$

$\Rightarrow \qquad X = 20 \text{ km}$

Area of triangle OPQ × 2 + Area of square NOQR

$$= 2 \times \frac{1}{2} \times 20 \times 20 + 20 \times 20$$

$$= 400 + 400$$

$$= 800 \text{ km}^2$$

73. (3) R – M ÷ D × T:

R$^-$——M$^+$

D$^+$——T

+ → Male

– → Female

Clearly, 'D is nephew of R'.

74. (1) M × R + T:

M$^+$——R$^-$

T

+ → Male

– → Female

75. (5) Gentleman —— Brother (Deepak's father)

Deepak's daughter's father (Deepak)

Deepak's daughter

Hence, the gentleman is uncle of Deepak.

76. (3) $H \$ J \Rightarrow H \geq J$

$J*T \Rightarrow J = T$

$T \delta K \Rightarrow T < K$

Hence, $H \geq J = T < K$

Conclusions:

I. $T * H \Rightarrow T = H$ (Not true)

II. $T \delta H \Rightarrow T < H$ (Not true)

Conclusions I and II form complementary pair. Hence, either I or II is correct.

77. (4) $Z \% N \Rightarrow Z \leq N$

$N @ D \Rightarrow N > D$

$D \delta K \Rightarrow D < K$

Hence, $Z \leq N > D < K$

Conclusions:

I. $K @ N \Rightarrow K > N$ (Not true)

II. $Z \delta D \Rightarrow z < D$ (Not true)

78. (2) $W \delta K \Rightarrow W < K$

$K \% M \Rightarrow K \leq M$

$M \$ H \Rightarrow M \geq H$

Hence, $W < K \leq M \geq H$

Conclusions:

I. $H * K \Rightarrow H = K$ (Not true)

II. $W \delta M \Rightarrow W < M$ (True)

79. (2) $M * R \Rightarrow M = R$

$R \% N \Rightarrow R \leq N$

$N \$ B \Rightarrow N \geq B$

Hence, $M = R \leq N \geq B$

Conclusions:

I. $B \delta R \Rightarrow B < R$ (Not true)

II. $N \$ M \Rightarrow N \geq M$ (True)

80. (5) $D \% T \Rightarrow D \leq T$

$T \delta K \Rightarrow T < K$

$K * W \Rightarrow K = W$

Hence, $D \leq T < K = W$

Conclusions:

I. $W @ T \Rightarrow W > T$ (True)

II. $K @ D \Rightarrow K > D$ (True)

For questions 81 to 85: The given information can be shown as:

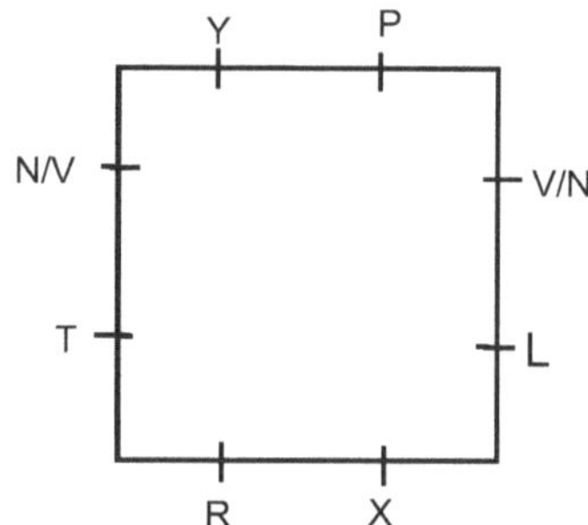

For question 86 to 90: The given information can be shown as:

little	pa
flower	li
school	ka
beautiful	bi
garden	gu
girl	sa
reopens	ha / ru
tomorrow	ru / ha

For question 91 to 95: The given information can be shown as:

Car I:
| Manish-Kareena |
| Deepak-Heena |

Car II:
| Ramesh-Shalini |
| Keshav-Divya |

Car III:
| Harish-Monika |
| Sameer-Ritika |

91. (1) Deepak and Kareena traveled along with Manish and Heena.

92. (2) Ramesh-Shalini is the correct combination of a husband wife couple.

93. (3) Deepak and Manish traveled in the same car.

96. (1)

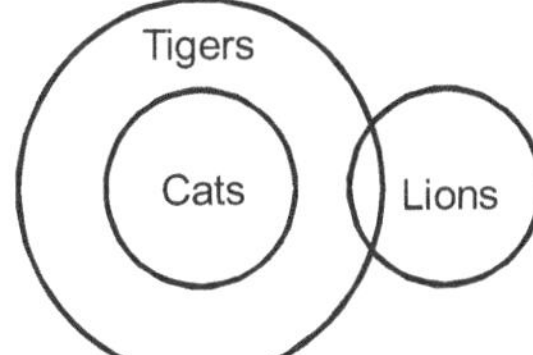

Fig (a)

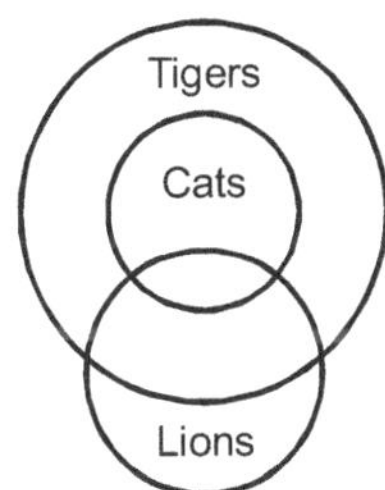

Fig (b)

None of the given conclusions follow.

97. (4)

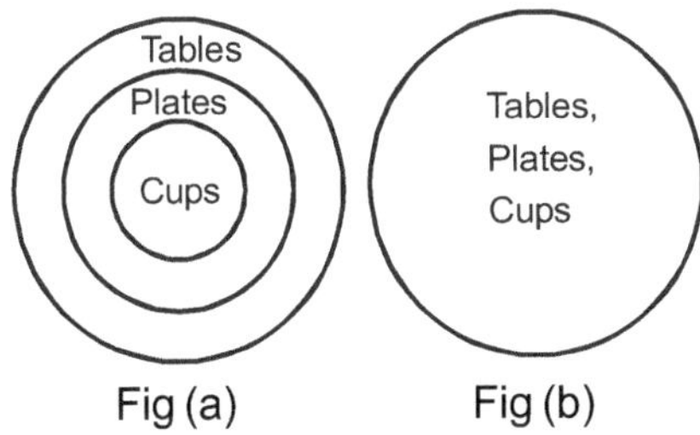

Fig (a)   Fig (b)

Only conclusions I and III follow.

98. (3)

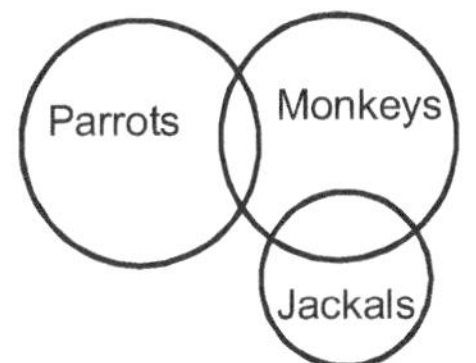

Fig (a)

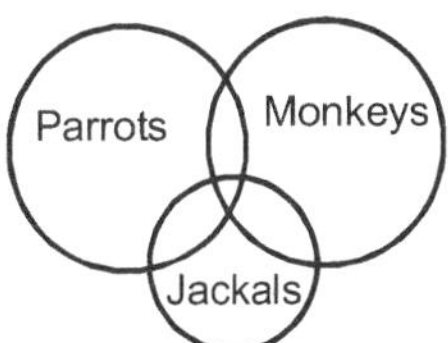

Fig (b)

Only conclusions III and IV follow.

99. (5)

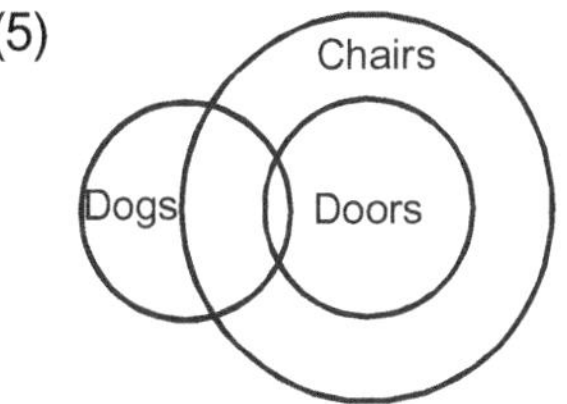

Fig (a)

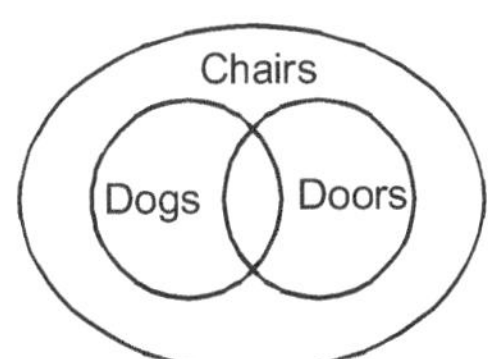

Fig (b)

Only conclusions I and II follow.

100. (4)

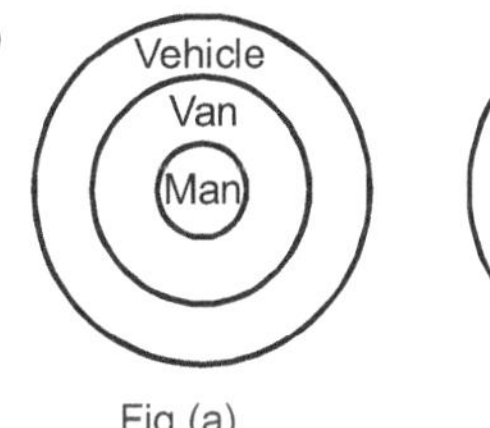

Fig (a)   Fig (b)

Only conclusions I, II and III follow.

PRACTICE PAPER – 6

ENGLISH LANGUAGE

Directions for questions 1 to 5: Read each sentence to find out whether there is any grammatical or idiomatic error in it. The error, if any, will be in one part of the sentence. The number of that part is the answer. If there is no error, the answer is 5 (Ignore errors of punctuation, if any).

1. Banks are on the verge (1) / of facing a formidable challenge (2) /of losing over fifty per cent of (3) / their employees due to retirement. (4) / No error

2. Not only has the commerce ministry fixed (1) / extraordinarily high minimum prices for onion exports (2) /but also made licences mandatory (3) / for every consignment. (4) / No error (5)

3. A new study found that while weight loss (1) / via surgery may reduce knee pain (2) / there may be permanent damage to the knee in obese patients (3) / from being severely overweight. (4) / No error (5)

4. In order to streamline (1) / the movement of vehicles during (2) / the festival, traffic police have (3) / chalked out diversion plans. (4) / No error (5)

5. With a view to avoid another caste conflict, (1) / the administration has deployed additional police force (2) / on the village, while the administration as well as police officials (3) / are monitoring the situation. (4) / No error (5)

Directions for questions 6 to 10: Each question below has two blanks, each blank indicating that something has been omitted. Choose the set of words for each blank which best fits the meaning of the sentence as a whole.

6. Much of the ___ that cricket has is due to the fact it is a ___ sport.
   - (1) allure, lucrative
   - (2) criticism, controversial
   - (3) attraction, unpopular
   - (4) flak, great
   - (5) comments, unusual

7. Since foggy weather ___ visibility by several metres, the railways has either ___ or diverted some of the trains.
   - (1) improves, started
   - (2) impairs, called off
   - (3) hampers, withdrawn
   - (4) decrease, stopped
   - (5) reduces, cancelled

8. The once ___ district is gradually being ___ of its green cover.
   - (1) remote, eroded
   - (2) arid, replenished
   - (3) beautiful, devoid
   - (4) picturesque, depleted
   - (5) lush, rob

9. The pilot knew she would be able to see the ___ lights of the city from her cockpit window, but she would not see the fireworks explode to welcome the new year as she would have ___ to cruising altitude.
   - (1) few, soared
   - (2) divine, escalate
   - (3) glistening, jumped
   - (4) shining, reached
   - (5) glittering, climbed

10. The New Year has ___ in good news for city hotels as most properties are ___ for the whole month.
    - (1) brought, deserted
    - (2) ushered, packed
    - (3) pushed, full
    - (4) steered, renovating
    - (5) escorted, vacant

Directions for questions 11 to 15: Rearrange the following six sentences (A), (B), (C), (D), (E) and (F) in the proper sequence to form a meaningful paragraph; then answer the questions given below them.

(A) To their surprise, however, the reward went to a beggar who had contributed only a rupee instead of a wealthy donor.

(B) He received funds from many people as rich and poor donated generously to this trust.

(C) The man explained that the one rupee given by the beggar was worth millions of rupees as that was all the money he possessed and that he had made a much greater sacrifice than the others.

(D) During the function everyone waited with bated breath to hear who had made the maximum contribution.

(E) A man went from town to town to collect money for his charitable trust.

(F) On returning he decided to hold a function and reward the person whose contribution had been the maximum

11. Which of the following should be the **FIRST** sentence after rearrangement?

(1) A   (2) B

(3) D   (4) E

(5) F

12. Which of the following should be the **SECOND** sentence after rearrangement?

(1) B   (2) C

(3) D   (4) E

(5) F

13. Which of the following should be the **THIRD** sentence after rearrangement

(1) A   (2) B

(3) D   (4) E

(5) F

14. Which of the following should be the **FOURTH** sentence after rearrangement

(1) B   (2) C

(3) D   (4) E

(5) F

15. Which of the following should be the **LAST (SIXTH)** sentence after rearrangement

(1) A   (2) C

(3) D   (4) E

(5) F

Directions for questions 16 to 25: Read the following passage carefully and answer the questions given below it. Certain words/phrases have been given in **bold** to help you locate them while answering some of the questions.

Nevertheless, with the hunt for resources turning inwards history begins to repeat itself, but this time perhaps as a **farce**. Development again becomes a class project despite attempts at giving it the face of a nationalist project. Attempts converge on projecting "national prestige" on the international scene as the main goal, and market- driven rapid growth for which the hunt for natural resource becomes the essential means. This class project is made to appear inclusive and nationalistic by privileging a select minority which gains disproportionately from this pattern of rapid growth. A new post-colonial comprador class soon emerges from the old privileged comprador class. However this time the task is easier because their mind has already been suitably colonized. It supports this process through the control of the bureaucracy, the media, while domestic and foreign big business, multilateral agencies like the World Bank, the International Monetary Fund (IMF) and the World Trade Organization (WTO) make collaboration

exceptionally attractive in financial terms in the poor countries. In the process, the show of democracy becomes a form that is increasingly devoid of popular content, a shadow without substance.

By its own logic, the violent hunt follows the international pecking order of power. Among the new entrants to this race, a relatively more powerful country like China has greater ability to externalize its hunt for resources compared to a less powerful country like India. In this perverted "nationalist" project, achieving a higher rate of economic growth becomes synonymous with the speed with which the country climbs up the ladder of power. However, higher growth driven by this logic also means greater pressure for procuring natural resources by dispossessing those fellow citizens who are unfortunate enough to live in areas of abundant natural resources.

With effortless ease the old colonial logic of "a white man's burden" returns to haunt the one time colonies. A "civilized" class consisting of corporate leaders, sleek media persons and the wheeler-dealer politicians with a **pliant** class of bureaucrats, join hands to "civilize" and "develop" the uncivilized. Even ethnic details of the old colonial ideology are not left out. The centuries old ancient homeland of the adivasis (about 8% of the population) in resource rich regions and the dalits (16%) who are treated as rejects of the Hindu society together are among the poorest in rural India.

Together they constitute just about a quarter of the total population, but account for more than half of those who fell prey to the violently predatory growth process. Dispossessed of their land, homes, livelihoods, families, close-knit communities and common properties, this ethnic war of the "master race" continues to relentlessly civilize the "primitives". This is done legally or illegally, with or without the façade of democracy by using state power. When the law of the land protects inalienable land rights to tribal communities (the Fifth Schedule of the Constitution, PESA 1996, etc), corporations with the aid of state power overcomes this hurdle to "development" by manufacturing consent at gun point or, simply by ignoring it. When dalits are dispossessed, our democracy consoles them with the false compassion of "reservation".

Developmental terrorism on this massive scale is **camouflaged** by a liberalized and globalized market economy. Irrespective of the ideological colour of the political party in power, the states and the center join this hunt with great patriotism to dispossess the poor for making India (or their respective states) an emerging global power. National and multinational corporations are viewed as the muscle powers needed to win the race in countries like India. They are enabled with special economic steroids by granting them almost free land, water bodies and rivers, mineral resources, forests, mountains, coast lines and anything else they might fancy, with the democratic government in India at their service to acquire for them mining resources and provide special economic zones (SEZs). This becomes the public purpose for private wealth, and corporate wealth grows at a dizzying rate with poverty stricken India producing billionaires at an alarmingly high rate. They are presented as the face of emergent India which the world is expected to admire.

Irrevocably, however, the balance of power must shift in this process. Increasingly powerful corporations take charge of this **gangrenous** growth process with their money power to further cripple a sick democracy. Under the empty shell of a multiparty democracy, a new script is written to reverse the balance of power. The principal becomes the agent and the agent the principal. Corporations do not merely stop at bribing operators of the state apparatus, the politicians, the judges and the bureaucrats; they begin to dictate terms and replace them openly. Laws proposed for the SEZs where corporations would rule supreme, read almost like the chronicle of the death of Indian democracy foretold.

And, yet, unprecedented growth in a hollow democracy is dangled before the people, while both government and corporations systematically **deform** every aspect of the democratic polity. A new script has been written about India's miraculous achievements, combining high growth with democracy that is presented to the audience.

16. What is the tone of the author?

(1) derogatory   (2) rhetorical

(3) critical   (4) objective

(5) analytical

17. What can be inferred from the words "developmental terrorism"?

(1) Development being done in the name of terrorism.

(2) Terrorism spreading too fast.

(3) Terrorism being practiced in the name of development.

(4) Development and terrorism are going hand-in-hand.

(5) Terrorists having an increased access to the new technology.

18. The author is most likely to support which of the following statements?

(1) Few colonizers are again trying to exploit the weak and poor people of the colonies.

(2) A few terrorists are gaining power and taking control in some countries.

(3) Politicians are causing harm to the countries.

(4) Imperialism turns inwards, and the colonies wage a war against their own citizens, in the name of developing them.

(5) None of these

19. Which of the following cannot be inferred from the passage?

(1) The State and the Center are working efficiently and diligently in making India a global power.

(2) The master class in some countries continues to relentlessly exploit the weak.

(3) The corporations are given undue favors and advantages by the ruling politicians in some countries.

(4) Corporate wealth is growing in India at the expense of the poor sections of the society.

(5) None of these

20. Why does the author feel that democracy is a shadow without substance?

(1) Democracy has become less charming.

(2) Democracy is losing its lusture.

(3) Democracy has failed to function by its ideology.

(4) Democracy is enrapturing the dejected.

(5) Democracy is beguiling the opulent.

Directions for questions 21 to 23: Choose the word that is closest in meaning to the word given in **bold**.

21. Farce

(1) Travesty   (2) Garrulous

(3) Gastronomic   (4) Diligent

(5) Holiday

22. Pliant

(1) Lethal   (2) Expert

(3) Finicky   (4) Eccentric

(5) Accommodating

23. Camouflaged

(1) Forbidden   (2) Attempted

(3) Hidden   (4) Forsaken

(5) Perennial

Directions for questions 24 and 25: In each of the following questions, choose the word that is most nearly the opposite in meaning to the word given in **bold**.

24. Deform

(1) Curlosity

(2) Manageable

(3) Noticeable

(4) Create

(5) Malleable

25. Gangrenous

    (1) Healthy   (2) Decaying

    (3) Battered   (4) Slow

    (5) Tardy

Directions for questions 26 to 30: In the following passage there are blanks, each of which has been numbered. These numbers are given below the passage and against each five words are suggested one of which fits the blank appropriately. Find out the appropriate word in each case.

Recently the World Bank and the Asian Development Bank (ADB) released separate reports on poverty. The World Bank Report __(26)__ its benchmark of extreme poverty by 25 percents from $1 per person per day to $1.25 per person a day. The ADB announced an even higher benchmark of $1.35 per person a day. These new benchmarks are __(27)__ on surveys in the world's poorest countries.

Experts often like to __(28)__ that poverty has declined because of economic growth in India and China. This is wrong and misleading. In the past twenty-five years the poverty rate in India has __(29)__ by less than one percentage point a year. Whether we use a poverty line of $1 per person per day or $1.25 per person per day makes little __(30)__ . The number of poor in India is large. The purpose of these statistics is not to dispute them but to study whether the benefits of economic growth are being shared with the poor.

26. (1) heightened   (2) announced

     (3) raised   (4) maintained

     (5) notified

27. (1) based   (2) collected

     (3) inferred   (4) derived

     (5) gathered

28. (1) realise   (2) claim

     (3) discover   (4) recommend

     (5) criticise

29. (1) deplete

     (2) declined

     (3) plunge

     (4) weaken

     (5) fell

30. (1) difference

     (2) effect

     (3) contrast

     (4) question

     (5) option

NUMERICAL ABILITY

Directions (Q. 31 to 35): In the following questions two equations numbered I and II are given. You have to solve both the equations and give answer

(1) if $x > y$

(2) if $x \geq y$

(3) if $x < y$

(4) if $x \leq y$

(5) if $x = y$ or the relationship between 'x' and 'y' cannot be established.

31. I. $\dfrac{15}{\sqrt{x}} - \dfrac{9}{\sqrt{x}} = (x)^{\frac{1}{2}}$

    II. $Y^{10} - (36)^5 = 0$

32. I. $5x + 2y = 96$

    II. $3(7x + 5y) = 489$

33. I. $(441)^{\frac{1}{2}} x^2 - 111 = (15)^2$

    II. $\sqrt{121}y^2 + (6)^3 = 260$

34. I. $17x = (13)^2 + \sqrt{196} + (5)^2 + 4x$

    II. $9y - 345 = 4y - 260$

35. I. $3x^2 - 13x + 14 = 0$

    II. $Y^2 - 7y + 12 = 0$

Directions (Q. 36 to 40): What approximate value should come in place of question mark (?) in each of the following questions.

36. $11.593 \times 31.118 \times 24.924 = ?$

    (1) 7783   (2) 8999

    (3) 6781   (4) 10987

    (5) 80491

37. $9938 \div 92 \div 9 = ?$

    (1) 12   (2) 21

    (3) 7   (4) 19

    (5) 5

38. $\sqrt[3]{750000} = ?$

    (1) 111   (2) 101

    (3) 91   (4) 81

    (5) 71

39. $(? \% \text{ of } 44.444) \times (21\% \text{ of } 66.666) = 136.89$

    (1) 11   (2) 22

    (3) 33   (4) 44

    (5) 55

40. $2\frac{3}{5} + 8\frac{1}{3} + 3\frac{7}{8} = ?$

(1) 10 (2) 23

(3) 37 (4) 15

(5) 60

41. Divide Rs. 6,168 into two parts such that the CI on the first part at 20% for 2 years is equal to the CI on the second part at 10% for 3 years. Find the two parts.

(1) Rs.2,658, Rs. 3,510

(2) Rs. 2,648, Rs. 3,520

(3) Rs. 3,000, Rs. 3,168

(4) Rs. 3,100, Rs. 3,068

(5) None of these

42. In a test, minimum passing percentage for girls and boys is 30% and 45% respectively. A boy scored 280 marks and failed by 80 marks. How many more marks did a girl require to pass in the test if she scored 108 marks?

(1) 132 (2) 160

(3) 140 (4) 112

(5) 228

43. The sum of the present ages of father and his son is 45 years. 5 years ago, the product of their ages was four times the father's age at that time. What is the present age of the father?

(1) 38 years (2) 39 years

(3) 40 years (4) 41 years

(5) 36 years

44. A vessel of 90 kg is filled with sugar and sand. 60% of sugar and 40% of sand is taken out of the vessel. It is found that the vessel is vacated by 50%. Find the initial quantity of sugar.

(1) 45 kg (2) 60 kg

(3) 30 kg (4) 40 kg

(5) 50 kg

45. A merchant has 115 kg of rice, part of which he sells at 7% loss and the rest at 16% profit. He gains 10% on the whole. How much is sold at 16% profit?

(1) 65 kg

(2) 55 kg

(3) 50 kg

(4) 85 kg

(5) 30 kg

Directions (Q. 46 to 50) : Answer the questions on the basis of the information given below.

Percentage of marks obtained by six students in six different subjects

Student \ Subject	History (Out of 50)	Geography (Out of 50)	Maths (Out of 150)	Science (Out of 100)	English (Out of 75)	Hindi (Out of 75)
Amit	76	85	69	73	64	88
Bharat	84	80	85	78	73	92
Umesh	82	67	92	87	69	76
Nikhil	73	72	78	69	58	83
Pratiksha	68	79	64	91	66	65
Ritesh	79	87	88	93	82	72

46. What is the approximate integral percentage of marks obtained by Umesh in all the subjects?

(1) 80% (2) 84%

(3) 86% (4) 78%

(5) 77%

47. What is the average percentage of marks obtained by all students in Hindi? (approximated to two places of decimal)

(1) 77.45%

(2) 79.33%

(3) 75.52%

(4) 7.52%

(5) None of these

48. What is the average marks of all the students in mathematics?

(1) 128 (2) 112

(3) 119 (4) 138

(5) 144

49. What is the average marks obtained by all the students in geography?

(1) 38.26 (2) 37.26

(3) 37.16 (4) 39.16

(5) None of these

50. What are the total marks obtained by Ritesh in all the subjects taken together?

(1) 401.75 (2) 410.75

(3) 402.75 (4) 420.75

(5) None of these

Directions (Q. 51 to 55): What will come in place of the question mark (?) in the following questions?

51. ?, 16, 28, 58, 114, 204

    (1) 7   (2) 9

    (3) 14   (4) 6

    (5) 10

52. 13.76, 14.91, 17.21, 20.66 , ? , 31.01

    (1) 25.66   (2) 24.36

    (3) 24.26   (4) 25.26

    (5) 25.36

53. 949, 189.8, ?, 22.776, 11.388, 6.8328

    (1) 48.24   (2) 53.86

    (3) 74.26   (4) 56.94

    (5) None of these

54. 41, 164, 2624, ?, 6045696

    (1) 104244   (2) 94644

    (3) 94464   (4) 102444

    (5) None of these

55. 121, 144, 190, 259, ?, 466

    (1) 351   (2) 349

    (3) 374   (4) 328

    (5) None of these

56. A train when increases its speed by 20% saves 1.5 hours to reach its destination. Find the usual time taken by the train.

    (1) 6 hours

    (2) 8 hours

    (3) 9 hours

    (4) 12 hours

    (5) 14 hours

57. 3 men, 4 women and 6 children can complete the same job in 4, 9 and 2 days respectively. In how many days will the same job be completed by a man, a woman and a child while working together?

    (1) $4\frac{1}{7}$ days   (2) $5\frac{1}{3}$ days

    (3) $5\frac{1}{7}$ days   (4) $6\frac{1}{3}$ days

    (5) None of these

58. If the area of a square is $3\sqrt{3}$ times the area of an equilateral triangle, then find the ratio of the side of the square to the side of this equilateral triangle?

    (1) 3 : 2   (2) 4 : 7

    (3) 2 : 3   (4) 5 : 6

    (5) $\sqrt{3}$: 2

59. In how many ways can the seven letters A, B, C, D, E, F and G be arranged so that both the vovels are together ?

    (1) 120   (2) 720

    (3) 450   (4) 540

    (5) None of these

60. A railway half ticket costs half the full basic fare, and the reservation charge is same as on full ticket. While travelling from Delhi to Bhopal, one half ticket reserved first class costs Rs. 432 and one full & one half ticket reserved first class costs Rs. 1,259. What is the basic first class full fare?

    [Note: Cost of ticket = Basic fare + Reservation charge]

    (1) Rs. 827   (2) Rs. 790

    (3) Rs. 395   (4) Rs. 810

    (5) Rs. 900

Directions (Q. 61 to 65): Study the following graphs carefully to answer the questions which follow:

The bar-graph shows the export and production of wheat (in million kg) in India during the period of 2010 to 2015.

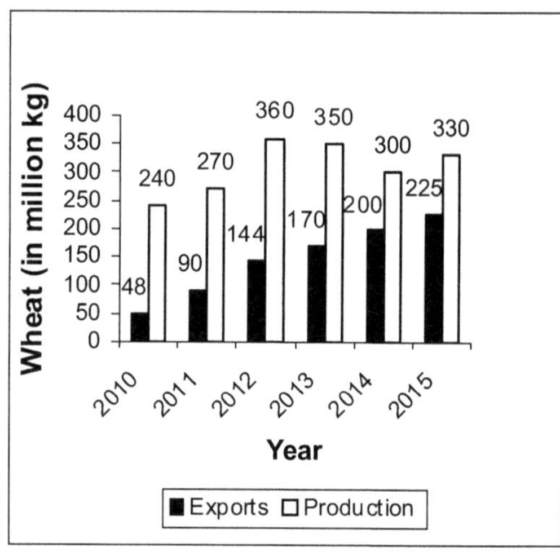

The line chart shows the per capita availability of wheat (in gm) during the given period.

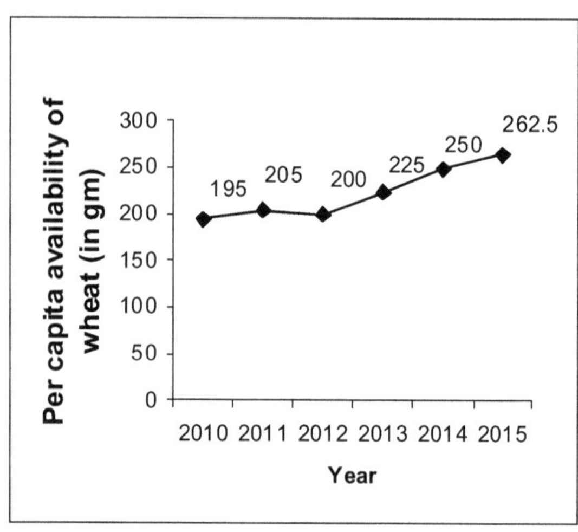

61. Which year shows the minimum percentage of export with respect to production?

(1) 2013   (2) 2011

(3) 2015   (4) 2010

(5) 2012

62. The percentage increase or decrease in the population from year 2012 to year 2014 was

(1) 56.48%   (2) 36.42%

(3) 62.96%   (4) 69.32%

(5) 47.92%

63. For how many years, the wheat production was more than the average wheat production over the given period?

(1) 1   (2) 2

(3) 3   (4) 4

(5) None of these

64. Which year had the maximum percentage growth in per capita availability of wheat as compared to the previous year?

(1) 2014   (2) 2015

(3) 2011   (4) 2013

(5) Cannot be determined

65. If population of India in a year K is represented as Pop (K), then which three set of years X, Y and Z satisfy the equation Pop (X) = Pop (Y) + Pop (Z)?

(1) 2011, 2013, 2015   (2) 2013, 2013, 2015

(3) 2012, 2013, 2014   (4) 2010, 2013, 2015

(5) 2010, 2011, 2012

REASONING ABILITY

66. I walked 20 m towards east from a point 'S' and then turned right and walked another 20 m. Now I turned to my left and walked 10 m and turning to my right I walked another 10 m. Finally I turned to my right and walked 30 m to reach a point 'F'. What is the shortest straight distance between points 'S' and 'F' ?

(1) 20 m   (2) 25 m

(3) 15 m   (4) 40 m

(5) 30 m

67. Shalloo drives 10 km towards south from her house and turns left and drives another 25 km. She again turns left and drives 40 km straight, then she turns right and drives another 5 km to reach her office. How far is her office from her house?

(1) $33\sqrt{2}$ km   (2) $40\sqrt{2}$ km

(3) $30\sqrt{2}$ km   (4) $39\sqrt{2}$ km

(5) 30 km

68. If Maya is the only daughter of Richa's grandmother's brother, how is Maya's daughter related to Richa?

(1) Niece   (2) Cousin

(3) Aunt   (4) Mother

(5) Sister

Directions (Q. 69 and 70): Read the following information carefully and answer the questions given below :

  i. A, B, C, D, E and F are six members of a family. Out of these, three are male members.

  ii. There are two married couples among them.

  iii. C is the father of A and F, and E is the mother of C.

  iv. B is the grandfather of F.

69. Which of the following pairs is one of the married couples?

(1) EF   (2) BD

(3) EB   (4) AB

(5) Cannot be determined

70. How is B related to A?

(1) Brother

(2) Son-in-law

(3) Husband

(4) Data inadequate

(5) Grandfather

Directions (Q. 71 to 75): Study the following information to answer the given questions:

A family of eight members – A, B, C, D, E, F, G and H – consists of three couples. There are three generations in the family. They form four groups of two members each and decide to go on foreign tour in four different countries – Canada, USA, UK and France. It is also known that:

  (i) A is the grandfather of one of the male members who go to the USA.

  (ii) Both members of a group go to the same country and each couple forms a group.

  (iii) H, a female, is married to E, who doesn't go to the UK.

  (iv) B and D form a group and agree to go to the USA after showing stiff resistance not to go to the same.

  (v) E's mother-in-law is mother of C, who is the father of B and brother of H.

  (vi) D is unmarried and niece of C.

  (vii) Oldest member of the family goes to Canada.

71. Who is the mother-in-law of F?

(1) D   (2) G

(3) H   (4) A

(5) Cannot be determined

72. How many male members are there in the family?

(1) 3   (2) 4

(3) 5   (4) 2

(5) None of these

73. Which of the following groups goes to the UK?

(1) A and F   (2) A and G

(3) C and G   (4) C and F

(5) Either (3) or (4)

74. How is D related to E?

(1) Son   (2) Daughter

(3) Niece   (4) Nephew

(5) None of these

75. How many children does A have?

(1) 1   (2) 3

(3) 2   (4) 4

(5) Cannot be determined

Directions (Q. 76 to 80) : Answer the questions on the basis of information given below.

In a certain code "untidy obese woman" is coded as "ni si ke", "lovely intelligent woman" is coded as "gu si di" , "lovely wild berries" is coded as "di pu ta" and "untidy wild boys" is coded as "yo pu ni".

76. What does the code "ni yo gu" stand for?

(1) intelligent wild woman

(2) untidy intelligent boys

(3) wild obese boys

(4) obese intelligent woman

(5) lovely obese boys

77. What does "pu si" represent?

(1) lovely berries   (2) wild boys

(3) obese woman   (4) lovely boys

(5) wild woman

78. What could be the code for "dull obese boys"?

(1) yo ke ta   (2) ke du yo

(3) di si yo   (4) yo gu ke

(5) ke yo pu

79. How can "lovely woman eats wild berries" be coded?

(1) "pu ta yo si di"   (2) "rudi si ni yo"

(3) "ha ru so di si"   (4) "pu we si di ta"

(5) "pu gu ta di si"

80. If boys hate berries is coded as "ta mo yo" then what will be the code for "woman hate untidy"?

(1) si mo ke   (2) mo ke gu

(3) si mo ni   (4) si pu ta

(5) mo si yo

Directions (Q. 81 to 85): Answer the questions on the basis of information given below.

A, B, C, D, E, F, G and H are eight friends travelling in three different cars, viz. X, Y and Z with at least two in one car to three different places, viz. Delhi, Chandigarh and Agra.

There is at least one female member in each car. D is travelling with G to Delhi but not in car Y. A is travelling with only H in car Z but not to Chandigarh. C is not travelling with either D or E. F and D are studying in the same only girls' college. H. B and G are studying in the same only boys' college.

81. Which of the following represents the group of females among them?

(1) F, C, A   (2) F, G, A

(3) D, C, A   (4) Data inadequate

(5) None of these

82. Which of the following combinations is correct?

(1) Delhi - X - C   (2) Chandigarh - X - G

(3) Agra - Z - E   (5) Delhi - Y - E

(5) None is correct

83. In which car are four of them travelling?

(1) X or Z   (2) Y

(3) X or Y   (4) Z

(5) None of these

84. In which of the following cars is C travelling?

(1) X   (2) Y

(3) Z   (5) Either X or Y

(5) Data inadequate

85. Passengers in which car are travelling to Agra?

(1) Y   (2) X

(3) Either X or Y   (4) Z

(5) None of these

Direction (Q. 86 to 90): In the following questions, the symbols @, ©, %, $ and * are used with the following meaning as illustrated below:

'P © Q' means 'P is either equal to or greater than Q'

'P % Q' means 'P is smaller than Q'.

'P * Q' means 'P is either equal to or smaller than Q'.

'P @ Q' means 'P is greater than Q'

'P $ Q' means 'P is equal to Q.'

Now in each of the following questions assuming the given statements to be true, find which of the two conclusions I and II given below them is/are definitely true.

Give answer (1) if only Conclusion I is true.

Give answer (2) if only Conclusion II is true.

Give answer (3) if either Conclusion I or II is true.

Give answer (4) if neither Conclusion I nor II is true.

Give answer (5) if both Conclusions I and II are true.

86. Statements: L * M,   M $ N,   N % K

Conclusions:

I.   K @ L

II. L * N

87. Statements: A © B,   B @ C,   C * D

Conclusions:

I.   A © B

II. C % A

88. Statements: H % G,   G © F,   F * E

Conclusions:

I.   F % H

II. G © E

89. Statements: R @ S,   S © T,   T $ V

Conclusions:

I.   R @ T

II. V * S

90. Statements: W * X,   X @ Y,   Y % Z

Conclusions:

I.   W % Y

II. Z @ W

Directions (Q. 91 to 95): Answer the question on the basis of the information given below.

Eight friends – P, Q, R, S, T, U, V and W – are sitting at equidistant positions around a circular table. Exactly three friends are facing towards the center and the rest five are facing away from the center.

It is also known that:

(i) V who is facing outside, is not sitting opposite to either T or U. However, the person sitting opposite to V is facing the center.

(ii) Q who is facing the center is sitting to the immediate right of W and opposite to R.

(iii) P is sitting fourth to the left of W and to the immediate right of V.

91. Who is sitting opposite to T?

(1) P   (2) S

(3) U   (4) Q

(5) Cannot be determined

92. Who is sitting opposite to V?

(1) W   (2) Q

(3) R   (4) S

(5) Cannot be determined

93. Who among the given friends are definitely facing the center?

(1) P and W   (2) S and Q

(3) R and T   (4) U and W

(5) R an Q

94. Who are the immediate neighbors of P?

(1) V and U   (2) S and U

(3) W and Q   (4) V and R

(5) U and T

95. If R is 3rd to the right of U, then who among the following is definitely not facing the center?

(1) U   (2) S

(3) R   (4) P

(5) T

Directions (Q. 96 to 100): In each of the following questions, statements are given followed by conclusions. You have to consider the given statements to be true even if they seem to be at variance with commonly known facts. Read all the conclusions and decide which of the following conclusion(s) logically follow(s) from the given statements disregarding commonly known facts.

96. Statements: No player is singer. Some singers are Gandhian. All players are Gandhian.

Conclusions:

I.   All Gandhians are players.

II. Some Gandhians are not players.

III. Some singers are players.

IV. Some Gandhians singers are players.

(1) None follow

(2) Only I follows

(3) Only II and III follow

(4) Only II follows

(5) Only IV follows

97. Statements: Green are strong. Amit is green. Green plays football.

Conclusions:

I.   Amit plays football.

II. Football are green.

III. Some footballs are strong.

IV. The English love football.

(1) None follow

(2) Only I and III follow

(3) Only II and III follow

(4) Only II follows

(5) Only III follow

98. Statements: All trains run late. Rajdhani is a train. Some trains are fine.

Conclusions:

I. Some Rajdhani are fine.

II. All Rajdhani are late.

III. All fine are trains.

IV. All trains are Rajdhani.

(1) None follow

(2) Only I and III follow

(3) Only II and IV follow

(4) Only II follows

(5) Only III follows

99. Statements: Teachers teach in school. Only postgraduates are teachers. All postgraduates are graduates.

Conclusions:

I. Some graduates teach in school.

II. All teachers are postgraduates.

III. Some postgraduates are graduates.

IV. Schools employ only postgraduates.

(1) None follow

(2) Only I, II and III follow

(3) Only II and III follow

(4) Only II follows

(5) Only IV follows

100. Statements: Britons are islanders. Islanders are fishes. Fishes are water.

Conclusions:

I. Some Britons are water.

II. Britons are fishes.

III. Some fishes are islanders.

IV. No islander is a European.

(1) Only II follows

(2) Only I and III follow

(3) Only II and III follow

(4) Only III follows

(5) Only I, II and III follow

ANSWERS

1. (4)	**2.** (3)	**3.** (1)	**4.** (3)	**5.** (1)	**6.** (1)	**7.** (5)	**8.** (4)	**9.** (5)	**10.** (2)
11. (4)	**12.** (1)	**13.** (5)	**14.** (3)	**15.** (2)	**16.** (3)	**17.** (3)	**18.** (4)	**19.** (1)	**20.** (3)
21. (1)	**22.** (5)	**23.** (3)	**24.** (4)	**25.** (1)	**26.** (3)	**27.** (1)	**28.** (2)	**29.** (2)	**30.** (1)
31. (2)	**32.** (1)	**33.** (5)	**34.** (3)	**35.** (3)	**36.** (2)	**37.** (1)	**38.** (3)	**39.** (2)	**40.** (4)
41. (2)	**42.** (1)	**43.** (5)	**44.** (1)	**45.** (4)	**46.** (1)	**47.** (2)	**48.** (3)	**49.** (4)	**50.** (5)
51. (3)	**52.** (4)	**53.** (4)	**54.** (3)	**55.** (1)	**56.** (3)	**57.** (3)	**58.** (1)	**59.** (5)	**60.** (2)
61. (4)	**62.** (3)	**63.** (3)	**64.** (4)	**65.** (2)	**66.** (5)	**67.** (3)	**68.** (2)	**69.** (3)	**70.** (5)
71. (5)	**72.** (2)	**73.** (5)	**74.** (2)	**75.** (3)	**76.** (2)	**77.** (5)	**78.** (2)	**79.** (4)	**80.** (3)
81. (4)	**82.** (5)	**83.** (5)	**84.** (2)	**85.** (4)	**86.** (5)	**87.** (2)	**88.** (4)	**89.** (5)	**90.** (4)
91. (3)	**92.** (4)	**93.** (2)	**94.** (4)	**95.** (1)	**96.** (4)	**97.** (2)	**98.** (4)	**99.** (2)	**100.** (5)

EXPLANATIONS

1. (4) The given sentence suggests that banks are facing a challenge due to retirement. To make the sentence logically correct, 'due to' should be replaced by 'on account of'. Now the sentence means that the challenge faced by banks is that they are loosing people and the reason for this is that they are retiring.

2. (3) There is a parallelism error in the given sentence. 'But' in part (3) should be followed by 'has'.

3. (1) The correct phrase is 'a new study has found that'.

4. (3) 'Traffic police' is taken as a single unit in this sentence. So, 'have' should be replaced by 'has'.

5. (1) The correct phrase is 'view to avoiding'.

6. (1) The first blank can take either 'allure' or 'attraction'. Out of the two options, the second blank will take 'lucrative' only since 'unpopular' in the second blank will make the sentence logically incorrect.

7. (5) Foggy whether cannot improve visibility. So, option (1) is incorrect. 'Impair' means to make (something) weaker or worse. It is incorrect in the given context as we do not know if the visibility is already weak or not. 'Hamper', which means to restrict movement or progress of something, is again incorrect. Option (4) is incorrect. Had it been 'decreases', it would have been correct. 'Foggy weather' is singular, and hence, requires a singular verb after it. Only option (5) grammatically fits in the meaning of the sentence.

8. (4) Option (1) does not make much sense. So, it is negated. Option (2) is incorrect. 'Replenish' means to fill or build up (something) again. If the district was once 'raid', then it cannot be made green again. 'being devoid' is incorrect and therefore, option (3) is also incorrect. Option (5) is incorrect because the second blank will take 'robbed' and not 'rob'. Only option (4) grammatically fits in the meaning of the sentence.

9. (5) 'Glisten' means to shine with light reflected off a wet surface. 'Lights' will either 'shine' or 'glitter'. So, options (1) and (2) and (3) are incorrect. 'Climbed' is correct here. 'Reached to' will make the sentence grammatically incorrect.

10. (2) Since the sentence talks about good news for hotels, the properties will either be 'packed' or 'full' for the whole month. 'Pushed in good news' seems logically incorrect. 'Usher' means to lead someone to a place.

11. (4) The correct sequence is EBFDAC. E starts the paragraph by introducing the man who went from town to town to collect money for his trust. It is followed by B that says that everyone, rich and poor, donated generously. B is followed by F that says that the man decided to hold a function to reward the person who had donated most generously. F is followed by D that says everyone waited eagerly to find out who had had donated most generously. DA is a mandatory pair. 'To their surprise' is the key word here. The paragraph ends with C that says that the man explained why he thought that the beggar had donated most generously.

16. (3) The author criticizes the present scenario of democracy and development in countries like China and India and tries to reveal the real picture hidden behind the veil of growth. Hence, his tone is critical.

17. (3) Refer to the fifth paragraph of the passage. 'Developmental terrorism' refers to terrorism being practiced in the name of development.

18. (4) Option (4) is the statement which the author is trying to explain by this passage.

19. (1) Refer to the fifth paragraph of the passage. Option (1) is contrary to the information provided in the paragraph. Hence, it cannot be inferred from this passage.

20. (3) The author feels that 'democracy is shadow without substance' because democracy has failed to function by its ideology.

26. (3) The benchmark has been increased from $1 to $1.35. So, the blank will take 'raised'.

27. (1) Only 'based' fit in the meaning of the sentence.

28. (2) The sentence means that experts assert that poverty has declined. So, option (2), claim, fits in the blank.

29. (2) The first sentence of the second paragraph talks about economic growth in India and China and the next sentence says that the claim is misleading. So, the blank will take 'declined', to make the sentence logically correct.

30. (1) Only 'difference' fits in the meaning of the sentence.

31. (2) I. $\dfrac{15}{\sqrt{x}} - \dfrac{9}{\sqrt{x}} = (x)^{\frac{1}{2}}$

$\Rightarrow \dfrac{15-9}{\sqrt{x}} = x^{\frac{1}{2}} = \sqrt{x}$

$\Rightarrow x = 6$

II. $y^{10} - (36)^5 = 0$

$\Rightarrow y^{10} = (36)^5 = 0$

$\Rightarrow y = (36)^{\frac{5}{10}} = 36^{\frac{1}{2}}$

$\Rightarrow y = \sqrt{36} = \pm 6$

$\therefore x \geq y.$

32. (1) $\quad 5x + 2y = 96 \qquad\qquad ...(i)$

$21x + 15y = 489 \qquad\qquad ...(ii)$

By solving equations (i) and (ii) we get,

$\qquad x = 14$ and $y = 13$

$\therefore x > y.$

33. (5) I. $\quad (441)^{\frac{1}{2}} x^2 - 111 = (15)^2$

$\Rightarrow (21)^{2 \times \frac{1}{2}} x^2 = 225 + 111 = 336$

$\Rightarrow 21x^2 = 336$

$\Rightarrow x^2 = \dfrac{336}{21} = 16$

$\Rightarrow x = \pm 4$

II. $\sqrt{121} y^2 + 6^3 = 260$

$\Rightarrow 11y^2 + 6^3 = 260$

$\Rightarrow 11y^2 = 260 - 216 = 44$

$\Rightarrow y^2 = 4$

$\Rightarrow y = \pm 2$

Hence, relationship between x and y cannot be established.

34. (3) I. $\quad 17x = 169 + 14 + 25 + 4x$

$\Rightarrow 13x = 208$

$\Rightarrow x = \dfrac{208}{13} = 16$

II. $9y - 4y = 345 - 260 = 85$

$\Rightarrow 5y = 85$

$\Rightarrow y = 17$

$\therefore x < y.$

35. (3) I. $\quad 3x^2 - 13x + 14 = 0$

$\Rightarrow 3x^2 - 7x - 6x + 14 = 0$

$\Rightarrow 3x(x - 2) - 7(x - 2) = 0$

$\Rightarrow (3x - 7)(x - 2) = 0$

$\therefore x = \dfrac{7}{3}, 2$

II. $y^2 - 7y + 12 = 0$

$\Rightarrow y^2 - 4y - 3y + 12 = 0$

$\Rightarrow y(y - 4) - 3(y - 4) = 0$

$\Rightarrow (y - 3)(y - 4) = 0$

$\therefore y = 4, 3$

$\therefore x < y.$

36. (2) $11.593 \times 31.118 \times 24.924$

$\approx 11.6 \times 31 \times 25 \approx 8999.$

37. (1) $9938 \div 92 \div 9 = 9938 \times \dfrac{1}{92} \times \dfrac{1}{9}$

$\approx 1104.22 \times \dfrac{1}{92}$

$\approx 12.$

38. (3) $(750000)^{\frac{1}{3}} = (10^3 \times 5^3 \times 6)^{\frac{1}{3}} = 10 \times 5 \times (6)^{\frac{1}{3}}$

$\approx 10 \times 5 \times 1.82 \approx 91.$

39. (2) $(?\% \text{ of } 44.444) \times (21\% \text{ of } 66.666) = 136.89$

$\Rightarrow \left(\dfrac{?}{100} \times 44.444\right) \times \left(\dfrac{21}{100} \times 66.666\right) = 136.89$

$\Rightarrow (?) \times 0.44 \times 0.21 \times 67 \approx 136.89$

$\Rightarrow (?) \times 6.1908 \approx 136.89$

$\Rightarrow (?) \approx \dfrac{136.89}{6.1908}$

$\Rightarrow (?) \approx 22.$

40. (4) $2\dfrac{3}{5} + 8\dfrac{1}{3} + 3\dfrac{7}{8} = \dfrac{13}{5} + \dfrac{25}{3} + \dfrac{31}{8}$

$\approx 2.6 + 8.3 + 3.9$

$\approx 14.8 \approx 15.$

41. (2) First part = Rs. x and second part = 6168 – x

$\Rightarrow 0.44x = 33.1 (6168 - x)$

Thus, x = Rs. 2,648 and second part = 3,520.

42. (1) If the maximum marks of examination be x. Then,

$\dfrac{x \times 45}{100} = 280 + 80 = 360$

$\Rightarrow \qquad x = \dfrac{360 \times 100}{45} = 800$

Therefore, minimum marks to pass for girls

$= 30\% \text{ of } 800 = 240$

$\therefore$ Required difference = 240 – 108 = 132.

43. (5) Let present age of father be 'x'.

So age of son = 45 – x

According to question,

$(x - 5)(40 - x) = 4(x - 5)$

$\Rightarrow x = 36$ years

Present age of father = 36 years.

44. (1)
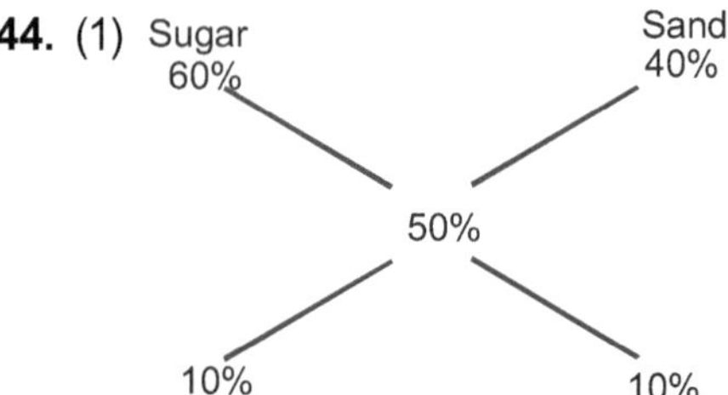

Ratio of sugar to sand = 10 : 10 = 1 : 1

$\therefore$ Quantity of sugar $= \dfrac{90 \times 1}{2} = 45$ kg

45. (4) Let he sold x kg of rice at 16% profit.

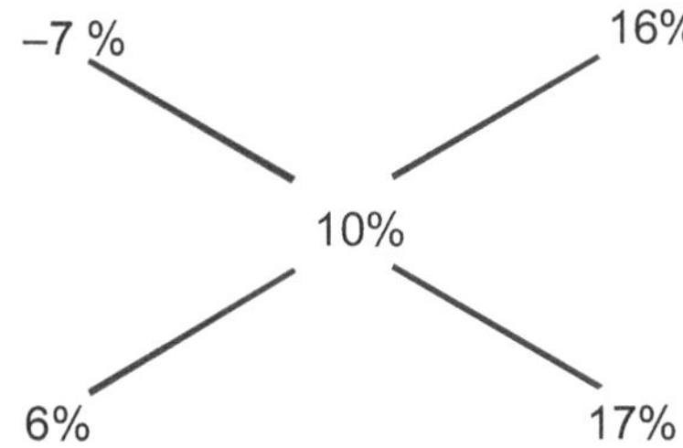

Ratio of the two parts = 6 : 17

Since he made overall 10% profit on selling 115 Kg of rice

$\therefore$ Merchant must have sold $\dfrac{115}{6+17} \times 17 = 85$ kg of rice at 16% profit.

46. (1) Total marks obtained by Umesh

$$= 41 + 33.5 + \dfrac{92}{100} \times 150 + 87$$

$$+ \dfrac{69}{100} \times 75 + \dfrac{76}{100} \times 75$$

$$= 41 + 33.5 + 138 + 87 + 51.75 + 57$$

$$= 408.25$$

Required percentage $= \dfrac{408}{500} \times 100 \approx 80\%$

47. (2) Required average of percentage in Hindi

$$= \dfrac{88 + 92 + 76 + 83 + 65 + 72}{6}$$

$$= \dfrac{476}{6} = 79.33\%$$

48. (3) Average marks in Mathematics

$$= \dfrac{(69 + 85 + 92 + 78 + 64 + 88)}{100 \times 6} \times 150$$

$$= \dfrac{150 \times 476}{100 \times 6} = 119$$

49. (4) Average marks in Geography

$$= \dfrac{(85 + 80 + 67 + 72 + 79 + 87)}{6} \times \dfrac{1}{100} \times 50$$

$$= 50 \times \dfrac{470}{6} \times \dfrac{1}{100} = 39.16$$

50. (5) Marks obtained by Ritesh

$$= 79 \times \dfrac{50}{100} + 87 \times \dfrac{50}{100} + 88 \times \dfrac{150}{100} + 93 + 82$$

$$\times \dfrac{75}{100} + 72 \times \dfrac{75}{100}$$

$$= 39.50 + 43.50 + 132 + 93 + 61.50 + 54$$

$$= 423.50$$

51. (3) The pattern of the number series is :

$$14 + 1 \times 2 = 16$$

$$16 + 3 \times 4 = 16 + 12 = 28$$

$$28 + 5 \times 6 = 28 + 30 = 58$$

$$58 + 7 \times 8 = 58 + 56 = 114$$

$$114 + 9 \times 10 = 114 + 90 = 204$$

52. (4) The pattern of the number series is :

$$13.76 + 1 \times 1.15 = 14.91$$

$$14.91 + 2 \times 1.15 = 14 + 2.30 = 17.21$$

$$17.21 + 3 \times 1.15 = 17.21 + 3.45 = 20.66$$

$$20.66 + 4 \times 1.15 = 20.66 + 4.60 = 25.26$$

$$25.26 + 5 \times 1.15 = 25.26 + 5.75 = 31.01$$

53. (4) The given number series is based on the following pattern :

949		189.8		56.94	22.776	11.388	6.8328
	× 0.2		× 0.3	× 0.4	× 0.5	× 0.6	

Hence, 56.94 will replace the question mark.

54. (3) The given number series is based on the following pattern :

$$41 \times 2^2 = 164$$

$$164 \times 4^2 = 2624$$

$$2624 \times 6^2 = \mathbf{94464}$$

$$94464 \times 8^2 = 6045696$$

Hence, 94464 will replace the question mark.

55. (1) The given number series is based on the following pattern :

$$121 + 23 \times 1 = 144$$

$$144 + 23 \times 2 = 190$$

$$190 + 23 \times 3 = 259$$

$$\Rightarrow \quad ? = 259 + 23 \times 4$$

$$= 259 + 92 = 351$$

Hence, 351 will replace the question mark.

56. (3) We know that : S1 × T1 = S2 × T2

Now, $S2 = \dfrac{6}{5}S1 \Rightarrow T2 = \dfrac{5}{6}T1$

Given that, $\dfrac{1}{6}T1 = 1.5$ hours

Hence, T1 = 9 hours.

57. (3) Let the job consists of W units of work.

Number of units completed by a man in one day

$$= \dfrac{W}{(3 \times 4)} = \dfrac{W}{12}$$

Number of units completed by a woman in one day

$$= \frac{W}{(4 \times 9)} = \frac{W}{36}$$

Number of units completed by a child in one day

$$= \frac{W}{(6 \times 2)} = \frac{W}{12}$$

Total number of units completed by a man, a woman and a child in one day

$$= W\left(\frac{1}{12} + \frac{1}{36} + \frac{1}{12}\right) = \frac{7W}{36}$$

So the work will get completed in

$$\frac{W}{\left(\frac{7W}{36}\right)} = \frac{36}{7} = 5\frac{1}{7} \text{ days.}$$

58. (1) Let the side of the square be x m and the side of the equilateral triangle be y m, then

$$x^2 = 3\sqrt{3}\,\frac{\sqrt{3}}{4}\,y^2$$

$$\Rightarrow \frac{x^2}{y^2} = \frac{3\sqrt{3} \times \sqrt{3}}{4} = \frac{3 \times 3}{4} = \frac{9}{4}$$

$$\Rightarrow \frac{x}{y} = \sqrt{\frac{9}{4}} = \frac{3}{2}$$

So, the ratio between their sides is 3 : 2.

59. (5) Considering A and E as one unit, the six things can be arranged in 6! = 720 ways. Now A and E can be arranged among themselves in 2! ways i.e. AE and EA.

Total number of arrangements = 720 × 2 = 1440 ways.

60. (2) Let the basic fare for reserved first class and reservation charges are Rs. F and Rs. R respectively.

Full Ticket Fare = F + R

and Half Ticket Fare $= \dfrac{F}{2} + R$

$$\therefore \ \frac{F}{2} + R = 432 \qquad \text{...(i)}$$

Also, as per the condition given in the question

$$(F + R) + \left(\frac{F}{2} + R\right) = 1259 \qquad \text{...(ii)}$$

On solving equations (i) and (ii), we get, F = Rs. 790

Hence, the basic fare for the reserved full first class ticket is Rs. 790.

61. (4) Percentage of export with respect to production is given by $\left(\dfrac{\text{Export}}{\text{Production}}\right) \times 100$

which is minimum for the year 2010.

Short cut: It is clearly evident from the graph that export as a percentage of production is minimum in the year 2010.

62. (3) Population in year 2012

$$= \frac{360 - 144}{0.200} = 1080 \text{ million}$$

Population in year 2014

$$= \frac{300 - 200}{0.250} = 400 \text{ million}$$

Percentage decrease

$$= \frac{1080 - 400}{1080} \times 100 = 62.96\%.$$

63. (3) Average wheat production

$$= \frac{1850}{6} \approx 308.33 \text{ million kg.}$$

The production is greater than the average production in 3 years viz. 2012, 2013 and 2015.

64. (4) Percentage growth in year 2011

$$= \frac{205 - 195}{195} \times 100 \approx 5.13\%$$

Percentage growth in year 2013

$$= \frac{225 - 200}{200} \times 100 = 12.5\%$$

Percentage growth in year 2014

$$= \frac{250 - 225}{225} \times 100 \approx 11.11\%$$

Percentage growth in year 2015

$$= \frac{262.5 - 250}{250} \times 100 = 5\%$$

Thus, the maximum percentage growth was registered in the year 2013.

65. (2) Population in year 2010

$$= \frac{240 - 48}{0.195} = 984.6 \text{ million}$$

Population in year 2011

$$= \frac{270 - 90}{0.205} = 878 \text{ million}$$

Population in year 2012

$$= 1080 \text{ million}$$

Population in year 2013

$$= \frac{350 - 170}{0.225} = 800 \text{ million}$$

Population in year 2014

$$= 400 \text{ million}$$

Population in year 2015

$$= \frac{330 - 225}{0.2625} = 400 \text{ million}$$

Thus, we can see that the given condition satisfies for years 2013, 2014 and 2015.

66. (5)

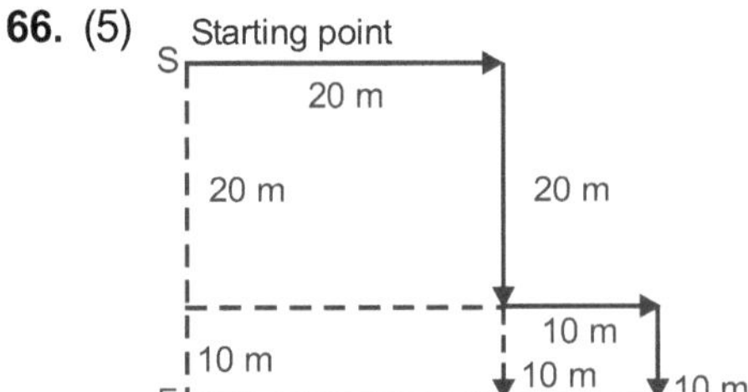

It is clear from the diagram that the distance between S and F is 30 metres.

67. (3)

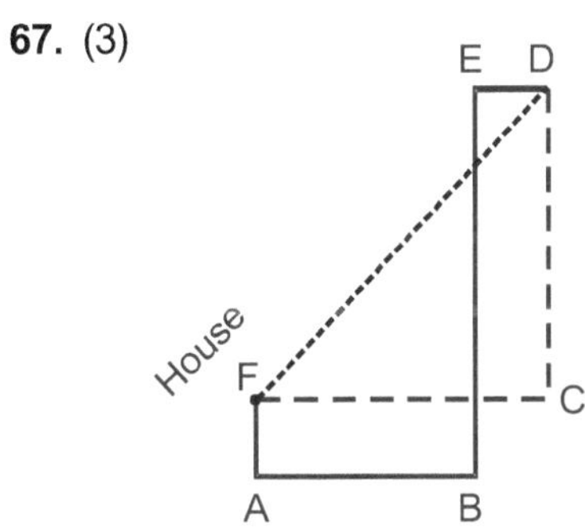

$$FC = AB + ED$$
$$= 25 + 5 = 30$$
$$CD = BE - AF$$
$$= 40 - 10 = 30$$
$$FD = \sqrt{30^2 + 30^2}$$
$$= 30\sqrt{2} \text{ km}$$

68. (2)

Brother ——— Richa's granddaughter

Maya   X

Maya's Daughter —Cousin— Richa

From the figure above, it can be clearly concluded that Maya's daughter is the cousin of Richa.

For questions 69 and 70 :

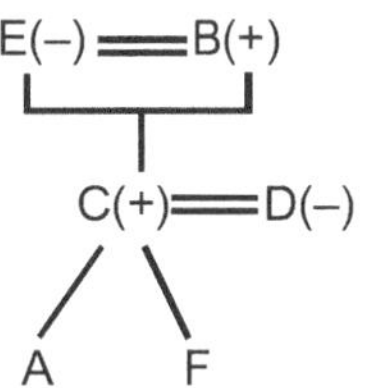

══ = Married couple

(+) Male

(−) Female

69. (3) EB is one of the married couples

70. (5) B is the grandfather of A.

For questions 71 to 75: The given information can be shown as:

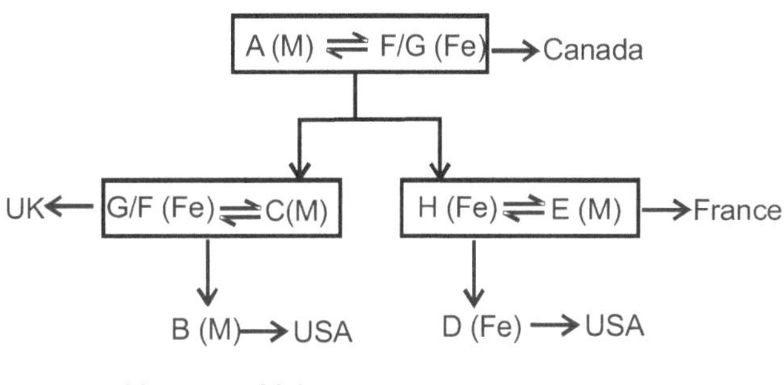

For questions 76 to 80: The given information can be shown as:

untidy	ni
obese	ke
woman	si
lovely	di
intelligent	gu
wild	pu
berries	ta
boys	yo

For questions 81 to 85: Given information can be summarized in the table as shown below

Friend	Sex	Car	Destination
A	Female	Z	Agra
B	Male	Y	Chandigarh
C	M/F	Y	Chandigarh
D	Female	X	Delhi
E	M/F	X	Delhi
F	Female	X/Y	Delhi or Chandigarh
G	Male	X	Delhi
H	Male	Z	Agra

81. (4) The sex of C and E is not known.

82. (5) None of the combinations is true.

83. (5) Four of them may be travelling in Car X.

84. (2) C is travelling in Car Y.

85. (4) The passengers of Car Z are travelling to Agra.

86. (5)

$$L \leq M \qquad \text{... (i)}$$
$$M = N \qquad \text{... (ii)}$$
$$N < K \qquad \text{... (iii)}$$

Combining these, we get $L \leq M = N < K$

Hence, $K > L$ (true)

Also, $L \leq N$ (true).

87. (2)

$$A \geq B \qquad \text{... (i)}$$
$$B > C \qquad \text{... (ii)}$$
$$C \leq D \qquad \text{... (iii)}$$

Combining these, we get $A \geq B > C \leq D$.

Clearly, D and B can't be compared. Hence, I does not true.

But $C < A$ (true).

88. (4)

$$H < G \qquad \text{... (i)}$$
$$G \geq F \qquad \text{... (ii)}$$
$$F \leq E \qquad \text{... (iii)}$$

Combining these, we get $H < G \geq F \leq E$

No comparisons can be made.

89. (5)

$$R > S \qquad \text{... (i)}$$
$$S \geq T \qquad \text{... (ii)}$$
$$T = V \qquad \text{... (iii)}$$

Combining these, we get $R > S \geq T = V$

Hence, $R > T$ (true).

Also, $V \leq S$ (true).

90. (4)

$$W \leq X \qquad \text{... (i)}$$
$$X > Y \qquad \text{... (ii)}$$
$$Y < Z \qquad \text{... (iii)}$$

Combining these, we get $W \leq X > Y < Z$

No comparisons can be made.

Solution for questions 91 to 95:

The given arrangement can be shown as:

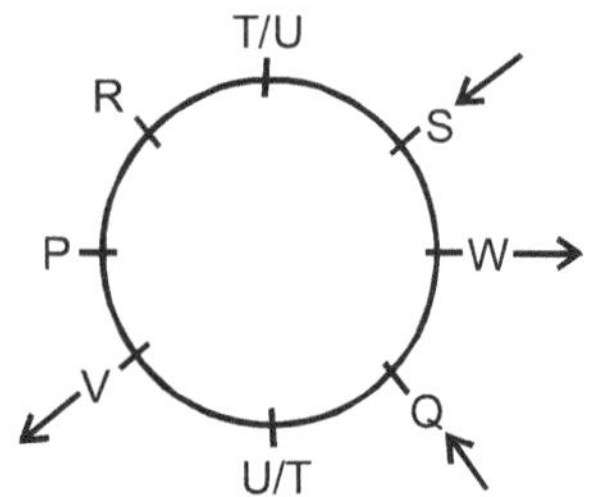

95. (1) If R is third to the right of U then the given arrangement can be shown as:

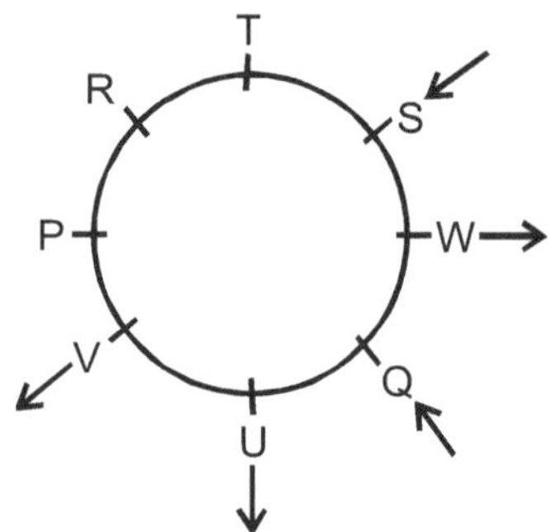

Hence, U must be facing outside

96. (4)

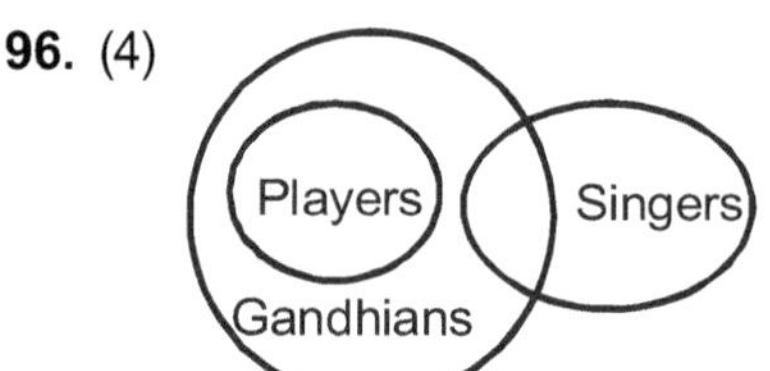

97. (2)

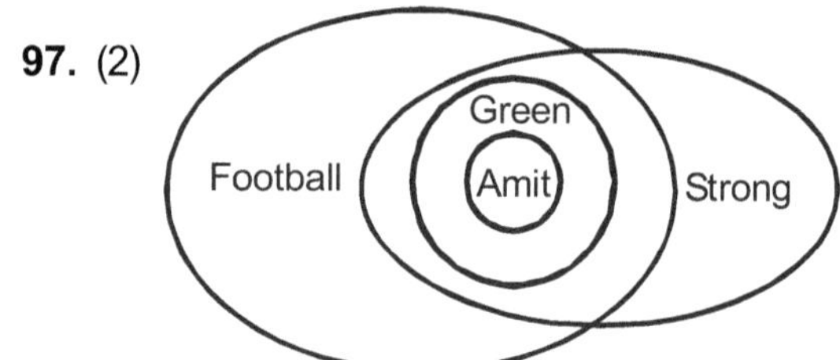

98. (4)

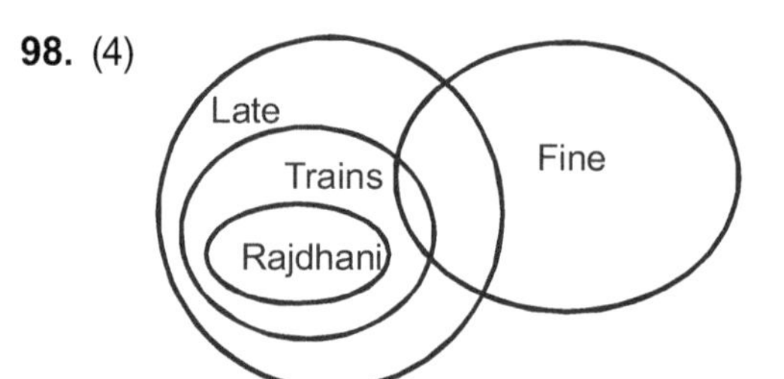

99. (2)

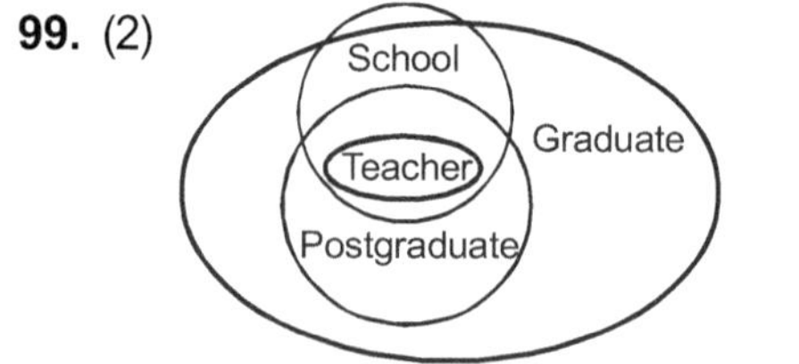

From the given information, we can surmise that teachers are graduates and postgraduates and they teach in a school. Hence, option (2) is correct.

100. (5)

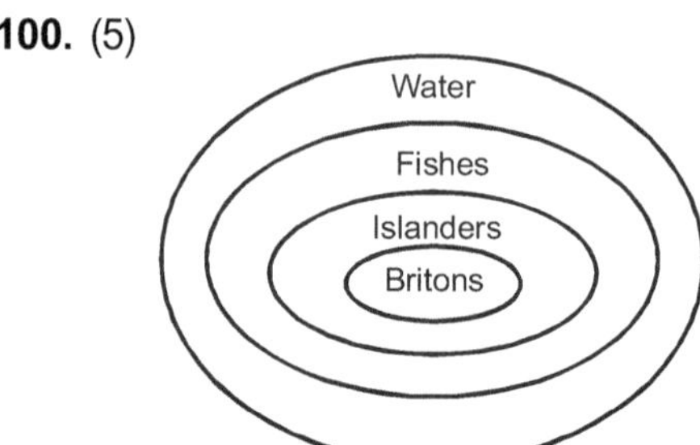

PRACTICE PAPER – 7

ENGLISH LANGUAGE

Directions (Q. 1 to 10): The questions in this section are based on a single passage. The questions are to be answered on the basis of what is stated or implied in the passage. Kindly note that more than one of the choices may conceivably answer some of the questions. However, you are to choose the most appropriate answer, that is, the response that most accurately and completely answers the question.

The unique geopolitical significance of Bangladesh results from myriad interwoven strands, each representing facets of this nation's complex historical evolution which, in turn, are crucially influenced by specific features of its geographical location.

The geographical features of this deltaic nation have evolved in tandem with the changing courses of three of Asia's great rivers: the Ganges, the Brahmaputra and the Meghna. The ancient city of Pundranagara (known today as Mahasthangarh in Bangladesh's Bogra district) and Vanga (south and south-east districts of present-day Bangladesh) find mention in the epics Ramayana and Mahabharata.

By the 5th century BC, the Indo-Aryan civilization, moving eastward along the Ganges river, was at the doorstep of the Bengal region. The 'Aryanization' of Bengal was a gradual process rarely displacing the already deep-rooted local traditions. Little surprise that even today the people of Bengal successfully retain many elements which are non-Aryan and even pre-Aryan in their life and culture.

The first Indo-Aryan empire, the Mauryan (321-181 BC) incorporated Varendra, with the capital at Pundranagara, as its easternmost province. Written during this reign, Kautilya's treatise, Arthasastra (third century BC) has references to the fine cotton fabric of Vanga as an important item of trade throughout India.

Beginning with Emperor Ashoka (273-236 BC) Buddhism put down deep roots in Bengal. Subsequently, the Buddhist Pala dynasty ruled Bengal for 400 years beginning in the mid-eighth century. The powerful kingdoms of deltaic Bengal flourished and prospered as a result of their **maritime** trade with China and other countries, equally when they were part of a pan-Indian empire, such as under Samudragupta in the fourth century AD, or in later centuries, when these kingdoms asserted their independence. This region was renowned for religious tolerance and coexistence where a succession of Hindu and Buddhist rulers patronized the other's religion.

The deltaic region of Bengal was the hub of two overlapping trade **diasporas**. The one extending westward towards the Arabian Peninsula was dominated by Arabs or Persians; the other extending eastward from the Bay of Bengal was dominated by the Bengalis.

The tenth century Arab geographer Masudi recorded the first evidence of Muslims residing in the Pala domains involved in the textile trade. The conquest of Bengal in 1204 by the Turkish cavalry officer Muhammad Bakhtiyar Khalji (operating in the service of Muhammad Ghuri who had conquered Delhi in 1193) signalled the initiation of the independent Bengal Sultanate that continued right up to the Mughal conquest of Bengal. Bakhtiyar Khalji constructed mosques, madrasas and khanaqahs (shelter for the Sufis and saints).

Under the Bengal Sultanate the influence of Islam remained primarily in the urban areas. Bakhtiyar Khalji's conquest in 1204 was followed by the arrival of thousands of immigrants from Turkey, Iran, Abyssinia, Arabia, Afghanistan, Central Asia and North India. They came as noblemen, judges (qazi), administrators, religious officials (ulema), traders, soldiers and Sufi saints and their followers. They were all part of the Muslim elite or ashraf where foreign origin, either their own or that of their ancestors, was the key element of their identity. Their presence was concentrated in the major towns and cities.

Side by side but socially distinct from the ashraf was the increasing number of Muslim urban artisans or industrial workers, grouped into communities according to their occupation, not unlike the jatis of Hindu society. These included weavers, loom-makers, paper-makers, tailors, bow and other weaponry makers, fishmongers and wandering holy men (kalandars). These were the earliest known groups of Bengali Muslims.

All this indicates a process of religious conversion that was slow, even leisurely and above all, interactive. The Sufis who came to Bengal were pious mystics rather than holy warriors or ghazis. There is hardly any contemporary evidence of violent conflicts or wars. Rather, there is evidence that the early Sufis of Bengal, attracted by the yogic and **cosmological** traditions that were widely practiced in Kamrup (Assam), sought to integrate elements of these into their religious lives.

The consolidation of Mughal rule in Bengal was a gradual process, begun under Emperor Humayun, pursued with vigour under Emperor Akbar, but completed only under Emperor Jahangir (1605-1627). The provincial capital was moved to Dhaka, which was renamed Jahangirnagar. The incorporation of Bengal as part of the vast Mughal empire in India effectively ended the region's isolation from the rest of the subcontinent. This brought economic prosperity to Bengal as it greatly stimulated demand for textiles and other manufactured goods. It also hastened agricultural development in Bengal's huge forested hinterlands.

Bengal's Mughal rulers maintained a clear distinction between matters of religion and matters of state. Mughal officials did not **patronize** Islam as a state religion. They followed a strictly non-interventionist position in religious matters despite pressure from local mullahs (Muslim preachers) and Sufis to support Islam over other religions.

It seems paradoxical that despite a policy of non-intervention, it is precisely during this period that Islam spread beyond the urban areas to become the religion of the cultivators in the vast rural hinterland of Bengal. This is particularly true of East Bengal, the present-day Bangladesh. Prior to the 1550s, the lack of direct riverine contact between East Bengal and the areas to the West, including upper India, had **inhibited** the development of this region. After this, however, the Ganga intensified its steady move eastwards and by the late 17th century had linked up with the Padma river and begun flowing through the heart of Bengal.

This had a dramatic impact on the development of East Bengal. The alluvial silt of the Ganga allowed wet rice cultivation in increasingly large tracts of land. Cash crops such as cotton and silk flourished. The easy availability of fertile land led to the rapid expansion of rice-production and of population-density in the East as compared to the western regions of Bengal.

1. Which of the following is true according to the passage?

   (1) Arthasastra refers to different kinds of cotton and woolen fabrics.

   (2) The 'Aryanisation' of Bengal happened all of a sudden and drastic changes were felt throughout India.

   (3) It is greatly astonishing to note that people in Bengal follow rituals borrowed from both pre-Aryan and non-Aryan life and culture.

   (4) The Indo-Aryan civilization reached Bengal by 5th century BC.

   (5) The deltaic region of Bengal was characterized by the activities of the Malays.

2. Out of the following options, which one can be an appropriate title for the passage?

   (1) Accounts of the Arab explorer Masudi

   (2) An overview of the Mughal rule in Bengal

   (3) An overview of the Mauryan influence on Bengal

   (4) An account of agricultural practices followed in Bengal during the Mauryan rule

   (5) A socio-economic overview of Bengal under different dynasties

3. What can be assumed about the author's profession?

   (1) A scientist   (2) A historian

   (3) A philosopher   (4) A thinker

   (5) An agricultural scientist

4. What, according to the author, is the reason behind the prosperity of the kingdoms of deltaic Bengal?

   (1) Land trade with the Deccan

   (2) Cultural influence of the Marathas

   (3) Socio economic development

   (4) Influence of Buddhism

   (5) Sea trade with China and other countries

5. Out of the given statements, the author would agree with which one of the following?

   (1) Agricultural development took place in Bengal after the Mughal came to power.

   (2) Bengal's Mughal rulers often mixed matters of religion and governance.

   (3) Islam was mainly confined within urban limits during the Mughal period.

   (4) Cotton was the only cash crop that flourished in Bengal during the Mughal rule.

   (5) Bengal faced a dearth of fertile lands despite the presence of major rivers in the region.

Which of the following options would come closest to the word printed in bold as used in the passage?

6. Maritime

   (1) Islands   (2) Topography

   (3) Land trade   (4) Nautical

   (5) Mountainous

7. Diaspora

   (1) Expatriate community

   (2) Exiled persons

   (3) Factory workers

   (4) Nobility

   (5) Merchants

8. Cosmology

   (1) Study of electro-magnets

   (2) Analysis of atmosphere

   (3) Study of paranormal aliens

   (4) Origin and evolution of Spirituality

   (5) Origin and development of the universe

Which of the following options would come opposite to the word printed in bold as used in the passage?

9. Patronize

   (1) Oppose   (2) Reign

   (3) Feign   (4) Bolster

   (5) Support

10. Inhibit

   (1) Intensify   (2) Promote

   (3) Hesitation   (4) Partial

   (5) Inhabit

Directions (Q. 11 to 15): Given below are the jumbled sentences of a paragraph. The first and the last sentence of the jumbled paragraph are given in correct order. Arrange the middle sentences in the correct sequence.

11. i. Until 50 or 60 years ago, saving some of your own seeds was an integral part of the gardening year for most vegetable gardeners.

   ii. This is a shame.

   iii. Knowledge of how to save seeds has largely been lost by amateur gardeners and today many of us assume that they are something you have to buy in packets from seed suppliers.

   iv. Not least because there is something immensely rewarding about saving a few of your own seeds.

   v. Over generations, their dedication helped to create a rich diversity of vegetable varieties, adapted to suit the local soil and climate.

   vi. You get to watch them grow the following year.

   (1) iv, iii, ii, v   (2) iv, v, iii, ii

   (3) v, iii, ii, iv   (4) v, ii, iv, iii

   (5) iv, ii, iii, v

12. i. Change, as they say, is the only constant.

   ii. The Planning Commission, established 64 years ago, brings up the issues of time, context and environment.

   iii. What is relevant in a certain context at a given period of time and environment may cease to be so in a different context, a different time or a changed environment.

   iv. And so, when confronted with change the choices are limited to just two — change with the times, or risk being consigned to the dustbin of history.

   v. This applies as much to institutions and organisations as to people, ideas and concepts.

   vi. Between 1950, when it was established, and now, the times have changed.

   (1) v, iii, iv, ii   (2) iii, v, iv, ii

   (3) iv, iii, ii, v   (4) iii, ii, v, iv

   (5) v, iii, ii, iv

13. i. There are times when state and citizen are so hopelessly locked in conflict that one of them will have to give in.

   ii. Whatever the state does — be it arresting and force-feeding her or ignoring her demand for an end to military impunity by repealing the Armed Forces Special Powers Act, 1958 — the Manipuri activist, now 42, seems to triumph.

   iii. In normal circumstances, the state prevails.

   iv. It is a sign of the government's defeat that it has been forced to arrest Ms. Sharmila again, two days after she was released by a court.

   v. But Irom Sharmila Chanu's 14-year-long hunger strike is no ordinary circumstance.

   vi. The ostensible objective is to save her life, as she insists on continuing her indefinite fast even after her release.

   (1) ii, iii, v, iv   (2) iii, iv, v, ii

   (3) iii, v, ii, iv   (4) v, ii, iv, iii

   (5) iv, v, iii, ii

14. i. There she slept, a puckered little bundle of DNA fighting to organise.

   ii. Her breathing rattled less than it had when she was born; I could hardly tell she was alive apart from that relentless ticking.

   iii. She looked and smelled like a lump of dough.

   iv. The ticks were supposed to be reassuring, but to me they sounded like a countdown.

   v. There was an electronic pad tucked beneath her baby mattress that sensed her breathing, translating each inhalation and exhalation into a metronomic tick.

   vi. Everything about the last year had been a countdown. Waiting to conceive, watching the bump grow, buying everything we thought we needed.

   (1) ii, iii, iv, v   (2) v, iv, ii, iii

   (3) ii, v, iii, iv   (4) iii, ii, v, iv

   (5) iii, v, iv, ii

15. i. Shaun Wright, Labour's South Yorkshire police and crime commissioner, who was Rotherham's cabinet member for children and young people's services from 2005 until 2010, is refusing to resign.

   ii. He should have gone at once.

   iii. He apologises unreservedly for the grotesque abuse that 1,400 children or more may have endured on his watch, but he says the scale of the abuse has come as a surprise to him.

   iv. His lack of leadership, his reluctance to ask difficult questions or to intervene proactively, allowed the exploitation itemised in Professor Alexis Jay's grim report on Tuesday to grow from what an earlier investigator called gang abuse for personal gratification into "financial and career opportunities" for young, mainly Asian, men.

v.　The chorus of voices raised against him, which includes the leadership of his own party, is, rightly, swelling.

vi.　His failure to take responsibility now, in the face of the evidence, suggests a dangerous reluctance to address what went so damagingly wrong for so many vulnerable young women.

(1) iii, v, ii, iv　　　　　(2) v, iv, iii, ii

(3) ii, v, iii, iv　　　　　(4) iv, ii, v, iii

(5) v, iii, ii, iv

Directions (Q. 16 to 20): Which of the phrases (1), (2), (3) and (4) given below each sentence should replace the phrases printed in bold in the following sentences to make the sentence grammatically correct. If the sentence is correct as it is and 'No correction is required', mark (5) as the answer.

16. He didn't want **risking to get wet** as he had only one suit.

(1) risking for getting wet

(2) risking at getting wet

(3) to risk getting wet

(4) to get wet at the risk of

(5) No correction required

17. He postponed making a decision **until he been given** complete information.

(1) till he had been given

(2) until he will get

(3) till he would be giving

(4) till he could be giving

(5) No correction required

18. They came in **quiet so as not** to wake the others in the dormitory.

(1) as quiet as not

(2) so quiet as not

(3) so quiet that not

(4) quietly so as not

(5) No correction required

19. If you were rule bound as you claim to be, you **should stop at** the signal.

(1) should stop before

(2) would have stopped at

(3) should be stopped at

(4) would have been stopped

(5) No correction required

20. He refused to sign till he **would read** the text of the agreement.

(1) had read

(2) will read

(3) would have read

(4) should be reading

(5) No correction required

Directions (Q. 21 to 25): Fill in the blanks by choosing the most appropriate options.

21. _____ rice, they had paneer _____ mutton.

(1) with, and　　　　　(2) besides, or

(3) apart, aside　　　　(4) under, above

(5) and, with

22. He may be right _____ wrong in his opinion, _____ he is too clearheaded to be unjust.

(1) and, with　　　　　(2) or, but

(3) besides, although　(4) but, with

(5) besides, above

23. A regular bath ___ the morning, has always an _____ effect.

(1) at, depressing　　　(2) on, suicidal

(3) from, fresh　　　　(4) in, invigorating

(5) since, disastrous.

24. A fog rolled _____ the city ___ the small hours.

(1) at, above　　　　　(2) in, around

(3) beneath, across　　(4) under, on

(5) over, in

25. Akbar was known _____ his expertise _____ governance and administration.

(1) at, for　　　　　　(2) on, with

(3) until, till　　　　　(4) about, still

(5) for, in

Directions (Q. 26 to 30): In the following passage there are blanks, each of which has been numbered. These numbers are printed below the passage and against each, five words are suggested, one of which fits the blank appropriately. Find out the appropriate word in each case.

Long time ago, there lived a group of rats under a tree _(26)_. One day a group of tigers in search of water passed that way and destroyed the homes of the rats. As a result, many of them were crushed to _(27)_. The king of rats decided to approach the tiger king and requested him to use another route.

The tiger king _(28)_ to this and took another route to the water, so the lives of the rats were saved. One day a group of _(29)_ came to the forest and trapped the tigers in huge nets. Then, the tiger king suddenly remembered the king of rats. He summoned one of the tigers of his herd which had not been trapped to go and **_(30)_** the king of rats.

On listening to the tiger, the king of the rats took his entire group of mice and they cut open the nets which trapped the tiger herd, in this way the tigers were set free by the rats.

26. (1) destructively   (2) coldly
     (3) peacefully   (4) silently
     (5) mildly

27. (1) sleep   (2) death
     (3) torture   (4) fall
     (5) powder

28. (1) convinced   (2) ignorant
     (3) tempted   (4) rejoiced
     (5) agreed

29. (1) animals   (2) hunters
     (3) kings   (4) friends
     (5) fishermen

30. (1) banish   (2) rescue
     (3) contact   (4) address
     (5) glorify

NUMERICAL ABILITY

Directions (Q. 31 to 35): What approximate value will come in place of question mark (?) in the following questions? (You are not expected to calculate the exact value.)

31. 68% of 1288 + 26% of 734 – 215 = ?
     (1) 620   (2) 930
     (3) 540   (4) 850
     (5) 710

32. $(32.05)^2 - (18.9)^2 - (11.9)^2 = ?$
     (1) 670   (2) 530
     (3) 420   (4) 780
     (5) 960

33. 6578 ÷ 67 × 15 = ? × 6
     (1) 200   (2) 250
     (3) 150   (4) 100
     (5) 300

34. $\dfrac{679}{45} \div \dfrac{23}{2130} \times \dfrac{126}{169} = ?$
     (1) 540   (2) 760
     (3) 800   (4) 1260
     (5) 1040

35. $\sqrt{5687} \times \sqrt{1245} \div \sqrt{689} = ? \div 13$
     (1) 840   (2) 910
     (3) 1320   (4) 1120
     (5) 1550

Directions for questions 36 to 40: In the following questions two equations numbered I and II are given. You have to solve both the equations and

Give answer

(1) if x > y   (2) if x ≥ y

(3) if x < y   (4) if x ≤ y

(5) if x = y or the relationship cannot be established

36. I. $\sqrt{x + 18} = \sqrt{144} - \sqrt{49}$
    II. $y^2 + 409 = 473$

37. I. $x^2 - 7x + 12 = 0$
    II. $y^2 - 9y + 20 = 0$

38. I. $y^2 - x^2 = 32$
    II.   y – x = 2

39. I. $\sqrt{x} - \dfrac{\sqrt{5}}{\sqrt{x}} = 0$
    II. $y^3 - 5^{(3/2)} = 0$

40. I.   3x + 5y = 28
    II.   8x – 3y = 42

41. Two runners A and B, are running on a circular track of length 14 km. If A and B started simultaneously from the same point but in opposite direction with speeds 15m/s and 20m/s respectively, what is the distance covered by A when they cross each other for the first time?
     (1) 6 km   (2) 8 km
     (3) 5 km   (4) 9 km
     (5) 4 km

42. A alone can do a piece of work in 6 days and B alone in 8 days. A and B undertook to do it for Rs. 3,200. With the help of C, they completed the work in 3 days. How much is to be paid to C?
     (1) Rs. 375   (2) Rs. 400
     (3) Rs. 600   (4) Rs. 800
     (5) Rs. 500

43. Vaishali wants to get the floor of her room covered with tiles. The length and the breadth of her room are 20 m and 16 m respectively. What will be the minimum number of square tiles required to cover the floor?
     (1) 20   (2) 25
     (3) 16   (4) 24
     (5) None of these

44. Out of five boys and two girls, a group of 4 is to be selected. The number of ways, group consists three boys and a girl, are

(1) 10   (2) 35

(3) 30   (4) 12

(5) 20

45. The average weight of five persons sitting in a boat is 38 kg. The average weight of the boat and the persons sitting in the boat is 52 kg. What is the weight of the boat?

(1) 228 kg   (2) 122 kg

(3) 232 kg   (4) 242 kg

(5) 235 kg

Directions (Q. 46 to 50): In each of the following questions complete the given series.

46. 2, 11, 27, 52, 88, 137, ?

(1) 209   (2) 207

(3) 205   (4) 203

(5) 201

47. 405, 135, 54, 27, 18, 18, ?

(1) 30   (2) 48

(3) 42   (4) 24

(5) 36

48. 64, 512, 1728, 4096, 8000, 13824, ?

(1) 15625   (2) 21952

(3) 19683   (4) 17576

(5) 12167

49. 18, 32, 58, 108, 206, 400, ?

(1) 786   (2) 784

(3) 782   (4) 780

(5) 778

50. 8, 14, 30.5, 79.25, 241.25, 848.375, ?

(1) 3397.5   (2) 3819

(3) 3398   (4) 4241.75

(5) 4050

Directions (Q. 51 to 55): Answer the following questions based on the given information.

The given table shows the number or percentage of children, women and men playing six different games.

GAMES	NUMBER OR PERCENTAGE		
	Children	Women	Men
Squash	99	138	21%
Hockey	35%	159	166
Tennis	632	168	20%
Baseball	163	36%	221
Badminton	261	34%	37%
Cricket	36%	77	435

51. What is the total number of children playing all the games together ?

(1) 1618   (2) 1064

(3) 1418   (4) 1264

(5) None of these

52. What is the average number of men playing all the games together ? (rounded off to two digits after decimal)

(1) 177.33   (2) 236.33

(3) 210.67   (4) 269.67

(5) None of these

53. What is the respective ratio of the total number of women playing baseball to the men playing badminton?

(1) 2 : 3   (2) 23 : 36

(3) 24 : 37   (4) 11 : 18

(5) None of these

54. Number of children playing hockey forms what percent of children playing cricket ? (rounded off to two digits after decimal)

(1) 54.76%   (2) 56.76%

(3) 58.76%   (4) 60.76%

(5) None of these

55. Total number of women playing badminton forms approximately what percent of the total number of women playing all the games together ?

(1) 45   (2) 41

(3) 37   (4) 33

(5) 29

56. Suresh invested Rs.10000 at a certain rate of simple interest for 2 years. Had he invested the amount at the same rate of compound interest, compounded annually, for the same period, the interest accrued would have been Rs.400 more. Find the value of the rate of interest.

(1) 10%   (2) 15%

(3) 20%   (4) 25%

(5) None of these

57. By selling a goat for Rs.3,520, a man loses 12%. At what price must he sell it to gain 12%?

(1) Rs.4,260   (2) Rs.4,480

(3) Rs.4,080   (4) Rs.4,660

(5) None of these

58. If the total cost of four tube lights and three bulbs is Rs.260 and the ratio between the cost of a tube light and a bulb is 5 : 2 respectively, what is the total cost of one tube light and six bulbs?

(1) Rs. 210   (2) Rs. 130

(3) Rs. 180   (4) Rs. 170

(5) None of these

59. In a water and alcohol mixture, at 10 a.m, the amount of water was twice of that of alcohol. On the same day at 4:00 p.m. amount of water was half of that of alcohol. If 100 m³ volume of water is lost due to evaporation each hour, then what was the percentage of alcohol in the mixture at 9 a.m. on the same day?

(1) 30.17% (2) 30.76%

(3) 31.57% (4) 32.27%

(5) None of these

60. Milka purchased an item for Rs. 7,200 and sold it at the gain of 25%. From that amount he purchased another item and sold it at the loss of 25%. What is his overall gain/loss?

(1) Loss of Rs. 540

(2) Gain of Rs.420

(3) Loss of Rs.450

(4) Neither gain nor loss

(5) None of these

Directions (Q. 61 to 65) : Answer the questions on the basis of the information given below.

The bar graph given below shows the total number of students appeared and qualified from various colleges – P, Q, R, S and T.

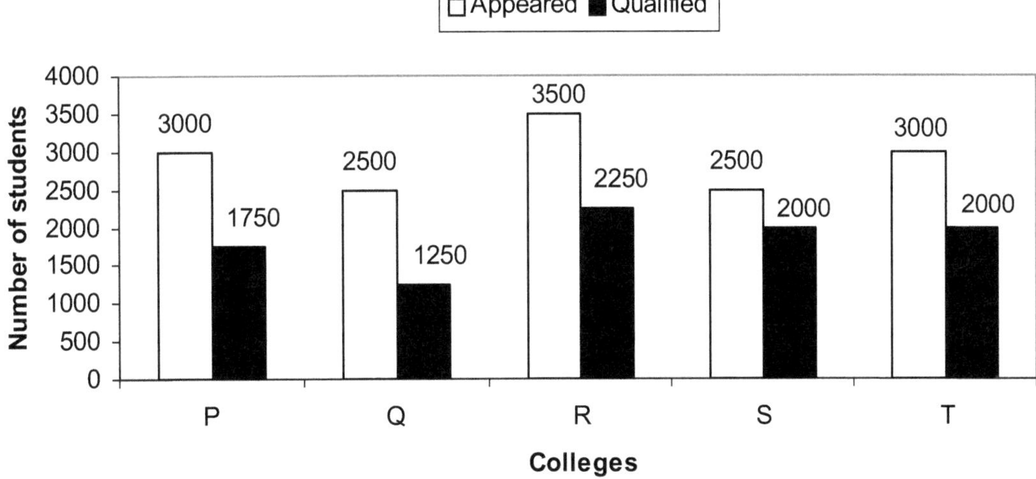

61. The average number of students qualified in the examination from colleges R and S is what percent of the average number of students appeared for the examination from the same colleges? (rounded off to two digits after decimal)

(1) 58.62 (2) 70.83

(3) 62.58 (4) 58.96

(5) None of these

62. What is the ratio of the number of students appeared to the number of students qualified in the examination from college R?

(1) 7 : 12 (2) 6 : 5

(3) 9 : 13 (4) 9 : 10

(5) None of these

63. What is the ratio of the number of students qualified in the examination from college P and the number of students qualified in the examination from college Q?

(1) 8 : 3 (2) 5 : 7

(3) 7 : 3 (4) 9 : 5

(5) None of these

64. The number of students appeared for the exam from college S is approximately what percent of the total number of students appeared for the exam from all the colleges together?

(1) 12 (2) 24

(3) 29 (4) 18

(5) 8

65. What is the difference between the average number of students appeared in the exam from all the given colleges and the average number of students qualified from all the colleges together?

(1) 1050 (2) 1100

(3) 990 (4) 1020

(5) None of these

REASONING ABILITY

66. Both Pran and Khan start from their office and drive for 14 km to reach their respective homes. Pran turns left and drives for 7 km before turning left again to drive the remaining distance to his home. Khan turns right and drives for 5 km before turning right again to drive the remaining distance to his home. What is the distance between their homes?

(1) 10 km   (2) 28 km

(3) 14 km   (4) 25 km

(5) 20 km

67. In an apartment complex there are several blocks. The residential block is at the centre and the gym is 200m to the north of it. The school is $200\sqrt{2}$ m to the south west of the gym whereas the playground is 400 m to the east of the school. The temple is $200\sqrt{2}$ m to the south west of the playground. The store is at a distance of $200\sqrt{2}$ m towards the south east of the residential block. How far is the temple from the store?

(1) $300\sqrt{2}$ m   (2) 200m

(3) $200\sqrt{2}$ m   (4) 400m

(5) None of these

68. Kusuma is the wife of Ravi. Govind and Prabhu are brothers. Govind is the brother of Ravi. Prabhu is Kusuma's

(1) Cousin   (2) Borhter

(3) Brother-in-law   (4) Uncle

(5) None of these

69. Vijay says "Anand's mother is the only daughter of my mother". How is Anand related to Vijay?

(1) Brother   (2) Father

(3) Nephew   (4) Grandfather

(5) None of these

70. Pointing to Mala, Kala said "She is my brother's only sister's daughter". How is Mala related to Kala?

(1) Mother   (2) Daughter

(3) Aunt   (4) Niece

(5) None of these

Directions (Q. 71 to 75) : Answer the questions on the basis of information given below.

In a certain code "pencils and erasers" is coded as "tables or chairs", "tables and chairs"is coded as "trucks or buses" , "trucks and buses" is coded as "pencils or erasers" and "chairs and pencils" is coded as "trucks or tables".

71. What does the code "chairs" stand for?

(1) pencils   (2) erasers

(3) chairs   (4) buses

(5) None of these

72. What is the code for "buses and erasers"?

(1) pencils or buses

(2) pencils or chairs

(3) chairs and erasers

(4) erasers or chairs

(5) Either (2) or (4)

73. If "sharp knives" is coded as "big spoons", then what can be the code for "sharp pencils"?

(1) spoons tables   (2) high chairs

(3) big trucks   (4) big tables

(5) Either (1) or (4)

74. How can "tables and erasers" be coded?

(1) chairs or buses

(2) buses and chairs

(3) trucks or chairs

(4) pencils or trucks

(5) Either (2) or (3)

75. If any number "n" is coded as "50-n" then what will be the code for "27 pencils"?

(1) 50 trucks   (2) 27 chairs

(3) 23 tables   (4) 33 buses

(5) 27 erasers

Directions (Q. 76 to 80): Answer the following questions based on the given information.

Vinay, Ravi, Anamika, Yogesh, Abhay and Rihana stay on different floors of a six-storey building (ground floor is numbered as floor 1 and top floor is numbered as floor 6).

Each of them plays one of the following games: Football, Hockey, Cricket, Tennis, Chess and Volleyball, but not necessarily in the same order.

Ravi stays on floor 4 and he plays neither Chess nor Volleyball. The one who plays Hockey stays on floor 3. Abhay plays Tennis and he doesn't stay on either floor 1 or 6. Anamika stays on floor 2 and plays Cricket. Yogesh plays Volleyball but neither he nor Rihana stays on floor 1.

76. Who plays Football?

(1) Rihana   (2) Yogsh

(3) Ravi   (4) Vinay

(5) None of these

77. Which game does Vinay play?

(1) Cricket   (2) Chess

(3) Hockey   (4) Football

(5) None of these

78. On which floor does Abhay stay?

(1) 5   (2) 4

(3) 3   (4) 2

(5) None of these

79. Who plays Hockey?

(1) Ravi   (2) Vinay

(3) Rihana   (4) Anamika

(5) None of these

80. Which of the following combinations is true?

  (1) Vinay-Floor 1-Hockey

  (2) Abhay-Floor 5-Chess

  (3) Yogesh-Floor 6 -Volleyball

  (4) Ravi-Floor 4-Chess

  (5) None of these

Directions (Q. 81 to 85): Answer the questions on the basis of the information given below.

(a) Six plays are to be organised from Tuesday to Monday —one play each day with one day when there is no play. 'No play' day is not Monday or Tuesday.

(b) The plays are held in sets of 3 plays each in such a way that 3 plays are held without any break, ie 3 plays are held in such a way that there is no 'No play' day between them but immediately before this set or immediately after this set it is 'No play' day.

(c) Play N was held on 26th and play A was held on 31st of the same month.

(d) Play P was not held immediately after play R (but was held after R, not necessarily immediately) and play S was held immediately before T.

(e) All the six plays were held in the same month.

81. Which play was organised on Monday?

  (1) N   (2) S

  (3) T   (4) P

  (5) None of these

82. Which day was play N organised?

  (1) Wednesday   (2) Monday

  (3) Tuesday   (4) Friday

  (5) None of these

83. Which date was a 'No play' day?

  (1) 26th   (2) 28th

  (3) 29th   (4) 27th

  (5) None of these

84. Which of the following is true?

  (1) Play P is held immediately before play S.

  (2) Play N is held after play P.

  (3) There was a gap after 2 plays and then 4 plays were organised.

  (4) First play was organised on the 25th.

  (5) Play P was held on Thursday.

85. Which day was play T organised?

  (1) Friday   (2) Wednesday

  (3) Sunday   (4) Tuesday

  (5) None of these

Directions (Q. 86 to 90): In the following questions the symbols %, &, ϕ, $\Leftrightarrow$ and Ω are used with following meaning as illustrated below:

P % Q means 'P is not less than Q'.

P & Q means 'P is neither less than nor equal to Q'.

P ϕ Q means 'P is neither less than nor greater than Q'.

P $\Leftrightarrow$ Q means 'P is neither greater than nor equal to Q'.

P Ω Q means 'P is not greater than Q'.

Based on the statements given in each of the questions below, find out which of the conclusion follows.

Mark:

(1) If only conclusion I follows.

(2) If only conclusion II follows.

(3) Both the conclusion follows.

(4) If either conclusion I or conclusion II follows.

(5) If neither conclusion I nor conclusion II follows.

86. **Statement** : L % N, L $\Leftrightarrow$ K, M ϕ K

  Conclusion : I. N $\Leftrightarrow$ K

                II. M % N

87. **Statement** : Q ϕ P, P Ω S, S & R

  Conclusion : I. R $\Leftrightarrow$ P

                II. S ϕ Q

88. **Statement** : X & Y, Y % Z, Z Ω A

  Conclusion : I. Y ϕ A

                II. X & Z

89. **Statement** : G $\Leftrightarrow$ H, J ϕ H, J Ω O

  Conclusion : I. J & G

                II. O % H

90. **Statement** : S & T, T % U, V ϕ U

  Conclusion : I. T & V

                II. V ϕ T

Directions (Q. 91 to 95): Answer the questions on the basis of the information given below.

Eight friends, Arzan, Gautam, David, Rizwan, Sunil, Gurleen, Chetan and Ravi, are sitting around a square table in such a way that four of them sit at four corners of the square while four sit in the middle of each of the four sides. The ones who sit at the four corners face the centre while those who sit in the middle of the sides face outside.

Ravi sits second to the right of David. Ravi does not sit at any of the corners. Arzan sits third to the right of Sunil. Sunil is not an immediate neighbour of David. Gautam and Chetan are immediate neighbours of each other but Gautam does not sit at any of the corners of the table. Gurleen is an immediate neighbour of neither Sunil nor David.

91. Four of the following five are alike in a certain way and so form a group. Which is the one that does not belong to that group?

(1) Sunil   (2) Gautam

(3) Gurleen   (4) David

(5) Ravi

92. Who sits third to the left of Rizwan?

(1) Ravi   (2) Gautam

(3) David   (4) Sunil

(5) Cannot be determined

93. What is the position of Sunil with respect to Arzan?

(1) Immediate to the left   (2) Second to the left

(3) Third to the left   (4) Third to the right

(5) Second to the right

94. Who amongst the following sits second to the right of Chetan?

(1) David   (2) Rizwan

(3) Ravi   (4) Gurleen

(5) Arzan

95. Who amongst the following represent the immediate neighbours of Gurleen?

(1) Arzan, Chetan   (2) Ravi, Gautam

(3) Ravi, Arzan   (4) Rizwan, Gautam

(5) Rizwan, Chetan

Directions (Q. 96 to 100): In each question below are three statements followed by two conclusions numbered I and II. You have to take the three given statements to be true even if they seem to be at variance from commonly known facts and then decide which of the given conclusions logically follows from the three statements disregarding commonly known facts.

Give answer (1) if only conclusion I follows.

Give answer (2) if only conclusion II follows.

Give answer (3) if either conclusion I or II follows.

Give answer (4) if neither conclusion I nor II follows.

Give answer (5) if both conclusions I and II follow.

96. Statements:

All packets are tents.

All tents are houses.

Some boxes are houses.

Conclusions:

I. Some houses are packets.

II. Some boxes are tents.

97. Statements:

Some nuts are bolts.

Some bolts are hammers.

Some hammers are nails.

Conclusions:

I. Some nails are bolts.

II. No nail is bolt.

98. Statements:

All windows are doors.

No door is mountain.

Some mountains are roads.

Conclusions:

I. Some roads are windows.

II. Some roads are doors.

99. Statements:

Some phones are bangles.

Some bangles are rings.

All rings are sticks.

Conclusions:

I. Some rings are phones.

II. Some sticks are bangles.

100. Statements:

All bricks are walls.

All stones are walls.

All candles are walls.

Conclusions:

I. Some walls are bricks.

II. Some walls are candles.

ANSWERS

1. (4)	**2.** (5)	**3.** (2)	**4.** (5)	**5.** (1)	**6.** (4)	**7.** (1)	**8.** (5)	**9.** (1)	**10.** (2)
11. (3)	**12.** (2)	**13.** (3)	**14.** (4)	**15.** (1)	**16.** (3)	**17.** (1)	**18.** (4)	**19.** (2)	**20.** (1)
21. (1)	**22.** (2)	**23.** (4)	**24.** (5)	**25.** (5)	**26.** (3)	**27.** (2)	**28.** (5)	**29.** (2)	**30.** (3)
31. (4)	**32.** (2)	**33.** (2)	**34.** (5)	**35.** (3)	**36.** (5)	**37.** (4)	**38.** (3)	**39.** (5)	**40.** (1)
41. (1)	**42.** (2)	**43.** (1)	**44.** (5)	**45.** (2)	**46.** (5)	**47.** (5)	**48.** (2)	**49.** (1)	**50.** (3)
51. (1)	**52.** (2)	**53.** (3)	**54.** (4)	**55.** (5)	**56.** (3)	**57.** (2)	**58.** (4)	**59.** (2)	**60.** (3)
61. (2)	**62.** (5)	**63.** (5)	**64.** (4)	**65.** (1)	**66.** (5)	**67.** (2)	**68.** (3)	**69.** (3)	**70.** (2)
71. (2)	**72.** (5)	**73.** (5)	**74.** (1)	**75.** (3)	**76.** (3)	**77.** (2)	**78.** (1)	**79.** (3)	**80.** (3)
81. (5)	**82.** (1)	**83.** (2)	**84.** (4)	**85.** (3)	**86.** (1)	**87.** (5)	**88.** (2)	**89.** (3)	**90.** (4)
91. (3)	**92.** (1)	**93.** (4)	**94.** (4)	**95.** (2)	**96.** (1)	**97.** (3)	**98.** (4)	**99.** (2)	**100.** (5)

EXPLANATIONS

1. (4) Refer to the third paragraph for the answer. The author states that the Indo-Aryan civilization reached Bengal's doorstep by the 5th century BC. The other options are incorrect as per the passage.

2. (5) The passage deals with the socio-economic parameters of Bengal that have evolved over the ages. Hence, option (5) is the answer. The other options are narrow in scope.

3. (2) The author is most likely a historian. The passage contains innumerable historical details which only a historian can be aware of.

4. (5) Refer to the third sentence of the fifth paragraph for the answer. The author mentions that the kingdoms of deltaic Bengal mainly flourished because of maritime trade with China and other countries.

5. (1) Refer to the last sentence of the eleventh paragraph where the author mentions that agricultural development started taking place after the Mughals came to power in Bengal. The other options are incorrect as per the passage.

6. (4) 'Maritime' refers to anything that is related to sea or the navy.

7. (1) 'Diaspora' refers to the expatriate community.

8. (5) 'Cosmology' refers to the origin and development of the universe.

9. (1) 'Patronize' in the passage has been used to mean 'support'. Hence, 'oppose' would be its antonym.

10. (2) 'Inhibit' means 'to oppose'. Hence, its antonym would be 'to promote'.

11. (3) Statement (v) carries forward the idea mentioned in statement (i). Statement (iii) states that the situation has changed now and the knowledge of how to save seeds has been lost. Statement (ii) describes the situation now as a shame. This makes (iii) and (ii) a mandatory pair. Statement (iv) should precede statement (vi) because the 'rewarding' factor mentioned in statement (iv) is explained in statement (vi).

12. (2) Statement (iii) logically follows statement (i) because it further elaborates on the idea introduced in statement (i). The demonstrative pronoun 'this' in (v) refers to the relevance of an idea in a certain context, and hence follows (iii). Statement (iv) talks of available choices when faced with change. Statement (ii) then introduces the institutions and organizations mentioned in (v) and therefore follows (ii).

13. (3) Statement (iii) continues the thought introduced in statement (i). Statement (v) states that there is an exception to the situation, wherein the state prevails in the standoff between it and the citizens, by quoting the case of Irom Sharmila Chanu and hence it logically follows statement (iii). Statement (ii) further elaborates the reason why the case of Irom Sharmila is not an ordinary one.

14. (4) Statement (iii) logically follows statement (i) because the latter further describes the condition of the girl who was sleeping. Statement (ii) further describes her breathing and introduces a ticking sound. Statement (v) explains the source of the ticking sound and hence follows statement (ii). Statement (iv) follows statement (v) as it further elaborates on the 'ticks'.

15. (1) Statement (iii) logically follows statement (i) because it gives the reason behind Shaun Wright refusing to resign as mentioned in statement (i). Statement (v) talks about the voices being raised against Shaun Wright. Along with that, the author is of the opinion that the dissent against Wright is justified. Statement (ii) talks about the action that should have happened, according to the author. Hence, statements (v) and (ii) is a mandatory pair and this is present only in option (1).

16. (3) 'to risk' is grammatically correct in the context of the sentence.

17. (1) The past perfect tense should be used.

18. (4) 'quietly' is correct because the adverbial form should be used to make the sentence correct.

19. (2) Since the sentence starts with a condition, 'would have' is the correct form.

20. (1) Past perfect tense should be used.

21. (1) 'with', 'and' are the right words for the blanks.

22. (2) 'or', 'but' are the right words.

23. (4) 'In' is the correct preposition. A regular bath in the morning will certainly have an 'invigorating' effect. The other options are out of context.

24. (5) 'over' and 'in' are the correct prepositions.

25. (5) 'For' and 'in' are the correct prepositions.

26. (3) 'Peacefully' goes with the context of the sentence.

27. (2) 'Crushed to death' makes sense.

28. (5) 'Agreed' is the correct word in the context of the sentence.

29. (2) 'Hunters' is the right word because they trapped the tigers.

30. (3) 'Contact' is the correct word in the context of the sentence.

31. (4) $? = \dfrac{68 \times 1288}{100} + \dfrac{26 \times 734}{100} - 215$

$\qquad = 875.84 + 190.84 - 215$

$\qquad \approx 876 + 191 - 215$

$\qquad = 852 \approx 850$

32. (2) $(32.05)^2 - (18.9)^2 - (11.9)^2$

$\qquad \approx 1027 - 357 - 144$

$\qquad = 526 \approx 530$

33. (2) $? = \dfrac{6578 \times 15}{67 \times 6} = 245.45 \cong 250$

34. (5) $? = \dfrac{680}{45} \times \dfrac{2130}{23} \times \dfrac{126}{170}$

$\qquad\qquad = 1043 \approx 1040$

35. (3) $\sqrt{5687} \times \sqrt{1245} \div \sqrt{689} = ? \div 13$

$\qquad \therefore \ ? = \dfrac{\sqrt{5687} \times \sqrt{1245} \times 13}{\sqrt{689}}$

$\qquad\qquad = \dfrac{74.4 \times 35.2 \times 13}{26.2} \approx 1320$

36. (5) **From statement I:**

$$\sqrt{x + 18} = \sqrt{144} - \sqrt{49}$$

$$\Rightarrow \ \sqrt{x + 18} = 12 - 7 = 5$$

$$\Rightarrow \ x + 18 = 25$$

$$\Rightarrow \ x = 25 - 18 = 7$$

From statement II:

$$y^2 = 473 - 409 = 64$$

$$\Rightarrow \qquad y = \sqrt{64} = \pm 8$$

Hence, the relationship cannot be established.

37. (4) **From statement I:**

$x^2 - 7x + 12 = 0$

$\Rightarrow \ x^2 - 4x - 3x + 12 = 0$

$\Rightarrow \ x(x - 4) - 3(x - 4) = 0$

$\Rightarrow \ (x - 3)(x - 4) = 0$

$\therefore \ \ x = 3$ or 4

From statement II:

$y^2 - 9y + 20 = 0$

$\Rightarrow \ y^2 - 5y - 4y + 20 = 0$

$\Rightarrow \ y(y - 5) - 4(y - 5) = 0$

$\Rightarrow \ (y - 4)(y - 5) = 0$

$\therefore \ \ y = 4$ or 5

Clearly, $x \leq y$.

38. (3) By dividing equation I by II,

$$\dfrac{(y - x)(y + x)}{y - x} = \dfrac{32}{2}$$

$\Rightarrow \qquad y + x = 16 \qquad\qquad\qquad ...(i)$

$\qquad\qquad\quad y - x = 2 \qquad\qquad\qquad ...(ii)$

From equations (i) and (ii),

$\qquad\qquad y = 9$ and $x = 7$

Hence, $\qquad x < y$.

39. (5) **From statement I:**

$$\sqrt{x} - \dfrac{\sqrt{5}}{\sqrt{x}} = 0$$

$$\Rightarrow \ \sqrt{x} \times \sqrt{x} - \sqrt{5} = 0$$

$$\Rightarrow \qquad\qquad x = \sqrt{5}$$

From statement II:

$$y^3 = 5^{3/2}$$
$$\Rightarrow \quad y^3 = (\sqrt{5})^3$$
$$\Rightarrow \quad y = \sqrt{5}$$

Hence, $x = y$.

40. (1) We have,

$$3x + 5y = 28 \qquad \ldots \text{(i)}$$
$$8x - 3y = 42 \qquad \ldots \text{(ii)}$$

From equations (i) and (ii),

$$x = 6 \text{ and } y = 2$$

Hence, $x > y$

41. (1)

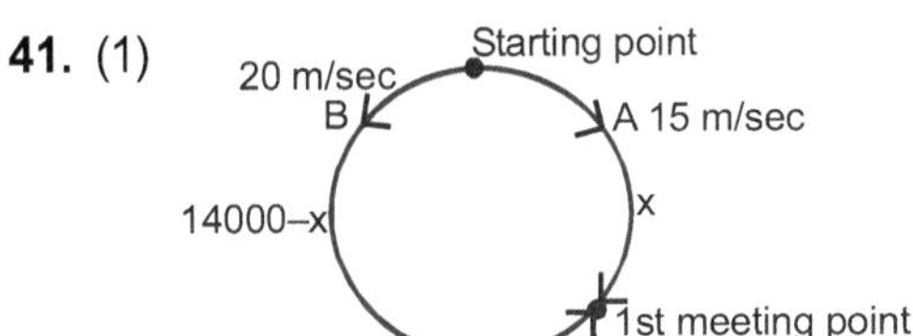

Let the distance covered by A be x km.

$$\text{Time} = \frac{\text{Distance}}{\text{Speed}}$$

$$\therefore \quad \frac{x}{15} = \frac{14000 - x}{20}$$

$$\Rightarrow 35x = 14000 \times 15$$

$$\Rightarrow x = 6000 \text{ m} = 6 \text{ km}$$

42. (2) Let the amount of work be 24 units.

A does 4 units per day and B does 3 units per day.

As the work done is one day is 8 units, so C does 1 unit per day.

Amount paid to $C = \dfrac{1}{8} \times 3200 = \text{Rs.}400$

43. (1) HCF of (20, 16) = 4

Thus, the largest side of the square tile would be 4 m.

Total number of tiles required

$$= \frac{20}{4} \times \frac{16}{4} = 4 \times 5 = 20$$

44. (5) Number of ways of selecting 3 boys out of 5 boys $= {}^5C_3$

Number of ways of selecting a girl out of 2 girls $= {}^2C_1$

$\therefore$ Total number of ways

$$= {}^5C_3 \times {}^2C_1 = \frac{5!}{2!3!} \times \frac{2!}{1!1!}$$
$$= 10 \times 2 = 20.$$

45. (2) Weight of the boat

$$= 6 \times 52 - 5 \times 38$$
$$= 312 - 190 = 122 \text{ kg}$$

46. (5) 2 11 27 52 88 137 **?(201)**

$$+3^2 \quad +4^2 \quad +5^2 \quad +6^2 \quad +7^2 \quad +8^2$$

47. (5) 405 135 54 27 18 18 **?(36)**

$$\div 3 \quad \div 2.5 \quad \div 2 \quad \div 1.5 \quad \div 1 \quad \div 0.5$$

48. (2) 64 512 1728 4096 8000 13824 ?(21952)

$$4^3 \quad 8^3 \quad 12^3 \quad 16^3 \quad 20^3 \quad 24^3 \quad 28^3$$

49. (1)

18 32 58 108 206 400 **?(786)**

14 26 50 98 194 **(386)**

12 24 48 96 192

50. (3)

8 14 30.5 79.25 241.25 848.375 **?(3398)**

$$\times 1.5 + 2 \quad \times 2 + 2.5 \quad \times 2.5 + 3 \quad \times 3 + 3.5 \quad \times 3.5 + 4 \quad \times 4 + 4.5$$

For questions 51 to 55:

Number of men playing squash $= 237 \times \dfrac{21}{79} = 63$.

Number of children playing hockey $= 325 \times \dfrac{35}{65} = 175$.

Number of men playing tennis $= 800 \times \dfrac{20}{80} = 200$.

Number of women playing baseball $= 384 \times \dfrac{36}{64} = 216$.

Number of women playing badminton $= 261 \times \dfrac{34}{29} = 306$.

Number of men playing badminton $= 261 \times \dfrac{37}{29} = 333$.

Number of children playing cricket $= 512 \times \dfrac{36}{64} = 288$.

Games	Number		
	Children	Women	Men
Squash	99	138	63
Hockey	175	159	166
Tennis	632	168	200
Baseball	163	216	221
Badminton	261	306	333
Cricket	288	77	435
Total	1618	1064	1418

52. (2) Average number of men $= \dfrac{1418}{6} \approx 236.33$.

53. (3) Required ratio = 216 : 333 or 24 : 37.

54. (4) Required percentage = $\dfrac{175}{288} \times 100 \approx 60.76\%$.

55. (5) Required percentage = $\dfrac{306}{1064} \times 100 \approx 29\%$.

56. (3) Difference between CI and SI = ₹400

We know that

$$D = P\left(\dfrac{R}{100}\right)^2$$

Where   D → Difference between SI and CI

P → Principal

R → Rate of interest

$\Rightarrow\ 400 = 10000\left(\dfrac{R}{100}\right)^2$

$\Rightarrow\ \left(\dfrac{2}{10}\right)^2 = \left(\dfrac{R}{100}\right)^2$

$\Rightarrow\ R = 20$

Hence, the required rate = 20%.

57. (2) Cost price $= \dfrac{\text{Selling price.} \times 100}{100 - \text{loss}\%} = ₹\,\dfrac{3520 \times 100}{100 - 12}$

$= ₹\,\dfrac{3520 \times 100}{88} = ₹\,4{,}000$

Now, selling price $= \left(\dfrac{100 + \text{profit}\%}{100}\right) \times \text{Cost price}$

$= ₹\left(\dfrac{100 + 12}{100}\right) \times 4000 = ₹\,4{,}480$

58. (4) Let the cost of each tube light and each bulb be Rs. 5x and 2x respectively.

Now, 4× 5x + 3× 2x = 260

$\Rightarrow\quad 20x + 6x = 260$

$\Rightarrow\qquad\qquad x = 10$

∴   Cost of tube light = Rs. 50

Cost of bulb = Rs. 20

Total cost = 50 + 6× 20 = Rs. 170

59. (2) Let the volume of alcohol at 10 a.m. = v m³

Therefore, the volume of water at 10 a.m. = 2v m³

Volume of water lost between 10 a.m. and 4 p.m

= 6 × 100 = 600 m³

Volume of water at 4 p.m. = 2v − 600 = $\dfrac{1}{2}$v

$\Rightarrow \dfrac{3v}{2} = 600$ or v = 400 m³

∴   Volume of water at 9 a.m. = 2v + 100 = 900 m³

Volume of alcohol at 9 a.m. = 400 m³.

Hence, required percentage

$= \dfrac{400}{400 + 900} \times 100 = 30.76\%$.

60. (3) CP of the item = Rs. 7200

SP of the item $= \dfrac{125}{100} \times 7200 = $ Rs. 9,000

SP of another item $= \dfrac{75}{100} \times 9000 = $ Rs. 6,750

Overall Loss = Rs. 7200 − 6750 = Rs. 450

61. (2) The average number of students qualified for the examination from college R and S

$= \dfrac{2250 + 2000}{2} = 2125$

The average number of students appeared for the examination from college R and S

$= \dfrac{3500 + 2500}{2} = 3000$

∴   Required percentage

$= \dfrac{2125}{3000} \times 100 = 70.83\%$.

62. (5) Required ratio = 3500 : 2250 = 14 : 9

63. (5) Required ratio = 1750 : 1250 = 7 : 5

64. (4) Required percentage

$= \dfrac{2500 \times 100}{(3000 + 2500 + 3500 + 2500 + 3000)}$

$= \dfrac{2500}{14500} \times 100 = 17.24\% \approx 18\%$.

65. (1) Average number of students appeared in all the colleges together $= \dfrac{14500}{5} = 2900$

Average number of students qualified from all the colleges together

$= \dfrac{1750 + 1250 + 2250 + 2000 + 2000}{5}$

$= \dfrac{9250}{8} = 1850$

∴   Required difference = 2900 − 1850 = 1050

66. (5)

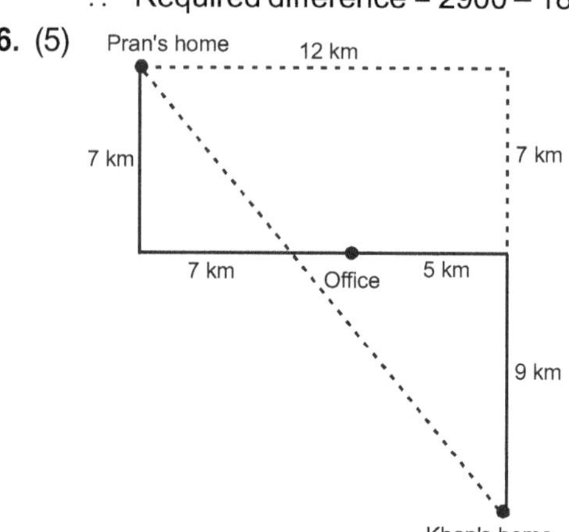

Distance $= \sqrt{12^2 + 16^2} = 20$ km

67. (2)

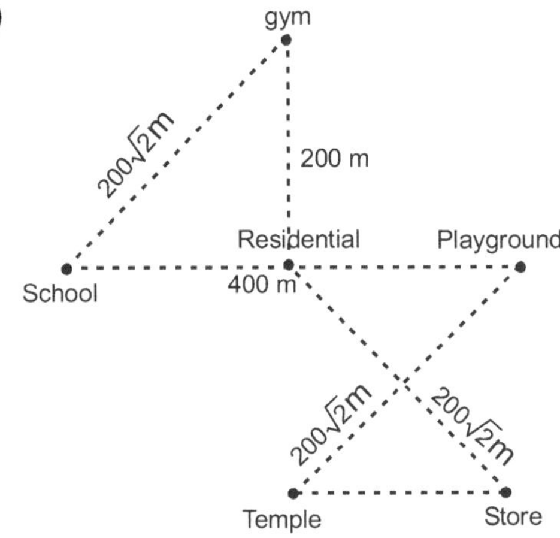

Distance between temple and store = 200 m.

68. (3) Ravi is brother of Govind and Prabhu. Prabhu is brother-in-law of Kusuma.

69. (3) Only daughter of Vijay's mother means sister of Vijay.

Sister of Vijay is mother of Anand.

Therefore, Anand is nephew of Vijay.

70. (2) Only sister of Kala's brother means Kala herself.

Therefore, Mala is daughter of Kala.

For questions 71 to 75:

pencils	tables
erasers	chairs
tables	buses
chairs	trucks
trucks	pencils/erasers
buses	erasers/pencils
and	or

For questions 76 to 80:

Person	Floor	Game
Vinay	1	Chess
Ravi	4	Football
Anamika	2	Cricket
Yogesh	6	Volleyball
Abhay	5	Tennis
Rihana	3	Hockey

For questions: 81 to 85:

Date	Day	Play
25	Tuesday	R
26	Wednesday	N
27	Thursday	P
28	Friday	No play
29	Saturday	S
30	Sunday	T
31	Monday	A

81. (5) Play A was organized on Monday.

82. (1) Play N was organized on Wednesday.

83. (2) On 28th , it was a No play day .

84. (4) First play was organized on 25th.

85. (3) Play T was organized on Sunday.

86. (1) L % N, L $\Leftrightarrow$ K, M ϕ K

$\Rightarrow$ L $\geq$ N, L < K, M = K

$\Rightarrow$ N $\leq$ L < K = M

Conclusion I: N $\Leftrightarrow$ K $\Rightarrow$ N < K follows.

Conclusion II: M % N $\Rightarrow$ M $\geq$ N does not follow.

Only conclusion I follows.

87. (5) Q ϕ P, P Ω S, S & R

$\Rightarrow$ Q = P, P $\leq$ S, R < S

$\Rightarrow$ Q = P $\leq$ S and R < S

Conclusion I: R $\Leftrightarrow$ P $\Rightarrow$ R < P does not follow.

Conclusion II: S ϕ Q $\Rightarrow$ S = Q may or may not follow.

$\therefore$ Neither conclusion I nor conclusion II follows.

88. (2) X & Y, Y % Z, Z Ω A

$\Rightarrow$ X >Y, Y $\geq$ Z, Z $\leq$ A

$\Rightarrow$ X >Y $\geq$ Z and Z $\leq$ A

Conclusion I: Y ϕ A $\Rightarrow$ Y=A may or may not follow.

Conclusion II: X & Z $\Rightarrow$ X > Z follows.

Only conclusion II follows.

89. (3) G $\Leftrightarrow$ H, J ϕ H, J Ω O

$\Rightarrow$ G < H, J = H, J $\leq$ O

$\Rightarrow$ G < H = J $\leq$ O

Conclusion I: J & G $\Rightarrow$ J > G follows.

Conclusion II: O % H $\Rightarrow$ O $\geq$ H follows.

$\therefore$ Both conclusions follow.

90. (4) S & T, T % U, V ϕ U

$\Rightarrow$ S > T, T $\geq$ U, V = U

$\Rightarrow$ S > T $\geq$ U = V

Conclusion I: T & V $\Rightarrow$ T > V may or may not follow.

Conclusion II: V ϕ T $\Rightarrow$ V =T may or may not follow.

$\therefore$ Either conclusion I or conclusion II follows.

For questions 91 to 95:

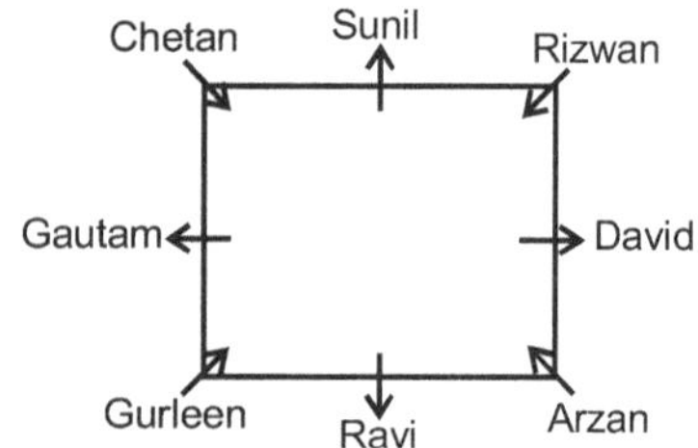

91. (3) All others sit in the middle of the sides.

92. (1) Ravi sits third to the left of Rizwan.

93. (4) Sunil is third to the right of Arzan

94. (4) Gurleen sits second to the right of Chetan

95. (2) Ravi and Gautam are neighbors of Gurleen.

96. (1)   Case I   Case II

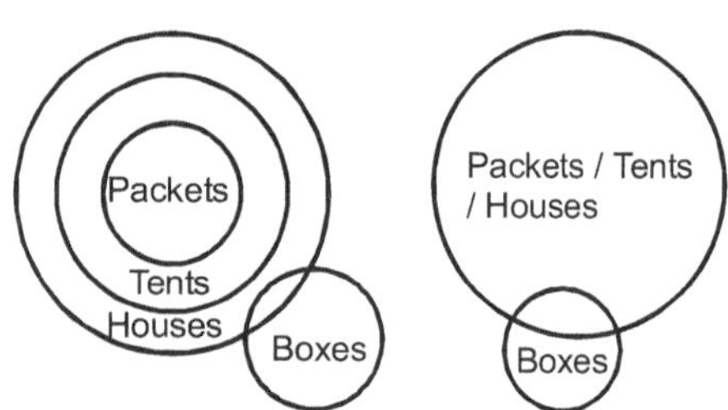

97. (3)

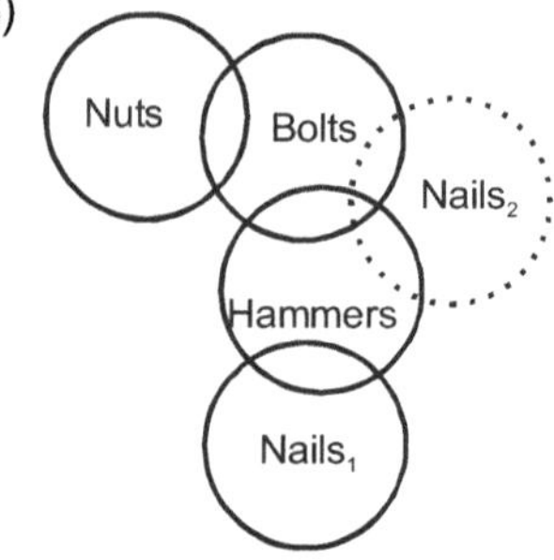

98. (4)   Case I

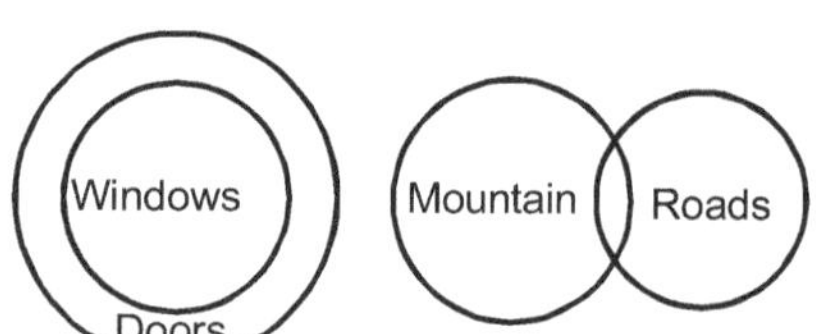

99. (2)   Case I   Case II

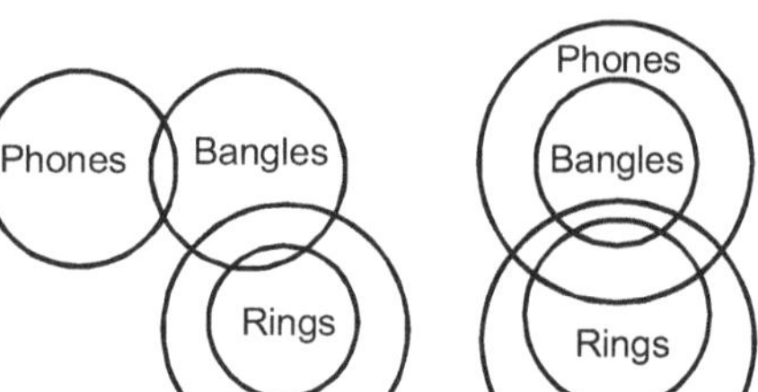

100. (5)   Case I

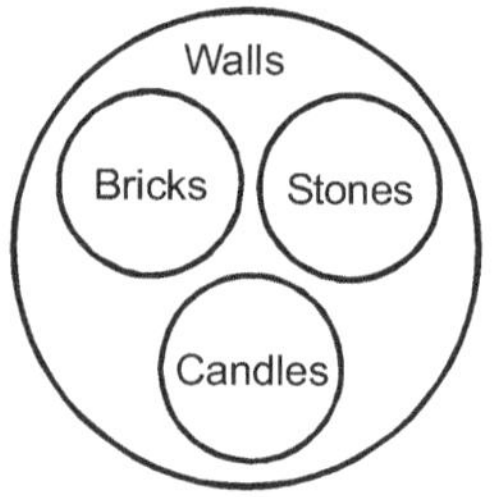

Case II

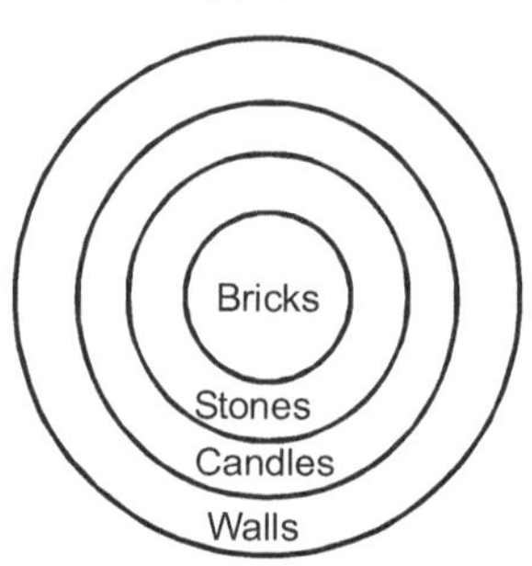

PRACTICE PAPER – 8

Directions (Q. 1 to 10): Read the following passage carefully and answer the questions given below it. Certain words are printed in bold to help you to locate them while answering some of the questions.

Every morning the men of the village would nick into a **hearty** breakfast and then gather in groups. If the men had spent even a little time on their land, they would have **reaped** wonderful crops but they spent the day telling each other tall tales about the food they would have at the next meal. They returned home only at lunch and dinnertime. All responsibilities fell on the women. They cooked, cleaned, sent the children to school, worked in the fields, took the crops to the market - in short, they did everything. The women grew tired of this. Some one suggested writing to the King, who was known to be fair and kind. So a letter was written and sent. The women went back to their work, but were on the lookout to see if the King would solve their problem. Many days passed, and slowly the women began to lose hope. After all, why would the King of such a vast empire be concerned about the plight of a few women in a tiny village like theirs?

One night, when the men gathered to chat and boast after dinner, a tall and handsome stranger joined them. Each man wanted to prove he was better than the others to impress him. One said, "As soon as I was bom, I ran to the capital and met the King.' Not to be outdone, a second man said, "When I was a day old, I rode a horse all the way to the King's palace and we had the most delicious breakfast together." At the thought of food everyone began to applaud. Now a third man said, "I sat on an elephant when I was a week old and had lunch with the King in his palace. "Before the **admiring** murmurs could die down, a fourth one said, "When I was a month old I flew to the King's garden. He let me sit with him on his throne!"

The stranger then spoke up. "Do you four men know the King very well?" "Of course we do !" they replied together. "In fact, he is proud to have supernatural beings like us in his kingdom." The stranger looked thoughtful and said, "Some time ago, the king called four supermen to the city in order to repair the city walls. Since the largest, toughest stones were used, this could be done only by these supermen. The four asked to be paid in gold and the King gave them the money. But they disappeared and I have been wandering the kingdom looking for them. The King has ordered me to find them and bring them

back to the capital to finish the work. They will also have to return the gold they ran away with. It looks like my search has finally ended. I will take you four to the King, along with the gold you stole from him. I shall be the rich one now."

By the time the stranger **finished** telling this amazing story, the men's faces were ashen. What trouble had their lies landed them in? They **dived** at the stranger's feet. 'Forget what we said!' they wailed. Those were all lies. We are just lazy men." the stranger smiled. "I will tell the king there are no supermen in this village, only hard-working, ordinary men and women. But he will come to verify this himself!" The men promised to stop telling tales and do some honest work. That night the stranger left the village on a white horse fit to belong to the King!

1. Which of the following can be said about the men of the village?

   (A) They were lazy and spent the whole day doing nothing.

   (B) They were supportive if their wives or daughters wanted to work.

   (C) They were well acquainted with the King.

   (1) Only (A)   (2) Both (B) & C)

   (3) Only (B)   (4) Both (A) & (C)

   (5) None of these

2. What did the men discuss when they gathered in groups?

   (1) The food they would eat at the next meal

   (2) They boasted about the wealth they had cheated the King out of

   (3) Their wife's accomplishments

   (4) Impossible tasks that they were able to accomplish

   (5) The problems facing the village

3. What motivated the men to begin working?

   (A) They felt bad that the women were overworked.

   (B) The stranger threatened them with imprisonment for their idleness.

   (C) They wanted to impress the stranger.

   (1) Both (A) & (B)

   (2) Only (A)

   (3) Only (C)

   (4) Only (B)

   (5) None of these

4. Which of the following describes the King?

(1) He was sensitive and concerned about the needs of his subjects

(2) He did not trust anyone and verified facts for himself

(3) He was wealthy and fond of horse riding

(4) The King was kind but foolish and people easily deceived him

(5) He was merciless and severely punished those who did wrong

5. What reason did the stranger give for visiting the village?

(1) The King had asked him to verify if the women's letter was accurate

(2) He wanted to meet the people with superior abilities in the village

(3) He was passing through looking for four men who had deceived the King

(4) He wanted to steal the gold that the villagers had taken from the King

(5) After a long journey he wanted to rest along with his horse

Directions (Q. 6 to 8): Choose the word which ts most nearly the SAME in meaning as the word printed in bold as used in the passage.

6. hearty

(1) warm (2) enthusiastic

(3) strong (4) substantial

(5) energetic

7. reaped

(1) grown (2) harvested

(3) sown (4) receipt

(5) secured

8. dived

(1) jump (2) fell

(3) descend (4) submerged

(5) leap

Directions (Q. 9 and 10): Choose the word which is most OPPOSITE in meaning to the word printed in bold as used in the passage.

9. finished

(1) completed (2) interrupted

(3) began (4) rough

(5) dark

10. admiring

(1) rejecting (2) disapproving

(3) harmful (4) frightening

(5) threatening

Directions (Q. 11 to 15) : In each of the following sentences there are two blank spaces. Below each sentence there are five pairs of words denoted by (1), (2), (3), (4) and (5). Find out which pair of words can be filled up in the blanks in the sentence in the same sequence to make the sentence grammatically correct and meaningfully complete.

11. If the system _____ to yield the desired result, try to _____ the whole procedure in the given sequence.

(1) entitles, dump (2) ignores, reproduce

(3) fails, reoperate (4) imitates, generate

(5) equips, encompass

12. He is so _____ in his approach that not a single point ever _____ his attention.

(1) meticulous, escapes

(2) casual, erodes

(3) fanatic, brings

(4) deliberate, attracts

(5) nasty, coincides

13. Generally, _____ students _____ those who are mediocre.

(1) humble, surmount (2) meritorious, surpass

(3) bright, overestimate (4) intelligent, surrender

(5) studious, respect

14. _____ and _____ should not be tolerated in our country which boasts of 'Ahimsa' as its way of life.

(1) Politicking, elections

(2) Dishonour, efficiency

(3) Lethargy, procrastination

(4) Nepotism, selfishness

(5) Hatred, violence

15. He _____ a wrong act because it was _____ for him to do so due to circumstantial forces.

(1) compelled, necessary

(2) refused, dangerous

(3) did, avoidable

(4) committed, inevitable

(5) simplified, harmful

Directions (Q. 16 to 20) : Rearrange the following six sentences (A), (B), (C), (D), (E) and (F) in the proper sequence to form a meaningful paragraph; then answer the questions given below them.

A. It is no wonder that a majority of these excluded and low-achievers come from the most deprived sections of society.

B. They are precisely those who are supposed to be empowered through education.

C. With heightened political consciousness about the plight of these to-be-empowered people, never in the history of India has the demand for inclusive education been as fervent as today.

D. They either never enrol or they drop out of schools at different stages during these eight years.

E. Of the nearly 200 million children in the age group between 6 and 14 years, more than half do not complete eight years of elementary education.

F. Of those who do complete eight years of schooling, the achievement levels of a large percentage, in language and mathematics, is unacceptably low.

16. Which of the following should be the THIRD sentence after rearrangement?

    (1) A   (2) B
    (3) C   (4) D
    (5) F

17. Which of the following should be the FIRST sentence after rearrangement?

    (1) A   (2) B
    (3) C   (4) D
    (5) E

18. Which of the following should be the SECOND sentence after rearrangement?

    (1) F   (2) E
    (3) D   (4) C
    (5) B

19. Which of the following should be the FOURTH sentence after rearrangement?

    (1) A   (2) B
    (3) C   (4) D
    (5) E

20. Which of the following should be the FIFTH sentence after rearrangement?

    (1) F   (2) E
    (3) D   (4) B
    (5) A

Directions (Q. 21 to 25) : Read each sentence to find out whether there is any grammatical error in it. The error, if any, will be in one part of the sentence. The number of that part is the answer. If there is no error, the answer is (5). i.e. 'No error'. (Ignore the errors of punctuation, if any.)

21. These companies have been asked (1) / to furnish their financial details (2) / and information (3) / to its board members. (4) / No error (5)

22. The scheme which will be launched (1) / during the next two years (2) / require an additional investment (3) / of one hundred crores. (4) / No error (5).

23. Road developers unable (1) / to complete their projects (2) / on time will not be (3) / awarded new ones. (4) / No error (5)

24. We have taken on (1) / the responsibility of (2) / arranging the required training (3) / and supervise the new staff. (4) / No error (5)

25. The government has signed (1) / a memorandum of understanding with (2) / the company to set up (3) / a plant in the state. (4) / No error (5)

Directions (Q. 26 to 30) : In the following passage there are blanks, each of which has been numbered. These numbers are given below the passage and against each, five words are suggested, one of which fits the blank appropriately. Find out the appropriate word in each case.

All over the world, rights related to information technology that are already legally recognised are daily being violated, __(26)__ in the name of economic advancement, political stability or for personal greed and interests. Violations of these rights have created new problems in human social systems, such as the digital divide, cybercrime, digital security and privacy concerns, all of which have __(27)__ people's lives either directly or indirectly.

It is important that countries come up with the guidelines for action to combat the incidences of malicious attacks on the confidentiality, integrity and availability of electronic data and systems, computer related crimes, content related offences and violations of intellectual property rights. __(28)__ threats to critical infrastructure and national interests arising from the use of the internet for criminal and terrorist activities are of growing concern. The harm incurred to businesses, governments and individuals in those countries in which the internet is used __(29)__ is gaining in fear and importance, while in other countries: cybercrime threatens the application of information and communication technology for government services, health care, trade, and banking. As users start losing __(30)__ in online transactions and business, the opportunity costs may become substantial.

26. (1) scarcely   (2) whether
    (3) and   (4) for
    (5) hardly

27. (1) distanced   (2) affected
    (3) exaggerated   (4) advanced
    (5) cropped

28. (1) But   (2) More
    (3) Addition   (4) Beside
    (5) Further

29. (1) really   (2) figuratively
     (3) widely   (4) never
     (5) tandem

30. (1) tracks   (2) measure
     (3) confidence   (4) mind
     (5) grip

NUMERICAL ABILITY

31. A stream runs at 1 km/hr. A boat goes 35 km upstream and comes back again in 12 hr. The speed of the boat in still water is
     (1) 6 km/hr   (2) 4.5 km/hr
     (3) 3 km/hr   (4) 7.5 km/hr
     (5) None of these

32. A and B can complete a piece of work in 45 days and 40 days respectively. They begin together but A leaves after some days and B completes the rest in 23 days. For how many days did A work?
     (1) 6 days   (2) 9 days
     (3) 8 days   (4) 12 days
     (5) None of these

33. The cost of leveling a square ground at the rate of Rs. 0.80 per 100 m^2 is Rs. 28.80. Find the cost of fencing the same at Rs.0. 60 per metre.
     (1) Rs. 144   (2) Rs. 196
     (3) Rs. 225   (4) Rs. 250
     (5) Rs. 204

34. There are 17 coins in a bag numbered from 1 to 17. Raju picks up a coin at random and puts it back in the bag. He continues this process untill he gets a coin which shows an odd number. What is the probability that the coin shows a prime number when he stops?
     (1) $\dfrac{1}{2}$ (2) $\dfrac{1}{3}$
     (3) $\dfrac{1}{4}$ (4) $\dfrac{4}{5}$
     (5) None of these

35. An amount of money is distributed amongst A, B and C in such a way that A gets half of that of B and B gets twice that of C. What is ratio of money that B gets to that of the sum money that A and B get together?
     (1) 2 : 5   (2) 2 : 3
     (3) 3 : 2   (4) 4 : 3
     (5) 3 : 4

Directions (Q. 36 to 40): Answer the questions on the basis of the information given below.

The number of persons visiting six different super-markets and the percentage of men, women and children visiting those super markets.

Name of the Super markets	Total Number of Persons	Percentage of		
		Men	Women	Children
M	34560	35	55	–
N	65900	37	–	20
I	45640	35	45	20
J	55500	–	26	33
Y	42350	06	70	24
Z	59650	24	–	14

36. The number of men visiting super market J forms approximately what percent of the total number of persons visiting all the super markets together?
     (1) 11%   (2) 5.5%
     (3) 13%   (4) 9%
     (5) 7.5%

37. The number of children visiting super market I forms what percent of the number of children visiting super market Z? (rounded off to two digits after decimal)
     (1) 91.49%   (2) 49.85%
     (3) 121.71%   (4) 109.30%
     (5) None of these

38. What is the total number of children visiting super markets N and J together?
     (1) 18515   (2) 28479
     (3) 31495   (4) 22308
     (5) None of these

39. What is the average of women visiting all the super markets together?
     (1) 24823.5   (2) 22388.5
     (3) 26432.5   (4) 20988.5
     (5) None of these

40. What is the ratio of the number of women visiting super market M to that of those visiting super market I?
     (1) 35 : 37   (2) 245 : 316
     (3) 352 : 377   (4) 1041 : 1156
     (5) None of these

41. If the difference between the compound interest, compounded half-yearly and the simple interest on a sum at 10% p.a. for one year is Rs. 25, the sum is
     (1) Rs. 7,000   (2) Rs. 8,000
     (3) Rs. 9,000   (4) Rs. 25,000
     (5) Rs. 10,000

42. In an examination, A got 10% marks less than B; B got 25% marks more than C and C got 20% less than D. If A got 360 marks out of 500, the percentage of marks obtained by D was
(1) 60%   (2) 20%
(3) 80%   (4) 40%
(5) None of these

43. Four years ago, the ratio of the ages of Rahul and Deepak was 3 : 4. Four years hence, the ratio of their ages will be 11 : 12. What is Deepak's age at present?
(1) 3 years   (2) 4 years
(3) 7 years   (4) 8 years
(5) None of these

44. A producer of tea blends two varieties costing Rs. 18 per kilogram and another Rs. 20 per kilogram in the ratio 5 : 3. If he sells the blended variety at Rs. 21 per kilogram, then what is his gain percentage?
(1) 12%   (2) 10%
(3) 14%   (4) 15%
(5) None of these

45. Sneh buys X eggs to resell them at a profit of 10% but unfortunately she loses 10% of the eggs. By how much should she mark up the selling price in order to retain 10% profit?
(1) 11%   (2) 12.25%
(3) 22.22%   (4) 22.8%
(5) 20%

Directions (Q.46 to 50): What will come in place of the question mark (?) in the following number series?

46. 5 , 11, 19, 29, ?
(1) 40   (2) 45
(3) 41   (4) 39
(5) None of these

47. 7, 15, ?, 63, 127
(1) 32   (2) 29
(3) 33   (4) 30
(5) 31

48. 2, 3, 10, ?, 172
(1) 45   (2) 39
(3) 36   (4) 42
(5) None of these

49. 8, 4, 6, ?, 52.5
(1) 9   (2) 12.5
(3) 14.5   (4) 16
(5) 15

50. 5, 6, ?, 45, 184
(1) 15   (2) 12
(3) 16   (4) 9
(5) None of these

Directions (Q. 51 to 55) : In each of the following questions two equations are given. Solve these equations and give answer :
(1) if $x \geq y$, i.e., x is greater than or equal to y
(2) if $x > y$, i.e., x is greater than y
(3) if $x \leq y$, i.e., x is less than or equal to y
(4) if $x < y$. i.e., x is less than y
(5) if $x = y$ or no relation can be established between x and y

51. I. $x^2 + 5x + 6 = 0$
II. $y^2 + 7y + 12 = 0$

52. I. $x^2 + 20 = 9x$
II. $y^2 + 42 = 13y$

53. I. $2x + 3y = 14$
II. $4x + 2y = 16$

54. I. $x = \sqrt{625}$
II. $y = \sqrt{676}$

55. I. $x^2 + 4x + 4 = 0$
II. $y^2 - 8y + 16 = 0$

Directions (Q. 56 to 60): What approximate value will come in place of the question mark (?) in the following questions?

56. $324.995 \times 15.98 \div 4.002 + 36.88 = ?$
(1) 1300   (2) 1230
(3) 1440   (4) 1380
(5) 1340

57. 69.008% of 699.998 + 32.99% of 399.999 = ?
(1) 615   (2) 645
(3) 675   (4) 715
(5) 725

58. $\sqrt{624.98} + \sqrt{729.25} = ?$
(1) 58   (2) 56
(3) 52   (4) 63
(5) 61

59. $175 \times 28 + 275 \times 27.98 = ?$
(1) 11800   (2) 12600
(3) 12800   (4) 11600
(5) 12200

60. $1164 \times 128 \div 8.008 + 969.007 = ?$
(1) 18800   (2) 19000
(3) 19600   (4) 19200
(5) 18600

Directions (Q. 61 to 65): Answer the following questions based on the given information.

The bar graph given below represents the total number of vehicles in two cities X and Y respectively during the period of 2009 to 2014.

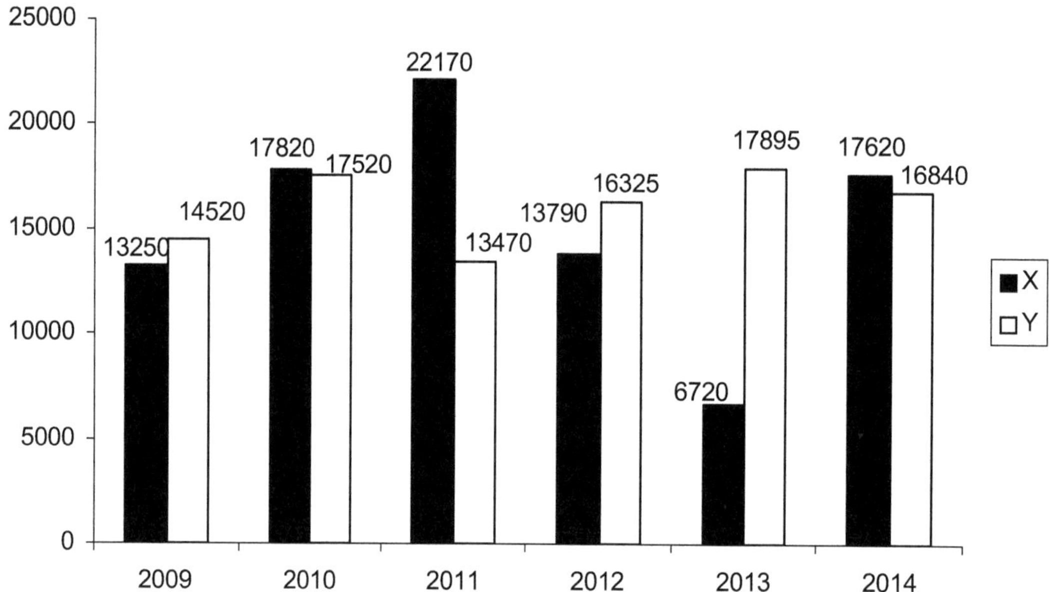

61. What was the total number of vehicles in city 'X' over the given period?

(1) 89,710
(2) 91,370
(3) 90,840
(4) 97,470
(5) None of these

62. For how many years, were the total number of vehicles in city 'X' more than the total number of vehicles in city 'Y'?

(1) 1
(2) 2
(3) 3
(4) 4
(5) None of these

63. The maximum number of vehicles in city 'X', was by what percentage more or less than the minimum number of vehicles in city 'Y', in any of the given years?

(1) 64.58%, more
(2) 60.75%, less
(3) 64.58%, less
(4) 60.75%, more
(5) 35.42%, less

64. What was the growth rate in terms of the total number of vehicles in the two cities put together during the given period?

(1) 27.67%
(2) 12.28%
(3) 23.87%
(4) 4.82%
(5) None of these

65. If on an average a vehicle consumes 1.1 liters of petrol every day, then in which year was the maximum petrol consumed? (Assume that all the vehicles running on the road consume petrol only and all vehicles in each year run from start day of the year to end day of that year)

(1) 2009
(2) 2010
(3) 2011
(4) 2012
(5) 2013

<h2 style="text-align:center">REASONING ABILITY</h2>

66. Uttam ran 40 m east, then turned right and ran 20 m and then turned to right and ran 18 m and again turned to left and ran 10 m and then turned to left, ran 24 m and finally turned to left and ran 12 m. Now he is running towards which direction?

(1) West
(2) North
(3) South
(4) East
(5) North-east

67. Narendra travels 20 km to the north, turns left and travels 8 km and then again turns right and covers another 10 km and then turns right and travels another 8 km. How far is he from the starting point?

(1) 8 km
(2) 40 km
(3) 30 km
(4) 20 km
(5) 28 km

68. If Lekha says, "Neha's father Neeraj is the only son of my father-in-law Rajesh", then how is Bindu, who is the sister of Neha, related to Rajesh?

(1) Daughter

(2) Wife

(3) Daughter-in-law

(4) Granddaughter

(5) Niece

Directions (Q. 69 and 70) : In the following questions, the symbols +, @, $ and % are used with the following meaning as illustrated below:

'P + Q' means 'P is the sister of Q'.

'P @ Q' means 'P is the wife of Q'.

'P $ Q' means 'P is the son of Q'.

'P % Q' means 'P is the mother of Q'.

69. What is the relation between 'J and A' in the expression 'A @ F $ M % J + T' ?

(1) J is the mother-in-law of A

(2) A is the aunt of J

(3) J is the sister-in-law of A

(4) A is the husband of J

(5) None of these

70. What will come in the place of question mark(?), if it is provided that 'J is the daughter-in-law of T' in the expression 'J % B ? K $ T' ?

(1) @   (2) %

(3) +   (4) $

(5) % or +

Directions (Q. 71 to 75): Answer the questions on the basis of the information given below.

There are 5 people – Amaya, Bhavya, Chavi, Diya and Eisha – working in an organization in five different departments viz. Finance, Human Resource (HR), Marketing, Operations and Production (not necessarily in this order) at five different levels of seniority viz. 1, 2, 3, 4 and 5 (not necessarily in this order). Levels of seniority decreases as the numeric value increases.

  i. Eisha does not work either in HR or Production department. She is working at level of seniority 3.

 ii. Diya does not work either in Finance or Production department.

iii. Bhavya works in Operations.

iv. Chavi works at one level of seniority below Eisha.

 v. Amaya does not work at senior-most level and she works in Marketing.

vi. The person who works in HR, works at two levels of seniority below Eisha.

71. Who works in HR department?

(1) Amaya   (2) Bhavya

(3) Chavi   (4) Diya

(5) Eisha

72. Which department does the senior-most employee work in?

(1) Operations

(2) Finance

(3) HR

(4) Production

(5) Cannot be determined

73. Which level of seniority does Amaya work?

(1) 1   (2) 2

(3) 3   (4) 4

(5) 5

74. Which department does Chavi work in?

(1) Finance   (2) Operations

(3) Production   (4) HR

(5) Marketing

75. Which of the following combination is wrong?

(1) Amaya-2   (2) Bhavya-1

(3) Diya-5   (4) Eisha-Finance

(5) None of these

Directions (Q. 76 to 80): Answer the questions on the basis of the information given below.

Eight friends - Ayan, Badal, Chitra, Durga, Ekta, Fred, Gyan and Hira - studying in various classes from 1st to 8th are sitting around a circular table facing the centre.

 (i) Ayan sits third to the right of the one, studying in 8th standard, who is an immediate neighbour of Durga.

 (ii) Chitra studies in 6th standard and sits second to the right of the one studying in 8th standard.

(iii) The one in 2nd standard faces Gyan and sits on the immediate right of Hira.

(iv) Gyan does not study in 4th standard and sits to the immediate right of Ekta who is second to the left of Badal.

 (v) The one in 1st standard sits to the immediate right of the one in 6th standard, who faces the one in 5th standard.

(vi) Durga faces the one in 1st standard and is third to the right of the one in 3rd standard.

76. Who sits opposite to Fred?

(1) Chitra   (2) Durga

(3) Fred   (4) Ekta

(5) Gyan

77. If Hira and Fred form a pair and Ayan and Ekta also form a pair then select a similar pair from the given options.

(1) Gyan and Badal

(2) Durga and Chitra

(3) Hira and Ekta

(4) Gyan and Ekta

(5) None of these

78. Starting from the one studying in 1st standard all the eight friends are made to sit clockwise, in ascending order of the classes that they study in. Find the number of persons, (excluding the one in 1ststd) whose seats remain unchanged.

(1) Five   (2) Four

(3) Two   (4) One

(5) Three

79. Who sits to the immediate left of the one who is third to the right of the one studying in 3rd standard?

(1) The one in 7th standard

(2) Hira

(3) Badal

(4) Ekta

(5) None of these

80. Select the pair in which the student and class combination is not correct.

(1) Ekta - 3rd   (2) Durga - 8th

(3) Badal - 5th   (4) Chitra - 6th

(5) Ayan - 1st

Directions (Q. 81 to 85): Answer the questions on the basis of the information given below.

Pihu, Qadir, Ruhi, Sania, Tej, Usha, Vani and Wafi are standing in a row facing west. Only Tej is between Sania and Usha, whereas only Vani is between Usha and Wafi. Pihu and Ruhi are Qadir's neighbours. Neither Pihu nor Sania is at an extreme end of the row. Wafi is to the right of Pihu but not necessarily immediate right.

81. Who among the following are neighbours?

(1) Ruhi, Sania   (2) Pihu, Ruhi

(3) Pihu, Sania   (4) Wafi, Ruhi

(5) None of these

82. Which of the following defines the position of Vani?

(1) Vani is second to the left of Tej.

(2) Vani is the neighbour of Sania.

(3) Vani is at one of the extreme ends.

(4) Vani is on the immediate right of Wafi.

(5) None of these

83. Which of the following is true?

(1) Tej is on the immediate right of Sania.

(2) Ruhi is not at either extreme end.

(3) Pihu is at one of the extreme ends.

(4) Pihu is between Qadir and Ruhi.

(5) None of these

84. If Ruhi is related to Pihu in a way and Qadir is related to Sania in the same way, then to whom is Tej related?

(1) Sania   (2) Usha

(3) Vani   (4) Wafi

(5) Pihu

85. Who is standing at an extreme end of the row?

(1) Sania   (2) Tej

(3) Usha   (4) Pihu

(5) Wafi

Directions (Q. 86 to 90): Answer the questions on the basis of the information given below.

In a certain code "hill top castle" is coded as "wu ai oe", "haunted old castle" is coded as "au do ai" , "top class cottage" is coded as "oe pa sa" and "haunted hill cottage" is coded as "sa wu au".

86. What does the code "sa" stand for?

(1) Class   (2) Top

(3) Haunted   (4) Cottage

(5) None of these

87. What is the code for "old castle" ?

(1) do wu   (2) ai do

(3) ai oe   (4) oe sa

(5) None of these

88. If "bright new cottage" is code as "ti sa ef" then what will be the code for "new castle"?

(1) ti ai   (2) ai sa

(3) ef sa   (4) ef ai

(5) Either (1) or (4)

89. How can "climb haunted hill" be coded?

(1) au wu ai   (2) wu ai sa

(3) au pa wu   (4) wu li au

(5) do ai wu

90. What is the code for "old"?

(1) pa

(2) do

(3) sa

(4) wu

(5) Cannot be determined

Directions (Q. 91 to 95) : In the following questions, the symbols ©, #, @, δ and \$ are used with the following meaning as illustrated below :

'P © Q' means 'P is not greater than Q'.

'P # Q' means 'P is neither greater than nor equal to Q'

'P @ Q' means 'P is neither greater than nor smaller than Q'

'P δ Q' means 'P is neither smaller than nor equal to Q'

'P \$ Q' means 'P is not smaller than Q'

Now in each of the following questions assuming the given statements to be true, find which of the conclusions given below them are **definitely true?**

91. Statements:

A δ N, S \$ N, S δ W, W © R

Conclusions:

I. R \$ A

II. S δ R

III. S δ A

IV. W © A

(1) Only I and II are true
(2) Only II, III and IV are true
(3) None is true
(4) All I, II, III and IV are true
(5) None of these

92. Statements:

D # E, E © T, T @ C, C # A

Conclusions:

I. D # A

II. C © D

III. A δ E

IV. T # A

(1) Only I, III and IV are true
(2) Only I, II and IV are true
(3) Only I, II and III are true
(4) Only I, and III are true
(5) All I, II, III and IV are true

93. Statements

O \$ B, B @ S, S # E, E © R

Conclusions

I. S © O

II. R δ S

III. B # R

IV. B # E

(1) Only I and II are true
(2) Only III is true
(3) Only I, III and IV are true
(4) All I, II, III and IV are true
(5) Only III and IV are true

94. Statements

D © S, S δ P, P \$ I, P @ T

Conclusions

I. P # D

II. P \$ T

III. T # S

IV. I © D

(1) Only I and III are true
(2) Only III is true
(3) Only III and IV are true
(4) Only II, III and IV are true
(5) Only I, III and IV are true

95. Statements

U @ N, N \$ F, F \$ A, A δ R

Conclusions

I. A @ U

II. N δ R

III. R © U

IV. U δ A

(1) Only II is true
(2) Only I and II are true
(3) Only I, II and IV are true
(4) Only III and IV are true
(5) Only II and either I or IV are true

Directions (Q. 96 to 100) : In each question below are two or three statements followed by two or three statements followed by two conclusions numbered I and II. You have to take the two given statements to be true if they seem to be at variance from commonly known facts and then decide which of the given conclusions logically follows from the given statements disregarding commonly known facts.

Give answer (1) if only conclusion I follows.

Give answer (2) if only conclusion II follows.

Give answer (3) if either conclusion I or conclusion II follows.

Give answer (4) if neither conclusion I nor conclusion II follows.

Give answer (5) if both conclusion I and conclusion II follow.

Statements for Q. 96 and 97:

No cow is a bull.

All bulls are animals.

Some animals are mammals.

96. Conclusions :

    I.   At least some mammals are animals.

    II. Some mammals being bulls is a possibility.

97. Conclusions :

    I.   At least some animals are bulls.

    II. No animal is a cow.

98. Statements :

    Some pencils are pens.

    No pen is eraser.

    All sharpeners are erasers.

Conclusions :

    I.   No eraser is a pencil.

    II. All pencils can never be sharpeners.

Statements for Q. 99 and 100:

Some stars are planets.

Some planets are moons.

No moon is a sun.

99. Conclusions :

    I.   No star is a sun.

    II. All planets being suns is a possibility.

100. Conclusions :

    I.   All suns being stars is a possibility.

    II. Some stars are planets.

ANSWERS

1. (1)	**2.** (1)	**3.** (5)	**4.** (1)	**5.** (3)	**6.** (4)	**7.** (2)	**8.** (2)	**9.** (3)	**10.** (2)
11. (3)	**12.** (1)	**13.** (2)	**14.** (5)	**15.** (4)	**16.** (5)	**17.** (5)	**18.** (3)	**19.** (2)	**20.** (5)
21. (4)	**22.** (3)	**23.** (5)	**24.** (4)	**25.** (5)	**26.** (2)	**27.** (2)	**28.** (5)	**29.** (3)	**30.** (3)
31. (1)	**32.** (2)	**33.** (1)	**34.** (5)	**35.** (2)	**36.** (5)	**37.** (4)	**38.** (3)	**39.** (1)	**40.** (5)
41. (5)	**42.** (3)	**43.** (4)	**44.** (1)	**45.** (3)	**46.** (3)	**47.** (5)	**48.** (2)	**49.** (5)	**50.** (5)
51. (1)	**52.** (4)	**53.** (4)	**54.** (4)	**55.** (4)	**56.** (5)	**57.** (1)	**58.** (3)	**59.** (2)	**60.** (3)
61. (2)	**62.** (3)	**63.** (1)	**64.** (5)	**65.** (3)	**66.** (2)	**67.** (3)	**68.** (4)	**69.** (3)	**70.** (4)
71. (4)	**72.** (1)	**73.** (2)	**74.** (3)	**75.** (5)	**76.** (5)	**77.** (1)	**78.** (4)	**79.** (3)	**80.** (2)
81. (3)	**82.** (5)	**83.** (1)	**84.** (3)	**85.** (5)	**86.** (4)	**87.** (2)	**88.** (5)	**89.** (4)	**90.** (2)
91. (3)	**92.** (1)	**93.** (4)	**94.** (2)	**95.** (5)	**96.** (5)	**97.** (1)	**98.** (2)	**99.** (4)	**100.** (5)

EXPLANATIONS

1. (1) Only statement A is correct. Had the men been supportive, their wives wouldn't have complained to the king. Statement C is incorrect in the context of the passage.

2. (1) Refer to the second sentence of the passage for the answer. The other options are incorrect.

3. (5) None of the statements is true in the context of the passage.

4. (1) Options 3,4 and 5 are incorrect as per the passage. Option 2 cannot be inferred. However, option 1 is correct because the king was definitely sensitive towards the needs of his subjects.

5. (3) Refer to the third paragraph for the answer.

6. (4) 'Hearty' in the context of the passage means substantial.

7. (2) 'Reaped' means to produce or harvest.

8. (2) In the context of the passage, 'dived' means 'to fell'.

9. (3) 'Began' is the opposite of 'Finished'.

10. (2) 'Disapproving' is the opposite of 'admiring'.

11. (3) The tone of the sentence suggests that the first blank will take 'fails'.

12. (1) The second blank can only take 'escapes' or 'attracts'. 'Deliberate' in the first blank will make the sentence logically incorrect. Only 'meticulous' fits here.

13. (2) Option (2) is incorrect because of the word 'generally'. 'Meritorious' students always surpass mediocre students. Bright students overestimating mediocre students also seem logically incorrect. Only option (5) fits in the blank to make it logically and grammatically correct.

14. (5) The word 'Ahimsa' suggests that the blanks will take 'hatred' and 'violence'.

15. (4) The only word that fits in the first blank is 'committed'.

16. (5) The correct sequence is EDFBAC. E starts the sequence by stating the number of children who do not complete their elementary education. D follows E. 'They' in D links it to E. It refers to the children who do not complete their education. It is followed by F which talks about children who did complete their 8 years of education. FBA is a mandatory sequence. 'They' in B refers to the children who complete their 8 years of education. 'These' in A also refer to the same. C concludes the paragraph by talking about political consciousness.

21. (4) The subject of the sentence 'these companies' is plural. Hence, 'to its board members' should be replaced by 'to their board members'.

22. (3) The subject of the sentence is 'the scheme' that is singular and it will take singular verb. Hence, 'require an additional investment' should be replaced by 'requires an additional investment'.

23. (5) The sentence is correct in its given form

24. (4) Replace 'and supervise the new staff' by 'and supervising the new staff' to make the structure parallel.

25. (5) The sentence is correct in its given form.

26. (2) Only 'whether' fits in grammatically.

27. (2) The listed problems have directly or indirectly, 'affected' people's lives.

28. (5) Only 'further', which means in addition to what has been said, fits in grammatically.

29. (3) 'Widely', which means by a large number of people, fits in the meaning of the sentence.

30. (3) 'To lose confidence' is the correct phrase. It means to lose trust.

31. (1) Let the speed of boat in still water be x km/hr.

$$\therefore \quad 12 = \frac{35}{x-1} + \frac{35}{x+1}$$

$$= 35\left[\frac{1}{x-1} + \frac{1}{x+1}\right] = 35\left[\frac{2x}{x^2-1}\right]$$

$$\Rightarrow \quad 12x^2 - 70x - 12 = 0$$

$$\Rightarrow \quad x = \frac{70 \pm \sqrt{4900+576}}{24}$$

$$= \frac{70 \pm \sqrt{5476}}{24} = \frac{70 \pm 74}{24}$$

$$\Rightarrow \quad x = \frac{144}{24} = 6 \text{ km/hr.}$$

32. (2) B's work lasts for 23 days after A leaves.

$$\therefore \quad \text{Work done in 23 days by B} = \frac{23}{40}.$$

$$\text{Remaining work} = \left(1 - \frac{23}{40}\right) = \frac{17}{40}.$$

$$(A + B)\text{'s 1 day's work} = \left(\frac{1}{45} + \frac{1}{40}\right)$$

Number of days required to finish $\frac{17}{40}$ th of work

$$= \frac{17}{40} \times \frac{(40 \times 45)}{(45+40)} = \frac{17 \times 40 \times 45}{40 \times 85} = 9 \text{ days}$$

33. (1) Cost of 1 sq. m = $\dfrac{0.8}{100}$ = Rs. $\dfrac{80}{10000}$

Area of square ground = $\dfrac{\text{Total Cost}}{\text{Cost per m}^2}$

$$= \dfrac{28.8}{80} \times 10000 = 3600 \text{ m}^2$$

$\therefore$ Side of square = $\sqrt{\text{Area of sq.}}$

$$= \sqrt{3600} = 60 \text{ m}$$

Perimeter of square = 4 × side = 4 × 60 = 240 m

Hence, cost of fencing = 0.6 × 240 = Rs. 144.

34. (5) From 1 to 17, there will be 9 odd numbers among which 6 numbers will be odd prime.

Now, it is given that the man will stop putting the coins back in the bag, once he gets an odd numbered coin.

So the required probability = $\dfrac{6}{9}$ = $\dfrac{2}{3}$.

35. (2) A = $\dfrac{1}{2}$B or $\dfrac{A}{B} = \dfrac{1}{2}$ and B = 2C or $\dfrac{B}{C} = \dfrac{2}{1}$

$\Rightarrow$ A : B : C = 1 : 2 : 1

Let shares of A, B and C are x, 2x and x respectively.

$$\Rightarrow \dfrac{B}{A+B} = \dfrac{2x}{x+2x} = \dfrac{2x}{3x} = \dfrac{2}{3} \text{ i.e. } 2 : 3.$$

36. (5) Total number of persons

= 34560 + 65900 + 45640 + 55550 + 42350 + 59650

= 303600

Required percentage = $\dfrac{\dfrac{41}{100} \times 55500}{303600} \times 100$

$$= 7.5\%$$

37. (4) Required percentage

$$= \dfrac{\dfrac{20}{100} \times 45640}{\dfrac{14}{100} \times 59650} \times 100$$

= 109.30%

38. (3) Total number of children

$$= \dfrac{20}{100} \times 65900 + \dfrac{33}{100} \times 55500$$

= 31495

39. (1) Number of women visiting

$$= \dfrac{55}{10} \times 3456 + \dfrac{43}{10} \times 6590 + \dfrac{45}{10} \times 4564 + \dfrac{26}{10}$$

$$\times 5550 + \dfrac{70}{10} \times 4235 + \dfrac{62}{10} \times 5965$$

= 19008 + 28337 + 20538 + 14430 + 29645 + 36983

= 148941

Required average = $\dfrac{148941}{6}$ = 24823.5

40. (5) Required ratio = $\dfrac{55}{100} \times 34560 : \dfrac{45}{100} \times 45640$

$$= 1056 : 1141.$$

41. (5) Let the sum be x. Then,

$$CI = x\left(1+\dfrac{5}{100}\right)^2 - x = \left(\dfrac{441\,x}{400} - x\right) = \dfrac{41\,x}{400}$$

$$SI = \dfrac{x \times 10 \times 1}{100} = \dfrac{x}{10}$$

$$CI - SI = \dfrac{41x}{400} - \dfrac{x}{10} = \dfrac{x}{400}$$

$$\therefore \dfrac{x}{400} = 25 \Rightarrow x = \text{Rs.}\,10,000$$

42. (3) A = $\dfrac{90}{100}$B, B = $\dfrac{125}{100}$C and C = $\dfrac{80}{100}$D

B = $\dfrac{10}{9}$A, C = $\dfrac{4}{5}$B and D = $\dfrac{5}{4}$C

B = $\dfrac{10}{9} \times 360 = 400$, C = $\dfrac{4}{5} \times 400 = 320$

and D = $\dfrac{5}{4} \times 320 = 400$

Percentage of D = $\dfrac{400}{500} \times 100 = 80\%$

43. (4) Let 4 years ago, the ages of Rahul and Deepak be 3x and 4x respectively.

Then, $\dfrac{3x+4+4}{4x+4+4} = \dfrac{11}{12}$

$\Rightarrow$ 44x + 88 = 36x + 96

$\Rightarrow$ 8x = 8

$\Rightarrow$ x = 1.

Hence, Deepak's present age = 4 × 1 + 4 = 8 years.

44. (1) CP of first = Rs. 18 per kilogram.

CP of second = Rs. 20 per kilogram.

Suppose he mixes 5 kg of first variety and 3 kg of second variety for 8 kg tea.

Total CP = 18 × 5 + 20 × 3 = 90 + 60 = Rs. 150.

Total SP = 21 × 8 = Rs. 168.

Profit $= \dfrac{18}{150} \times 100 = 18\dfrac{2}{3} = 12\%$.

45. (3) Let CP_1 per egg initially = Rs. 1 (Assuming she had 100 eggs)

Due to loss of 10% eggs, CP of remaining 90 eggs increases.

$$CP_2 = \frac{100}{90} = \text{Rs. 1.11 per egg}$$

To retain 10% profit,

$$SP_2 = 1.11 \times 1.1$$
$$= 1.222 \text{ or a mark-up of } 22.2\%.$$

46. (3) The series is as follows:

$$2^2 + 1 = 5$$
$$3^2 + 2 = 11$$
$$4^2 + 3 = 19$$
$$5^2 + 4 = 29$$
$$6^2 + 5 = 41$$
$$\therefore\ ? = 41$$

47. (5) The series is as follows:

$$7 \times 2 + 1 = 15$$
$$15 \times 2 + 1 = 31$$
$$31 \times 2 + 1 = 63$$
$$63 \times 2 + 1 = 127$$
$$\therefore\ ? = 31$$

48. (2) The series is as follows:

$$(2 + 1) \times 1 = 3$$
$$(3 + 2) \times 2 = 10$$
$$(10 + 3) \times 3 = 39$$
$$(39 + 4) \times 4 = 172$$
$$\therefore\ ? = 39$$

49. (5) The series is as follows:

$$8 \times 0.5 = 4$$
$$4 \times 1.5 = 6$$
$$6 \times 2.5 = 15$$
$$15 \times 3.5 = 52.5$$
$$\therefore\ ? = 15$$

50. (5) The series is as follows:

$$5 \times 1 + 1 = 6$$
$$6 \times 2 + 2 = 14$$
$$14 \times 3 + 3 = 45$$
$$45 \times 4 + 4 = 184$$
$$\therefore\ ? = 14$$

51. (1) I. $x^2 + 5x + 6 = 0$

$\Rightarrow\ x^2 + 2x + 3x + 6 = 0$

$\Rightarrow\ x(x + 2) + 3(x + 2) = 0$

$\Rightarrow\ (x + 3)(x + 2) = 0$

$\Rightarrow\ x = -3 \text{ or } -2$

II. $y^2 + 7y + 12 = 0$

$\Rightarrow\ y^2 + 4y + 3y + 12 = 0$

$\Rightarrow\ y(y + 4) + 3(y + 4) = 0$

$\Rightarrow\ (y + 3)(y + 4) = 0$

$\Rightarrow\ y = -3 \text{ or } -4$

52. (4) I. $x^2 - 9x + 20 = 0$

$\Rightarrow\ x^2 - 5x - 4x + 20 = 0$

$\Rightarrow\ x(x - 5) - 4(x - 5) = 0$

$\Rightarrow\ (x - 4)(x - 5) = 0$

$\Rightarrow\ x = 4 \text{ or } 5$

II. $y^2 - 13y + 42 = 0$

$\Rightarrow\ y^2 - 7y - 6y + 42 = 0$

$\Rightarrow\ y(y - 7) - 6(y - 7) = 0$

$\Rightarrow\ (y - 6)(y - 7) = 0$

$\Rightarrow\ y = 6 \text{ or } 7$

53. (4)

$$2x + 3y = 14 \quad \dots (i)$$
$$4x + 2y = 16 \quad \dots (ii)$$

By equation (i) × 2 – equation (ii),

$$4x + 6y - 4x - 2y = 28 - 16$$
$$\Rightarrow\ 4y = 12$$
$$\Rightarrow\ y = 3$$

From equation (i), $2x + 3 \times 3 = 14$

$$\Rightarrow\ 2x = 14 - 9 = 5 \Rightarrow x = \frac{5}{2}$$

Hence, $x < y$.

54. (4) I. $x = \sqrt{625} = 25$

II. $y = \sqrt{676} = 26$

Hence, $x < y$.

55. (4) I. $x^2 + 4x + 4 = 0$

$(x + 2)^2 = 0 \Rightarrow x = -2$

II. $y^2 - 8y + 16 = 0$

$\Rightarrow\ (y - 4)^2 = 0$

$\Rightarrow\ y = 4$

Hence, $x < y$.

56. (5) $? = 324.995 \times 15.98 \div 4.002 + 36.88$

$$\approx 325 \times 16 \div 4 + 37$$
$$= 325 \times 4 + 37$$
$$= 1337 \approx 1340$$

57. (1) ? = 69.008% of 699.998 + 32.99% of 399.999

$$\approx \frac{69}{100} \times 700 + \frac{33}{100} \times 400$$

$$= 483 + 132 = 615$$

58. (3) $? = \sqrt{624.98} + \sqrt{729.25}$

$$\approx \sqrt{625} + \sqrt{729}$$

$$= 25 + 27 = 52$$

59. (2) ? = 175 × 28 + 275 × 27.98

$$\approx 175 \times 28 + 275 \times 28$$

$$= (175 + 275) \times 28$$

$$= 450 \times 28 = 12600$$

60. (3) ? = 1164 × 128 ÷ 8.008 + 969.007

$$\approx 1164 \times 128 \div 8 + 970$$

$$= 18624 + 970 = 19594 \approx 19600$$

61. (2) Total number of vehicles in city 'X' over the given period = 13,250 + 17,820 + 22,170 + 13,790 + 6,720 + 17,620 = 91,370

62. (3) The total number of vehicles in city 'X' is more than the total number of vehicles in city 'Y' in the year 2010, 2011 and 2014 i.e. 3.

63. (1) The maximum number of vehicles in city 'X' is maximum in the year 2011 = 22,170

The minimum number of vehicles in city 'Y' is minimum in the year 2011 = 13,470

$$\text{Required percentage value} = \frac{22,170}{13,470} = 1.6458$$

or 64.58% more.

64. (5) Total number of vehicles in the two cities put together in year 2009 = 13,250 + 14,520 = 27,770

Total number of vehicles in two cities put together in the year 2014 = 17,620 + 16,840 = 34,460

$$\text{Required growth rate} = \left(\frac{34,460}{27,770}\right) = 1.2409 \text{ or}$$

24.09%

65. (3) In this question, there is no need to calculate the answer. As it is evident that the total number of vehicles are maximum in the year 2011. Thus, the consumption of petrol will be maximum in the that year.

66. (2)

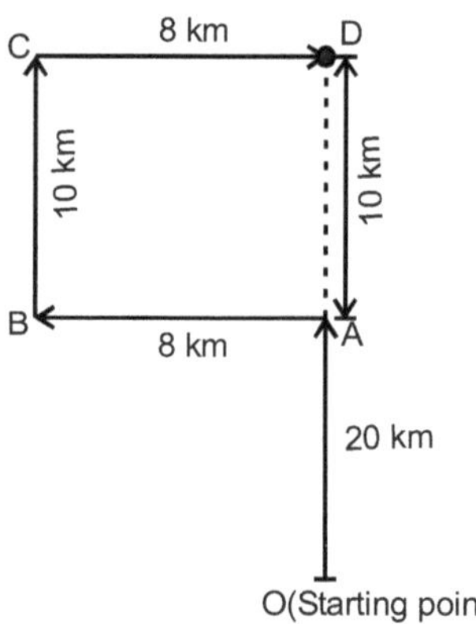

The path traversed by Uttam is OABCDEF, obviously Uttam is heading towards NORTH.

67. (3)

The path traversed by Narendra is OABCD.

The distance from O to D is OA + AD.

∵   AD = BC = 10 km

Therefore, OD = OA + AD

$$= 20 + 10 = 30 \text{ km}$$

68. (4)

Hence, Bindu is granddaughter of Rajesh.

69. (3)

J is the sister-in-law of A.

+ → Male

− → Female

= → Married couple.

70. (4)

+ → Male

− → Female

= → Married couple.

∴   \$ will come in place of question mark.

For questions 71 to 75:

Level of seniority	Name of person	Department
1	Bhavya	Operations
2	Amaya	Marketing
3	Eisha	Finance
4	Chavi	Production
5	Diya	HR

For questions 76 to 80:

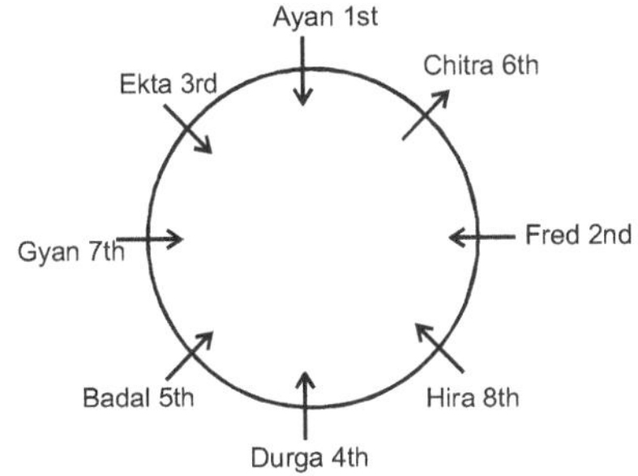

For questions 81 to 85:

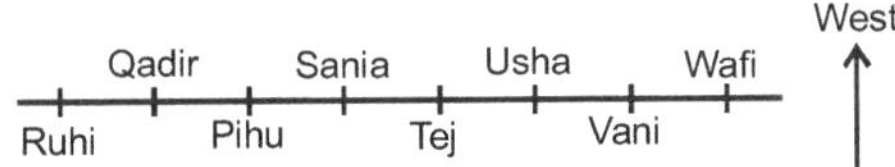

For questions 86 to 90:

hill	wu
top	oe
castle	ai
haunted	au
old	do
top	oe
class	pa
cottage	sa

91. (3) Statements:

$A > N$ ... (i)

$S \geq N$ ... (ii)

$S > W$ ... (iii)

$W \leq R$ ... (iv)

Combining all these, we get $A > N \leq S > W \leq R$

Conclusions:

I. $R \geq A$ (Not true)

II. $S > R$ (Not true)

III. $S > A$ (Not true)

IV. $W \leq A$ (Not true)

92. (1) Statements:

$D < E$ ... (i)

$E \leq T$ ... (ii)

$T = C$ ... (iii)

$C < A$ ... (iv)

Combining all these, we get $D < E \leq T = C < A$

Conclusions:

I. $D < A$ (True)

II. $C \leq D$ (Not true)

III. $A > E$ (True)

IV. $T < A$ (True)

93. (4) Statements:

$O \geq B$ ... (i)

$B = S$ ... (ii)

$S < E$ ... (iii)

$E \leq R$ ... (iv)

Combining all these, we get $O \geq B = S < E \leq R$

Conclusions:

I. $S \leq O$ (True)

II. $R > S$ (True)

III. $B < R$ (True)

IV. $B < E$ (True)

94. (2) Statements:

$D \leq S$ ... (i)

$S > P$ ... (ii)

$P \geq I$ ... (iii)

$P = T$ ... (iv)

Combining all these, we get $D \leq S > P = T \geq I$

Conclusions:

I. $P < D$ (Not true)

II. $P \geq T$ (Not true)

III. $T < S$ (True)

IV. $I \leq D$ (Not true)

95. (5) Statements:

$U = N$ ... (i)

$N \geq F$ ... (ii)

$F \geq A$ ... (iii)

$A > R$ ... (iv)

Combining all these, we get $U = N \geq F \geq A > R$

Conclusions:

I. $A = U$ (May or may not be true.)

II. $N > R$ (True)

III. $R \leq U$ (Not true)

IV. $U > A$ (May or may not be true.)

U is either greater than or equal to A. Therefore, either I or IV is true.

For questions 96 and 97:

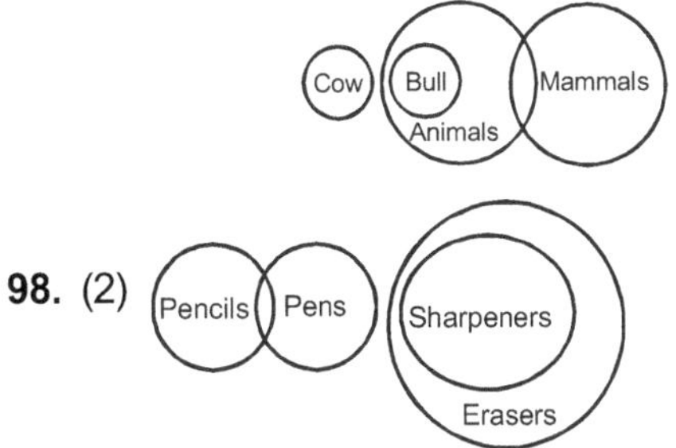

98. (2)

For questions 99 and 100:

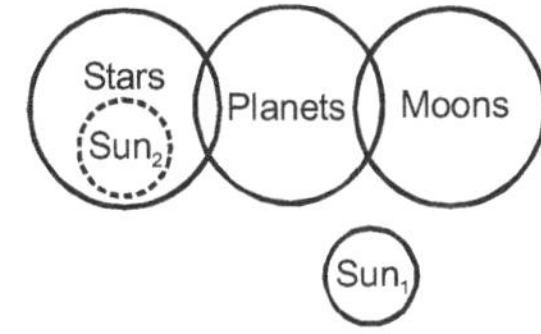

PRACTICE PAPER – 9

Directions (Q. 1 to 5): Read each sentence to find out whether there is any grammatical error in it. The error, if any, will be in one part of the sentence. The number of that part will be the answer. If there is no error, mark (5) as the answer. (Ignore errors of punctuation, if any.)

1. The oppostion leader tried (1) / to bolster his position (2) / with the voters by pressing (3) / corruption charges against rivals.(4) / No error (5)

2. The recently imposed dress code (1) / in the university has enraged (2) / the students who will be going (3) / on strike since tomorrow. (4) / No error (5)

3. Ever since he took over (1) / as the chief minister of the state, (2) / rate for unemployment (3) / has drastically increased.(4) / No error (5)

4. Although the brilliant writer,(1) / an underlying (2) / pessimism pervails in (3) / all her novels.(4) / No error (5)

5. Changed social setting (1) / demands the schools to teach (2) / moral and social values (3) / among with the academic skills. (4) / No error (5)

Directions (Q. 6 to 10): In the following passage, there are blanks, each of which has been numbered. These numbers are printed below the passage and against each, five words are suggested, one of which fits the blank appropriately. Find out the appropriate word in each case.

Birbal was in Persia at the invitation of the king of that country. During his stay parties were given in his honour. On the eve of his __6__ for home, a nobleman asked him how he would compare the king of Persia to his own king. "Your king is a full moon," said Birbal. "Whereas mine could be __7__ of as the quarter moon." The Persians were very happy. But when Birbal got home he found that Emperor Akbar was furious win him. "How could you belittle your own king?" demanded Akbar, "You are a traitor!".

"No, Your Majesty," said Birbal, "I did not belittle you. The full moon __8__ and disappears whereas the quarter moon grows with strength. What I, in fact, proclaimed to the world is that your power is __9__ from day to day whereas that of the king of Persia is about to go into decline." Akbar smiled in satisfaction and welcomed Birbal back __10__ a warm embrace.

6. (1) arrival   (2) depart
   (3) leave   (4) departure
   (5) exit

7. (1) pass   (2) celebrated
   (3) imagined   (4) wished
   (5) thought

8. (1) appear   (2) decrease
   (3) diminishes   (4) reduce
   (5) vanish

9. (1) sure   (2) fixed
   (3) growing   (4) new
   (5) increase

10. (1) with   (2) giving
   (3) granting   (4) shaving
   (5) by

Directions (Q. 11 to 15): Choose the correct option out of the four choices given.

11. The net losses clearly indicate that the company is ________ bankrupt.
   (1) gone   (2) going
   (3) went   (4) coming
   (5) getting

12. The author has been ________ plagiarism.
   (1) charged with   (2) accused in
   (3) blamed to   (4) convicted on
   (5) accused by

13. The ________ that the earth is being visited by at least one extraterrestrial civilization is extensive both in scope and detail.
   (1) authority   (2) evidence
   (3) apprehension   (4) speculation
   (5) doubt

14. Adventure tourism ________ involves travelling into remote, inaccessible and possibly hostile areas.
   (1) typically   (2) logically
   (3) technically   (4) easily
   (5) incidentally

15. The escape route for large economies with technological ________ is to develop and make their own weapon systems.
   (1) liberty
   (2) locomotion
   (3) limitation
   (4) prowess
   (5) intelligence

Directions for questions 16 to 25: Read the given passage carefully and attempt the questions that follow.

It is the air of vulnerability that strikes you more than anything else. He is reserved, a man of few words – between conversations that is. For Upamanyu Chatterjee, making small talk does not come easy. He is a self-confessed recluse of sorts - "I hardly meet any people." But, on the other hand, he is verbose enough in the books he writes. A dichotomy? Perhaps. But then, Chatterjee's life seems full of dichotomies. Two separate selves working at two different levels. "For the last 20 years, I've lived two completely different lives," says Chatterjee.

It is not easy getting him into a controversy. Like a seasoned bureaucrat, he avoids it with a general answer. Ask him why he's never thought of giving up his job, now that he's an established writer, and he replies that he's not sure that it would help him write more. "I am not sure if I would produce more if I become a writer full time. Here you have a 9-to-5 and then when you do get down to work - it's nice to switch off and get onto something else. Whereas I imagine if I was writing fulltime, I'd always be looking for distractions to prevent me from getting the job done. Writing is sort of both tiresome and tiring, don't you think so?" He readily agrees that it is also the subconscious need to have the security of not having to worry about the next meal that keeps him at his job with the government.

Weight Loss is autobiographical, claims Chatterjee. "In the sense that the concerns in this book are autobiographical." He quickly clarifies: "In the spiritual aspect that Bhola seeks, that is." Chatterjee is convinced that a deep sense of "futility" is inevitable in every being. When asked why, he murmurs, "May be, I should meet more people." But on a more serious note, he says that the concerns in Weight Loss revolve around the notion of a wasted life. "Bhola follows this degrading sensual life because the spiritual life is more difficult to follow. It's downhill all the way because he gives up the battle even before he starts." Explaining the dark humor that underlies almost all his writing, Chatterjee says that his books are "both dark and light. I see Weight Loss also as a funny book but it is also about a wasted life." Bhola, according to him, is very much a modern character and the world he inhabits "is very much the world here, it's not as though he's transposed from any other milieu," he says.

As a writer, he is influenced by everything around him. Ask him if he is a spiritual person, he pauses and admits that he has a sense of morality, a code of ethics and then surprisingly says, "I don't think anyone can believe in God anymore but to me, increasingly, it has seemed that to find God you only need time. All you need is literally superhuman patience, the time for it to unfold itself out. But, otherwise, I think I'm suspicious of religious tenets and **mumbo jumbo**."

While he is unwilling to be drawn into any arguments about the debate on Indians writing in English, Chatterjee's major concern is that he would just want more and more people to read and for that, he would not mind considering a ban on television. He also does not agree with the notion that it is the marketing and the hype that push a book's sales. Neither is he convinced that the face of an author can help sell a book. It's another matter that he has been chosen as one of the "hot babes" by a gossip magazine for not only his looks but also for his **whacky** sense of humour. "In the end, it is the content that will survive. I don't want to sound callous but it's obviously something (the hype) that publishers want to do. But had it not been there I wouldn't have insisted on it for my books," he added.

From his first book English, August to his fourth, Weight Loss, Chatterjee's journey has been long and sometimes, in his own words, slow. He says that when he started writing, he gave himself a deadline of sorts - one book to coincide with every Olympics. Obviously that hasn't quite happened but he is satisfied and feels that a book sets its own pace. Weight Loss took him five years, but then Chatterjee is unperturbed. Asked to comment on his literary journey, he **quips**, "It is difficult for me to rate my own books... exactly like a parent with four children." Yet, the first book is special to him. At the same time, he's also very happy with the way the others turned out. Though, while re-reading The Last Burden after a gap of 10 years, he says he was surprised and taken aback at the "rage and anger" in his writing.

Is he writing something else already? "Yes, but I don't want to talk about it now." Persist and he reveals, "Well, it's really like a companion book to the last one. By companion book, I mean it's like a spiritual book. You know what I mean... it's about wasted lives."

As the shadows lengthen, Chatterjee returns to his favourite theme of dark melancholy. Is he affected? "Yes, very much so." For him time is the boss and he cannot see how anybody can escape this sense of the **inevitable**.

16. According to the passage, Upamanyu Chatterjee is

    (1) a gregarious person.

    (2) very verbose.

    (3) a blabber mouth.

    (4) someone who loves to make small talk.

    (5) an introvert and speaks only when necessary.

17. According to the passage, what is the dichotomy in the author's character?

   (1) While he is a man of few words and hardly meets people, he is verbose in the books he writes.

   (2) He is a self-confessed recluse who thinks he should meet more people.

   (3) He is completely averse to the idea of spirituality and yet, he has written about it exhaustively in his new book.

   (4) None of the above

   (5) All of the above

18. According to the passage, why does Chatterjee not quit his job and take to full-time writing?

   (1) It is difficult for him to leave his 9 to 5 job because of his sense of commitment.

   (2) He feels that writing is both tiresome and tiring.

   (3) He likes to dabble in many activities at the same time.

   (4) He feels that it may not help him to write more as he would be looking for distractions and a job gives him financial security too.

   (5) He is not a very good writer.

19. From the passage, it can be inferred that Upamanyu Chatterjee

   (1) secretly believes in religious tenets.

   (2) thinks that spirituality lies in having a sense of right and wrong and a code of conduct.

   (3) does not believe in God.

   (4) believes that with patience any one can become spiritual.

   (5) None of the above

20. In Chatterjee's opinion, what helps in the sale of a book?

   (1) Good marketing

   (2) Face value of the author

   (3) A good sense of humour in the author

   (4) Good content of the book

   (5) Theme of the book

21. Which of the following about Upamanyu Chatterjee is not true according to the passage?

   (1) He is a person who welcomes the idea of social gatherings.

   (2) He feels time is the ultimate master.

   (3) He is a spiritual person.

   (4) His fourth book is Weight Loss.

   (5) All are true

Directions (Q. 22 and 23): Choose the word which ts most nearly the **SAME** in meaning as the word printed in bold as used in the passage.

22. Mumbo jumbo

   (1) Analytical   (2) Insightful

   (3) Complicated   (4) Gibberish

   (5) Meaningful

23. Quip

   (1) Gaze   (2) Joke

   (3) Frown   (4) Scowl

   (5) Glower

Directions (Q. 24 and 25): Choose the word which is most **OPPOSITE** in meaning to the word printed in bold as used in the passage.

24. Whacky

   (1) Zany   (2) Surreal

   (3) Sensible   (4) Cranky

   (5) Bizarre

25. Inevitable

   (1) Imminent   (2) Impending

   (3) Fortuitous   (4) Inexorable

   (5) Undeniable

Directions for questions 26 to 30: In each of the questions below, four sentences are given. Arrange these sentences labeled i, ii, iii and iv in a logical order so that together they make a coherent passage. From the given options, choose the one with the most appropriate sequence.

26. i. This is one IT professional who always wanted to get into movies and writing was "just a hobby".

   ii. Sixteen Malayalam short stories compiled in a book titled *Pension* has made Jayan Rajan an author.

   iii. "It just happened," says Jayan, on his new avatar.

   iv. Nevertheless, his first book, published by DC Books, has found a space on bookshelves.

   (1) iv, i, ii, iii   (2) ii, iii, i, iv

   (3) i, iv, iii, ii   (4) ii, iv, i, iii

   (5) i, ii, iii, iv

27. i. After an increasing number of drowning incidents, the authorities have banned people from entering the water.

   ii. They have also posted community lifeguards to enforce the ban.

   iii. However, the rough seas combined with a rocky coastline and a natural gradient make it an unsafe place to swim.

iv. Vizag's picturesque beaches attract many tourists and the promenade is a popular place to relax and unwind.

(1) iv, iii, i, ii   (2) iv, ii, i, iii

(3) iv, i, iii, ii   (4) ii, i, iii, iv

(5) i, ii, iii, iv

28. i. The India Surf Festival was conducted in February this year near Puri, Orissa.

ii. It advocates the freedom of expression and will also host cultural evenings.

iii. The organizers plan to host the festival again between January 25 and 27, next year.

iv. The festival hopes to promote a wholesome surf culture in the country.

(1) i, iii, ii, iv   (2) ii, i, iii, iv

(3) ii, iv, iii, i   (4) i, iii, iv, ii

(5) i, ii, iii, iv

29. i. I first read it at 14 or so and, it has remained my favourite novel ever since.

ii. By some miracle, a story written in the mid-1850s had captured much of how I felt in a small provincial town at the end of the 1970s.

iii. Read a book at the right age and it will stay with you for life.

iv. For some people it's *Pride and Prejudice*, *Jane Eyre* or *Wuthering Heights*, but for me it is *Great Expectations*.

(1) iii, ii, iv, i   (2) iv, i, ii, iii

(3) iii, iv, i, ii   (4) iii, i, ii, iv

(5) i, ii, iii, iv

30. i. It was used by a doctor who was examining my older brother, Timothy.

ii. In 1961, my parents heard the word "autism" for the first time.

iii. He had frequent screaming tantrums for no obvious reason.

iv. He was a handsome but very troubled five year old with little speech and fixed obsessions.

(1) ii, iv, i, iii   (2) ii, i, iv, iii

(3) i, ii, iii, iv   (4) i, iv, iii, ii

(5) iv, iii, ii, i

NUMERICAL ABILITY

Directions (Q. 31 to 35) : In the following table, the number of employees working in five companies and the corresponding ratio of male and female employees have been given. You are required to study the table carefully and answer the questions.

Company	Number of Employees
L	400
M	600
N	800
O	1000
P	1200

Company	Male : Female
L	12 : 8
M	15 : 5
N	4 : 1
O	13 : 12
P	7 : 5

31. What is the respective ratio between the number of females in company P and number of females in company L?

(1) 8 : 25   (2) 25 : 8

(3) 3 : 16   (4) 16 : 3

(5) None of these

32. The number of female employees working in company O is what percent of total employees working in that company?

(1) 24   (2) 12

(3) 48   (4) 13

(5) None of these

33. What is the average number of employees in all companies together?

(1) 800   (2) 775

(3) 760   (4) 600

(5) None of these

34. The number of female employees in company M is

(1) 450   (2) 150

(3) 250   (4) 350

(5) None of these

35. The total number of male employees working in companies N and P together is

(1) 1240   (2) 1360

(3) 1340   (4) 1260

(5) None of these

36. Two trains start from opposite directions at the same time towards each other to cover a distance of 200 km. They cross each other at a distance of 110 km from one of the stations. What is the ratio of their speeds?

(1) 11 : 20   (2) 9 : 20

(3) 11 : 9   (4) 17 : 9

(5) None of these

37. Aman and Chintu can complete a job in 40 days and 25 days respectively. How long will they take to complete the work if they work on alternate days?

(1) 8 days　　　　　　　(2) 10 days

(3) 12 days　　　　　　(4) 27 days

(5) Cannot be determined

38. Find the area of a right-angled triangle if radius of its circumcircle is 3 cm and altitude drawn to hypotenuse is 2 cm.

(1) 4 cm^2　　　　　　(2) 4.5 cm^2

(3) 5.2 cm^2　　　　　(4) 6 cm^2

(5) None of these

39. If a dice is rolled twice and the two results are multiplied, then what is the probability of getting a number which is a multiple of 12?

(1) $\dfrac{7}{36}$　　　　　　　(2) $\dfrac{1}{6}$

(3) $\dfrac{5}{36}$　　　　　　　(4) $\dfrac{1}{12}$

(5) None of these

40. Rs. 385 has been divided among Amar, Byom and Chiru such that Amar receives 2/9 th of what Byom and Chiru receive together. What is the share of Amar?

(1) Rs. 70　　　　　　(2) Rs. 50

(3) Rs. 85　　　　　　(4) Rs. 35

(5) Rs. 75

Directions (Q. 41 to 45): In each questions below one or more equation(s) is/are provided. On the basis of these, you have to find out relation between p and q.

Give answer (1) if p = q

Give answer (2) if p > q

Give answer (3) if q > p

Give answer (4) if p $\geq$ q and

Give answer (5) if q $\geq$ p.

41. I.　$4q^2 + 8q = 4q + 8$

II.　$p^2 + 9p = 2p - 12$

42. I.　$2p^2 + 40 = 18p$

II.　$q^2 = 13q - 42$

43. I.　$6q^2 + \dfrac{1}{2} = \dfrac{7}{2}q$

II.　$12p^2 + 2 = 10p$

44. I.　$2p^2 - 7p + 3 = 0$

II.　$15q^2 - 5q = 6q - 2$

45. I.　$q^2 - 8q = 12q - 99$

II.　$2p^2 - 24p = 10p - 144$

46. A certain amount of money at r% interest compounded annually becomes Rs. 1,440 and Rs. 1,728 after 2 and 3 years respectively. Find the value of r.

(1) 5　　　　　　　　(2) 10

(3) 15　　　　　　　(4) 20

(5) None of these

47. A person gets 3 successive discounts of 28.56%, 12.5% and 60%. The net discount is

(1) 68%　　　　　　(2) 74.23%

(3) 75%　　　　　　(4) 75.65%

(5) 72.71%

48. The average salary of 20 workers in an office is Rs. 1,900 per month. If the manager's salary is added, then the average salary becomes Rs. 2,000 per month. What is the manager's annual salary?

(1) Rs. 24,000

(2) Rs. 25,200

(3) Rs. 45,600

(4) Rs. 42,000

(5) None of these

49. A solution containing milk and water in the ratio 3 : 2 is mixed with another milk and water solution with respective ratio as 4 : 1. If the volumes are 400 ml and 1,000 ml respectively, then what is the ratio of milk to water in the resultant solution?

(1) 9 : 5　　　　　　(2) 26 : 9

(3) 5 : 26　　　　　(4) 8 : 21

(5) 9 : 26

50. A sells a bicycle to B at a profit of 5% and B sells it to C at a profit of 25%. If C pays Rs. 1,050 for the bicycle. What did A pay for it?

(1) Rs. 800　　　　　(2) Rs. 840

(3) Rs. 630　　　　　(4) Rs. 945

(5) None of these

Directions (Q. 51 and 52): Find out the number that would replace the question mark (?) in each of the following questions.

51. 6, 15, 35, 77, 143, _?_

(1) 283　　　　　　(2) 292

(3) 221　　　　　　(4) 305

(5) 195

52. 4, 18, 48, 100, 180, _?_

(1) 222　　　　　　(2) 242

(3) 320　　　　　　(4) 294

(5) 343

Direction (Q. 53): What should come in place of the question mark (?) in the following number series?

53. 25,   30,   70,   260,   1280, ?
- (1) 6400
- (2) 7680
- (3) 6380
- (4) 7660
- (5) None of these

Directions (54 and 55): In each of these questions a number series is given. In each series only one number is wrong. Find out the wrong number.

54. 3601, 3602, 1803, 604, 154, 36, 12
- (1) 3602
- (2) 1803
- (3) 604
- (4) 154
- (5) 36

55. 4, 12, 42, 196, 1005, 6066, 42511
- (1) 12
- (2) 42
- (3) 1005
- (4) 196
- (5) 6066

Directions (Q. 56 to 60): Read the given information carefully and answer the questions based on it.

The bar-graph given below represents the yearly AIR's Commercial Earnings (in Rs. crore) from the two All India Radio Channels, viz. Vividh Bharati and Primary Channel for different years.

56. By approximately how many times has AIR's commercial earnings increased in 1995-96 over 1975-76?
- (1) 10.9 times
- (2) 11.9 times
- (3) 12.9 times
- (4) 13.9 times
- (5) 12.6 times

57. What was the percentage increase of AIR's commercial earnings from 1985-86 to 1995-96 (Approximately)?
- (1) 250%
- (2) 275%
- (3) 301%
- (4) 325%
- (5) 201%

58. What is the difference between Vividh Bharati's percentage increase in revenue from 1985-86 to 1995-96 and that of from 1975-76 to 1985-86?

- (1) 60%
- (2) 62%
- (3) 65%
- (4) 68%
- (5) None of these

59. What was the annual percentage increase in revenue of the Primary channel since its inception?
- (1) 20.5%
- (2) 205%
- (3) 250%
- (4) 2.05%
- (5) Cannot be determined

60. What is the average earnings of Primary Channel during the given time period?
- (1) 20.13 crores
- (2) 22.13 crores
- (3) 21.15 crores
- (4) 23.16 crores
- (5) None of these

Directions (Q. 61 to 65): What should come in place of the question mark (?) in the following questions?

61. $74844 \div ? = 54 \times 63$

    (1) 34   (2) 42

    (3) 22   (4) 54

    (5) None of these

62. $(21.35)^2 + (12.25)^2 = ?$

    (1) 171.4125   (2) 605.885

    (3) 604.085   (4) 463.8125

    (5) None of these

63. $124 + 56 \times 1.5 - 12 = ?$

    (1) −1890   (2) 252

    (3) 230   (4) 196

    (5) None of these

64. $\sqrt[3]{1092727} = ?$

    (1) 108   (2) 99

    (3) 97   (4) 107

    (5) None of these

65. $(46351 - 36418 - 4505) \div ? = 1357$

    (1) 4   (2) 6

    (3) 3   (4) 2

    (5) None of these

REASONING ABILITY

Directions (Q. 66 to 70): Answer the following questions based on the given information.

One day three friends namely Girish, Ram and Lokesh whose surnames are Achrekar, Karmarkar and Wandrekar (not necessarilly in the given order) met in 'Cafe Coffee Day'. Each of them was wearing a different garment of a different color. The garments they were wearing was Sweater, Jacket and Raincoat and the color of the garment was among blue, brown and grey (not necessarily in the given order). Further it is given as:

  (i) Neither Ram nor Wandrekar was wearing the grey sweater.

  (ii) Achrekar wasn't wearing the raincoat.

 (iii) Lokesh was wearing the brown jacket.

 (iv) The garment worn by Karmarkar or Achrekar was not of brown color.

66. Who wore the sweater?

    (1) Girish   (2) Ram

    (3) Lokesh   (4) Girish or Lokesh

    (5) Cannot be determined

67. Karmarkar was the surname of the person wearing

    (1) Sweater   (2) Jacket

    (3) Raincoat   (4) Sweater or Raincoat

    (5) None of these

68. Lokesh's surname was

    (1) Achrekar   (2) Karmarkar

    (3) Wandrekar   (4) Achrekar or Karmarkar

    (5) None of these

69. The raincoat was of which colour?

    (1) Grey   (2) Brown

    (3) Blue   (4) Grey or Blue

    (5) None of these

70. Which of the given combination is correct?

    (1) Sweater-Karmarkar

    (2) Lokesh-Brown

    (3) Raincoat-Girish

    (4) Jacket-Grey

    (5) Ram-Archrekar

71. A travels a distance of 5 km towards the west, then he travels a distance of 3 km towards the south and then he travels a distance of 4 km, 7 km and 8 km towards the west, north and west respectively. At what horizontal distance is he from the starting point?

    (1) 12 km   (2) 15 km

    (3) 17 km   (4) 19 km

    (5) None of these

72. A person is facing east. He turns 45° in the clockwise direction and then another 135° in the same direction and then 225° in the anticlockwise direction. Which direction is he facing now?

    (1) South-west   (2) East

    (3) North-west   (4) North-east

    (5) None of these

73. A person said to me, "I am the only son of only brother of one of your parents whose parent have only one son". What is the relation of the person's father with me?

    (1) Paternal uncle

    (2) Cousin

    (3) Brother-in-law

    (4) Maternal uncle

    (5) No relation

74. A person in my family once said to me "Instead of having two sons if I had a son and a daughter, then you would have an aunt instead of uncle". What is the relation between the person and me?

    (1) Grandfather

    (2) Grandmother

    (3) Father

    (4) Uncle

    (5) Cannot be determined

75. Pointing towards a person in the photograph Leela said, "He is the only son of the father of my sister's brother". How is that person related to Leela?

   (1) Mother

   (2) Father

   (3) Brother

   (4) Maternal uncle

   (5) Cousin brother

Directions (Q. 76 to 80): Answer the following questions based on the given information.

Eight members of a family - Raja, Rani, Lucky, Vicky, Vina, Sweety, Bunny and Sunny - sit around a circular table such that no two persons sitting next to each other face the same side.

   i. There are two married couples in the family.

   ii. The father of the family, Raja faces the centre and sits exactly in between his son and daughter.

   iii. The sons Lucky and Vicky sit on the right of each other.

   iv. Raja's wife Rani sits third to the right of her daughter in law Vina.

   v. Vina faces her husband and her daughter, Bunny sits opposite to Lucky.

   vi. Sweety sits third to the left of Sunny, the grandson of Rani.

76. What is the grandmother's position with respect to her grandson?

   (1) Third to the left

   (2) Immediate left

   (3) Second to the right

   (4) Immediate right

   (5) None of these

77. If Bunny and Lucky form a pair and Vina and Vicky form a similar pair then select a similar pair from the given options.

   (1) Sweety and Sunny

   (2) Raja and Rani

   (3) Vicky and Lucky

   (4) Rani and Vina

   (5) None of these

78. Who sits third to the left of the person who sits third to the right of Bunny?

   (1) Rani   (2) Vicky

   (3) Sunny   (4) Sweety

   (5) Lucky

79. Who are the unmarried children of Rani?

   (1) Vina and Sweety

   (2) Bunny and Sunny

   (3) Vicky and Llucky

   (4) Lucky and Sweety

   (5) Rani and Bunny

80. Whom does Rani face?

   (1) Her unmarried son

   (2) Her daughter-in-law

   (3) Her grand-daughter

   (4) Her daughter

   (5) None

Directions (Q. 81 to 85): Answer the following questions based on the given information.

In a certain code "cup of orange juice" is coded as "qu eo ga ud", "fresh orange pulp" is coded as "ga lu es", "fresh cup coffee" is coded as "fe qu es" and "pulp and juice" is coded as "lu ud la".

81. What does the code "lu" stand for?

   (1) cup   (2) pulp

   (3) juice   (4) orange

   (5) None of these

82. What is the code for "fresh orange juice"?

   (1) ud es fe   (2) qu es fe

   (3) ud es ga   (4) es ga la

   (5) None of these

83. If "hot tea" is coded as "to mi" then what will be the code for "hot cup of coffee"?

   (1) qu to ga fe   (2) qu lu eo fe

   (3) ud to eo ga   (4) qu to eo fe

   (5) None of these

84. How can "sweet orange pulp" be coded?

   (1) ws ga lu

   (2) lu ga fe

   (3) eo ga ud

   (4) ws ga qu

   (5) ws ga ni

85. What does the code "qu es" stand for?

   (1) orange pulp

   (2) cup fresh

   (3) pulp of

   (4) and juice

   (5) None of these

Directions (Q. 86 to 90): In each of the following questions, symbols %, £, = , ? and + are used with the following meaning as illustrated below:

A % B means 'A is equal to B'.

A £ B means 'A is less than or equal to B'.

A = B means 'A is greater than B'.

A ? B means 'A is greater than or equal to B'.

A + B means 'A is less than B'.

Based on the statements given in each of the questions below, find out which of the conclusion follows.

Mark:

(1) if only conclusion I follows.

(2) if only conclusion II follows.

(3) if either conclusion I or II follows.

(4) if both conclusions follow.

(5) if neither conclusion I nor II follows

86. Statement: A ? B, B = C, C % D

   Conclusion:

   I.   A ? D

   II. D £ B

87. Statement: X £ Z, Z + Y, Y = W

   Conclusion:

   I.   X + Y

   II. Z % W

88. Statement: X % Y, Y = Z, Z ? W

   Conclusion:

   I.   X = W

   II. Y + W

89. Statement: A + B, B £ C, C % D

   Conclusion:

   I.   B % D

   II. D = B

90. Statement: A = B, B ? C, C + D, D £ E

   Conclusion:

   I.   A ? D

   II. B % E

Directions (Q. 91 to 95): Read the information carefully and answer the questions based on it.

Twelve friends – I, J, K, L, M, N, O, P, Q, R, S and T – are sitting in two parallel rows such that six friends are sitting in each row and each friend in a particular row is facing to one of the friends in the other row.

(i) I is sitting at the left end of the row and facing S.

(ii) Only two friends are sitting between S and Q, who is facing M.

(iii) T is facing J and shares the same row with I, O and N.

(iv) Niether O nor K is sitting at any extreme end of the row.

(v) Only two friends are sitting between T and P. O is facing the north direction.

(vi) R is third to the left of L, who is an immediate neighbor of J.

91. Who is facing R?

   (1) N   (2) P

   (3) O   (4) T

   (5) None of these

92. How many friends are sitting between O and M?

   (1) Two   (2) One

   (3) Three   (4) Four

   (5) None

93. Who is sitting between Q and J?

   (1) M   (2) O

   (3) K   (4) L

   (5) None of these

94. If Q is related to I in a certain way and same is true for T and K, then O is related to whom following the same pattern?

   (1) S   (2) P

   (3) R   (4) N

   (5) None of these

95. Which of the following pairs of friends are sitting at the extreme ends of the row?

   (1) S – P   (2) R – N

   (3) R – P   (4) N – T

   (5) None of these

Directions (Q. 96 and 97): Each question comprises two statements, numbered I and II. You have to take the statements as true even if they seem to be at variance with commonly known facts. Read all the conclusions and then decide which of the given conclusions logically follow from the given statements, disregarding commonly known facts.

96. (I) Some whites are black.

   (II) No whites are green.

   Which of the following derivations is correct?

   (1) Some whites are green

   (2) Some whites are not green

   (3) Some black are green.

   (4) All green are black.

   (5) No black is white.

97. (I)   All flowers are stems.

(II)   All stems are roots.

Which of the following derivations is correct?

(1) All roots are flowers.

(2) All stems are flowers.

(3) Some stems are not roots.

(4) Some roots might not be flowers.

(5) Some flowers are not stems.

Directions (Q. 98 to 100): Two statements followed by two conclusions, numbered I and II are given below . You have to consider the two statements to be true even if they seem to be at variance with commonly known facts. You have to decide which of the conclusions, if any, follow from the given statements.

98. Statements:

Some kites are green.

All green are cow.

Conclusions:

I.   Some kites are not green.

II.   Some kites are not cow.

(1) Only (I) follows

(2) Only (II) follows

(3) Both (I) and (II) follow

(4) None follows

(5) Either (I) or (II) follows

99. Statements:

All good are girls.

All studious are girls.

Conclusions:

I.   Some studious are good.

II.   All girls maybe studious.

(1) Only (I) follows

(2) Only (II) follows

(3) Both (I) and (II) follow

(4) None follows

(5) Either (I) or (II) follows

100. Statements:

Some cities are villages.

Some towns are villages.

Conclusions:

I.   Some cities are towns.

II.   No town is a village.

(1) Only (I) follows

(2) Only (II) follows

(3) Both (I) and (II) follow

(4) None follows

(5) Either (I) or (II) follows

ANSWERS

1. (3)	**2.** (4)	**3.** (3)	**4.** (1)	**5.** (4)	**6.** (4)	**7.** (5)	**8.** (3)	**9.** (3)	**10.** (2)
11. (2)	**12.** (1)	**13.** (2)	**14.** (1)	**15.** (4)	**16.** (5)	**17.** (1)	**18.** (4)	**19.** (2)	**20.** (4)
21. (1)	**22.** (4)	**23.** (2)	**24.** (3)	**25.** (3)	**26.** (2)	**27.** (1)	**28.** (4)	**29.** (3)	**30.** (2)
31. (2)	**32.** (3)	**33.** (1)	**34.** (2)	**35.** (3)	**36.** (3)	**37.** (5)	**38.** (4)	**39.** (1)	**40.** (1)
41. (3)	**42.** (3)	**43.** (4)	**44.** (2)	**45.** (5)	**46.** (4)	**47.** (3)	**48.** (5)	**49.** (2)	**50.** (1)
51. (3)	**52.** (4)	**53.** (4)	**54.** (4)	**55.** (2)	**56.** (2)	**57.** (3)	**58.** (4)	**59.** (5)	**60.** (1)
61. (3)	**62.** (2)	**63.** (4)	**64.** (5)	**65.** (1)	**66.** (1)	**67.** (3)	**68.** (3)	**69.** (3)	**70.** (2)
71. (3)	**72.** (4)	**73.** (4)	**74.** (5)	**75.** (3)	**76.** (4)	**77.** (5)	**78.** (1)	**79.** (4)	**80.** (5)
81. (2)	**82.** (3)	**83.** (4)	**84.** (1)	**85.** (2)	**86.** (5)	**87.** (1)	**88.** (1)	**89.** (3)	**90.** (5)
91. (1)	**92.** (5)	**93.** (4)	**94.** (3)	**95.** (2)	**96.** (2)	**97.** (4)	**98.** (4)	**99.** (2)	**100.** (4)

EXPLANATIONS

1. (3) Use 'among' instead of 'with'.

2. (4) 'Since' will be replaced by 'from'.

3. (3) It should be 'the rate of'.

4. (1) Replace 'the' with 'a'.

5. (4) Replace 'among' with 'along.'

6. (4) 'Departure for home' sounds correct.

7. (5) 'Thought' is the correct word in the context of the sentence.

8. (3) In the context of the sentence, 'diminishes' is the correct word.

9. (3) 'Growing' is the correct word in the context of the sentence.

10. (2) An embrace can only be 'given'.

11. (2) The sentence requires the verb to be in present continuous form and the correct phrase is 'going bankrupt'.

12. (1) 'Charged with' is the correct phrasal verb.

13. (2) 'Scope and detail' defines the blank. Only option 2 logically fits in the blank.

14. (1) 'Typically' means characteristically.

15. (4) 'Prowess' refers to extraordinary ability.

16. (5) The second sentence of the first paragraph describes Upamanyu Chatterjee to be 'reserved' and 'a man of few words'. 'A man of few words' is one who speaks only when necessary. Option (2) is negated because he is only verbose in his books and not in general.

17. (1) While Upamanyu Chatterjee is reserved and a recluse by nature, his books are verbose. Therefore, there is a dichotomy (things that are totally opposite to each other) in his persona.

18. (4) According to Upamanyu Chatterjee, a full-time occupation of writing is monotonous, whereas a 9-5 job could help him get back to writing and also provide him financial security.

19. (2) In the fourth paragraph, when asked if he is spiritual by nature, Upamanyu Chatterjee admits that he may not be religious in the ritualistic sense, but he has a sense of morality and a code of ethics. He is circumspect in his religious beliefs.

20. (4) In the fifth paragraph, Chatterjee quotes that, "In the end, it is the content that will survive".

21. (1) Chatterjee is a self-declared recluse and hence cannot be expected to welcome the idea of social gathering.

26. (2) (i) and (iv) form a mandatory pair as (i) states that writing was 'just a hobby' for this person and then (iv) goes on to say that in spite of writing being a hobby, his book has successfully found its way to the bookshelves. So, options (1) and (4) can be negated as they do not have this pair in its proper sequence. Further, the paragraph cannot abruptly start with (i). (ii) is a better start as it also introduces the subject properly. Therefore, option (2) is the correct answer.

27. (1) (i) and (ii) form a mandatory pair as (i) talks about a ban that had been imposed by the authorities and (ii) goes on to talk about what steps have been taken to enforce that ban. 'They' in (ii) refers to the authorities in (i). The 'it' in (iii) refers to Vizag's picturesque beaches. Only option (1) has this sequence in its proper order and therefore, it is the correct answer.

28. (4) The paragraph has to start with (i) as it is only in this sentence that the subject has been introduced. So, options (2) and (3) can be easily negated. (iii) and (iv) follow as they talk about a series of ideas regarding the festival. The 'and will also' in (ii) makes it the concluding sentence and thus the correct sequence is i, iii, iv, ii. Hence, option (4) is the answer.

29. (3) (iii), (iv) is a mandatory pair with (iii) introducing the topic of books that stay with you lifelong and (iv) giving examples of such books. (iv) and (i) form another mandatory pair as the 'it' in (i) refers to the author's favorite book mentioned in (iv) - *Great Expectations*. Further, (ii) has to follow (i) as it carries the idea forward by stating the reason why it was the author's favorite novel. This sequence is given in option (3) which is the correct answer.

30. (2) (ii), (i) forms a mandatory pair as the 'it' in (i) refers to the word "autism" mentioned in (ii). (iv) and (iii) have to come after (i) as they describe the 'elder brother, Timothy' mentioned in (i). Therefore, option (2) is the correct answer.

31. (2) Females in company P $= \dfrac{5}{12} \times 1200 = 500$

Females in company L $= 400 \times \dfrac{8}{20} = 160$

Required ratio $= 500 : 160 = 25 : 8$.

32. (3) Required percentage $= \dfrac{12}{25} \times 100 = 48\%$.

33. (1) Required average $= \dfrac{4000}{5} = 800$.

34. (2) Females in company M $= \dfrac{5}{20} \times 600 = 150$

35. (3) Males in company N and company P

$$= \dfrac{4}{5} \times 800 + 1200 \times \dfrac{7}{12}$$

$$= 640 + 700$$

$$= 1340.$$

36. (3) By the time the trains cross each other,

let one cover 110 km and the second covers 90 km

Ratio of speeds = Ratio of the distances covered

$$= \dfrac{110}{90} = 11 : 9$$

37. (5) We cannot determine the required number of days as it is not known that who among the two started the work.

38. (4)

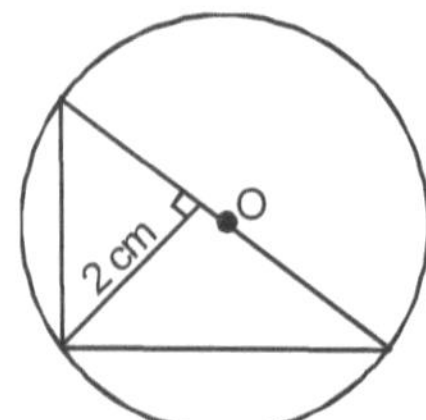

Hypotenuse of right-angled triangle

$$= 2 \times \text{radius of circle}$$

$$= 2 \times 3 = 6 \text{ cm}$$

$$\text{Altitude} = 2 \text{ cm}$$

$$\text{Area} = \dfrac{1}{2} \times \text{base} \times \text{height}$$

$$= \dfrac{1}{2} \times 6 \times 2 = 6 \text{ cm}^2 .$$

39. (1) Total cases = 36

Favourable cases = (2, 6), (3, 4), (4, 3), (4, 6), (6, 4), (6, 2) and (6, 6) = 7

$$\therefore \text{ Probability} = \dfrac{7}{36}.$$

40. (1) Let the amounts received, in rupees, by Amar, Byom and Chiru be A, B and C respectively.

Since A + B + C = 385 and $A = \dfrac{2}{9}(B + C) = \dfrac{2}{9}$

$(385 - A)$

Solving the above equations for A, we get A = Rs. 70.

41. (3) Solving the equations

$$q = 1, -2$$

$$p = -3, -4$$

$$\Rightarrow \qquad q > p$$

42. (3) After solving the equations

$$p = 4, 5$$

$$q = 6, 7$$

$$\Rightarrow \qquad q > p$$

43. (4) After solving the equations

$$q = \dfrac{1}{3}, \dfrac{1}{4}$$

$$p = \dfrac{1}{2}, \dfrac{1}{3}$$

$$\Rightarrow p \geq q.$$

44. (2) After solving the equations

$$p = \dfrac{1}{2}, 3$$

$$q = \dfrac{1}{3}, \dfrac{2}{5}$$

$$\Rightarrow p > q.$$

45. (5) After solving the equations, we get

$$q = 9, 11$$

$$p = 8, 9$$

$$\Rightarrow q \geq p$$

46. (4) Difference between the amount is

$$= (1728 - 1440)$$

$$= \text{Rs. } 288$$

Rs. 288 is the simple interest on Rs. 1,440 for one year.

$$288 = \dfrac{1440 \times r \times 1}{100} \Rightarrow r = 20\% .$$

47. (3) Let the amount on which the discounts are being offered be Rs. 100.

Now after the discounts the final amount will be

$$= 100 \times \dfrac{5}{7} \times \dfrac{7}{8} \times \dfrac{2}{5}$$

$$= 100 \times \dfrac{1}{4} = 25.$$

Hence, the net discount is $= \left(\dfrac{100 - 25}{100} \right) \times 100$

$$= 75\%.$$

48. (5) Total salary of 20 workers for a month

$$= 20 \times 1900 = \text{Rs. } 38,000$$

Total salary of 20 workers and a manager for a month

$$= 21 \times 2000 = \text{Rs. } 42,000$$

$\therefore$ Managers salary for a month = Rs. 4,000

$\therefore$ Manager's annual salary = 12×4000

$$= \text{Rs. } 48,000.$$

49. (2) Quantity of milk in first solution

$$= \frac{3}{5} \times 400 = 240 \text{ ml}$$

Quantity of water in first solution

$$= 400 - 240 = 160 \text{ml}$$

Quantity of milk in second solution

$$= \frac{4}{5} \times 1000 = 800 \text{ ml}$$

Quantity of water in second solution

$$= 1000 - 800$$
$$= 200 \text{ ml}$$

Hence, total milk = 240 + 800 = 1040 ml and total water = 160 + 200 = 360 ml.

∴ Required milk to water ratio

$$= 1040 : 360$$
$$= 26 : 9.$$

50. (1) If C pays Rs.1,050, then selling price for B = Rs.1,050.

Hence, cost price for B $= 1050 \times \dfrac{100}{125} = $ Rs. 840

Selling price for A = Rs. 840

Cost price for A $= 840 \times \dfrac{100}{105} = $ Rs.800 .

51. (3)
$$6 = 2 \times 3$$
$$15 = 3 \times 5$$
$$35 = 7 \times 5$$
$$77 = 7 \times 11$$
$$143 = 11 \times 13$$

So next number should be 13 × 17 = 221.

52. (4)
$$4 = 2^2 \times 1$$
$$18 = 3^2 \times 2$$
$$48 = 4^2 \times 3$$
$$100 = 5^2 \times 4$$
$$180 = 6^2 \times 5$$
$$294 = 7^2 \times 6$$

53. (4)

25   30   70   260   1280   **?(7660)**

×2–20   ×3–20   ×4–20   ×5–20   ×6–20

54. (4)

3601   3602   1803   604   155   36   12

+1+1   ÷2+2   ÷3+3   ÷4+4   ÷5+5   ÷6+6

154 is written in place of 155.

55. (2)

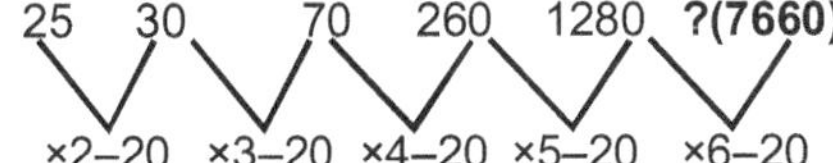

4   12   45   196   1005   6066   42511

×2+(2)²   ×3+(3)²   ×4+(4)²   ×5+(5)²   ×6+(6)²   ×7+(7)²

42 is written in place of 45.

56. (2) Commercial earning in 1975-76

$$= \text{Rs. } 6.26 \text{ crore}$$

Commercial earning in 1995-96

$$= 43.7 + 37.3$$
$$= \text{Rs. } 81 \text{ crore}$$

Increase in commercial earning

$$= 81 - 6.26$$
$$= \text{Rs. } 74.74 \text{ crore}$$

So, required $= \dfrac{74.74}{6.26} = 11.9$ times.

57. (3) Commercial earnings in 1985-86

$$= 17.55 + 2.64 = 20.19 \text{ crore}$$

Commercial earnings in 1995-96 = 81 crore

Percentage increase $= \dfrac{81 - 20.19}{20.19} \times 100$

$$= 301.19\%.$$

58. (4) Percentage increase in revenue of Vivid Bharti from 1985-86 to 1995-96

$$= \frac{37.3 - 17.55}{17.55} \times 100 = 112.53\%$$

Percentage increase in revenue of Vivid Bharti from 1975-76 to 1985-86

$$= \frac{17.55 - 6.26}{6.26} \times 100 = 180.35\%$$

Difference = 180.35 − 112.53 ≈ 68%.

59. (5) It cannot be determined because we don't know from which year to which year we have to find percentage increase.

60. (1) Required average

$$= \frac{2.64 + 14.05 + 43.07}{3} = 20.13 \text{ crores}$$

61. (3) 74844 ÷ ? = 54 × 63

$$? = \frac{74844}{54 \times 63} = 22$$

62. (2) ? = (21.35)² + (12.25)²

$$= 455.8225 + 150.0625$$
$$= 605.885$$

63. (4) ? = 124 + 56 × 1.5 – 12

$$= 124 + 84 - 12$$
$$= 196$$

64. (5) $? = \sqrt[3]{1092727} = 103$

65. (1) (46351 − 36418 − 4505) ÷ ? = 1357

$$? = \frac{5428}{1357} = 4$$

For questions 66 to 70: From the given information the following table deduced as:

Name	Surname	Garment	Colour
Ram	Karmarkar	Raincoat	Blue
Lokesh	Wandrekar	Jacket	Brown
Girish	Achrekar	Sweater	Grey

71. (3)

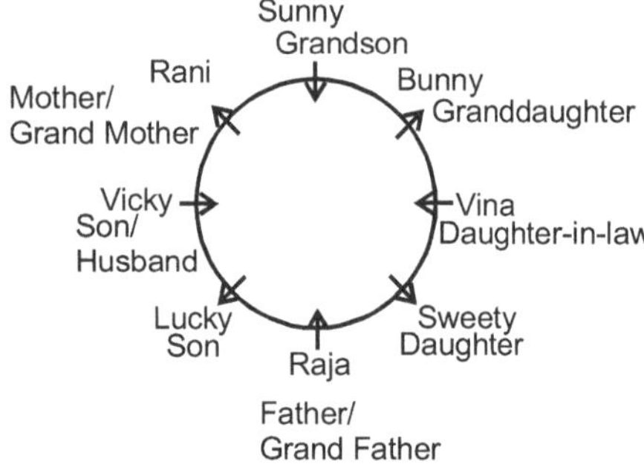

Horizontal distance of A from starting point

$$O = O'D = O'P' + P'C + CD = 5 + 4 + 8 = 17 \text{ km}$$

72. (4)

Hence, he is facing north-east direction.

73. (4) The person is the son of the only brother of one of my parents whose parents have only one son. Therefore, person's father is the brother of my mother. Hence, person's father is my maternal uncle.

74. (5) According to the statement of the person, I am the grandson of the person. Since the gender of the person is not mentioned so the person could be my grandfather or grandmother.

75. (3) The father of Leela's sister's brother is Leela's father. The only son of Leela's father is Leela's brother. Hence, the person is the brother of Leela.

For questions 76 to 80: From the given information the following table deduced as:

For questions 81 to 85: From the given information the following table deduced as

cup	qu
of	eo
orange	ga
juice	ud
fresh	es
pulp	lu
and	la
coffee	fe

86. (5) Given statement:

$$A \geq B, B > C, C = D$$

$$\Rightarrow A \geq B > C = D$$

Conclusion I : $A \geq D$ does not follow

Conclusion II : $D \leq B$ does not follow

Hence, option (5) is the answer.

87. (1) Given statement:

$$X \leq Z, Z < Y, Y > W$$

$$\Rightarrow X \leq Z < Y, Y > W$$

Conclusion I: $X < Y$ follows

Conclusion II: $Z = W$ does not follow

Hence, option (I) is the answer.

88. (1) Given statement:

$$X = Y, Y > Z, Z \geq W$$

$$\Rightarrow X = Y > Z \geq W$$

Conclusion I: $X > W$ follows

Conclusion II: $Y < W$ does not follow

Hence, option (1) is the answer.

89. (3) Given statement:

$$A < B, B \leq C, C = D$$

$$\Rightarrow A < B \leq C = D$$

Conclusion I: $B = D$ may or may not follow

Conclusion II: $B < D$ may or may not follow

Hence, option (3) is the answer.

90. (5) Given statement

$$A > B, B \geq C, C < D, D \leq E$$

$$\Rightarrow A > B \geq C, C < D \leq E$$

Conclusion I: $A \geq D$ does not follow.

Conclusion II: $B = E$ does not follow.

Hence, option (5) is the answer.

For questions 91 to 95: From the given information the following table deduced as

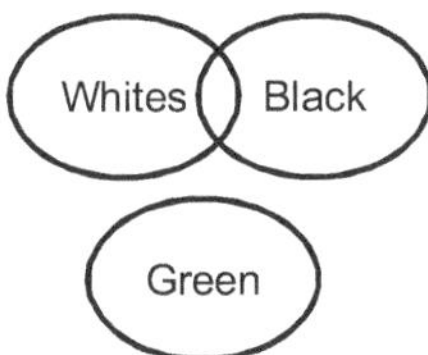

	S	J	L	Q	K	R	↓South
↑North	I	T	O	M	P	N	

96. (2) As we can see from the venn diagram given below, the correct answer is option (2).

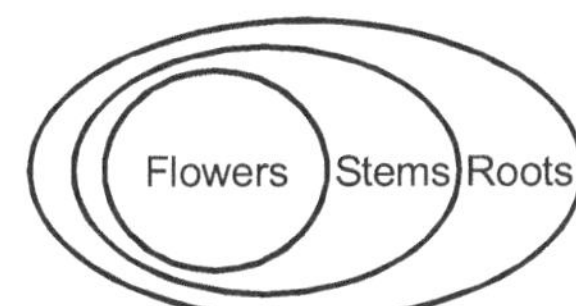

97. (4) As we can see from the venn diagram given below, the correct answer is option (4).

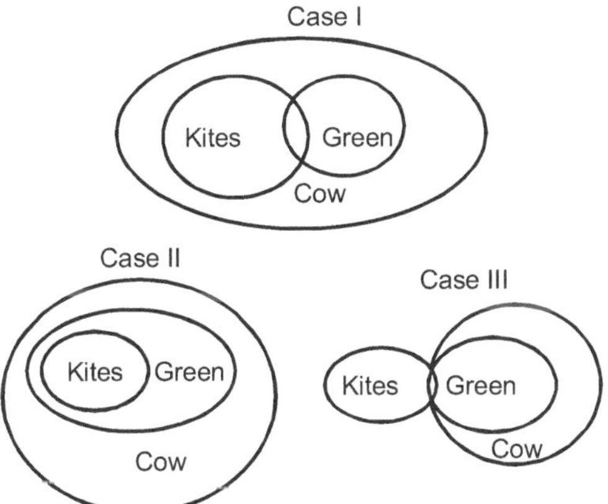

98. (4) As we can see from the venn diagrams given below, the correct answer is option (4).

Case I

Case II

Case III

99. (2) As we can see from the venn diagrams given below, the correct answer is option (2).

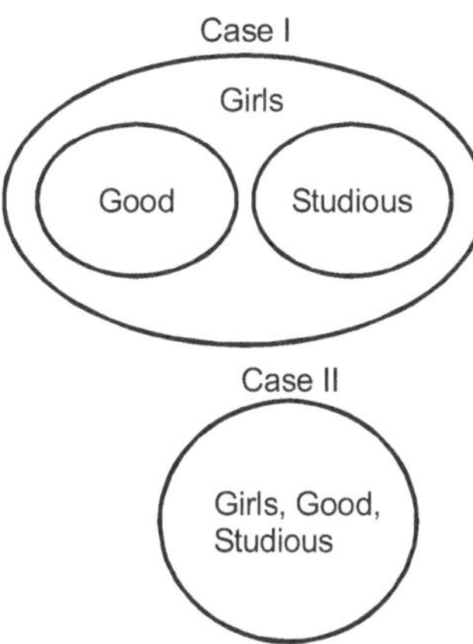

Case I

Case II

100. (4) As we can see from the venn diagram given below, the correct answer is option (4).

PRACTICE PAPER – 10

Directions (Q. 1 to 5): Fill in the blanks by choosing the most appropriate options.

1. It was very difficult to dig as the ground was very __________.

   (1) rigid   (2) soft

   (3) hard   (4) hardly

   (5) strong

2. This was a dangerous method of _________ popular support.

   (1) extracting   (2) expecting

   (3) soliciting   (4) asking

   (5) devising

3. The teller in the bank _________ the money and signed a receipt for it.

   (1) divided   (2) remitted

   (3) credited   (4) saw

   (5) counted

4. Two of the fugitives managed to flee by adeptly avoiding the ____ of the police.

   (1) pursuit   (2) torture

   (3) following   (4) repression

   (5) shadow

5. Diseases are easily _________ through contact with infected animals.

   (1) transmitted   (2) transported

   (3) transacting   (4) transplanted

   (5) transportable

Directions (Q. 6 to 10) Which of the phrases (1), (2), (3) and (4) given below each statement should replace the phrase printed in bold in the sentence to make it grammatically correct? If the sentence is correct as it is given and no correction is required, mark (5) as the answer.

6. One of the **main function of** the State is maintenance of law and order.

   (1) main function for

   (2) main functions of

   (3) main functions for

   (4) main functions off

   (5) No correction required

7. Setbacks and failures **has always been** an integral part of science.

   (1) has always being

   (2) were always been

   (3) has been always

   (4) have always been

   (5) No correction required

8. The sword of Tipu Sultan was recently **brought at an** auction by an Indian for Rs.2 crores.

   (1) brought in a

   (2) brought in an

   (3) bought in an

   (4) bought at a

   (5) No correction required

9. Alcohol in moderate quantity boosts concentration of good cholesterol and **inhibiting blood clots**.

   (1) inhibits blood clots

   (2) inhibit blood clots

   (3) inhibited blood clots

   (4) inhabiting blood clots

   (5) No correction required

10. We must realize that learning from **mistakes is an** important part of life.

    (1) mistakes are an

    (2) mistakes are a

    (3) mistake are a

    (4) mistakes has an

    (5) No correction required

Directions (Q. 11 to 15): In the following passage there are blanks, each of which has been numbered. These numbers are printed below the passage and against each, five words are suggested, oireof which fits the blank appropriately. Find out the appropriate word in each case.

Clement Atlee became the Prime Minister of England after the Second World War. Winston Churchill who had successfully __(11)__ England and the allies to victory over Hitler was now rejected by the English people at the hustings. Labour Party was swept to power and Atlee became the Prime Minister, One of his memorable tasks was that he was __(12)__ in granting India its freedom, Atlee was born in a well-to-do family but he always had __(13)__ for the poor and the downtrodden. He is known for keeping faith and cooperation among his cabinet colleagues. Not that there were no differences of opinion __(14)__ his cabinet members, but Atlee by his gentle nature and positive approach, always managed to keep them together and had control over them. __(15)__ , being sympathetic to the cause of India, granted India freedom. He did many a constructive activity for his country too, like nationalization of some industries, and starting national health scheme.

11. (1) isolated   (2) established
     (3) conquered   (4) marginalized
     (5) led

12. (1) interested   (2) instrumental
     (3) eager   (4) reluctant
     (5) particular

13. (1) concern   (2) reverence
     (3) apathy   (4) jobs
     (5) indifference

14. (1) among   (2) within
     (3) between   (4) from
     (5) with

15. (1) Although   (2) without
     (3) He   (4) beside
     (5) after

Directions (Q. 16 to 20): Rearrange the following six sentences (A), (B), (C), (D), (E) and (F) in the proper sequence to form a meaningful paragraph; then answer the questions given below them.

(A) When this boy was twelve years old he attended a party given by his parents.

(B) A boy was considered a dunce and his usual place in class was standing in a corner as punishment.

(C) The boy timidly quoted the rest of the poem and named the author.

(D) The guest, a famous writer, was delighted and said "You are a bright boy who will achieve a lot one day".

(E) This one word of encouragement changed the boy's life - he went on to become a famous poet.

(F) One of the guests saw two lines of poetry underneath a painting and wanted to know who the poet was, but no one knew.

16. Which of the following should be the **FIFTH** sentence after rearrangement?
     (1) (B)   (2) (C)
     (3) (D)   (4) (E)
     (5) (F)

17. Which of the following should be the **LAST (SIXTH)** sentence after rearrangement?
     (1) (B)   (2) (A)
     (3) (C)   (4) (D)
     (5) (E)

18. Which of the following should be the **FIRST** sentence after rearrangement?
     (1) (A)   (2) (B)
     (3) (C)   (4) (D)
     (5) (E)

19. Which of the following should be the **SECOND** sentence after rearrangement?
     (1) (A)   (2) (B)
     (3) (C)   (4) (D)
     (5) (E)

20. Which of the following should be the **THIRD** sentence after rearrangement?
     (1) (B)   (2) (C)
     (3) (D)   (4) (E)
     (5) (F)

Directions (Q. 21 to 30): Read the given passage carefully and answer the questions that follow.

If I were to give a summary of the tendency of our times, I would say, Quantity. The multitude, the mass spirit, dominates everywhere, destroying quality. Our entire life—production, politics, and education—rests on quantity, on numbers. The worker who once took pride in the thoroughness and quality of his work, has been replaced by brainless, incompetent automatons, who turn out enormous quantities of things, valueless to themselves, and generally injurious to the rest of mankind. Thus quantity, instead of adding to life's comforts and peace, has merely increased man's burden.

In politics, naught but quantity counts. In proportion to its increase, however, principles, ideals, justice, and uprightness are completely swamped by the **array** of numbers. In the struggle for supremacy, the various political parties outdo each other in trickery, deceit, cunning, and shady machinations, confident that the one who succeeds is sure to be hailed by the majority as the victor. That is the only God — Success. As to what expense, what terrible cost to character, is of no moment. We have not far to go in search of proof to verify this sad fact.

Never before did the corruption, the complete rottenness of our government stand so thoroughly exposed; never before were the American people brought face to face with the Judas nature of that political body, which has claimed for years to be absolutely beyond reproach, as the mainstay of our institutions, the true protector of the rights and liberties of the people.

Yet when the crimes of that party became so brazen that even the blind could see them, it needed but to muster up its minions, and its supremacy was assured. Thus the very victims, duped, betrayed, outraged a hundred times, decided, not against, but in favor of the victor. Bewildered, the few asked how could the majority betray the traditions of American liberty? Where was its judgment, its reasoning capacity? That is just it, the majority cannot reason; it has no judgment. Lacking utterly in originality and moral courage, the majority has always placed its destiny in the hands of others. Incapable of standing responsibilities, it has followed its leaders even unto destruction. Dr. Stockman was right: "The most dangerous enemies of truth and justice in our midst are the compact majorities, the damned compact majority." Without ambition or initiative, the compact mass hates nothing so much as innovation. It has always opposed, condemned, and hounded the innovator, the pioneer of a new truth.

The oft repeated slogan of our time is, among all politicians, the Socialists included, that ours is an era of individualism, of the minority. Only those who do not probe beneath the surface might be led to entertain this view. Have not the few accumulated the wealth of the world? Are they not the masters, the absolute kings of the situation? Their success, however, is due not to individualism, but to the inertia, the cravenness, the utter submission of the mass. The latter wants but to be dominated, to be led, to be coerced. As to individualism, at no time in human history did it have less chance of expression, less opportunity to assert itself in a normal, healthy manner.

The individual educator **imbued** with honesty of purpose, the artist or writer of original ideas, the independent scientist or explorer, the non-compromising pioneers of social changes are daily pushed to the wall by men whose learning and creative ability have become decrepit with age.

Educators of Ferrer's type are nowhere tolerated, while the dieticians of predigested food, a la Professors Eliot and Butler, are the successful perpetuators of an age of nonentities, of automatons. In the literary and dramatic world, the Humphrey Wards and Clyde Fitches are the idols of the mass, while but few know or appreciate the beauty and genius of an Emerson, Thoreau, Whitman; an Ibsen, a Hauptmann, a Butler Yeats, or a Stephen Phillips. They are like **solitary** stars, far beyond the horizon of the **multitude**.

Publishers, theatrical managers, and critics ask not for the quality inherent in creative art, but will it meet with a good sale, will it suit the palate of the people? Alas, this palate is like a dumping ground; it relishes anything that needs no mental mastication. As a result, the mediocre, the ordinary, the commonplace represents the chief literary output.

21. Which of the following cannot be inferred from the passage?

(1) There are a few who question the judgment of the masses.

(2) Masses are not the victims of their own choices.

(3) Present times do not give the opportunity to express individualism in a healthy manner.

(4) People do not seek quality that is inherent in the creative arts.

(5) None of the above

22. Why does the author summarize his time as that of 'quantity'?

(1) Quality, generally, is injurious to mankind.

(2) Workers are more concerned with quantity than quality.

(3) Automatons are competent enough to produce high quantity and not high quality products.

(4) Quantity dominates all spheres of life.

(5) None of the above

23. What does the author mean by 'the Judas nature of that political body'?

(1) The present nature of the political body is that of rendering honest service to the public.

(2) The present trait of the political body is to safeguard the traditions of American liberty and maintain their supremacy.

(3) The present nature of the political body is being pretentious in protecting peoples' rights while, actually, working for the party's advancement to supremacy.

(4) The present nature of the political body is openly portrayed as that of a party which is working for its mass supporters.

(5) None of the above

24. The author favours individual educators because

(1) they accept that their creative abilities have diminished with age.

(2) they are honest about publicly accepting their mistakes.

(3) they, unlike politicians, are challenged by their readers or masses.

(4) they are honest.

(5) they do not compromise their ideas for anybody.

25. The author gives examples from the spheres of politics and literature because

(1) he wants to reveal the state of the individual educator of the present time.

(2) he wants to show the importance given to quantity over quality.

(3) he is upset by the lack of appreciation given to writers like Ibsen.

(4) he wants to condemn the corrupt ways of politicians and the lack of concern for authors by publishers and critics.

(5) he knows more about these two

26. According to the author, it can be inferred that:

(1) minorities are afraid to question the authorities in power.

(2) writers like Emerson are not creative enough to write for the masses.

(3) that which does not require reasoning is preferred by the masses.

(4) corruption and deceit are acceptable as long as they are for the benefit of the minority.

(5) All of the above

Directions (Q. 27 to 29): Choose the word which ts most nearly the **SAME** in meaning as the word printed in bold as used in the passage.

27. Multitude

(1) Minority   (2) Zero

(3) Portion   (4) Horde

(5) Single

28. Solitary

(1) Regal   (2) Natural

(3) Forsaken   (4) General

(5) Common

29. Imbued

(1) Deteriorate   (2) Suffuse

(3) Alleviate   (4) Ameliorate

(5) Drain

30. Choose the word which is most **OPPOSITE** in meaning to the word printed in bold as used in the passage.

Array

(1) Multiple

(2) Individual

(3) Pattern

(4) Bundle

(5) Bunch

31. The average speed of a bus is $2\frac{1}{2}$ times the average speed of a tractor. The tractor covers 336 kms in 21 hours. How much distance will the bus cover in 12 hours?

(1) 380 km   (2) 440 km

(3) 360 km   (4) 460 km

(5) None of these

32. A can do a piece of work in 4 hours; B and C can do it in 3 hours. A and C can do it in 2 hours. How long will B alone take to do it?

(1) 10 hours   (2) 12 hours

(3) 8 hours   (4) 24 hours

(5) 15 hours

33. The perimeters of two similar triangles ABC and PQR are 36 cm and 24 cm respectively. If PQ = 10 cm, then AB is equal to:

(1) 12 cm   (2) 16 cm

(3) 15 cm   (4) 10 cm

(5) None of these

34. The midpoints of the sides of a square, of side 4 cm, are joined to form another square. A circle is inscribed in the thus formed square. The ratio of the area of the circle to that of the original square is

(1) $\pi : 8$ (2) $\pi : 4$

(3) $\pi : 16$ (4) $\pi : 6$

(5) None of these

35. The sum of five consecutive odd numbers is equal to 125. What is the sum of the product of the largest and the smallest numbers and the second largest number?

(1) 512   (2) 535

(3) 634   (4) 636

(5) None of these

36. The simple interest accrued in 5 years on a principal of Rs. 24,000 is one-tenth the principal. What is the rate of simple interest p.c.p.a.?

(1) 5   (2) 4

(3) 6   (4) 2

(5) None of these

37. Out of two numbers, 40% of the greater number is equal to 60% of the smaller. If the sum of the numbers is 150, then the greater number is

(1) 70   (2) 80

(3) 90   (4) 60

(5) 50

38. The average of 5 positive integers is 436. The average of first two numbers is 344 and the average of last two numbers is 554. What is the third number?

(1) 482   (2) 346

(3) 556   (4) 384

(5) None of these

39. The ratio between the present ages of Dheeraj and Raman is 2 : 3 respectively. Four years ago, the ratio between their ages was 5 : 8 respectively. What will be Dheeraj's age after 7 years?

(1) 29 years   (2) 35 years

(3) 31 years   (4) 33 years

(5) 41 years

40. The cost price of a radio is Rs. 600. The 5% of the cost price is charged towards transportation. After adding that, if the net profit to be made is 15%, then the selling price of the radio must be

(1) Rs. 704.50

(2) Rs. 724.50

(3) Rs. 664.50

(4) Rs. 684.50

(5) Rs. 790.50

Directions (Q. 41 to 45): Answer the following questions based on the given information.

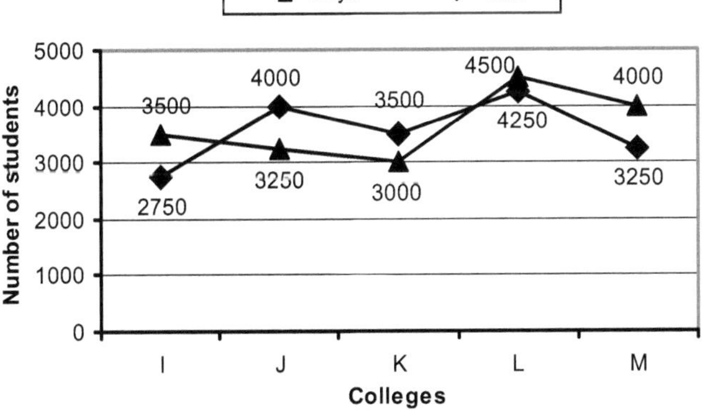

Total number of boys and girls in five different colleges

41. What is the average number of boys from all the colleges together?

(1) 3350   (2) 3450

(3) 3550   (4) 3650

(5) None of these

42. The number of girls from college I is approximately what percent of the total number of girls from all the colleges together?

(1) 21   (2) 17

(3) 23   (4) 19

(5) 15

43. What is the difference between the total number of boys and the total number of girls from all the colleges together?

(1) 500   (2) 650

(3) 725   (4) 800

(5) None of these

44. What is the respective ratio of the number of girls from college K to the number of girls from college M?

(1) 13 : 14   (2) 14 : 13

(3) 7 : 6   (4) 6 : 7

(5) None of these

45. The total number of boys from colleges J and L together is approximately what percent of the total number of boys from colleges I, K and M together?

(1) 135   (2) 65

(3) 128   (4) 97

(5) 74

Direction for questions 46 to 50: Two equations I and II are given in each question. On the basis of these equations you have to decide the relation between p and q and give the answer.

(1) if $p \leq q$

(2) if $p > q$

(3) if $q > p$

(4) if $p = q$

(5) if $p \geq q$

46. I. $p^2 + 13p + 40 = 0$

II. $q^2 + 7q + 12 = 0$

47. I. $p = (-10)^2$

II. $q^2 + q - 9900 = 0$

48. I. $p^2 - 5p + 6 = 0$

II. $q^2 - 3q + 2 = 0$

49. I. $p = 10$

II. $q = \sqrt{100}$

50. I. $p = \pm 100$

II. $q = (10000)^{1/2}$

Directions (Q. 51 to 55): In the following number series, only one number is wrong. Find out the wrong number.

51. 32,   34,   37,   46,   62,   87,   123

(1) 34   (2) 37

(3) 62   (4) 87

(5) 46

52. 7,   18,   40,   106,   183,   282,   403

(1) 18   (2) 282

(3) 40   (4) 106

(5) 183

53. 850,   843,   829,   808,   788,   745,   703

(1) 843   (2) 829

(3) 808   (4) 788

(5) 745

54. 33,   321,   465,   537,   573,   590,   600

(1) 321   (2) 465

(3) 573   (4) 537

(5) 590

55. 37,   47,   52,   67,   87,   112,   142

(1) 47   (2) 52

(3) 67   (4) 87

(5) 112

Directions (Q. 56 to 60): Answer the following questions based on the given information.

The bar graph shows the number of cars (in thousand) sold by three companies over the given period.

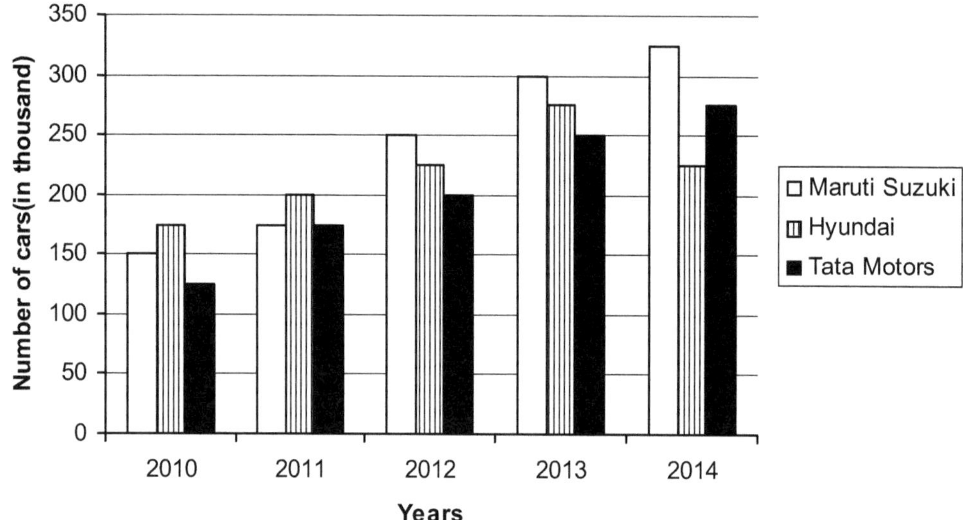

56. What is the percentage increase in the number of cars sold by Hyundai from year 2012 to year 2013?

(1) 20.20%   (2) 1.82%

(3) 22.22%   (4) 12.12%

(5) 32%

57. What is the average number of cars sold by Tata Motors over the given period?

(1) 200000   (2) 105000

(3) 205200   (4) 225000

(5) 205000

58. What is the respective ratio of the total number of cars sold by all the three given companies in the years 2011 and 2013?

(1) 2 : 3   (2) 7 : 11

(3) 11 : 17   (4) 11 : 7

(5) 3 : 2

59. What is the difference between the total number of cars sold by Maruti-Suzuki and the total number of cars sold by Hyundai over the given period?

(1) 75000   (2) 150000

(3) 125000   (4) 10000

(5) None of these

60. The total number of cars sold by all the three given companies in the year 2010 is what percent the total number of cars sold by all the three given companies in the year 2014?

(1) 83.33%   (2) 54.55%

(3) 45.45%   (4) 58.58%

(5) 48.24%

Directions (Q. 61 to 65): Find the value of question mark (?) in the following questions.

61. 2110 ÷ 25 + 350 ÷ 50 = ?

(1) 91.4   (2) 8.688

(3) 86.2   (4) 86.4

(5) None of these

62. 6999 + 3555 − 2333 = ?

(1) 8337   (2) 8444

(3) 7338   (4) 8221

(5) None of these

63. $49 \times 64 = (?)^2$

(1) 54   (2) 56

(3) 52   (4) 63

(5) None of these

64. 6.8 × ? × 7.9 = 161.16

(1) 2　　　　　　　　(2) 7

(3) 5　　　　　　　　(4) 4

(5) 3

65. 16% of 380 × 5 = ?

(1) 276　　　　　　　(2) 284

(3) 304　　　　　　　(4) 312

(5) None of these

REASONING ABILITY

66. Anil and Mohit are facing each other and are separated by some distance. Anil moves 15 km in North-East direction while Mohit moves 15 km in South-West direction. After reaching their respective places the distance between them remains the same as it was at the start. So, what is the distance between them?

(1) 15 km　　　　　　(2) $\dfrac{15}{\sqrt{2}}$ km

(3) $15\sqrt{2}$ km　　　　(4) $20\sqrt{2}$ km

(5) Cannot be determined

67. Joe starts from her house and walks 6 km in the East direction and reaches college. She then walks 6 km in North direction and reaches mall. From here she goes in South-West direction and covers $6\sqrt{2}$ km to reach a place where she had been before. She finally covers 8 km in North direction to reach gymnasium. What is the shortest distance between gymnasium and her college?

(1) 10 km　　　　　　(2) $\dfrac{8}{\sqrt{2}}$ km

(3) $6\sqrt{2}$ km　　　　(4) 6 km

(5) 8 km

Directions (Q. 68 to 70): Answer the questions on the basis of the information given below.

A, B, C, D, J, K, L, M and N are members of a family in which there are 3 generations. Among them 3 are children.

 i. B is J's son in law.

 ii. A has two children who are both married.

 iii. C loves her uncle D who is J's son.

 iv. M is A's grandson and N's cousin.

 v. N does not like his uncle B.

68. How is N related to D?

(1) Father　　　　　　(2) Daughter

(3) Son　　　　　　　(4) Brother

(5) Son or Daughter

69. How is L related to M?

(1) Mother　　　　　　(2) Aunt

(3) Nephew　　　　　(4) Son

(5) Cannot be determined

70. If K is B's wife, then how is L related to J?

(1) Daughter-in-law

(2) Son-in-law

(3) Daughter

(4) Son

(5) Daughter or Daughter-in-law

Directions (Q. 71 to 75): Answer the question on the basis of the information given below.

Five friends, namely Punit, Manav, Saurabh, Ashu and Sahil with their surnames being Sharma, Mahajan, Gemini, Singh and Tiwari (not necessarily in that order), went for shopping. Each friend prefers an apparel of a particular brand. The brands are Colour plus, Pepe, Numero Uno, Levis, and Raymonds (not necessarily in that order). They purchased Jeans, T-shirt, Shirt, Suit and Pant. The amounts spent by each of them is Rs. 300, Rs. 800, Rs. 900, Rs. 1600 and Rs. 2100 (not necessarily in that order).

 i. Mr Singh spent more than Punit and the man who purchased brand Color plus, but less than the man who purchased the brand Numero Uno.

 ii. Saurabh spent thrice as much as the man who purchased the T-shirt.

 iii. The Numero Uno item purchased cost 7 times as much as the Levis item.

 iv. The person who purchased Jeans spent less than the man who buys brand Raymonds but more than the man who bought Color plus brand.

 v. Mr Gemini spent more than man who bought brand Levis and one who bought Shirt but less than Ashu and Mr. Tiwari.

 vi. Suit was the costliest item.

 vii. Person who purchased Pant spent less than Sahil.

 viii. One person is having the name and surname starting with same alphabet.

71. Who purchased Jeans?

(1) Punit　　　　　　(2) Manav

(3) Saurabh　　　　　(4) Ashu

(5) Sahil

72. Suit is from which Brand?

(1) Levis　　　　　　(2) Color plus

(3) Pepe　　　　　　(4) Numero Uno

(5) Raymonds

73. Mr. Sharma purchased
   (1) Shirt   (2) T-shirt
   (3) Jeans   (4) Pant
   (5) Suit

74. How much money spent by Ashu?
   (1) Rs. 300   (2) Rs. 800
   (3) Rs. 900   (4) Rs. 1,600
   (5) Rs. 2,100

75. Gemini is the surname of?
   (1) Punit   (2) Manav
   (3) Saurabh   (4) Ashu
   (5) Sahil

Directions (Q. 76 to 80): Answer the question on the basis of the information given below.

In a certain code "blue fountain pens" is coded as "fa re ub", "designs in pens" is coded as "no me re", "beautiful designs available" is coded as "tu me wi" and "blue drink available" is coded as "ub lo wi".

76. What does the code "ub" stand for?
   (1) blue   (2) fountain
   (3) designs   (4) available
   (5) drink

77. What does "no re" represent?
   (1) designs available
   (2) in pens
   (3) pens blue
   (4) blue fountain
   (5) drink blue

78. What is the code for "beautiful designs"?
   (1) ub wi   (2) lo ub
   (3) re me   (4) ub tu
   (5) tu me

79. How can "water fountain" be coded?
   (1) "fa re"   (2) "re wi"
   (3) "me re"   (4) "fa wa"
   (5) "re li"

80. What is the code for "drink"?
   (1) wi   (2) ub
   (3) lo   (4) li
   (5) Cannot be determined

Directions (Q. 81 to 85): Answer the question on the basis of the information given below.

At a meeting of executives of a company there are ten people sitting in two rows on two sides of a conference table. In each row there is one executive from each of the following departments - Finance, Administration, IT, HR and Marketing.

Akshay, Bhaskar, Chandan, Dhairya and Eshan are sitting in row I and Harsh, Jai, Karan, Laksh and Mohan are sitting in row 2.

   i. Dhairya sits to the right of Chandan and to the left of the Marketing executive.

   ii. Mohan sits at the extreme left end of his row and is not from HR or Finance.

   iii. Chandan, who is not from Finance sits to the right of Eshan, who is from Administration.

   iv. The marketing executive in row 2 sits to the right of Laksh and to the second left of Harsh who is from IT.

   v. Eshan sits opposite to Jai who is not from HR.

   vi. Bhaskar from HR faces Harsh.

81. Which department is Dhairya from?
   (1) Administration   (2) IT
   (3) HR   (4) Marketing
   (5) Finance

82. Who sits third to the right of the one who faces the person on the left of Harsh?
   (1) Akshay   (2) Bhaskar
   (3) Chandan   (4) Dhairya
   (5) Eshan

83. Which pair of person and department is correct?
   (1) Chandan - HR
   (2) Jai - Adminisration
   (3) Mohan - IT
   (4) Dhairya - Finance
   (5) None of these

84. If Eshan and Mohan form a pair and Jai and Dhairya form a pair then selecte a similar pair from the given options.
   (1) Chandan and Karan
   (2) Bhaskar and Jai
   (3) Akshay and Karan
   (4) Harsh and Dhairya
   (5) None of these

85. If the people in row 1 are made to sit in alphabetical order of their names from right to left, then which of the following persons in row 2 will face the same person as in the original seating arrangement?
   (1) Jai
   (2) The person from Marketing
   (3) Laksh
   (4) The IT executive
   (5) Mohan

Directions (Q. 86 to 90): In the following questions, the symbols %, &, @, # and $ are used with the following meaning as illustrated below:

'A%B' means 'A is neither smaller than nor greater than B'.

'A&B' means 'A is not greater than B'.

'A@B' means 'A is not smaller than B'.

'A#B' means 'A is neither greater than nor equal to B'.

'A$B' means 'A is neither smaller than nor equal to B'.

Now in each of the following questions assuming that the given statements to be true, find which of the four conclusions I, II, III and IV given below them is/are definitely true and give your answer accordingly.

86. Statements: Y&C, C@K, K$L, H#L.

Conclusions:

I.   K%Y

II. K$H

III. C%Y

IV. L#C

(1) Only II   (2) Only IV

(3) Both II & III   (4) Both II & IV

(5) All I, II, III & IV

87. Statements: W#V, V%R, R@T, T$S

Conclusions:

I.   V$S

II. W%T

III. V@T

IV. R#W

(1) Only I   (2) Only IV

(3) Both I & II   (4) I, II & III

(5) Both I & III

88. Statements: L@M, M%N, N&P, P#U

Conclusions:

I.   N#L

II. U$M

III. P%M

IV. L%P

(1) Only I   (2) Only II

(3) Only III   (4) Only IV

(5) None of these

89. Statements: D#F, F&G, G%J, K@J

Conclusions:

I.   K$D

II. J%F

III. G&K

IV. D#J

(1) Both I & II   (2) Both III & IV

(3) I, III & IV   (4) I, II & IV

(5) All I, II, III & IV

90. Statements: Z%H, H$K, K@M, M&X

Conclusions:

I.   K#Z

II. H$M

III. X%K

IV. M&K

(1) Both I & II   (2) Both I & IV

(3) Both II & IV   (4) I, II & IV

(5) None of these

Directions (Q. 91 to 95): Answer the question on the basis of the information given below.

Eight women members of a family - Avani, Bhumi, Chavi, Drishti, Gita, Hema, Indu and Jaya - sit around a circular table such that no two ladies sitting next to each other face the same side.

i. Indu sits to the left of her mother-in-law, Jaya who faces the centre and also to the left of her sister-in-law, Gita.

ii. Gita has only two daughters Drishti and Avani who sit on either side of Chavi who is their paternal aunt.

iii. Hema faces Jaya and sits to the left of Avani who is her great grand daughter.

iv. Indu has only one daughter who sits to the left of her aunt Gita.

91. Who is the eldest member sitting at the table?

(1) Jaya   (2) Hema

(3) Gita   (4) Indu

(5) Bhumi

92. If Jaya and Indu form a pair and Chavi and Drishti form a pair then select a similar pair from the given options.

(1) Avani and Bhumi   (2) Indu and Chavi

(3) Gita and Hema   (4) Hema and Avani

(5) None of these

93. Who is sitting second to the left of the one facing Drishti?

(1) Indu   (2) Avani

(3) Bhumi   (4) Hema

(5) Chavi

94. How many generations of women are sitting at the table?

(1) Two   (2) Three

(3) Four   (4) One

(5) None of these

95. If Jaya is related to Chavi in a particular way and Gita is related to Avani then who Indu related to?

    (1) Chavi   (2) Hema

    (3) Jaya   (4) Bhumi

    (5) Gita

Directions (Q. 96 to 100): In each question below, a set of statements and conclusions is given. Accept the given statements to be true, even if they appear to be at variance from commonly known facts. Read all the conclusions and then decide which of the given conclusions logically follows from the statements.

96. Statement I: Some ducks are brown.

    Statement II: All brown are biscuits.

    Conclusions:

    (1) All ducks are biscuits.

    (2) Some ducks are biscuits.

    (3) All biscuits are brown.

    (4) Some ducks are not brown.

    (5) Both (1) and (2)

97. Statement I: Tigers are pandas.

    Statement II: Only lions are pandas.

    Conclusions:

    (1) Some tigers are lions.

    (2) All pandas are tigers.

    (3) All lions are tigers.

    (4) All lions are pandas.

    (5) Some tigers are not lions.

98. Statement I: Some animals are reptiles.

    Statement II: Some reptiles are mammals.

    Conclusions:

    (1) Some mammals are animals.

    (2) No animal is mammal.

    (3) Both (1) and (2)

    (4) None of the above

    (5) Either (1) or (2)

99. Statement I: Some Situ are Simran.

    Statement II: Some Simran are Sita.

    Conclusions:

    (1) Some Situ are Sita.

    (2) All Situ are not Sita.

    (3) Some Sita may be Situ.

    (4) Both (2) and (3)

    (5) None of the above

100. Statement I: Lion is light.

    Statement II: Elephant is light.

    Conclusions:

    (1) Some light is lion.

    (2) Some lion is elephant.

    (3) Both (1) and (2)

    (4) None of the above

    (5) Either (1) or (2)

ANSWERS

1. (3)	**2.** (3)	**3.** (5)	**4.** (1)	**5.** (1)	**6.** (2)	**7.** (4)	**8.** (3)	**9.** (1)	**10.** (5)
11. (5)	**12.** (2)	**13.** (1)	**14.** (1)	**15.** (3)	**16.** (3)	**17.** (5)	**18.** (2)	**19.** (1)	**20.** (5)
21. (2)	**22.** (4)	**23.** (3)	**24.** (5)	**25.** (2)	**26.** (3)	**27.** (4)	**28.** (3)	**29.** (2)	**30.** (2)
31. (5)	**32.** (2)	**33.** (3)	**34.** (1)	**35.** (4)	**36.** (4)	**37.** (3)	**38.** (4)	**39.** (3)	**40.** (2)
41. (4)	**42.** (5)	**43.** (1)	**44.** (2)	**45.** (5)	**46.** (3)	**47.** (2)	**48.** (5)	**49.** (4)	**50.** (1)
51. (1)	**52.** (3)	**53.** (4)	**54.** (5)	**55.** (1)	**56.** (3)	**57.** (5)	**58.** (1)	**59.** (5)	**60.** (2)
61. (1)	**62.** (4)	**63.** (2)	**64.** (5)	**65.** (3)	**66.** (3)	**67.** (1)	**68.** (3)	**69.** (5)	**70.** (1)
71. (3)	**72.** (4)	**73.** (2)	**74.** (4)	**75.** (3)	**76.** (1)	**77.** (2)	**78.** (5)	**79.** (4)	**80.** (3)
81. (5)	**82.** (1)	**83.** (4)	**84.** (3)	**85.** (2)	**86.** (4)	**87.** (5)	**88.** (2)	**89.** (3)	**90.** (4)
91. (2)	**92.** (4)	**93.** (1)	**94.** (3)	**95.** (4)	**96.** (2)	**97.** (1)	**98.** (5)	**99.** (3)	**100.** (1)

EXPLANATIONS

1. (3) A person can be rigid while the ground can be hard.

2. (3) 'To solicit' means *to try to obtain by usually urgent requests or pleas*.

3. (5) Only option (5) logically fits in the sentence as the sentence suggests that the teller has signed a document that confirmed the receipt of a certain amount of money.

4. (1) 'Pursuit' refers to a chase in order to catch someone or something.

5. (1) Spread of diseases can be described as 'transmit' of diseases. Hence, the correct option is 'transmitted'.

6. (2) There are many functions of the State out of which one is maintenance of law and order.

7. (4) 'Setbacks' and 'failures' are two different things and so, the verb should be plural.

8. (3) The correct word should be 'bought'.

9. (1) It is an issue of parallelism. Keeping in mind the usage of 'boost' in the sentence, the other verb should be 'inhibits'.

10. (5) The sentence is grammatically correct.

11. (5) 'Led' is the correct word because Churchill is being referred to as a leader.

12. (2) 'Instrumental' refers to serving as a means of pursuing an aim. Hence, it is the correct word.

13. (1) 'Concern' for the poor makes sense.

14. (1) 'Among' is the correct preposition because more than one member is being referred to in the sentence.

15. (3) 'He' refers to Atlee.

16. (3) The correct sequence should be BAFCDE

21. (2) Option (1) can be inferred by the line, "Bewildered, the few asked….traditions of American liberty?" Option (3) is supported by the last line of the fifth paragraph while option (4) is mentioned in the first line of the last paragraph. The fourth paragraph mentions that the despite the publicly known crimes of the political parties, the masses continue to support them. This suggests that the masses are the victims of their own choices, negating option (2).

22. (4) The author explains in the first paragraph that quantity is predominant in all spheres of life.

23. (3) The third and fourth paragraphs clearly explain that on one hand, parties claim to protect rights and liberties of the people while on the other, they work only to gain their supremacy. Options (1), (2) and (4) are contrary to the passage because the author explains that political parties are interested in neither safeguarding peoples' rights nor working for their mass supporters.

24. (5) Option (1) is incorrect because individual educators are different from those men whose creative abilities have diminished with age. Options (2), (3) and (4) are irrelevant. Option (5) is supported by the sixth paragraph of the passage as it states that they are the "noncompromising pioneers of social change" who are daily pushed to the wall by men whose learning and creative ability has become decrepit with age.

25. (2) Refer to the seventh paragraph. The author has mentioned the spheres of politics and literature in order to give examples for the fact that quality and character are compromised in the present time in order to cater to the masses. This supports option (2). Options (1) and (3), though true, are narrow in scope. Options (4) and (5) are not supported by the passage.

26. (3) Options (1) and (4) cannot be inferred from the passage. Option (2) contradicts the passage as the author states that that writers like Emerson are not appreciated by the masses that prefer predigested food over mental mastication. Option (3) can be inferred from the passage because the last lines of the passage confirm the author's views about mass mentality – 'it relishes anything that needs no mental mastication'.

31. (5) Speed of the tractor = $\dfrac{336}{21}$ = 16 km/hr

Speed of the bus = $\dfrac{5}{2} \times 16$ km/hr

Distance travelled in 12 hours
$$= 40 \times 12 = 480 \text{ km}.$$

32. (2) A's 1 hour's work = $\dfrac{1}{4}$

(B + C)'s 1 hour's work = $\dfrac{1}{3}$

(A + C)'s 1 hour's work = $\dfrac{1}{2}$

∴ C's 1 hour's work

$$= \dfrac{1}{2} - \dfrac{1}{4} = \dfrac{2-1}{4} = \dfrac{1}{4}$$

and B's 1 hour's work

$$\dfrac{1}{3} - \dfrac{1}{4} = \dfrac{4-3}{12} = \dfrac{1}{12}$$

Hence, B alone can do the work in 12 hours.

33. (3) As the two triangles are similar, then the corresponding sides will be in the same proportion.

$$\because \quad \frac{AB}{PQ} = \frac{BC}{QR} = \frac{AC}{PR}$$

Then the perimeter will be given as:

$$\frac{AB + BC + AC}{PQ + QR + PR} = \frac{36}{24} = \frac{AB}{PQ}$$

$$\Rightarrow \frac{36}{24} = \frac{AB}{10}$$

$$\Rightarrow AB = 36 \times \frac{10}{24}$$

$$\Rightarrow AB = 15 \text{ cm}$$

34. (1) The side of the smaller square $= \dfrac{4}{\sqrt{2}} = 2\sqrt{2}$ cm

The radius of the circle $= \dfrac{2\sqrt{2}}{2} = \sqrt{2}$ cm

Hence, the required ratio $= \dfrac{\pi(\sqrt{2})^2}{4^2} = \dfrac{\pi}{8}$.

35. (4) Let the numbers be x, x + 2 , x + 4 , x + 6 and x + 8

x + x + 2 + x + 4 + x + 6 + x + 8 = 125

$\Rightarrow$ x = 21

Required sum = 21 × 29 + 27 = 636.

36. (4) Let R be the rate of interest per annum.

$$\text{Given, } \frac{1}{10} \times 24000 = \frac{24000 \times R \times 5}{100}$$

$\Rightarrow$ R = 2%

37. (3) Let greater number be x.

$\therefore$ Smaller number = 150 – x

According to the question,

$$\frac{40 \times x}{100} = \frac{60(150 - x)}{100}$$

$\Rightarrow \qquad 2x = 3 \times 150 - 3x$

$\Rightarrow \qquad 5x = 3 \times 150$

$\Rightarrow \qquad x = 90.$

38. (4) Third number = 436 × 5 – 344 × 2 – 554 × 2

$\qquad\qquad = 2180 - 688 - 1088 = 384$

39. (3) Let the present ages of Dheeraj and Raman be 2x and 3x years respectively.

$$\text{Given, } \frac{2x - 4}{3x - 4} = \frac{5}{8}$$

$\Rightarrow$ x = 12

Dheeraj's age after 7 years = 2 × 12 + 7 = 31 years.

40. (2) Actual CP of radio

$$= 600 + \frac{600 \times 5}{100} = \text{Rs } 630$$

$\therefore$ Required S.P

$$= \frac{630 \times 115}{100} = \text{Rs } 724.50$$

41. (4) The average number of boys

$$= \frac{3500 + 3250 + 3000 + 4500 + 4000}{5}$$

$$= \frac{18250}{5} = 3650.1$$

42. (5) Number of girls from college I = 2750.

Total number of girls

$$= 2750 + 4000 + 3500 + 4250 + 3250$$

$$= 17750.$$

Required percentage

$$= \frac{2750}{17750} \times 100 \approx 15.49\% \approx 15\%.$$

43. (1) Required difference = 18250 – 17750 = 500.

44. (2) Number of girls from college K = 3500.

Number of girls from college M = 3250.

Required ratio = 3500 : 3250 i.e. 14 : 13.

45. (5) Total number of boys from college J and L

$$= 3250 + 4500 = 7750.$$

Total number of boys from college I, K and M

$$= 3500 + 3000 + 4000 = 10500.$$

Required percentage

$$= \frac{7750}{10500} \times 100 \approx 73.8\% \approx 74\%.$$

46. (3) I. $p^2 + 13p + 40 = 0$

$\Rightarrow$ (p + 5) (p + 8) = 0

$\Rightarrow$ p = –5 or p = –8

II. $q^2 + 7q + 12 = 0$

$\Rightarrow$ (q + 3) (q + 4) = 0

$\Rightarrow$ q = –3 or q = –4

$\therefore$ q > p.

47. (2) I. $p = (-10)^2$

$\Rightarrow$ p = 100

II. $q^2 + q - 9900 = 0$

$\Rightarrow$ (q + 100) (q – 99) = 0

$\Rightarrow$ q = –100 or q = 99

$\therefore$ p > q.

48. (5) I. $p^2 - 5p + 6 = 0$

$\Rightarrow$ (p – 2) (p – 3) = 0

$\Rightarrow$ p = 2 or p = 3

II. $q^2 - 3q + 2 = 0$

$\Rightarrow$ $(q - 2)(q - 1) = 0$

$\Rightarrow$ $q = 2$ or $q = 1$

$\therefore$ $p \geq q$.

49. (4) I. $p = 10$

II. $q = \sqrt{100} = 10$

$\Rightarrow$ $p = q$.

50. (1) I. $p = \pm 100$

II. $q = (10000)^{\frac{1}{2}} = 100$

$\therefore$ $p \leq q$.

51. (1) The series is as follows:

$32 + 1^2 = 33$

$33 + 2^2 = 37$

$37 + 3^2 = 46$

$46 + 4^2 = 62$

$62 + 5^2 = 87$

$87 + 6^2 = 123$

$\therefore$ 34 is the wrong number and will be replaced by 33.

52. (3) The series is as follows:

$7 + 11 \times 1 = 18$

$18 + 11 \times 3 = 51$

$51 + 11 \times 5 = 106$

$106 + 11 \times 7 = 183$

$183 + 11 \times 9 = 282$

$282 + 11 \times 11 = 403$

$\therefore$ 40 is the wrong number and will be replaced by 51.

53. (4) The series is as follows:

$850 - 7 = 843$

$843 - 14 = 829$

$829 - 21 = 808$

$808 - 28 = 780$

$788 - 35 = 745$

$745 - 42 = 703$

$\therefore$ 788 is the wrong number and will be replaced by 780.

54. (5) The series is as follows:

$33 + 288 = 321$

$321 + 144 = 465$

$465 + 72 = 537$

$537 + 36 = 573$

$573 + 18 = 591$

$591 + 9 = 600$

$\therefore$ 590 is the wrong number and will be replaced by 591.

55. (1) The series is as follows:

$37 + 5 = 42$

$42 + 10 = 52$

$52 + 15 = 67$

$67 + 20 = 87$

$87 + 25 = 112$

$112 + 30 = 142$

$\therefore$ 47 is the wrong number and will be replaced by 42.

56. (3) Number of cars sold by Hyundai in the year 2012 = 225000.

Number of cars sold by Hyundai in the year 2013 = 275000.

Percentage increase

$= \dfrac{275000 - 225000}{225000} \times 100 \approx 22.22\%$.

57. (5) The average number of cars sold by Tata Motors over the given period

$= \dfrac{(125 + 175 + 200 + 250 + 275) \times 1000}{5}$

$= \dfrac{1025000}{5} = 205000$.

58. (1) Total number of cars sold in the year 2011

$= (175 + 200 + 175) \times 1000$

$= 550000$.

Total number of cars sold in the year 2013

$= (300 + 275 + 250) \times 1000$

$= 825000$.

Required ratio = 550000 : 825000 i.e. 2 : 3.

59. (5) Total number of cars sold by Maruti-Suzuki

$= (150 + 175 + 250 + 300 + 325) \times 1000$

$= 1200000$.

Total number of cars sold by Hyundai

$= (175 + 200 + 225 + 275 + 225) \times 1000$

$= 1100000$.

Required difference = 1200000 − 1100000

$= 100000$.

60. (2) Total number of cars sold in the year 2010

$= (150 + 175 + 125) \times 1000$

$= 450000$.

Total number of cars sold in the year 2014

$= (325 + 225 + 275) \times 1000$

$= 825000$.

Percentage value

$$= \frac{450000}{825000} \times 100 \approx 54.55\%.$$

61. (1)　　　$? = 2110 \div 25 + 350 \div 50$

　　　　　　　$= 84.4 + 7$

　　　　　　　$= 91.4$

62. (4)　　　$? = 6999 + 3555 - 2333$

　　　　　　　$= 8221$

63. (2)　　　$(?)^2 = 49 \times 64$

　　　　　　　$? = 7 \times 8 = 56$

64. (5)　　　$? = \dfrac{161.16}{6.8 \times 7.9} = 3$

65. (3)　　　$? = \dfrac{16}{100} \times 380 \times 5 = 304$

66. (3)

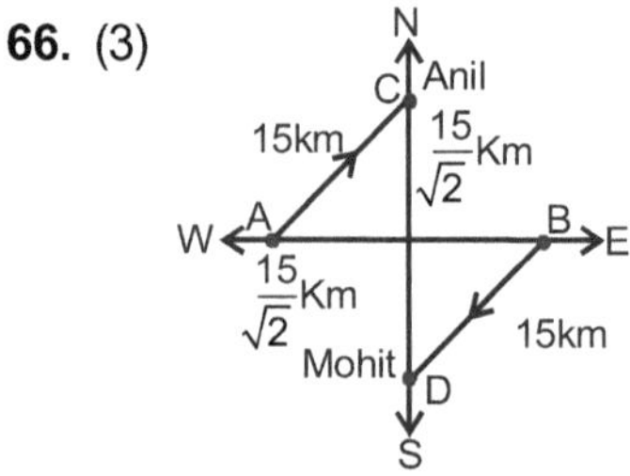

Distance between Anil and Mohit

$$= \frac{15}{\sqrt{2}} + \frac{15}{\sqrt{2}} = 15\sqrt{2} \text{ km}$$

67. (1)

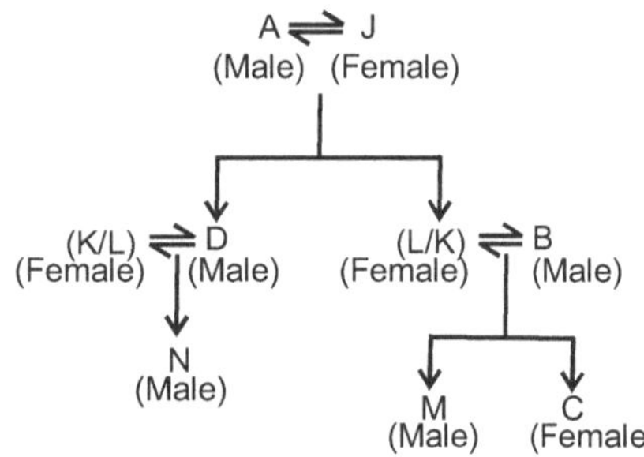

Distance between gymnasium and her college

$$= \sqrt{8^2 + 6^2} = 10 \text{ km}$$

For questions 68 to 70:

$$A \rightleftharpoons J$$
$$\text{(Male)} \quad \text{(Female)}$$

```
                    A ⇌ J
                 (Male) (Female)
                       |
           ┌───────────┴───────────┐
           ↓                       ↓
  (K/L) ⇌ D              (L/K) ⇌ B
 (Female) (Male)        (Female) (Male)
           ↓                       |
           N              ┌────────┴────────┐
        (Male)            M                 C
                        (Male)          (Female)
```

For questions 71 to 75: All the information given in the question can be tabulated as:

Rs. 300	Rs. 800	Rs. 900	Rs. 1600	Rs. 2100
Punit	Manav	Saurabh	Ashu	Sahil
Sharma	Mahajan	Gemini	Singh	Tiwari
T-shirt	Shirt	Jeans	Pant	Suit
Levis	Color plus	Pepe	Raymonds	Numerouno

For questions 76 to 80: All the information given in the question can be tabulated as:

blue	ub
fountain	fa
pens	re
designs	me
in	no
beautiful	tu
available	wi
drink	lo

For questions 81 to 85: All the information given in the question can be tabulated as:

Akshay	Dhairya	Chandan	Eshan	Bhaskar
Marketing	Finance	IT	Administration	HR
Mohan	Laksh	Karan	Jai	Harsh
Administration	HR	Marketing	Finance	IT

86. (4) Y&C, C@K, K\$L, H#L

　　　$\Rightarrow$ Y $\leq$ C, C $\geq$ K, K > L, H < L

　　　$\Rightarrow$ C $\geq$ K > L > H; C $\geq$ Y.

　　　Conclusions:

　　　I.　K%Y $\Rightarrow$ K = Y is not true.

　　　II.　K\$H $\Rightarrow$ K > H is true.

　　　III.　C%Y $\Rightarrow$ C = Y may or may not be true.

　　　IV.　L#C $\Rightarrow$ L < C is true.

　　　Hence, statements II and IV are true.

87. (5) W#V, V%R, R@T, T\$S

　　　$\Rightarrow$ W < V, V = R, R $\geq$ T, T > S

　　　$\Rightarrow$ R = V > W; V = R $\geq$ T > S.

　　　Conclusions:

　　　I.　V\$S $\Rightarrow$ V > S is true.

　　　II.　W%T $\Rightarrow$ W = T is not true.

　　　III.　V@T $\Rightarrow$ V $\geq$ T is true.

　　　IV.　R#W $\Rightarrow$ R < W is not true.

　　　Hence, statements I and III are true.

88. (2) L@M, M%N, N&P, P#U

　　　$\Rightarrow$ L $\geq$ M, M = N, N $\leq$ P, P < U

　　　$\Rightarrow$ L $\geq$ M = N; U > P $\geq$ N = M.

　　　Conclusions:

　　　I.　N#L $\Rightarrow$ N < L may or may not be true.

　　　II.　U\$M $\Rightarrow$ U > M is true.

　　　III.　P%M $\Rightarrow$ P = M may or may not be true.

　　　IV.　L%P $\Rightarrow$ L = P is not true.

　　　Hence, only statement II is true.

89. (3) D#F, F&G, G%J, K@J

　　　$\Rightarrow$ D < F, F $\leq$ G, G = J, K $\geq$ J

　　　$\Rightarrow$ K $\geq$ J = G $\geq$ F > D.

Conclusions:

I.   K$D $\Rightarrow$ K > D is true.

II. J%F $\Rightarrow$ J = F may or may not be true.

III. G&K $\Rightarrow$ G $\leq$ K is true.

IV. D#J $\Rightarrow$ D < J is true.

Hence, statements I, III and IV are true.

90. (4) Z%H, H$K, K@M, M&X

$\Rightarrow$ Z = H, H > K, K $\geq$ M, M $\leq$ X

$\Rightarrow$ Z = H > K $\geq$ M; X $\geq$ M.

Conclusions:

I.   K#Z $\Rightarrow$ K < Z is true.

II. H$M $\Rightarrow$ H > M is true.

III. X%K $\Rightarrow$ X = K is not true.

IV. M&K $\Rightarrow$ M $\leq$ K is true.

Hence, statements I, II and IV are true.

For questions 91 to 95: All the information given in the question can be tabulated as:

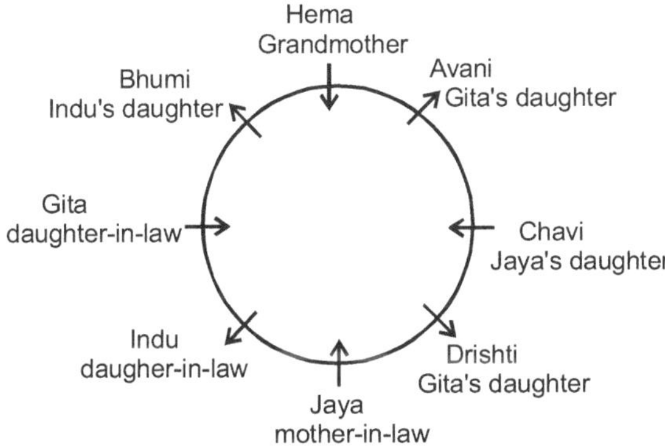

96. (2)
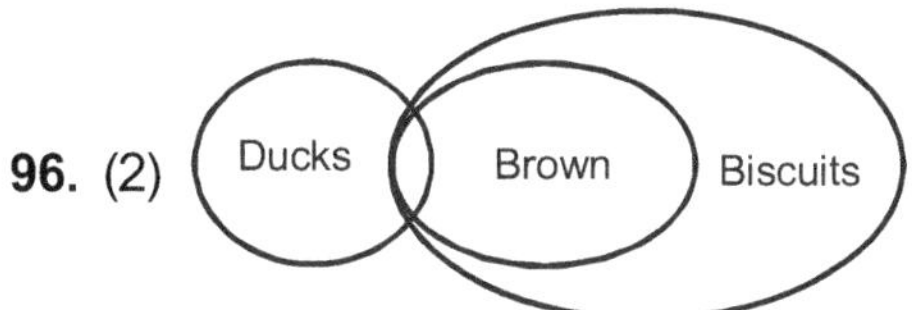

97. (1)
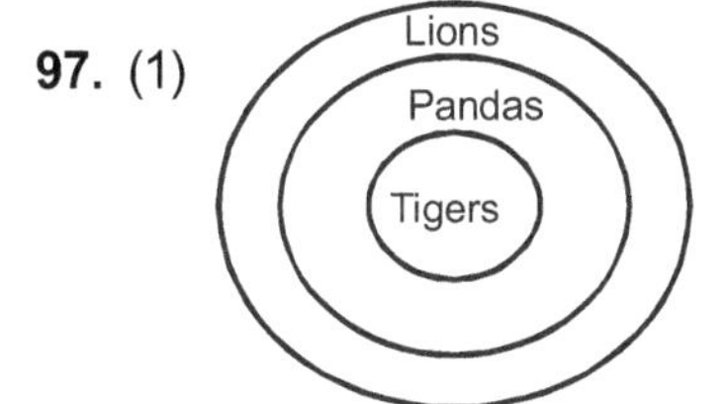

98. (5)
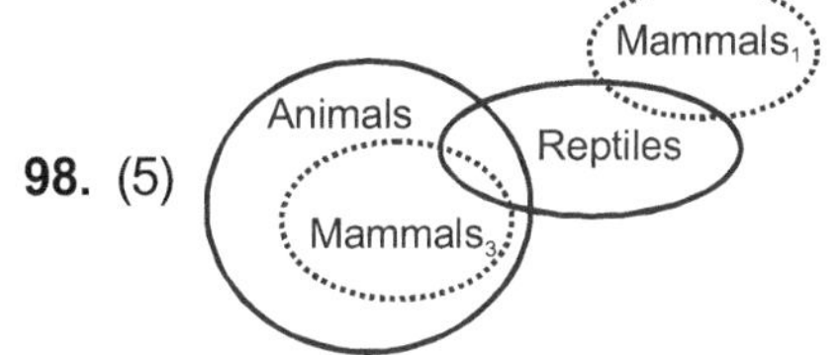

99. (3)
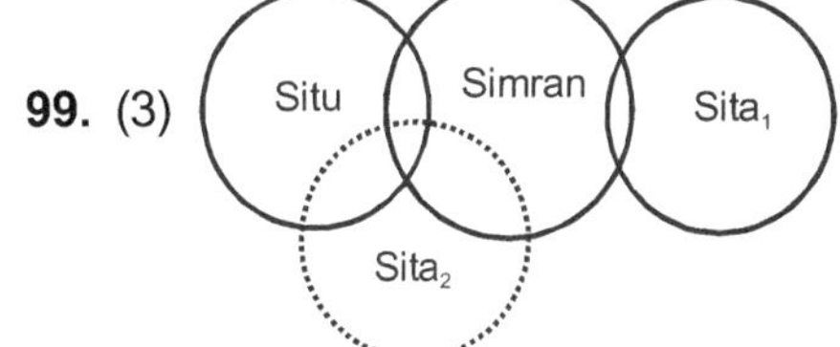

100. (1)
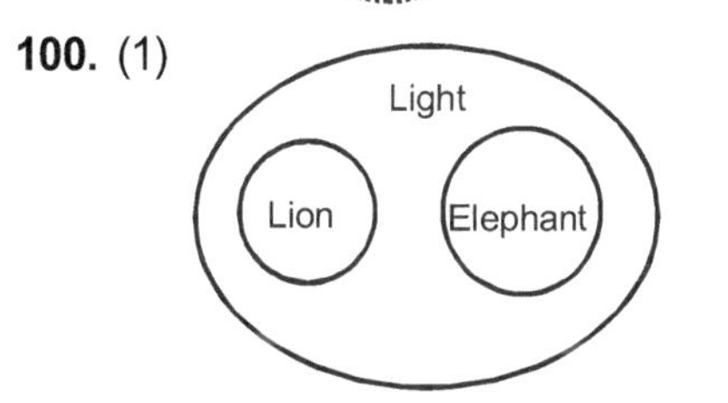

ENGLISH LANGUAGE

Directions (Q. 1 to 10) : Read the following passage carefully and answer the questions given below it. Certain words/phrases have been printed in **bold** to help you locate them while answering some of the questions.

In India, innovation is emerging as one of the most important rubrics in the discourse on how to bring about greater and more consistent economic and social development. One observes steadily growing investments in R & D across the country, the setting up of national and state innovation bodies, as well as the introduction of government sponsored innovation funds. There have also been several conferences and debates on innovation and how to best promote and accomplish it in India, and a number of articles on the subject, written for newspapers and magazines, as well as more informal platforms like online forums and blogs.

Academic engagement and Indian authorship on the subject have also exploded in the last five years. Despite widespread agreement on the importance of innovation in India, there are wide gulfs between different conceptions of innovation and the path India should take towards securing benefits through investments in innovation.

Many Indian conversations around innovation begin by talking about jugaad, that uniquely Indian approach to a temporary fix when something complex, like an automobile or a steam engine stops working. However, many observers have pointed out that while jugaad is certainly innovative, it is a response to the **lack** of an innovation culture-more a survival or coping mechanism at a time of need than a systematic methodology to effectively address a wide-ranging, complex set of problems.

Another specifically Indian approach to innovation that has entered into wide **currency** of late is so called 'frugal innovation,' deemed by many to be the most appropriate for the Indian context. In its midterm assessment of the 11 th five-year plan, the Planning Commission stressed the need for innovation in India in order to accelerate its growth and to make growth more inclusive as well as environmentally sustainable. The document went on to say that 'India needs more frugal innovation that produces more frugal cost products and services that are affordable by people at low levels of incomes without **compromising** the safety, efficiency. and utility of the products. The country also needs processes of innovation that are frugal in the resources required to produce the

innovations. The products and processes must also have **frugal impact on the earth's resources**.

Two people formulated a similar theory called the More-from-Less-for-More (MLM theory of Innovation) theory of Innovation which advocates a focus on innovations that allow for more production using fewer resources but benefit more people. Under this rubric come products that are more affordable versions of existing technologies. While both frugal innovation and the MLM theory are certainly valuable in terms of bringing affordable products and services to a greater number of people, and may even be considered a necessary first step on India's innovation path, they barely graze the surface of what innovation can accomplish. That is, innovation is capable of bringing about complete paradigm-shifts and redefining the way we perceive and interact with the world.

Take the cell phone, for example : it revolutionized communication in a previously **inconceivable** way. provided consumers with a product of unprecedented value and created an entirely new market. The cell phone was a result of years of directed, intentional innovation efforts and large investments, and would not have ever been created if the people responsible simply set out to make the existing telephone cheaper and more accessible to all.

While jugaad and frugal innovation may be **indicative** of the Indian potential for innovativeness, this potential is not utilised or given opportunity to flourish due to the lack of an enabling culture.

India's many diverse and complex needs can be met only through systematic innovation, and major shifts have to first take place-in our educational institutions, government policies and commercial firms in order for such an innovation-enabling culture to come about.

The one thing that India's innovation theorists have not said is that the absence of a culture of innovation is **intrinsically** linked to many of the most intractable problems facing India as a nation. These include poor delivery of government services, inadequate systems of personal identification and the absence of widely available financial services for rural poor, health and sanitation failures. This list can go on. Cumulatively, the inability of India as a nation, society and economy to adequately provide for its own population no longer reflects a failure of implementation, but rather of a failure of innovation, for there are not immediately-available off- the-shelf solutions that would make it possible for these grand challenges facing India to be **redressed.** Rather, we need to look at these intractable problems from the more sophisticated and empowering lens of innovation, for them to begin to be solved.

1. Which of the following depict/s the growing importance of innovation in India?

A. Increased investment in research.

B. Initiation of Government backed funds for innovation

C. Increase in the number of conferences arranged and articles written on innovation.

(1) Only (B)　　　　(2) Only (A) and (B)

(3) Only (C)　　　　(4) Only (B) and (C)

(5) All (A), (B) and (C)

2. Which of the following is possibly the most appropriate title for the passage?

(1) Innovation At Its Best

(2) India And The Elixir Called Innovation

(3) Innovation Around The World vis-a-vis India And Other Neighbouring Countries

(4) Worldwide Developments In Innovation

(5) Innovation - The History

3. Why, according to the author, is India unable to adequately provide for its people?

(1) Failure to implement schemes and initiatives meant for the Indian populace.

(2) Absence of regulatory authorities to oversee the implementation process.

(3) Failure to innovate in order to find solutions.

(4) Lack of governmental schemes and initiatives to redress the challenges faced by India.

(5) Hesitance of the Indian people in trying out different schemes provided by the Government for upliftment.

4. Which of the following is/are true about the cell phone?

A. The innovation of the cell phone required investment of huge capital.

B. The cell phone, when invented was meant to be affordable to all.

C. The cell phone was made available to the public in a very short time from its ideation.

(1) Only (A)

(2) Only (A) and (B)

(3) Only (B) and (C)

(4) Only (B)

(5) All (A), (B) and (C)

5. What does the author mean by 'frugal impact on the earth's resources' as given in the passage?

(1) The damage to the environment should be assessable.

(2) There should be more consumption of natural resources as compared to manmade ones.

(3) There should be minimum impact on the environment in terms of pollution.

(4) The impact on the environment should be such that it is reversible.

(5) Minimum usage of earth's natural resources should be done.

Directions (Q. 6 to 8) : Choose the word/group of words which is most similar in meaning to the word/ group of words given in **bold** as used in the passage.

6. REDRESSED

(1) Cure　　　　　　(2) Equalised

(3) Restored　　　　(4) Redone

(5) Rearranged

7. INTRINSICALLY

(1) Entirely　　　　(2) Whole-heartedly

(3) Essentially　　　(4) Virtually

(5) Unavoidably

8. COMPROMISING

(1) Cooperating with

(2) Reducing the quality

(3) Hampering the progress

(4) Conciliating in order to

(5) Adjusting for the better

Directions (Q. 9 to 10): Choose the word/group of words which is most opposite in meaning to the word/group of words given in bold as used in the passage.

9. LACK

(1) Presence　　　　(2) Sufficient

(3) Charisma　　　　(4) Adequacy

(5) Dearth

10. INCONCEIVABLE

(1) Visible　　　　　(2) Truthful

(3) Incredible　　　(4) Apparent

(5) Complex

Directions (Q. 11 to 15): Which of the phrases (1), (2), (3) and (4) given below each sentence should replace the word/phrase given in bold in the sentence to make it grammatically correct? If the sentence is correct as it is given and no correction is required, mark (5) as the answer.

11. The poor Brahmin led a **hand to mouthful existence** and could use any job which paid him a little.

    (1) handful to mouthful existence

    (2) hand to mouth existence

    (3) handing for mouthful existing

    (4) hand and mouth exist

    (5) No correction required

12. In order to **earning decent living** we need to have a good job which pays a substantial amount of money.

    (1) earned decency life

    (2) earning decency live

    (3) earn a decent living

    (4) earned decently life

    (5) No correction required

13. We went to the famous restaurant to eat and were **served piped hot** food.

    (1) served piping hotter

    (2) serving pipe hot

    (3) served piping hot

    (4) serve pipe hot ten

    (5) No correction required

14. Akshay considered Suresh a complete **pain in the neck** as he kept asking baseless questions.

    (1) paining in the neck

    (2) painless neck

    (3) painful necks

    (4) pain in necking

    (5) No correction required

15. I **jump through hoop** to finish this project in time but was not rewarded adequately.

    (1) jumped through hoops

    (2) jumping for hooping

    (3) jumped on hoop

    (4) jumping from hoop

    (5) No correction required

Directions (Q. 16 to 20): Rearrange the following six sentences (A), (B), (C), (D), (E) and (F) in the proper sequence to form a meaningful paragraph; then answer the questions given below them

(A) However if this happens it will cause problems for the elderly who mainly use cheques.

(B) The use of cheques has fallen dramatically in the past few years.

(C) Thus cheques may be phased out gradually making sure that the needs of all consumers including the elderly are met.

(D) This is because more and more consumers are transferring money electronically by direct debit or credit cards.

(E) Without cheques they are likely to keep large amounts of cash in their homes making them vulnerable to theft.

(F) British banks have thus voted to phase cheques out in favour of these more modern payment methods.

16. Which of the following should be the **last (sixth)** sentence after rearrangement ?

    (1) B   (2) C

    (3) D   (4) E

    (5) F

17. Which of the following should be the **third** sentence after rearrangement ?

    (1) B   (2) C

    (3) D   (4) E

    (5) A

18. Which of the following should be the **fifth** sentence after rearrangement ?

    (1) A   (2) B

    (3) C   (4) D

    (5) E

19. Which of the following should be the **first** sentence after rearrangement ?

    (1) B   (2) C

    (3) D   (4) E

    (5) F

20. Which of the following should be the **second** sentence after rearrangement ?

    (1) A   (2) B

    (3) C   (4) D

    (5) F

Directions (Q. 21 to 25): Read each sentence to find out whether there is any grammatical error in it. The error, if any, will be in one part of the sentence. The number of that part is the answer. If there is no error, the answer is (5), i.e. 'No Error' (Ignore the error of punctuation, if any).

21. People who intend (1) / to visit the tourist spots (2) / are always thrilling (3) / to see the scenario here.(4) / No error (5)

22. In such delicate matters, (1) / we often go with (2) / his advice as he has (3) / been handling such cases effectively.(4) / No error (5)

23. You should think that (1) / of all the possibilities (2) / before you take (3) / any decision. (4) No error (5)

24. He was too tired that (1) / he could not cross (2) / the street even with (3) / the help of a porter. (4) / No error (5)

25. Whenever a man attain fame, (1) / his personal qualities are (2) / imitated by others who (3) / are close to him.(4) / No error (5)

Directions (Q. 26 to 30): In the following passage there are blanks, each of which has been numbered. These numbers are given below the passage and against each, five words are suggested, one of which fits the blank appropriately. Find out the appropriate word in each case.

Initially, the Grameen Bank did not __(26)__ to get involved with the education of its borrowers. But as time went by, they began to feel the need for it. Most of the borrowers had no formal education __(27)__ the ability to read and write. The borrowers had difficulty in expanding their business. They wanted to be able to keep accounts, read __(28)__ about business, health, new ways of farming etc. They sent their children to school and their children in turn helped their parents to keep accounts, read instructions and __(29)__ else needed to be read.

But this is not enough for the future. So the bank has set out to make sure that their borrowers __(30)__ a hundred per cent literacy rate within five years.

26. (1) meant   (2) deserve
      (3) plan   (4) intent
      (5) realise

27. (1) except   (2) having
      (3) besides   (4) unless
      (5) without

28. (1) knowledge   (2) awareness
      (3) information   (4) fact
      (5) circular

29. (1) above   (2) nothing
      (3) any   (4) whatever
      (5) something

30. (1) acquire   (2) qualify
      (3) collect   (4) reaching
      (5) fulfilling

NUMERICAL ABILITY

Directions (Q. 31 to 35): What should come in place of the question mark (?) in the following questions?

31. 460 × 15 – 5 × 20 = ?
      (1) 9200   (2) 4600
      (3) 13780   (4) 7000
      (5) None of these

32. 5163 – 4018 + 3209 = ?
      (1) 4174   (2) 4264
      (3) 4804   (4) 4354
      (5) None of these

33. 4848 ÷ 24 × 11 – 222 = ?
      (1) 200   (2) 2444
      (3) 2000   (4) 115
      (5) None of these

34. 475 + 64% of 950 = 900 + ?
      (1) 183   (2) 233
      (3) 1983   (4) 1863
      (5) None of these

35. $(0.064) \times (0.4)^7 = (0.4)^? \times (0.0256)^2$
      (1) 17   (2) 2
      (3) 18   (4) 3
      (5) None of these

Directions (Q. 36 to 40): In the following graph the number of laptops manufactured by six different companies in the years 2015 and 2016 has been given. Read the graph carefully and answer the questions.

Number of laptops (in thousands) manufactured by 6 different companies

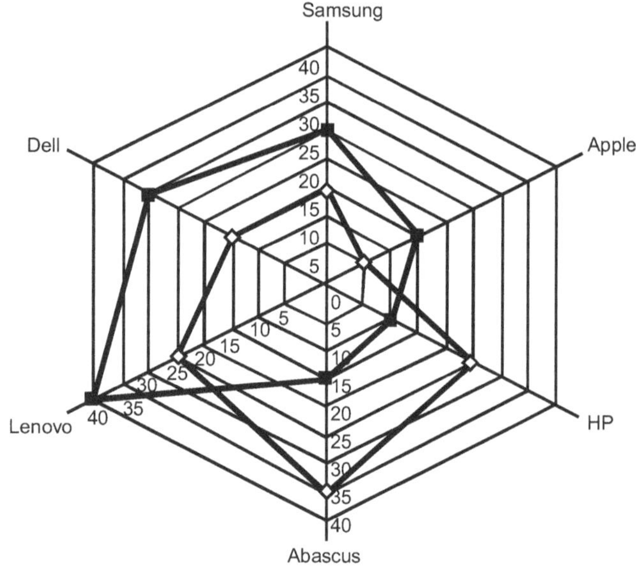

36. The respective ratio between the number of laptops manufactured by Lenovo in 2015 and that by Abascus in 2016 is
      (1) 8 : 7   (2) 7 : 8
      (3) 3 : 5   (4) 5 : 3
      (5) None of these

37. What is the average number of laptops (in thousands) manufactured by all companies taken together in 2015 ?
      (1) 22   (2) 22.5
      (3) 32.5   (4) 23.5
      (5) 27.5

38. What is the percentage increase in production of laptops by HP in 2016 in comparison to that in 2015 ?

(1) 125   (2) 100

(3) 150   (4) 250

(5) None of these

39. The difference between the number of laptops manufactured by Apple, Lenovo and Samsung in 2015 and that by Dell, HP and Abascus in 2016 is

(1) 5500   (2) 4550

(3) 3550   (4) 4500

(5) 5000

40. In 2016, which company manufactured the maximum number of laptops ?

(1) Abacus   (2) Lenovo

(3) Dell   (4) Samsung

(5) HP

41. The number of boys in a class of 48 students is 18. The students are to be seated in rows such that the number of students in all the rows is equal. If none of the rows contain both boys and girls, then what is the maximum number of students sitting in one row?

(1) 4   (2) 6

(3) 9   (4) 8

(5) Cannot be determined

42. Amit's salary increased at the rate of 12%, 14% and 16% for three consecutive years. If his final salary after three consecutive increases is Rs. 2,457, then what was his initial salary (in Rs.) approximately?

(1) 1659   (2) 1720

(3) 1432   (4) 1960

(4) None of these

43. By selling 10 marbles for a rupee, a shopkeeper loses 20%. In order to gain 60% in the transaction, at what rate should he sell the marbles for a rupee?

(1) 2   (2) 6

(3) 4   (4) 3

(5) 5

44. A shopkeeper makes 20% profit on selling a Pizza. Had there been a hike of Rs. 10 in the cost price, he would have made a profit of 10%. If the selling price remains constant, at what price does he sell a Pizza?

(1) Rs. 132   (2) Rs. 110

(3) Rs. 100   (4) Rs. 120

(5) Rs. 142

45. If a sum of money, when compounded annually, becomes three times in 4 years, then in how many years will the sum become 81 times?

(1) 8 years   (2) 16 years

(3) 12 years   (4) 24 years

(5) 20 years

46. The weights of three heaps of sand are in the ratio of 6 : 7 : 8. By what fraction of themselves should the respective weights of the first two heaps be increased such that the new ratio becomes 7 : 8 : 9?

(1) $\dfrac{1}{63}, \dfrac{1}{27}$ (2) $\dfrac{1}{36}, \dfrac{1}{72}$

(3) $\dfrac{1}{27}, \dfrac{1}{63}$ (4) $\dfrac{1}{72}, \dfrac{1}{36}$

(5) None of these

47. How much amount of pure milk must be added to a 20% milk-water solution to make 32 litres of 45% milk-water solution?

(1) 5 litres   (2) 10 litres

(3) 16 litres   (4) 11 litres

(5) 12 litres

48. An amount of Rs.3,000 is to be divided among P, Q, R and T such that the ratio of share of Q to that of R is 1 : 2, the share of P to that of T is 2 : 1. If the share of P was Rs.1,100 more than that of Q, then what was the difference between the share of T and the share of R?

(1) Rs. 100   (2) Rs. 200

(3) Rs. 300   (4) Rs. 400

(5) Rs. 500

49. The average age of a family of 6 members is 22 years. If the age of the youngest member is 7 years, then find the average age of the family, one day before the birth of the youngest member.

(1) 15 years   (2) 19 years

(3) 16 years   (4) 17 years

(5) 18 years

50. Three years ago, the average age of a man, his wife and his son was 27 years. If five years ago, the average age of his wife and his son was 20 years, then how old the man is at present?

(1) 40 years

(2) 41 years

(3) 42 years

(4) 43 years

(5) 50 years

Directions (Q. 51 to 55): In each of these questions, two equations I and II with variables a and b are given. You have to solve both the equations to find the values of a and b.

Mark answer:

(1) If a < b

(2) If a > b

(3) If a $\leq$ b

(4) If a $\geq$ b

(5) If a = b or relationship between a and b cannot be established.

51. I. $35a^2 - 46a + 15 = 0$

II. $14b^2 - 17b + 5 = 0$

52. I. $4a^2 - 8a + 3 = 0$

II. $3b^2 - 14b + 15 = 0$

53. I. $a^2 - 4a - 221 = 0$

II. $b^2 + 2b - 195 = 0$

54. I. $a^2 + 24a + 143 = 0$

II. $b^2 + 29b + 210 = 0$

55. I. $a^2 - 3\sqrt{3}a + 6 = 0$

II. $b^2 - 2 = 0$

Directions (Q. 56 to 58): In each question below, a number series is given in which one number is wrong. Find out the wrong number.

56. 6, 7, 16, 41, 90, 154, 292

(1) 7

(2) 16

(3) 41

(4) 90

(5) 154

57. 5, 7, 16, 57, 244, 1245, 7506

(1) 7

(2) 16

(3) 57

(4) 244

(5) 1245

58. 4 , 2.5, 3.5, 6.5, 15.5, 41.25, 126.75

(1) 2.5

(2) 3.5

(3) 6.5

(4) 15.5

(5) 41.25

Directions (Q. 59 and 60): In each question below, a number series is given in which one number is missing. Find the missing number.

59. 124 228 436 ? 1684 3348

(1) 844

(2) 851

(3) 872

(4) 834

(5) 852

60. 1108 1117 1142 1191 ? 1481

(1) 1204

(2) 1300

(3) 1272

(4) 1312

(5) None of these

Directions (Q. 61 to 65): Study the given table carefully to answer the questions that follow.

Number of people staying in five different localities and the percentage break-up of men, women and children in them

Locality	Total No. of People	Percentage		
		Men	Women	Children
F	5640	55	35	10
G	4850	34	44	22
H	5200	48	39	13
I	6020	65	25	10
J	4900	42	41	17

61. Total number of people staying in locality J forms approximately what percent of the total number of people staying in locality F?

(1) 81

(2) 72

(3) 78

(4) 89

(5) 87

62. What is the total number of children staying in localities H and I together?

(1) 1287

(2) 1278

(3) 1827

(4) 1728

(5) 1378

63. The number of women staying in which locality is the highest?

(1) H

(2) J

(3) F

(4) G

(5) I

64. What is the total number of men and children staying in locality I together?

(1) 4115

(2) 4551

(3) 4515

(4) 4155

(5) None of these

65. What is the ratio of the number of men staying in locality F to the number of men staying in locality H?

(1) 517 : 416

(2) 403 : 522

(3) 416 : 517

(4) 522 : 403

(5) None of these

REASONING ABILITY

66. Pointing to a woman in a photograph a man said "Her sister's father is the only child of my grandfather". How is the man related to woman in the photograph?

(1) Uncle

(2) Father

(3) Son

(4) Cousin

(5) Brother

67. Pointing to the man in the photograph, Ram said, "His mother has only one grandchild whose mother is my sister". How is Ram related to the man in the photograph?

    (1) Brother

    (2) Father-in-law

    (3) Brother-in-law

    (4) Sister

    (5) None of these

Directions (Q. 68 and 69): Answer the following questions based on the given information.

Each of the five friends – Jaggu, Kallu, Lallu, Mallu and Nattu has a different weight. Jaggu is heavier than Lallu but lighter than Kallu. Mallu is lighter than Lallu. Kalllu is lighter than Nattu.

68. Who among them is the heaviest?

    (1) Nattu   (2) Kallu

    (3) Lallu   (4) Mallu

    (5) Cannot be determined

69. Who among them is the second lightest?

    (1) Nattu   (2) Kallu

    (3) Lallu   (4) Mallu

    (5) Cannot be determined

70. In certain military code, 'SYSTEM' is written as 'SYSMET' and 'NEARER' as 'AENRER', what will be the code for 'FRACTION'?

    (1) CRAFNOIT   (2) FRCAITNO

    (3) CARFNOIT   (4) FRACNOIT

    (5) CRFANOIT

71. In a certain code language

    I. 'Mit Ju Push' means 'Orange is red'

    II. 'Ju Ba Dum' means 'Red and black'

    III. 'Sa Push Num' means 'Watch is white'

    Which word in that language means 'Orange'?

    (1) Push   (2) Ju

    (3) Mit   (4) Sa

    (5) None of these

72. How many such pairs of letters are there in the word RECRUIT each of which has as many letters between them in the word as they have in the English alphabet series?

    (1) None

    (2) One

    (3) Two

    (4) Three

    (5) More than three

73. Four girls are sitting on a bench to be photographed. All four girls are facing north. Shikha is to the left of Reena. Manju is to the right of Reena. Rita is between Reena and Manju. Who would be the second from the left in the photograph?

    (1) Reena   (2) Shikha

    (3) Manju   (4) Rita

    (5) Cannot be determine

74. How many such digits are there in the number 3246759, which will occupy the same position when the digits of the number are rearranged in ascending order?

    (1) None   (2) One

    (3) Two   (4) Three

    (5) More than three

75. The following question is based upon the alphabetical series given below:

    S L U A Y J V E I O N Q G Z B D R H

    If 'SU is related 'HD' and 'UY' is related to 'DZ' in a certain way, then which of the following is YV related to, following the same pattern?

    (1) ZQ   (2) IN

    (3) BG   (4) QO

    (5) DZ

Directions (Q. 76 to 80) : Answer the questions on the basis of the information given below.

J, P, Q, R, S, T, U and V are four married couples sitting in a circle facing the centre. The profession of the males within the group are lecturer, lawyer, doctor and scientist. Among the males, only R (the lawyer) and V (the scientist) are sitting together. Each man is seated besides his wife. U, the wife of the lecturer is seated second to the right of V. T is seated between U and V. P is the wife of the doctor. Q is not the doctor. S is a male.

76. Which of the following is P's position with respect to S?

    (1) Second to the right

    (2) Second to the left

    (3) Immediate right

    (4) Immediate left

    (5) Third to the left

77. Which of the following is J's position with respect to T?

    (1) Third to the left

    (2) Fourth to the right

    (3) Third to the right

    (4) Opposite T

    (5) Second to the right

78. Which of the following is not true regarding the couples?

(1) P is the wife of S

(2) T is the wife of Q

(3) R is the husband of J

(4) J and S are seated adjacent to each other

(5) All are true

79. The wives of which two husbands are immediate neighbours?

(1) UT

(2) SR

(3) VQ

(4) RV

(5) None of these

80. Four of the following five are alike in a certain way based on their seating position in the above arrangement and so form a group. Which is the one that does not belong to the group?

(1) RSJ (2) TRV

(3) UTV (4) SQP

(5) UPQ

Direction (Q. 81 to 85): Answer the questions on the basis of the information given below.

Twelve members of a family are sitting in two parallel rows facing north-south, containing 6 members each, in such a way that there is an equal distance between the adjacent members. The family is spread across three generations. There are six male members and six female members in this family.

(i) U, who faces his brother, sits adjacent to both his son and his mother. U is facing towards north.

(ii) P sits opposite to his wife and immediate left of his grand-daughter.

(iii) T, who is the son-in-law of D, sits second to the left of his wife facing one of his two daughters but R is not one of them. T is facing towards south.

(iv) F, who is facing Q, sits adjacent to both her brother and her daughter.

(v) E sits third to the left of her grandfather.

(vi) B who is mother of Q sits second to the right of her husband.

(vii) S, who faces his sister, C, sits second to the left of his father, U.

81. Who are the two daughters of T?

(1) C and A (2) A and E

(3) C and E (4) U and C

(5) D and E

82. Who is B's husband?

(1) Q (2) P

(3) R (4) U

(5) Cannot be determined

83. Who among the following are siblings?

(I) U, R and F

(II) A and E

(III) C, Q and S

(1) Only (I)

(2) Only (II)

(3) Only (I) and (II)

(4) Only (II) and (II)

(5) All (I), (II) and (III)

84. Who is sitting second to the right of E's mother?

(1) T's brother-in-law

(2) T's nephew

(3) F's father

(4) F's sister-in-law

(5) Cannot be determined

85. Which of the following is true?

(1) P has three grandsons.

(2) R is brother-in-law of F.

(3) There are four married couples in the family.

(4) F is the father of E.

(5) U is the maternal uncle of A.

Directions (Q. 86 to 90): In each question below are given three statements followed by four conclusions -I, II, III and IV. You have to take the given statements to be true even if they seem to be at variance with commonly known facts. Read all the conclusions and then decide which of the given conclusions logically follow(s) from the given statements disregarding commonly known facts.

86. Statements :

Some ships are pens.

All pens are rockets.

Some rockets are science.

Conclusions :

I. Some ships are rockets.

II. Some rockets are ships.

III. All science are rockets.

IV. Some science are rockets.

(1) All follow

(2) Only I, II and III follow

(3) Only I, II and IV follow

(4) Only II, III and IV follow

(5) None of these

87. Statements :

All cars are jeeps.

All jeeps are buses.

All buses are trucks.

Conclusions :

I.   All trucks are buses.

II. All buses are jeeps.

III. All jeeps are cars.

IV. All cars are trucks.

(1) Only I and III follow

(2) All follow

(3) Only III and IV follow

(4) Only IV follows

(5) None follows

88. Statements :

Some trees are flows.

Some flows are purse.

Some purse are tables.

Conclusions :

I.   Some tables are flows.

II. Some purse are trees.

III. Some tables are trees.

IV. Some trees are purse.

(1) All follow

(2) Only II follows

(3) Only I and III follow

(4) Only II and IV follow

(5) None follows

89. Statements :

All roads are red.

Some red are white.

All white are doors.

Conclusions :

I.   Some roads are doors.

II. Some doors are whites.

III. Some roads are not doors.

IV. All doors are roads.

(1) Only I and II follow

(2) Only I, II and III follow

(3) Only either I or III and II follow

(4) Only either I or III and IV follow

(5) None of these

90. Statements :

Some books are pens.

Some pens are watches.

All watches are radios.

Conclusions :

I.   Some radios are watches.

II. Some radios are pens.

III. Some watches are books.

IV. Some books are watches.

(1) All follow

(2) Only I and III follow

(3) Only II and IV follow

(4) Only I and IV follow

(5) Only I and II follow

Directions (Q.91 to 95): Read the following information and answer the questions based on it.

There are five persons P, Q, R, S and T. One is a footballer, one is a cricketer and one a table tennis player.

P & S are unmarried ladies and do not take part in any game. None of the ladies play football or cricket. There is a married couple in which T is a husband. Q is the brother of R and Q is neither a cricketer nor a table tennis player.

91. Who is the footballer?

(1) Q   (2) R

(3) S   (4) T

(5) P

92. Who is the table tennis player?

(1) Q   (2) R

(3) S   (4) T

(5) P

93. Who is the cricketer?

(1) Q   (2) R

(3) S   (4) P

(5) T

94. Who is the wife of T?

(1) P   (2) S

(3) T   (4) Q

(5) R

95. The three ladies in the group are.

(1) PQR   (2) PRS

(3) QRS   (4) PST

(5) QTP

Directions (Q.96 to 100): In the following questions, the symbols @, ©, % and * are used with the following meaning as illustrated below:

P © Q means P is not smaller than Q.

P * Q means P is not greater than Q.

P @ Q means P is neither greater than nor smaller than Q.

P $ Q means P is neither smaller than nor equal to Q.

P % Q means P is neither greater than nor equal to Q.

Now in each of the following questions assuming the given statements to be true, find which of the conclusions I, II, III and IV given below them is/are definitely true and give your answer accordingly.

96. Statements:

K © L, L % O, O @ M, M * N

Conclusions:

I. N © O

II. M $ L

III. K * N

IV. L @ N

(1) Only II is true

(2) None is true

(3) Only I is true

(4) Either I or II is true

(5) Only I and II are true

97. Statements:

A * B, B $ C, C % D, D © E

Conclusions:

I. D $ A

II. B $ D

III. E % C

IV. A @ E

(1) Only I is true

(2) Only either I or II is true

(3) Only I and IV are true

(4) None is true

(5) Only IV is true

98. Statements:

F $ P, P @ R, R © S, S % T

Conclusions:

I. R % F

II. S * P

III. P © T

IV. S % F

(1) Only I, II, and III are true

(2) Only I and II are true

(3) Only III and IV are true

(4) Only I, II and IV are true

(5) All are true

99. Statements:

G % H, H * I, I $ J, J @ K

Conclusions:

I. G % I

II. G % J

III. K $ I

IV. H * J

(1) Only I is true

(2) Only II is true

(3) Only I, II and III are true

(4) Only either I or II and III are true

(5) All are true

100. Statements:

V @ W, W % X, X * Y, Y $ Z

Conclusions:

I. Z $ X

II. Y © V

III. W % Y

IV. Y @ W

(1) Only I and II are true

(2) Only II is true

(3) Only III and IV are true

(4) None is true

(5) Only III is true

ANSWERS

1. (5)	**2.** (2)	**3.** (3)	**4.** (2)	**5.** (5)	**6.** (1)	**7.** (3)	**8.** (2)	**9.** (4)	**10.** (4)
11. (2)	**12.** (3)	**13.** (3)	**14.** (5)	**15.** (1)	**16.** (5)	**17.** (5)	**18.** (3)	**19.** (1)	**20.** (4)
21. (3)	**22.** (2)	**23.** (1)	**24.** (1)	**25.** (1)	**26.** (3)	**27.** (1)	**28.** (3)	**29.** (4)	**30.** (1)
31. (5)	**32.** (4)	**33.** (3)	**34.** (1)	**35.** (2)	**36.** (1)	**37.** (2)	**38.** (3)	**39.** (5)	**40.** (1)
41. (2)	**42.** (1)	**43.** (5)	**44.** (1)	**45.** (2)	**46.** (3)	**47.** (2)	**48.** (1)	**49.** (5)	**50.** (1)
51. (4)	**52.** (1)	**53.** (5)	**54.** (2)	**55.** (2)	**56.** (5)	**57.** (1)	**58.** (3)	**59.** (5)	**60.** (4)
61. (5)	**62.** (2)	**63.** (4)	**64.** (3)	**65.** (1)	**66.** (5)	**67.** (3)	**68.** (1)	**69.** (3)	**70.** (3)
71. (3)	**72.** (2)	**73.** (4)	**74.** (3)	**75.** (1)	**76.** (4)	**77.** (1)	**78.** (2)	**79.** (3)	**80.** (3)
81. (2)	**82.** (4)	**83.** (5)	**84.** (3)	**85.** (5)	**86.** (3)	**87.** (4)	**88.** (5)	**89.** (3)	**90.** (5)
91. (1)	**92.** (2)	**93.** (5)	**94.** (5)	**95.** (2)	**96.** (5)	**97.** (4)	**98.** (4)	**99.** (1)	**100.** (5)

EXPLANATIONS

1. (5) All (A), (B) and (C) depict the growing importance of innovation in India.

2. (2) The passage talks about the need of innovation in India. So, the appropriate title of the passage is India And The Elixir Called Innovation.

3. (3) Refer to the first sentence of the last paragraph. Clearly, failure to innovate in order to find solutions is the reason behind India's inability to adequately provide for its people.

4. (2) Refer to the sixth paragraph. We can conclude from it that statements A and B are true about the cell phone.

5. (5) 'frugal impacts on earth's resources' means that there should be minimum usage of earth's natural resources.

6. (1) The word 'redress' means to correct or cure something that is unfair or wrong.

7. (3) The word 'intrinsically' means occurring as a natural part of something.

8. (2) The word 'compromise' means reducing the quality.

9. (4) The word 'lack' means dearth, the state of not having excess of something. Its antonym should be adequacy.

10. (4) The word 'inconceivable' means impossible to imagine or believe; unthinkable. Its antonym should be apparent.

11. (2) The correct idiom is 'hand to mouth' which means satisfying only one's immediate needs because of lack of money for future plans and investments.

12. (3) The correct phrase is 'earn a decent living'.

13. (3) The correct phrase is 'piping hot', which means very hot.

14. (5) The sentence is correct in its given form.

15. (1) The correct idiom is 'jumped through hoops', which means to perform a difficult and grueling series of tests at someone else's request or command.

For questions 16 - 20 :

The correct sequence is BDAECF. B starts the passage by introducing the topic of the passage - fall in the use of cheques. D follows B by stating the reason for the fall in its use. AE is a mandatory pair that follows D by saying how the fall in the use of cheques will prove to be a disadvantage for the elderly. C follows AE by saying that the needs of all consumers including the elderly should be taken care of. F ends the passage by saying that because of the reason stated in the passage, British banks have voted to phase cheques out.

21. (3) 'Always thrilling' is grammatically incorrect. The correct phrase is 'always thrilled'.

22. (2) 'Go by' is a standard phrase.

23. (1) 'That' is redundant.

24. (1) 'Too' should be replaced by 'so'.

25. (1) 'Attain' should be replaced by 'attains' since man is singular.

26. (3) The sentence means that earlier the Gramin Bank did not think of getting involved with the education of its borrowers, but later they realised that it was needed. Only 'plan' fits in the context of the sentence and hence, is the answer.

27. (1) The sentence implies that many customers did not have a formal education, they only knew how to read and write. So, 'except' fits in the blank.

28. (3) Only 'circular' and 'information' can be read. Since more than one topics are listedto be read, viz., business, health, etc., the blank will take 'information'. Had option (5) been 'circulars', it would have been correct.

29. (4) 'Whatever' here refers to that which needs to be done out of all the things. Other options will make the sentence grammatically incorrect.

30. (1) 'Acquire' means gain.

31. (5) $460 \times 15 = 460 \times 10 + \dfrac{1}{2} \times 4600$

$$= 4600 + 2300 - 100$$
$$= 6900 - 100$$
$$= 6800$$

32. (4) $5163 + 3209 - 4018 = 8372 - 4018$
$$= 4354$$

33. (3) $4848 \div 24 = 202,$
$$202 \times 11 = 2222$$
$$2222 - 222 = 2000$$

34. (1) 64% of 950

$$= 60\% \text{ of } 950 + 4\% \text{ of } 950$$
$$= 570 + 38 = 608$$
$$\therefore \quad ? = 475 + 608 - 900$$
$$= 1083 - 900 = 183.$$

35. (2) $(0.4)^? = \dfrac{0.064 \times (0.4)^7}{(0.0256)^2}$

$$= \dfrac{64 \times 10^{-3} \times (4 \times 10^{-1})^7}{(256 \times 10^{-4})^2}$$

$$= \dfrac{64 \times 4^7 \times 10^{-3} \times 10^{-7}}{256 \times 256 \times 10^{-8}}$$

$$= \dfrac{64 \times 4 \times 4 \times 4 \times 4 \times 4 \times 4^2}{256 \times 256} \times 10^{-2}$$

$$= (0.4)^2$$
$$\therefore \ ? = 2$$

36. (1) Required ratio = 40 : 35 = 8 : 7

37. (2) Required average

$$= \left(\dfrac{15 + 25 + 30 + 40 + 15 + 10}{6} \right) \text{thousand}$$

$$= \dfrac{135}{6} = 22.5 \text{ thousand}$$

38. (3) Required percentage increase

$$= \dfrac{25 - 10}{10} \times 100 = 150\%$$

39. (5) Laptops manufactured by Apple, Lenovo and Samsung in 2014

$$= 15 + 40 + 25 = 80 \text{ thousand}$$

Laptops manufactured by Dell, HP and Abascus in 2015

$$= 15 + 25 + 35 = 75 \text{ thousand}$$

Difference = 5000.

40. (1) Abascus $\Rightarrow$ 35000

41. (2) Number of boys in the class = 18

Number of girls in the class = 48 – 18 = 30

H.C.F of 18 and 30 = 6

So, a row can have a maximum of 6 students.

42. (1) Let A's salary be a.

So, A's salary after increase

$$= a\,(1.12)\,(1.14)\,(1.16)$$
$$= 2457$$

$$\Rightarrow \qquad a = \dfrac{2457}{1.481} = \text{Rs.1,659.}$$

43. (5) Selling price of one marble $= \dfrac{100}{10} = 10 \text{ paise}$

Given, cost price of one marble × 0.80 = selling price of one marble.

$\therefore$ Cost price of one marble

$$= \dfrac{10}{0.80} = 12.5 \text{ paise}$$

In order to gain 60%, selling price of one marble

$$= 12.5 \times 1.6 = 20 \text{ paise.}$$

$\therefore$ Number of marbles in one rupee

$$= \dfrac{100}{20} = 5 \text{ marbles.}$$

44. (1) Let the cost of pizza be Rs. x.

Now, $\quad$ SP = 1.2x

The cost price after hike is Rs. (x + 10) and he made 10% profit on this new CP,

$$\text{SP} = 1.1 \times (x + 10)$$
$$\Rightarrow \qquad 1.2x = 1.1x + 11$$
$$\Rightarrow \qquad x = \text{Rs. } 110$$

So, $\quad$ SP = 110 × 1.2

$$= \text{Rs. } 132.$$

Hence, selling price of pizza is Rs. 132.

45. (2)

$$3P = P\left(1+\frac{r}{100}\right)^4$$

$$\Rightarrow \left(1+\frac{r}{100}\right) = 3^{\frac{1}{4}}$$

Now, $81P = P\left(1+\frac{r}{100}\right)^n$

$$\Rightarrow 3^4 = 3^{\frac{n}{4}}$$

$\Rightarrow$ n = 16 years.

Alternative method:

Amount becomes 3 times in 4 years

and we know that $3^4 = 81$

So, amount will be 81 times in 4 × 4 = 16 years.

46. (3) Let the initial weights of the three heaps be 6x, 7x and 8x respectively and let the final weights be 7y, 8y and 9y respectively.

Since the third heap has not been changed

$\Rightarrow$ 8x = 9y

Now, fractional change in the first heap

$$= \frac{(7y-6x)}{6x} = \frac{1}{27},$$

and fractional change in the second heap

$$= \frac{(8y-7x)}{7x} = \frac{1}{63}.$$

47. (2) Using alligation, the ratio between pure milk to 20% milk water solution is

$$\frac{(100-45)}{(45-20)} = \frac{55}{25} = \frac{11}{5}$$

$\Rightarrow$ 11x + 5x = 32

$\Rightarrow$ x = 2.

Hence, 10 litres of pure milk is required.

48. (1) Let Q's share be Rs. x

$\therefore$ R's share = Rs. 2x

Let P's share = Rs. 2y

Hence, T's share = Rs. y

Overall sum = (x + 2x + 2y + y)

            = 3(x + y) = Rs. 3,000

$\Rightarrow$ x + y = 1,000   ... (i)

Also given, 2y – x = Rs. 1,100   ... (ii)

From (i) and (ii),

3y = 2,100 or y = 700 and x = 1000 – 700 = 300

Answer is 700 – 2 × 300 = Rs. 100.

49. (5) Total age of the family

          = 6 × 22 = 132 years

Total age of the family 7 years ago

          = 132 – (7 × 6) = 90 years

But there were only 5 members.

So the average age of family 7 years ago

$$= \frac{90}{5} = 18 \text{ years.}$$

50. (1) Total age of husband, wife and son 3 years ago

          = 3 × 27 = 81 years

Their present total age

          = 81 + 3 × 3 = 90 years

Present age of wife and son

          = 2 × 20 + 2 × 5 = 50 years

Present age of the husband

          = 90 – 50

          = 40 years.

51. (4) On solving (I), we get a = $\frac{5}{7}$ and $\frac{3}{5}$

On solving (II), we get b = $\frac{5}{7}$ and $\frac{1}{2}$

Clearly, $a \geq b$.

52. (1) On solving (I), we get a = $\frac{3}{2}$ and $\frac{1}{2}$

On solving (II), we get b = $\frac{5}{3}$ and 3

Clearly, b > a.

53. (5) On solving (I), we get a = 17 and –13

On solving (II), we get b = 13 and –15

Since, 17 is greater than both 13 and –15 but –13 is less than 13 and greater than –15.

Clearly, variables are not comparable.

54. (2) On solving (I), we get a = –13 and –11

On solving (II), we get b = –15 and –14

Clearly, a > b.

55. (2) On solving (I), we get $a = \sqrt{3}$ and $2\sqrt{3}$

On solving (II), we get $b = \sqrt{2}$ and $-\sqrt{2}$

Clearly, a > b.

56. (5) The given series is

+ $(1)^2$, + $(3)^2$, + $(5)^2$, + $(7)^2$, + $(9)^2$, + $(11)^2$

$\therefore$ The correct answer is 171 instead of wrong number 154.

57. (1) The given series is

× 1 + (1)^2, × 2 + (2)^2, × 3 + (3)^2, × 4 + (4)^2, × 5 + (5)^2, × 6 + (6)^2

∴ The correct answer is 6 instead of wrong number 7.

58. (3) The given series is

$\times\dfrac{1}{2}+\dfrac{1}{2}$, ×1+1, ×1.5+1.5, +2+2, ×2.5+2.5, ×3+3

∴ The correct answer is 6.75 instead of wrong number 6.5.

59. (5) 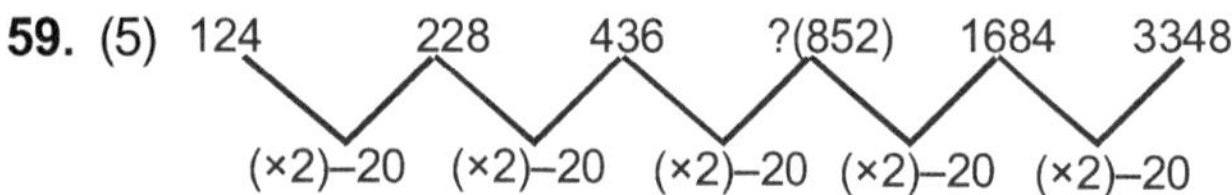

60. (4) 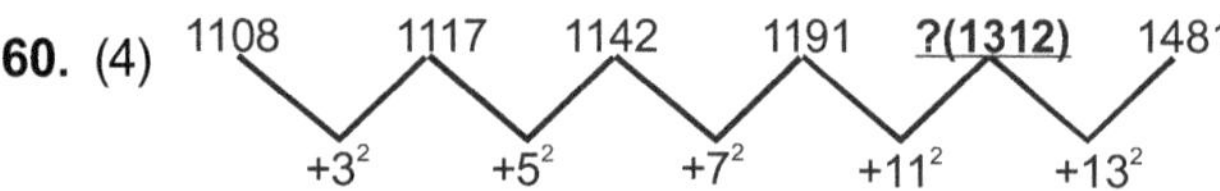

Where 3, 5, 7, 11 and 13 are prime numbers.

61. (5) Required % = $\dfrac{4900}{5640} \times 100 \approx 87\%$.

62. (2) Required number of children

$$= 52 \times 13 + 602 = 1278.$$

63. (4) Number of women living in the locality

F : 56.4 × 35 = 56 × 35 + 0.4 × 35

$\qquad\qquad = 1960 + 14 = 1974$

G : 48.5 × 44 = 2112 + 222 = 2134

H : 52 × 39 = 2028

I : 6020 × $\dfrac{1}{4}$ = 1505

J : 49 × 41 = 2009

64. (3) Total number of men and children in locality I,

$$= 6020 \times \dfrac{(65+10)}{100}$$

$$= 6020 \times \dfrac{3}{4} = 4515.$$

65. (1) Required ratio = $\dfrac{5640 \times 55}{5200 \times 48}$ = 517 : 416.

66. (5) 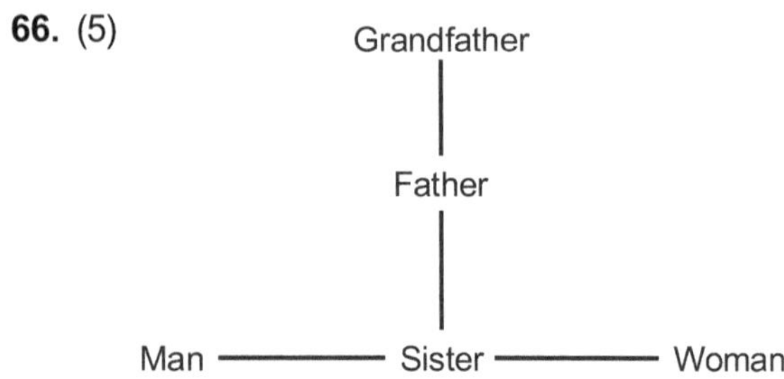

67. (3) 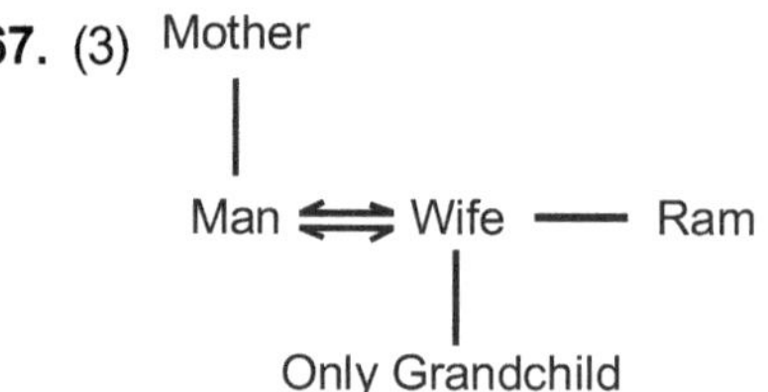

For questions 68 and 69:

Order of their weights is given below

Nattu > Kallu > Jaggu > Lallu > Mallu

70. (3) The word is divided into two equal parts and the letters of each part are written in reverse order as

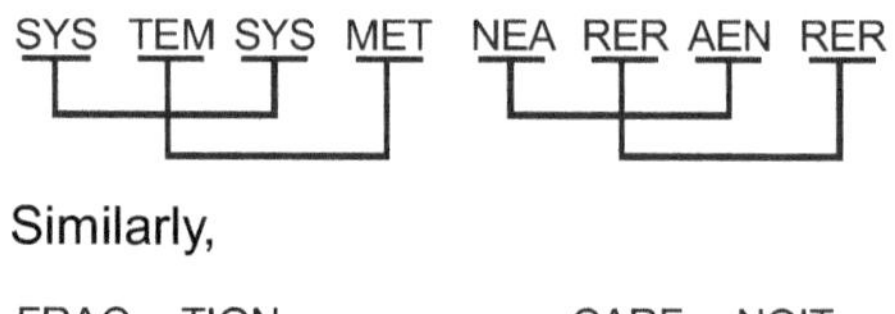

Similarly,

71. (3) By comparing (I) and (II) 'Ju' means 'Red'. By Comparing (I) and (III) 'Push' means 'is'

∴ Orange means Mit.

72. (2) R E C R U I T

Only one pair, EI.

73. (4) Shikha is to the left of Reena and Manju is to her right. Rita is between Reena and Manju. So the order is: Shikha, Reena, Rita, Manju. In the photograph, Rita will be second from left.

74. (3) Given number:

3 2 4 6 7 5 9

Ascending order:

2 3 4 5 6 7 9

Two digits, 4 and 9, will occupy the same place.

75. (1) The group of letters are at the same position from left as the corresponding group of letters are from the right end.

For questions 76 to 80: Sitting arrangement

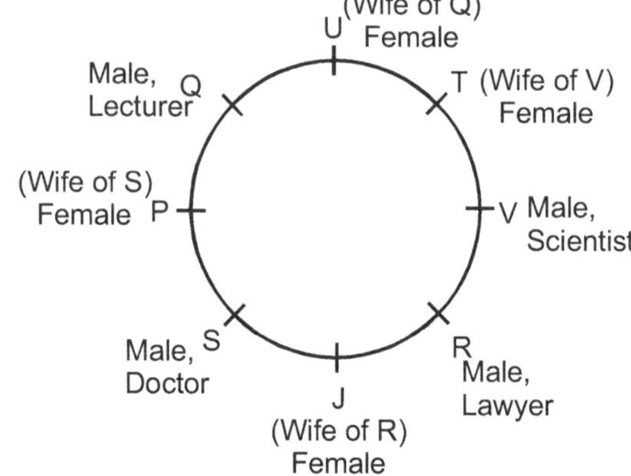

76. (4) P is to the immediate left of S.

77. (1) J is third to the left of T.

78. (2) T is the wife of Q.

79. (3) Wives of Q and V are immediate neighbours.

80. (3) Except in UTV, in all others the third person is sitting between the first and the second persons. In UTV, the second person is sitting between the first and the third persons.

For questions 81 to 85:

Female	Male	Male	Female	Female	Male
C	P	R	F	E	T
S	D	U	Q	B	A
Male	Female	Male	Male	Female	Female

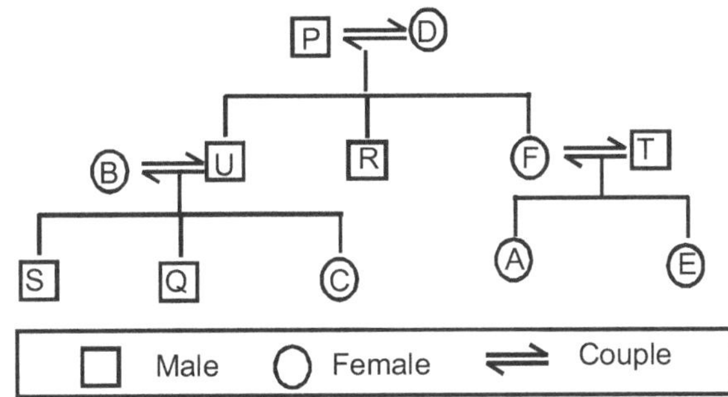

86. (3)

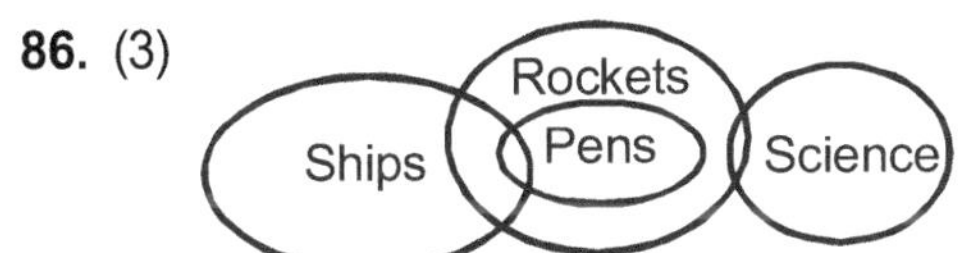

87. (4)

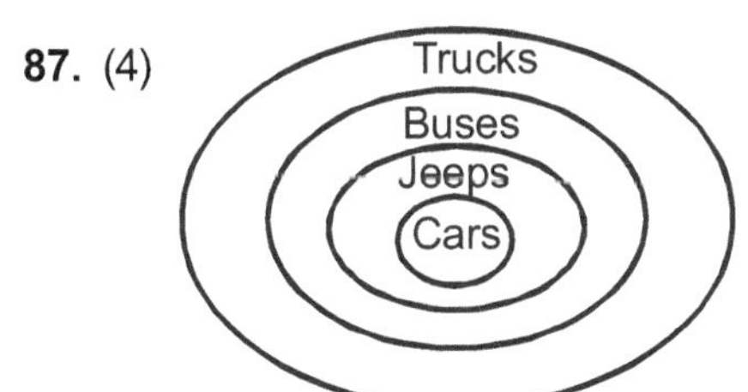

88. (5)

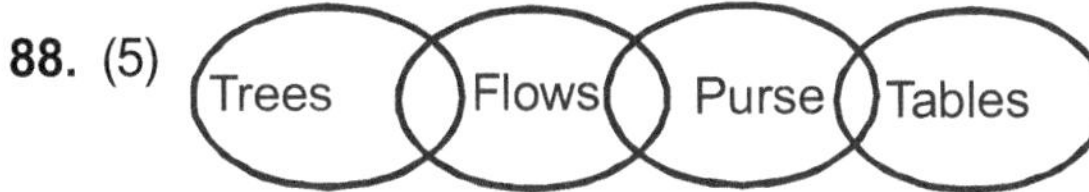

89. (3)

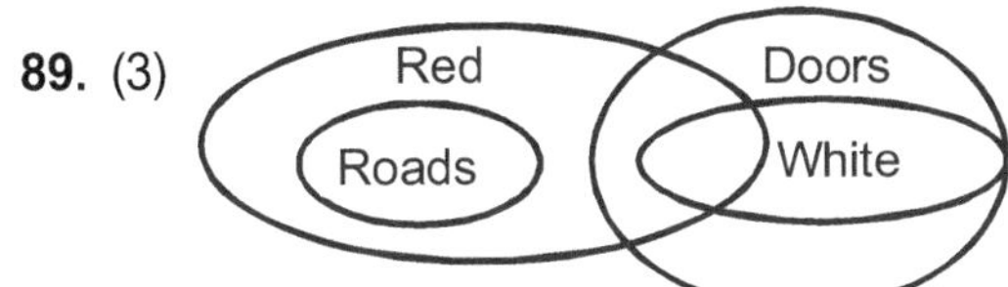

90. (5)

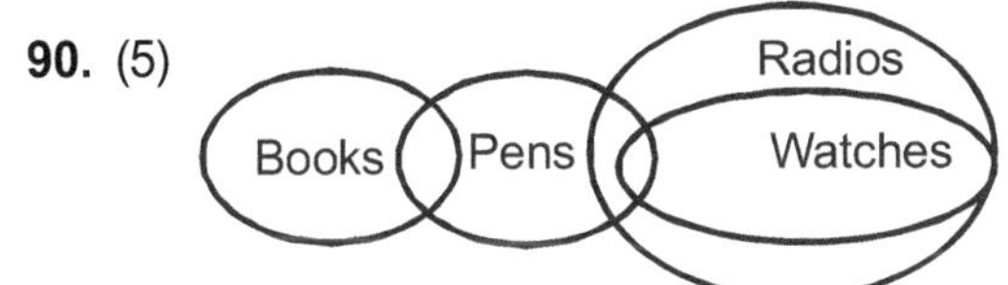

For questions 91 to 95:

The information can be collated in the form of a table as shown below.

Person	Gender	Game	Wife/Husband
P	Female	–	–
Q	Male	Footballer	–
R	Female	T.T.	Wife of T
S	Female	–	–
T	Male	Cricketer	Husband of R

91. (1) Q is the footballer.

92. (2) R is the Table Tennis player.

93. (5) T is the cricketer.

94. (5) R is the wife of T.

95. (2) P and S are ladies as given in the initial information. R is the wife of T. Hence, the ladies in the group are P, R and S.

96. (5) $K © L \Rightarrow K \geq L$

$L \% O \Rightarrow L < O$

$O @ M \Rightarrow O = M$

$M * N \Rightarrow M \leq N$

$\therefore K \geq L < O = M \leq N$

Conclusions:

I. $N © O \Rightarrow N \geq O$ (True)

II. $M \$ L \Rightarrow M > L$ (True)

III. $K*N \Rightarrow K \leq N$ (Not true)

IV. $L @ N \Rightarrow L = N$ (Not true)

97. (4) $A * B \Rightarrow A \leq B$

$B \$ C \Rightarrow B > C$

$C \% D \Rightarrow C < D$

$D © E \Rightarrow D \geq E$

$\therefore A \leq B > C < D \geq E$

Conclusions:

I. $D \$ A \Rightarrow D > A$ (Not true)

II. $B \$ D \Rightarrow B > D$ (Not true)

III. $E \% C \Rightarrow E < C$ (Not true)

IV. $A @ E \Rightarrow A = E$ (Not true)

98. (4) $F \$ P \Rightarrow F > P$

$P @ R \Rightarrow P = R$

$R © S \Rightarrow R \geq S$

$S \% T \Rightarrow S < T$

$\therefore F > P = R \geq S < T$

Conclusions:

I. $R \% F \Rightarrow R < F$ (True)

II. $S * P \Rightarrow S \leq P$ (True)

III. $P © T \Rightarrow P \geq T$ (Not true)

IV. $S \% F \Rightarrow S < F$ (True)

99. (1) $G \% H \Rightarrow G < H$

$H * I \Rightarrow H \leq I$

$I \$ J \Rightarrow I > J$

$J @ K \Rightarrow J = K$

$\therefore G < H \leq I > J = K$

Conclusions:

I. $G \% I \Rightarrow G < I$ (True)

II. $G \% J \Rightarrow G < J$ (Not True)

III. $K \$ I \Rightarrow K > I$ (Not true)

IV. $H * J \Rightarrow H \leq J$ (Not true)

100. (5) $V @ W \Rightarrow V = W$

$W \% X \Rightarrow W < X$

$X * Y \Rightarrow X \leq Y$

$Y \$ Z \Rightarrow Y > Z$

$\therefore V = W < X \leq Y > Z$

Conclusions:

I. $Z \$ X \Rightarrow Z > X$ (Not true)

II. $Y © V \Rightarrow Y \geq V$ (Not true)

III. $W \% Y \Rightarrow W < Y$ (True)

IV. $Y @ W \Rightarrow Y = W$ (Not true)

ENGLISH LANGUAGE

Directions (Q. 1 to 5): Pick out the most effective word/words from the given word/s to fill in the blanks to make the sentence meaningfully complete in the context of the sentence.

1. I have given myself _______ the end of September to finish my research.
   (1) between   (2) until
   (3) to   (4) for
   (5) near

2. It is _______ that John did not hurt himself when he fell off his motorbike.
   (1) luckily   (2) fortunate
   (3) understanding   (4) found
   (5) knowing

3. You must not look directly at the sun _______ the eclipse.
   (1) during   (2) in
   (3) on   (4) to
   (5) at

4. The mist was so thick, it was like walking _______ a cloud.
   (1) beyond   (2) by
   (3) along   (4) through
   (5) against

5. I told my friend that he could not catch a big fish _______ a small rod like the one he was carrying, but he insisted _______ trying.
   (1) with, on   (2) by, about
   (3) with, about   (4) by, on
   (5) on, for

Directions (Q. 6 to 15): Read the following passage carefully and answer the questions given below it. Certain words/phrases have been printed in bold to help you locate them while answering some of the questions.

A large number of branches of banks have been set up in the villages. The main purpose of setting up these banks is to develop the habit of saving among the villagers and also to give loans to farmers for **boosting** production in one way or the other. So far banks had been **concentrated** in the bigger cities and Indian villagers had no faith in them. The new banks also intend to re-channel bank credit-from the big industries to the small sectors. With the intention of promoting rural banking, regional rural banks were established. These aligned the local field with the rural problems. These banks are not to replace the other credit-giving bodies but to supplement them.

The Steering Committee of the Regional Rural Banks considered some structural changes. First of all they gave thought to the staffing spectrum, then to effective coordination among banks - rural cooperatives and commercial, and the possibility of bringing credit within the **access** of weaker sections. They wanted to recruit staff for the rural banks at lower salaries. But this type of discrimination would have been unfruitful. So it was given up.

A problem with regard to the rural banks is the creditworthiness of the poor. The Indian farmers are so poor that they cannot pay back their loans. The rural Indian surveys make it quite clear that practically rural farmers have no creditworthiness. Their socio-economic mobility is almost zero. That is why banks fear that their credit will never be paid back.

Another difficulty for the rural banks is that loans cannot be processed so easily. Processing loans also **entails** heavy expenditure. This was also going to affect their financial position. Still the establishment of the rural banks was decided because the social advantages were more important than the commercial consideration.

Rural banks definitely encourage savings. No doubt the villagers do not have to pay income tax and they get many other concessions, yet their saving is not **significant**. Despite all the hurdles, the rural banking system will boost up the economy of villages, and thereby the economy of the country.

6. Which of the following is/are the purpose/s of setting up banks in rural areas?
   (A) Replacing other credit-giving bodies
   (B) Giving loans to farmers
   (C) Increasing the amount of savings of villagers.
   (1) Only (B)
   (2) Only (A) and (B)
   (3) Only (B) and (C)
   (4) Only (A)
   (5) All (A), (B) and (C)

7. The structural changes made by the Steering Committee were in respect of
   (1) staffing, co-ordinating and providing access to weaker sections
   (2) building smaller buildings to house the banks
   (3) investing very little in terms of infrastructure required to start a bank
   (4) discriminating between urban bank staff and rural bank staff
   (5) None of these

8. Which of the following is possibly the most appropriate title for the passage?
   (1) Regional Rural Banks
   (2) The Rural Consumer
   (3) Microfinance In Rural India
   (4) Characteristics Of Indian Villages
   (5) Banking Concepts In India

9. Which of the following is NOT TRUE according to the passage?
   (1) Processing of loans by rural banks is difficult
   (2) Staff of the rural banks is paid a lower salary as compared to urban banks
   (3) Rural banks may not make as much profit as their urban counterparts
   (4) Processing of loans by banks is not cheap
   (5) Rural farmers are, many a time, unable to pay back the loans they avail

10. Which of the following is one of the benefits of living in the village, as mentioned in the passage?
    (1) People living in the villages enjoy a higher income than their urban counterparts
    (2) People living in villages do not have to pay income tax and they also get other concessions.
    (3) People living in villages have a better quality of life
    (4) Villages are self-sufficient; hence they do not need outside help for any activity
    (5) People living in villages are rarely in need of a loan

Directions (Q. 11 to 13): Choose the word which is most similar in meaning to the word printed in bold as used in the passage.

11. **CONCENTRATED**
    (1) clustered   (2) rigorous
    (3) attentive   (4) diluted
    (5) intense

12. **ACCESS**
    (1) admittance   (2) reach
    (3) admission   (4) entry
    (5) permission

13. **ENTAILS**
    (1) recommends   (2) lasts
    (3) lists   (4) involves
    (5) filters

Directions (Q. 14 and 15): Choose the word which is most opposite in meaning to the word printed in bold as used in the passage.

14. **BOOSTING**
    (1) reducing   (2) managing
    (3) overwhelming   (4) smoothening
    (5) heightening

15. **SIGNIFICANT**
    (1) forgettable   (2) untrustworthy
    (3) reliable   (4) irregular
    (5) little

Directions (16 to 20): Read each sentence to find out whether there is any grammatical error in it. The error if any will be in one part of the sentence, the number of that part will be the answer. If there is 'No error', mark (5) as the answer. (Ignore errors of punctuation, if any.)

16. Angered over the delay in giving compensation, (1)/ the factory workers shouted (2)/ slogans against the president (3)/ when he reaches the office. (4)/ No error (5)

17. The cascading effect of economic slowdown (1)/ has brought a much unnerving gloom (2)/ to the real estate industry last year (3)/ but the industry is looking up this year. (4)/ No error (5)

18. A recycling plant in close proximity to (1)/ the residential area can pose (2)/ serious threats from residents (3)/ by leaving behind persistent pollutants. (4)/ No error (5)

19. The government has the obligation (1)/ to provide basic infrastructure facilities (2)/ to regulating the process of (3) / urbanization in the country. (4)/ No error (5)

20. Bharatpur is transforming into (1)/ India's most fastest growing bird sanctuary (2)/ attracting thousands of rare migratory birds (3)/ from Europe and Siberia. (4)/ No error (5)

Directions (Q.21 to 25): In the following passage there are blanks, each of which has been numbered. These numbers are given below the passage and against each, five words are suggested, one of which fits the blank appropriately. Find out the appropriate word in each case.

This happened thousands of years ago. Life was hard as people had to do all the work by themselves. A large number of people were __(21)__ . They would travel from one place to another in search of food and shelter. While travelling one day, a man arrived at the edge of a desert. He was walking on the sand, when suddenly he came across a frightening creature - it had extremely long, thin legs, a giant hump and a long neck. It was this neck that he extended towards the man, who, scared out of his __(22)__, ran away from the spot. The following day, he met the creature again. It was standing near a lake, drinking water. This time, the man was fascinated at what he saw --- the creature putting its long neck into the lake and drinking water continuously. Then suddenly the giant creature looked up and stared straight into the eyes of the man standing across. But this time, an __(23)__ of water separated the two, and the man did not run away. He stood and watched the animal, which made no effort to come closer. In the following weeks, the man saw more such creatures, again and again. It seemed they were all over the desert, aimlessly walking about for miles on end. The man began to observe the creatures very closely. He saw that they were vegetarian. Moreover, despite their huge size, they were remarkably meek and gentle. And the stamina the creatures had was __(24)__. They could walk the entire length of the desert without being exhausted. Observing them, the man thought, "What if I tame this creature and make it ferry all my stuff? I could then make the desert my home." So, one day, while one of the creatures' was dozing, the man went up to it and put a bridle in its mouth. Then he rode around on it, after placing an enormous amount of load on its back. With that, the taming of the camel was complete (for that was who the creature was). And ever since that day, the camel has faithfully __(25)__ up to its title of 'Ship of the Desert'.

21. (1) masons   (2) cobblers
   (3) farmers   (4) nomads
   (5) potters

22. (1) humor   (2) mind
   (3) wits   (4) life
   (5) face

23. (1) expanse   (2) stretch
   (3) wedge   (4) pond
   (5) element

24. (1) unarguable   (2) unbelievable
   (3) unforgivable   (4) unbearable
   (5) unavailable

25. (1) been   (2) ran
   (3) seen   (4) lived
   (5) stood

Directions (Q. 26 to 30): Rearrange the following six sentences (A), (B), (C), (D), (E) and (F) in the proper sequence to form a meaningful paragraph; then answer the questions given below them.

(A) He instructed his stable master to give him the fastest of all the horses he had.

(B) Akhar was embarrassed and in turn gifted the sage a horse cart and made the stable master its driver in order to punish him.

(C) After a few days Akbar saw the sage walking again and asked him where the horse was.

(D) Once Akbar saw a sage walking and decided to gift him a horse.

(E) The sage answered, "My Lord, the horse gifted to me was so fast that it crossed the distance from earth to heaven in one night."

(F) However, it so happened that the stable master gave him a frail and sick horse which died the same night it was gifted to the sage.

26. Which of the following should be the FIRST sentence after rearrangement?
   (1) A   (2) B
   (3) C   (4) D
   (5) E

27. Which of the following should be the SECOND sentence after rearrangement?
   (1) B   (2) A
   (3) D   (4) F
   (5) E

28. Which of the following should be the THIRD sentence after rearrangement?
   (1) A   (2) B
   (3) C   (4) D
   (5) F

29. Which of the following should be the FOURTH sentence after rearrangement?
   (1) C   (2) E
   (3) D   (4) B
   (5) F

30. Which of the following should be the LAST (SIXTH) sentence after rearrangement?
   (1) A   (2) B
   (3) C   (4) D
   (5) E

NUMERICAL ABILITY

Direction (Q. 31 to 35): What approximate value will come in place of the question mark (?) in the following questions? (You are not expected to calculate the exact value)

31. $7999.99 + 72 \times 49.99 = ?$

  (1) 12000   (2) 12600

  (3) 12500   (4) 11600

  (5) 11000

32. $(25.01)^2 - (15.99)^2 = ?$

  (1) 361   (2) 381

  (3) 369   (4) 375

  (5) 356

33. $380 \times 12.25 - 365 \div 15 = ?$

  (1) 4500   (2) 4550

  (3) 4800   (4) 4850

  (5) 4650

34. 180% of 25501 + 50% of 28999 = ?

  (1) 62400   (2) 64000

  (3) 60400   (5) 64200

  (5) 61600

35. $171.995 \times 14.995 \div 25 = ?$

  (1) 105   (2) 115

  (3) 110   (4) 125

  (5) 120

36. Three bells B1, B2 and B3 started tolling together and they kept tolling at intervals of 6, 8 and 10 seconds respectively. How many times did exactly two of three bells toll together in the first 5 minutes from the start?

  (1) 21   (2) 22

  (3) 23   (4) 24

  (5) 25

37. Due to an increase in the price of mangoes by 20%, a person is able to purchase 5 less mangoes for Rs. 60. What is the original price per mango?

  (1) Rs. 4   (2) Rs. 3

  (3) Rs. 2   (4) Rs. 2.40

  (5) Rs. 2.50

38. A shopkeeper gives a discount of 35% on the marked price of goods. If he makes a profit of 30% after the completion of transaction, then which of the following statements is true?

  (1) Marked price is 1.65 times of the cost price.

  (2) Marked price is 1.3 times of the cost price.

  (3) Marked price is 2 times of the cost price.

  (4) Marked price is equal to the cost price.

  (5) Marked price is 1.5 times of the cost price.

39. An importer of cereals got a consignment of coarse rice. He had to sell his goods at 10% loss to the distributor who sold it to the retailer at 9% loss. However, the retailer manages to sell it to the customer at 8% profit. If the cost price per kg for the importer is Rs. 200, then what is the approximate cumulative loss?

  (1) Rs. 47   (2) Rs. 23

  (3) Rs. 27   (4) Rs. 33

  (5) Rs. 35

40. Find the compound interest on Rs. 4,500 for 9 months at 16% per annum compounded quarterly.

  (1) Rs. 432.85   (2) Rs. 561.88

  (3) Rs. 616.44   (4) Rs. 714.22

  (5) None of these

Directions (Q. 41 to 45): In each of the following series, find the wrong number.

41. 13, 67, 405, 2840, 22717

  (1) 13   (2) 67

  (3) 405   (4) 2840

  (5) 22717

42. 48, 240, 1440, 10080, 80740

  (1) 48   (2) 1440

  (3) 80740   (4) 10080

  (5) 240

43. 218, 345, 515, 731, 1002

  (1) 1002   (2) 218

  (3) 731   (4) 515

  (5) 345

44. 6, 120, 504, 1320, 2830

  (1) 120   (2) 504

  (3) 1320   (4) 2830

  (5) None of these

45. 13, 40, 85, 145, 221

  (1) 13   (2) 40

  (3) 85   (4) 145

  (5) 221

46. The ratio of the medals won by Aditi and Punam in school is 3 : 7 respectively and the medals won by them in college is 7 : 8 respectively. If the ratio of the total number of medals won by them is 1 : 2 respectively, then what fraction of medals are won by Punam in the school?

  (1) $\dfrac{8}{7}$ (2) $\dfrac{21}{25}$

  (3) $\dfrac{25}{21}$ (4) $\dfrac{7}{8}$

  (5) None of these

47. Forty litres of a water-alcohol mixture comprising 40% alcohol is mixed with 100 litres of another water-alcohol mixture such that the amount of alcohol in 40 litres of the new mixture formed is 8 litres. What is the ratio of water to alcohol in the second mixture?

(1) 22 : 3   (2) 21 : 4

(3) 19 : 6   (4) 17 : 8

(5) 3 : 22

48. Anil (A), Byom (B), Charu (C) and Disha (D) enter into a joint venture in which the ratios of the investments are given as A : B = 2 : 5, B : C = 3 : 4 and C : D = 5 : 7. If the total profit at the end of the year is Rs. 46,000, then what is the share of Anil?

(1) Rs. 4,500

(2) Rs. 5,000

(3) Rs. 3,000

(4) Rs. 4,000

(5) Rs.10,000

49. The average weight of a class of 35 students is 40 kg. If a group of five students having an average weight of 42 kg leave the class, then what will be the average weight of the remaining 30 students?

(1) $40\dfrac{2}{3}$ kg   (2) $39\dfrac{2}{3}$ kg

(3) $38\dfrac{2}{3}$ kg   (4) $37\dfrac{2}{3}$ kg

(5) $39\dfrac{1}{3}$ kg

50. Ten years ago Sachin was twice as old as Ajay. If Sachin will be 38 years old after 12 years, then what is the present age of Ajay?

(1) 22 years

(2) 20 years

(3) 16 years

(4) 13 years

(5) 18 years

Directions (Q. 51 to 55) : Answer the questions on the basis of the information given below.

The bar-graph given below shows the number of employees working in different departments of an organization and table shows the ratio of males and females in those departments.

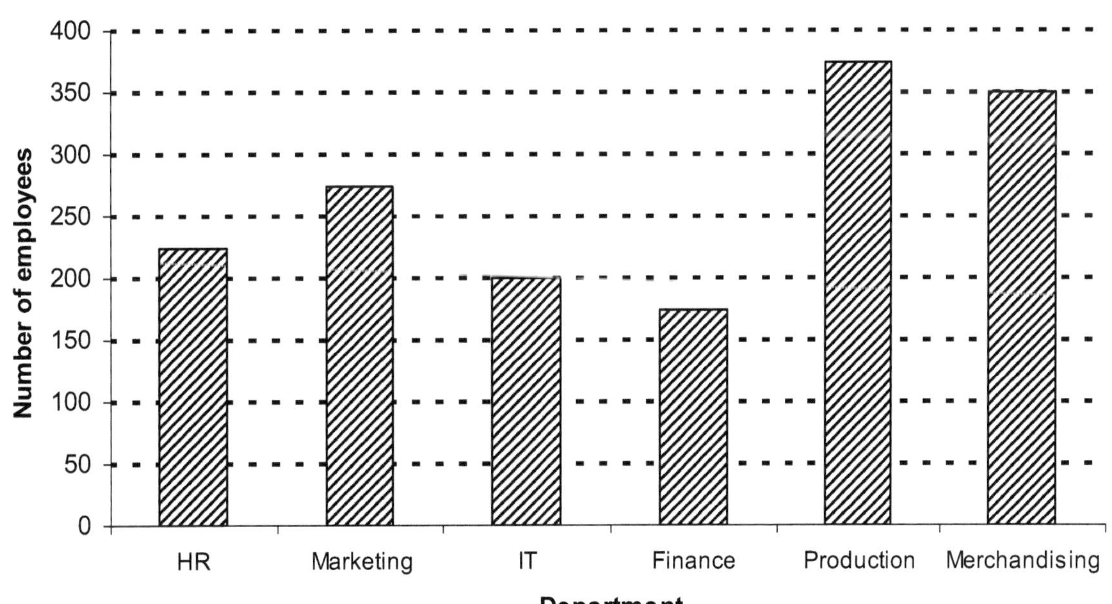

Department	Males	Females
HR	9	16
Marketing	3	2
IT	9	31
Finance	2	3
Production	11	4
Merchandising	4	3

51. What is the total number of males working in all the departments together?

(1) 755   (2) 925

(3) 836   (4) 784

(5) None of these

52. What is the number of females working in the HR department?

(1) 158   (2) 128

(3) 136   (4) 144

(5) None of these

53. What is the respective ratio of total number of employees working in the production department to those working in the Merchandising department?

(1) 15 : 14   (2) 8 : 7

(3) 14 : 15   (4) 7 : 8

(5) None of these

54. In which department are the lowest number of females working?

(1) Marketing   (2) Production

(3) HR   (4) Finance

(5) None of these

55. What is the total number of employees from all departments together in the organization?

(1) 1500   (2) 1575

(3) 1525   (4) 1625

(5) None of these

Directions (Q. 56 to 60) : In each of these questions, two equations I and II with variables a and b are given. You have to solve both the equations to find the values of a and b.

Mark answer if:

(1) $a < b$

(2) $a \leq b$

(3) Relationship between a and b cannot be established.

(4) $a > b$

(5) $a \geq b$

56. I. $2a^2 + a - 1 = 0$

    II. $12b^2 - 17b + 6 = 0$

57. I. $a^2 - 5a + 6 = 0$

    II. $2b^2 - 13b + 21 = 0$

58. I. $a^2 + 5a + 6 = 0$

    II. $b^2 + 7b + 12 = 0$

59. I. $16a^2 = 1$

    II. $3b^2 + 7b + 2 = 0$

60. I. $a^2 + 2a + 1 = 0$

    II. $b^2 = 4$

Directions (Q. 61 to 65) : Answer the questions on the basis of information given below.

The table given below shows the number of candidates interviewed by five firms on different working days.

Working Day	Firms				
	A	**B**	**C**	**D**	**E**
Monday	17	18	23	25	18
Tuesday	21	19	14	28	25
Wednesday	23	22	23	12	18
Thursday	24	14	12	23	18
Friday	10	10	16	15	22
Saturday	17	26	20	20	24

61. What is the respective ratio between the number of candidates interviewed by firm D on Friday and Saturday together and that of candidates interviewed by firm B on the same days?

(1) 35 : 38   (2) 39 : 40

(3) 43 : 44   (4) 45 : 46

(5) 35 : 36

62. The number of candidates interviewed by firm C on Wednesday is approximately what percent of total number of candidates interviewed by all the firms on the same day?

(1) 24   (2) 23

(3) 38   (4) 29

(5) 28

63. In which firm the number of candidates interviewed decreased consistently from Monday to Saturday?

(1) B   (2) None

(3) D   (4) C

(5) A

64. What is the number of candidates interviewed by all the firms on Monday?

(1) 101   (2) 102

(3) 114   (4) 98

(5) 96

65. By what percent the number of candidates interviewed by firm E on Tuesday increased with respect to that of interviewed on the preceding day?

(1) 45   (2) 26

(3) 61   (4) 56

(5) 39

REASONING ABILITY

Directions (Q. 66 to 70): Read the following information carefully and answer the questions given below it.

I. Eight persons E, F, G, H, I, J, K and L are seated around a square table — two on each side.

II. There are three lady members and they are not seated next to each other.

III. J is between L and F.

IV. G is between I and F.

V. H, a lady member, is second to the left of J.

VI. L, a male member, is seated opposite to E, a lady member.

VII. There is a lady member between F and I.

66. Who among the following is seated between E and H?

(1) F   (2) I

(3) J   (4) L

(5) None of these

67. How many persons are seated between K and F?

(1) None   (2) One

(3) Four   (4) Two

(5) Three

68. Who among the following are the three lady members?

(1) E, G and J   (2) E, H and G

(3) G, H and J   (4) G, E and K

(5) E, J and F

69. Who among the following is to the immediate left of F?

(1) G   (2) I

(3) H   (4) K

(5) J

70. Four of the following are alike in a certain way and form a group. Which is the one that does not belong to that group?

(1) JI   (2) LE

(3) FH   (4) GK

(5) LK

71. Pointing to a photograph a lady tells Mohan, "I am the only daughter of this lady and her son is your maternal uncle." How is the speaker related to Mohan's father?

(1) Wife

(2) Sister-in-law

(3) Mother

(4) Sister

(5) Either (1) or (2)

72. A man starts moving in north direction and after traveling 20 km takes a right turn to travel 30 km. He again turns to his right then left and again left to travel 35 km, 15 km and 15 km respectively. Finally he takes a left turn again to travel 15 km. In which direction and at what distance is he from his starting position?

(1) East, 45 km   (2) East, 30 km

(3) West, 15 km   (4) West, 30 km

(5) East, 60 km

73. There are five persons: Ram, Keshav, Lalit, Pawan and Prabhat. Lalit is older than Pawan but not younger than Keshav. Ram is older than Keshav but younger than Pawan. Who is the eldest?

(1) Lalit   (2) Prabhat

(3) Ram   (4) Cannot be determined

(5) None of these

74. Among P, Q, R, S and T each having different height. Q is shorter than only T and P is taller than only S. Who will be third when they are arranged in descending order of their height?

(1) R   (2) S

(3) T   (4) Q

(5) Data inadequate

75. In a certain code, if SCHOOL is coded as 123445 and TEAM as 6078, then how would HOTEL be coded in that code?

(1) 34065   (2) 43605

(3) 60734   (4) 34785

(5) 34605

Directions (Q. 76 to 80): In the following questions, the symbols δ, %, *, @ and © are used with the following meaning as illustrated below:

'P % Q' means P is not smaller than Q'.

'P© Q' means P is not greater than Q'..

'P δ Q' means 'P is neither greater than nor equal to Q'

'P @Q' means 'P is neither smaller than nor equal to Q'

'P * Q' means 'P is neither greater than nor smaller than Q'.

Now in each of the following questions, assuming the given statements to be true, find which of the two conclusions I and II given below them is/are definitely true. Give answer

(1) if only Conclusion I is true.

(2) if only Conclusion II is true.

(3) if either Conclusion I or II is true.

(4) if neither Conclusion I nor II is true.

(5) if both Conclusions I and II are true.

76. Statements:

M @ T, T % R, R * K

Conclusions:

I. K © T

II. M @ K

77. Statements:

J © N, N % D, D δ M

Conclusions:

I. M @ N

II. J δ D

78. Statements:

W δ F, F @ N, N © H

Conclusions:

I. N δ W

II. H @ F

79. Statements:

K % R, R @ M, M δ W

Conclusions:

I. M @ R

II. M δ K

80. Statements:

H * D, D © T, T @ N

Conclusions:

I. T * H

II. T @ H

81. If 'FINANCE' is coded as 'GKQESIL', then how will 'BANK' be coded in the same manner?

(1) CBOL (2) CDRP

(3) CCQO (4) CCPN

(5) None of these

82. How many such pairs of letters are there in the word DOCUMENTARY each of which has as many letters between them in the word as there are between them in the English alphabet?

(1) None (2) One

(3) Two (4) Three

(5) More than three

83. In a march past, seven persons are standing in a row facing north. Q is standing to the left of R and to the right of P. O is standing to the right of N and to the left of P. Similarly, S is standing to the right of R and to the left of T. Who is standing in the middle?

(1) P (2) Q

(3) R (4) O

(5) T

84. How many meaningful English words can be made with the letters DREO using each letter only once in each word?

(1) None (2) One

(3) Two (4) Three

(5) More than three

85. All the alphabets of the word BOARJDTNG are arranged in alphabetical order from left to right. Thereafter, if each vowel is changed to the next letter in the English alphabet and each consonant is changed to the previous letter in the English alphabet, then which of the following will be third from left

(1) M (2) C

(3) F (4) B

(5) Q

Directions (Q. 86 to 90): Answer the questions on the basis of the information given below.

Andy, Bhola, Chandan, Dinkar, Ehsan and Fredrick are six male players who sit in row-1 while facing North, while Parveen, Kali, Reshma, Sarita, Tanu and Urmila are six female players who sit in row-2 while facing South such that they constitute six teams that participated in a Table Tennis Mixed Doubles tournament; each team consists of one male player and one female player. Each player of a particular row is facing a player of the other row and the distance between any two adjacent players of each row is same. The names of the teams are - RCB, GKI, KKR, LNS, DVL and REX – but not necessarily in the same order. It is also known that:

Players from GKI sit opposite to each other. Dinkar plays for RCB and sits at equidistant positions from the players belonging to LNS and KKR. None of the players from REX and DVL is an immediate neighbor of each other. Each player of the KKR team sits at the extreme end of his/her row; same is true for Chandan and Urmila. Parveen sits second to the left of Tanu. Sarita plays for REX and is an immediate neighbor of the players from both RCB and GKI. Reshma sits third to the left of Kali, who plays for LNS, and sits opposite to Ehsan who is an immediate neighbor of the player from REX and Andy. Urmila is from DVL and she is facing Fredrick who is sitting third to the right of the player from DVL.

86. Who is sitting third to the left of the player from RCB in row 2?

(1) Chandan

(2) Ehsan

(3) Andy

(4) Bhola

(5) Fredrick

87. How many players are sitting between Kali and the one from DVL?

(1) None   (2) One

(3) Two   (4) Three

(5) Four

88. Four of the five are alike in a certain way and thus form a group. Find the one that does not belong to the group.

(1) Tanu   (2) Chandan

(3) Urmila   (4) Fredrick

(5) Kali

89. Players of which team sit opposite to each other?

(1) LNS   (2) KKR

(3) RCB   (4) DVL

(5) REX

90. Who are the immediate neighbors of the person from REX in row-2?

(1) Kali and Tanu

(2) Kali and Parveen

(3) Parveen and Reshma

(4) Urmila and Reshma

(5) Urmila and Kali

Directions (91 to 95): In each of the questions below, four statements are followed by four conclusions numbered I, II, III and IV. You have to take the given statements to be true even if they seem to be at variance with commonly known facts. Read all the conclusions and then decide which of the given conclusions logically follow(s) from the given statements disregarding commonly known facts.

91. Statements:

Some stoves are ovens.

All ovens are cylinders.

Some engines are stoves.

Some metals are cylinders.

Conclusions:

I. Some ovens are metals

II. Some cylinders are stoves.

III. Some ovens are engines.

IV. No engine is a cylinder.

(1) None follows

(2) Only II and IV follow

(3) Only II and III follow

(4) Only III follows

(5) Only II follows

92. Statements:

Some cars are buses.

Some buses are trains.

All aeroplanes are trains.

All trucks are buses.

Conclusions:

I. Some aeroplanes are trucks.

II. Some cars are trains.

III. Some trucks are aeroplanes.

IV. No truck is a train.

(1) All follow

(2) Only II and IV follow

(3) Only III and IV follow

(4) Only I and III follow

(5) None of these

93. Statements:

Some tools are hammers.

All tools are trees.

Some trees are flowers.

No hammer is a flower.

Conclusions:

I. All hammers are tools

II. No tool is a flower.

III. Some hammers are trees.

IV. Some flowers are tools

(1) All follow

(2) Only I and either II or IV follow

(3) Only II and IV follow

(4) Only III and either II or IV follow

(5) None of these

94. Statements:

Some bags are pockets.

Some pockets are trousers

All skirts are pockets.

Some belts are bags.

Conclusions:

I. Some trousers are belts.

II. Some skirts are bags.

III. No trouser is a belt.

IV. Some skirts are trousers.

(1) All follow

(2) Only II and IV follow

(3) Only III follows

(4) Only either I or III follows

(5) None of these

95. **Statements:**

Some cats are tigers.

All lions are cats.

Some horses are lions.

All horses are animals.

Conclusions:

I.   Some lions are tigers.

II. No horse is a tiger.

III. Some horses are cats.

IV. Some horses are tigers.

(1) All follow

(2) Only III follows

(3) Only I and IV follow

(4) Only III and either II or IV follow

(5) None of these

Directions (Q. 96 to 100) : Answer the following questions on the basis of the information given below.

Anu, Bhanu, Chanak, Dhruv, Ekta, Firoz, Gauri and Hamit are eight employees of an organization working in three departments viz. Personnel, Administration and Marketing with not more than three of them in any department. Each of them has a different choice of sports from football, cricket, volleybal, badminton, lawn tennis, basketball, hockey and table tennis, not necessarily in the same order.

Dhruv works in Administration and does not like either football or cricket. Firoz works in Personnel with only Anu who likes table tennis. Ekta and Hamit do not work in the same department as Dhruv. Chanak likes hockey and does not work in Marketing. Gauri does not work in Administration and does not like either cricket or badminton. One of those who work in Administration likes football. The one who likes volleyball works in Personnel. None of those who work in Administration likes either badminton or lawn tennis. Hamit does not like cricket.

96. Which of the following groups of employees work in Administration department?

(1) Ekta, Gauri, Hamit

(2) Anu, Firoz

(3) Bhanu, Chanak, Dhruv

(4) Bhanu, Gauri ,Dhruv

(5) Data inadequate

97. In which department does Ekta work ?

(1) Personnel

(2) Marketing

(3) Administration

(4) Data inadequate

(5) None of these

98. What is Ekta's favourite sport ?

(1) Cricket

(2) Badminton

(3) Basketball

(4) Lawn Tennis

(5) None of these

99. Which of the following combinations of employee-department-favourite sport is correct?

(1) Ekta - Administration - Cricket

(2) Firoz - Personnel - Lawn Tennis

(3) Hamit - Marketing - Lawn Tennis

(4) Bhanu - Administration - Table Tennis

(5) None of the above

100. What is Gauri's favourite sport ?

(1) Cricket

(2) Badminton

(3) Basketball

(4) Lawn Tennis

(5) None of these

ANSWERS

1. (2)	**2.** (2)	**3.** (1)	**4.** (4)	**5.** (1)	**6.** (3)	**7.** (1)	**8.** (1)	**9.** (2)	**10.** (2)
11. (1)	**12.** (2)	**13.** (4)	**14.** (1)	**15.** (5)	**16.** (4)	**17.** (2)	**18.** (3)	**19.** (3)	**20.** (2)
21. (4)	**22.** (3)	**23.** (1)	**24.** (2)	**25.** (4)	**26.** (4)	**27.** (2)	**28.** (3)	**29.** (2)	**30.** (2)
31. (4)	**32.** (3)	**33.** (2)	**34.** (3)	**35.** (1)	**36.** (3)	**37.** (3)	**38.** (3)	**39.** (2)	**40.** (2)
41. (4)	**42.** (3)	**43.** (4)	**44.** (4)	**45.** (2)	**46.** (2)	**47.** (1)	**48.** (4)	**49.** (2)	**50.** (5)
51. (3)	**52.** (4)	**53.** (1)	**54.** (2)	**55.** (5)	**56.** (1)	**57.** (2)	**58.** (5)	**59.** (4)	**60.** (3)
61. (5)	**62.** (2)	**63.** (2)	**64.** (1)	**65.** (5)	**66.** (5)	**67.** (5)	**68.** (2)	**69.** (5)	**70.** (5)
71. (1)	**72.** (2)	**73.** (4)	**74.** (1)	**75.** (5)	**76.** (5)	**77.** (4)	**78.** (4)	**79.** (2)	**80.** (3)
81. (3)	**82.** (3)	**83.** (2)	**84.** (2)	**85.** (2)	**86.** (1)	**87.** (4)	**88.** (5)	**89.** (1)	**90.** (3)
91. (5)	**92.** (5)	**93.** (4)	**94.** (4)	**95.** (4)	**96.** (3)	**97.** (2)	**98.** (1)	**99.** (5)	**100.** (4)

EXPLANATIONS

1. (2) 'Until' here means up to the time or point.

2. (2) Only 'fortunate' fits in the blank. Rest of the options will make the sentence grammatically incorrect.

3. (1) 'During' here means throughout the entire time of occurrence.

4. (4) 'Through' is used as a function word to indicate movement within a large expanse.

5. (1) 'With' here means through the help of. 'Insisted' takes the preposition 'on' after it.

6. (3) Refer to the second sentence in the first paragraph for the answer.

7. (1) Refer to the second sentence of the second paragraph for the answer.

8. (1) The entire passage deals with regional rural banks. Hence, option (1) is the most appropriate title.

9. (2) Option (2) is incorrect. Refer to the last three sentences of the second paragraph.

10. (2) Refer to the second last sentence of the passage for the answer.

16. (4) The sentence talks of an action in the past and hence, it should be 'when he reached the office'.

17. (2) The phrase talks of the situation of the industry in the previous year and hence, should use the past tense. So, it should be 'had brought a much'.

18. (3) The threat is not from the residents but a threat to them.

19. (3) It should be 'to regulate' or 'for regulating'.

20. (2) 'Fastest' is a superlative degree of comparison and hence, it should not be 'most fastest' but only 'fastest'.

21. (4) People who travel in search of food and shelter are called nomads.

22. (3) The correct idiom is "to be scared out of one's wits", which means to be extremely frightened.

23. (1) "Expanse" refers to a great extent of something spread out.

24. (2) The man is amazed at the stamina of the creatures. So, "unbelievable" correctly fits in the blank.

25. (4) "Live up to something" means to fulfill.

For questions 26 - 30 :

The correct sequence is DACEFB. D opens the paragraph by saying that a Sage once visited Akbar and Akbar decided to give him a horse. A follows D by saying that Akbar instructed the stable master to give him the fastest horse. CE is a mandatory pair. C says that Akbar asked the Sage a question and E says that the Sage replied to him. F follows E by stating what had happened to the horse. B ends the paragraph by saying that the actual reason embarrassed Akbar.

31. (4)
$$? = 7999.99 + 72 \times 49.99$$
$$\approx 8000 + 72 \times 50$$
$$= 8000 + 3600$$
$$= 11600$$

32. (3)
$$? = (25.01)^2 - (15.99)^2$$
$$\approx 25^2 - 16^2$$
$$= (25 - 16)(25 + 16)$$
$$= 9 \times 41$$
$$= 369$$

33. (2)
$$? = 380 \times 12.25 - 365 \div 15$$
$$\approx 4560 - 24$$
$$= 4536 \approx 4550$$

34. (3)

$$? = \frac{180}{100} \times 25501 + \frac{50}{100} \times 28999$$

$$\approx \frac{180}{100} \times 25500 + \frac{50}{100} \times 29000$$

$$= 45900 + 14500$$

$$= 60400$$

35. (1)

$$? = 171.995 \times 14.995 \div 25$$

$$\approx 172 \times 15 \div 25$$

$$= 103.2 \approx 105$$

36. (3) All the three bells tolled together after every 120 sec.i.e. L.C.M. (6, 8, 10)

B1 and B2 tolled together after every 24 sec. i.e. L.C.M. (6, 8)

B2 and B3 tolled together after every 40 sec. i.e. L.C.M. (8, 10)

B1 and B3 tolled together after every 30 sec. i.e. L.C.M. (6, 10)

In every 120 sec, B1 and B2 tolled 4 times, B2 and B3 tolled 2 times and B1 and B3 tolled 3 times.

So in 5 minutes (i.e., 120 sec × 2 + 60 sec), the number of times exactly two of three bells tolled together was (4 + 2 + 3) × 2 + (2 + 1 + 2) = 23.

37. (3) Let the original price of each mango be Rs. x.

Then, new price = 1.2x

Original quantity – new quantity = 5

$$\Rightarrow \frac{60}{x} - \frac{60}{1.2x} = 5$$

$$\Rightarrow x = 2$$

Hence, the price of a mango = Rs. 2

38. (3) Marked price $= \left(\dfrac{1+p\%}{1-d\%}\right) CP = \dfrac{1.3}{0.65} CP = 2\ CP$

39. (2) Given that the CP for the importer is Rs. 200

His SP $= \dfrac{90}{100} \times 200$ = Rs. 180

This is the CP for the distributor

∴ The SP for the distributor

$$= \frac{91}{100} \times 180 = \text{Rs. } 163.80$$

This SP is the CP for the retailer

∴ SP of the retailer

$$= \frac{108}{100} \times 163.80 = \text{Rs. } 176.90$$

∴ Cumulative loss

$$= 200 - 176.90$$

$$= \text{Rs. } 23.10.$$

40. (2) P = Rs. 4,500, Time = 9 months = 3 quarters. R = 16% p.a. = 4% per quarter.

$$\therefore \quad \text{Amount} = 4500 \times \left(1 + \frac{4}{100}\right)^3$$

$$= 4500 \times \left(\frac{26}{25}\right)^3 = \text{Rs. } 5061.88.$$

$$\therefore \quad \text{C.I.} = 5061.88 - 4500$$

$$= \text{Rs. } 561.88.$$

41. (4) The series follows as:

$$3 \times 4 + 1 = 13$$
$$13 \times 5 + 2 = 67$$
$$67 \times 6 + 3 = 405$$
$$405 \times 7 + 4 = 2840\ (2839)$$
$$2839 \times 8 + 5 = 22717$$

Hence, the wrong term in the series is 2840.

Alternate method: 2840 is only even number and others are odd.

42. (3) The series follows as:

$$48 \times 5 = 240$$
$$240 \times 6 = 1440$$
$$1440 \times 7 = 10080$$
$$10080 \times 8 = 80740\ (80640)$$

Hence, the wrong term in the series is 80740.

43. (4) The series follows as:

$$6^3 + 2 = 218$$
$$7^3 + 2 = 345$$
$$8^3 + 2 = 515\ (514)$$
$$9^3 + 2 = 731$$
$$10^3 + 2 = 1002$$

Hence, the wrong term in the series is 515.

44. (4) The series follows as:

$$1 \times 2 \times 3 = 6$$
$$4 \times 5 \times 6 = 120$$
$$7 \times 8 \times 9 = 504$$
$$10 \times 11 \times 12 = 1320$$
$$13 \times 14 \times 15 = 2830\ (2730)$$

Hence, the wrong term in the series is 2830.

45. (2) The series follows as:

$$2^2 + 3^2 = 13$$
$$4^2 + 5^2 = 41\ (40)$$
$$6^2 + 7^2 = 85$$
$$8^2 + 9^2 = 145$$
$$10^2 + 11^2 = 221$$

Hence, the wrong term in the series is 40.

46. (2) Medals won by Aditi in school = 3x

Medals won by Punam in school = 7x

Medals won by Aditi in college = 7y

Medals won by Punam in college = 8y

$$\therefore \quad \frac{(3x + 7y)}{(7x + 8y)} = \frac{1}{2}$$

$$\Rightarrow \quad x = 6y.$$

Required fraction $= \dfrac{7x}{(7x + 8y)} = \dfrac{21}{25}$.

47. (1) Let the quantity of alcohol in second mixture be x litre.

Hence, overall quantity of alcohol in the new mixture $= \left(\dfrac{(0.4 \times 40) + x}{40 + 100}\right) = \dfrac{(16 + x)}{140}$

$$\therefore \quad \frac{(16 + x)}{140} = \frac{8}{40}$$

$$\Rightarrow \quad 16 + x = 28$$

$$\Rightarrow \quad x = 12 \text{ litres.}$$

Hence, the required ratio is = 88 : 12 = 22 : 3.

48. (4) Since A : B = 2 : 5, B : C = 3 : 4 and C : D = 5 : 7

So, we get the combined ratio as A : B : C : D

$$= 6 : 15 : 20 : 28$$

Thus, Anil's share $= \dfrac{6}{69} \times 46000 = \text{Rs.}4,000$.

49. (2) Total weight of 35 students

$$= 35 \times 40 = 1400 \text{ kg.}$$

Total weight of 5 students

$$= 5 \times 42 = 210 \text{ kg.}$$

Total weight of 30 remaining students

$$= 1400 - 210$$

$$= 1190 \text{ kg.}$$

Average weight of 30 students

$$= \frac{1190}{30} = 39\frac{2}{3} \text{ kg.}$$

50. (5) Let present age of Sachin be 'x' years.

Age of Ajay 10 years ago $= \dfrac{(x - 10)}{2}$.

After 12 years, age of Sachin = x + 12 = 38

$$\Rightarrow \quad x = 26$$

$\therefore$ Present age of Ajay

$$= \frac{x - 10}{2} + 10 = 18 \text{ years.}$$

51. (3) Number of males in HR

$$= \frac{9}{25} \times 225 = 81$$

Number of males in Marketing

$$= \frac{3}{5} \times 275 = 165$$

Number of males in IT

$$= \frac{9}{40} \times 200 = 45$$

Number of males in Finance

$$= \frac{2}{5} \times 175 = 70$$

Number of males in Production

$$= \frac{11}{15} \times 375 = 275$$

Number of males in Merchandising

$$= \frac{4}{7} \times 350 = 200$$

Total number of males working in all the departments

$$= 81 + 165 + 45 + 70 + 275 + 200$$

$$= 836$$

52. (4) Number of females working in HR department

$$= \frac{16}{25} \times 225 = 144$$

53. (1) Required ratio = 375 : 350 = 15 : 14

54. (2) Number of females in HR

$$= \frac{16}{25} \times 225 = 144$$

Number of females in Marketing

$$= \frac{2}{5} \times 275 = 110$$

Number of females in IT

$$= \frac{31}{40} \times 200 = 155$$

Number of females in Finance

$$= \frac{3}{5} \times 175 = 105$$

Number of females in Production

$$= \frac{4}{15} \times 375 = 100$$

Number of females in Merchandising

$$= \frac{3}{7} \times 350 = 150$$

55. (5) Total number of employees in the organization
= 225 + 275 + 200 + 175 + 375 + 350
= 1600

56. (1) After solving equation I, $a = -1, \dfrac{1}{2}$

After solving equation II, $b = \dfrac{2}{3}, \dfrac{3}{4}$

Thus, a < b.

57. (2) After solving equation I, a = 2, 3

After solving equation II, $b = 3, \dfrac{7}{2}$

Thus, $a \leq b$.

58. (5) After solving equation I, a = –2, – 3
After solving equation II, b = –3, –4
Thus, $a \geq b$.

59. (4) After solving equation I, $a = \pm \dfrac{1}{4}$

After solving equation II, $b = -\dfrac{1}{3}, -2$

Thus, a > b.

60. (3) After solving equation I, $a = \pm 1$

After solving equation II, $b = \pm 2$

Thus, relation between a and b cannot be established.

61. (5) Number of candidates interviewed by firm D on Friday and Saturday together = 15 + 20 = 35

Number of candidates interviewed by firm B on Friday and Saturday together = 10 + 26 = 36

∴   Required ratio = 35 : 36

62. (2) Required percentage

$$= \frac{23}{(23 + 22 + 23 + 12 + 18)} \times 100$$

$$= \frac{23}{98} \times 100$$

$$= 23.46 \approx 23\%$$

64. (1) Number of candidates interviewed by all the firms on Monday = 17 + 18 + 23 + 25 + 18 = 101

65. (5) Percentage increase

$$= \left(\frac{25 - 18}{18} \right) \times 100$$

$$= 38.88 \approx 39\%$$

For questions 66 to 70: On the basis of the given information, we arrive at the following sitting plan that does not violate any of the given conditions.

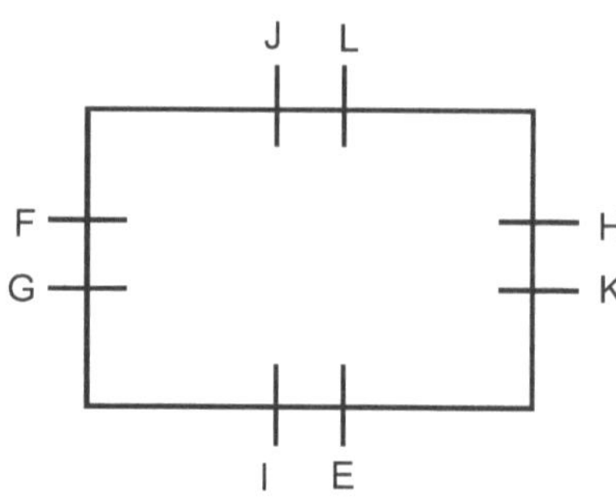

And on the basis of the above figure rest of the questions are solved as follows:

66. (5) K is seated between E and H.

67. (5) Three persons H, L and J or G, I and E are seated between K and F.

68. (2) The three lady members are E, H and G.

69. (5) J is to the immediate left of F.

71. (1) The lady who is speaking is the only daughter of the lady in photograph. The son of the lady in photograph is the brother of lady who is speaking. If the brother of the lady speaker is the maternal uncle of Mohan, then the lady speaker is the mother of Mohan, and so she is also the wife of Mohan's father.

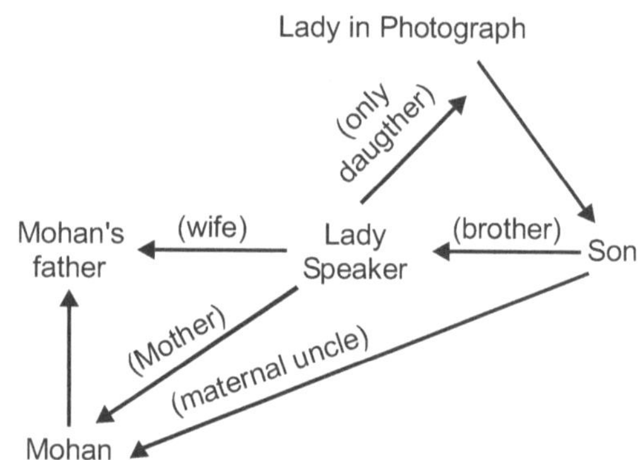

72. (2)

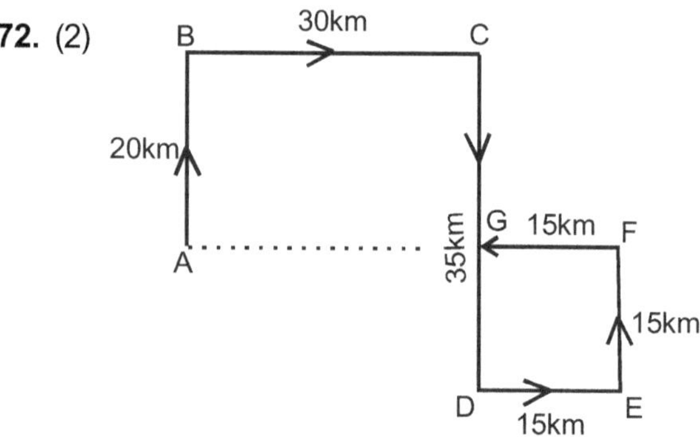

The starting point is A and the terminal point is G.

73. (4) Cannot be determined because there is no information about Prabhat.

74. (1) According to the information,

$$T > Q > R > P > S$$

∴ Required answer is R.

75. (5) S C H O O L and T E A M

1 2 3 4 4 56 0 7 8

Hence, H O T E L → 3 4 6 0 5

76. (5) M > T ≥ R = K

(i) K ≤ T (True)

(ii) M > K (True)

Both (i) and (ii) are true.

77. (4) J ≤ N ≥ D < M

(i) M > N (False)

(ii) J < D (False)

Both (i) and (ii) are false.

78. (4) W < F > N ≤ H

(i) N < W (False)

(ii) H > F (False)

Both (i) and (ii) are false.

79. (2) K ≥ R > M < W

(i) M > R (False)

(ii) M < K (True)

Only (ii) is true.

80. (3) H = D ≤ T > N

(i) T = H

(ii) T > H

Either (i) or (ii) is true.

81. (3) The letters of the word are coded by moving one step ahead and increasing the difference by one.

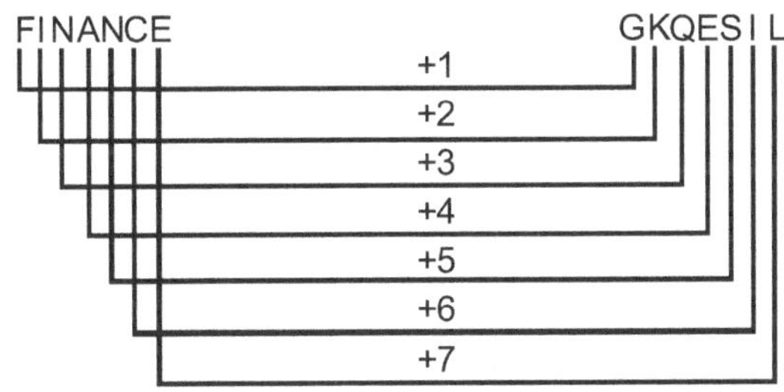

Similarly,

82. (3) 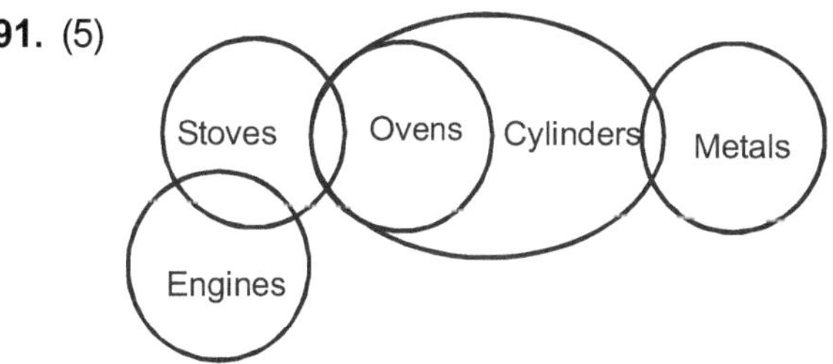

83. (2) 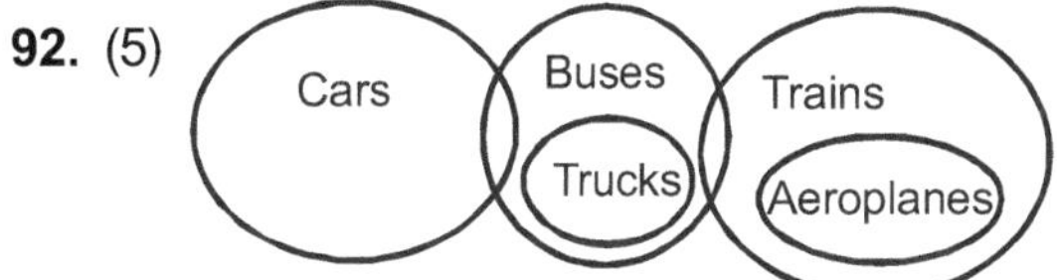

Q is to the left of R and to the right of P, i.e. P, Q, R.

O is to the right of N and to the left of P, i.e. N, O, P.

S is to the right of R and to the left of T, i.e. R, S, T.

So the order is: N, O, P, Q, R, S, T.

Clearly, Q is in the middle.

84. (2) RODE

85. (2) 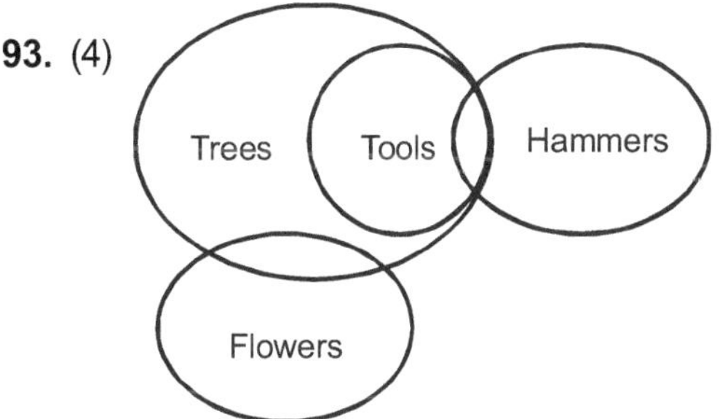

Third from the left = C.

For questions 86 to 90:

Row-2	KKR	LNS	RCB	REX	GKI	DVL
	Tanu	Kali	Parveen	Sarita	Reshma	Urmila
Row-1	Chandan	Ehsan	Andy	Dinkar	Bhola	Fredrick
	REC	LNS	DVL	RCB	GKI	KKR

91. (5) 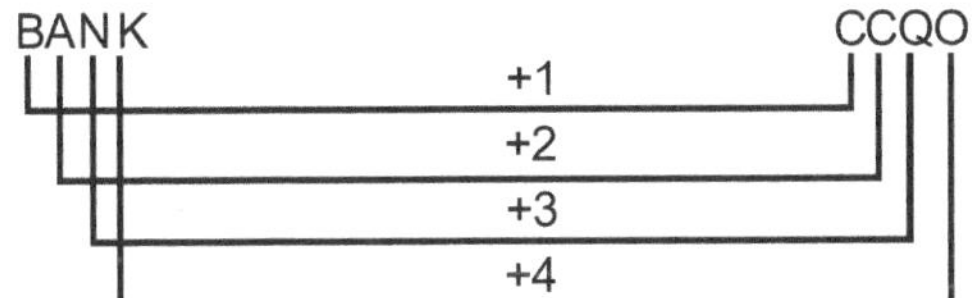

92. (5)

93. (4)

94. (4)

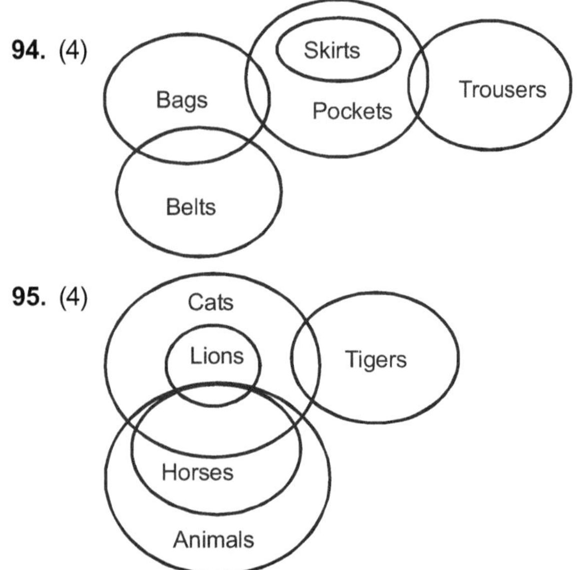

95. (4)

For questions 96 to 100:

Person	Department	Game
Anu	Personnel	Table Tennis
Bhanu	Administration	Football
Chanak	Administration	Hockey
Dhruv	Administration	Basketball
Ekta	Marketing	Cricket
Firoz	Personnel	Volleyball
Gauri	Marketing	Lawn Tennis
Hamit	Marketing	Badminton

PRACTICE PAPER – 13

ENGLISH LANGUAGE

Directions (Q. 1 to 5): Read each sentence to find out whether there is any grammatical or idiomatic error in it. The error, if any, will be in one part of the sentence. The number of that part is the answer. If there is no error, the answer is 5 (Ignore errors of punctuation, if any).

1. The biggest (1) / health burden that India (2)/ is set to face in the coming years (3) / is tackle cancer. (4) / No error (5)

2. Illegal sand mining in the peripheral areas (1) / of the district continues to remain a big problem for (2) / forest-range officers as yet another instance illegal (3) /mining was reported yesterday.(4) / No error (5)

3. The policemen, who (1) / was deployed heavily (2) / in the area, did nothing to (3) / dissuade the protesters. (4) / No error (5)

4. Festivals are prime occasions (1) / for splurging on presents and owing to improved economic situation, (2) / the youths is gung-ho (3)/ about breaking all previous records. (4) / No error (5)

5. It is important to recruit personnel at (1) / different levels in the organisation so that (2) / the ensuing human resource gap is bridged (3) / at least for the critical operations. (4) / No error (5)

Directions (Q. 6 to 10): In the following passage there are blanks, each of which has been numbered. These numbers are printed below the passage and against each, five words/phrases are suggested, one of which fits the blank appropriately. Find out the appropriate word/phrase in each case.

Global healthcare is a \$4.5 trillion industry, second only to the agro industry. Even then healthcare __(6)__ only eight percent of world's population. Policymakers should __(7)__ at healthcare industry as not only an industry which addresses pain but also as one which can __(8)__ the economy. The last century was driven by machines that addressed human toil and it is strongly __(9)__ that this century will be driven by healthcare. This, however, will only happen if policymakers make a conscious effort to __(10)__ the right policies in place soon.

6. (1) affords   (2) cures
   (3) visits   (4) reaches
   (5) provides

7. (1) look   (2) plan
   (3) weigh   (4) admire
   (5) consider

8. (1) persuade   (2) ascertain
   (3) influence   (4) drive
   (5) estimate

9. (1) thought   (2) credited
   (3) identified   (4) believed
   (5) supposed

10. (1) derive
    (2) frame
    (3) figure
    (4) consider
    (5) put

Directions (Q. 11 to 15): Rearrange the following six sentences (A), (B), (C), (D), (E) and (F) in the proper sequence to form a meaningful paragraph; then answer the questions given below them.

(A) When it comes to the number of tigers though, I think it is too small a number representing a species.

(B) These days, everywhere I go, I see hoardings saying 'Just 1411 Left'.

(C) The three being, the Caspian, Balinese and Javan.

(D) Besides the small number, we are steadily losing a few species of these animals as well.

(E) Normally, I would groan and grumble on seeing this figure of 1411 on my shopping bills as it sounds too much.

(F) At the end of the last century we had lost 3 out of 8 tiger species.

11. Which of the following should be the **FIRST** sentence after rearrangement?
    (1) A   (2) B
    (3) F   (4) D
    (5) E

12. Which of the following should be the **SECOND** sentence after rearrangement?
    (1) F   (2) D
    (3) C   (4) E
    (5) A

13. Which of the following should be the **THIRD** sentence after rearrangement?
    (1) A   (2) B
    (3) F   (4) D
    (5) E

14. Which of the following should be the **FIFTH** sentence after rearrangement?

(1) A   (2) B

(3) D   (4) F

(5) E

15. Which of the following should be the **SIXTH (Last)** sentence after rearrangement?

(1) E   (2) C

(3) F   (4) B

(5) A

Directions (Q. 16-25): Read the following passage carefully and answer the questions given below it. Certain words/phrases have been printed in bold to help you locate them while answering some of the questions.

Mahatma Gandhi, the father of the nation, was a practitioner of "green politics" far ahead of his times. His politics in the first half of the last century embraced the six principles of green politics, namely social justice, ecological wisdom, grass-roots democracy, non-violence, ecological wisdom and **sustainability**, that were adopted in 2001 at the first Global Greens Congress at Canberra, Australia.

Despite Gandhi's green politics, no established political party in India can claim to be a "green party" in the accepted sense of the term. Perhaps, a vibrant middle class of reasonable size, necessary to support such a green party, has emerged or is emerging in India only in the last couple of decades. In this context, two questions of considerable interest are: Why has a green party not occupied more political space in India for so long? How green is the politics of the Indian middle class? This article is an attempt at answering these questions. It is not about the right approach to the environment and associated lifestyle, including such important issues as consumerism, large-scale industrialisation and urbanisation. It is a simple attempt at examining whether, with the emerging Indian middle class, a conventional political party contesting elections is likely to champion environmental issues in the same way as green parties do in the developed North.

Gandhi had a significant impact on the new social movements in Europe and America, whose participants were middle-class people concerned about nature. In India also, the environmental groups, for example, the Chipko (embrace) movement and Narmada Bachao Andolan (NBA), have adopted Gandhi's methods of protests such as demonstrations and hunger strikes. But the protesters have been generally the people at the margin-peasants, tribal communities, fishermen and other underprivileged people-"empty-belly" environmentalists in Ramachandra Guha's spectacular words, very different from the "full-stomach" environmentalists in the North.

The classification of people into "full-stomach" and "empty-belly" environmentalists, or omnivores, ecological refugees and ecosystem people perhaps does not deal adequately with the emerging middle class in India in the context of green politics. The Indian middle class is neither rich nor poor, nor ecological refugees, nor ecosystem people. With their education and access to the media, they have some awareness of the ecological issues. At the receiving end of many environmental problems, day to day, they suffer problems of unsafe and inadequate water supply, poor air quality and sewerage. Furthermore, ecological wisdom and sustainability are two critical, but only two of the six pillars of green politics. The Indian middle class has a strong commitment to the other four pillars, namely social justice, grass-roots democracy, non-violence, and respect for diversity.

Before taking up the two questions under discussion, it is useful to recall that the term "green" of green parties comes from a heightened concern for the environment and its sustainability. "Greenpeace"-the well-known organisation that carries out non-violent campaigns and creative confrontations to expose global environmental problems-has "green" in its name. The term "green" also became popular worldwide with the "green bans" movement in Australia in the early 1970s. Workers under the New South Wales Builders' Labourers' Federation (NSWBLF), on a large scale, refused to work on ecologically unsound projects. It came to be known as the "green bans" movement after the term was used by the Australian trade union leader and environmentalist Jack Mundey in May 1973. Soon the term "greenies" designated not only supporters of the NSWBLF green bans but also environmentally concerned people in general.

Single-issue parties find it difficult to **mobilise** popular support. Thus, given the reach of politics beyond just the environment, green parties slowly came to embrace a few more fundamental agendas. Environmentalists and peace activists in erstwhile West Germany came together to form the political party "The Greens" on 13 January 1980 and adopt the "Four Pillars of Green Politics" – social justice, ecological wisdom, grass-roots democracy, and non-violence. Soon, these became the four accepted pillars of green politics. The four pillars got expanded to six principles in 2001 at the first Global Greens Congress at Canberra. The additional two principles were sustainability and respect for diversity.

The emergence of the six principles is partly explained by the roots of the green parties. These parties were established in countries across Western Europe in the 1980s and arose from four different social movements-the environmental movement, the labour movement, the civil rights movement, and the peace movement. The philosophy of the four movements got enshrined in the six principles. There is widespread popular support in India across classes for four of the six pillars of green politics, namely social justice, grass-roots democracy, non-violence and respect for diversity, and these are endorsed by almost all political parties in India. Thus, in what follows, the discussion on green politics in India focuses on the residual two environmental pillars, namely ecological wisdom and sustainability.

Green parties are a characteristic of Western Europe, Australia, New Zealand, and of some Latin American and East Asian countries. All of them have a sizeable middle class. A post-materialist philosophy is **congenial** for the growth of a green party. The appeal of such a philosophy gained in popularity with humanity's demand on nature exceeding, for over four decades, what nature can **replenish**. The danger from the regenerative capacity of 1.5 Earths required to supply the ecological goods and services that mankind needs every year has more **resonance** in the middle class placed comfortably far beyond the poverty line. Poverty is not conducive for such a world view. That brings us to the important development: the recent emergence of the Indian middle class.

The median, a technical term in statistics, refers to the entity that separates the lower half of a sample or population from the upper half. The celebrated "median voter rule" states that, in a majoritarian democracy, political parties and leaders will select the policy or outcome most preferred by the median voter. Thus, the middle class, separating the poor from the rich, often play a critical role in many countries in determining not only who wins the election but also the nature of policies promised by political parties in manifestos and even the nature of political parties. What is important to note, however, is that the median voter will not be from the middle class unless the class is reasonably large. With say more than a half the population in poverty, it will be a poor at the median separating the even poorer from the richer in two equal halves. This brings us to the problem of defining the middle class itself.

16. According to the passage, Mahatma Gandhi practised Green Politics

(1) because Gandhi wanted to examine ecological policies.

(2) because he wanted to integrate Indians through Green Politics.

(3) because Gandhi believed that Green Politics consists of a dozen principles.

(4) since Green Politics was considered to be fashionable in those days.

(5) and was far ahead of his contemporaries.

17. Which of the following statements is incorrect according to the passage?

(1) Green parties were established in Western Europe in the 1980s.

(2) The term 'green' became popular in Australia in the early 1970s.

(3) The Indian middle class is conversant with ecological issues.

(4) The Indian middle class respects diversity.

(5) Green parties are found in some African countries as well.

18. Among the given options, what can be a suitable title for the passage?

(1) The role of the middle class in Green parties.

(2) The evolution of Green parties

(3) The regeneration of Green parties

(4) The role of Gandhi in the Green party movement.

(5) The principles of Green parties

19. According to the author, single-issue parties

(1) do not find it easy to garner mass support.

(2) often foment communal trouble.

(3) are not very popular in Australia.

(4) have been instrumental in achieving India's freedom from the British rule.

(5) are often supported by the middle classes.

20. According to the author, Mahatma Gandhi

(1) was myopic in his vision of green politics.

(2) formulated certain principles of green politics which were never adopted by the world community.

(3) influenced the new social movements in European countries and America.

(4) helped formed green parties in India just after independence.

(5) never thought that green politics could be self-sustainable.

Directions (Q. 21-23): Choose the word which is most similar in meaning to the word printed in bold as used in the passage.

21. Sustainability

(1) Ability to maintain

(2) Ability to justify

(3) Ability to compete

(4) Ability to complete

(5) Ability to grow

22. Mobilise

(1) A type of fuel

(2) To marshal

(3) To order

(4) To implement

(5) To apply

23. Resonance

(1) Requirement

(2) Emergence

(3) Huge

(4) Service

(5) Relevance

Directions (Q. 24 and 25): Choose the word which is most opposite in meaning to the word printed in bold as used in the passage.

24. Replenish

(1) Refill   (2) Deplete

(3) Restore   (4) Reload

(5) Make up

25. Congenial

(1) Compatible

(2) Affable

(3) Cordial

(4) Mellow

(5) Discordant

Directions (Q. 26 to 30): Each question below has two blanks, each blank indicating that something has been omitted. Choose the set of words for each blank which best fits the meaning of the sentence as a whole.

26. Adding to a growing body of research _______ cutting back on sweetened beverages it is now found that drinking _______ sugary drinks may help lower blood pressure.

(1) for, all

(2) sustaining, increased

(3) against, lesser

(4) behind, more

(5) supporting, fewer

27. The blame game for the air tragedy is already in full _______ with the authorities involved making attempts to _______ for themselves.

(1) sway, defend

(2) view, try

(3) fledged, protect

(4) swing, cover

(5) roll, hide

28. The actress, wearing a dark gray suit and open necked shirt, sat _______ the proceedings looking nervous throughout, occasionally frowning as her lawyer _______ with the judge.

(1) through, spoke

(2) on, argued

(3) for, addressed

(4) with, discussed

(5) along, lectured

29. It was an excellent social evening with people from all _______ of life getting a chance to let their hair _______.

(1) areas, drop   (2) realms, flow

(3) arena, undone   (4) walks, down

(5) types, loose

30. There can be no denying the fact that in sports, star coaches have the _______ to get something extra out of their _______.

(1) apprehension, work

(2) ability, teams

(3) fear, member

(4) capability, house

(5) desirous, players

NUMERICAL ABILITY

Directions for questions 31 to 35: In each of the questions given below, a series is given following a specific pattern. Select from answer choices an appropriate term to fill in the blank to continue the on-going pattern.

31. 6, 24, 60, 120, ?

(1) 180   (2) 210

(3) 240   (4) 204

(5) 150

32. 2, 6, 33, 49, ?

(1) 74   (2) 64

(3) 84   (4) 174

(5) 144

33. 2704, 3844, 5184, 6724, ?

(1) 8454   (2) 8474

(3) 8464   (4) 8964

(5) None of these

34. 400, 100, 50, 50, 100, 400, ?

(1) 800   (2) 400

(3) 200   (4) 1200

(5) None of these

35. 23, 29, 40, 40, 44, 60, 66, ?

(1) 72   (2) 82

(3) 78   (4) 102

(5) None of these

36. The ratio of the number of boys and girls in a class of 400 students is 1 : 24. How many girls need to be removed from the class, so that the percentage of boys in the class becomes 64%?

(1) 383   (2) 377

(3) 375   (4) 359

(5) 385

37. Three-fourth part of a tank is filled with water. 50% of the water is removed from the tank and 60 litres of pure milk is added to it. If now the ratio of milk to water in the tank becomes 5 : 4, then the capacity (in litres) of the tank will be:

(1) 120 litre   (2) 128 litre

(3) 112 litre   (4) 136 litre

(5) None of these

38. A, B and C invested in a partnership in the ratio of 8 : 7 : 5. A withdraws half her money after 5 months. If the profit was Rs. 26,500 for the year, then find B's share.

(1) Rs. 9,800   (2) Rs. 10,200

(3) Rs. 11,500   (4) Rs. 12,600

(5) Rs. 10,500

39. The average score in 8 different subjects is 87. Of these scores, the highest score is 2 more than the next highest score. If these two highest scores are eliminated, then the average of the remaining scores comes out to be 85. What is the highest score?

(1) 93   (2) 94

(3) 95   (4) 96

(5) 92

40. The respective ratio between the present ages of son, mother, father and grandfather is 2 : 7 : 8 : 12. The average age of son and mother is 27 years. What will be mother's age after 7 years?

(1) 40 years   (2) 41 years

(3) 48 years   (4) 49 years

(5) 50 years

Directions (Q.41 to 45): What will come in place of question mark (?) in the following questions?

41. $5^{8.9} \times 25^{7.2} \div 125^{4.6} = 5^{?}$

(1) 10.5   (2) 9.5

(3) 7.6   (4) 8.7

(5) None of these

42. $(1024 - 362 - 214) \div (786 - 730) = ?$

(1) 7   (2) 6

(3) 9   (4) 12

(5) None of these

43. 699.14 + 478.23 + 174.69 = ?

(1) 1322.06   (2) 1352.06

(3) 1205.02   (4) 1235.03

(5) None of these

44. 25% of 965 – 69% of ? = 210.2

(1) 50   (2) 49

(3) 55   (4) 45

(5) None of these

45. $2704 \div 2 \times ? = 31096$

(1) 21   (2) 33

(3) 23   (4) 26

(5) None of these

46. The sum of the digits of a two-digit number is 11. When 27 is added to the number, its digits gets reversed to that of the original number. What is the original number?

(1) 83   (2) 65

(3) 74   (4) 56

(5) None of these

47. In a department there are only two categories of employees i.e, officers and clerks. Out of which 40% are officers. Further, the percentage of female employees in the respective categories is 65% and 40%. If the total number of female employees in the department is 500, then what is the strength of the department?

(1) 940   (2) 680

(3) 1050   (4) 860

(5) 1000

48. A shopkeeper purchased 6 kg rice at Rs. 12 per kg and mixed it with 2 kg white grains of Rs. 14 per kg. The mixture needs to be grinded before selling. Grinding of the mixture cost 20 paise per kg. At what price (in Rs. per kg) should the shopkeeper sell the mixture so as to gain 20% on the whole transaction?

(1) Rs. 14.25

(2) Rs. 13.20

(3) Rs. 14.72

(4) Rs. 15.24

(5) None of these

49. How much adulteration per kg should a vendor of pulses do so that he ends up making a profit of 25%, if the price of unadulterated pulse is Rs.40 per kg and the adulterated pulse is also sold on the same price.

(1) $\dfrac{1}{6}$ kg   (2) $\dfrac{1}{5}$ kg

(3) 250 gm   (4) 225 gm

(5) None of these

50. Divide Rs. 1,105 between A and B, so that the amount of A after 5 years is equal to the amount of B after 7 years, the interest being compounded at 10% per annum.

(1) Rs. 705, Rs. 400

(2) Rs. 605, Rs. 500

(3) Rs. 650, Rs. 455

(4) Rs. 655, Rs. 450

(5) None of these

Directions (Q. 51 to 55): Answer the questions on the basis of the information given below.

In a college, 150 students of MBA are enrolled. The ratio of boys and girls is 7 : 8 respectively. There are three disciplines namely marketing, HR and finance in the college. In marketing discipline there are 50% girls of their total number and the boys are 40% of their total number. In HR discipline, girls are 30% of their total number. Finance discipline has girls 20% of their total number and boys 30% of their total number. 7 boys and 9 girls are in HR and marketing both. 6 boys and 7 girls are in HR and finance both. 5 boys and 8 girls are in marketing and finance both. 2 boys and 3 girls are enrolled in all three disciplines.

51. What percentage of students are enrolled in all three disciplines?

(1) 3.33%   (2) 7.28%

(3) 8.56%   (4) 9.32%

(5) 3.67%

52. What is the respective ratio of boys and girls only in marketing discipline?

(1) 13 : 9   (2) 9 : 13

(3) 9 : 11   (4) 11 : 9

(5) None of these

53. The ratio of number of boys in marketing and finance both and that of girls in finance only is

(1) 5 : 3   (2) 3 : 5

(3) 5 : 4   (4) 4 : 7

(5) None of these

54. By what percent is the number of boys in marketing more than the number of girls in HR discipline?

(1) $13\dfrac{1}{3}\%$ (2) $33\dfrac{1}{3}\%$

(3) $14\dfrac{2}{3}\%$ (4) $16\dfrac{2}{3}\%$

(5) None of these

55. The respective ratio of boys and girls enrolled in HR discipline only is

(1) 11 : 10   (2) 9 : 10

(3) 7 : 5   (4) 5 : 7

(5) 10 : 11

Directions (Q. 56 to 60): Answer the questions on the basis of the information given below.

The pie charts given below show the percentage break-up of the white goods market for 2015 and 2016. The 8 companies given in the pie-charts are the only companies in this market.

Total production 26,93,000 units in market (2015)

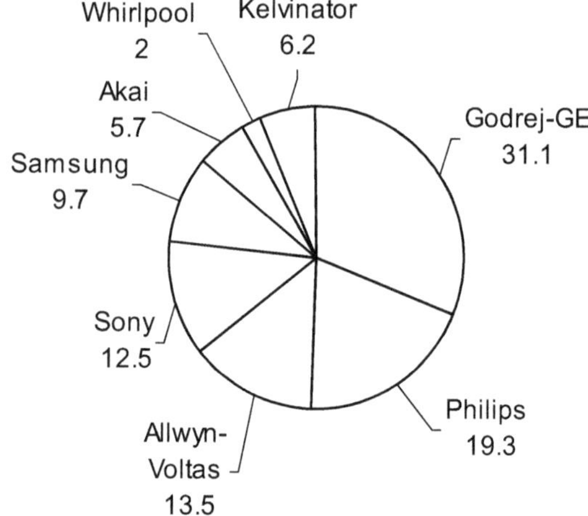

Total production 37,63,000 units in market (2016)

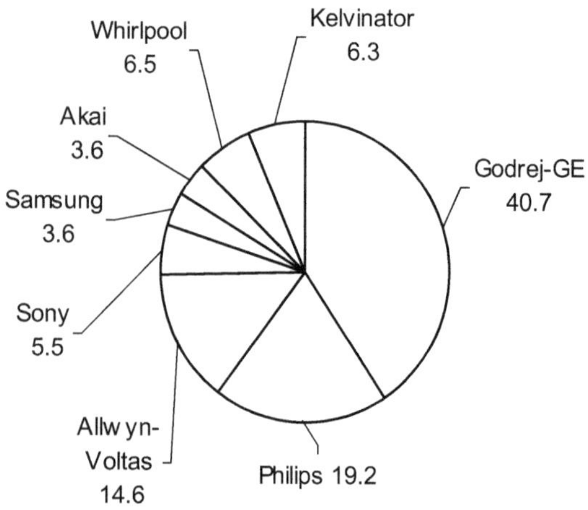

56. Which company shows the best performance in terms of the percentage increase in the market share (in units) from 2015 to 2016?

(1) Godrej-GE (2) Allwyn-Voltas

(3) Whirlpool (4) Kelvinator

(5) None of these

57. If the price of the goods sold by Allwyn-Voltas is lower than that sold by Kelvinator, what is the difference in the sales revenues when the total sales revenue is Rs. 15,00,000 from these companies in 2016?

(1) Rs. 3,425 (2) Rs. 4,576

(3) Rs. 4,537 (4) Rs. 6,238

(5) Cannot be determined

58. Which company ranks second last in the production of total number of goods in 2016? Also mention the number of units produced by that company.

(1) Sony, 2,06,965 units

(2) Samsung, 2,06,965 units

(3) Akai, 2,06,965 units

(4) Kelvinator, 2,06,965 units

(5) Whirlpool, 2,44,595 units

59. If the market continues to grow at the same rate in 2017, while the percentage market share of each company remains the same as for 2016, what is the total number of goods produced by the least five performers (performance measured in terms of number of goods produced) in 2017?

(1) 1.56 millions (2) 1.34 millions

(3) 1.43 millions (4) 1.64 millions

(5) 1.46 millions

60. Which company shows the least performance in terms of the percentage decrease in the market share (in units) from 2015 to 2016?

(1) Philips (2) Sony

(3) Samsung (4) Akai

(5) None of these

Directions (Q. 61 to 65): In each questions, two equations numbered I and II are given. You have to solve both the equations and mark the appropriate answer.

Give answer

(1) If $x < y$

(2) If $x > y$

(3) If $x \leq y$

(4) If $x \geq y$

(5) If relationship between x and y cannot be determined

61. I. $4x^2 - 15x + 14 = 0$

II. $6y^2 - 10y + 4 = 0$

62. I. $3x^2 + 10x + 3 = 0$

II. $2y^2 + 15y + 27 = 0$

63. I. $7x^2 + 12x + 5 = 0$

II. $3y^2 + 7y + 2 = 0$

64. I. $16x^2 - 14x + 3 = 0$

II. $6y^2 - 19y + 15 = 0$

65. I. $x^2 + 11x + 18 = 0$

II. $y^2 - \sqrt{81} = 0$

REASONING ABILITY

Directions (Q. 66 to 70): In the following questions, the symbols δ, @, ©, % and * are used with the following meaning as illustrated below:

'P © Q' means 'P is not smaller than Q'

'P % Q' means 'P is neither smaller than nor equal to Q'

'P * Q' means 'P is neither greater than nor equal to Q'

'P δ Q' means 'P is not greater than Q'

'P @ Q' means 'P is neither greater than nor smaller than Q'

Now in each of the following questions assuming the given statements to be true, find which of the four conclusions I, II, III and IV given below them is/are definitely true and give your answer accordingly.

66. Statements:

R * K, K % D, D @ V, V δ M

Conclusions:

I. R * D

II. V * R

III. D @ M

IV. M % D

(1) None is true

(2) Only III is true

(3) Only IV is true

(4) Only either III or IV is true

(5) Only either III or IV and II are true

67. Statements:

B © T, T * R, R % F, F @ K

Conclusions:

I. B % R

II. F * T

III. R % K

IV. K * T

(1) None is true (2) Only I is true

(3) Only II is true (4) Only III is true

(5) Only IV is true

68. Statements:

F % N,   N © W,   W δ Y,   Y * T

Conclusions:

I.   F % W

II. T % N

III. N % Y

IV. T % W

(1) Only I and III are true

(2) Only I and IV are true

(3) Only II and III are true

(4) Only I, II and IV are true

(5) None of these

69. Statements:

D δ T,   T @ R,   R © M,   M % K

Conclusions:

I.   R @ D

II. R % D

III. K * T

IV. M δ T

(1) Only either I or II is true

(2) Only III and IV are true

(3) Only either I or II and III are true

(4) Only either I or II and IV are true

(5) Only either I or II and III and IV are true

70. Statements:

J @ F,   F δ N,   N % H,   H © G

Conclusions:

I.   G * N

II. N © J

III. F * J

IV. J δ G

(1) Only I and II are true

(2) Only I, II and III are true

(3) Only II, III and IV are true

(4) All I, II, III and IV are true

(5) None of these

71. A family of six members A, B, C, D, S and K consist of three females and a married couple. A is the mother of C, and D is the son of C. B is the husband of A, and C is his son, while K is his daughter. Female members in the family are

(1) S, K, A   (2) A, B, C

(3) A, S, D   (4) S, A, C

(5) K, A, D

72. Deepak walks 20 m towards north. Then he turns right and walks 30 m. Now he turns right and walks 35 m. Now turning left, he walks 15 m. Finally he turns left and moves 15 m. In which direction and how far is he from his original position?

(1) East, 15 m   (2) North east, 5 m

(3) West, 15 m   (4) West, 45 m

(5) East, 45 m

73. Six friends – P, Q, R, S, T and U are sitting in a row. P and Q are sitting at the two middle positions. R and S are sitting at the extreme ends. T is sitting to the immediate left of R. Who is sitting adjacent to S?

(1) Q   (2) P

(3) T   (4) Cannot be determined

(5) None of these

74. In a class of thirty students, Mahesh is fourteenth from the left end and Ramesh is twentieth from the right end. How many students are there between Ramesh and Mahesh?

(1) 3   (2) 2

(3) 4   (4) 5

(5) Data inadequate

75. 'PLANNING' is coded in a certain language as a 'UFFHSCSA'. How will 'AUTHORITY' be coded in the same language?

(1) FOYBTLNND   (2) FYOTBNNLT

(3) FBOYTLNTN   (4) FBOYTNLTN

(5) FOYBTLMMD

Directions (Q. 76 to 80): Answer the questions on the basis of the information given below.

Eight friends - Mohan, Sohan, Nayan, Pavan, Lakhan, Hasan, Raman and Aman - are playing different games sitting around a circular table. Four of them are facing the centre and the rest are facing away from the centre. The eight games are Temple Run, Candy Crush, Grand Theft, Mine Craft, Tetris Blitz, Subway Surfers, Angry Birds and Hungry Shark.

The person playing Mine Craft is sitting second to the left of the person who is playing Temple Run. Nayan is playing Tetris Blitz and sitting third to the right of Lakhan, who is playing Hungry Shark. Hasan is playing Grand Theft, and is sitting diametrically opposite to Mohan, who is facing away from the table. Pavan is playing Mine Craft and he is sitting second to the right of Lakhan. Both Hasan and Nayan are facing away from the centre. Mohan is not playing Subway Surfers. Sohan is sitting second to the right of Raman, who is playing Angry Birds. Raman is facing away from the centre and he is sitting third to the right of Hasan.

76. Who is playing Subway Surfers?

   (1) Sohan   (2) Nayan

   (3) Aman   (4) Mohan

   (5) Hasan

77. How many people sit between the person who plays Candy Crush and the one who plays Tetris Blitz in the clockwise direction?

   (1) Two   (2) Three

   (3) None   (4) One

   (5) None of these

78. Select the option with the right combination of person and game.

   (1) Pavan, Temple Run

   (2) Aman, Candy Crush

   (3) Lakhan, Grand Theft

   (4) Raman, Mine Craft

   (5) Nayan, Tetris Blitz

79. Which two friends face each other?

   (1) Mohan, Hasan   (2) Aman, Nayan

   (3) Raman, Pavan   (4) Sohan, Lakhan

   (5) None of these

80. Select the group which consists of persons facing towards the centre of the table.

   (1) Aman, Lakhan, Pavan, Sohan

   (2) Hasan, Mohan, Pavan, Sohan

   (3) Raman, Nayan, Pavan, Raman

   (4) Nayan, Aman, Pavan, Sohan

   (5) None of these

81. If BD4167 is coded as YW5832, what will be the code for PK0099?

   (1) CE4967   (2) KP9900

   (3) KP1188   (4) PK9900

   (5) QR2244

82. How many such pairs of letters are there in the word CONTRAST each of which has as many letters between them in the word as in the English alphabet?

   (1) None   (2) One

   (3) Two   (4) Three

   (5) More than three

83. There are five persons G, H, I, J and K of different heights. I, who is taller than K is not the tallest. K is not as tall as H. G, who is not as tall as J, is not the shortest. Who is the shortest of all?

   (1) J   (2) I

   (3) G   (4) Cannot of determined

   (5) None of these

84. How many such digits are there in the number 62591483 each of which is as far away from the beginning of the number as when the digits are arranged in ascending order within the number?

   (1) None   (2) One

   (3) Two   (4) Three

   (5) More than three

85. Find the missing term in the following question.

   ced, gih, kml, __, sut, wyx

   (1) npo   (2) noq

   (3) oqp   (4) qro

   (5) opq

Directions (Q. 86-90): Answer the questions on the basis of the information given below.

In a certain code 'facing problems with health' is coded as 'mlp hlt ngi snk', 'health problems on rise' is coded as 'hlt sa rtv mlp', 'rise with every challenge' is coded as 'snk rtv lne riy' and 'facing challenge each day' is coded as 'ngi riy nop hus'.

86. What could be a code for "lne"?

   (1) facing   (2) with

   (3) every   (4) rise

   (5) challenge

87. "riy rtv roi" could be a code for which of the following?

   (1) rise above challenge   (2) rise health challenge

   (3) day rise challenge   (4) with rise challenge

   (5) challenge every rise

88. Which of the following is the code for 'facing'?

   (1) nop   (2) rtv

   (3) ngi   (4) snk

   (5) sa

89. "riy snk mlp" could be a code for which of the following?

   (1) problem every day   (2) challenge with health

   (3) with health day   (4) every challenge facing

   (5) challenge facing with

90. Which of the following is the code for 'day'?

   (1) riy   (2) nop

   (3) ngi   (4) hus

   (5) Cannot be determined

Directions (Q. 91 to 93): Each question below has two statements followed by four conclusions I, II, III and IV. You have to accept the given statements to be true, even if they appear to be at variance from commonly known facts. Read all the conclusions and then decide which of the given conclusions logically follows from the two statements:

91. Statements: All streets are watches.

All watches are eagles.

Conclusions:

I. All streets are eagles.

II. All watches are streets.

III. All eagles are streets.

IV. Some watches are streets.

(1) Only I and IV follow   (2) Only II and III follow

(3) Only IV follows   (4) Only III follows

(5) None follows

92. Statements: All bubbles are dazzling ones.

Some dazzling ones are crystals.

Conclusions:

I. Some crystals are not dazzling ones.

II. All dazzling ones are not bubbles.

III. All crystals are bubbles.

IV. All crystals are not bubbles.

(1) Only III and II follow   (2) Only II and IV follow

(3) Only III follows   (4) Only I follows

(5) None follows

93. Statements: Horse is a bird.

Some birds are clouds.

Conclusions:

I. Horse is a cloud.

II. Some clouds are birds.

III. No horse is a cloud.

IV. Some birds are horses.

(1) Only I follows   (2) Only I and II follow

(3) Only II and IV follow   (4) Only I, II and III follow

(5) Only III follows

Directions (Q. 94 and 95): Select the statement which logically follows the two given statements.

94. Statements:

I. No dove is a sparrow.

II. Some sparrows are crows.

III. Therefore, _________________

(1) Some crows are not dove.

(2) All sparrows are crow.

(3) No crow is a dove.

(4) All crows are doves.

(5) None follows

95. Statements:

I. Some philosophers are old.

II. All old are wise.

III. Therefore, _________________

(1) All wise are philosophers.

(2) Some philosophers are wise.

(3) All philosophers are wise.

(4) Some wise are not old.

(5) None follows

Directions (Q. 96 to 100): Answer the questions on the basis of the information given below.

Six airplanes – P_1, P_2, P_3, P_4, P_5 and P_6 – took off from six different airports – Dubai, Mexico, Kuala-Lumpur, Boston, Geneva and Cairo and landed on six different airports Houston, Belgium, Las-Vegas, Shanghai, Atlanta and Tokyo not necessarily in that order. It is also known that:

I. The airplane that took off from Dubai airport landed on Tokyo airport.

II. P_3 took off from Mexico airport and landed on Shanghai airport.

III. P_6 took off from Geneva airport, but not landed on Houston airport.

IV. P_4 took off from Kuala-Lumpur airport. P_5 landed on Belgium airport.

V. The airplane which took off from Boston airport landed on Las-Vegas airport.

96. Which airplane took off from Boston airport?

(1) P_1 (2) P_2

(3) P_5 (4) Either P_1 or P_2

(5) Either P_2 or P_5

97. On which airport did the airplane P_4 land?

(1) Houston   (2) Tokyo

(3) Atlanta   (4) Las-Vegas

(5) None of these

98. Which airplane landed on Atlanta airport?

(1) P_4 (2) P_2

(3) P_6 (4) P_1

(5) Data inadequate

99. Which of the following combinations cannot be true?

(1) P_1 – Dubai – Tokyo

(2) P_4 – Kuala-Lumpur – Atlanta

(3) P_2 – Boston – Las-Vegas

(4) P_6 – Geneva – Atlanta

(5) All are true

100. If airplane P_1 took off from Dubai, then on which airport airplane P_2 land?

(1) Tokyo

(2) Shanghai

(3) Tokyo or Las-Vegas

(4) Houston

(5) Las-Vegas

ANSWERS

1. (4)	**2.** (3)	**3.** (2)	**4.** (3)	**5.** (5)	**6.** (4)	**7.** (1)	**8.** (4)	**9.** (4)	**10.** (5)
11. (2)	**12.** (4)	**13.** (1)	**14.** (4)	**15.** (2)	**16.** (5)	**17.** (5)	**18.** (2)	**19.** (1)	**20.** (3)
21. (1)	**22.** (2)	**23.** (5)	**24.** (2)	**25.** (5)	**26.** (5)	**27.** (4)	**28.** (1)	**29.** (4)	**30.** (2)
31. (2)	**32.** (4)	**33.** (3)	**34.** (5)	**35.** (4)	**36.** (3)	**37.** (2)	**38.** (5)	**39.** (2)	**40.** (4)
41. (2)	**42.** (5)	**43.** (2)	**44.** (4)	**45.** (3)	**46.** (5)	**47.** (5)	**48.** (4)	**49.** (2)	**50.** (2)
51. (1)	**52.** (2)	**53.** (3)	**54.** (4)	**55.** (5)	**56.** (3)	**57.** (5)	**58.** (1)	**59.** (2)	**60.** (3)
61. (2)	**62.** (4)	**63.** (5)	**64.** (1)	**65.** (5)	**66.** (4)	**67.** (4)	**68.** (2)	**69.** (5)	**70.** (1)
71. (1)	**72.** (5)	**73.** (5)	**74.** (2)	**75.** (1)	**76.** (3)	**77.** (4)	**78.** (5)	**79.** (4)	**80.** (1)
81. (2)	**82.** (4)	**83.** (5)	**84.** (3)	**85.** (3)	**86.** (3)	**87.** (1)	**88.** (3)	**89.** (2)	**90.** (5)
91. (1)	**92.** (5)	**93.** (3)	**94.** (1)	**95.** (2)	**96.** (4)	**97.** (1)	**98.** (3)	**99.** (2)	**100.** (5)

EXPLANATIONS

1. (4) 'Tackle' should be replaced by 'tackling'.

2. (3) The correct phrase is 'instance of illegal'.

3. (2) The correct phrase is "were heavily deployed"

4. (3) 'Youths' is plural while 'is' is used with a singular noun. So, 'youths' should be replaced by 'youth'.

5. (5) The sentence is correct in its given form

6. (4) The sentence means that even though healthcare industry is second biggest, it just reaches 8% of the world's population.

7. (1) 'At' suggests that the blank will take 'look'.

8. (4) Only 'drive' fits in the meaning of the sentence.

9. (4) The sentence means that there is a general perception that this year will be driven by healthcare. So, 'drive' fits in the blank perfectly.

10. (5) The only word that fits in the blank is 'puts'.

For questions 11 - 15 :

The correct sequence is BEADFC. B starts the statement by telling us how many tigers are left. E follows it by saying how the author would normally react to see this figure on his shopping list. EA is a mandatory pair. 'Though' in A is the key word here. It suggests that although the number appears big on a shopping list, it is too smallwhen it comes to representing a species. DF again is a mandatory pair. D tells us that we are steadily loosing a few species of tigers and F gives statistical information about the number of species that were lost by the end of the last century. FC is a mandatory pair.

16. (5) Refer to the first sentence of the passage where the answer is given.

17. (5) Refer to the first sentence of the eighth paragraph for the answer. Green parties are not present in African countries. Options (3) and (4) are correct.

Refer to the fourth paragraph. Option (2) is correct. Refer to the fifth paragraph. Option (1) is correct as well. Refer to the seventh paragraph.

18. (2) The entire passage talks about the history of the Green parties. The passage also talks about the role of Green parties in the society. The other options are narrow in scope.

19. (1) Refer to the first sentence of the sixth paragraph where the author makes a comment on single-issue parties.

20. (3) Refer to the first sentence of the third paragraph where the author mentions that Gandhi had a significant impact on the new social movements of Europe and America. The other options are incorrect as per the passage.

23. (5) 'Resonance' in the context of the sentence means 'relevance'.

26. (5) 'Adding' suggests that the two ideas stated in the sentence will not be contradicting. If the research supports cutting back on sweetened beverages then consuming less quantity of sugary drinks will help lower blood pressure and vice versa. Only option (5) supports this idea and hence is the correct answer.

27. (4) The idiom 'in full swing' means at the highest level of activity or operation.'Cover for' means to conceal someone's errors.

28. (1) You sit 'through' something. Also, a lawyer will speak with a judge and not argue with a judge.

29. (4) The idiom 'to let your hair down' means to relax and enjoy yourself without worrying what other people will think.

30. (2) The second blank will not take 'member' or 'house'. Therefore, options (3) and (4) are negated. Only 'ability' fits in the first blank, thereby making option (2) correct.

31. (2) The series is moving as $2^3 - 2 = 6$, $3^3 - 3 = 24$, $4^3 - 4 = 60$, $5^3 - 5 = 120$ and $6^3 - 6 = 210$

32. (4) The series is moving as $- +2^2, +3^3, +4^2, +5^3$

33. (3) The series is $52^2, 62^2, 72^2, 82^2, 92^2$

34. (5) If one can observe the series is 1st Term $\times \dfrac{1}{4}$, 2nd Term $\times \dfrac{1}{2}$, 3rd Term $\times 1$…and hence the seventh term would be $\times 8$, in other words the term which is multiplied to the number is simply getting doubled.

35. (4) 23 – Product of digits is 6. Therefore 23 + 6 = 29

29 – Sum of digits is 11. Therefore 29 + 11 = 40

40 – Product of digits is 0. Therefore 40 + 0 = 40

40 – Sum of digits is 4. Therefore 40 + 4 = 44

44 – Product of digits is 16. Therefore 44 + 16 = 60

60 – Sum of digits is 6. Therefore 60 + 6 = 66

66 – Product of digits is 36.

Therefore 66 + 36 = 102

36. (3) Number of boys $= \dfrac{1}{25} \times 400 = 16$

Number of girls $= \dfrac{24}{25} \times 400 = 384$

Let's say finally the number of students left be x.

$\therefore \dfrac{64}{100} x = 16$

$\Rightarrow x = 25$

$\therefore$ The number of girls that need to be removed
$= 400 - 25 = 375.$

37. (2) As the new ratio of milk and water is 5 : 4.

Hence, the quantity of milk = 60 litre and the quantity of water has to be 48 litre.

Now it is given that, $\dfrac{1}{2}$ of $\dfrac{3}{4}$th of the capacity of tank = 48 litre.

So, the net capacity of the tank = 128 litre.

38. (5) Let A's, B's and C's investments be Rs. 8x, Rs. 7x and Rs. 5x respectively.

A's investment
$$= (8x)5 + (4x)7$$
$$= 40x + 28x = \text{Rs. } 68x$$

B's investment
$$= 7x \times 12 = \text{Rs. } 84x$$

C's investment
$$= 5x \times 12 = \text{Rs.} 60x$$

B's share $= \dfrac{84}{212} \times 26500 = \text{Rs.} 10{,}500$

39. (2) Total marks scored in these two highest scores
$$= 8 \times 87 - 6 \times 85$$
$$= 696 - 510 = 186$$

If X is the highest score, then next highest score is (X – 2).

$\Rightarrow X + (X - 2) = 186$

$\Rightarrow 2X = 188$

$\quad X = 94.$

Hence, the highest score is 94.

40. (4) According to the question, $\dfrac{2x + 7x}{2} = 27$

$\Rightarrow \qquad 9x = 27 \times 2 = 54$

$\Rightarrow \qquad x = \dfrac{54}{9} = 6$

$\therefore$ Mother's age after 7 years $= 7x + 7$
$$= 7 \times 6 + 7$$
$$= 49 \text{ years.}$$

41. (2) $5^{8.9} \times 25^{7.2} \div 125^{4.6} = 5^?$

$\Rightarrow 5^{8.9 + 7.2 \times 2 - 4.6 \times 3} = 5^?$

$\Rightarrow ? = 9.5.$

42. (5) $\qquad ? = \dfrac{1024 - 362 - 214}{786 - 730}$

$\Rightarrow \qquad ? = 8$

43. (2) $\qquad ? = 699.14 + 478.23 + 174.69$
$$= 1352.06$$

44. (4) $\dfrac{25}{100} \times 965 - \dfrac{69}{100} \times ? = 210.2$

$\Rightarrow 241.25 - 210.2 = \dfrac{69}{100} \times ?$

$\Rightarrow ? = 45$

45. (3) $\qquad ? = \dfrac{31096 \times 2}{2704}$

$\Rightarrow \qquad ? = 23.$

46. (5) Let y be the digit at unit's place and x be the digit at ten's place.

$\therefore$ Number = 10x + y

According to the problem,

$\qquad x + y = 11 \qquad\qquad\qquad …\text{(i)}$

and $(10y + x) - (10x + y) = 27$

$\Rightarrow \qquad y - x = 3 \qquad\qquad\qquad …\text{(ii)}$

By solving (i) and (ii), we get y = 7 and x = 4.

∴ The two digit number

$$= 10x + y$$
$$= 40 + 7 = 47.$$

47. (5) Let the strength of the department be n.

Number of officers in the department = 0.4n

Number of clerks in the department

$$= n - 0.4n = 0.6n$$

Number of female officers in the department

$$= 0.4n × 0.65 = 0.26n$$

Number of female clerks in the department

$$= 0.6n × 0.4 = 0.24n$$

Total number of female employees in the department

$$= 0.24n + 0.26n = 0.50n$$

∴ Strength of the department = $\dfrac{500}{0.50}$ = 1000.

48. (4) Total cost = 6 × 12 + 2 × 14 + (6 + 2) (0.2) = Rs. 101.60

Total selling price = 101.60 × 1.2 = Rs. 121.92

∴ Selling price per kg = $\dfrac{121.92}{8}$ = Rs. 15.24.

49. (2) On selling Rs. 40 per kg he gets a profit of 25% so the C.P. of the adulterated pulse

$$= \dfrac{40}{1.25} = Rs.\ 32$$

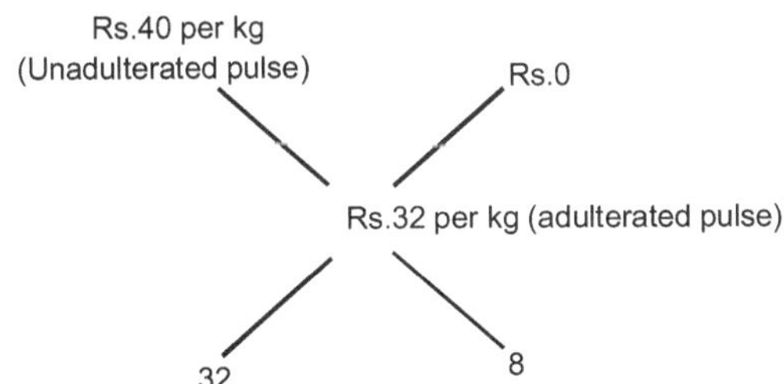

i.e. 4 : 1

So, the adulteration is 1 part out of 5

So, in 1 kg, adulteration will be = $\dfrac{1}{5}$ kg = 200 gm.

50. (2) Let two parts be Rs x and Rs. (1105 − x). Then,

$$x\left(1+\dfrac{10}{100}\right)^5 = (1105 - x)\left(1+\dfrac{10}{100}\right)^7$$

$$\Rightarrow \dfrac{x}{1105 - x} = \left(1+\dfrac{10}{100}\right)^2 = \dfrac{11}{10} \times \dfrac{11}{10}$$

$$\Rightarrow x = 605$$

So, the two parts are Rs. 605 and Rs. (1105 − 605) = Rs 500.

For questions 51 to 55 :

Number of boys = $\dfrac{7}{15} \times 150 = 70$

Number of girls = 150 − 70 = 80

	Boys	Girls
Marketing	28	40
HR	21	24
Finance	21	16
HR + Marketing	7	9
HR + Finance	6	7
Marketing + Finance	5	8

Boys

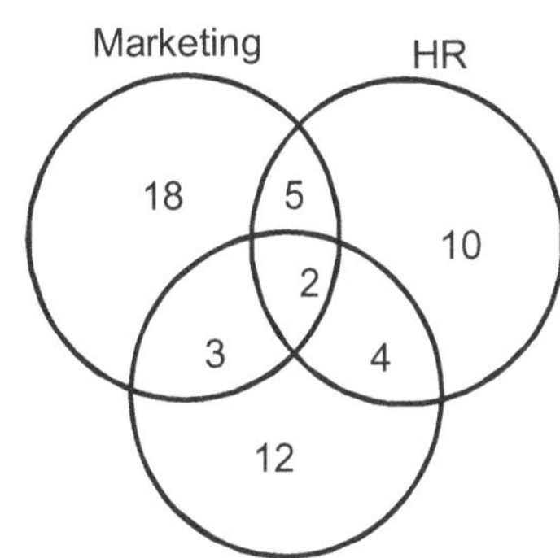

Girls

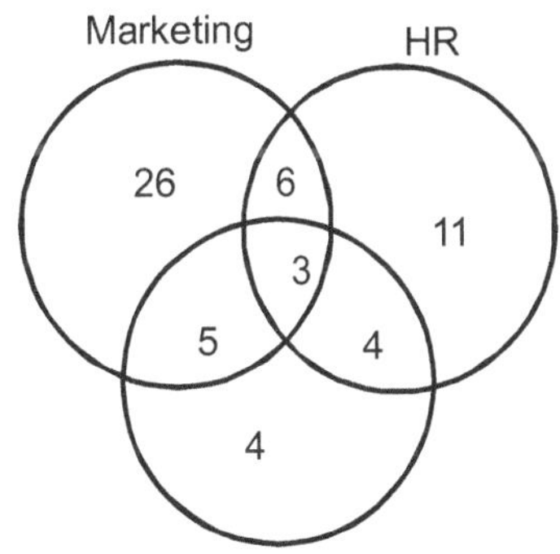

51. (1) Required percentage = $\dfrac{5}{150} \times 100 = \dfrac{10}{3} = 3\dfrac{1}{3}\%$

$$= 3.33\%$$

52. (2) Required ratio = 18 : 26 = 9 : 13

53. (3) Required ratio = 5 : 4.

54. (4) Required percentage = $\dfrac{28 - 24}{24} \times 100$

$$= \dfrac{50}{3} = 16\dfrac{2}{3}\% .$$

55. (5) Required ratio = 10 : 11

56. (3) Companies showing increase in market shares are Godrej-GE, Kelvinator, Allwyn-Voltas and Whirlpool, where Kelvinator and Allwyn-Voltas shows marginal increments.

Thus, percentage increase in Godrej-GE is

$$\frac{40.7 - 31.1}{31.1} \times 100 = \frac{9.6}{31.1} \times 100 = \frac{9600}{311}$$

$$= 30.868 \approx 31\%$$

Percentage increase in Whirlpool

$$= \frac{6.5 - 2}{2} \times 100 = \frac{4.5}{2} \times 100$$

$$= \frac{450}{2} = 225\%$$

Hence, the best performance is shown by Whirlpool.

57. (5) Since the total sales revenues of individual companies is not given.Besides this, the given pie chart is volume based pie chart. Therefore, difference cannot be determined.

58. (1) Sony ranks second last in the total production of goods with production = 3763 × 55 = 2,06,965 units

59. (2) Since percentage share of five least performers will remain same in 2017, which are Kelvinator with 6.3%, Whirlpool 6.5%, Akai 3.6% Samsung 3.6%, Sony 5.5%.

Thus, growth rate for the year 2016 is

$$= \frac{3763,000 - 2693,000}{2693,000} \times 100 = 39.7\%$$

Thus, the production for the year 2017

$$= \frac{3763,000 \times 39.7}{100} + 3763,000 = 5257,000$$

Thus, their respective production in 2017, will be

I.   Production for Kelvinator = 5257 × 63 = 3,31,191

II. Production for Whirlpool = 5257 × 65 = 3,41,705

III. Production for Akai = 5257 × 36 = 1,89,252

IV. Production for Samsung = 5257 × 36 = 1,89,252

V.   Production for Sony = 5257 × 55 = 2,89,135

Total production = I + II + III + IV + V

$$= 13,40,525$$

$$= 1.34 \text{ millions.}$$

60. (3) Percentage decrease in Samsung

$$= \frac{9.7 - 3.6}{9.7} \times 100 \approx 62.89\%.$$

61. (2) $4x^2 - 15x + 14 = 0$

$\Rightarrow 4x^2 - 8x - 7x + 14 = 0$

$\Rightarrow (4x - 7)(x - 2) = 0$

$\therefore \ x = \dfrac{7}{4}, 2$

$6y^2 - 10y + 4 = 0$

$\Rightarrow 6y^2 - 6y - 4y + 4 = 0$

$\Rightarrow (6y - 4)(y - 1) = 0$

$\therefore \ y = \dfrac{2}{3}, 1$

Clearly, x > y.

62. (4) $3x^2 + 10x + 3 = 0$

$\Rightarrow 3x^2 + 9x + 3 = 0$

$\Rightarrow (3x + 1)(x + 3) = 0$

$\therefore \ x = -3, -\dfrac{1}{3}$

$2y^2 + 15y + 27 = 0$

$\Rightarrow 2y^2 + 6y + 9y + 27 = 0$

$\Rightarrow (2y + 9)(y + 3) = 0$

$\therefore \ y = -3, -\dfrac{9}{2}$

Clearly x ≥ y.

63. (5) $7x^2 + 12x + 5 = 0$

$\Rightarrow 7x^2 + 7x + 5x = 0$

$\Rightarrow (7x + 5)(x + 1) = 0$

$\therefore \ x = -1, -\dfrac{5}{7}$

$3y^2 + 7y + 2 = 0$

$\Rightarrow 3y^2 + 6y + y + 2 = 0$

$\Rightarrow (3y + 1)(y + 2) = 0$

$\therefore \ y = -2, -\dfrac{1}{3}$

Clearly, variables are not comparable.

64. (1) $16x^2 - 14x + 3 = 0$

$\Rightarrow 16x^2 - 8x - 6x + 3 = 0$

$\Rightarrow (8x - 3)(2x - 1) = 0$

$\therefore \ x = \dfrac{3}{8}, \dfrac{1}{2}$

$6y^2 - 19y + 15 = 0$

$\Rightarrow 6y^2 - 9y - 10y + 15 = 0$

$\Rightarrow (2y - 3)(3y - 5) = 0$

$\therefore \ y = \dfrac{3}{2}, \dfrac{5}{3}$

Clearly, y > x.

65. (5) $x^2 + 11x + 18 = 0$

$\Rightarrow x^2 + 2x + 9x + 18 = 0$

$\Rightarrow (x + 9)(x + 2) = 0$

$\therefore$ x = – 2, –9

$y^2 = \sqrt{81} = 9$

$\therefore$ y = +3, –3

Clearly, variables are not comparable.

66. (4)

R < K	... (i)
K > D	... (ii)
D = V	... (iii)
V $\leq$ M	... (iv)

From (i) and (ii), R and D can't be compared.

Hence, I and II do not follow.

From (iii) and (iv), D = V $\leq$ M or D $\leq$ M.

Hence, either III (D = M) or IV (M > D) follows.

67. (4)

B $\geq$ T	... (i)
T < R	... (ii)
R > F	... (iii)
F = K	... (iv)

From (i) and (ii), B and R can't be compared. Hence, I does not follow.

From (iii) and (iv), R > F = K or R > K.

Hence, III follows.

68. (2)

F > N	... (i)
N $\geq$ W	... (ii)
W $\leq$ Y	... (iii)
Y < T	... (iv)

From (i) and (ii), F > N $\geq$ W or F > W. Hence, I follows

From (ii) and (iii), N and Y can't be compared. Hence, II and III do not follow.

From (iii) and (iv), W $\leq$ Y < T or T > W.

Hence, IV follow.

69. (5)

D $\leq$ T	... (i)
T = R	... (ii)
R $\geq$ M	... (iii)
M > K	... (iv)

From (i) and (ii), D $\leq$ T = R or D $\leq$ R.

Hence, either I (R = D) or II (R > D) follows,

From (ii) and (iii), T = R $\geq$ M or M $\leq$ T

Hence, IV follows,

From (iv) and IV, K < M $\leq$ T or K < T.

Hence, III follows.

70. (1)

J = F	... (i)
F $\leq$ N	... (ii)
N > H	... (iii)
H $\geq$ G	... (iv)

From (iii) and (iv), N > H $\geq$ G or G < N.

Hence, I follows.

From (i) and (ii), J = F $\leq$ N or N $\geq$ J.

Hence, II follows,

From (i), III (F < J) is false.

From I and II, G and J can't be compared.

Hence, IV does not follow.

71. (1) The given relation could be shown as:

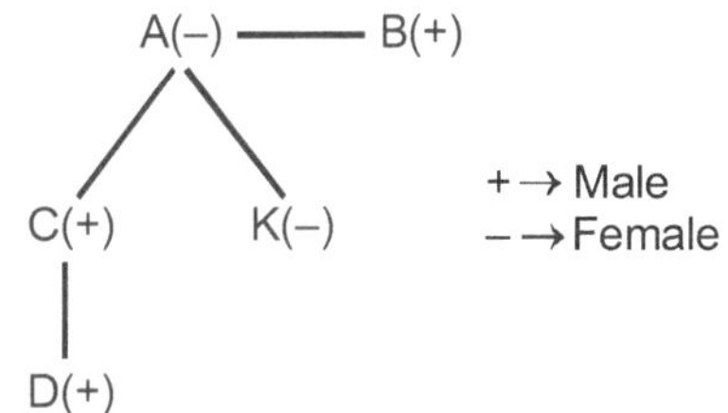

72. (5)

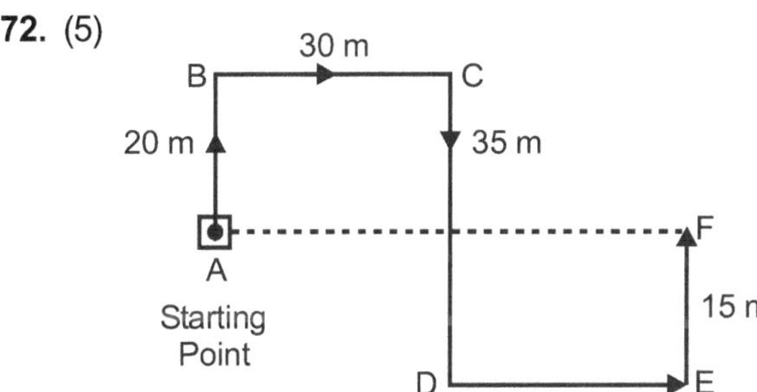

Deepak's distance from his original position.

AF = BC + DE

= 30 + 15 = 45.

Also 'F' lies to East of 'A'.

73. (5) The required arrangement is as follows:

S U P/Q Q/P T R

$\therefore$ U is sitting adjacent to S.

74. (2)

Total number of students = 30

Clearly, Ramesh is 11th from the left end.

Hence, there are 2 students between Ramesh and Mahesh.

75. (1) The letters of the word are coded by moving five steps forward and six steps backward alternately.

For questions 76 to 80:

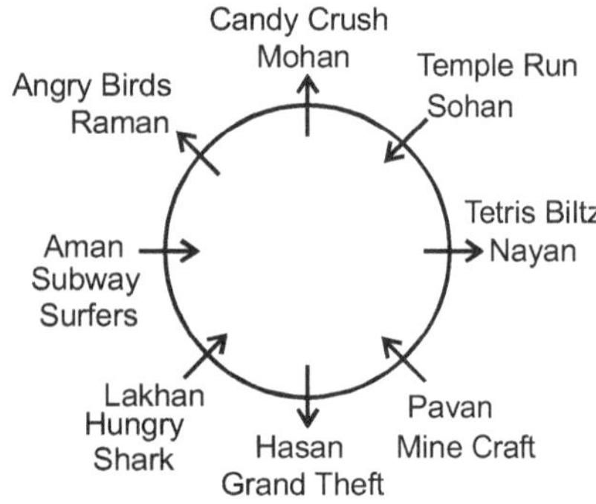

81. (2) B is 2nd letter from left in alphabet and Y is 2nd letter from right. Same is the case with D also, and for digits codes are complementary of 9.

$$PK0099 \rightarrow KP9900.$$

So right answer is option (2).

82. (4) C O N T R A S T

83. (5) The arrangement can be determined as: I, H > K, J > G . Since G is not the shortest, so K is the shortest of all.

84. (3) Numbers: 6 2 5 9 1 4 8 3
Arranged in ascending order: 1 2 3 4 5 6 8 9

85. (3) The respecitve letters in each term are 4 positions ahead in the English alphabet series, with respect to the letters in the previous term.

For questions 86-90:

facing problems with health → mlp hlt ngi snk ..(i)

health problems on rise → hlt sa rtv mlp...(ii)

rise with every challenge → snk rtv lne riy ...(iii)

facing challenge each day → ngi riy nop hus ...(iv)

From (i) and (iv), facing → ngi ...(v)

From (i) and (iii), with → snk ...(vi)

From (ii) and (iii), rise → rtv ...(vii)

From (iii) and (iv), challenge → riy ...(viii)

From (iii), (vi), (vii) and (viii), every → lne ...(ix)

From (i) and (ii), health → mlp or hlt

problems → mlp or hit ...(x)

From (iv), (v) and (viii), each → nop or hus

day → nop or hus ...(xi)

From (ii), (vii) and (x), on → sa ... (xii)

faci-ng	with	ris-e	challen-ge	ever-y	on	ea-ch	day	healt-h	proble-ms
ngi	snk	rtv	riy	lne	sa	nop or hus	nop or hus	mlp or hlt	mlp or hlt

87. (1) roi: given new code for 'above'.

91. (1) Refer to the venn diagrams given below.

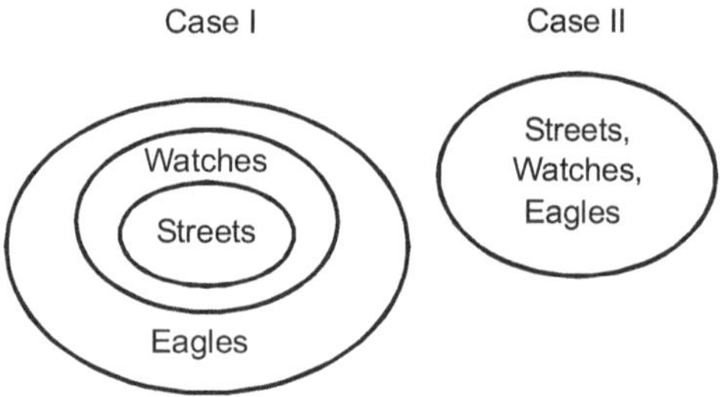

92. (5) Refer to the venn diagrams given below.

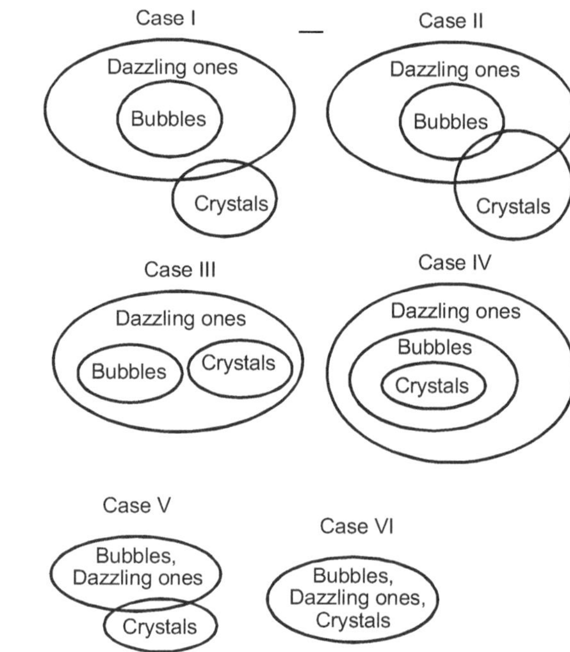

93. (3) Refer to the venn diagrams given below.

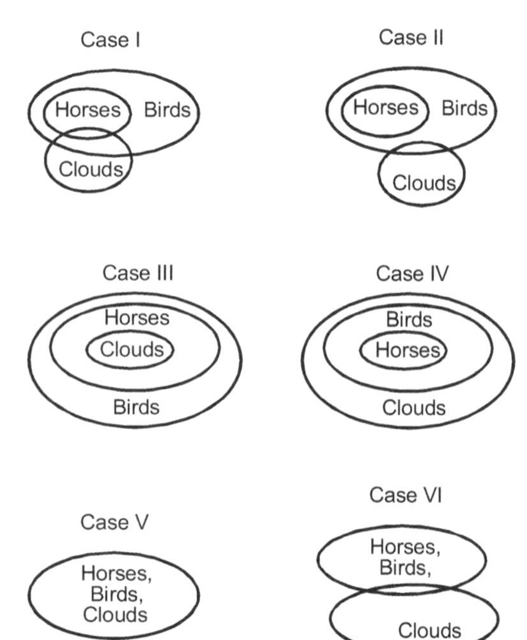

94. (1) As we can see from the venn diagrams given below, only option (1) follows.

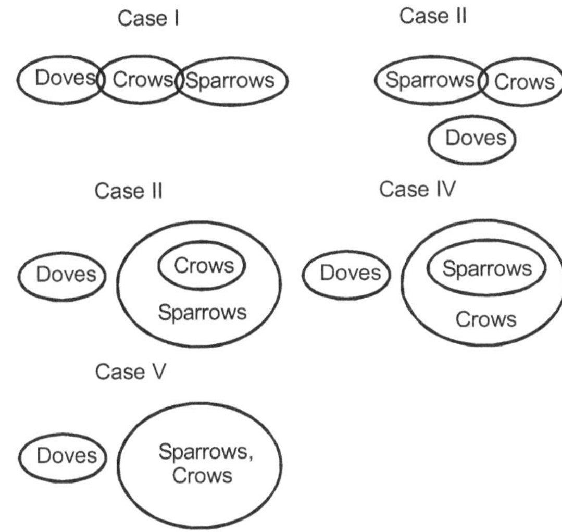

95. (2) As we can see from the venn diagrams given below, only option (2) follows.

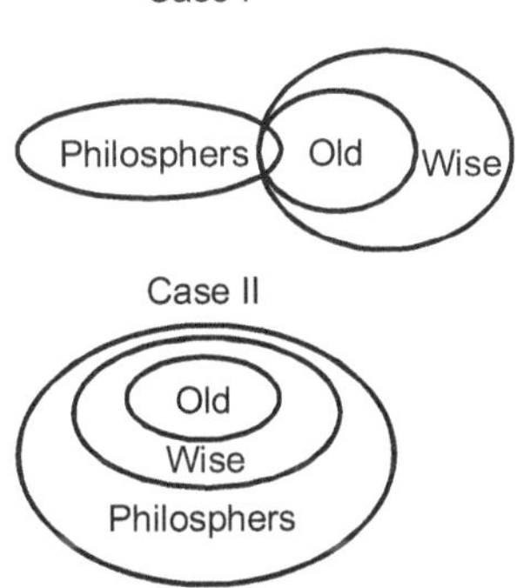

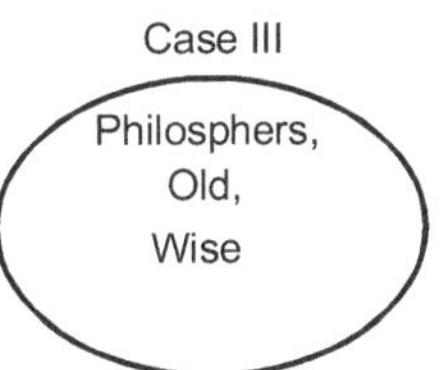

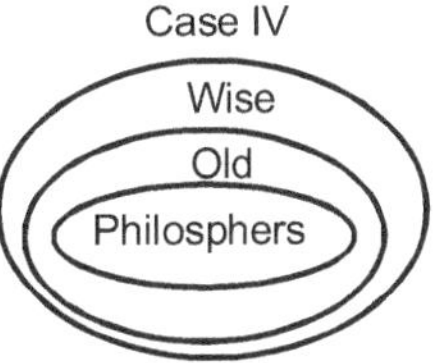

For questions 96 to 100: The given information can be tabulated as shown below:

Departure airport	Arrival airport	Airplane's name
Dubai	Tokyo	P_1/P_2
Mexico	Shanghai	P_3
Kuala-Lumpur	Houston	P_4
Boston	Las-Vegas	P_2/P_1
Geneva	Atlanta	P_6
Cairo	Belgium	P_5

PRACTICE PAPER – 14

ENGLISH LANGUAGE

Directions (Q. 1 to 5): Pick out the most effective pair of words from the given options to make the sentences meaningfully complete.

1. Never _____ its independence, had India witnessed such _____ growth.
   - (1) since, exponential
   - (2) from, fast
   - (3) after, fine
   - (4) before, brilliance
   - (5) through, slow

2. One of the best examples of a _____ maintained cricket ground is the MCG, one of the _____ cricket stadiums in the world.
   - (1) brilliant, firstly
   - (2) well, finest
   - (3) well, fine
   - (4) poorly, best
   - (5) moderately, best

3. Rinnegan, a village in Madhya Pradesh, _____ has vast _____ of bauxite.
   - (1) fondly, contains
   - (2) reportedly, reserves
   - (3) boldly, shelves
   - (4) coolly, ores
   - (5) solely, wells

4. The _____ of a soldier depends on his flexibility, _____ and power.
   - (1) guts, speed
   - (2) weight, food
   - (3) weapons, strength
   - (4) uniform, agility
   - (5) effectiveness, speed

5. In Siberia, temperatures can _____ to –40 degrees Celsius _____ winters.
   - (1) pile, through
   - (2) climb, around
   - (3) plunge, during
   - (4) drop, after
   - (5) hit, under

Directions (Q. 6 to 15): The questions in this section are based on a single passage. The questions are to be answered on the basis of what is stated or implied in the passage. Kindly note that more than one of the choices may conceivably answer some of the questions. However, you are to choose the most appropriate answer, that is, the response that most accurately and completely answers the question.

The use of bilateral investment treaties (BITs) has proliferated over the last three decades. The total number of newly ratified BITs by middle income countries multiplied more than 55 times, from 33 in 1985 to 1,854 in 2012.

BITs reduce political risk to foreign investors. They establish clear, simple and enforceable rules for foreign investment protection from expropriation, specify the circumstances under which expropriation takes place and the compensation standards, and design the necessary investment dispute settlement mechanisms between states and investors. BITs therefore reduce policy uncertainty and guarantee the presence and adoption of rules for foreign investment protection, which may boost foreign investor's confidence and promote foreign investment flows.

The domain of foreign investment BITs extends beyond FDI. FDI has been the only type of capital flows examined in the BITs literature. Foreign investment, in the 2012 U.S. Model Bilateral Investment Treaties for example, is defined as "every asset that an investor owns or controls, directly or indirectly, that has the characteristics of an investment, including such characteristics as the commitment of capital or other resources, the expectation of gain or profit, or the assumption of risk". An investment may take the form of an enterprise; shares, stock, and other forms of equity participation in an enterprise; bonds, debentures, other debt instruments, and loans; and futures, options, and other derivatives. Therefore, BITs provide political risk guarantees to portfolio equity, private non-guaranteed debt in addition to FDI. They may even provide guarantees to public and publicly guaranteed debt as far as multinational corporations seek guarantees on their loans from host country governments.

Public debt, as well as FDI, is particularly an important capital flow in low income countries. Hindered by low per capita income, financial underdevelopment and low credit ratings, governments and financial institutions of low income countries tend to rely more heavily on public debt to finance their investment and possibly consumption needs.

The capital flows determinants literature has developed over time. The development largely reflects the increasing financial globalization that has taken place over the past three decades and the role of external and domestic factors in mobilizing capital flows to recipient countries. Among the domestic factors, institutions and political risk has attracted special attention in the capital flows literature. Increasing corruption and weak rule of law were among the institutions that increased political risk and triggered the 1997 Asian financial crisis. In addition, the role of capital controls and financial development in attracting capital flows has been explored in the literature. In the FDI literature specifically the influence of BITs, as an investor protection mechanism, on FDI has also been examined.

The determinants of capital flows have been extensively examined in the capital flows literature. Some studies have distinguished between the role of external (push) and domestic (pull) factors explain capital flows during the 1990s in terms of external factors to the recipient economy and domestic factors. External factors to the recipient economy include declining world interest rates, which improve creditworthiness and reduce default risk in developing countries, global business cycle, integration of world capital markets, diversification of investments internationally and contagion effects.

Domestic factors include sound domestic monetary and **fiscal** policies, and trade and capital market liberalization.

Over the past three decades of increased global financial integration many governments adopted policies of financial liberalization in order to lure more capital flows and reap the benefits of smoothing consumption, boosting investment, and speeding up economic growth, while other governments adopted capital control measures to reduce the disruption that the high volumes and volatility of capital inflows and outflows create. A number of studies have focused on the impact of financial liberalization and capital controls examine the efficacy of capital controls in 74 countries during the period 1995–2005 in stemming inflows and outflows of equity, FDI, and debt holdings. They find that the efficacy of capital controls is on the outflow side but is very little or absent on the inflow side. In addition they find that the efficacy of capital controls is low in low and middle income countries. Okada attributes the efficacy of capital controls to institutional quality, and examines the effect of these two factors and their interaction on FDI and foreign private investment. He finds that while there is no individual impact of financial openness and institutional quality on capital inflows, the interaction between these two factors has a significant impact.

Recent studies have focused on the role of institutions and political risk as domestic factors in attracting capital flows explores the drivers of global portfolio investment flows using high frequency mutual funds data for the period 2005–2010 differentiating between financial crises and the subsequent recovery, and between common global shocks and country-specific factors. He finds that during crises there is a strong divergence in capital flows across countries with dynamics of capital flows primarily driven by safe-haven flows. He also finds that the effect of global shocks, in particular during the recovery period, was heterogeneous and depended on the recipient country's institutional quality, country risk, and the strength of macroeconomic fundamentals and policies. He contends that, "countries are far from innocent bystanders that are powerless in being exposed to **volatile** global markets, and that indeed they have tools to insulate to some extent their economies from adverse global shocks".

Opacity of the operating environment seems to matter for capital flows. Hooper and Kim examine the role of operating environment opacity in influencing FDI, portfolio investment, and international bank lending. They argue that opacity in general discourages capital flows. However, with the profit opportunities it creates, opacity may increase capital flows. For example, multinational corporations (MNCs) may concentrate on FDI to exploit accounting and reporting opacity in order to maximize profit. Other forms of capital flows may respond differently to accounting opacity.

Interestingly they point out that opacity in corruption might increase FDI or international bank lending. Corruption opacity can increase MNCs likelihood of obtaining loans, which are government guaranteed, or favorable tax treatments, thus increasing FDI flows to the country. Corruption opacity might take the form of government guarantees of crony capitalists' international loans, increasing the likelihood of obtaining loans and thus international bank lending. In contrast, legal opacity reduces contract enforcement and protection of property rights and thus capital flows in general.

In explaining the Lucas **paradox** on why capital flows from poor to rich countries, contrary to the neoclassical model prediction of capital flowing in the opposite direction, Papaioannou (2009) focuses on the role of institutions in explaining these flows and finds that weak institutions – weak property rights protection, inefficient legal system and high risk of investment **expropriation deter** banking flows. Similarly, in examining mainly the role of demographic structure in international portfolio flows, De Santis and Luhrmann (2009) find that lower quality institutions deter net portfolio inflows explaining the capital reallocation from developing to developed countries.

6. Which of the following options is true in the light of the passage?

    (1) Governments are often wary of introducing changes in the rural sector.

    (2) In the past thirty years, very few governments have adopted policies of financial liberalisation.

    (3) Domestic factors often result in contagion effects.

    (4) The factors of capital flows have been rarely analysed in literature.

    (5) Lack of transparency in the operating environment might affect flow of capital.

7. What can be an appropriate title for the passage?

    (1) Influence of bilateral investment treaties on foreign direct investment

    (2) Use of empirical model and data to analyse investment figures

    (3) The flow of capital from poor to rich countries

    (4) Effects of corruption on direct foreign lending

    (5) The role of bilateral investment treaties

8. The author of the passage is most likely a/an

(1) Sociologist   (2) Scientist

(3) Economist   (4) Anthropologist

(5) Political scientist

9. Out of the following options, the author is most likely to agree with

(1) Literature concerning factors of capital flows has never remained stagnant.

(2) The 1997 Asian financial crisis was triggered by political instability.

(3) Financial openness plays a pivotal role in geo-political stability.

(4) Opacity of the operating environment can never affect capital flows.

(5) Financial liberalisation was introduced in order to check unabated investment.

10. What, according to the author, is an important capital flow in a low income country?

(1) Non-guaranteed debt

(2) Institutional equity

(3) Loans based on demographic patterns

(4) Public debt

(5) Assistance rendered by international humanitarian organisations.

Which of the following options would come closest to the word printed in bold as used in the passage?

11. Fiscal

(1) Miserly   (2) Government policies

(3) Sociological data   (4) Social

(5) Related to revenue or taxes

12. Expropriation

(1) A situation when a political party almost goes bankrupt

(2) The act of taking of privately owned property by a government to be used for the benefit of the public.

(3) A hung parliament

(4) A form of governance where there are multiple heads

(5) A political party which has lost the vote of confidence

13. Paradox

(1) Satirical   (2) Ironical

(3) Erroneous   (4) Contradiction

(5) A kind of fable

Which of the following options would come opposite to the word printed in bold as used in the passage?

14. Deter

(1) Turn off   (2) Debar

(3) Encourage   (4) Restrain

(5) Forestall

15. Volatile

(1) Capricious   (2) Constant

(3) Erratic   (4) Flippant

(5) Ephemeral

Directions (Q. 16 to 20) Rearrange the following sentences (A), (B), (C), (D), (E) and (F) to make a meaningful paragraph and then answer the questions which follow:

A. For most managers of organizations, the external context, or environment, is represented by the market for which they are trying to provide a good or service.

B. Contextual conditions are important because they influence the methods by which managers can effectively use resources to plan, organize and staff, direct, and control organization activities

C. Similarly, governmental regulations, technological changes in unrelated industries, national events, and other organizations that provide information and entertainment may also affect the operations of the television station.

D. Yet the external context can also include events and activities that do not exist in the market the organization is serving.

E. For instance, a television station operates in a context in which viewers, advertisers, program producers, and news services all affect the broadcasting by the television station.

F. And this control of organizational activities is of prime importance.

16. Which of the following sentences should be the **FIRST** after rearrangement?

(1) A   (2) B

(3) C   (4) D

(5) F

17. Which of the following sentences should be the **FOURTH** after rearrangement?

(1) B   (2) F

(3) C   (4) D

(5) F

18. Which of the following sentences should be the **SECOND** after rearrangement?

(1) A   (2) B

(3) C   (4) D

(5) F

19. Which of the following sentences should be the **LAST** after rearrangement?

(1) D   (2) B
(3) C   (4) A
(5) F

20. Which of the following sentences should be the **THIRD** after rearrangement?

(1) A   (2) E
(3) C   (4) D
(5) F

Directions (Q. 21 to 25): In the following passage, there are blanks, each of which has been numbered. These numbers are printed below the passage and against each, five words are suggested, one of which fits the blank appropriately. Find out the appropriate word in each case.

Prima facie, there is much cause for cheer. Provisional data gleaned from the latest Census __(21)__ that India's literacy level has soared: India's effective literacy rate jumped by 9.2% to reach 74.04%.

Significantly, literacy rate improved sharply among females compared __(22)__ males. Thus, while effective literacy rate for males rose from 75.26% to 82.14% — a rise of 6.9% — literacy rates for females climbed from 53.67% to 65.48%, an 11.8% increase.

That is heartening news indeed. But this data masks a few worrying concerns. First, the data relates to effective literacy, and __(23)__ literacy. Measuring effective literacy in India means including anyone who can read and write his or her own name. Thus, if Ram knows how to read and write the three letters of his name, and Sita knows how to read and write the four letters of her name, they get included in the __(24)__ of effective literates. This is not the way developed countries define literacy.

Second, literacy becomes relevant if it leads to employability. Both the Confederation of Indian Industry and the Boston Consulting Group have estimated that India would face a "talent gap" of more than five million by 2012, as existing educational institutions do not impart employable skills. Just 20% of the engineering graduates are employable. A McKinsey report finds only 25% engineers, 15% finance graduates and less than 10% of the other graduates to be employable.

It is even __(25)__ alarming when one takes into account that graduates comprise only 3.5% of India's population. This includes graduates in all streams such as Arts, Commerce, Science, Engineering and Medicine. If 90% of the graduates are unemployable, it means that barely 0.5% of India's population comprises employable graduates.

21. (1) show   (2) speak
(3) site   (4) seek
(5) strive

22. (1) to   (2) against
(3) for   (4) of
(5) at

23. (1) also   (2) nor
(3) not   (4) ineffective
(5) masked

24. (1) process   (2) dynamic
(3) style   (4) development
(5) category

25. (1) less   (2) above
(3) more   (4) significant
(5) major

Directions (Q.26 to 30): Which of the phrases (1), (2), (3) and (4) given below each statement should replace the phrase given in bold in the sentence to make it grammatically correct? If the sentence is correct as it is given and 'No correction is required', mark (5) as the answer.

26. There are a lot **most right hand people** in the world than left handed people.

(1) more rightly hand people

(2) more right handed people

(3) more right handy people

(4) most rightly hand people

(5) No correction required.

27. Absinthe has been popularly known as the 'genius' drink **because it is** believed to induce creativity.

(1) because of its   (2) because of

(3) because it may   (4) because it might

(5) No correction required

28. The tallest man ever to have **walked in this** planet was almost nine feet tall.

(1) walked under this   (2) walked through this

(3) walked on this   (4) walked about

(5) No correction required

29. There has **been an eerie** silence since we have come.

(1) been on eerie   (2) been in eerie

(3) been through eerie   (4) been at eerie

(5) No correction required

30. Climbing Mount Everest **have been** a dream for many mountaineers.

(1) has been   (2) will been

(3) might been   (4) shall been

(5) No correction required

NUMERICAL ABILITY

Directions (Q. 31 and 32): In the following number series only one number is wrong. Find out the wrong number.

31. 7, 15, 36, 72, 117, 177
- (1) 7
- (2) 117
- (3) 36
- (4) 72
- (5) 177

32. 6, 91, 584, 2935, 11756, 35277, 70558
- (1) 91
- (2) 70558
- (3) 584
- (4) 2935
- (5) 35277

Directions (Q.33 to 35): What will come in place of question mark (?) in the following number series.

33. 123, 183, 213, 228, 235.5, ?
- (1) 238.25
- (2) 239.25
- (3) 275.50
- (4) 238.50
- (5) None of these

34. 311, 300, 278, 245, 201, 146, ?
- (1) 70
- (2) 90
- (3) 80
- (4) 110
- (5) None of these

35. 142, 119, 100, 83, ?, 59, 52
- (1) 70
- (2) 79
- (3) 65
- (4) 81
- (5) None of these

36. A man sells an article at a profit of 20%. If he had bought it at 20% less and sold it for Rs. 5 less, he would have gained 25%. Find the cost price of the article.
- (1) Rs. 20
- (2) Rs. 22
- (3) Rs. 24
- (4) Rs. 30
- (5) Rs. 25

37. Deepak goes to a shop to buy a radio costing Rs. 2,675. The rate of sales tax is 7%. He tells the shopkeeper to reduce the price of the radio to such an extent that he has to pay Rs. 2,675, inclusive of sales tax. Find the reduction needed in the price of the radio.
- (1) Rs. 179.76
- (2) Rs. 170
- (3) Rs. 175
- (4) Rs. 169
- (5) None of these

38. How many natural numbers between 200 and 400 are there which are divisible by both 4 and 5?
- (1) 9
- (2) 8
- (3) 7
- (4) 10
- (5) None of these

39. Two articles were sold at Rs. 350 each. After selling it was realized that on one, a profit of 30% was made, and on the other, a loss of 30% was made. What was the net result?
- (1) 15% loss
- (2) 3% loss
- (3) 9% loss
- (4) 15% profit
- (5) None of these

40. The difference between the compound interest and simple interest for two years on a certain sum of money is Rs. 208. If the rate of interest is 8% per annum, then find the sum.
- (1) Rs.32,800
- (2) Rs.30,500
- (3) Rs.32,500
- (4) Rs.16,250
- (5) Rs.15,250

Directions (Q. 41 to 45): What should come in place of question mark (?) in the following questions?

41. 12% of 450 + ?% of 200 = 83
- (1) 13 .5
- (2) 16
- (3) 14.5
- (4) 15
- (5) None of these

42. 726.34 + 888.12 − ? = 1001.88
- (1) 621.58
- (2) 602.64
- (3) 654.54
- (4) 618.78
- (5) None of these

43. 534.596 + 61.472 − 496.708 = ? + 27.271
- (1) 126.631
- (2) 62.069
- (3) 72.089
- (4) 132.788
- (5) None of these

44. 16 × 12 − 672 ÷ 21 = ? − 211
- (1) 381
- (2) 347
- (3) 372
- (4) 311
- (5) None of these

45. $(21)^2 − 3717 ÷ 59 = ? × 8$
- (1) 43.75
- (2) 42.25
- (3) 45.75
- (4) 47.25
- (5) None of these

46. The average age of husband and wife was 25 years when they were married 5 years ago. The average age of husband, wife and the child, who was born during the interval, is 21 years now. How old is the child now?
- (1) Less than 1 year
- (2) 1 year
- (3) 4 years
- (4) 2 years
- (5) 3 years

47. If 3 litre grape juice containing $\frac{2}{3}$ water and $\frac{1}{3}$ juice is mixed with 2 litre of grape juice containing $\frac{3}{8}$ water and $\frac{5}{8}$ juice, then what percentage of the new solution is juice?

(1) $47\frac{1}{2}\%$ (2) 50%

(3) 45% (4) $52\frac{1}{2}\%$

(5) None of these

48. The ratio of investments of 2 partners Prince and Deepak is 5 : 6 and the ratio of their profits is 4 : 3. If Deepak invested the money for 10 months, then for how many months did Prince invest his money?

(1) 12 months (2) 10 months

(3) 9 months (4) 8 months

(5) 16 months

49. The cost of manufacturing a product including labour, material and overheads are in the ratio 5 : 7 : 3. If the profits are calculated as 20% on costs, then what is the ratio of material costs to profit?

(1) 5 : 2 (2) 10 : 3

(3) 7 : 3 (4) 11 : 9

(5) 3 : 7

50. The ratio of the present ages of two persons is 2 : 1. After six years, their ages will be in the ratio 7 : 4. What is the age of the elder person?

(1) 18 years (2) 27 years

(3) 36 years (4) 24 years

(5) None of these

Directions (Q. 51 to 55): Answer the questions on the basis of the information given below.

Four different companies – Adidas, Bata, Century and Dabur trade their shares during the period 2012 to 2016. The table given below shows the numbre of shares sold by them and the line graph given below shows the price (in Rs. '00) of each share of these companies in a particular year.

Company	2012	2013	2014	2015	2016
Adidas	1200	1441	1237	1668	1586
Bata	1375	1231	1568	1241	1158
Century	1447	1528	1472	1078	1416
Dabur	1178	1382	1268	1122	1228

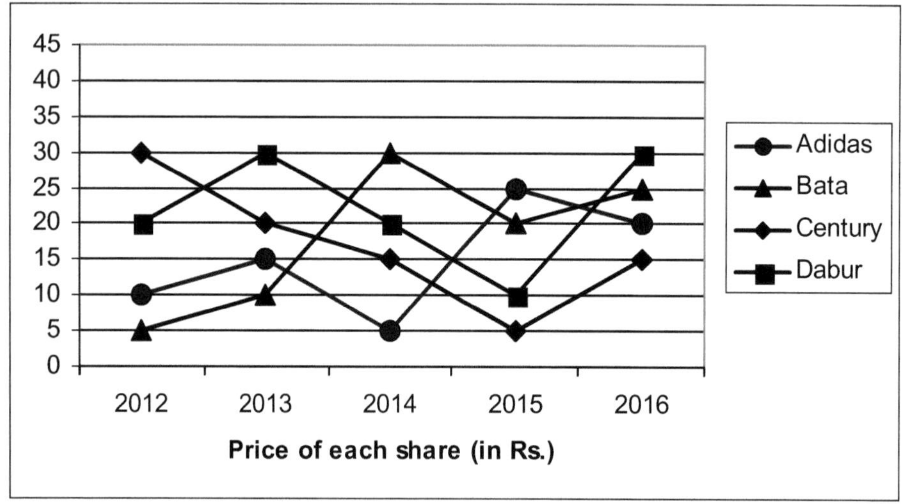

51. Find the total number of shares sold by Century in all the years together.

(1) 6941 (2) 6521

(3) 6851 (4) 6781

(5) None of these

52. What is the total revenue generated by Bata and Dabur in 2013?

(1) Rs. 53,870 (2) Rs. 47,180

(3) Rs. 49,170 (4) Rs. 53,770

(5) None of these

53. What is the overall percentage increase in the price of each share of Bata during the given period?

(1) 200% (2) 250%

(3) 300% (4) 350%

(5) None of these

54. By what percent is the number of shares sold by Century in 2016 more than that by Adidas in 2012?

(1) 18% (2) 18.5%

(3) 20% (4) 20.5%

(5) None of these

55. Which company sold the highest number of shares and in which year?

(1) Adidas – 2016
(2) Century – 2013
(3) Bata – 2014
(4) Dabur – 2013
(5) Adidas – 2015

Directions (Q. 56 to 60): Answer the questions on the basis of the information given below.

Each question given below consists of a statement followed by two quantities i.e. I and II. Solve both of them and mark your answer accordingly.

56. Quantity I: A and B together can complete a certain piece of work in 20 days. However, they started working together but A leaves the work after 10 days and B completed the remaining work in 30 days. Find the time taken by A to complete work alone.

Quantity II: A and B together can complete a certain piece of work in 18 days. B is 50% more efficient than A and he can complete 40% of the work in 12 days. Find the time taken by A to complete 67.5% of the work alone.

(1) Quantity I > Quantity II

(2) Quantity I ≥ Quantity II

(3) Quantity II > Quantity I

(4) Quantity II ≥ Quantity I

(5) Quantity I = Quantity II or relationship cannot be established

57. Quantity I: A shopkeeper makes a profit of 16.67%, if he allows a discount of 16.67% on the list price of an article. Find the profit percent that would have made by the shopkeeper if he had offered no discount.

Quantity II: The list price of an article is Rs. 1,50,000 and a shopkeeper sells it at 20% profit after giving a discount of 10%. Had the cost price of the article increased by 15% and it was sold at the same selling price then the profit made by the shopkeeper would have been?

(1) Quantity I > Quantity II

(2) Quantity I ≥ Quantity II

(3) Quantity II > Quantity I

(4) Quantity II ≥ Quantity I

(5) Quantity I = Quantity II or relationship cannot be established

58. Quantity I: What will be the equivalent discount of three successive discounts of 20%, 35% and 30%?

Quantity II: What will be the equivalent discount of three successive discounts of 25%, 40% and 20%?

(1) Quantity I > Quantity II

(2) Quantity I ≥ Quantity II

(3) Quantity II > Quantity I

(4) Quantity II ≥ Quantity I

(5) Quantity I = Quantity II or relationship cannot be established

59. Quantity I: Five years ago, the respective ratio of the ages of A and B was 5 : 6 and five years hence the respective ratio will be 6 : 7. Find the sum of the present ages of A and B.

Quantity II: Six years ago, the respective ratio of the ages of A and B was 4 : 5 and three years hence the respective ratio will be 5 : 6. Find the sum of the ages of A and B after twelve years.

(1) Quantity I > Quantity II

(2) Quantity I ≥ Quantity II

(3) Quantity II > Quantity I

(4) Quantity II ≥ Quantity I

(5) Quantity I = Quantity II or relationship cannot be established

60. Quantity I: What is the length of the train which crosses a pole in 18 seconds and a 220 m long platform in 40 seconds?

Quantity II: What will be the speed of the train in (km/hr) that crosses a platform of length 200 m in 25 seconds and a pole in 15 seconds?

(1) Quantity I > Quantity II

(2) Quantity I ≥ Quantity II

(3) Quantity II > Quantity I

(4) Quantity II ≥ Quantity I

(5) Quantity I = Quantity II or relationship cannot be established

Directions (Q. 61 to 65): Answer the following questions on the basis of the information given below.

The table given below shows the number of students studying in six different schools during the period 2009 to 2014.

Year \ School	A	B	C	D	E	F
2009	2500	2250	2450	2150	2020	2300
2010	2040	2300	2400	2200	2090	2120
2011	2100	2150	2330	2250	2180	2260
2012	2280	2600	2260	2340	2250	2490
2013	2540	2540	2120	2380	2310	2520
2014	2320	2440	2500	2480	2400	2440

61. What is the percent increase in the number of students in school E in the year 2012 from the previous year? (rounded off to two digits after decimal)

(1) 8.33
(2) 5.18
(3) 6.63
(4) 3.21
(5) None of these

62. What is the total number of students studying in all the schools together in the year 2010?

(1) 10350   (2) 13150

(3) 15311   (4) 11350

(5) None of these

63. What is the average number of students in all the schools together in the year 2009 (rounded off to the nearest integer)?

(1) 2208   (2) 2196

(3) 2144   (4) 2324

(5) 2278

64. The number of students in school A in the year 2013 forms approximately what percent of the total number of students in that school from all the years together?

(1) 11   (2) 31

(3) 18   (4) 26

(5) 23

65. What is the ratio of the total number of students in school D in the years 2011 and 2014 together to the total number of students in school F from the same years?

(1) 473 : 470

(2) 470 : 473

(3) 371 : 390

(4) 390 : 371

(5) None of these

REASONING ABILITY

Directions (Q. 66-70): In the following questions, the symbols @, *, δ, $ and % are used with the following meaning as illustrated below :

'P δ Q' means 'P is not smaller than Q'.

'P * Q' means 'P is not greater than Q'.

'P % Q' means 'P is neither greater than nor equal to Q'.

'P $ Q' means 'P is neither smaller than nor equal to Q'.

'P @ Q' means 'P is neither greater than nor smaller than Q'.

Now in each of the following questions assuming the given statements to be true, find which of the three conclusions I, II and III given below them is/are definitely true and give your answer accordingly.

66. Statements : B % N, N δ F, F * H

Conclusions :

I. H $ N

II. F% B

III. B% H

(1) Only I and II are true

(2) Only I and III are true

(3) Only II and III are true

(4) None of these

(5) All I, II and III are true

67. Statements : W δ F, F % K, K $ M

Conclusions :

I. M % F

II. M δ F

III. W $ K

(1) Only I is true

(2) Only II is true

(3) Only either I or II is true

(4) Only III is true

(5) None of these

68. Statements : W $ B, B @ M, M * R

Conclusions :

I. R $ B

II. R @ B

III. M%W

(1) Only either I or II is true

(2) Only eitherI or II and III are true

(3) Only III is true

(4) All I, II and III are true

(5) None of these

69. Statements : M * D, D $ K, K @ T

Conclusions :

I. T % D

II. K % M

III. M % T

(1) Only I is true

(2) Only II is true

(3) Only III is true

(4) Only I and III are true

(5) None of these

70. Statements : K @ F, F $ M, M δ T

Conclusions:

I. T % F

II. M % K

III. K $ T

(1) Only I and II are true

(2) Only I and III are true

(3) Only II and III are true

(4) All I, II and III are true

(5) None of these

71. In a certain code language, 'DRINK' is coded as 'JMHQC' and 'BLOTS' is coded as 'RSNKA'. In the same code language, 'HONEY' will be coded as '_____'.

(1) XDMOG (2) GNMDX

(3) XDMNG (4) DXMGN

(5) Cannot be determined

72. How many such pairs of letters are there in the word 'CHILDREN' each of which has as many letters between them in the word as there are between them in the English alphabet?

(1) 3 (2) 5

(3) 4 (4) 2

(5) None of these

73. Among M, N, T, R and D each having a different height, T is taller than D but shorter than M. R is taller than N but shorter than D. Who among them is the tallest?

(1) D (2) T

(3) M (4) R

(5) N

74. If the digits in the number 25673948 are arranged in ascending order from left to right, what will be the sum of the digits which are fourth from the right and third from the left in the new arrangement?

(1) 10 (2) 9

(3) 4 (4) 6

(5) 8

75. If each of the vowels in the word HONESTLY is changed to the next letter in the English alphabetical series and each consonant is changed to the previous letter in the English alphabetical series, and then the alphabets so formed are arranged in alphabetical order from left to right, which of the following will be fifth from the left of the new arrangement thus formed?

(1) S (2) R

(3) M (4) F

(5) P

Directions (Q. 76-80): Answer the questions on the basis of the information given below.

Ten people, Binu, Dipu, Gita, Hira, Mira, Pari, Rani, Sara, Tara and Vini, are sitting in two parallel rows containing five people each, in such a way that there is an equal distance between adjacent persons. Mira faces south and sits opposite to Vini who is at the centre of the row. Tara sits to the immediate left of Pari who sits opposite to Hira. Dipu sits third to the left of Hira and faces Rani who is second to the right of Vini. Rani, Tara, Dipu and Gita are alike in some way. Sara and Mira are not immediate neighbours.

76. Who is facing Binu?

(1) Dipu

(2) Sara

(3) Gita

(4) Hira

(5) Cannot be determined

77. Who is facing the person sitting exactly between Tara and Vini?

(1) Gita (2) Binu

(3) Hira (4) Dipu

(5) Cannot be determined

78. Which pair is the odd one out?

(1) Hira-Gita

(2) Binu-Mira

(3) Pari-Vini

(4) Dipu-Sara

(5) Cannot be determined

79. What is true regarding Binu?

(1) Binu is sitting exactly beween Pari and Dipu.

(2) Dipu is sitting second to the right of Binu.

(3) Binu is sitting at the extreme end of the line.

(4) Binu is the neighbour of the person facing Rani.

(5) None is true

80. Four of the following five are alike in a certain way based on their positions in the above arrangment and so form a group. Which is the one that does not belong to that group?

(1) Gita (2) Binu

(3) Hira (4) Sara

(5) Pari

81. If 'A × B' means 'B is father of A', 'A + B' means 'A is wife of B' and 'A ÷ B' means 'A is brother of B', then what is the relation of J with L in 'J + H ÷ R × L'?

(1) Daughter

(2) Daughter-in-law

(3) Sister-in-law

(4) Cannot be determined

(5) None of these

82. Ajay walked 2 m towards east, took a right turn and walked 7 m. He then took a left turn and walked 5 m before taking a left turn and walking 7 m. He then took a final right turn and walked 1 m before stopping. How far is Ajay from the starting point?

(1) 8 m (2) 7 m

(3) 6 m (4) 5 m

(5) 9 m

83. In a row of children facing North, Ritesh is twelfth from the left end. Sudhir who is twenty-second from the right end is fourth to the right of Ritesh.Total how many children are there in the row?

   (1) 35   (2) 36

   (3) 37   (4) 38

   (5) None of these

84. In a column of 20 boys, D is fourteenth from the top and F is ninth from the bottom. How many boys are there between D and F?

   (1) 2   (2) 3

   (3) 4   (4) Data inadequate

   (5) None of these

85. In a certain code DUPLICATE is written as MRVFJFVBE. How is CARTOUCHE written in that code?

   (1) UTBEPWDJF

   (2) UTBFQFJDW

   (3) UTBEQFJDW

   (4) UTBEPFJDW

   (5) None of these

Directions (Q. 86 to 90): Answer the questions on the basis of the information given below.

Eight people - A, B, C, D, E, F, G, and H - are sitting in a straight line such that three people face north and the others face south. G and H face in a direction opposite to F. A sits third to the left of E, who faces north. F is at an extreme end and he faces in a direction opposite to A. There is exactly one person between A and F and also between A and B. D and G face in opposite directions and there are exactly two people between them. G is not an immediate neighbour of B. H sits third to the left of B, who faces south. A and H face in the same direction as B.

86. Select the option that represents the persons facing north.

   (1) A, B, G   (2) C, F, E

   (3) F, D, E   (4) B, G, H

   (5) D, E, H

87. Who sits third to the right of F?

   (1) E   (2) B

   (3) A   (4) D

   (5) G

88. Who are the immediate neighbours of B?

   (1) A, C   (2) D, E

   (3) C, E   (4) F, H

   (5) E, G

89. Who sits second to the left of the person who is third to the right of the immediate neighbour of H.

   (1) G   (2) F

   (3) A   (4) E

   (5) C

90. How many persons are sitting between C and E?

   (1) Two   (2) Three

   (3) Four   (4) One

   (5) None

Directions (Q. 91 to 95): Answer the following questions based on the given information.

Representatives of eight different banks, viz Amit, Billu, Chinu, Dhiman, Ellu, Fakram, Gagan and Hari, are sitting around a circular table, facing the centre, but not necessarily in the same order. Each one of them is from a different bank, viz UCO Bank, Oriental Bank of Commerce, Bank of Maharashtra, Canara Bank, Syndicate Bank, Punjab National Bank, Bank of India and Dena Bank.

Fakram sits second to the right of the representative of Canara Bank. The representative of Bank of India is an immediate neighbour of the representative of Canara Bank. Two persons sit between the representative of Bank of India and Billu. Chinu and Ellu are immediate neighbours. Neither Chinu nor Ellu is an immediate neighbour of either Billu or the representative of Canara Bank. The representative of Bank of Maharashtra sits second to the right of Dhiman. Dhiman is the representative of neither Canara Bank nor Bank of India. Gagan and the representative of UCO Bank are immediate neighbours. Billu is not the representative of UCO Bank. Only one person sits between Chinu and the representative of Oriental Bank of Commerce.

Hari sits third to the left of the representative of Dena Bank. The representative of Punjab National Bank sits second to the left of the representative of Syndicate Bank.

91. Four of the following five are alike in a certain way based on the given arrangement and thus form a group. Which is the one that does not belong to that group?

   (1) Hari-UCO Bank

   (2) Amit-Canara Bank

   (3) Dhiman - Bank of Maharashtra

   (4) Ellu - Syndicate Bank

   (5) Fakram - Punjab National Bank

92. Which of the following is true with respect to the given seating arrangement?

   (1) Billu is the representative of Bank of Maharashtra.

   (2) Chinu sits second to the right of Hari.

   (3) The representative of Dena Bank sits on the immediate left of the representative of UCO Bank.

(4) Amit sits second to the right of the representative of Bank of India.

(5) The representatives of Bank of Maharashtra and Syndicate Bank are immediate neighbours.

93. Who among the following sit(s) exactly between Billu and the representative of Bank of India?

(1) Amit and the representative of UCO Bank

(2) Amit and Hari

(3) Ellu and the representative of Bank of Maharashtra

(4) Hari and Gagan

(5) Representatives of Syndicate Bank and Oriental Bank of Commerce

94. Who among the following is the representative of Oriental Bank of Commerce?

(1) Amit   (2) Chinu

(3) Hari   (4) Gagan

(5) Dhiman

95. Who among the following sits second to the left of Billu?

(1) Chinu

(2) Hari

(3) The representative of Canara Bank

(4) The representative of Punjab National Bank

(5) Gagan

Directions for questions (Q. 96 to 100): In each question below are two/three statements followed by two conclusions numbered I and II. You have to take the given statements to be true even if they seem to be at variance from the commonly known facts and then decide which of the given counclusions logically follow from the given statements disregarding commonly known facts.

Give Answer :

(1) If only conclusion I follows

(2) If only conclusions II follows

(3) If either conclusion I or conclusion II follows.

(4) If neither conclusion I nor conclusion II followes.

(5) If both conclusions I and conclusion II follw.

96. Statements :

All packets are envelopes.No envelop is a gift.

Some gifts are boxes.

Conclusions :

I. All envelopes are packets.

II. All boxes can never be envelopes.

97. Statements :

All diaries are novels.

All novels are biographies.

Some biographies are scripts.

Conclusions :

I. Some diaries are scripts.

II. No diary is a script.

98. Statements :

Some days are months.

Some months are weeks.

Conclusions :

I. Some weeks are days.

II. No week is a day.

99. Statements :

All packets are envelopes.No envelop is a gift.

Some gifts are boxes.

Conclusions :

I. All packets being boxes is a possibility.

II. No packet is a gift.

100. Statements :

All diaries are novels.

All novels are biographies.

Some biographies are scripts.

Conclusions :

I. All diaries are biographies.

II. Some scripts are definitely not novels.

ANSWERS

1. (1)	**2.** (2)	**3.** (2)	**4.** (5)	**5.** (3)	**6.** (5)	**7.** (5)	**8.** (3)	**9.** (1)	**10.** (4)
11. (5)	**12.** (2)	**13.** (4)	**14.** (3)	**15.** (2)	**16.** (1)	**17.** (3)	**18.** (4)	**19.** (5)	**20.** (2)
21. (1)	**22.** (1)	**23.** (3)	**24.** (5)	**25.** (3)	**26.** (2)	**27.** (5)	**28.** (3)	**29.** (5)	**30.** (1)
31. (4)	**32.** (3)	**33.** (2)	**34.** (3)	**35.** (1)	**36.** (5)	**37.** (3)	**38.** (1)	**39.** (3)	**40.** (3)
41. (3)	**42.** (5)	**43.** (3)	**44.** (5)	**45.** (4)	**46.** (5)	**47.** (3)	**48.** (5)	**49.** (3)	**50.** (3)
51. (1)	**52.** (4)	**53.** (5)	**54.** (1)	**55.** (5)	**56.** (3)	**57.** (5)	**58.** (3)	**59.** (1)	**60.** (5)
61. (4)	**62.** (2)	**63.** (5)	**64.** (3)	**65.** (1)	**66.** (4)	**67.** (3)	**68.** (2)	**69.** (1)	**70.** (4)
71. (3)	**72.** (3)	**73.** (3)	**74.** (1)	**75.** (5)	**76.** (2)	**77.** (3)	**78.** (4)	**79.** (4)	**80.** (1)
81. (2)	**82.** (1)	**83.** (3)	**84.** (5)	**85.** (4)	**86.** (3)	**87.** (4)	**88.** (2)	**89.** (5)	**90.** (2)
91. (2)	**92.** (5)	**93.** (2)	**94.** (5)	**95.** (4)	**96.** (2)	**97.** (3)	**98.** (3)	**99.** (5)	**100.** (1)

EXPLANATIONS

1. (1) The first blank can take either 'since' or 'before'. Out of the two options, the second blank can only take 'exponential'. 'Brilliance' will make the sentence grammatically incorrect.

2. (2) Both the blanks will take positive words. So, options (4) and (5) are negated. 'Brilliant maintained' is grammatically incorrect. Had it been 'brilliantly maintained', it might have been correct. Option (2) is correct because the correct phrase is 'one of the finest'.

3. (2) The option (2) is the only viable answer.

4. (5) Only 'effectiveness' goes with 'flexibility' and 'power'.

5. (3) Since we are talking about low temperatures, 'plunge' and 'drop' are the most appropriate options for the first blank. Between 'during' and 'after', the former fits the sentence better than the latter.

6. (5) Refer to the line "Opacity of the operating environment … flows' where the author mentions that opacity or lack of transparency affect capital flows. Option (3) is too generic and vague.

7. (5) The passage discusses the role of bilateral investment treaties and the political risks that come with it. The other options are narrow in scope.

8. (3) The passage talks about capital flows and bilateral investment treaties. These are topics of Economics and so, the author is most likely an economist.

9. (1) Refer to the line, "The capital flows determinants … developed over time." The other options are incorrect and hence, can be ruled out.

10. (4) Refer to the line "Public debt, as well as FDI … low income countries." The other options can be ruled out.

11. (5) The word 'fiscal' refers to revenue or taxes.

12. (2) 'Expropriation' refers to a situation when the government takes a privately owned property and uses it for the benefit of the public.

13. (4) 'Paradox' refers to an absurd or contradictory statement.

14. (3) 'Deter' means to discourage or dissuade. Hence, 'encourage' is an antonym. The other options are synonyms.

15. (2) 'Volatile' means 'unstable'. Hence, 'constant' is an antonym.

For questions 16 to 20:

A introduces the topic - external context and environment being represented by the market which the managers are trying to provide a good or service. Next comes D which says what else can be included in the external context. 'also' is the key word here. E follows D by giving an example of it. Thus, DE is a mandatory pair. C carries on the argument by citing other factors affecting the television stations. Next comes B which gives the importance of contextual conditions and F clearly concludes the argument.

21. (1) Data from census can 'show' and not 'speak', 'site', 'seek' or 'strive' India's literacy level.

22. (1) The correct preposition with 'compared' is 'to'.

23. (3) The sentence says that the data relates to effective literacy and not literacy as a whole.

24. (5) The sentence says that if one can read and write his/her name, then he/she comes in the group of effective literacy. So, 'category' is the correct answer here.

25. (3) The blank will take 'more'. The sentence suggests that when one takes into account the percentage of population that comprises graduates, it becomes even more shocking.

26. (2) The correct phrase is 'more right handed'.

27. (5) The sentence is correct in its given form.

28. (3) People walk 'on' something.

29. (5) The sentence is correct in its given form.

30. (1) Climbing 'has been' a dream and not 'have been' a dream.

31. (4) The pattern of number series is as follows:

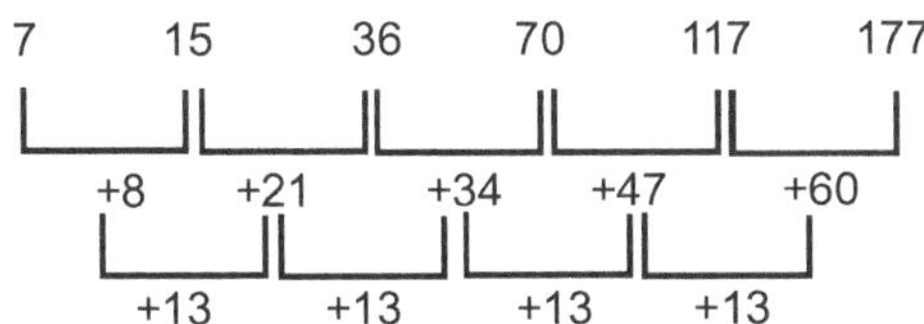

32. (3) The pattern of number series is as follows:

$6 \times 7 + 7^2 = 42 + 49 = 91$

$91 \times 6 + 6^2 = 546 + 36 = \underline{\textbf{582}}$

$582 \times 5 + 5^2 = 2910 + 25 = 2935$

$2935 \times 4 + 4^2 = 11740 + 16 = 11756$

$11756 \times 3 + 3^2 = 35268 + 9 = 35277$

$35277 \times 2 + 2^2 = 70554 + 4 = 70558$.

33. (2) The given series is:

$$+120, +\left(\frac{120}{2}\right), +\left(\frac{60}{2}\right), +\left(\frac{30}{2}\right), +\left(\frac{15}{2}\right), +\left(\frac{7.5}{2}\right)$$

34. (3) The given series is :

$(11 \times 1), -(11 \times 2), -(11 \times 3), -(11 \times 4),$

$-(11 \times 5), -(11 \times 6)$

35. (1) The series is

$-23, -19, -17, -13, -11, -7, \dots$

(Subtraction of prime numbers starting with 23 and following decreasing order)

36. (5) Let the CP be Rs. x.

$\therefore$ SP = Rs. 1.2 x

New CP = Rs. 0.8x

New SP = Rs. (1.2x – 5)

$\therefore$ 1.25 (0.8x) = 1.2x – 5

$\Rightarrow$ x = 1.2x – 5

$\Rightarrow$ x = Rs. 25

Hence, cost price of the article is Rs. 25.

37. (3) Let the reduced price be Rs. x.

According to the condition

$\Rightarrow$ x + 0.07x = 2675

$\Rightarrow$ 1.07x = 2675

$\Rightarrow$ x = Rs. 2500

So, Reduction = 2675 – 2500 = Rs. 175.

38. (1) LCM (4, 5) = 20

$\therefore$ Numbers divisible by both 4 and 5 must be divisible by 20. Hence, numbers will be 220, 240, … 380 i.e. 9 numbers.

39. (3) When SP of two article is same, one is sold at loss of x% and other at a gain of x%, then there is always an overall loss of $\dfrac{x^2}{100}$%.

Percentage loss $= \dfrac{30 \times 30}{100}$ = 9% loss.

40. (3) Difference between compound interest and simple interest for 2 years is given as:

$$CI - SI = \frac{PR^2}{100^2}$$

$$\Rightarrow 208 = \frac{P \times 8 \times 8}{100^2}$$

$$\Rightarrow P = \frac{208 \times 100^2}{8 \times 8} = Rs.\ 32,500.$$

Hence, sum is Rs. 32,500.

41. (3) 12% of 450 + ?% of 200 = 83

$\Rightarrow$?% of 200 = 83 – 54 = 29

$\Rightarrow ? = \dfrac{29}{200} \times 100 = 14.5.$

42. (5) ? = 726.34 + 888.12 – 1001.88

= 612.58.

43. (3) ? = 534.596 + 61.472 – 496.708 – 27.271

? = 596.068 – 523.979 = 72.089

44. (5) ? = 16 × 12 – 672 ÷ 21 + 211

$\Rightarrow$? = 192 – 32 + 211

$\Rightarrow$? = 160 + 211 = 371

45. (4) $441 - \dfrac{3717}{59} = ? \times 8$

$\Rightarrow ? = \dfrac{441 - 63}{8} = 47.25$

46. (5) Since the average age of husband and wife five years ago was 25 years.

$\therefore \dfrac{h + w}{2} = 25$ years

$\Rightarrow$ h + w = 50 years

At present, the sum of the ages of husband and wife is 60 years.

Let the present age of the baby be x years.

$$\therefore \frac{60+x}{3} = 21$$

$$\Rightarrow x = 3 \text{ years.}$$

47. (3) $\dfrac{\text{Quantity of Juice}}{\text{Quantity of Water}} = \dfrac{\frac{1}{3} \times 3 + \frac{5}{8} \times 2}{\frac{2}{3} \times 3 + \frac{3}{8} \times 2} = \dfrac{9}{11}$

$$= 9 : 11$$

$\therefore$ Percentage of juice content in new solution

$$= \frac{9}{20} \times 100 = 45\%.$$

48. (5) The amount of profit given at the end of the period is proportional to the capital invested and number of month i.e.

$$\frac{4}{3} = \frac{5}{6} \times \frac{t}{10}$$

$$\Rightarrow t = \frac{4}{3} \times \frac{6}{5} \times 10 \Rightarrow t = 16 \text{ months.}$$

49. (3) Let Labour cost be 5x, Material cost be 7x and overheads be 3x, Total cost = 15x

Profits = 20% of 15x = 3x

$$\frac{\text{Material cost}}{\text{Profit}} = \frac{7x}{3x} = \frac{7}{3} \text{ i.e. } 7 : 3$$

50. (3) Let the present age of elder person be x years and younger person be y years, then

$$\frac{x}{y} = \frac{2}{1}.$$

$$\Rightarrow x = 2y \qquad \qquad \cdots \text{(i)}$$

after six years the ratio will be 7 : 4.

$$\therefore \frac{x+6}{y+6} = \frac{7}{4} \qquad \qquad \cdots \text{(ii)}$$

By solving equations (i) and (ii),

we get x = 36 years, y = 18 years.

Hence, the age of elder person is 36 years.

51. (1) Required number of shares

= 1447 + 1528 + 1472 + 1078 + 1416

= 6941

52. (4) Required revenue

= 1231 × 10 + 1382 × 30

= Rs. 53,770

53. (5) Required increase = $\dfrac{25-5}{5} \times 100 = 400\%$

54. (1) Required difference = $\dfrac{1416-1200}{1200} \times 100 = 18\%$

55. (5) Adidas – 2015.

56. (3) Quantity I: Let the work done by A and B in one day be 'x' and 'y' units respectively.

$$\Rightarrow 20(x + y) = 10(x + y) + 30y$$

$$\Rightarrow x : y = 2 : 1$$

Hence, required time = $\dfrac{60}{2}$ = 30 days.

Quantity II: Let the work done by A and B in one day be 'x' and '1.5x' units respectively.

Thus, total work = 18 × 2.5x = 45x

Hence, required time = $\dfrac{45x \times 0.675}{x}$

$$= 30.375 \text{ days.}$$

Therefore, Quantity II > Quantity I.

57. (5) Percentage of profit in Quantity I cannot be compared with the absolute profit asked in Quantity II.

58. (3) Quantity I: Net discount = 1 – 0.8 × 0.65 × 0.7

$$= 63.6\%$$

Quantity II: Net discount = 1 – 0.75 × 0.6 × 0.8

$$= 64\%$$

Therefore, Quantity II > Quantity I.

59. (1) Quantity I: (A – 5) : (B – 5) = 5 : 6 and (A + 5) : (B + 5) = 6 : 7

Hence, A + B = 120 years.

Quantity II: (A – 6) : (B – 6) = 4 : 5 and (A + 3) : (B + 3) = 5 : 6

Hence, (A + 12) + (B + 12) = 117 years.

Therefore, Quantity I > Quantity II.

60. (5) Length of train in Quantity I cannot be compared with the speed of the train asked in Quantity II.

61. (4) Required percentage = $\dfrac{2250-2180}{2180} \times 100$

$$= 3.21\%$$

62. (2) Total number of students

= 2040 + 2300 + 2400 + 2200 + 2090 + 2120

= 13150

63. (5) Required average

$$= \frac{2500+2250+2450+2150+2020+2300}{6}$$

$$= 2278$$

64. (3) Required percentage

$$= \frac{2540}{2500+2040+2100+2280+2540+2320} \times 100$$

$$= 18\%$$

65. (1) Required ratio = (2250 + 2480) : (2260 + 2440)
= 473 : 470.

For solutions 66-70

$\delta \Rightarrow \geq$

$\$ \Rightarrow >$

$* \Rightarrow \leq$

$@ \Rightarrow =$

$\% \Rightarrow <$

66. (4) B % N $\Rightarrow$ B < N

N δ F $\Rightarrow$ N $\geq$ F

F * H $\Rightarrow$ F $\leq$ H

∴ B < N $\geq$ F $\leq$ H

Conclusions :

I.   H $ N $\Rightarrow$ H > N (Not True)

II. F % B $\Rightarrow$ F < B (Not True)

III. B % H $\Rightarrow$ B < H (Not True)

67. (3) W δ F $\Rightarrow$ W $\geq$ F

F % K $\Rightarrow$ F < K

K $ M $\Rightarrow$ K > M

∴ W $\geq$ F < K > B

Conclusions :

I.   M % F $\Rightarrow$ M < F (Not True)

II. M δ F $\Rightarrow$ M $\geq$ F (Not True)

III. W $ K $\Rightarrow$ W > K (Not True)

Conclusions I and II are complimentary pairs. Hence either I or II is true.

68. (2) W $ B $\Rightarrow$ W > B

B @ M $\Rightarrow$ B = M

M * R $\Rightarrow$ M $\leq$ R

∴ W > B = M $\leq$ R

Conclusions :

I.   R $ B $\Rightarrow$ R > B (Not True)

II. R @ B $\Rightarrow$ R = B (Not True)

III. M % W $\Rightarrow$ M < W (True)

Conclusions I and II form complimentary pair. Hence either I or II and III are true.

69. (1) M * D $\Rightarrow$ M $\leq$ D

D $ K $\Rightarrow$ D > K

K @ T $\Rightarrow$ K = T

∴ M $\leq$ D > K = T

Conclusions :

I.   T % D $\Rightarrow$ T < D (True)

II. K % M $\Rightarrow$ K < M (Not True)

III. M % T $\Rightarrow$ M < T (Not True)

70. (4) K @ F $\Rightarrow$ K = F

F $ M $\Rightarrow$ F > M

M δ T $\Rightarrow$ M $\geq$ T

∴ K = F > M $\geq$ T

Conclusions :

I.   T % F $\Rightarrow$ T < F (True)

II. M % K $\Rightarrow$ M < K (True)

III. K $ T $\Rightarrow$ K > T (True)

71. (3) Reverse all the letters of DRINK and then,

K N I R D
–1 –1 –1 –1 –1
J M H Q C

Similarly,

S T O L B
–1 –1 –1 –1 –1
R S N K A

Similarly,

Y E N O H
–1 –1 –1 –1 –1
X D M N G

Therefore, code of 'HONEY' is 'XDMNG'.

72. (3) 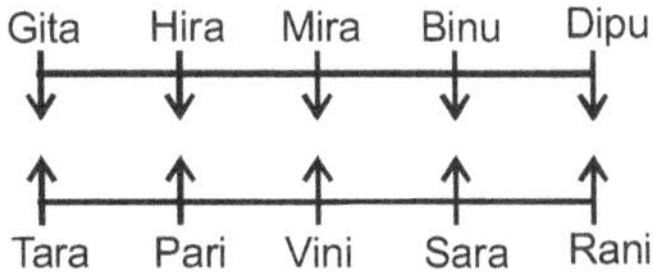

Such pairs are HI, EI, HN and IN.

73. (3) M > T > D > R > N

Hence, M is the tallest.

74. (1) 2 3 4 5 6 7 8 9

Now, 4 + 6 = 10.

75. (5) HONESTLY → GPMFRSKX → FGKMPRSX

For questions 76-80:

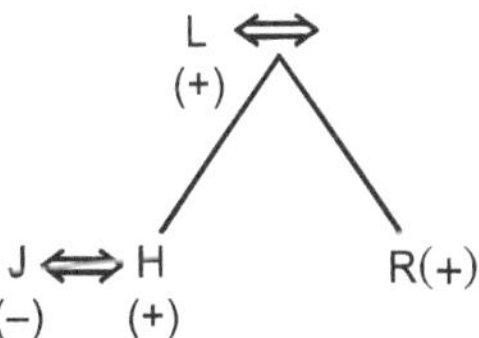

81. (2) J + H ÷ R × L : Drawing family tree

Hence, J is daughter-in-law of L.

82. (1)

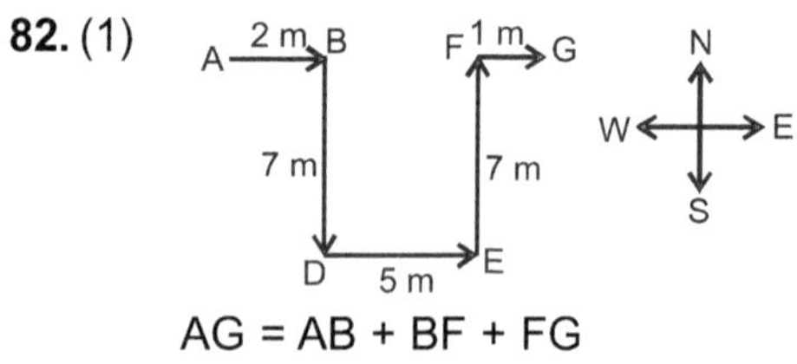

$$AG = AB + BF + FG$$
$$(\because BF = DE) = 2 + 5 + 1 = 8m.$$

83. (3) Total number of children in the row
$$= 12 + 4 + 22 - 1 = 37$$

84. (5)

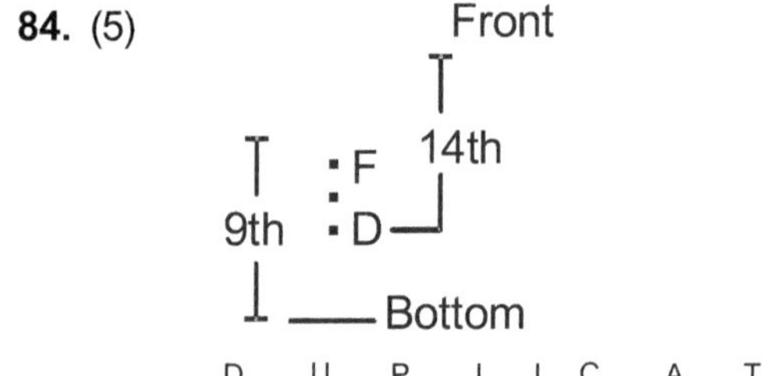

85. (4)

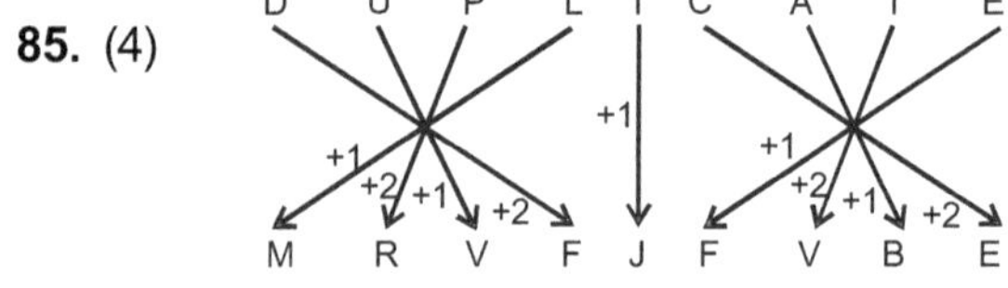

Similarly,

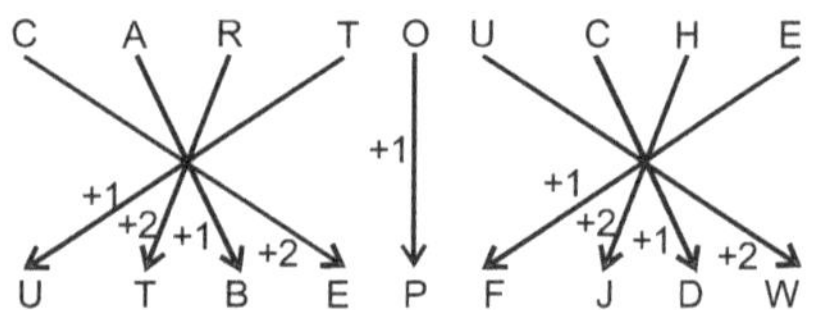

For questions 86 to 90:

F	C	A	D	B	E	G	H
↑	↓	↓	↑	↓	↑	↓	↓

For solutions 91 to 95:

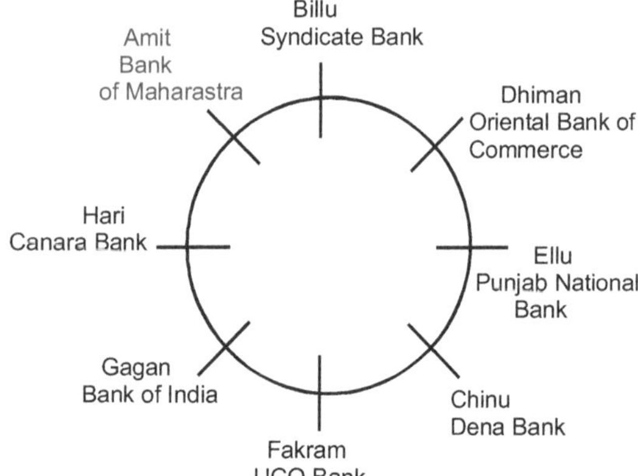

96. (2)

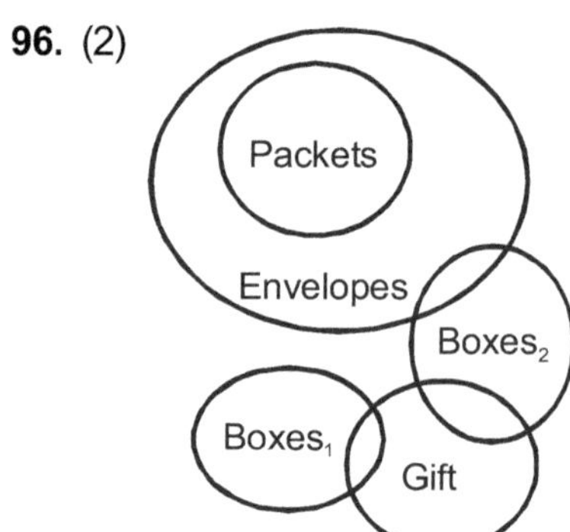

97. (3)

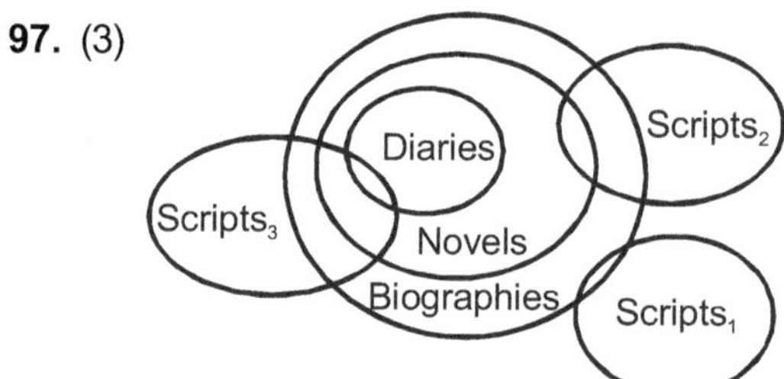

98. (3)

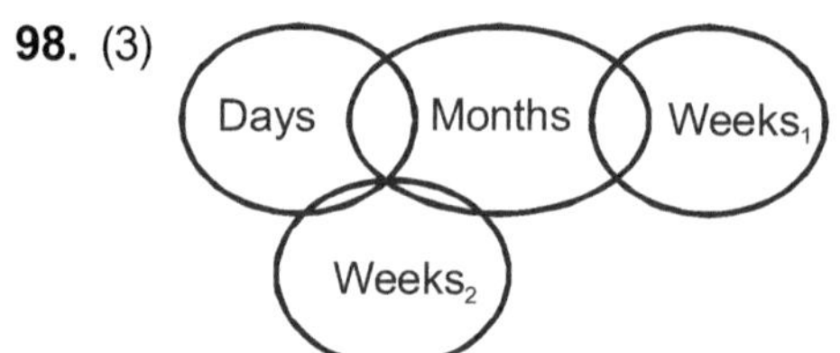

99. (5)

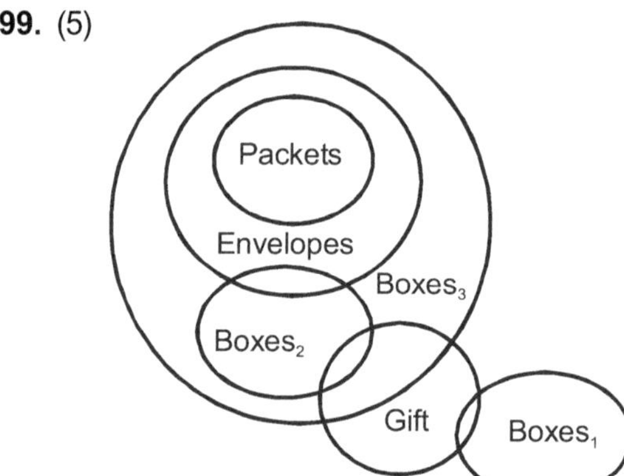

100. (1)

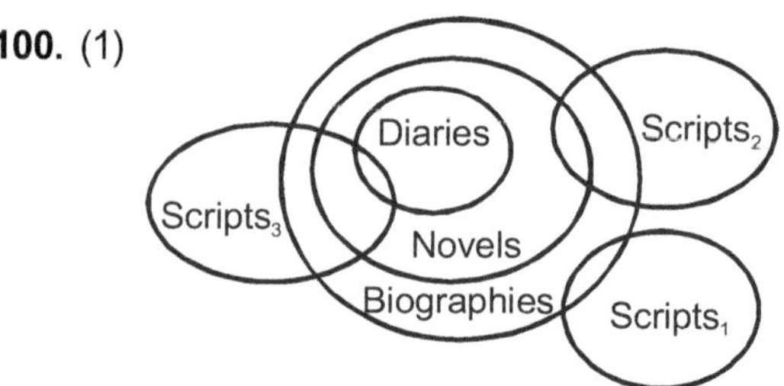

ENGLISH LANGUAGE

Directions for questions 1 to 10: Read the following passage carefully and answer the questions given below it. Certain words/phrases have been given in **bold** to help you locate them while answering some of the questions.

The long-term trend of an increasing share of service sector FDI has accelerated over the last twenty years. Nevertheless, empirical research on FDI is still concentrated on manufacturing. As the basic characteristics of services and goods differ - the main specifics of services are intangibility, inseparability of production and consumption, heterogeneity, perishability and restricted ownership one would expect that the determinants of internationalisation are not the same in the two sectors. This may hold true although the separation line between goods and services has become quite blurred reflecting the growing service content of manufacturing and a certain tendency towards the industrialisation of parts of the service sector. Against this background, it is surprising that firm-level econometric research dealing with the internationalisation of service firms by way of FDI is scarce. Particularly, only few studies cover the whole service sector, and there is hardly any **empirical** work investigating systematically the differences between manufacturing and services.

The analysis of the internationalisation of services companies is dominated until now by studies for specific industries. To mention are, in particular, financial services, ICT/software, the hotel industry, business services and retail trade. The majority of contributions are case studies or small-sample descriptive analyses focusing on one or very few service industries. Econometric studies dealing at firm level with specific service industries became available, with some exceptions, only in recent years. The concentration on industry-specific studies may be due to the absence of (large scale) datasets covering the whole service sector as is already pointed out in some earlier review articles. Another reason may be the presumption that the service sector is particularly heterogeneous as advocated, for example, by Dunning who argues that type and combination are integral to the service sector.

The present study contributes to filling this research gap by identifying and comparing for the two sectors (a) the drivers of the internationalisation of firm activity in terms of exports and FDI, and (b) the determinants of the choice among specific forms of FDI in terms of business functions. As mentioned, there is little evidence from econometric studies with respect to the first topic, and the second one, to the best of our knowledge, has never been investigated at all. In order to analyse these problems we formulate two empirical models using the well-known OLI paradigm as **theoretical** framework.

The present analysis is an extension of Hollenstein, who estimated, using data for 1998, OLI-based models that are structurally similar to model I and II but did so only for the entire business sector. The present research also goes beyond who disaggregated the business sector in manufacturing and services and estimated a model comparable to our model I which distinguishes between "exporting only" and "direct foreign presence". However, this author did not further differentiate within the category of firms with FDI as we do in model II. The paper is based on a large dataset containing information from 1921 companies of the Swiss business sector that responded to a comprehensive survey we conducted in 2010 among a random sample drawn from the official enterprise census of 2008. The available data allow a rich specification of the explanatory part of the two models. By estimating model I and II we are able to significantly add to previous evidence on the differences between manufacturing and service companies with respect to the determinants of international activities - a topic strongly neglected in empirical research. In line with our hypotheses, we find, for both sectors, that an OLI-based model is well suited not only for explaining the **propensity** of firms to go international by means of exports and/or FDI (model I) but also differences between specific forms of FDI in terms of business functions (model II). In all models, the explanatory power of the OLI approach is stronger for manufacturing than for services. The results for manufacturing are in line with the stages view of internationalization, what is only partly the case for the services sector.

As early as in the 1970s, Dunning argued that no single approach is able to explain a firm's international activities. He proposed an **eclectic** theory of international production, the well-known OLI **paradigm**, which he further developed over the years to account for changing features of the international economy and new theoretical approaches. In the most recent version the OLI model applies not only to international production but also to other business functions. In addition, it emphasizes the strategic aspects of internationalization more explicitly by drawing on the "resource-based" or "dynamic capability" view of the firm, or the concept of the "knowledge-based company".

1. According to the author, what dominates the examination of the internationalization of services companies?

(1) Studies for specific industries

(2) Studies for every industry

(3) Studies for agro-based industry

(4) Studies for automobile industry

(5) Studies for textile industry

2. According to the author, empirical research on FDI is focused on

(1) Equities   (2) Foreign exchange

(3) Manufacturing   (4) Agriculture

(5) None of the above

3. What did Dunning propose in the 1970s?

(1) A theory that revolves around the export industry

(2) A theory that revolves around the international activities of Swiss companies

(3) A unilateral theory of international production

(4) A heterogeneous theory of international production

(5) Both 1 and 2

4. What is the tone of the author in the passage?

(1) Diffusive   (2) Detailed

(3) Meandering   (4) Wandering

(5) Discursive

5. According to the author, when did econometric studies become available?

(1) In the 1980s

(2) In the early years of this century

(3) In the first decade of this century

(4) In the recent past

(5) In the 1990s

6. Choose the word which is **most similar** in meaning to the word given in **bold** as used in the passage.

PROPENSITY

(1) Expository   (2) Cursory

(3) Proclivity   (4) Indignation

(5) Discrete

7. Choose the word which is **most similar** in meaning to the word given in **bold** as used in the passage.

ECLECTIC

(1) Pursuit

(2) Handiwork

(3) Cross-disciplinary

(4) Unitary

(5) Readily

8. Choose the word which is **most similar** in meaning to the word given in **bold** as used in the passage.

PARADIGM

(1) Catholic   (2) Diverse

(3) Liberal   (4) Archetype

(5) Universal

9. Choose the word which is **opposite** in meaning to the word given in **bold** as used in the passage

THEORETICAL

(1) Metaphysical   (2) Experimental

(3) Abstract   (4) Philosophical

(5) Terrestrial

10. Choose the word which is **opposite** in meaning to the word given in **bold** as used in the passage

EMPIRICAL

(1) Conjectural   (2) Experiential

(3) Observational   (4) Employable

(5) Acumen

Directions (Q. 11 to 15): Fill in the blanks by choosing the most appropriate options.

11. The lion sprang _____ Mr. Robertson and knocked him _____

(1) at, down   (2) upon, up

(3) above, till   (4) in, on

(5) till, about.

12. Sheela is always _______ about showing up for her tutorials because she believes that _____ is a sign of irresponsibility.

(1) Sound, illiterate   (2) conscious, commotion

(3) chaos, fast   (4) late, early

(5) punctual, tardiness

13. Sincerity is an ______ part of one's success ____ life.

(1) initial, for

(2) immediate, till

(3) insightful, above

(4) integral, in

(5) inimical, towards

14. The most important factor in today's social context is the ____ of social security measures which have been initiated ____ the government.

(1) allowance, to

(2) emergence, by

(3) abolition, for

(4) facilitate, on

(5) introduce, till

15. Millions of dollars have been _____ on welfare measures and yet, most of them are _____ the purview of the people of this region.

(1) credited, for   (2) allowed, allocated

(3) documented, well   (4) spent, outside

(5) earned, inside

Directions (Q. 16 to 20): Rearrange the following six sentences (1), (2), (3), (4), (5)and (6) in the proper sequence to form a meaningful paragraph; then answer the questions given below them-

(1) The man immediately got off the car, slapped the young boy who had thrown the brick and asked him why he did so.

(2) The boy then requested the driver to help him since he was unable to lift his injured brother alone.

(3) The driver stood to watch the young boy push the wheelchair down the road and decided to never repair the dent.

(4) A man was driving down a highway when a brick smashed on the side of his expensive, brand new car.

(5) Moved beyond words, the driver apologised to the young boy and quickly lifted his brother and provided first aid to him.

(6) The boy was in tears and said that he had to do so as no one on the highway had stopped to help his handicapped brother who had slipped from his wheelchair.

16. Which of the following should be the **FIRST** sentence after rearrangement?

(1) 1   (2) 2

(3) 3   (4) 4

(5) 5

17. Which of the following should be the **SECOND** sentence after rearrangement?

(1) 2   (2) 1

(3) 4   (4) 6

(5) 5

18. Which of the following should be the **THIRD** sentence after rearrangement?

(1) 1

(2) 2

(3) 3

(4) 4

(5) 6

19. Which of the following should be the **FOURTH** sentence after rearrangement?

(1) 2   (2) 3

(3) 4   (4) 5

(5) 6

20. Which of the following should be the **LAST (SIXTH)** sentence after rearrangement?

(1) 1   (2) 2

(3) 3   (4) 4

(5) 5

Directions (Q. 21 to 25): Read each sentence to find out whether there is any grammatical error or idiomatic error in it. The error, if any, will be in one part of the sentence. The letter of that part is the answer. If there is 'No error', the answer is (5). (Ignore errors of punctuation, if any.)

21. The administration has conclusive (1)/ that it is retailers who are (2)/ responsible for upsetting (3)/ the city's household budget.(4)/No error (5)

22. The assurances, unfortunately, (1)/ remained on paper, as (2)/ neither the Centre or the state initiated steps (3)/ for the development of the backward region. (4)/ No error (5)

23. Sediment deposit along the coast (1)/ may be the primary reason for (2)/ the change in conditions, (3)/ buta lot more remains to be understand. (4)/ No error (5)

24. A committee will be set up (1)/ to explore pros and cons by (2)/ a common fee structure, and will (3)/ take a final decision on it within a week. (4)/ No error (5)

25. The infection which causes (1)/ gums to bleed and teeth to fall out (2)/ results from the build-up of (3)/ a particular bacteria in the mouth. (4)/ No error (5)

Directions (Q. 26 to 30): In the following passage there are blanks, each of which has been numbered. These numbers are printed below the passage and against each, five words are suggested, one of which fits the blank appropriately. Find out the appropriate word in each case.

From the beginning, we __(26)__ that we would trust our clients and never involve the judiciary in seeking repayment of our loans. We feel that our relationship is with people __(27)__ than with papers. We succeed or fail depending on how strong our personal relationship is with our borrowers. Today, the __(28)__ in other banks is that every borrower is going to run away with their money so they tie him or her up in legal documents to make certain that the borrower cannot escape the reach of the bank. In __(29)__ cases the borrower does end up defaulting but this is less than one per cent. To us this represents a __(30)__ reminder of what we need to improve to succeed.

26. (1) clear   (2) decided
     (3) determine   (4) firm
     (5) emphatic

27. (1) instead   (2) preferable
     (3) prior   (4) rather
     (5) less

28. (1) assumption   (2) guess
     (3) undertaking   (4) responsibility
     (5) guarantee

29. (1) open   (2) hardly
     (3) often   (4) seldom
     (5) rare

30. (1) past   (2) eager
     (3) compulsorily   (4) constant
     (5) persisted

NUMERICAL ABILITY

Directions for questions 31 to 35: What will come in place of question mark (?) in the following questions?

31. $\left(\sqrt{5}-\sqrt{10}\right)^2+\left(\sqrt{2}+5\right)^2=(?)^3-22$

     (1) $\sqrt{2}$ (2) 2
     (3) 16   (4) 8
     (5) None of these

32. 55% of $\sqrt{2116}\div 0.01=?\times 20$

     (1) 126.5   (2) 126.6
     (3) 124.6   (4) 125.4
     (5) None of these

33. $\sqrt{12^2\times 16\div 24+193+7\times 5}=(?)^2$

     (1) $3\sqrt{2}$ (2) $4\sqrt{2}$
     (3) $5\sqrt{2}$ (4) 18
     (5) None of these

34. $\sqrt{31.36}\div\sqrt{0.64}\times 252=(?)^2\times 36$

     (1) 81   (2) 64
     (3) -8 (4) -7
     (5) 9

35. $(1.69)^4\div(2197\div 1000)^3\times(0.13\times 10)^3=(1.3)^?$

     (1) 6   (2) 2
     (3) 4   (4) 0
     (5) None of these

36. The simple interest obtained on a sum of certain principal is Rs.2,000 in five years at the rate of 4% per annum. What would be the compound interest obtained on same principal at same rate in two years?

     (1) Rs.716   (2) Rs.724
     (3) Rs.824   (4) Rs.816
     (5) None of these

37. A candidate scores an average of 60% marks in all his subjects scoring an average of 56% marks in four of the subjects and an average of 68% marks in the remaining subjects. What are the total number of subjects?

     (1) 6   (2) 7
     (3) 10   (4) 8
     (5) None of these

38. Find a two digit number such that the product of its digits is 18, and when 63 is added to this number, then the digits interchange their places.

     (1) 63   (2) 36
     (3) 29   (4) 92
     (5) None of these

39. A milkman makes a profit of 20% on the sale of milk. If he added 10% water to the milk, by what percent would his profit increase?

     (1) 25%   (2) 60%
     (3) 40%   (4) 45%
     (5) 32%

40. In two alloys, aluminium and iron are in the ratio 4 : 1 and 1 : 3 respectively. After mixing together 10 kg of the first alloy, 16 kg of the second and several kilograms of pure aluminium, an alloy was obtained in which the ratio of aluminium to iron was 3 : 2. Find the weight of the new alloy.

     (1) 15 kg   (2) 25 kg
     (3) 65 kg   (4) 95 kg
     (5) 35 kg

Directions for questions 41 to 45: In each of these questions a number series is given. In each series only one number is wrong. Find out wrong number.

41. 5531, 5506, 5425, 5304, 5135, 4910, 4621

     (1) 5531   (2) 5435
     (3) 4621   (4) 5135
     (5) 5506

42. 6, 7, 9, 13, 26, 37, 69

     (1) 7   (2) 26
     (3) 69   (4) 37
     (5) 9

43. 1, 3, 10, 36, 152, 760, 4632
  (1) 3 (2) 36
  (3) 4632 (4) 760
  (5) 152

44. 4, 7, 12, 20, 28, 39, 50
  (1) 4 (2) 7
  (3) 39 (4) 20
  (5) 28

45. 157.5, 45, 15, 6, 3, 2, 1
  (1) 1 (2) 2
  (3) 6 (4) 157. 5
  (5) 45

46. The average age of five children of a family is eleven years. The average age of their parents and their grandfather is 35 years. Find the average age of the family if the family has only given eight members.
  (1) 18 years (2) 19 years
  (3) 20 years (4) 21 years
  (5) Cannot be determined

47. The marked price of an article is Rs. 100. If it is sold at a discount of 10%, a profit of 35% is made. What loss or profit will be made if it is sold for Rs. 30 less than marked price?
  (1) 10% loss (2) 8% gain
  (3) 4.5% loss (4) 6.34% gain
  (5) 5.01% gain

48. In a college seats for Maths, Physics and Biology are in the ratio of 5 : 7 : 8 respectively. There is a proposal to increase these seats by 40%, 50% and 75% respectively. What will be the respective ratio of increased seats?
  (1) 2 : 3 : 4 (2) 6 : 7 : 8
  (3) 6 : 8 : 9 (4) Cannot be determined
  (5) None of these

49. A man can row at 22 kmph in still water. It takes him thrice as long to row up as to row down the river. Find the rate at which stream is running.
  (1) 20 km/hr (2) 9 km/hr
  (3) 11 km/hr. (4) 8 km/hr
  (5) 12 km/hr

50. The ages of Gyani and Mani were in the ratio 2 : 3 in 1996. Their ages were in the ratio 7 : 10 in 2001. What will be the ratio of their ages in 2011?
  (1) 5 : 6 (2) 3 : 4
  (3) 4 : 5 (4) 6 : 7
  (5) 1 : 3

Directions for questions 51 to 55: Answer the questions on the basis of the information given below.

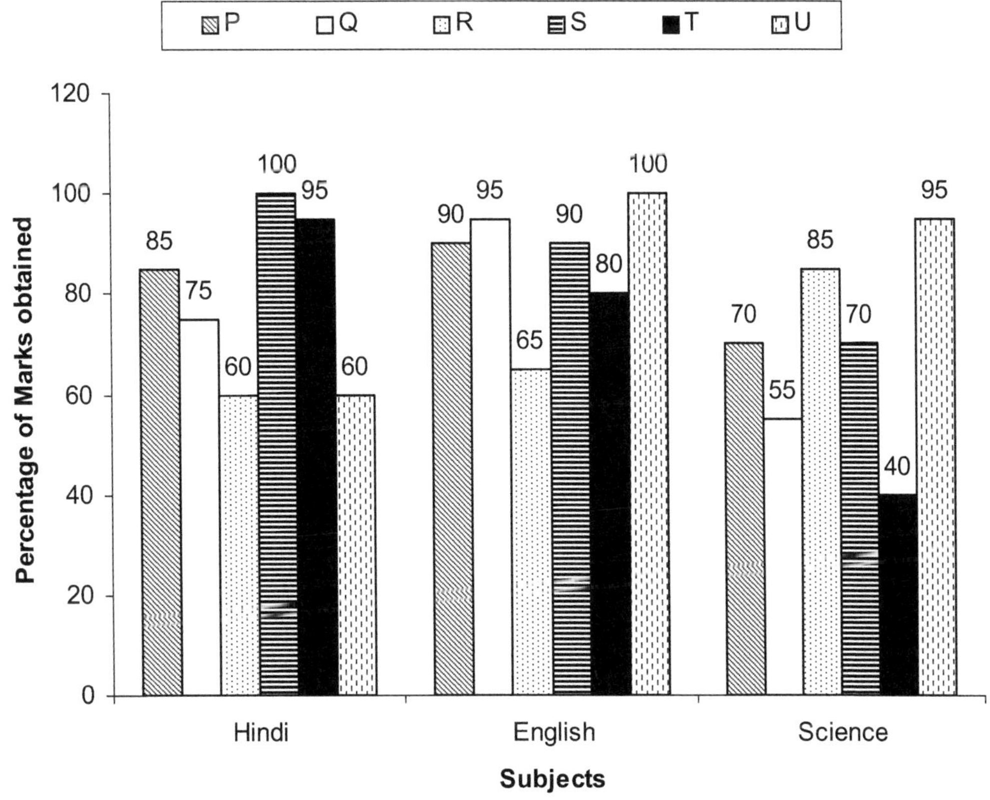

The bar-graph given above shows the percentage of marks obtained by six students namely P, Q, R, S, T and U in a class test. There were three class tests viz. Hindi, English and Science and each test was of 20 marks. Any student scoring less than 58% marks is considered failed in the exams.

51. What is the average score of the class in these three tests?

(1) 15.9   (2) 17.8

(3) 18.4   (4) 16.6

(5) Cannot be determined

52. The marks scored by P in Hindi is what percentage more or less than that scored by T in Science?

(1) 112.5%   (2) 52.94%

(3) 136.67%   (4) 109.5%

(5) 98.5%

53. What is the average of marks scored by U in all the tests?

(1) 15   (2) 17

(3) 18   (4) 16.3

(5) 15.8

54. Among the given six students, who has topped in all tests?

(1) P   (2) Q

(3) U   (4) S

(5) T

55. The average marks scored by S in all three tests is what percentage more or less than that scored by T in all tests?

(1) 21.93%   (2) 26.52%

(3) 20.93%   (4) 26%

(5) 23.94%

Directions (Q. 56 to 60) : In each questions, two equations numbered I and II are given. You have to solve both the equations and mark the appropriate answer.

Give answer

(1) If $a > b$

(2) If $a \geq b$

(3) If $a < b$

(4) If $a \leq b$

(5) If relationship between a and b cannot be determined

56. I. $a^2 - 4a - 621 = 0$

     II. $b^2 + 56b + 783 = 0$

57. I. $15a^2 - 34a + 15 = 0$

     II. $15b^2 - 22b + 8 = 0$

58. I. $14a^2 - 41a + 15 = 0$

     II. $56b^2 - 54b + 10 = 0$

59. I. $a^3 = -6859$

     II. $b^2 - 7b - 494 = 0$

60. I. $14a - 27b = 16$

     II. $32b - 11a = 9$

Directions (Q. 61 to 65) : Answer the questions on the basis of the information given below.

Number of people (in thousands) participating in the annual fair from six different towns during the period 2011 to 2016.

Years	Town					
	Patnipur	Kolapur	Roshipur	Sholapur	Tundlapur	Udhampur
2011	4.2	5.5	4.5	5.8	6.0	5.7
2012	5.1	5.3	6.2	5.7	6.1	6.2
2013	6.3	5.1	6.5	5.3	5.9	6.6
2014	4.4	5.0	5.9	5.1	5.3	5.1
2015	5.8	5.4	5.4	4.9	5.5	4.4
2016	6.2	6.8	4.9	4.8	5.7	4.3

61. Number of people participating in the fair from Patnipur in the year 2016 forms approximately what per cent of the total number of people participating in the fair from that town during the period 2011 to 2016?

(1) 19   (2) 24

(3) 27   (4) 12

(5) 15

62. What is the respective ratio of the total number of people participating in the fair from Sholapur in the years 2012 and 2013 together to the number of people participating in the fair from Roshipur in the same years ?

(1) 8 : 9   (2) 110 : 127

(3) 136 : 143   (4) 11 : 12

(5) None of these

63. What is the per cent increase in the number of people participating in the fair from Tundlapur in the year 2015 from the previous year? (Rounded off to two digits after decimal)

(1) 4.15   (2) 3.77

(3) 1.68   (4) 2.83

(5) None of these

64. What is the average number of people participating in the fair from Udhampur during the period 2011 to 2016? (Rounded off to the nearest integer)

(1) 5153   (2) 5234

(3) 5672   (4) 5411

(5) 5383

65. How many people participated in the fair from all the towns together in the year 2011?

(1) 32900   (2) 31000

(3) 32400   (4) 31700

(5) None of these

REASONING ABILITY

Directions for questions 66 to 71: Answer the following questions based on the given information. Twelve people are sitting in two parallel rows such that each row contains six people and each of the persons in the parallel rows is sitting opposite to another person.

In row 1: P, Q, R, S, T and V are seated and all of them are facing South. In row 2: A, B, C, D, E and F are seated and all of them are facing North.

It is also known that:

S sits third to the right of Q. Either S or Q sits at one of the extreme ends of a row. The one who faces Q sits second to the right of E. Two people sit between B and F. Neither B nor F sits at the extreme ends. The immediate neighbour of B faces the person who sits third to the left of P. R and T are immediate neighbours. C sits second to the left of A. T does not face the immediate neighbour of D.

66. Who among the following sit at the extreme ends of the row?

(1) S and D   (2) Q and A

(3) V and C   (4) P and D

(5) Q and F

67. Who among the following faces S?

(1) A   (2) B

(3) C   (4) D

(5) F

68. How many persons are sitting between V and R?

(1) One   (2) Two

(3) Three   (4) Four

(5) None of these

69. P is related to A in the same way as S is related to B based on the given arrangement. Who among the following is T related to, following the same pattern?

(1) C   (2) D

(3) E   (4) F

(5) Cannot be determined

70. Which of the following is true regarding T?

(1) F faces T.

(2) V is an immediate neighbour of T.

(3) F faces the one who is second to the right of T.

(4) T sits at one of the extreme ends of the row.

(5) Q sits second to the right of T.

71. Four of the following five are alike in a certain way based on the given arrangement and so form a group. Which is the one that does not belong to that group?

(1) A-T   (2) B-Q

(3) F-S   (4) D-R

(5) E-R

Directions for questions 72 to 76: Read the given information and answer the following questions based on it.

Five friends Pankaj, Purushottam, Pulkit, Parinita and Prerna wrote test in Zoology, Botany and Chemistry. They got different ranks according to the performance by them in their respective test. Rank 1 is the best rank followed by rank 2, 3, 4 and 5. No two persons got the same rank in same test and got different ranks in different subjects.

(A) Pulkit got better rank than Parinita in Zoology and Pankaj in Chemistry

(B) Prerna didn't get the best rank in any of the subjects and got third rank in Zoology.

(C) Person with rank 5 in Chemistry got rank 2 in Botany.

(D) Purushottam got rank 5 in Botany and his best possible rank is 3.

(E) Parinita got best rank in Botany but her Chemistry rank is lower than Purushottam.

(F) Both Parinita and Pankaj got a best rank and a worst rank each.

(G) Pankaj got rank 1 in Zoology and Parinita got rank 4 in Chemistry.

72. Who got rank 3 in Botany?

(1) Pulkit   (2) Purushottam

(3) Parinita   (4) Pankaj

(5) Canot be determined

73. Who got best rank in Chemistry?

(1) Pulkit   (2) Prerna

(3) Purushottam   (4) Either (2) or (3)

(5) Either (1)   or (3)

74. Who got rank 2 in Botany?

   (1) Pulkit   (2) Prerna

   (3) Purushottam   (4) Parinita

   (5) Pankaj

75. Who got lowest rank in Zoology?

   (1) Pulkit   (2) Prerna

   (3) Purushottam   (4) Parinita

   (5) Pankaj

76. Who got rank 3 in chemistry?

   (1) Pulkit   (2) Prerna

   (3) Purushottam   (4) Parinita

   (5) Pankaj

77. How many such pairs of letters are there in the word POSITIVE each of which has as many letters between them in the word as in the English alphabet?

   (1) None   (2) One

   (3) Two   (4) Three

   (5) More than three

78. Starting from O, Vivek walked 40 m towards south, then he turned left and walked 60 m. He again turned left and walked 40 m. He once again turned left and walked 80 m and reached at D. How far and in which direction is D from O?

   (1) 20 m, east   (2) 40 m, west

   (3) 20 m, west   (4) 20 m, south

   (5) 20 m, north

79. The positions of the first and the fifth digits in the number 83416759 are interchanged. Similarly, the positions of the second and the sixth digits are interchanged, and so on. Which of the following will be the fourth digit from the right end after the rearrangement?

   (1) 3   (2) 8

   (3) 4   (4) 6

   (5) None of these

80. Each consonant in the word TEMPORAL is changed to the previous letter in the English alphabet and each vowel is changed to the next letter in the English alphabet and then the letters so arrived are arranged in alphabetical order, which of the following will be the fourth from the right end?

   (1) E

   (2) P

   (3) L

   (4) K

   (5) None of these

Directions for questions 81 to 85: In the following questions, the symbols @, \$,*,# and δ are used with the following meaning as illustrated below:

'P \$ Q' means 'P is not smaller than Q'.

'P @ Q' means 'P is neither smaller than nor equal to Q'.

'P # Q' means 'P is neither greater than nor equal to Q'.

'P δ Q' means' P is neither greater than nor smaller than Q'.

'P * Q' means 'P is not greater than Q'.

Now in each of the following questions assuming the given statements to be true, find which of the four conclusions I, II, III and IV given below them is/are definitely true and give your answer accordingly.

81. Statements:

   H @ T, T # F, F δ E, E*V

   Conclusions:

   I. V \$ F

   II. E @ T

   III. H @ V

   IV. T # V

   (1) Only I, II and III are true

   (2) Only I, II and IV are true

   (3) Only II. III and IV are true

   (4) Only I, III and IV are true

   (5) All I, II, III and IV are true

82. Statements:

   D # R, R * K, K @ F, F \$ J

   Conclusions:

   I. J # R

   II. J # K

   III. R # F

   IV. K @ D

   (1) Only I, II and III are true

   (2) Only II, III and IV are true

   (3) Only I, III and IV are true

   (4) All I, II, III and IV are true

   (5) None of these

83. Statements:

   N δ B, B \$ W, W # H, H*M

   Conclusions:

   I. M @ W

   II. H @ N

   III. W δ N

   IV. W # N

(1) Only I is true

(2) Only III is true

(3) Only IV is true

(4) Only either III or IV is true

(5) Only either III or IV and I are true

84. Statements:

R * D, D $ J, J # M, M @ K

Conclusions:

I.   K # J

II. D @ M

III. R # M

IV. D @ K

(1) None is true   (2) Only I is true

(3) Only II is true   (4) Only III is true

(5) Only IV is true

85. Statements:

M $ K, K @ N, N * R, R# W

Conclusions:

I.   W @ K

II. M $ R

III. K @W

IV. M.@N

(1) Only I and II are true

(2) Only I. II and III are true

(3) Only III and IV are true

(4) Only II, III and IV are true

(5) None of these

86. Pointing to a woman in a photograph a man says, "This woman is the mother-in-law of the only daughter of my mother-in-law". How is the man related to the woman?

(1) Son   (2) Husband

(3) Brother   (4) Father-in-law

(5) Father

87. Kavita walks 3 km towards north and then she turns left and moves 2 km. She again turns left and goes 3 km and turns to her right and starts walking straight. In which direction is she walking now?

(1) North-west

(2) South

(3) West

(4) North

(5) None of these

Directions for questions 88 and 89: Read the following information carefully and answer the questions given below it.

I.   There are five friends.

II. They are standing in a row facing south.

III. Jayesh is to the immediate right of Alok.

IV. Pramod is between Bhagat and Subodh.

V.   Subodh is between Jayesh and Pramod.

88. Who is at the extreme left end?

(1) Alok   (2) Bhagat

(3) Subodh   (4) Either (1) or (2)

(5) Jayesh

89. Who is in the middle?

(1) Bhagat   (2) Jayesh

(3) Pramod   (4) Subodh

(5) Either (3) or (4)

90. In a certain code 'MOMENT' is written as 'OMOCPR'. How would 'THERMO' be written in that code?

(1) VFGQOM   (2) VFGPPM

(3) VEGPON   (4) VFGPOM

(5) None of these

Directions for questions 91 to 95: Study the following information carefully and answer the given questions.

P, Q, R, S, T, W, V and Y are sitting around a circular table with four of them facing the centre and four others facing away from the centre.

(1) V sits second to left of Y.

(2) Only two people sit between T and R.

(3) Q sits third to the left of P, who is facing away from the centre.

(4) P is not an immediate neighbour of V

(5) T and Y are immediate neighbours of each other.

(6) Only one person sits between Y and R.

(7) S is not an immediate neighbour of P or R.

(8) The immediate neighbours of V face the opposite direction as that of V.

(9) R and W face the same direction as that of Y.

91. What is the position of R with respect to P?

(1) Third to the left

(2) Immediately to the right

(3) Second to the left

(4) Immediately to the left

(5) Third to the right

92. If all the persons are made to sit in alphabetical order in clockwise direction starting, from P, the positions of how many (excluding P) will remain unchanged as compared to their original seating positions?

    (1) One   (2) Two

    (3) None   (4) Three

    (5) Four

93. Who sits between Y and R?

    (1) W   (2) P

    (3) T   (4) Q

    (5) None of these

94. How many persons sit between S and V when counted in clockwise direction from S?

    (1) Three   (2) Five

    (3) Six   (4) None

    (5) Four

95. Four of the following five are alike in a certain way based on their seating positions in the above arrangement and so form a group. Which is the one that does not belong to that group?

    (1) SR   (2) YW

    (3) QT   (4) WV

    (5) SP

Directions (Q. 96 to 100): Answer the questions on the basis of the information given below.

Six persons – Ram, Raka, Ravan, Raheem, Ramulal and Ranvijay– live in the same building. They own cars– Zen, City, Palio, Safari, Scorpio and Fortuner– not necessarily in this order. They park their cars in different garages 1 to 6(from left to right), not necessarily in this order. It is also known that:

(i) Ram owns Palio.

(ii) Persons parking their cars in Garage 1 and Garage 6 have a difference of one in the name length of their cars.

(iii) Safari is being parked in Garage 2 and City is being parked in Garage 5.

(iv) Raka parks his car to the immediate left of Raheem.

(v) Car owner of car parked in Garage 3 has same name length as garage number.

(vi) No car owner owns a car with same name length as his name. i.e. Raka does not own City– similarly for others.

Note : Name length means total number of letters in the name.

96. If Ravan parks his car in Garage 6, then who parks his car in Garage 1?

    (1) Ranvijay   (2) Ramulal

    (3) Raka   (4) Raheem

    (5) Cannot be determined

97. City is owned by:

    (1) Ravan   (2) Ramulal

    (3) Raheem   (4) Raka

    (5) Cannot be determined

98. If Ravan owns Fortuner, then who parks his car in Garage 2?

    (1) Ram   (2) Ravan

    (3) Raka   (4) Ramulal

    (5) Cannot be determined

99. If the difference between the Garage No. and the Name Length of the car owned by Ravan is 2 then find the number of cars parked between City and the car owned by Ramulal.

    (1) One   (2) Two

    (3) Three   (4) Four

    (5) Cannot be determined

100. How many cars have their fixed parkings?

    (1) Three   (2) Two

    (3) Five   (4) Four

    (5) All six

ANSWERS

1. (1)	**2.** (3)	**3.** (4)	**4.** (2)	**5.** (4)	**6.** (3)	**7.** (3)	**8.** (4)	**9.** (2)	**10.** (1)
11. (1)	**12.** (5)	**13.** (4)	**14.** (2)	**15.** (5)	**16.** (5)	**17.** (2)	**18.** (5)	**19.** (1)	**20.** (3)
21. (1)	**22.** (3)	**23.** (5)	**24.** (2)	**25.** (5)	**26.** (2)	**27.** (5)	**28.** (1)	**29.** (5)	**30.** (5)
31. (5)	**32.** (1)	**33.** (1)	**34.** (5)	**35.** (2)	**36.** (5)	**37.** (1)	**38.** (3)	**39.** (2)	**40.** (5)
41. (1)	**42.** (2)	**43.** (5)	**44.** (5)	**45.** (1)	**46.** (3)	**47.** (5)	**48.** (1)	**49.** (3)	**50.** (2)
51. (5)	**52.** (1)	**53.** (2)	**54.** (5)	**55.** (3)	**56.** (1)	**57.** (5)	**58.** (5)	**59.** (4)	**60.** (1)
61. (1)	**62.** (2)	**63.** (2)	**64.** (5)	**65.** (4)	**66.** (5)	**67.** (1)	**68.** (2)	**69.** (2)	**70.** (3)
71. (5)	**72.** (1)	**73.** (1)	**74.** (5)	**75.** (5)	**76.** (3)	**77.** (5)	**78.** (3)	**79.** (2)	**80.** (5)
81. (2)	**82.** (5)	**83.** (5)	**84.** (1)	**85.** (5)	**86.** (1)	**87.** (3)	**88.** (1)	**89.** (5)	**90.** (5)
91. (5)	**92.** (1)	**93.** (2)	**94.** (3)	**95.** (5)	**96.** (5)	**97.** (3)	**98.** (4)	**99.** (2)	**100.** (4)

EXPLANATIONS

1. (1) Refer to the first sentence of the second paragraph for the answer.

2. (3) Refer to the second sentence of the passage for the answer.

3. (4) Refer to the second sentence of the last paragraph for the answer.

4. (2) The author of the passage approaches the subject in great detail. The author cites case studies and quotes scholars to substantiate his arguments. Hence, his tone can be termed as detailed.

5. (4) Refer to the sentence in the second paragraph beginning with "Econometric studies dealing at firm level with specific service industries …."

11. (1) 'At' and 'down' are the correct prepositions.

12. (5) 'Punctual' and 'tardiness' convey a meaning. 'Tardiness' refers to the quality of being late.

13. (4) 'Integral' and 'in' are making sense in the context of the passage.

14. (2) 'Emergence' and 'by' are making sense in the context of the passage.

15. (4) 'Spent' and 'outside' are the only words that fit the blanks correctly.

For questions 16 - 20 :

The correct sequence is 416253.

21. (1) 'Conclusive' is incorrect here. It means showing that something is certainly true. The correct word to use here is 'concluded', which means decided.

22. (3) With 'neither' we use 'nor' and not 'or'.

23. (4) The correct phrase is 'remains to be understood'.

24. (2) We do not explore pros and cons'with the help of'common fee structure; we explore pros and cons 'for'common fee structure.

25. (5) The sentence is correct in its given form.

26. (2) The line talks about a decision.

27. (4) 'Rather' is the most appropriate word because a comparison is being made.

28. (1) The line talks about an assumption.

29. (5) 'Rare' is the only word that is making sense.

30. (4) 'Constant' reminder is appropriate for the given blank.

31. (5) $(?)^3 = \left(\sqrt{5} - \sqrt{10}\right)^2 + \left(\sqrt{2} + 5\right)^2 + 22$

$\qquad = 5 - 2\sqrt{50} + 10 + 2 + 10\sqrt{2} + 25 + 22$

$\qquad = 5 - 10\sqrt{2} + 10 + 2 + 10\sqrt{2} + 25 + 22 = 64$

$\quad (?)^3 = 64$ or $? = 4$.

32. (1) $\dfrac{55 \times \sqrt{2116}}{100} \div 0.01 = ? \times 20$

$\qquad\qquad\qquad \left(\because \sqrt{2116} = \sqrt{46 \times 46} = 46\right)$

$\quad \Rightarrow ? \times 20 = \dfrac{55 \times 46}{100 \times 0.01} = \dfrac{55 \times 46}{1} = 2530$

$\quad \Rightarrow ? = \dfrac{2530}{20} = 126.5$

33. (1) $(?)^2 = \sqrt{12^2 \times 16 \div 24 + 193 + 7 \times 5}$

$\qquad = \sqrt{144 \times \dfrac{16}{24} + 193 + 35}$

$\qquad = \sqrt{96 + 193 + 35} = \sqrt{324}$

$\quad \Rightarrow (?)^2 = \sqrt{324} = 18$

$\quad \therefore \ ? = \sqrt{18} = \sqrt{3 \times 3 \times 2} = 3\sqrt{2}$

34. (4) $(?)^2 = \dfrac{\sqrt{31.36} \div \sqrt{0.64} \times 252}{36}$

$\qquad = \dfrac{\dfrac{5.6}{0.8} \times 252}{36} = \dfrac{7 \times 252}{36} = 49$

$\quad \therefore ? = \pm\sqrt{49} = \pm 7$

$\quad$ Hence, $? = -7$.

35. (2) $\because (1.69)^4 \div \left(\dfrac{2197}{1000}\right)^3 \times (1.3)^3 = 1.3^?$

$\quad \Rightarrow (1.3)^8 \div (1.3)^{3 \times 3} \times 13^3 = 13^?$

$\quad \Rightarrow 1.3^{8 - 9 + 3} = 13^?$

$\quad \Rightarrow 13^2 = 13^?$ or $? = 2$.

36. (4) Principal $= \dfrac{SI \times 100}{Time \times Rate} = \dfrac{2000 \times 100}{5 \times 4} = Rs.\,10,000$

$\quad \therefore$ CI for two years

$\qquad = 10000\left(1 + \dfrac{4}{100}\right)^2 - 10000 = Rs.\,816.$

37. (1) Let there be X number of subjects

$\quad \Rightarrow 60X = 56 \times 4 + 68\,(X - 4)$

$\quad \Rightarrow 60X = 224 + 68X - 272$

$\quad \Rightarrow 68X - 60X = 272 - 224$

$\quad \Rightarrow 8X = 48$

$\quad \Rightarrow X = \dfrac{48}{8}$

$\quad \Rightarrow X = 6$

$\quad \therefore$ Total number of subjects are 6.

38. (3) Let the tens digit be x and units digit be y, then

$\qquad\qquad x\,y = 18 \qquad\qquad\qquad \text{...(i)}$

$\quad 10x + y + 63 = 10\,y + x$

$\quad \Rightarrow \quad 9x - 9y = -63$

$\qquad\quad x - y = -7 \qquad\qquad \text{...(ii)}$

$\quad$ By (i), $y = \dfrac{18}{x}$ putting in (ii), we get

$\qquad x - \dfrac{18}{x} = -7$

$\quad \Rightarrow \quad x^2 - 18 = -7x$

$\quad \Rightarrow x^2 + 7x - 18 = 0$

$\quad \Rightarrow \qquad\qquad x = 2 \text{ or } -9$

$\quad$ Putting $x = 2$ in (i) , $y = 9$

$\quad \therefore$ The two digit number is 29.

39. (2) Let the cost of 10 litres of milk be Rs.100.

$\quad$ {Rate = Rs.10/lt}

$\quad$ SP would be Rs. 120 for 20% gain.

$\quad$ {Rate = Rs. 12 / lt}

$\quad$ 10% water means now amount of milk is 11 litre and its SP would be = 11 × 12 = Rs. 132.

$\quad \therefore$ Profit increases $= \dfrac{32 - 20}{20} \times 100 = 60\%.$

40. (5) Quantity of aluminium in first alloy

$\qquad = \dfrac{4}{5} \times 10 = 8 \text{ kg.}$

$\quad$ Quantity of aluminium in second alloy

$\qquad = \dfrac{1}{4} \times 16 = 4 \text{ kg.}$

$\quad$ Let, x kg of pure aluminium is mixed.

$\quad$ So, $8 + 4 + x = \dfrac{3}{5}\,(10 + 16 + x)$

$\quad \Rightarrow 60 + 5x = 78 + 3x$

$\quad \Rightarrow 2x = 18$

$\quad \Rightarrow x = 9 \text{ kg.}$

$\quad$ So, the weight of the new alloy = 10 + 16 + 9

$\qquad\qquad\qquad\qquad = 35 \text{ kg.}$

41. (1) The series follows the given pattern:

$\quad -7^2, -9^2, -11^2, -13^2, -15^2, -17^2 \,...$

$\quad$ Hence, 5531 should be replaced with 5555.

42. (2) The series follows the given pattern:

+1, +2, +4, +8, +16, +32

Hence, 26 should be replaced with 21.

43. (4) The series follows the given pattern:

×1 + 2, ×2 + 4, ×3 + 6, ×4 + 8,

×5 + 10, × 6 + 12, ...

Hence, 760 should be replaced with 770.

44. (4) The series follows the given pattern:

$2^2 - 0, 3^2 - 2, 4^2 - 4, 5^2 - 6, 6^2 - 8,$

$7^2 - 10, 8^2 - 12$

Hence, 20 should be replaced with 19.

45. (1) The series follows the given pattern:

The number should be 2 in place of 1.

÷3.5, ÷3, ÷2.5, ÷2, ÷1.5, ÷1, ...

Hence, 1 should be replaced with 2.

46. (3) Average age of given 8 members

$$\Rightarrow \frac{11 \times 5 + 3 \times 35}{5 + 3} = \frac{160}{8} = 20 \text{ years.}$$

47. (5) MP = Rs. 100

SP = Rs. 90

$$CP = \frac{90}{1.35} = Rs.66.66$$

If it is sold Rs.30 less than MP, SP = Rs.70.

$$\text{Gain} = \frac{70 - 66.66}{66.66} \times 100 = 5.01\% .$$

48. (1) Let the initial seats for Maths, Physics and Biology be 5x, 7x and 8x respectively.

∴ Required ratio = 5 × 140 : 7 × 150 : 8 × 175

= 2 : 3 : 4.

49. (3) Let the speed of the man when rowing upstream be x kmph, then his downstream speed = 3x kmph.

$$\therefore \text{ Rate in still water} = \frac{1}{2}\left(3x + x\right) = 2x \text{ kmph}$$

So, 2x = 22 ⇒ x = 11

∴ Rate upstream = 11 km/hr.

Rate downstream = 33 km/hr.

$$\text{Hence, rate of stream} = \frac{1}{2}\left(33 - 11\right) = 11\,\text{km}/\text{hr.}$$

50. (2) Let the ages of Gyani and Mani in 1996 be 2x and 3x respectively. Then,

$$\frac{2x + 5}{3x + 5} = \frac{7}{10}$$

⇒ x = 15.

$$\frac{2x + 15}{3x + 15} = \frac{45}{60} = 3 : 4.$$

51. (5) As we don't know the total number of student in the class. Hence, we cannot determine the average of marks of the class.

52. (1) Marks scored by P in Hindi = 20 × 0.85 = 17

Marks scored by T in Science = 20 × 0.40 = 8

$$\therefore \text{ Percentage value } = \frac{17 - 8}{8} \times 100 = 112.5\%$$

53. (2) Average marks scored by U

$$= \frac{20 \times 0.60 + 20 \times 1.00 + 20 \times 0.95}{3}$$

$$= \frac{12 + 20 + 19}{3} = \frac{51}{3} = 17 .$$

54. (4) Total marks scored by P = 17 + 18 + 14 = 49

Total marks scored by Q = 15 + 19 + 11 = 45

Total marks scored by R = 12 + 13 + 17 = 42

Total marks scored by S = 20 + 18 + 14 = 52

Total marks scored by T = 19 + 16 + 8 = 43

Total marks scored by U = 12 + 20 + 19 = 51

It is evident that S topped among given six students.

55. (3) Average marks scored by S $= \dfrac{52}{3}$

Average marks scored by T $= \dfrac{43}{3}$

∴ Percentage value

$$= \frac{\dfrac{52}{3} - \dfrac{43}{3}}{\dfrac{43}{3}} \times 100 = \frac{9}{43} \times 100 = 20.93\%$$

56. (1) Solving I we get:

$a^2 - 27a + 23a - 621 = 0$

$\Rightarrow a(a - 27) + 23(a - 27) = 0$

$\Rightarrow (a - 27) + (a + 23) = 0$

Thus, a = –23, 27

Solving II we get:

$b^2 + 56b + 783 = 0$

$\Rightarrow b^2 + 29b + 27b + 783 = 0$

$\Rightarrow b(b + 29) + 27(b + 29) = 0$

Thus, b = –27, –29

Hence, a > b.

57. (5) Solving I we get:

$15a^2 - 34a + 15 = 0$

$\Rightarrow 15a2 - 25a - 9a + 15 = 0$

$\Rightarrow 5a(3a - 5) - 3(3a - 5) = 0$

$\Rightarrow (5a - 3)(3a - 5) = 0$

Thus, $a = \dfrac{3}{5}, \dfrac{5}{3}$

Solving II we get:

$15b^2 - 22b + 8 = 0$

$\Rightarrow 15b^2 - 10b - 12b + 8 = 0$

$\Rightarrow 5b(3b - 2) - 4(3b - 2) = 0$

$\Rightarrow (5b - 4)(3b - 2) = 0$

Thus, $b = \dfrac{4}{5}, \dfrac{2}{3}$

Hence, relationship between 'a' and 'b' cannot be established.

58. (5) Solving I we get:

$14a^2 - 41a + 15 = 0$

$\Rightarrow 14a^2 - 35a - 6a + 15 = 0$

$\Rightarrow 7a(2a - 5) - 3(2a - 5) = 0$

$\Rightarrow (7a - 3)(2a - 5) = 0$

Thus, $a = \dfrac{3}{7}, \dfrac{5}{2}$

Solving II we get:

$56b^2 - 54b + 10 = 0$

$\Rightarrow 56b^2 - 40b - 14b + 10 = 0$

$\Rightarrow 8b(7b - 5) - 2(7b - 5) = 0$

$\Rightarrow (8b - 2)(7b - 5) = 0$

Thus, $b = \dfrac{1}{4}, \dfrac{5}{7}$

Hence, relationship between 'a' and 'b' cannot be established.

59. (4) Solving I we get:

$a = -19$

Solving II we get:

$b^2 - 7b - 494 = 0$

$\Rightarrow b^2 - 26b + 19b - 494 = 0$

$\Rightarrow b(b - 26) + 19(b - 26) = 0$

$\Rightarrow (b - 26)(b + 19) = 0$

Thus, $b = 26, -19$

Hence, $a \leq b$.

60. (1) Solving the two linear equations we get $a = 5$ and $b = 2$

Hence, $a > b$.

61. (1) Number of people participating from Patnipur in 2016 (in thousands) = 6.2

Total number of people participating from that town during all the years (in thousands)

$= 4.2 + 5.1 + 6.3 + 4.4 + 5.8 + 6.2$

$= 32$

$\therefore$ Required percentage = $\dfrac{6.2}{32} \times 100 \approx 19\%.$

62. (2) Total number of people participating from Sholapur in year 2012 and 2013 (in thousands) = $5.7 + 5.3 = 11.0$

Total number of people participating from Roshipur in year 2012 and 2013 (in thousands) = $6.2 + 6.5 = 12.7$

$\therefore$ Required ratio = 11.0 : 12.7

$= 110 : 127.$

63. (2) Number of people participating from Tundlapur in 2015 (in thousands) = 5.5

Number of people participating from Tundlapur in 2014 (in thousands) = 5.3

$\therefore$ Required percentage = $\dfrac{5.5 - 5.3}{5.3} \times 100$

$= 3.77\%$

64. (5) Number of people participating from Udhampur in all the years (in thousands) = $5.7 + 6.2 + 6.6 + 5.1 + 4.4 + 4.3 = 32.3$

$\therefore$ Required average = $\dfrac{32.3}{6} \times 100$

$= 538.$

65. (4) Number of people participating from all the towns in 2011 (in thousands) = $4.2 + 5.5 + 4.5 + 5.8 + 6.0 + 5.7 = 31.7$

For questions 66 to 71:

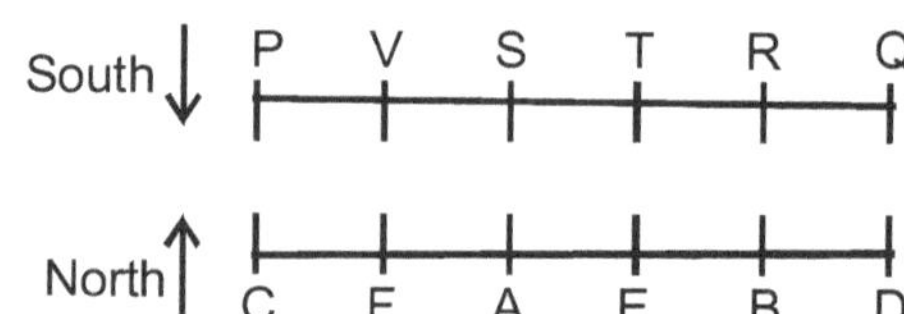

For questions 72 to 76: The given information can be tabulated as:

Rank	Zoology	Botany	Chemistry
1	Pankaj	Parinita	Pulkit
2	Pulkit	Pankaj	Prerna
3	Prerna	Pulkit	Purushottam
4	Purushottam	Prerna	Parinita
5	Parinita	Purushottam	Pankaj

77. (5) POSITIVE

78. (3) The movement of Vivek is like this.

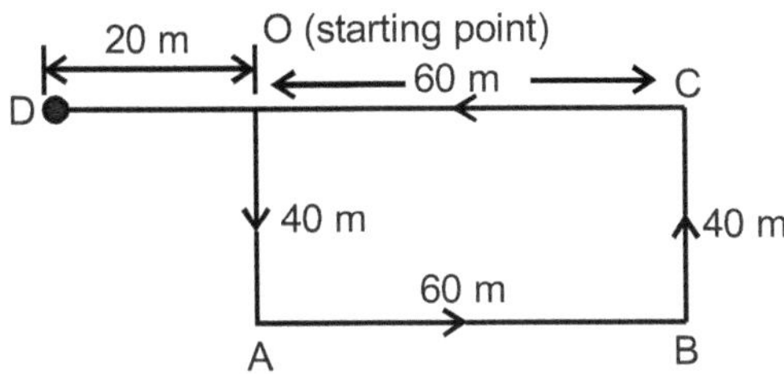

So, finally Vivek is moving towards west and is 20 m away from the starting point.

79. (2) The fourth digit from the right end is the fifth digit from the left. But the first digit becomes the fifth.

80. (5) According to question,

$$\begin{array}{cccccccc} T & E & M & P & O & R & A & L \\ {\scriptstyle -1\downarrow} & {\scriptstyle +1\downarrow} & {\scriptstyle -1\downarrow} & {\scriptstyle -1\downarrow} & {\scriptstyle +1\downarrow} & {\scriptstyle -1\downarrow} & {\scriptstyle +1\downarrow} & {\scriptstyle -1\downarrow} \\ S & F & L & O & Q & B & K \end{array}$$

After arranging in alphabetical order, we get

B F K L [O] P Q S

4th from the right

81. (2) H > T … (i)

T < F … (ii)

F = E … (iii)

E ≤ V … (iv).

Combining (ii), (iii) and (iv), we get

T < F = E ≤ V … (v)

Hence, V ≥ F and I is true.

Also, E > T and II is true.

Again, T < V and IV is true.

From (i) and (iv), H and V cannot be compared.

Hence, III is not true.

82. (5) D < R … (i)

R ≤ K … (ii)

K > F … (iii)

F ≥ J … (iv)

Combining these, we get D < R ≤ K > F ≤ J.

Now, J and R cannot be compared. Hence, I does not follow.

J < K and II follows.

R and F cannot be compared. Hence, III does not follow. K > D and IV follows.

83. (5) N = B … (i)

B ≥ W … (ii)

W < H … (iii)

H ≤ M … (iv)

Combining these, we get N = B ≥ W < H ≤ M.

Hence, M > W and I is true.

H and N cannot be compared. Hence, II does not follow.

Again, W ≤ N. Which means either III (W = N) or IV (W < N) is true.

84. (1) R ≤ D … (i)

D ≥ J … (ii)

J < M … (iii)

M > K … (iv)

None of these given conclusion can be compared.

85. (5) M ≥ K … (i)

K > N … (ii)

N ≤ R … (iii)

R < W …(iv)

From (i) and (ii), M ≥ K > N or M > N … (v)

From (iii) and (iv), N ≤ R < W or N < W … (vi)

Now, from (ii) and (vi), W and K cannot be compared. Hence, I is not true.

From (iii) and (v), M and R cannot be compared. Hence, II is not true.

From (ii) and (vi), K and W cannot be compared. Hence, III is not true.

IV is definitely true from from (v).

86. (1) Only daughter of my mother-in-law ⇒ my wife. Mother-in-law of my wife → my mother.

Hence, man is son of the woman.

87. (3)

For questions 88 and 89:

Jayesh is to the right of Alok, i.e. J, A. Pramod is between Bhagat and Subodh, i.e. B, P, S. Subodh is between Jayesh and Pramod. So the sequence is:

Bhagat Pramod Subodh Jayesh Alok

88. (1) Alok is at the extreme left end.

89. (4) Subodh is in the middle.

90. (4)

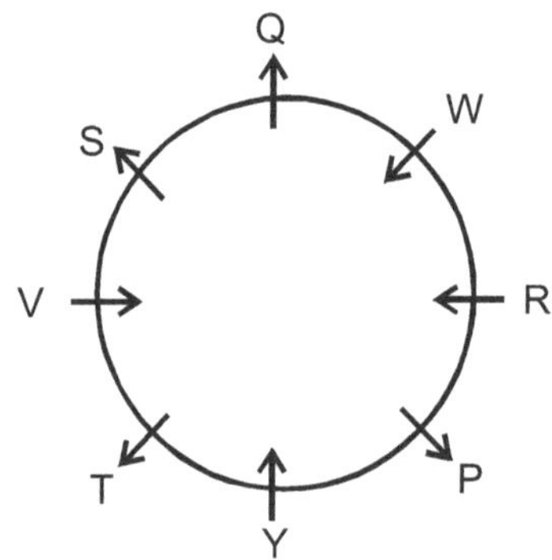

Similarly

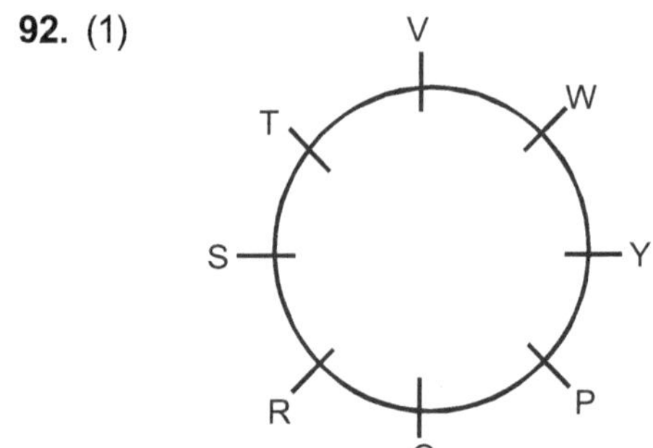

For questions 91 to 95:

92. (1)

For questions 96 to 100:

Given Information can be tabulated as follows.

As Car owner of Car parked in Garage 3 has name length of 3, it must be Ram and hence the car is Palio.

And as Raka can't own City and Raheem Can't own safari because of name length restrictions, they must park their cars in Garage 4 and Garage 5 respectively.

Cars parked in Garage1 and Garage 6 have a difference of one in their name lengths. Hence, the possible pairs are (Fortuner, Scorpio) and (Scorpio,Fortuner). Only (Scorpio, Fortuner) pair is left as a valid option as cars with name length 3,4,5,6 have been already parked in other garages.

Garage Number	Car Name (Name Length)	Car Owner (Name Length)
1	Scorpio(7) /Fortuner(8)	
2	Safari (6)	
3	Palio(5)	Ram(3)
4	Zen (3)	Raka(4)
5	City(4)	Raheem(6)
6	Fortuner(8) /Scorpio(7)	

96. (5) Even if Ravan parks his car in Garage 6 we can't determine owner of car parked in Garage 1 as we don't know about owner of car parked in Garage 2.

98. (4) Since it is understood that Ravan owns Fortuner and Ramulal can't own Scorpio (from statement vi), we can conclude that Ranvijay owns Scorpio. Also since Scorpio and Fortuner are parked in garage numbers 7 and 8, we can deduce that Ramulal owns a Safari.

PRACTICE PAPER – 16

ENGLISH LANGUAGE

Directions (Q. 1 to 5): Rearrange the following sentences into a meaningful paragraph and then answer the questions given below it.

(A) Development of drought resistance could benefit large numbers of farmers.

(B) Hence the human race will have no choice but to adapt to these impacts.

(C) India has to be concerned about climatic changes.

(D) This impact can run into decades and centuries.

(E) Environment day is thus an important occasion to assess the past and our future.

(F) There is a possibility of adverse impact on agriculture which could deter growth.

1. Which of the following is the **FIFTH** sentence of the passage?
   - (1) F
   - (2) D
   - (3) E
   - (4) A
   - (5) C

2. Which of the following is the **THIRD** sentence of the paragraph?
   - (1) A
   - (2) D
   - (3) B
   - (4) C
   - (5) E

3. Which of the following is the **SECOND** sentence of the paragraph?
   - (1) B
   - (2) D
   - (3) F
   - (4) C
   - (5) E

4. Which of the following is the **LAST (SIXTH)** sentence of the paragraph?
   - (1) C
   - (2) B
   - (3) F
   - (4) D
   - (5) E

5. Which of the following is the **FIRST** sentence of the paragraph?
   - (1) A
   - (2) D
   - (3) C
   - (4) B
   - (5) E

Directions (Q. 6 to 10): Which of the phrases (1), (3) and (4) given below each sentence should replace the phrase printed in bold in the sentence to make it grammatically; correct ? If the sentence is correct as it is given and no correction is required, mark (5) as the answer.

6. As Anuj was familiar with the road to Neeraj's house, he **lead the way**.
   - (1) led the way
   - (2) led away
   - (3) leading ways
   - (4) lead ways
   - (5) No correction required

7. Although he was new to the field of painting, Sharad **give it a go**.
   - (1) gave goes
   - (2) gives his go
   - (3) gave it a go
   - (4) giving it goes
   - (5) No correction required

8. The performance of the band on New Year's eye was **not of worlds**.
   - (1) but of the worldly
   - (2) outing of worlds
   - (3) out from the world
   - (4) out of this world
   - (5) No correction required

9. Parents are **changing with the times** and are friends and more open to their children's views.
   - (1) changed timings
   - (2) changed to the time
   - (3) changing times
   - (4) change with time
   - (5) No correction required

10. Many people do not like to **switch at** one brand to another.
    - (1) switched in
    - (2) switches at
    - (3) switch from
    - (4) switching on
    - (5) No correction required

Directions (Q. 11 to 20): Read the following passage carefully and answer the questions given below it. Certain words have been given in bold to help you locate them while answering some of the questions.

Once upon a time, there lived an old lion. The lion, the king of the forest, had grown old. He became **frail** and due to this, he could not hunt for food. With each passing day he became more and more weak. He realised that he would not live for long if it continued like that. He thought how he could arrange for his food. After pondering over it for quite some time, he decided that he should have an assistant.

The lion thought that a fox would be the best person to **handle** this position as he was intelligent and clever. He summoned for fox and said, "Dear friend, I have always liked you because you are smart. I want to appoint you as my minister and advise me on all the affairs of the forest." The old lion also asked the fox that since he was the king of the forest he should not have to hunt for his food. With respect to this, the fox's first duty as minister was to bring him an animal to eat everyday. The fox could not refuse the king and accepted the offer.

After the conversation, the fox went out to find an animal for the lion. On the way, he met a fat donkey. He said, "My friend, I have got good news for you. You are very lucky. Our king, the lion, has chosen you to be his chief minister. He asked me to meet you and inform you about his decision." The donkey was scared of the lion and said, "I am afraid of the lion. He might kill me and eat me up. Why has he chosen me as his chief minister? I am not even **fit** enough to be a minister as I am not as intilligent as other animals." The clever fox laughed and said, "Dear you don't know your qualities. **Our king is dying to meet you**. He has chosen you because you are wise, gentle, and hardworking. By serving the king, you will be the second most powerful animal of our forest. Imagine, all the other animals will respect you and seek favours from you. You must not **lose** your greatest chance in life." So, the poor donkey was convinced and got ready to go along with the fox.

In this way, the fox managed to attract the donkey to the den. When the fox and the donkey approached, the lion was hungrier than ever. But he kept a smiling face and said, "Welcome, my dear friend. Come near me. You are my chief minister." As the donkey came closer, the lion **pounced** upon him and killed him instantly. The lion thanked the clever fox and was happy to get the food. As the lion sat down to eat his meal, the fox said, "Your majesty, I know you are very hungry but a king must take a bath before a meal." Lion thought it was a good idea and told the fox to keep a watch on the carcass of the donkey. The fox silently sat down to keep a watch on the donkey and thought to himself, "I took all the trouble of getting the donkey here. It is I who deserve the best portion of the meal." Thus, the fox cut open the head of the donkey and ate up the whole brain. When the lion returned he shouted, "What happened to the donkey's brain? I wanted to eat the brain first." The fox smilingly replied, "Your Majesty, donkeys have no brains. If he had any, he would not have come near a lion at all."

11. Why did the lion decided to have an assistant for himself?

    (1) He was too lazy to hunt for himself.

    (2) He was old and weak and could not hunt anymore.

    (3) He wanted someone to help him kill the fat donkey.

    (4) He could not handle the affairs of the forest alone.

    (5) None of these

12. Which of the following is the moral of the story?

    (1) An idle brain is the devil's workshop.

    (2) Fools are deaf to wise words.

    (3) Never believe an enemy's sweet talks.

    (4) Morality can be best tested while one has power.

    (5) One can only lead a horse to water, not make him drink it.

13. Why did the fox say 'our king is dying to meet you' to the donkey?

    (1) The king would have died of hunger if the donkey did not meet him.

    (2) The king desperately wanted the donkey to be his chief minister as he was gentle and hardworking

    (3) The fox wanted to convince the donkey to come with him to the lion so that the lion could eat him.

    (4) The king wanted to meet the donkey since all other animals respected the donkey more than the king.

    (5) None of these

14. What did the fox do when the lion went to take a bath before having his meal?

    (1) He secretly told the donkey to run away as the lion had planned to kill him.

    (2) He ate up the donkey's brain as he had done all the hard work of bringing him to the lion's den.

    (3) He held himself responsible for the death of the poor donkey and did not let the lion eat the donkey.

    (4) He killed the lion with the help of the donkey and became the king of the forest

    (5) None of these

15. Which one of the phrases given below the following statements should be placed in the blank space provided so as to make a meaningfully correct sentence in the context of the passage?

When the lion did not see any brain in the donkey's head______.

    (1) he spared his life and let him go

    (2) he got upset with the fox for having selected such a donkey

    (3) he took his decision to make him the chief minister back

    (4) the fox explained to him that donkeys do not have any brains.

    (5) None of these

Directions (Q.16 to 18): Choose the word which is most similar in meaning to the word given in bold as used in the passage

16. FIT

(1) Healthy   (2) Deserving

(3) Strong   (4) Valuable

(5) Important

17. LOSE

(1) Misplace   (2) Suffer

(3) Dispose   (4) Defeat

(5) Miss

18. POUNCED

(1) Climbed   (2) Grew

(3) Attacked   (4) Plunged

(5) Roared

Directions (Q. 19 and 20): Choose the word which is most opposite in meaning to the word given in bold as used in the passage.

19. HANDLE

(1) Mismanage   (2) Drop

(3) Confront   (4) Decline

(5) Uncover

20. FRAIL

(1) Unhealthy   (2) Massive

(3) Rich   (4) Strong

(5) Civilised

Directions (Q. 21 to 25): Read each sentence to find out whether there is any grammatical error or idiomatic error in it. The error, if any, will be in one part of the sentence. The letter of that part is the answer. If there is no error, the answer is (5). (Ignore errors of punctuation, if any).

21. Sugar-sweetened drinks does not (1) /pose any particular health risk, and (2) / are not a unique risk factor (3) / for obesity or heart disease. (4)/ No error (5)

22. Airline managements should note (1) / that the ultimate passenger unfriendliness (2) / is to have their planes crash (3) / due to the adopted of unsafe procedures.(4) / No error (5)

23. Celebrating its ten long years (1) / in the industry, a private entertainment channel (2) / announce a series of (3) / programmes at a press conference. (4) / No error (5)

24. The award ceremony ended (1) / on a note of good cheer (2) / with audiences responding warmly (3) / to its line up of film. (4) / No error (5)

25. The actress was ordered for (1) / wear an alcohol monitoring bracelet and (2) / submit to random weekly drug testing after (3) / she failed to appear for a court date last week. (4) / No error (5)

Directions (Q. 26 to 30): In the following passage there are blanks, each of which has been numbered. These numbers are given below the passage and against each, five words are suggested, one of which fits the blank appropriately. Find out the appropriate word in each case.

The World Diabetes Congress has determined that India has the largest number of diabetics in the world. Apart from the loss of productivity, the __(26)__ burden is alarming – $ 2.8 billion annually. Sedentary jobs, __(27)__ of electronic entertainment, changing diet patterns and increasing dependence on automobiles have driven the activity __(28)__ of Indians' lives especially in cities.

The challenge is, therefore, to make people physically active and requires interventions which impact a large __(29)__ of the population. Admittedly physical activity is a matter of choice and is strongly driven by personal preferences. But policy making needs to shift to __(30)__ moderate levels of physical activity in the daily lives of people. One way to accomplish this is to create walk able communities that give residents a variety of destinations within walking distance.

26. (1) health   (2) economic

    (3) finance   (4) subsidy

    (5) physical

27. (1) widespread   (2) broadcast

    (3) spread   (4) prevalent

    (5) expand

28. (1) outside   (2) most

    (3) out   (4) from

    (5) through

29. (1) piece   (2) section

    (3) scale   (4) degree

    (5) per cent

30. (1) attract   (2) pursuit

    (3) indulge   (4) introduce

    (5) insist

NUMERICAL ABILITY

Directions (Q. 31 to 35): In the following number series only one number is wrong. Find out the wrong number.

31. 2, 10, 18, 54, 162, 486, 1458

    (1) 18   (2) 54

    (3) 162   (4) 10

    (5) None of these

32. 850, 600, 550, 500, 475, 462.5, 456.25

    (1) 600   (2) 550

    (3) 500   (4) 462.5

    (5) None of these

33. 9050, 5675, 3478, 2147, 1418, 1077, 950

    (1) 3478   (2) 1418

    (3) 5675   (4) 2147

    (5) 1077

34. 1, 4, 25, 256, 3125, 46656, 823543

    (1) 3125   (2) 823543

    (3) 46656   (4) 25

    (5) 256

35. 484, 240, 120, 57, 26.50, 11.25, 3.625

    (1) 240   (2) 120

    (3) 57   (4) 26.50

    (5) 11.25

36. If the simple interest on a sum of money at 10% per annum for 2 years is Rs. 1000, then find the compound interest on the same sum for the same period at the same rate.

    (1) Rs. 1,105   (2) Rs. 950

    (3) Rs. 1,280   (4) Rs. 1,150

    (5) Rs. 1,050

37. Out of 200 fish in an aquarium, 99% are red. How many red fish must be removed in order to reduce the percentage of red fish to 98%?

    (1) 10   (2) 50

    (3) 2   (4) 100

    (5) 98

38. Kanika goes to school at 20 km/hr and reaches the school 4 min late than the scheduled time. Next time she goes at 25 km/hr and reaches the school 2 min earlier than scheduled time. What is the distance of her school from her house?

    (1) 10 km   (2) 12 km

    (3) 14 km   (4) 17 km

    (5) 15 km

39. If selling price of three diamonds of MG Diamond Works is equal to cost price of four diamonds, what is the profit or loss percentage?

    (1) 50% profit   (2) 40% loss

    (3) 33.33% profit   (4) 30% loss

    (5) 25% profit

40. A cask full of soda-water solution contains 70% soda. Some part of this solution is taken out from the cask and is replaced with another solution containing 35% soda. Now the percentage of soda in new solution was found to be 45%. The proportion of solution replaced is

    (1) $\dfrac{2}{5}$ (2) $\dfrac{3}{5}$

    (3) $\dfrac{2}{7}$ (4) $\dfrac{5}{7}$

    (5) None of these

Directions (Q. 41 to 45): What approximate values will come in place of the question mark (?) in the following questions? (You are not expected to calculate the exact value)

41. $[(7.99)^2 - (13.001)^2 - (-4.01)^3]^2 = ?$

    (1) 1800   (2) 1450

    (3) −1660   (4) 1660

    (5) −1450

42. $(21.5\% \text{ of } 999)^{1/3} + (42\% \text{ of } 601)^{1/2} = ?$

    (1) 18   (2) 22

    (3) 26   (4) 30

    (5) 33

43. $331.8 \div 23.7 + (-21)^2 - 94 = (?)^2$

    (1) 15   (2) 16

    (3) 18   (4) 19

    (5) 17

44. 34% of 576 + 18% of 842 = ?% of 400 + 83.4

    (1) 75   (2) 72

    (3) 62   (4) 65

    (5) 66

45. 24.99% of 5001 − 65.01% of 2999 = ?

    (1) 840   (2) 500

    (3) 700   (4) −500

    (5) −700

46. The average age of A and B is 20 years, of B and C is 19 years and that of A and C is 21 years. What are the respective ages of A, B and C?

    (1) 18 years, 20 years, 22 years

    (2) 18 years, 22 years, 20 years

    (3) 22 years, 20 years, 18 years

    (4) 22 years, 18 years, 20 years

    (5) None of these

47. Mr. Vimlesh gains 15% by selling his car for Rs. 20, 700. How much would he lose or gain if he sells it for Rs. 19, 800?

    (1) 10% Profit   (2) 10% Loss

    (3) 9% Profit   (4) 9% Loss

    (5) No profit, no loss

48. The ratio of the incomes of 'P' to 'Q' is 6 : 7 and that of their expenditure is 7 : 8. If their savings are in the ratio of 2 : 3 respectively, then what is the ratio of the savings of 'P' to that of his income?

    (1) 1 : 10   (2) 1 : 15

    (3) 15 : 1   (4) 10 : 1

    (5) None of these

49. When digits of a two-digit even number is reversed, the resulting two-digit number is 54 less than the original number. What is the sum of the digits of this number?

    (1) 10   (2) 11

    (3) 12   (4) 14

    (5) 16

50. A train 100 m long moving at a speed of 50 km/hr crosses a train 120 m long coming from opposite direction in 6 seconds. The speed of the second train is
   (1) 60 km/hr   (2) 82 km/hr
   (3) 70 km/hr   (4) 74 km/hr
   (5) None of these

Directions (Q. 51 to 55) : What approximate value will come in place of the question mark (?) in the following questions? (You are not required to find the exact value).

51. $3\dfrac{1}{4} + 6\dfrac{2}{7} + ? = 13\dfrac{3}{28}$
   (1) $3\dfrac{2}{7}$ (2) $3\dfrac{4}{7}$
   (3) $3\dfrac{3}{7}$ (4) $3\dfrac{5}{7}$
   (5) $3\dfrac{6}{7}$

52. 134% of 3894 + 20% of 134 = ?
   (1) 11452   (2) 10000
   (3) 10452   (4) 1100
   (5) None of these

53. $10^3 \times 100^3 + 999999999 = 10^9 + 10^?$
   (1) 6   (2) 9
   (3) 7   (4) 10
   (5) 12

54. 4568.6531 – 2431.3178 + 134.675 = ?
   (1) 2272   (2) 2372
   (3) 2172   (4) 2200
   (5) None of these

55. $(6.99)^2 + (8.01)^2 - \sqrt{85}$ = ?
   (1) 95   (2) 115
   (3) 110   (4) 104
   (5) None of these

56. 10 men can complete a piece of work in 10 days, whereas it takes 12 women to complete the work in 10 days. If 15 men and 6 women undertake to complete the work, then how many days will they take to complete it?
   (1) 2 days   (2) 4 days
   (3) 5 days   (4) 11 days
   (5) 6 days

57. The salaries of A, B and C are in the ratio 1 : 2 : 5 respectively. If the increments of 20%, 15% and 10% respectively are allowed in their salaries, then what will be the new respective ratio of their salaries?
   (1) 12 : 23 : 55   (2) 11 : 23 : 55
   (3) 23 : 11 : 55   (4) 12 : 55 : 23
   (5) None of these

58. Five years ago, the average age of a family of 6 members is 27 years. What would be the average age of the family at present?
   (1) 40 years   (2) 31 years
   (3) 30 years   (4) 32 years
   (5) None of these

59. There is a flower bed in the shape of a trapezium. Its parallel sides are 60 m and 80 m respectively. If the distance between them is 20 m, then find the area of the flower bed.
   (1) 1296 m^2 (2) 1400 m^2
   (3) 1325 m^2 (4) 1700 m^2
   (5) 1425 m^2

60. Triangles ABC and DEF are similar. If their areas are 64 cm^2 and 49 cm^2 and if AB is 7 cm, find the value of DE.
   (1) 50 cm   (2) $\dfrac{49}{8}$ cm
   (3) $\dfrac{50}{4}$ cm   (4) $\dfrac{25}{3}$ cm
   (5) $\dfrac{49}{4}$ cm

Directions (Q. 61 to 65): Answer the questions on the basis of the information given below.

Table given below shows the percentage of Marks obtained by different students in different subjects of MBA.

SUBJECTS (Maximum Marks)						
Students	Strategic Management (150)	Brand Management (100)	Compensation Management (150)	Consumer Behaviour (125)	Service Marketing (75)	Training & Development (50)
Anushka	66	75	88	56	56	90
Archit	82	76	84	96	92	88
Arpan	76	66	78	88	72	70
Garvita	90	88	96	76	84	86
Gunit	64	70	68	72	68	74
Pranita	48	56	50	64	64	58

61. How many marks did Anushka get in all the subjects together?
    (1) 369   (2) 463
    (3) 558   (4) 496
    (5) None of these

62. The marks obtained by Garvita in Brand Management is what percent of the marks obtained by Archit in the same subject? (rounded off to two digits after decimal)
    (1) 86.36   (2) 101.71
    (3) 111.79   (4) 133.33
    (5) None of these

63. What is the average marks obtained by all students together in Compensation Management?
    (1) 116   (2) 120
    (3) 123   (4) 131
    (5) None of these

64. Who has scored the highest total marks in all the subjects together?
    (1) Archit   (2) Gunit
    (3) Pranita   (4) Garvita
    (5) Arpan

65. How many students have scored the highest marks in more than one subject?
    (1) three   (2) two
    (3) one   (4) none
    (5) None of these

REASONING ABILITY

Directions (Q. 66 to 70) : Study the following information carefully and answer the given question.

One of the seven subjects, viz., Fluid dynamics, Thermodynamics, Computer networks, Instrumentation, Biotechnology, Nanotechnology and Power electronics, is taught on one day in a week starting from Monday and ending on Sunday. Instrumentation is taught on Thursday. Nanotechnology is taught the day immediately next to the day when Thermodynamics is taught. Nanotechnology is taught neither on Tuesday nor on Saturday. Only one lecture is held between Instrumentation and Computer networks. Two lectures are scheduled between Fluid dynamics and Thermodynamics. Power electronics is taught neither on Monday nor on Sunday.

66. On which of the following days is Biotechnology taught?
    (1) Monday   (2) Tuesday
    (3) Wednesday   (4) Thursday
    (5) Friday

67. How many subjects are taught between Computer networks and Thermodynamics?
    (1) None   (2) One
    (3) Two   (4) Three
    (5) Four

68. Which of the following subjects is taught on Saturday?
    (1) Computer networks   (2) Power electronics
    (3) Thermodynamics   (4) Fluid dynamics
    (5) Biotechnology

69. On which of the following days is Power electronics taught?
    (1) Tuesday   (2) Wednesday
    (3) Thursday   (4) Friday
    (5) Cannot be determined

70. If Power electronics is related to Thermodynamics and Biotechnology is related to Computer networks in a certain way, then which of the following would Instrumentation be related to, following the same pattern?
    (1) Fluid dynamics   (2) Power electronics
    (3) Biotechnology   (4) Nanotechnology
    (5) Cannot be determined

Directions (Q. 71-75): Answer the questions on the basis of the information given below.

P, Q, R, S, T, U, V & W live on different floors in the same building having eight floors numbered one to eight (the ground floor is numbered 1, the floor above it, number 2 ..., the top most floor is numbered 8).

There are only two floors between the floors on which P and R live. R lives on an odd numbered floor.

There are four floors between the floors on which P and W live. T lives on a floor immediately above the floor on which U lives. There are only two floors between the floors on which V and S live. V lives on a floor above the floor of S. Q does not live on a floor immediately above or immediately below the floor on which R lives.

71. On which of the following floors does Q live?
    (1) Fifth   (2) Third
    (3) Second   (4) Fourth
    (5) Sixth

72. Who amongst the following live on the floors exactly between S and R?
    (1) V, W and Q   (2) V, U and W
    (3) U, V and Q   (4) T, U and Q
    (5) U, Q and W

73. Who amongst the following live on the odd numbered floors excluding R?
    (1) U, W and S   (2) Q, V and U
    (3) U, T and S   (4) T, W and S
    (5) None of these

74. Who amongst the following lives on the topmost floor?
    (1) T   (2) P
    (3) V   (4) Q
    (5) W

75. On which of the following floors does R live?
    (1) Fifth   (2) First
    (3) Seventh   (4) Third
    (5) Either third or fifth

76. How many such pairs of letters are there in the word 'ENTHUSIASTIC' each of which has as many letters between them in the word as there are between them in the English alphabet?
    (1) Two   (2) Three
    (3) Four   (4) More than four
    (5) None of these

77. If it is possible to make only one meaningful English word with the second, the fourth, the fifth and the seventh letters of the word COURTESY, using each letter only once in the word, which of the following will be the third letter of that word? If more than one such word can be formed, give M as the answer. If no such word can be formed give N as the answer.
    (1) R   (2) O
    (3) S   (4) N
    (5) M

78. Sandeep walks 40 m West from point A, and then takes a left turn and walks 50 m. He then takes a right turn and walks 40 m, and then walks 50 m towards North. He finally takes a left turn and walks another 20 m to reach point B. In which direction and how far is he from point A?
    (1) North, 80 m   (2) West, 100 m
    (3) East, 100 m   (4) South, 80 m
    (5) West, 60 m

79. How much time after 8:00 p.m., will the hour hand and the minute hand of a clock make an angle of 153 degrees for the first time?
    (1) 5 minutes 45 seconds
    (2) 6 minutes 30 seconds
    (3) 5 minutes
    (4) 5 minutes 30 seconds
    (5) 6 minutes

80. EDBA, KJHG, QPNM, __
    (1) KIGH   (2) QOMK
    (3) WVTS   (4) ZXVU
    (5) VUSR

Directions (Q. 81-85): Answer the questions on the basis of the information given below.

Six delegates – P, Q, R, S, T and U – from different countries – are sitting at a circular table facing the centre. All of them are sitting diagonally opposite to some other members. It is also known that:

(i) T is sitting to the immediate left of Indian delegate S.

(ii) Delegate from UK is sitting between delegates from USA and China.

(iii) Delegate from USA and R from France are sitting at diametrically opposite positions.

(iv) Indian delegate is not sitting opposite to delegate from UK.

(v) Q who is not immediate neighbor of R, is not from USA.

(vi) The sixth country is Russia.

81. Person from which of the following countries is sitting opposite to delegate from India?
    (1) China   (2) UK
    (3) Russia   (4) Either (1) or (2)
    (5) Cannot be determined

82. Delegates from which of the following countries are sitting adjacent to R?
    (1) USA and China   (2) UK and Russia
    (3) Russia and China   (4) India and Russia
    (5) None of these

83. Which of the following persons is from UK?
    (1) P   (2) Q
    (3) T   (4) U
    (5) Cannot be determined

84. If delegate from USA is not sitting immediate right to delegate from India, then which of the following persons is from Russia?
    (1) Q   (2) P
    (3) U   (4) Either (1) or (2)
    (5) Either (2) or (3)

85. If U is from China, then which of the following persons can be the immediate neighbors of S?
    (1) P and Q   (2) T and R
    (3) Q and R   (4) T and P
    (5) None of these

Directions (Q. 86 and 87): Read the following information carefully and answer the questions given below.

i.   'A + B' means 'A is the father of B'.

ii. 'A – B' means 'A is the wife of B'.

iii. 'A × B' means 'A is the brother of B'.

iv. 'A ÷ B' means 'A is the daughter of B'.

86. If 'P ÷ R + S + Q', then which of the following statements is true?

    (1) P is the daughter of Q.

    (2) Q is the aunt of P.

    (3) P is aunt of Q.

    (4) P is the mother of Q.

    (5) R is the aunt of Q.

87. If 'P – R + Q', then which of the following statements is true?

    (1) P is the daughter of Q.

    (2) Q is the aunt of P.

    (3) P is the aunt of Q.

    (4) P is the father of Q.

    (5) P is the mother of Q.

88. Ram and Sita started walking from a point towards the north direction. After traveling a distance of 10 km, Sita turned towards left to travel 5 km while Ram to his right to move by 3 km . Sita again took one left turn and Ram a right turn to travel 15 km. How far is Sita from Ram now?

    (1) 15 km   (2) 10 km

    (3) 8 km   (4) 12 km

    (5) 6 km

89. If the digits of the number 26839514 are arranged in descending order, the position of how many digits will remain unchanged?

    (1) One   (2) Two

    (3) Three   (4) Four

    (5) None

90. In a certain code '786' means 'Bring Me Apple', '958' means 'Peel Green Apple' and '645' means 'Bring Green Fruit', which of the following is the code for 'Me'?

    (1) 8

    (2) 6

    (3) 7

    (4) Cannot be determined

    (5) 5

Directions (Q. 91 to 95): In the following question @, ©, %, $ and * are used the following meanings as illustrated below:

'P©Q' means 'P is smaller than Q.'

'P%Q' means 'P is equal to Q.'

'P*Q' means 'P is greater than Q.'

'P@Q' means 'P is either equal to or smaller than Q'.

'P$Q' means 'P is either equal to or greater than Q'.

Now in each of the following questions assuming the given statements to be true, find which of the two conclusions I and II given below them is/are definitely true?

Give answer (1): if only conclusion I is true.

Give answer (2): if only conclusion II is true.

Give answer (3): if either conclusion I or II is true.

Give answer (4): if neither conclusion I nor II is true.

Give answer (5): if both conclusions I and II are true.

91. **Statement:**

    J $ H, H © F, F * G

    Conclusions

    I.   F * J

    II. H © G

92. **Statement:**

    R % S, S @ T, T © U

    Conclusions

    I.   U * S

    II. T $ R

93. **Statement:**

    M @ N, N % L, L © K

    Conclusions

    I.   L $ M

    II. K * M

94. **Statement:**

    Z © Y, Y $ W, W * V

    Conclusions

    I.   Z @ W

    II. V © Y

95. **Statement:**

    A * B, B % C, C @ D

    Conclusions

    I.   B @ D

    II. A * D

Directions (Q. 96-100): In these questions a group of letters is given followed by four combinations of digits and symbols numbered (1), (2), (3) and (4).

Letters are to be coded by digits/symbols as per the scheme and the conditions given below. Serial number of the combination of digits/symbols that represents the group of letters is your answer. If none of the combinations is correct your answer is (5) i.e. 'None of these'.

Letter	E	K	S	N	C	L	P	O	D	I	U	R	T	A	G
Digit/ Symbol Code	9	@	3	#	4	5	2	%	7	&	8	$	!	6	1

(i) If first letter is a consonant and the last letter is a vowel their codes are to be interchanged.

(ii) If the first and last letter is a vowel, both are to be coded as 'δ'.

(iii) If first as well as last letter is a consonant and in between there are two or more vowels, then all the vowels are coded as '£'.

(iv) If first letter is vowel and last letter is a consonant, both are to be coded as the code for consonant.

96. SNOPAD
  (1) 7#£2£3   (2) 3#δ2δ7
  (3) 3#£2£7   (4) 3#%267
  (5) None of these

97. ITGERL
  (1) &!19$5   (2) 5!19$5
  (3) 5!15$5   (4) &!19$&
  (5) None of these

98. NCKATU
  (1) 84@61#   (2) 84@6$#
  (3) #6@4!8   (4) 84@6!#
  (5) None of these

99. ALSRDO
  (1) δ53$7δ   (2) 653$7%
  (3) £53$7£   (4) δ53$&δ
  (5) None of these

100. PIGEUK
  (1) £&198£   (2) 2£1££@
  (3) 2£18@   (4) 2£19£@
  (5) None of these

ANSWERS

1. (4)	**2.** (2)	**3.** (3)	**4.** (5)	**5.** (3)	**6.** (1)	**7.** (3)	**8.** (4)	**9.** (5)	**10.** (3)
11. (2)	**12.** (3)	**13.** (3)	**14.** (2)	**15.** (4)	**16.** (2)	**17.** (5)	**18.** (3)	**19.** (1)	**20.** (4)
21. (1)	**22.** (4)	**23.** (3)	**24.** (3)	**25.** (1)	**26.** (2)	**27.** (3)	**28.** (3)	**29.** (2)	**30.** (4)
31. (4)	**32.** (1)	**33.** (5)	**34.** (4)	**35.** (2)	**36.** (5)	**37.** (4)	**38.** (1)	**39.** (3)	**40.** (4)
41. (4)	**42.** (2)	**43.** (4)	**44.** (5)	**45.** (5)	**46.** (4)	**47.** (1)	**48.** (2)	**49.** (1)	**50.** (2)
51. (2)	**52.** (5)	**53.** (2)	**54.** (1)	**55.** (4)	**56.** (3)	**57.** (1)	**58.** (4)	**59.** (2)	**60.** (2)
61. (2)	**62.** (5)	**63.** (1)	**64.** (4)	**65.** (2)	**66.** (1)	**67.** (4)	**68.** (3)	**69.** (4)	**70.** (2)
71. (3)	**72.** (1)	**73.** (4)	**74.** (2)	**75.** (1)	**76.** (1)	**77.** (5)	**78.** (2)	**79.** (5)	**80.** (3)
81. (1)	**82.** (3)	**83.** (2)	**84.** (5)	**85.** (4)	**86.** (3)	**87.** (5)	**88.** (3)	**89.** (5)	**90.** (3)
91. (4)	**92.** (5)	**93.** (5)	**94.** (2)	**95.** (1)	**96.** (3)	**97.** (2)	**98.** (4)	**99.** (1)	**100.** (2)

EXPLANATIONS

1. (4) The correct sequence is CFDBAE. C introduces the topic climatic changes and says that India should be concerned about it. F follows C by giving a reason so as to why India should be concerned. FDB is a mandatory pair. 'This impact' in D refers to the 'adverse impact' talked about in F and B concludes it by saying that if this impact takes place, human race will have to adapt to these impacts. A follows B as it says one of the ways by which humans can adapt to these changes. E concludes the passage by stating the importance of environment day.

6. (1) Past tense of 'lead' is 'led'.

7. (3) Past tense of 'give' is 'gave'.

8. (4) 'Out of this world' is an idiom which means wonderful and exciting.

9. (5) The sentence is correct in its given form.

10. (3) The correct phrase is 'from one to another'. So, the correct phrase will be 'switch from'.

11. (2) Refer to the first paragraph of the passage. It clearly says that the lion decided to have an assistant for himself because he was old and weak and could not hunt at all.

12. (3) The donkey was fooled by the lion's and the fox's sweet talks, even though he knew that the lion would kill him. So, the moral of the story is that we should not be befooled by an enemy's sweet talks.

13. (3) The lion appointed the fox as his assistant. The fox was tasked with bringing an animal to the lion, for him to eat. So, the fox made such a statement so that he could convince the donkey to come with him to the lion, so that he could eat him up.

14. (2) Refer to the last paragraph. The fox thought to himself that he had done all the work and therefore deserves the best part of the meal. So, he sent the lion to take a bath and in the lion's absence, ate the donkey's brain.

15. (4) As per the passage, when the lion did not see any brain in the donkey's head, the fox explained to him that donkeys do not have brains.

16. (2) 'Fit' here means deserving.

17. (5) 'Lose' here means miss.

18. (3) 'Pounced' here means attacked.

19. (1) Here the antonym of 'handle' will be mismanaged.

20. (4) 'Frail' means very weak. So its antonym is strong.

21. (1) 'Drinks' is plural. Therefore, 'does' should be replaced by 'do', which is used with plural nouns.

22. (4) 'Adopted' should be replaced by 'adoption' because a noun and not a verb is required here.

23. (3) 'Announce' should be replaced by 'announced' since the announcement was made in the past.

24. (3) An 'audience' is a single group of people that are attending a single event. Since the awards show is a single event, 'audience' will be used instead of 'audiences'.

25. (1) One can be ordered 'to' wear something and not ordered 'for' wear something.

26. (2) The blank will take 'economic' since the sentence ends with a figure that tells us how much is expended on diabetes or diabetics annually.

27. (3) The sentence gives the reasons for the reduction in activity. One of the reasons is spread of electronic entertainment. So, the blank will take 'spread'. A 'media' is not 'broadcast', something can be 'broadcast' by means of a media.

28. (3) Only 'out' fits the blank to make it a grammatically correct sentence.

29. (2) The correct option to fill in the blank is 'section'. It means a distinct part of a territorial or political area, community, or group of people.

30. (4) A shift in policy will not 'attract' but 'introduce' physical activity in daily life.

31. (4) In the given series, each term is 3 times of the previous term. Hence, 10 is the wrong number.

32. (1) The series is $-200, -100, -50, -25, -12.5,$ $-6.25, ...$

33. (5) The pattern of number series is as follows:

$9050 - 15^3 = 9050 - 3375 = 5675$

$5675 - 13^3 = 5675 - 2197 = 3478$

$3478 - 11^3 = 3478 - 1331 = 2147$

$2147 - 9^3 = 2147 - 729 = 1418$

$1418 - 7^3 = 1418 - 343 = \textbf{1075 (1077)}$

34. (4) The pattern of number series is as follows:

$1^1 = 1; \ 2^2 = 4; \ 3^3 = \textbf{27 (25)};$

$4^4 = 256; \ 5^5 = 3125; \ 6^6 = 46656;$

$7^7 = 823543$

35. (2) The given series is

$$\times \frac{1}{2} - 2, \times \frac{1}{2} - 2, \times \frac{1}{2} - 2, \times \frac{1}{2} - 2, \times \frac{1}{2} - 2, \times \frac{1}{2} - 2, \times \frac{1}{2} - 2.$$

Correct number is 118.

Hence, wrong number is 120.

36. (5) Rate = 10% p.a., time = 2 years, S.I. = Rs. 1,000

$$\text{Principal} = \frac{100 \times 1000}{10 \times 2} = \text{Rs. 5,000.}$$

$$\text{Amount} = 5000 \times \left(1 + \frac{10}{100}\right)^2 = 5000 \times \frac{11}{10} \times \frac{11}{10}$$

$$= \text{Rs. 6,050.}$$

$$\text{C.I.} = 6050 - 5000$$

$$= \text{Rs. 1,050.}$$

37. (4) Let the number of red fishes to be removed be n.

Hence, $\dfrac{198 - n}{200 - n} = \dfrac{98}{100} \Rightarrow n = 100.$

38. (1) Let the distance of school from house and time taken at 20 km/hr be D and T respectively,.
As speed increases from 20 km/hr to 25 km/hr i.e. speed becomes $\dfrac{5}{4}$ times, hence time taken will become $\dfrac{4}{5}$ of the time taken at 20 km/hr.

So, $T - \dfrac{4}{5}T = 6$ min $\Rightarrow$ T = 30 min

Hence, D = $20 \times \dfrac{1}{2}$ = 10 km

39. (3) Let the C.P. of 1 diamond be Rs. 1.
C.P. of 3 diamonds = Rs. 3.
S.P. of 3 diamonds = C.P. of 4 diamonds = Rs. 4

$\therefore$ Profit% $= \left(\dfrac{4 - 3}{3}\right) \times 100$ = 33. 33%.

40. (4) By the rule of allegation, we have:

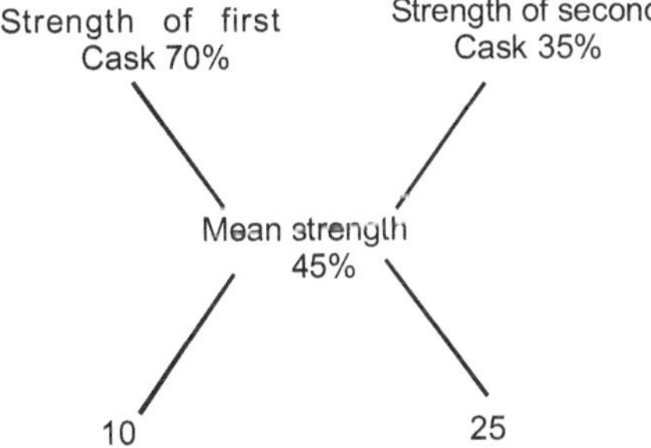

Hence, the required ratio is 2 : 5, which means in a solution with 7 parts, there should be 5 parts from the second solution. So, 5 parts out of 7 will be replaced by the second solution from the first.

Hence, the proportion of solution replaced is $\dfrac{5}{7}$.

41. (4) $? \approx [8^2 - 13^2 + 4^3]^2$

$\Rightarrow ? \approx [64 - 169 + 64]^2$

$\Rightarrow ? \approx (41)^2 \approx 1681$

$\therefore$ Required answer = 1660.

42. (2) $? \approx \left(\dfrac{1000 \times 21.5}{100}\right)^{\frac{1}{3}} + \left(\dfrac{600 \times 43}{100}\right)^{\frac{1}{2}}$

$\Rightarrow ? \approx (215)^{\frac{1}{3}} + (258)^{\frac{1}{2}} \approx 6 + 16 \approx 22.$

43. (4) $(?)^2 = 331.8 \div 23.7 + (-21)^2 - 94$

$\Rightarrow (?)^2 = 14 + 441 - 94 = 361$

$\Rightarrow ? = \sqrt{361} = 19$

44. (5) $\dfrac{576 \times 34}{100} + \dfrac{842 \times 18}{100} = \dfrac{400 \times ?}{100} + 83.4$

$\Rightarrow$ 195.84 + 151.56 = 4 × ? + 83.4

$\Rightarrow$ 347.4 = 4 × ? + 83.4

$\Rightarrow$ 4 ×? = 347.4 − 83.4 = 264

$\Rightarrow ? = \dfrac{264}{4} = 66$

45. (5) $? = \dfrac{5000 \times 25}{100} - \dfrac{3000 \times 65}{100}$

$\Rightarrow$? = 1250 − 1950 = − 700

46. (4) $\dfrac{A + B}{2} = 20 \Rightarrow A + B = 2 \times 20 = 40$ ... (i)

$\dfrac{C + B}{2} = 19 \Rightarrow C + B = 2 \times 19 = 38$ ... (ii)

$\dfrac{A + C}{2} = 21 \Rightarrow A + C = 2 \times 21 = 42$ ... (iii)

After solving equations (i), (ii) and (iii) for A, B and C we get
A = 22, B = 18, C = 20.

$\therefore$ Respective ages of A, B and C are 22 years, 18 years and 20 years.

47. (1) Let the cost price of car be Rs. x.
Then the selling price = 1.15x

$\Rightarrow$ 1.15x = 20700

x = Rs. 18000

If the selling price is Rs. 19,800
then, the profit = 19800 − 18000 = Rs 1,800

Percentage profit = $\dfrac{1800}{18000} \times 100 = 10\%.$

48. (2) Let the incomes of 'P' and 'Q' be 6x and 7x respectively and their expenditure be 7y and 8y respectively.

Therefore, $\dfrac{6x - 7y}{7x - 8y} = \dfrac{2}{3}$

$\Rightarrow y = \dfrac{4x}{5}$

$\therefore$ Required ratio = $\dfrac{6x - 5.6x}{6x} = 1 : 15.$

49. (1) Let the number be (10x + y).

So the number when reversing the digits should be (10y + x).

Now, (10x + y) − (10y + x) = 54

$\Rightarrow 9(x - y) = 54$

Hence x − y = 6.

The only possible even number is 82.

Hence, sum of the digits of number is 10.

50. (2) Let the speed of second train be x km/hr

$$\frac{100+120}{(50+x)1000}=\frac{6}{60\times60}$$

$\Rightarrow 0.22 \times 600 = 50 + x$

$\Rightarrow x = 82$ km/hr.

51. (2) $\dfrac{13}{4}+\dfrac{44}{7}+\,?=13+\dfrac{3}{28}$

$\Rightarrow \dfrac{91+176}{28}+\,?=13+\dfrac{3}{28}$

$\Rightarrow \dfrac{267}{28}+\,?=13+\dfrac{3}{28}$

$\Rightarrow \dfrac{264}{28}+\,?=13$

$\Rightarrow \dfrac{66}{7}+\,?=13$

$\Rightarrow\,?=\dfrac{25}{7}=3\dfrac{4}{7}$

52. (5) $?=\dfrac{134\times3894}{100}+\dfrac{20}{100}\times134$

$\Rightarrow\,?=\dfrac{134}{100}(3894+20)$

$\Rightarrow\,?=\dfrac{134}{100}\times3914=5244.76\approx5245.$

53. (2) $10^3\times10^6+10^9=10^9+10^?$

$\Rightarrow 10^?=10^9$

$\Rightarrow\,?=9$

54. (1) $?=4568.6531+134.675-2431.3178$

$\Rightarrow\,?=2272.0103\approx2272$

55. (4) $?=7^2+8^2-\sqrt{81}$

$\Rightarrow\,?\approx49+64-9\approx104$

56. (3) $\because$ 1 man will complete the work in 100 days

$\therefore$ Work done by one man in one day $=\dfrac{1}{100}$

$\because$ 1 Woman will complete the work in 120 days

$\therefore$ Work done by one woman in one day $=\dfrac{1}{120}$

Work done by 15 men and 6 women in one day

$$=\dfrac{15}{100}+\dfrac{6}{120}=\dfrac{1}{5}$$

$\therefore$ Time taken by 15 men and 6 women to complete the work = 5 days.

57. (1) Let the salary of A, B and C be k, 2k and 5k respectively.

$\therefore$ A's new salary $=\dfrac{120}{100}$of k$=\dfrac{120}{100}\times$k$=\dfrac{6}{5}$k

B's new salary $=\dfrac{115}{100}$ of 2k$=\dfrac{115}{100}\times$2k$=\dfrac{23}{10}$k

C's new salary $=\dfrac{110}{100}$ of 5k$=\dfrac{110}{100}\times$5k$=\dfrac{11}{2}$k

$\therefore$ New ratio $=\dfrac{6}{5}$k$:\dfrac{23}{10}$k$:\dfrac{11}{2}$k $= 12 : 23 : 55.$

58. (4) Five years ago, average age of the family

$\qquad$ = 27 years

At present, the average age will be

$\qquad$ = 27 + 5

$\qquad$ = 32 years.

59. (2)

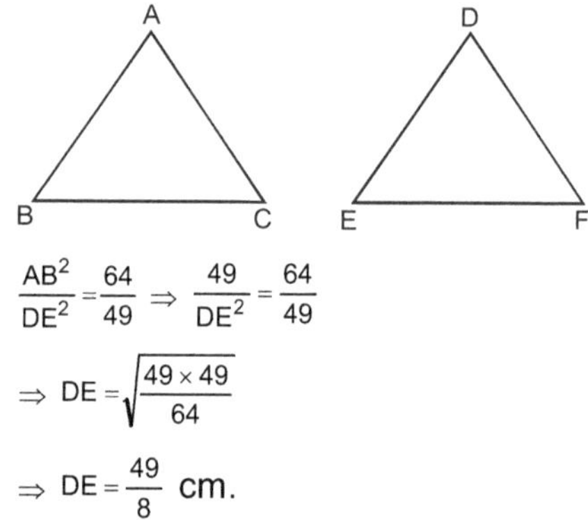

Area of a trapezium

$\qquad=\dfrac{1}{2}$ (Sum of the parallel sides) × Height.

Hence, area of the trapezium

$\qquad=\dfrac{1}{2}$ (60 + 80) × 20

$\qquad=\dfrac{1}{2}$ × 140 × 20 = 1400 m².

60. (2) $\dfrac{\text{Area of }\Delta\,ABC}{\text{Area of }\Delta\,DEF}=\dfrac{\text{Square of side}}{\text{Square of side}}=\dfrac{AB^2}{DE^2}$

(When two triangles ABC and DEF are similar)

$\dfrac{AB^2}{DE^2}=\dfrac{64}{49}\Rightarrow\dfrac{49}{DE^2}=\dfrac{64}{49}$

$\Rightarrow DE=\sqrt{\dfrac{49\times49}{64}}$

$\Rightarrow DE=\dfrac{49}{8}$ cm.

61. (2) Total marks of Anuska

$=\dfrac{150\times66}{100}+75+\dfrac{150\times88}{100}+\dfrac{56\times125}{100}+\dfrac{56\times75}{100}+45$

= 99 + 75 + 132 + 70 + 42 + 45

= 463

62. (5) Marks obtained by Garvita in Brand Management

$\qquad$ = 88% of 100 = 88

Marks obtained by Archit in Brand Management

$\qquad$ = 76% of 100 = 76

$\therefore$ Required percentage $=\dfrac{88}{76}\times100\approx115.79\%$

63. (1) Average marks obtained by all students together in Compensation Management

$$= \frac{\left(\begin{array}{c}\text{Total percentage of marks} \\ \text{obtained by all the students} \\ \text{in Compensation Management}\end{array}\right) \times \left(\begin{array}{c}\text{Maximum marks in} \\ \text{Compensation} \\ \text{Management}\end{array}\right)}{100 \times \text{Total number of students}}$$

$$= \left(\frac{88 + 84 + 78 + 96 + 68 + 50}{6 \times 100}\right) \times 150$$

$$= \frac{464}{600} \times 150 = 116$$

64. (4) Total marks scored in all the subjects together by

Arapan: 76% of 150 + 66% of 100 + 78% of 150 + 88% of 125 + 72% of 75 + 70% of 50

$$= \frac{76 \times 150}{100} + \frac{66 \times 100}{100} + \frac{78 \times 150}{100} + \frac{88 \times 125}{100} + \frac{72 \times 75}{100} + \frac{70 \times 50}{100}$$

= 114 + 66 + 117 + 110 + 54 + 35 = 496

Total marks scored in all the subjects together by

Archit: 82% of 150 + 76% of 100 + 84% of 150 + 96% of 125 + 92% of 75 + 88% of 50

$$= \frac{82 \times 150}{100} + \frac{76 \times 100}{100} + \frac{84 \times 150}{100} + \frac{96 \times 125}{100} + \frac{92 \times 75}{100} + \frac{88 \times 50}{100}$$

123 + 76 + 126 + 120 + 69 + 44 = 558

Total marks scored in all the subjects together by

Garvita: 64% of 150 + 88% of 100 + 96% of 150 + 76% of 125 + 84% of 75 + 86% of 50

$$= \frac{90 \times 150}{100} + \frac{88 \times 100}{100} + \frac{96 \times 150}{100} + \frac{76 \times 125}{100} + \frac{84 \times 75}{100} + \frac{86 \times 50}{100}$$

135 + 88 + 144 + 95 + 63 + 43 = 568

Total marks scored in all the subjects together by

Gunit: 64% of 150 + 70% of 100 + 68% of 150 + 72% of 125 + 68% of 75 + 74% of 50

$$= \frac{64 \times 150}{100} + \frac{75 \times 100}{100} + \frac{68 \times 150}{100} + \frac{72 \times 125}{100} + \frac{68 \times 75}{100} + \frac{74 \times 50}{100}$$

= 96 + 70 + 102 + 90 + 51 + 37 = 446

Total marks scored in all the subjects together by

Pranita: 48% of 150 + 56% of 100 + 50% of 150 + 64% of 125 + 64% of 75 + 58% of 50

$$= \frac{48 \times 150}{100} + \frac{56 \times 100}{100} + \frac{50 \times 150}{100} + \frac{64 \times 125}{100} + \frac{64 \times 75}{100} + \frac{58 \times 50}{100}$$

= 75 + 56 + 75 + 80 + 48 + 29 = 360

Clearly, Garvita scored the highest total marks in all the subjects together.

65. (2) Archit (consumer behaviour and service marketing) and Garvita (strategic management, brand management and compensation management).

For questions 66 to 70:

Day	Subject
Monday	Biotechnology
Tuesday	Computer networks
Wednesday	Fluid dynamics
Thursday	Instrumentation
Friday	Power electronics
Saturday	Thermodynamics
Sunday	Nanotechnology

For questions 71 to 75:

Floor Number	Person
8	P
7	T
6	U
5	R
4	V
3	W
2	Q
1	S

71. (3) Q lives on the floor number 2.

72. (1) V, W and Q live on floors exactly between the floors of S and R.

73. (4) T → Floor Number 7

W → Floor Number 3

S → Floor Number 1

74. (2) P lives on the topmost floor.

75. (1) R lives on the floor number 5.

76. (1)
```
  ┌──────────┐      ┌─────┐     ┌──┬──┐
  ↓          ↓      ↓     ↓     ↓  ↓
  E  N  T  H  U  S  I  A  S  T  I  C
```

77. (5) Second, fourth, fifth and seventh letter are O, R, T and S respectively. Words that can be formed with these letters are SORT and ROTS.

78. (2)

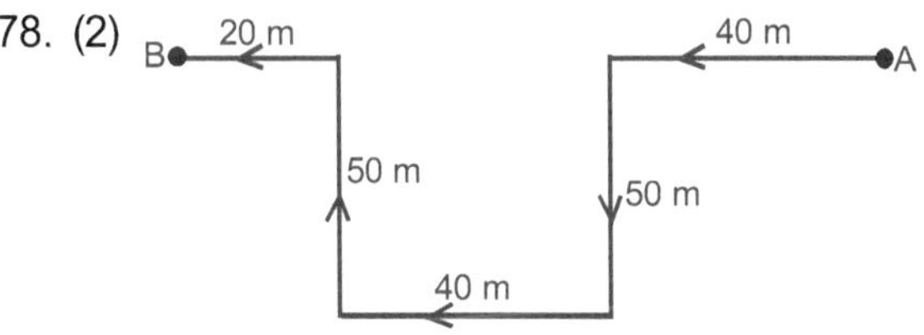

Sandeep is in West direction and 100 m away from point A.

79. (5) Angle between the two hands at 8:00 pm

= 120 degrees

Speed of the minute hand with respect to the hour hand

= 5.5 degrees/minute

Hence, the amount of time needed to increase the angle between the two hands by 33 degrees

$$= \frac{33}{5.5} = 6 \text{ minutes.}$$

80. (3) The terms are arranged in reverse alphabetical order without the 3, 6, 9, ... position number alphabets.

For questions 81 to 85: Given information can be shown as below:

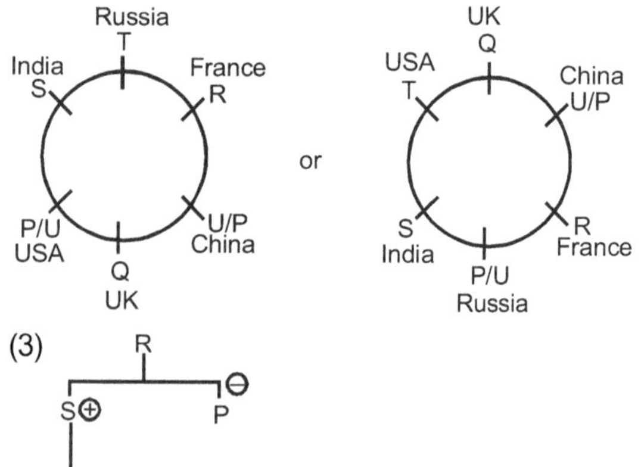

86. (3)

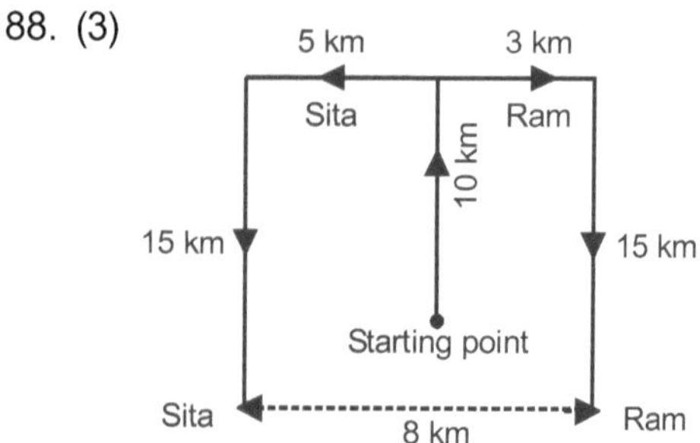

This clearly means P is the aunt (Father's sister) of Q.

87. (5)

$$P^{\ominus} = R^{\oplus}$$
Q

It is clear that P is the mother of Q.

88. (3)

Therefore the distance between Sita and Ram is 8 km.

89. (5) The given number: 2 6 8 3 9 5 1 4

In descending order: 9 8 6 5 4 3 2 1

90. (3) '8' means 'apple', '6' means 'bring', '7' means 'me'

For questions 91 to 95:

© ⇒ <   % ⇒ =   * ⇒ >
@ ⇒ ≤ $ ⇒ ≥

91. (4) J $ H ⇒ J ≥ H

H © F ⇒ H < F

F * G ⇒ F > G

Therefore, J ≥ H < F > G

Conclusions:

I.   F * J ⇒ F > J (Not True)

II. H © G ⇒ H < G (Not True)

92. (5) R % S ⇒ R = S

S @ T ⇒ S ≤ T

T © U ⇒ T < U

Therefore, R = S ≤ T < U

Conclusions:

I.   U * S ⇒ U > S (True)

II. T $ R ⇒ T ≥ R (True)

93. (5) M @ N ⇒ M ≤ N

N % L ⇒ N = L

L © K ⇒ L < K

Therefore, M ≤ N = L < K

Conclusions:

I.   L $ M ⇒ L ≥ M (True)

II. K * M ⇒ K > M (True)

94. (2) Z © Y ⇒ Z < Y

Y $ W ⇒ Y ≥ W

W * V ⇒ W > V

Therefore, Z < Y ≥ W > V

Conclusions:

I.   Z @ W ⇒ Z ≤ W (Not true)

II. V © Y ⇒ V < Y (True)

95. (1) A * B ⇒ A > B

B % C ⇒ B = C

C @ D ⇒ C ≤ D

Therefore, A > B = C ≤ D

Conclusions:

I.   B @ D ⇒ B ≤ D (True)

II. A * D ⇒ A > D (Not True)

96. (3) SNOPAD is coded as 3#£2£7.

97. (2) ITGERL is coded as 5!19$5.

98. (4) NCKATU is coded as 84@6!#.

99. (1) ALSRDO is coded as δ53$7δ.

100. (2) PIGEUK is coded as 2£1££@.

ENGLISH LANGUAGE

Directions (Q. 1 to 5): Fill in the blanks by choosing the most appropriate options.

1. This operation will start _____ immediate effect and carried ____ at no cost to the customer.

   (1) with, out   (2) on, in

   (3) about, till   (4) until, on

   (5) from, on

2. The head of the German Football Federation (DFB), has called _____ Thursday ____ an emergency meeting of Fifa's executive committee.

   (1) in, at   (2) on, for

   (3) by, to   (4) in, from

   (5) at, on

3. ONGC had filed a petition _______ Reliance India Limited _____ the Delhi high court last year.

   (1) from, on   (2) since, on

   (3) in, under   (4) from, at

   (5) against, in

4. Transfer pricing is a method wherein pricing is done _____ an arm's length basis _____ transactions taking place between two related entities.

   (1) on, till   (2) to, at

   (3) for, on   (4) on, for

   (5) in, until

5. It is argued that the sale of the call centre business was _______ two domestic companies and the transfer pricing officer had no jurisdiction _____ the transaction.

   (1) on, about   (2) between, over

   (3) among, in   (4) in, to

   (5) from, at

Directions (Q. 6 to 10): The sentences given in each question, when properly sequenced, form a coherent paragraph. Each sentence is labeled with a letter. Choose the most logical order of sentences from among the given choices to construct a coherent paragraph.

6. a. The Egyptians believed that life after death was the greatest accomplishment of all.

   b. So, the people of Egypt would spend most of their time preparing for the cross-over between life and death.

   c. In ancient Egypt, life after death was an enormous part of the Egyptian life.

   d. In preparation for the cross-over, people would spend hours of time and large amounts of money to ensure that they will have a good mummification process and funeral.

   (1) dabc   (2) cabd

   (3) acbd   (4) dbac

   (5) cbda

7. a. I am not suggesting that one of these ways of estimating is preferable to the other.

   b. There are two very different ways of estimating any human achievement.

   c. I am only concerned to point out that they give very different scales of importance.

   d. You may estimate it by what you consider its intrinsic excellence; or you may estimate it by its causal efficiency in transforming human life and human institutions.

   (1) cdab   (2) abcd

   (3) dcab   (4) bdac

   (5) dabc

8. a. Such also is the attitude of those who, in our own day, base their morality upon the struggle for survival, maintaining that the survivors are necessarily the fittest.

   b. Gradually, as morality grows bolder, the claim of the ideal world begins to be felt; and worship, if it is not to cease, must be given to gods of another kind than those created by the savage.

   c. Such is the attitude inculcated in God's answer to Job out of the whirlwind: the divine power and knowledge are paraded, but of the divine goodness there is no hint.

   d. Some, though they feel the demands of the ideal, will still consciously reject them, still urging that naked Power is worthy of worship.

   (1) bdac   (2) dacb

   (3) dbac   (4) cabd

   (5) bdca

9. a. It tells the story of the campaign to repeal the estate tax (what we would call inheritance tax) in the United States, which culminated in the inclusion of the measure in George Bush's massive tax-cutting legislation of 2001.

b. Politics of another country's tax system is unlikely to be of much interest to anyone with any sort of normal life.

c. Listening to the ins and outs of other people's fiscal battles can be like listening to other people's dreams: interminable and almost completely unreal.

d. *Death by a Thousand Cuts* is something different.

(1) badc   (2) bcda

(3) cbad   (4) cabd

(5) cbda

10. a. Lottery officials suspected a scam until they traced the sequence to a fortune printed with the digits "22-28-32-33-39-40" and Donald Lau's prediction: "All the preparation you've done will finally be paying off."

b. As a vice-president at Wonton Food, Inc., in Long Island City, Donald Lau manages the company's accounts payable and receivable, negotiates with insurers, and, somewhat incidentally, composes the fortunes that go inside the fortune cookies, of which Wonton is the world's largest manufacturer.

c. Each day, Wonton's factory churns out four million Golden Bowl-brand cookies, which are sold to several hundred vendors, who, in turn, sell them to most of the forty thousand Chinese restaurants across the country.

d. Wonton's primacy in the industry and, for that matter, in the gambler's imagination is such that when, in March, five of six lucky numbers printed on a fortune happened to coincide with the winning picks for the Powerball lottery, a hundred and ten people, instead of the usual handful, came forward to claim prizes of around a hundred thousand dollars.

(1) cbad   (2) cbda

(3) adcb   (4) dcab

(5) cadb

Directions (Q. 11 to 15): Read the following passage carefully and answer the questions given below it. Certain words have been printed in bold to help you locate them while answering some of the questions.

Once upon a time, there lived a herd of elephants at the bottom of the majestic Himalayas. Their leader was a rare white elephant who was an extremely kind-hearted soul. He greatly loved his mother who had grown blind and **feeble** and could not look out for herself. Each day this white elephant would go deep into the forest in search of food. He would look for the best of fruits to send to his mother through other elephants of the herd. But his mother never received any. This was because the other members of the herd would always eat them up themselves. Each night, when he returned home he would be surprised to hear that his mother had been starving all day. He was absolutely disgusted with his herd. Then one day, he decided to leave them all behind and **disappeared** in the middle of the night along with his dear mother. He took her to Mount Candorana to live in a cave besides a beautiful lake.

It so happened that one day, when the white elephant was feeding, he heard loud cries. A forester from Benaras had lost his way in the forest and was absolutely terrified. The white elephant told him not to worry as he knew every inch of this forest and could take him to safety. He then lifted him on to his back and carried him to the **edge** of the forest from where the forester went on his merry way back to Benaras.

On reaching the city, he heard that King's personal elephant had just died and the King was looking for a new elephant. His heralds were roaming the city, announcing that any man who had seen or heard of an elephant fit for a king should come forward with the information. The forester was very excited and immediately went up to the King and told him about the white elephant that he had seen on Mount Candorana. The King was quite pleased with the information and immediately dispatched a number of soldiers and elephant trainers along with the forester. After travelling for many days, the group reached the lake besides which the elephants resided. They slowly crept down to the edge of the lake and hid behind the bushes. The white elephant was collecting lotus shoots for his mother's meal and could sense the presence of humans. When he looked up, he **spotted** the forester and realized that it was he who had led the King's men to him. He was very upset at the ingratitude but decided not to put up a **struggle** as many of the men would be killed. And he was just too kind to hurt anyone. So he decided to go along with them to Benaras and then seek a solution to this problem.

On reaching the beautiful city of Benaras, the trainers laid out a feast for their new State elephant but he refused to touch a morsel. He did not respond to any kind of stimuli, be it the fragrant flowers or the beautiful and comfortable stable. He just sat there looking completely despondent. The King was extremely concerned. He offered the elephant food from the royal table and asked him why he grieved in this manner. The white elephant replied that he would not eat a thing until he met his mother back home on Mount Candorana as she must be hungry because she was blind and had no one to feed her and take care of her. He was afraid that she would die. The compassionate King was touched by the elephant's story and assured him that his soldiers would bring his old mother to the palace as soon as possible. The king kept his promise and his soldiers took good care of his mother as well for as long as she lived. She blessed the kind King with peace, prosperity and joy till the end of his days. In this way the white elephant could serve the king and also enjoy the royal perks at the king's palace along with his mother.

11. What did the white elephant do when he realised that his mother had been starving even though he had been sending food for her?

    (1) He punished his herd members and told them to leave the jungle

    (2) He went to Benaras to report the happenings of the herd to the King

    (3) With the help of the King's soldiers, he got the herd members killed

    (4) He and his mother left the herd behind

    (5) None of these

12. Why did the white elephant's mother never receive the fruits sent by her son?

    (1) The other members of the herd would eat up the fruits themselves instead of taking them to her

    (2) The King's soldiers blocked her food supply in order to make her weak and capture her to be taken to the King

    (3) Because the King would never let any food sent by the white elephant reach his mother

    (4) Because the ungrateful forester sold the fruits collected by the white elephant in Benaras

    (5) None of these

13. Why did the white elephant collect food for his mother daily?

    (1) The king did not provide food to the elephant's mother

    (2) All the elephants from the herd refused to collect food for the old mother elephant

    (3) The elephant's mother could not fend for herself

    (4) The white elephant's mother would not accept food from anyone but her son

    (5) None of these

14. Why was the white elephant upset to see the forester along with the King's soldiers?

    (1) He had invited only the forester and not the King's soldiers to the forest

    (2) The king's soldiers had arrested the forester for concealing the where abouts of the white elephant

    (3) He did not expect such ingratitude from the forester as he had helped him once

    (4) The forester, along with the soldiers had captured the white elephant's mother

    (5) None of these

15. Which of the following is TRUE in the context of the passage?

    (1) The forester could never go back to Benaras from the forest

    (2) The white elephant's herd members were co-operative and honest

    (3) The forester ultimately became a good friend of the white elephant

    (4) The white elephant's mother was finally left alone in the forest

    (5) None is true

Directions (Q. 16 to 18): Choose the word which is MOST SIMILAR in MEANING to the word printed in bold as used in the passage.

16. **DISAPPEARED**

    (1) Hid   (2) Departed

    (3) Escaped   (4) Disintegrated

    (5) Strayed

17. **SPOTTED**

    (1) Blemished   (2) Experienced

    (3) Appeared   (4) Projected

    (5) Saw

18. **STRUGGLE**

    (1) Hardship   (2) Adversity

    (3) Fight   (4) Striving

    (5) Argument

Directions (Q. 19 and 20): Choose the word which is MOST OPPOSITE in MEANING to the word printed in bold as used in the passage.

19. **FEEBLE**

    (1) Strong   (2) Intense

    (3) Unbreakable   (4) Preserved

    (5) Substantial

20. **EDGE**

    (1) Blunt   (2) Beginning

    (3) Indoors   (4) Interiors

    (5) Rim

Directions (Q. 21 to 25): In the following passage there are blanks, each of which has been numbered. These numbers are printed below the passage and against each, five words are suggested, one of which fits the blank appropriately. Find out the appropriate word in each case.

As you all know Emperor Akbar was very __(21)__ with Birbal's wisdom and greatly enjoyed his quick wit. One fine morning when Akbar was especially pleased with Birbal, as a gesture of appreciation, he promised to reward him with many valuable and beautiful gifts.

However, many days passed, and still there was no sign of even one gift. Birbal was quite __(22)__ with the king. Then one day, when Akbar was strolling down the banks of River Yamuna with his ever faithful Birbal at his side, he happened to notice a camel passing by. He asked Birbal why the neck of the camel was crooked. Birbal __(23)__ for a second and promptly replied that it might be because the camel may have forgotten to honour a promise. The holy books mention that those who break their word get punished with a crooked neck. Perhaps that was the reason for the camel's crooked neck.

Akbar soon __(24)__ his folly of making a promise to Birbal for gifts and not honouring it. He was ashamed of himself. As soon as they returned to the palace he immediately gave Birbal his much __(25)__ reward. In this way Birbal managed to get what he wanted without directly asking for it.

21. (1) impressed   (2) liked
    (3) interested   (4) jealous
    (5) enthusiastic

22. (1) jealous   (2) said
    (3) hated   (4) happy
    (5) disappointed

23. (1) thought   (2) scared
    (3) answered   (4) said
    (5) talked

24. (1) reminded   (2) mistook
    (3) realized   (4) apologized
    (5) understand

25. (1) accumulated   (2) expensive
    (3) extorted   (4) awaited
    (5) wanted

Directions (Q. 26 to 30): Read each sentence to find out whether there is any grammatical error or idiomatic error in it. The error, if any, will be in one part of the sentence. The letter of that part is the answer. If there is not error, the answer is (5). (Ignore errors of punctuation, if any.)

26. Some of our staff is worried (1) / that as soon as (2) / the project is over they (3) / will lose their jobs. (4) No error (5)

27. If you decide to hold (1) / the function in Kolkata (2) / not much of us (3) / will be able to attend. (4) No error (5)

28. In case you need five people (1) / to run a branch you (2) / should be selected (3) / ten since some may leave. (4) No error (5)

29. Although he approached (1) / many private businesses to invest (2) / in his printing business (3) / nobody of them was interested. (4) No error (5)

30. How can you give up (1) / this job when you are (2) / just about to be (3) / appointed for the position of General Manager ? (4) No error (5)

NUMERICAL ABILITY

Directions (Q. 31 to 35): In the following number series only one number is wrong. Find out the wrong number.

31. $8529 - (49)^2 - 125 - (9)^3 = ?$
    (1) 5994   (2) 5274
    (3) 7626   (4) 5922
    (5) None of these

32. $748 \times 362 = (520)^2 + ?$
    (1) 382   (2) 374
    (3) 365   (4) 376
    (5) None of these

33. $1720 - 258 + 428 \times 5.5 = ?$
    (1) 3431   (2) 3716
    (3) 3816   (4) 3388
    (5) None of these

34. $1895 - 225 \div 50 = ?$
    (1) 1890.5   (2) 1720
    (3) 33.4   (4) 2170
    (5) None of these

35. $6432 \div 16 \div ? = 6$
    (1) 69   (2) 57
    (3) 63   (4) 56
    (5) None of these

36. An amount of Rs. 7,000 was divided into two equal parts. The first part was deposited in a bank at the rate of 8% per annum simple interest for three years. The second part was deposited in another bank at the rate of 10% per annum compound interest, compounded annually for 2 years. What is the difference in the interests earned from the two amounts?
    (1) Rs. 105
    (2) Rs. 0
    (3) Rs. 150
    (4) Rs. 95
    (5) Rs. 115

37. In an examination it is required to get 55% of the aggregate marks to pass. A student gets 520 marks and is declared failed by 5% marks. What are the maximum aggregate marks a student can get?
    (1) 960   (2) 1250
    (3) 1040   (4) 1120
    (5) None of these

38. A boat takes 10 minutes to reach a place upstream. It comes back to the same place down the stream in 5 minutes. If the speed of the stream is 2 m/sec, what is the speed of the boat?

(1) 6 m/s   (2) 4 m/s

(3) 8 m/s   (4) 5 m/s

(5) 2.5 m/s

39. A shopkeeper sells 25 books such that after allowing a discount of 20% on the marked price, he manages to make a profit which is equal to the selling price of 5 books. Find the percentage profit that he made in the entire transaction.

(1) 20%   (2) 25%

(3) 30%   (4) 33.33%

(5) 10%

40. In a mixture of milk and water having volume 30 litres, the ratio of milk and water is 7 : 3. What quantity of water is to be added to the mixture to make the ratio of milk and water 1 : 2?

(1) 30 litres   (2) 32 litres

(3) 33 litres   (4) 35 litres

(5) None of these

Directions (Q. 41 to 45): What should come in place of question mark (?) in following number series.

41. 121, 117, 108, 92, 67, ?

(1) 31   (2) 29

(3) 41   (4) 37

(5) None of these

42. 748, 737, 715, 682, 638, ?

(1) 594   (2) 572

(3) 581   (4) 583

(5) None of these

43. 1, 121, 441, 961, 1681, ?

(1) 2701   (2) 2511

(3) 2601   (4) 2801

(5) None of these

44. 668, 656, 632, 584, 488, ?

(1) 294   (2) 296

(3) 300   (4) 396

(5) None of these

45. 2, 4, 12, 48, ?

(1) 240

(2) 192

(3) 144

(4) 288

(5) None of these

46. The average age of seven boys sitting in a row facing North is 26 years. If the average age of first four boys is 19 years and the average age of last four boys is 32 years. What is the age of boy who is sitting in the middle of the row?

(1) 28 years

(2) 29 years

(3) 24 years

(4) 31 years

(5) None of these

47. Manoj incurred a loss of 25% on selling an article for Rs. 6,300. If the cost price of the article is reduced by 20% and the selling price of the article is increased by 50% , then what is the approximate new loss or gain percentage?

(1) 40% loss

(2) 40% profit

(3) 35% profit

(4) 30% loss

(5) None of these

48. By mistake, instead of dividing Rs. 117 among A, B and C in the ratio of $\frac{1}{2} : \frac{1}{6} : \frac{1}{5}$, it was divided in the ratio of 2: 6: 5. Who gains the most and by how much?

(1) A, Rs 28   (2) B, Rs 31.50

(3) B, Rs 20   (4) C, Rs 25

(5) None of these

49. Gulshan, Shakti and Om start running around a circular stadium and complete one round in 14 sec, 8 sec and 15 sec respectively. In how much time will they meet again at the starting point?

(1) 23 min   (2) 14 min

(3) 13 min   (4) 21 min

(5) None of these

50. The distance travelled by a train is 1830 km. The magnitude of the speed of the train is 1 more than twice the time taken to travel the distance. What will be the respective ratio of the speed of the train and the time taken to travel?

(1) 30 : 61

(2) 61 : 30

(3) 25 : 51

(4) 51 : 25

(5) None of these

Directions (Q. 51 to 55): Read the following information and answer the questions given

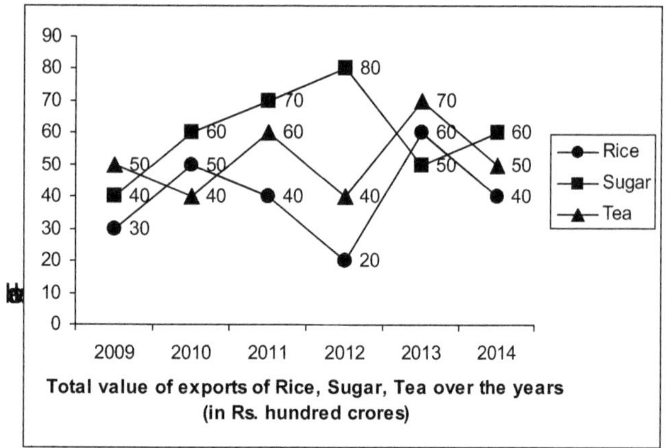

The line graph given above shows the exports of three commodities viz. Rice, Sugar and Tea over the years from 2009 to 2014.

51. In which year was the export value of Tea maximum among the given years?

(1) 2009
(2) 2011
(3) 2012
(4) 2013   (5) 2014

52. What was the difference in the export value of Rice and Tea in the year of 2012?

(1) Rs. 20 crore
(2) Rs. 2000 crore
(3) Rs. 200 lakh
(4) Rs. 200 crore
(5) None of these

53. What was the percentage decrease in export value of sugar from 2012 to 2013?

(1) 37.5%
(2) 63.5%
(3) $266\frac{2}{3}$ %
(4) 30%
(5) None of these

54. What was the percentage increase in the export value of Tea from 2012 to 2013?

(1) 175%
(2) 25%
(3) 125%
(4) 50%
(5) None of these

55. In which of the following year, the total export value of Tea, Rice and Sugar together the minimum among the given years?

(1) 2010
(2) 2012
(3) 2009
(4) 2014
(5) None of these

56. 10 men and 8 women together can complete a work in 5 days. Work done by one woman in a day is equal to half the work done by a man in one day. How many days will it take for 4 men and 6 women to complete that work?

(1) 12 days
(2) 10 days
(3) $8\frac{2}{3}$ days
(4) $9\frac{3}{4}$ days
(5) None of these

57. In a town, 80% of the population are adults, out of which the men and women are in the ratio of 9 : 7 respectively. If the number of adult women is 4.2 lakh. What is the total population of the village?

(1) 12 lakh
(2) 9.6 lakh
(3) 9.8 lakh
(4) 11.6 lakh
(5) None of these

58. At present Sheetal is three times Surabhi's age. Palash's present age is twice the age of Surabhi after 4 years. If the age of Surabhi three years ago was 9 years, how many imes will Sheetal's age be after 14 years with respect to the age of Palash seven years ago?

(1) 1
(2) 3
(3) 2
(4) 2.5
(5) None of these

59. The area of a square is thrice the area of a rectangle. If the area of the square is 324 cm^2 and the length of the rectangle is 12 cm more than the breadth, what is the difference between the breadth of the rectangle and the side of the square?

(1) 8 cm
(2) 10 cm
(3) 12 cm
(4) 6 cm
(5) None of these

60. What is the probability that a card drawn at random from a pack of 52 cards is either a King or a Spade?

(1) $\frac{17}{52}$
(2) $\frac{4}{13}$
(3) $\frac{3}{13}$
(4) $\frac{13}{52}$
(5) None of these

Directions (Q. 61 to 65): What should come in place of question mark (?) in the following questions?

61. 58.621 – 13.829 – 7.302 – 1.214 = ?

(1) 37.281
(2) 35.272
(3) 36.276
(4) 31.254
(5) None of these

62. ? % of 450 + 46% of 285 = 257.1

(1) 34
(2) 32
(3) 21
(4) 28
(5) None of these

63. $(81)^4 \div (9)^5 = ?$

(1) 6561   (2) 729

(3) 81   (4) 9

(5) None of these

64. $618 + 62 \times 0.50 - 29 = ?$

(1) 625   (2) 660

(3) 640   (4) 655

(5) None of these

65. $282 \times 82 \times 0.2 = ?$

(1) 4624.8   (2) 4734.6

(3) 4604.4   (4) 4324.2

(5) None of these

REASONING ABILITY

Directions (Q. 66 to 70): Answer the following questions on the basis of the information given below.

66. Which of the following expressions will not be true if the expression' $A = C \geq B > D$' is definitely true?

(1) $B > A$ (2) $D < C$

(3) $A \geq B$ (4) $D < A$

(5) All are true

67. In which of the following expressions will the expression '$L > M$' be definitely true?

(1) $M \geq N \geq P > L$

(2) $L > N \leq M > P$

(3) $M \leq N = P \geq L$

(4) $L > N \geq M < P$

(5) None of these

68. Which of the following expressions will be true if the expression '$Z < Y \geq W = V$ is definitely true?

(1) $V > Y$ (2) $Z < W$

(3) $V \geq Z$ (4) $W \leq Z$

(5) None is true

69. Which of the following expressions will be true if the expression '$B < A \leq M \geq W$' is definitely true?

(1) $M = A$ (2) $B < M$

(3) $B > M$ (4) $A = W$

(5) All are true

70. Which of the following expressions will be true if the expression '$K \leq O \leq R \geq T$' is definitely true?

(1) $K > R$

(2) $T < O$

(3) $K \leq R$

(4) $K = T$

(5) All are true

Directions (Q. 71 to 75): Answer the following questions based on the given information.

Five professors P, Q, R, S and T, residing in five different cities, teach five different subjects.

1. P does not live in either Bangalore or Lucknow and he teaches Philosophy.

2. Q lives neither in Hyderabad nor in Lucknow. He teaches Mathematics.

3. S lives in Jaipur and does not teach Economics.

4. T lives neither in Bangalore nor in Delhi. He teaches Geography.

5. R does not teach History and he lives in Delhi.

71. Who lives in Bangalore?

(1) P   (2) Q

(3) R   (4) S

(5) None of these

72. Which of the following subjects does R teach?

(1) Philosophy   (2) Mathematics

(3) History   (4) Economics

(5) None of these

73. In which of the following cities does T live?

(1) Bangalore   (2) Hyderabad

(3) Lucknow   (4) Delhi

(5) None of these

74. Which of the following subjects does S teach?

(1) Mathematics   (2) Philosophy

(3) Economics   (4) History

(5) None of these

75. Which of the following combinations is wrong?

(1) P-Hyderabad   (2) Q-Geography

(3) R-Delhi   (4) S-History

(5) All are true

76. How many such pairs of letters are there in the word TACKLE, each of which has as many letters between them in the word (in both forward and backward directions) as they have between them in the English alphabetical series?

(1) None   (2) One

(3) Two   (4) Three

(5) More than three

77. How many meaningful English words can be made with the letters 'OEHM' using each letter only once in each word?

(1) None   (2) One

(3) Two   (4) Three

(5) More than three

78. A boy walked 10 m towards South. He then turned to his right and walked 10 m. He again turned to his right and walked 10 m. Then he turned to his right and walked 15 m. Then he turned to his right and walked 10 m. Again he turned to his right and walked 5 m. How far was he from the starting point and in which direction ?

(1) $5\sqrt{5}$ m South-East

(2) 10 m West

(3) 5 m East

(4) 10 m South

(5) $10\sqrt{5}$ m North

79. Among J, K, L, M and N each having different height, M is shorter only than J. K is not as tall as N and N is shorter than L. Who among them is the shortest?

(1) J   (2) N

(3) K   (4) L

(5) Cannot be determined

80. The positions of first and the fourth letters of the word **WORTHY** are interchanged, similarly, the positions of second and fifth letters and third and sixth letters are interchanged. In the new arrangement thus formed, how many letters are there between the letter which is third from the right and the letter which is third from the left, in the English alphabetical order?

(1) None   (2) One

(3) Two   (4) Three

(5) More than three

Directions (Q. 81 to 85): Answer the questions on the basis of the information given below.

Akansha, Bhavya, Chavi, Dolly, Elena, Feroz, Gauri and Hema are sitting around a circle facing the centre. Chavi is fourth to the left of Feroz who is fifth to right of Elena. Dolly is third to the right of Akansha who is not immediate neigbhour of Elena or Feroz, Bhavya is third to left of Hema who is not immediate neighbour of Elena.

81. Four of the following five are alike in a certain way based on their positions in the above sitting arrangement and so form a group. Which is the one that does not belong to that group?

(1) Hema, Feroz, Elena

(2) Dolly, Chavi, Gauri

(3) Bhavya, Hema, Feroz

(4) Akansha, Elena, Feroz (5) Chavi, Gauri, Bhavya

82. Which of the following pairs are sitting between Akansha and Dolly?

(1) Feroz and Bhavya   (2) Gauri and Bhavya

(3) Feroz and Gauri   (4) Feroz and Elena

(5) Gauri and Elena

83. Who is third to the right of Elena?

(1) Bhavya   (2) Feroz

(3) Dolly   (4) Gauri

(5) None of these

84. What is Dolly's position with respect to Bhavya?

(A) Immediate right

(B) Fourth to the right

(C) Third to the left

(D) Immediate left

(1) Only A   (2) Only B

(3) Only B and C   (4) Only D

(5) Only either A or D

85. In which of the following pairs is the first person sitting to the immediate left of the second person?

(1) Chavi - Hema   (2) Gauri - Akansha

(3) Bhavya - Dolly   (4) Feroz - Gauri

(5) None of these

Directions (Q. 86 and 87): Answer the following questions on the basis of the information given below.

'A $\times$ B' means 'A is the son of B'.

'A + B' means 'A is the daughter of B'.

'A $\div$ B' means 'A is the brother of B'.

'A – B ' means 'A is the wife of B'.

86. How is C related to F if 'C + D – E $\times$ F' ?

(1) Daughter-in-law

(2) Father-in-law

(3) Granddaughter

(4) Grandson

(5) Mother

87. Which of the following means 'P is the father of K'?

(1) K × L ÷ P – R

(2) K ÷ L + R – P

(3) K + R – L × P

(4) R – P ÷ L + K

(5) None of these

88. A boy starts from home in early morning and walks straight for 8 km facing the sun. Then he takes a right turn and walks 3 km. Then he takes an about turn and walks 7 km and then turns right and walks 4 km. Then he takes a right turn walks 7 km. Then he takes a right turn and walks 8 km. How far is he from the starting point?

(1) 5 km   (2) 4 km

(3) 6 km   (4) 2 km

(5) None of these

89. Among A, B, C, D and E, each having a different height, C is taller than only A and B is taller than D and E. Who among them is the tallest?

   (1) C   (2) B

   (3) E   (4) Data inadequate

   (5) None of these

90. If HEEMA is coded as JHIRG, what will be the code for ELOQUENT?

   (1) GOSUALVC   (2) GOSVALVC

   (3) GOSVZLVC   (4) GOSVZLTC

   (5) GOSUZLVC

Directions (Q. 91 to 95) : Answer the following questions based on the given information.

There are six people sitting in each of the two parallel rows such that the distance between the any two neighbours is same. Ayush, Bhavna, Chirag, David, Eisha and Fiza are sitting in the first row and are facing the east direction. Punit, Manoj, Ridhima, Samar, Tanya and Vishu are sitting in the second row and are facing the west direction. Also, each member of the first row is sitting opposite to a member of the second row. Punit is sitting at one of the ends and to the immediate right of Tanya. Ayush is not facing either Punit or Tanya and is sitting third to the left of Fiza. There are two people sitting between Manoj and Vishu while only one person is sitting between Chirag and David. Bhavna is sitting next to Chirag. Samar which is not facing Chirag is not sitting next to Manoj while Chirag is not facing Tanya.

91. Among the following, who is facing Fiza?

   (1) Vishu   (2) Tanya

   (3) Samar   (4) Ridhima

   (5) Manoj

92. How many people are sitting between Eisha and Chirag?

   (1) One

   (2) Two

   (3) Three

   (4) Four

   (5) None of these

93. If Eisha is related to Punit and Bhavna is related to Samar according to a pattern, to whom Chirag is related?

   (1) Vishu   (2) Punit

   (3) Tanya   (4) Samar

   (5) None of these

94. In the following, which statement is true with relation to Bhavna?

   (1) Manoj is sitting to that person's left side which is facing to Bhavna.

   (2) Chirag is not nearest neighbour to Bhavna.

   (3) Eisha is sitting at second place to Bhavna's right.

   (4) Tanya is facing to Bhavna.

   (5) Bhavna is sitting at second place from one extreme end.

95. Who among the following are sitting at the ends of rows?

   (1) Punit, Vishu   (2) Fiza, Ayush

   (3) David, Eisha   (4) Punit, Samar

   (5) None of these

Directions (Q. 96 to 100): Answer the following questions based on the given information.

In a certain code 'colours of the sky' is written as 'ki la fa so', 'rainbow colours' is written as 'ro ki' and 'sky high rocket' is written as 'la pe jo' and 'the rocket world' is written as 'pe so ne'.

96. Which of the following is the code for 'colours sky high'?

   (1) ro jo la   (2) fa la jo

   (3) la ki so   (4) ki jo la

   (5) fa ki jo

97. Which of the following will/may represent 'the'?

   (1) Only 'fa'   (2) Either 'fa' or 'la'

   (3) Only 'so'   (4) Only 'la'

   (5) Either 'so' or 'fa'

98. What does 'pe' represent in the code?

   (1) colours   (2) sky

   (3) high   (4) rainbow

   (5) rocket

99. How can 'bird of the rainbow sky' be written in this code?

   (1) fa la tu ki jo   (2) fa so pe la ro

   (3) jo fa ro la tu   (4) so ro fa tu la

   (5) ki la fa tu ro

100. Which of the following is the code for 'high'?

   (1) Only 'la'

   (2) Only 'jo'

   (3) Either 'la' or 'jo'

   (4) Only 'ro'

   (5) None of these

ANSWERS

1. (1)	**2.** (2)	**3.** (5)	**4.** (4)	**5.** (2)	**6.** (2)	**7.** (4)	**8.** (5)	**9.** (2)	**10.** (2)
11. (4)	**12.** (1)	**13.** (3)	**14.** (3)	**15.** (5)	**16.** (3)	**17.** (5)	**18.** (3)	**19.** (1)	**20.** (4)
21. (1)	**22.** (5)	**23.** (1)	**24.** (3)	**25.** (4)	**26.** (1)	**27.** (3)	**28.** (3)	**29.** (4)	**30.** (5)
31. (2)	**32.** (4)	**33.** (3)	**34.** (1)	**35.** (5)	**36.** (1)	**37.** (3)	**38.** (1)	**39.** (2)	**40.** (3)
41. (1)	**42.** (4)	**43.** (3)	**44.** (2)	**45.** (1)	**46.** (5)	**47.** (2)	**48.** (2)	**49.** (2)	**50.** (2)
51. (4)	**52.** (2)	**53.** (1)	**54.** (5)	**55.** (3)	**56.** (2)	**57.** (1)	**58.** (3)	**59.** (3)	**60.** (2)
61. (3)	**62.** (4)	**63.** (2)	**64.** (5)	**65.** (1)	**66.** (1)	**67.** (4)	**68.** (5)	**69.** (2)	**70.** (3)
71. (2)	**72.** (4)	**73.** (3)	**74.** (4)	**75.** (2)	**76.** (3)	**77.** (2)	**78.** (4)	**79.** (3)	**80.** (2)
81. (4)	**82.** (3)	**83.** (5)	**84.** (4)	**85.** (1)	**86.** (3)	**87.** (2)	**88.** (1)	**89.** (2)	**90.** (2)
91. (1)	**92.** (2)	**93.** (5)	**94.** (5)	**95.** (1)	**96.** (4)	**97.** (3)	**98.** (5)	**99.** (4)	**100.** (2)

EXPLANATIONS

1. 1   'With' and 'out' are the correct adjectives.

2. 2   'On' and 'for' make sense in the context of the sentence.

3. 5   'Against' and 'in' are the most appropriate options.

4. 4   Only 'on' and 'for' make sense.

5. 2   'Between' and 'over' are the most appropriate options.

6. 2   Sentence c introduces the time and the topic the paragraph refers to. Sentence a goes on to explain why life after death was so important. Sentence a is the reason for sentence b which talks of what the Egyptians did for preparing themselves for the life after death. Sentence d carries forward the explanation about the preparation of cross-over. So, abd is a mandatory sequence.

7. 4   Out of the given options, sentence b is the obvious opener. bd is a mandatory pair, for d tells us what the 'two different ways' are. ac is again a mandatory pair for it gives the author's opinion on the use of these two ways.

8. 5   Out of the given options, sentence b is the best opener, for it refers to the topic of worship and the call of the ideal in a more general way than the others. Sentence d follows because it talks about an attitude that is contradictory to the one mentioned in sentence b. Sentence c definitely comes before sentence a because it starts with 'Such is', whereas sentence a starts with 'Such also is'.

9. 2   The best option for the first sentence is sentence b. It introduces the topic by talking about the disinterest regarding the politics of taxation of another country. Sentence c takes that further by elaborating upon why it is a cause of such disinterest and sentence d introduces a book that is 'different'. Sentence a is next and gives information about the content of the book. So, da is a mandatory pair.

10. 2   The author introduces the Wonton factory in sentence c and sentence b mentions its Vice President and his role. Sentence d talks about an interesting incident related to the company and sentence a provides the rationale behind it. So, da is a mandatory pair.

11. 4   Refer to the second last sentence of the first paragraph.

12. 1   Refer to the first paragraph for the answer. Refer to the sentence beginning with "This was because …."

13. 3   The elephant's mother was blind and feeble and so, could not search for food herself.

14. 3   Refer to the last three sentences of the third paragraph.

15. 5   None of the information is true in the context of the passage.

21. 1   'Impressed' is the appropriate word.

22. 5   'Disappointed' is the only word which rightly fits the blank.

23. 1   'Thought' is the correct word.

24. 3   Akbar 'realized' his folly.

25. 4   A reward is 'awaited.'

26. 1   Replace "is" with "are".

27. 3   Replace "much" with "many".

28. 3   Replace "should be selected" with "should select".

29. 4   Replace "nobody" with "none".

30. 5   The sentence is grammatically correct.

31. 2 $? = 8529 - (49)^2 - 125 - (9)^3$

$= 8529 - 2401 - 125 - 729$

$= 5274$

32. 4 $? = 748 \times 362 - (520)^2$

$= 270776 - 270400$

$= 376$

33. 3 $? = 1720 - 258 + 428 \times 5.5$

$= 1720 - 258 + 2354$

$= 3816$

34. 1 $? = 1895 - 225 \div 50$

$= 1895 - 4.5 = 1890.5$

35. 5 $\dfrac{6432}{16} \div ? = 6$

$402 \div ? = 6$

$? = 67$

36. 1   Interest earned on first part

$= 3500 \times 3 \times \dfrac{8}{100} = \text{Rs. } 840.00$

Interest earned on second part

$= 3500\left(1 + \dfrac{10}{100}\right)^2 - 3500$

$= 3500 \times \dfrac{11}{10} \times \dfrac{11}{10} - 3500 = 4235 - 3500 = \text{Rs. } 735$

Difference = Rs. $(840 - 735)$ = Rs.105

37. 3   55% marks is required to pass in the examination

According to the question, 50% of total marks = 520

Therefore, total marks = 1040.

38. 1   Let x be the speed of the boat.

	Upstream	Down stream
Speeds	$x - 2$	$x + 2$
Time (Mins)	10	5
Time (Ratio)	2	1
Speed (Ratio)	1	2

$\therefore \dfrac{x+2}{x-2} = \dfrac{2}{1}$

$\Rightarrow 2x - 4 = x + 2 \Rightarrow x = 6\,m/sec$

39. 2   Let the marked price of 25 books be Rs. 25.

Thus, the selling price of these books after 20% discount = 0.8 × 25 = Rs. 20.

Now, Rs. 20 also includes the profit which is equal to the selling price of 5 books that is Rs. 4.

Hence, the cost price of 25 books = 20 – 4 = Rs. 16.

So, profit percentage $= \dfrac{4}{16} \times 100 = 25\%$.

40. 3   Let the quantity of water to be added be x litres.

Milk in the mixture $= \dfrac{7}{10} \times 30 = 21$ litres

Water in the mixture = 9 litres

Now, $\dfrac{21}{9+x} = \dfrac{1}{2}$

$\Rightarrow 42 = 9 + x$

$\Rightarrow x = 33$ litres

41. 1   The series is as follows:

$121 - 2^2 = 117$

$117 - 3^2 = 108$

$108 - 4^2 = 92$

$92 - 5^2 = 67$

$67 - 6^2 = 31(?)$

42. 4   The series is as follows:

$748 - 11 = 737$

$737 - 22 = 715$

$715 - 33 = 682$

$682 - 44 = 638$

$638 - 55 = 583(?)$

43. 3   The series is as follows:

$(0 \times 10 + 1)^2 = 1$

$(1 \times 10 + 1)^2 = 121$

$(2 \times 10 + 1)^2 = 441$

$(3 \times 10 + 1)^2 = 961$

$(4 \times 10 + 1)^2 = 1681$

$(5 \times 10 + 1)^2 = 2601(?)$

44. 2   The series is as follows:

$668 - 12 = 656$

$656 - 24 = 632$

$632 - 48 = 584$

$584 - 96 = 488$

$488 - 192 = 296(?)$

45. 1   The series is as follows:

$2 \times 2 = 4$

$4 \times 3 = 12$

$12 \times 4 = 48$

$48 \times 5 = 240(?)$

46. 5 Let the average age of the boy sitting in the middle be x years.

Now, 26 × 7 = 19 × 4 + 32 × 4 − x

$\Rightarrow$ x = 22 years.

47. 2 Given , SP = Rs . 6,300 and loss = 25%

From this, we get CP = Rs. 8,400

New CP = $8400 \times \dfrac{4}{5}$ = Rs. 6,720

New SP = 6300 × $\dfrac{150}{100}$ = Rs. 9,450

Profit % = $\dfrac{9450 - 6720}{6720} \times 100$ ≈ 40%.

48. 2 Actual ratio of A, B and C = 15 : 5 : 6

Now, 15x + 5x + 6x = 117

$\Rightarrow 26x = 117$

$\Rightarrow x = 4.5$

Actual share of A, B and C is Rs. 67.5 , Rs. 22.5 and Rs. 27 respectively.

Let the amounts received by them be 2y, 6y and 5y respectively.

Now, 2y + 6y + 5y = 117

$\Rightarrow 13y = 117$ or $y = 9$

Share received by A = Rs. 18

Share received by B = Rs. 54

Share received by C = Rs. 45

B gains the most i.e. Rs. 31.5.

49. 2 They will meet at the starting point after 14 min (LCM of 14 sec , 8 sec and 15 sec)

50. 2 Let the time taken to travel be t hours

Given, 1830 = t (2t +1)

$\Rightarrow 2t^2 + t - 1830 = 0$

$\Rightarrow$ t = 30 hours

Speed = 2 × 30 + 1 = 61 km/hr

Required ratio = 61: 30.

51. 4 Export value of Tea is maximum in 2013.

52. 2 In year 2012,

Export value of Rice = Rs. 2000 crore and

Export value of Tea = Rs. 4000 crore

Difference = Rs. 2000 crore

53. 1 In 2012, export value of sugar = Rs. 8000 crore

In 2013, export value of sugar = Rs. 5000 crore

% decrease = $\dfrac{80 - 50}{80} \times 100 = \dfrac{30}{80} \times 100$

= $2\dfrac{300}{8} = 37.5\%$

54. 5 In 2012, export value of Tea = Rs. 4000 crore

In 2013, export value of Tea = Rs. 7000 crore

% increase = $\dfrac{70 - 40}{40} \times 100 = \dfrac{3}{4} \times 100 = 75\%$

55. 3 **Total export value of Tea, Rice and Sugar**

In 2009: 50 + 40 + 30 = Rs. 12000 crore

In 2010: 40 + 50 + 60 = Rs. 15000 crore

In 2011: 40 + 60 + 70 = Rs. 17000 crore

In 2012: 20 + 40 + 80 = Rs. 14000 crore

In 2013: 50 + 60 + 70 = Rs. 18000 crore

In 2014: 40 + 50 + 60 = Rs. 15000 crore

∴ The total is minimum for year 2009.

56. 2 Work done by one man = Work done by 2 women

$\Rightarrow$ 10 men and 8 women = 10 + 4 = 14 men

$\Rightarrow$ 4 men and 6 women = 7 men

Now, 14 men do a piece of work in 5 days

So, 7 men will complete the same piece of work in 10 days.

57. 1 Let the number of adult men, adult women and total population be 9x, 7x and p respectively.

Now, 7x = 4.2 lakh

$\Rightarrow$ x = 0.6 lakh

Total adult men and women = 16x = 9.6 lakh

Now, $\dfrac{80}{100} p = 9.6$

$\Rightarrow$ p = 12 lakh.

58. 3 Present age of Surabhi = 9 + 3 = 12 years

Present age of Sheetal = 36 years

Present age of Palash = 2(12 + 4) = 32 years

After 14 years, age of Sheetal = 36 + 14 = 50 Years

And age of Palash before 7 years = 25

∴ Age of Sheetal is 2 times the age of Palash 7 years ago.

59. 3 Area of square = 324 cm^2

Now, side = 18 cm

Area of the rectangle = $\dfrac{324}{3}$ = 108 cm^2

Let the breadth of the rectangle be b cms

∴ Length = (b+12) cms

b (b + 12) = 108

$\Rightarrow b^2 + 12b - 108 = 0$

$\Rightarrow (b + 18)(b - 6) = 0$

This gives breadth = 6 cm and length = 18 cm

Required difference = 18 − 6 = 12 cm

60. 2   Favorable cases = 4 + 12

Total number of cases = 52

Probability = $\dfrac{16}{52} = \dfrac{4}{13}$.

61. 3   ? = 58.621 – 13.829 – 7.302 – 1.214

= 58.621 – 22.345 = 36.276

62. 4   450 of ?% + 285 of 46% = 257.1

$\Rightarrow 450 \times \dfrac{?}{100} = 257.1 - 285 \times \dfrac{46}{100}$

$\Rightarrow ? = 126 \times \dfrac{100}{450}$

$\Rightarrow ? = 28$

63. 2   ? = $(81)^4 \div (9)^5$

= $(9)^8 \div (9)^5 = (9)^3$ or 729

64. 5   ? = 618 + 62 × 0.50 – 29

= 618 + 31 – 29 = 620

65. 1   ? = 282 × 82 × 0.2

= 4624.8

66. 1   B > A is false as A> B is true.

67. 4   In the expression, L > N ≥ M <P, L> M is definitely true.

68. 5   None of them is true.

69. 2   B < M is true.

70. 3   K ≤ R is true.

For questions 71 to 75:

Person	City	Subject
P	Hyderabad	Philosophy
Q	Bangalore	Mathematics
R	Delhi	Economics
S	Jaipur	History
T	Lucknow	Geography

76. 3

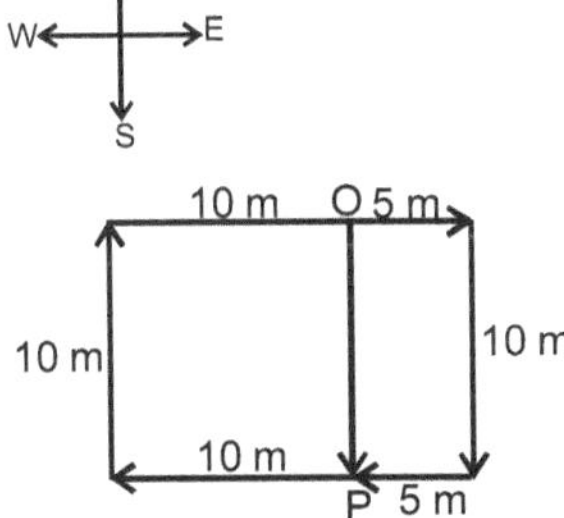

77. 2   The word that can be formed is HOME .

78. 4

He was 10 m in South from starting point.

79. 3   The order of heights is: J > M > L > N > K.

Hence, K is the shortest.

80. 2   The new word formed is: THYWOR

When arranged in alphabetical order, the word becomes : HORTWY

The letter third from the right is T and third from the left is R.

There is one letter 'S' in the English alphabet between R and T.

For questions 81 to 85:

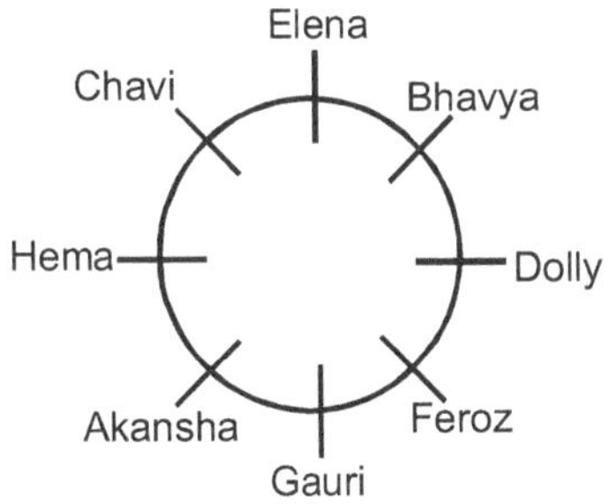

81. 4   Akansha- Elena- Feroz are sitting in the anticlockwise direction. Rest all are sitting in the clockwise direction.

86. 3   C + D – E × F → C is daughter of D, who is wife of E, who is son of F.

∴ C is granddaughter of F.

87. 2   K ÷ L + R - P → K is brother of L, who is daughter of R, who is wife of P.

This gives that P is the father of K.

88. 1

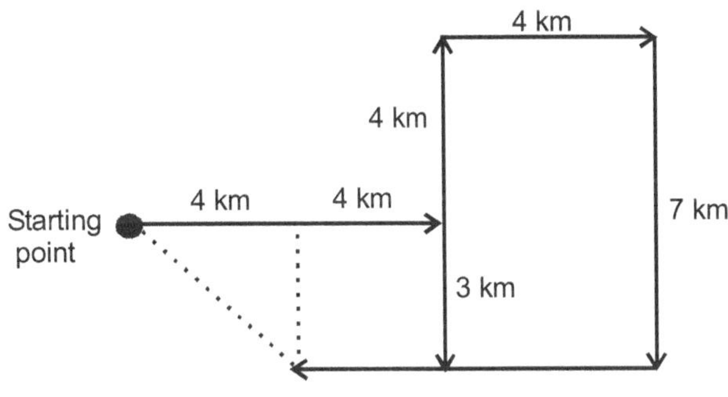

The required distance = $\sqrt{(3)^2 + (4)^2}$ = 5 km.

89. 2   C is taller than only A, so neither C nor A is the tallest. B is taller than D and E. So B is tallest among all of them.

90. 2 The position number of the respective alphabets is increased by 2, 3, 4, 5, and so on.

H(8) → J(10)	E(5) → G(7)
E(5) → H(8)	L(12) → O(15)
E(5) → I(9)	O(15) → S(19)
M(13) → R(18)	Q(17) → V(22)
A(1) → G(7)	U(21) → A(1)
	E(5) → L(12)
	N(14) → V(22)
	T(20) → C(3)

For solution 91 to 95:

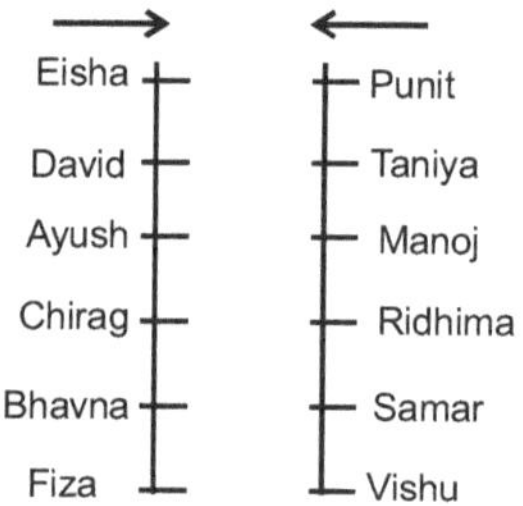

For solution 96 to 100:

word	colours	of	the	sky	rainbow	high	rocket	word
code	ki	fa	so	la	ro	jo	pe	ne

PRACTICE PAPER – 18

ENGLISH LANGUAGE

Directions for questions 1 to 5: Fill in the blanks given in the question using the most suitable options.

1. Akbar was renowned _______ his expertise _____ administration.
   - (1) for, in
   - (2) in, about
   - (3) regarding, to
   - (4) from, of
   - (5) before, on

2. He hindered me _____ going _____ the theatre.
   - (1) about, in
   - (2) for, inside
   - (3) in, towards
   - (4) of, at
   - (5) from, to

3. Contrary __ my instructions, he went ahead with the plan and would have certainly met ___ a fatal mishap but for the timely help rendered to him.
   - (1) against, to
   - (2) for, in
   - (3) about, on
   - (4) of, about
   - (5) to, with

4. When Ranjita .... me coming to her desk, she smiled and .... me a seat.
   - (1) saw, offered
   - (2) look, given
   - (3) heard, took
   - (4) got, gave
   - (5) looked, filled

5. We cannot........... with such a/an .... act of killing.
   - (1) control, clever
   - (2) happy, angry
   - (3) bear, shameful
   - (4) foresee, ordered
   - (5) feel, mindless

Directions for questions 6 to 10: Rearrange the following six sentences (A), (B), (C), (D), (E) and (F) in the proper sequence to form a meaningful paragraph, then answer the questions given below them.

A. "Certainly," said the wolf and began to howl.

B. "I know," said the sheep, "but please grant me my last wish."

C. Hearing him howl, the farmer's dogs rushed to the spot and drove him away.

D. A young wolf cornered a sheep in the farm.

E "My wish is for you to sing me a song so that I may dance one last time."

F. "You can't escape from me" said the proud wolf.

6. Which of the following should be the **SIXTH (LAST)** sentence after the rearrangement?
   - (1) E
   - (2) B
   - (3) D
   - (4) C
   - (5) F

7. Which of the following should be the **FIRST** sentence after the rearrangement?
   - (1) A
   - (2) D
   - (3) F
   - (4) C
   - (5) E

8. Which of the following should be the **FIFTH** sentence after the rearrangement?
   - (1) A
   - (2) D
   - (3) F
   - (4) B
   - , (5) E

9. Which of the following should be the **SECOND** sentence after the rearrangement?
   - (1) B
   - (2) C
   - (3) E
   - (4) D
   - (5) F

10. Which of the following should be the **FOURTH** sentence after the rearrangement?
   - (1) D
   - (2) F
   - (3) B
   - (4) E
   - (5) C

Directions for questions 11 to 20: The questions in this section are based on a single passage. The questions are to be answered on the basis of what is stated or implied in the passage. Kindly note that more than one of the choices may conceivably answer some of the questions. However, you are to choose the most appropriate answer, that is, the response that most accurately and completely answers the question.

Controlling the Internet censorship plays a role in everything that is portrayed on the Internet. However, due to its size and rapid growth, it has become almost impossible to control the Internet. In 1989, the World Wide Web was developed. This new technology enabled Internet users to exchange information on a global scale. With no restrictions on what information could be shared, the Internet has become home to an assortment of web sites consisting of topics that are shunned from the mainstream media. For example, literature that was banned from high schools and colleges for content that contained sexually explicit, anti-religious or immoral material has been made available through websites, such as "Banned Books On-Line". Over the last couple of decades, governments have struggled to regulate the content of the Internet. For example, in 1996 the Congress of the United States passed the "Communications Decency Act", which made it a crime to transmit indecent material over the Internet. Materials such as child-pornography were deemed offensive and thus distributors must be prosecuted.

To help catch Internet content violators, organizations such as the "Internet Police" were created. The "Internet Police", help to regulate the Internet by reporting illegal websites, pressuring governments to apply relevant legislation, blocking illegal material and reporting attempts by people to access child pornography. Many Internet users, industry experts and civil liberties groups were against the Communications Decency Act. Websites such as "The Electronic Frontier Foundation", were created to uphold the rights to free digital expression against political and legal threats. Anti-censorship followers feel that the government's actions are infringing on their freedom of speech. When taken to the Supreme Court in 1997, the court was forced to abolish the Act because it was unconstitutional. Internet censorship can sometimes vary depending on the country. For example, in communist countries such as China, western ideologies conveyed on the Internet are seen as harmful to the solidarity of the Chinese government. As such, all emails leaving and entering the country are screened and edited by government officials. But, sometimes messages are even deleted if they are seen as being harmful to national interests. Recently, the Chinese government tried to develop its own "China World Web" in order to censor any unwanted western messages.

The Internet is more like the everyday world, with all of its promises and problems, than a reflection of academia or an island village. While it's become a tremendous tool for commerce and information, it has also become a home to thieves, terrorists and vandals. The Internet conceals malicious users. The remote nature of the Internet also creates a false sense of security. Many users log on in blissful ignorance, believing they're okay because they can't see or feel any threats. Even after learning that their workstations or websites have been broken into multiple times, many fail to understand the threats lurking on the other end of the wire. Systems are routinely attacked by multiple vectors, worms carried in by e-mails, bandwidth consumed by floods of bogus traffic, and workstation CPUs hijacked through some unpatched vulnerability.

11. The above excerpt appears to have been taken from:
    (1) an encyclopedia   (2) a diary
    (3) an essay   (4) a novel
    (5) a play

12. Why does the author believe that it is almost impossible to control the Internet?
    (1) It is associated with technology.
    (2) Its present size and rapid tendency to expand.
    (3) Millions of users are using it.
    (4) Very few people understand the ill-effects of this technology.
    (5) Internet is difficult to be controlled because of viruses.

13. Why does the author give the Chinese government's example?
    (1) The author wants to show that different governments may follow different measures in order to censor the Internet.
    (2) The author specifically gives a communist country's example in order to show their bias towards western ideologies.
    (3) The author tries to explain that the people of China do not feel that their freedom of expression is endangered by these steps taken by their government.
    (4) The author just provides additional information on the issue in order to maintain the reader's interest.
    (5) The author wants to project China as a superpower.

14. Which of the following statements best expresses the author's opinion about Internet censorship?
    (1) The author is of the view that only specific content on the Internet should be censored.
    (2) The author believes that governments should not infringe upon the right to freedom of expression of the public.
    (3) The author does not take a definitive stand and suggests that there are advantages as well as disadvantages of this technology.
    (4) The author suggests that governments should not intervene in this issue at all.
    (5) The author believes that common people should keep a tab on the Internet.

15. According to the passage, which of the following is not included in the positive evaluations made by the author about the Internet?
    (1) Internet enables us to exchange information on a global scale.
    (2) Internet has given a huge boost to commerce.
    (3) Internet provides space to a number of web sites.
    (4) Internet is available round-the-clock.
    (5) The 'China World Web' has been formed by the Chinese government.

16. What is the meaning of the word 'lurking'?

    (1) Roaming   (2) Revealing

    (3) Crawling   (4) Slinking

    (5) Doubtful

17. Why does the author feel that the Internet has become 'a home for thieves'?

    (1) The Internet provides space for one to conceal his identity.

    (2) A number of crimes are committed due to a lack of screening process of the information exchanged.

    (3) The user-friendliness of the Internet encourages users to commit criminal acts.

    (4) The governments are unable to restrict cyber crimes.

    (5) It is easy to rob banks through Internet.

18. Which of the following statements best expresses the author's opinion regarding the Internet being similar to 'the everyday world'?

    (1) There are a number of things which are uncontrollable by human beings in the real world similarly it is the case with the Internet.

    (2) The real world provides us the opportunity to explore and this same opportunity is available to an internet user.

    (3) The Internet, just like the real world, presents both the advantages and the disadvantages to us.

    (4) The Internet, just like the real world, has only given us disadvantages and more issues which need to be resolved.

    (5) Internet often reflects sociological conditions.

19. The author's point regarding the restrictions on the Internet can be best reinstated by which of the following statements?

    (1) The Internet is remote in nature but can be accessed around the world.

    (2) The Internet has given a sense of security to its users due to the various restrictions placed on them.

    (3) The Internet does not restrict the various viruses and spams at all.

    (4) The Internet has given space to material which was considered immoral or anti-religious and did not find acceptance from any other source.

    (5) The Internet can be controlled from anywhere in the world.

20. According to the passage, which of the following is a disadvantage faced by an Internet user?

    (1) The sense of comfort established by the internet prevents the user from identifying the dangers that are lurking around him.

    (2) The amount of information available can easily confuse the user and lead to information overload.

    (3) All the sources of information available on the internet are not reliable and user-friendly.

    (4) The Internet provides a sense of security to the user which encourages misconduct and promotes blissful ignorance.

    (5) The Internet can be accessed only with a computer.

Directions for questions 21 to 25: In the following passing there are blanks, each of which has been numbered. These numbers are printed below the passage and against each, five words are suggested, one of which fits the blank appropriately. Find out the appropriate word in each case.

A poor washerman had a old donkey. He did not give it __(21)__ food. The donkey became thin and weak. The washerman had a wife and seven children. He said, "I am working hard. But I am not __(22)__ a lot of money. I can't feed my wife and children well. How can I feed this donkey?" Suddenly he remembered a tiger-skin in the house. It wa a gift to his father's good work. He thought. "I shall __(23)__ the donkey with the skin and drive it into the field and won't go near it. My donkey can eat a lot and grow fat too." The next day he dressed the donkey in the tiger-skin and drove it into the field of crops. The villagers saw the donkey in the tiger-skin and thought, "The tiger will kill us all. We shall write to the collector and he will __(24)__ it with the help of the police." Many days passed. The donkey ate a lot of crops every day and grew stout and strong. One day the villagers __(25)__ a letter from the collector saying. "There is no tiger in your village or in any place near your villagers." That evening the villagers went to the field with big sticks. The washerman's donkey in the tiger-skin was in the field. Suddenly another donkey brayed from some place near the field. The washerman's donkey lifted up his head and brayed too. The villagers saw this and beat the donkey.

21. (1) any   (2) too

    (3) many   (4) with

    (5) the

22. (1) accumulate   (2) spend

    (3) wasting   (4) earning

    (5) watching

23. (1) sew   (2) wrapped
    (3) enclose   (4) stuck
    (5) cover

24. (1) shoot   (2) stroke
    (3) shooed   (4) ask
    (5) feed

25. (1) granted   (2) tore
    (3) received   (4) shred
    (5) get

Directions for questions 26 to 30: Which of the phrases (1), (2), (3) and (4) given below each statement should replace the phrase printed in bold in the sentence to make it grammatically correction? If the sentenceis correct as it is given and no correction is required, mark (5) as the answer.

26. The grim job market has taken its toll on students, **many of those** had hoped for a much better future.

    (1) much of whom
    (2) many of whom
    (3) several of those
    (4) many of which
    (5) No correction required

27. The relationship we have with **our clients are** the cornerstone of our future.

    (1) our client are   (2) each elients is
    (3) our clients is   (4) all clients are
    (5) No correction required

28. Many developed countries **have been attempting** to buy agricultural land in other countries to meet their own demand.

    (1) has been attempting
    (2) have being attempting
    (3) are being attempting
    (4) have been attempted
    (5) No correction required

29. A nuclear testing fills the air with radioactive dust **and left the** area uninhabitable

    (1) and leaves the   (2) also leaves the
    (3) and leaving the   (4) and making the
    (5) No correction required

30. Modern ideas of governance **started back to** the time when people began to question kings.

    (1) started when
    (2) set back to
    (3) started back to
    (4) date back to
    (5) No correction required

NUMERICAL ABILITY

Directions (Q. 31 to 35): What should come in place of question mark (?) in following number series.

31. 256, 128, 64, 32, 16, 8, ?

    (1) 6   (2) 5
    (3) 3   (4) 4
    (5) 2

32. 49, 121, 169, 289, 361, ?

    (1) 576   (2) 347
    (3) 331   (4) 323
    (5) 529

33. 1728, 1000, 512, 216, 64, ?

    (1) 6   (2) 4
    (3) 27   (4) 8
    (5) 36

34. 1, 16, 81, 256, 625, ?

    (1) 1331   (2) 1296
    (3) 1728   (4) 1525
    (5) None of these

35. 1331, 11, 1728, 12, 2197, ?

    (1) 14   (2) 13
    (3) 16   (4) 17
    (5) None of these

36. The average age of 24 students and the principal is 15 years. When the principal's age is excluded, the average age decreases by 1 year. What is the age of the principal?

    (1) 38 years   (2) 40 years
    (3) 39 years   (4) Data inadequate
    (5) 41 years

37. Two pipes A and B can fill a tank in 24 minutes and 32 minutes respectively. If both the pipes are opened simultaneously, then after how much time should B be closed so that the tank is full in 16 minutes?

    (1) $\dfrac{32}{3}$ minutes   (2) 7 minutes
    (3) 9 minutes   (4) 33 minutes
    (5) None of these

38. Three utensils contain equal quantities of solution of milk and water in the ratios 6 : 1, 5 : 2 and 3 : 1. If all the three are mixed, then what will be the respective ratio of milk to water in the final mixture?

    (1) 19 : 65   (2) 14 : 4
    (3) 65 : 17   (4) 19 : 65
    (5) 65 : 19

39. An orchard has 48 apple trees, 60 mango trees and 96 banana trees. These have to be arranged in rows such that each row has the same number of trees and of the same type. Find the minimum possible number of such rows that can be formed.
    (1) 12   (2) 13
    (3) 14   (4) 18
    (5) 17

40. A train 100 m long moving at a speed of 54 kmph overtakes another train 120 m long moving in the same direction in 20 sec. The speed of second train is
    (1) 12.2 kmph   (2) 18.8 kmph
    (3) 14.4 kmph   (4) 10.4 kmph
    (5) 14 kmph

Directions (Q. 41 to 45): What approximate value should come in place of the question mark (?) in the following questions? (Note: You are not expected to calculate the exact value.)

41. $(12.997)^3$ = ?
    (1) 1800   (2) 2100
    (3) 2000   (4) 2500
    (5) 2200

42. $50550 \div 50 \div 5$ = ?
    (1) 350   (2) 150
    (3) 300   (4) 250
    (5) 200

43. $49.0003 \div 74.999$ = ?
    (1) 0.05   (2) 0.2
    (3) 1   (4) 0.7
    (5) 2

44. $23.005 \times 22.998 + 100.010$ = ?
    (1) 630   (2) 550
    (3) 700   (4) 720
    (5) 510

45. $125.008 + 69.999 + 104.989$ = ?
    (1) 420   (2) 300
    (3) 285   (4) 415
    (5) 325

46. A is thrice as efficient as B, and B is twice as efficient as C. If A, B and C work together, how long will they take to complete a job which B completes in 10 days?
    (1) $\dfrac{20}{9}$ days   (2) $\dfrac{16}{9}$ days
    (3) 2 days   (4) $\dfrac{17}{9}$ days
    (5) $2\dfrac{4}{9}$ days

47. The total profit of Rs. 3,600 is to be distributed amongst A, B and C such that the shares of A and B are in the ratio 5 : 4 and the shares of B and C are in the ratio 8 : 9. What is the share of C?
    (1) Rs. 1,066   (2) Rs. 1,350
    (3) Rs. 1,500   (4) Rs. 1,800
    (5) None of these

48. 5 years ago, the average age of A, B, C and D was 45. With E joining them now, the average age of all the five becomes 49 years. How old is E?
    (1) 25 years   (2) 40 years
    (3) 45 years   (4) 64 years
    (5) 49 years

49. A rectangular lawn of 40 m × 30 m has two roads, each with 5 m wide running in the middle of it; one is parallel to the length and the other is parallel to the breadth. Find the cost of gravelling them at 15 paise per sq. m.
    (1) Rs. 44.25   (2) Rs. 46.00
    (3) Rs. 48.75   (4) Rs. 50.25
    (5) None of these

50. In how many ways can the seven letters A, B, C, D, E, F and G be arranged so that B, C and G are always together?
    (1) 120   (2) 720
    (3) 450   (4) 540
    (5) None of these

51. $2110 \div 25 + 350 \div 50$ = ?
    (1) 91.4   (2) 8.688
    (3) 86.2   (4) 86.4
    (5) None of these

52. $6999 + 3555 - 2333$ = ?
    (1) 8337   (2) 8444
    (3) 7338   (4) 8221
    (5) None of these

53. $49 \times 64 = (?)^2$
    (1) 54   (2) 56
    (3) 52   (4) 63
    (5) None of these

54. $6.8 \times ? \times 7.9 = 161.16$
    (1) 2   (2) 7
    (3) 5   (4) 4
    (5) None of these

55. 16% of 380 × 5 = ?
    (1) 276   (2) 284
    (3) 304   (4) 312
    (5) None of these

56. Divide Rs. 3,650 into two parts such that the SI on the first part at 6% for 2 years is equals to the SI on the second part at 4% in 3 years. Find the two parts.

    (1) Rs.1,900, Rs. 1,750

    (2) Rs. 1,825, Rs. 1,825

    (3) Rs. 2,000, Rs. 1,650

    (4) Rs. 1,800, Rs. 1,850

    (5) None of these

57. A class is divided into three sections named as A, B, and C which comprises of 10, 20 and 30 students respectively. The percentage of students passing from the sections A, B, and C are 20%, 30%, and 40% respectively. What is the percentage of students who passed in the class?

    (1) 30%

    (2) 33.33%

    (3) 47%

    (4) 50%

    (5) 45%

58. Car x and car y are at points A and B respectively on a straight road such that the distance AB equals 1 km. Both start simultaneously towards each other at speeds of 20 m/s each. Car x increases its speed by 1 m/s while car y decreases its speed by 1 m/s after every two seconds. After how much time from the start will the two cars meet?

    (1) 22 seconds   (2) 23.86 seconds

    (3) 25 seconds   (4) 26.34 seconds

    (5) Cannot be determined

59. A merchant has 100 kg of sugar, part of which he sells at 7% profit and the rest at 17% profit. He gains 10% on the whole. How much is sold at 17% profit?

    (1) 70 kg   (2) 50 kg

    (3) 35 kg   (4) 30 kg

    (5) 25 kg

60. A mixture of 40 litres of fruit juice and water contains 10% water. How much water should be added to this so that water may be 20% in the new mixture?

    (1) 4 litres   (2) 5 litres

    (3) 6.5 litres   (4) 7.5 litres

    (5) 9 litres

Directions (Q. 61 to 65): Answer the following questions based on the given information.

The bar graph given below shows the number of candidates (in thousands) qualified in the written test for admission to two different institutions

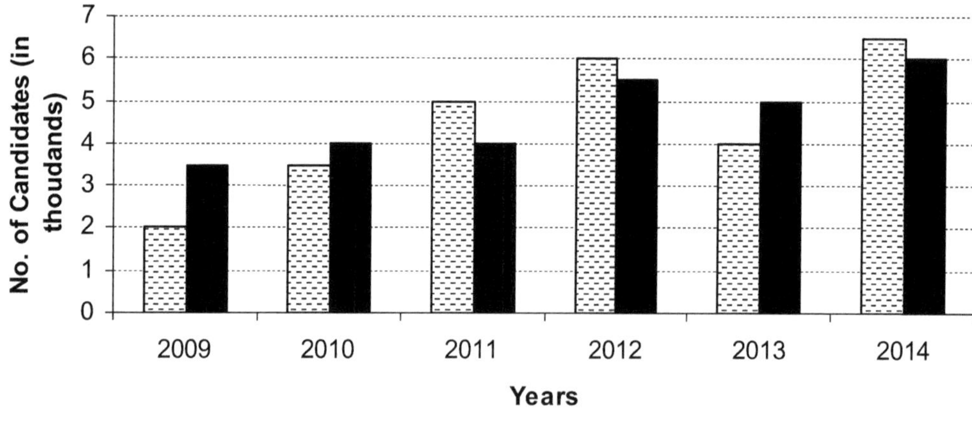

61. What was the respective ratio between the number of candidates qualified in the written test in the year 2009 for admission in institution Q and the number of candidates qualified in the written test in the year 2013 for admission to institution P?

    (1) 8 : 5   (2) 7 : 4

    (3) 7 : 8   (4) 7 : 5

    (5) 8 : 7

62. What was the approximate average number of candidates qualified in the written test for admission to institution Q over all the years ?

    (1) 4,555   (2) 4,200

    (3) 4,160   (4) 4,888

    (5) 4,667

63. In which year was the total number of candidates qualified in the written test for admission to both the institutions together the second highest ?

    (1) 2010   (2) 2011

    (3) 2012   (4) 2013

    (5) 2014

64. What is the difference between the total number of candidates qualified in written test in year 2013 for admission to institution P and Q together and the number of candidates qualified in written test in year 2010 for admission to institution P?

    (1) 5,000   (2) 3,500

    (3) 1,500   (4) 5,500

    (5) None of these

65. What was the total number of candidates qualified in the written test for admission to institution P over all the years together?

    (1) 27,000   (2) 26,500
    (3) 26,000   (4) 27,500
    (5) None of these

REASONING ABILITY

Directions for questions 66 to 70: In the following questions, symbols @ , • , \$, * and # have the following meanings:

A @ B means 'A is greater than B'

A • B means 'A is either greater than or equal to B'

A \$ B means 'A is equal to B'

A * B means 'A is smaller than B'

A # B means 'A is either smaller than or equal to B'

Based on the statements given in each of the questions below, find out which of the conclusions follows.

Mark:

(1) if only conclusion I follows

(2) if only conclusion II follows

(3) if either conclusion I or II follows

(4) if neither conclusion I nor II follows

(5) if both the conclusions follow

66. **Statement:** P # Q, M • N \$ P

   Conclusion: I. M @ P

                       II. N # Q

67. **Statement:** L • M,   R • T \$ L

   Conclusion: I. T • M

                       II. R @ L

68. **Statement :** X @ Y @ Z, U @ Z \$ V

   Conclusion :   I. V * U

                       II. X @ V

69. **Statement :** G * H # K, H @ Q \$ R

   Conclusion: I. G \$ Q

                       II. R • G

70. **Statement :** Z # P, T \$ M, M • Z

   Conclusion :   I. M \$ Z

                       II. M @ Z

Directions (Q. 71 to 75) : Answer the following questions based on the given information.

Punit, Qazi, Ramit, Sanya, Taruna, Urvashi, Vikas and Wazir are eight friends. Three of them play Hockey and Tennis each and two of them play Golf. They all are of different heights. The shortest does not play Hockey and the tallest does not play Golf. Urvashi is taller than Punit and Sanya, but shorter than Qazi and Wazir. Taruna, who does not play Hockey, is taller than Qazi and is second tallest. Vikas is shorter than Sanya, but taller than Punit. Wazir plays Tennis with Sanya, and is fourth from the top. Vikas does not play either Hockey or Golf. Qazi does not play Golf.

71. Who is the shortest?

   (1) Vikas   (2) Sanya

   (3) Punit   (4) Data inadequate

   (5) None of these

72. Who is the tallest?

   (1) Qazi   (2) Wazir

   (3) Ramit   (4) Data inadequate

   (5) None of these

73. Which of the following pairs of friends play Golf?

   (1) Taruna-Urvashi   (2) Tarun-Wazir

   (3) Wazir-Urvashi   (4) Data inadequate

   (5) None of these

74. What is Urvashi's position from the top, when they are arranged in descending order of their height?

   (1) Fifth   (2) Fourth

   (3) Sixth   (4) Cannot be determined
   (5) None of these

75. Which of the following groups of friends plays Hockey?

   (1) Ramit-Punit-Taruna

   (2) Ramit-Qazi-Urvashi

   (3) Ramit-Qazi-Punit

   (4) Ramit-Punit-Urvashi

   (5) None of these

Directions (Q. 76 to 80) : Answer the following questions based on the given information.

Eight friends, Pawan, Qureshi, Ranjit, Sonam, Tanisha, Vaishali, Wakram and Yasin are sitting around a square table in such a way that four of them sit at four corners of the square, while four sit in the middle of each of the four sides. The ones who sit at the four corners face the centre, while those who sit in the middle of the sides face outside.

Pawan who faces the centre sits third to the right of Vaishali. Tanisha, who faces the centre, is not an immediate neighbour of Vaishali. Only one person sits between Vaishali and Wakram. Sonam sits second to right of Qureshi. Qureshi faces the centre. Ranjit is not an immediate neighbour of Pawan.

76. Who sits second to the left of Qureshi?
    (1) Vaishali   (2) Pawan
    (3) Tanisha   (4) Yasin
    (5) Cannot be determined

77. What is the position of Tanisha with respect to Vaishali?
    (1) Fourth to the left
    (2) Second to the left
    (3) Third to the left
    (4) Third to the right
    (5) Second to the right

78. Four of the following five are alike in a certain way and so form a group. Which is the one that does not belong to that group?
    (1) Ranjit   (2) Wakram
    (3) Vaishali   (4) Sonam
    (5) Yasin

79. Which of the following will come in place of the question mark (?) based upon the given seating arrangement?
    Wakram-Pawan, Tanisha-Ranjit, Qureshi-Wakram, Ranjit-Sonam, ?
    (1) Yasin-Tanisha
    (2) Vaishali-Yasin
    (3) Vaishali-Qureshi
    (4) Pawan-Yasin
    (5) Qureshi-Vaishali

80. Which of the following is true regarding Ranjit?
    (1) Ranjit is an immediate neighbour of Vaishali
    (2) Ranjit faces the centre
    (3) Ranjit sits exactly between Tanisha and Sonam
    (4) Qureshi sits third to left of Ranjit
    (5) None is true

Directions (81-85) : Answer the questions on the basis of the information given below.

In a certain code language **'it is rush hour traffic'** is written as 'sa le do mi ru', **'go to school'** is written as 'be no pa',

'one hour to go' is written as 'mi fi pa be', **'rush to one'** is written as 'fi be sa' and **'traffic is fine'** is written as 'ga ru do'.

81. Which of the following represents 'school hour go fine'?
    (1) pa be fi ga   (2) no mi ra pa
    (3) pa no ga mi   (4) ga no mi le
    (5) None of these

82. 'mi fi le' would mean -
    (1) it one to   (2) to rush one
    (3) rush hour it   (4) it one hour
    (5) None of these

83. What does 'sa' stand for?
    (1) rush   (2) traffic
    (3) it   (4) is
    (5) None of these

84. Which of the following represents 'traffic is for one hour'?
    (1) fi ye no mi ru   (2) fi le do mi ru
    (3) fi ye do mi ru   (4) fi so do mi ro
    (5) None of these

85. What does 'do' stand for?
    (1) hour   (2) 'is' or 'traffic'
    (3) it   (4) is
    (5) None of these

Directions (Q. 86 to 90): Answer the following questions based on the given information.

A group of five boys, Krishna, Ajay, Vijay, Raju and Tinku, and five girls, Neha, Sony, Manju, Pammy and Tanu, are standing in two rows facing each other not necessarily in the same order. Boys are facing South. Tinku is not at any of the ends. Vijay is on the immediate right of Ajay. There are as many girls between Neha and Sony as between Manju and Pammy. Krishna is second to the left of Ajay. Pammy and Manju are not facing either Ajay or Raju. Tanu is on the immediate right of Neha, but not in the middle.

86. Who is standing to the immediate right of Krishna?
    (1) Tinku   (2) Vijay
    (3) Ajay   (4) Data inadequate
    (5) None of these

87. Which of the following indicate the pair of boys standing at the ends of the row?

   (1) Vijay, Ajay   (2) Raju, Ajay

   (3) Vijay, Raju   (4) Data inadequate

   (5) None of these

88. Which of the following is definitely true on the basis of the given information?

   (1) Vijay is second to the right of Raju.

   (2) Neha is third to the right of Sony.

   (3) Pammy is to the immediate right of Neha.

   (4) Raju is facing Tanu.

   (5) None of these

89. Who is facing Ajay?

   (1) Manju   (2) Pammy

   (3) Sony   (4) Data inadequate

   (5) None of these

90. Which of the following girls is standing in the middle of their row?

   (1) Manju   (2) Pammy

   (3) Manju or Pammy   (4) Neha

   (5) None of these

Directions (Q. 91 to 93): Answer the following questions based on the given information.

P is the son of Q. Q is the mother of R. R is the wife of T. T is the father of V. V is the brother of W. Y is the mother of T.

91. Which of the following is true based upon the relationships given above ?

   (1) W is the grand-daughter of Y

   (2) T is the brother of P

   (3) V is the son of Q

   (4) V is the brother-in-law of Y

   (5) R is the sister of P

92. How is T related to P ?

   (1) Son-in-law   (2) Brother

   (3) Father-in-law   (4) Brother-in-law

   (5) Cannot be determined

93. Which of the following is/are required to establish that W is the daughter of R ?

   (1) No extra information is required as the relation can be established from the given information

   (2) R has only three children, one son and two daughters

   (3) Q has only one grandson

   (4) Y has only two children, a son and a daughter

   (5) Either (2) or (3)

94. Rahul started from a point and walked straight to point Y at a distance of 90 meters. He turned right and walked 40 meters, then again turned right and walked 70 metres. Finally, he turned right and walked 40 metres. How far is he from the starting point?

   (1) 70 metres   (2) 10 metres

   (3) 20 metres   (4) 30 metres

   (5) None of these

95. Peter walks 5 m towards West, takes a right turn and walks 5 m again. He then takes another right turn and walks 20 m. He then takes a final right turn and walks 5 m before stopping. How far is he from the starting point?

   (1) 20 m   (2) 5 m

   (3) 25 m   (4) 15m

   (5) None of these

Directions (Q. 96 to 100): In each of the questions below are given four statements followed by three conclusions numbered, I, II and III. You have to take the given statements to be true even if they seem to be at variance from commonly known facts. Read all the conclusions and then decide which of the given conclusions logically follows from the given statements disregarding commonly known facts.

96. **Statements:**

   All coins are glasses

   Some glasses are cups

   Some cups are boxes

   All boxes are pins.

   Conclusions:

   I. Some coins are cups

   II. Some pins are glasses

   III. Some cups are pins

   (1) None follows   (2) Only I follow

   (3) Only III follows   (4) Only II and III follow

   (5) None of these

97. **Statements:**

   Some pens are pencils

   All pencils are caps

   All caps are buses

   Some buses are trains

   Conclusions:

   I. Some trains are caps

   II. Some pens are buses

   III. Some pencils are trains

   (1) Only I follows   (2) Only II follows

   (3) Only I and III follow   (4) None follows

   (5) Only I, II and III follow

98. **Statements:**

    All shirts are skirts

    All skirts are banks

    All banks are roads.

    All roads are brushes

    Conclusions:

    I. All banks are skirts

    II. All roads are banks

    III. Some brushes are shirts

    (1) Only I follows   (2) Only III follows

    (3) Only I and III follow   (4) Only I, II and III follow

    (5) None follows

99. **Statements:**

    Some fishes are plates

    Some plates are spoons

    Some spoons are plants

    All plants are crows.

    Conclusions:

    I. Some plates are crows

    II. Some crows are spoons

    III. Some plants are spoons

(1) Only I follows

(2) Only I and II follow

(3) None follows

(4) Only II and III follow

(5) Either I or III follows

100. **Statements:**

    Some eggs are hens

    Some hens are ducks

    All ducks are pigeons.

    All pigeons are sparrows

    Conclusions:

    I. All ducks are sparrows.

    II. No egg is duck

    III. Some sparrows are hens

    (1) Only I follows

    (2) Only I and II follow

    (3) Only III follow

    (4) Only I and III follow

    (5) All I, II and III follow

ANSWERS

1. (1)	**2.** (5)	**3.** (5)	**4.** (1)	**5.** (3)	**6.** (4)	**7.** (2)	**8.** (1)	**9.** (5)	**10.** (4)
11. (3)	**12.** (2)	**13.** (1)	**14.** (3)	**15.** (4)	**16.** (4)	**17.** (1)	**18.** (3)	**19.** (4)	**20.** (1)
21. (1)	**22.** (4)	**23.** (5)	**24.** (1)	**25.** (3)	**26.** (2)	**27.** (3)	**28.** (5)	**29.** (1)	**30.** (4)
31. (4)	**32.** (5)	**33.** (4)	**34.** (2)	**35.** (2)	**36.** (3)	**37.** (1)	**38.** (5)	**39.** (5)	**40.** (3)
41. (5)	**42.** (5)	**43.** (4)	**44.** (1)	**45.** (2)	**46.** (1)	**47.** (5)	**48.** (3)	**49.** (3)	**50.** (2)
51. (1)	**52.** (4)	**53.** (2)	**54.** (5)	**55.** (3)	**56.** (2)	**57.** (2)	**58.** (3)	**59.** (4)	**60.** (2)
61. (3)	**62.** (5)	**63.** (3)	**64.** (4)	**65.** (1)	**66.** (2)	**67.** (1)	**68.** (5)	**69.** (4)	**70.** (3)
71. (3)	**72.** (3)	**73.** (5)	**74.** (2)	**75.** (2)	**76.** (2)	**77.** (3)	**78.** (4)	**79.** (1)	**80.** (3)
81. (3)	**82.** (4)	**83.** (1)	**84.** (5)	**85.** (2)	**86.** (1)	**87.** (3)	**88.** (4)	**89.** (3)	**90.** (3)
91. (5)	**92.** (4)	**93.** (3)	**94.** (3)	**95.** (4)	**96.** (3)	**97.** (2)	**98.** (2)	**99.** (4)	**100.** (4)

EXPLANATIONS

1. (1) 'For, 'in correctly fills the blanks.

2. (5) 'from' follows 'hinder'.

3. (5) 'To', 'with' are the correct words that can fill the blanks.

4. (1) 'Saw' and 'offered' are the correct words.

5. (3) 'Bear with' means to tolerate. 'Shameful' appropriately fills the second blank.

6. (4) The correct sequence is DFBEAC.

11. (3) An encyclopedia is a comprehensive summary of information from either all branches of knowledge or a particular branch of knowledge. The given passage does not give a comprehensive summary of information. Option (2) is negated because a diary would have personal information while option (4) is negated because it is not a work of fiction. The passage could be an excerpt from an essay as it provides a detailed description of a particular topic, i.e. 'Controlling the Internet'.

12. (2) The second line of the passage clearly states that controlling the Internet has become impossible because of its size and rapid growth.

13. (1) Refer to the line, "Internet censorship can sometimes vary depending on the country." This supports option (1). Option (2) is negated because the main point is not the 'bias towards western ideologies'. Options (3) and (4) are irrelevant.

14. (3) It is clear from the passage that the author has not given his own opinion and has merely stated the facts and opinion of third parties. The author has suggested the advantages and disadvantages of the internet in the last paragraph of the passage. So, options (1), (2) and (4) can be negated.

15. (4) Options (1) and (3) are mentioned in the first paragraph while option (2) is mentioned in the third paragraph.

16. (4) 'Lurking' refers to *waiting in a secret place especially in order to do something wrong or harmful*. 'Slinking', which means *to move in a way that does not attract attention especially because you are embarrassed, afraid or doing something wrong*, is a synonym of the word in question.

17. (1) The third paragraph states that the Internet conceals malicious users and thus, it has become a home to thieves, terrorists and vandals. Options (2), (3) and (4) are not supported by the passage.

18. (3) The first line of the third paragraph clearly states that the Internet is like the everyday world with all of its promises and problems.

19. (4) Options (1) and (3) are not supported by the passage while option (2) is in negation of the passage. Option (4) is the correct answer because the passage states that the Internet contains material that is banned from the mainstream media due to the lack of restrictions on the Internet.

20. (1) Option (2) is negated because the passage does not talk of information overload. Option (3) is ruled out because the passage does not talk of sources of information available on the Internet. Option (4) is negated because the passage does not suggest that the false sense of security provided by the Internet encourages misconduct. Option (1) is the correct answer because the passage clearly states that the false sense of security leads the users to believe that they do not face any threats.

21. (1) "Any" is the most appropriate choice here because the author wants to say that the poor washer man could afford absolutely nothing for the donkey. The other options are incorrect in the context of the sentence.

22. (4) The poor washer man is obviously not "earning" enough money and so, he is poor. The other options are incorrect in the context of the sentence.

23. (5) The washer man can "cover" the donkey with the tiger skin. He cannot "wrap", "sew" or "enclose" the donkey with the tiger skin.

24. (1) Since the help of police is mentioned, it is obvious that "shoot" is the correct word. The other words are inappropriate.

25. (3) "Received" is the correct word because a letter can only be "received". It cannot be "granted", "tore", "shred" or "get". Furthermore, the word should be in the past tense and so, "get" and "shred" can be ruled out.

26. (2) 'Whom' refers to students.

27. (3) Subject is 'relationship' and so, the verb should be singular.

28. (5) The sentence is grammatically correct.

29. (1) Issue of parallelism: The second verb should be in the present tense because the first verb 'fills' is in the present tense.

30. (4) 'Date back to' is a better usage.

31. (4) The given series is as follows:

$256 \div 2 = 128$

$128 \div 2 = 64$

$64 \div 2 = 32$

$32 \div 2 = 16$

$16 \div 2 = 8$

$8 \div 2 = 4$

$\therefore\ ? = 4$

32. (5) The given series is the square of the prime numbers starting from 7.

$7^2 = 49$

$11^2 = 121$

$13^2 = 169$

$17^2 = 289$

$19^2 = 361$

$23^2 = 529$

$\therefore\ ? = 529$

33. (4) The given series is as follows:

$12^3 = 1728$

$10^3 = 1000$

$8^3 = 512$

$6^3 = 216$

$4^3 = 64$

$2^3 = 8$

$\therefore\ ? = 8$

34. (2) The given series is as follows:

$1^4 = 1$

$2^4 = 16$

$3^4 = 81$

$4^4 = 256$

$5^4 = 625$

$6^4 = 1296$

$\therefore\ ? = 1296$

35. (2) The given series is as follows:

$(11)^3,\ 11,\ (12)^3,\ 12,\ (13)^3,\ 13$

$\therefore\ ? = 13$

36. (3) Average age of 24 students and the principal = 15 years.

Total age of 24 students and the principal = 15 × 25 = 375 years.

New average age of 24 students = 15 – 1 = 14 years

Total age of 24 students = 14 × 24 = 336 years

$\therefore$ Age of the principal = 375 – 336 = 39 years.

37. (1) Let the pipe B be closed after t minutes.

Part of tank filled by A in one minute = $\dfrac{1}{24}$

and part of tank filled by B in one minute = $\dfrac{1}{32}$

So, $\dfrac{16}{24} + \dfrac{t}{32} = 1$

$\Rightarrow t = \dfrac{32}{3}$ min

Hence, pipe B is closed after $\dfrac{32}{3}$ minutes.

38. (5) As each mixture is of equal quantity. Let the quantity in each utensil be 28 litres.

In the final mixture,

$\dfrac{\text{Quantity of Milk}}{\text{Quantity of Water}} = \dfrac{24 + 20 + 21}{4 + 8 + 7} = \dfrac{65}{19}$ i.e. $65 : 19$.

39. (5) Total number of trees are $48 + 60 + 96 = 204$.

Given that each row has the same number of trees and all trees in a row are of the same type. Since we need to minimise the number of rows, we need to maximise the number of trees in each row.

Number of trees in each row = HCF of 48, 60 and 96

$= 12$

$\therefore$ Minimum number of rows $= \dfrac{204}{12} = 17$

40. (3) To cross the other train, first train has to cover $(100 + 120) = 220$ m.

Let the speed of the second train be x m/sec.

Then, $\dfrac{220}{54 \times \dfrac{5}{18} - x} = 20 \Rightarrow \dfrac{220}{15 - x} = 20$

$x = 4$ m/sec or 14.4 km/hr.

41. (5) $(12.997)^3$ or $(13)^3$

Now, $(13)^3 = 2197$

The integer nearest to 2197 is 2200.

42. (5) The expression can be written as: $\dfrac{50550}{50 \times 5}$

$= 202.50 \approx 200$

43. (4) The approximate expression will be: $\dfrac{49}{75} \approx 0.7$

44. (1) The expression could be written as:

$23 \times 23 + 100 = 629 \approx 630.$

45. (2) The expression could be written as:

$125 + 70 + 105 = 300$

46. (1) B takes 10 days to finish the job.

$\Rightarrow$ A will take $\dfrac{10}{3}$ days to finish the same job.

(As A is thrice as efficient as B)

$\Rightarrow$ C will take 20 days to finish the same job.

(As C is half as efficient as B)

$\therefore$ Together they will finish the job in

$\dfrac{1}{\dfrac{1}{10} + \dfrac{1}{20} + \dfrac{3}{10}} = \dfrac{20}{9}$ days

47. (5) $A : B = 5 : 4$

$B : C = 8 : 9$

$\therefore A : B : C = 40 : 32 : 36 = 10 : 8 : 9$

C's share is $= \dfrac{9}{27} \times 3600 = \text{Rs.} 1,200.$

48. (3) We have, $\dfrac{(A + B + C + D)}{4} = 45$

So, $A + B + C + D = 180$

In 5 years, the sum of ages of 4 persons will increase by 20 years. Lets assume age of the new person is E.

As per the question

$\dfrac{A + B + C + D + E + 20}{5} = 49$

$\dfrac{180 + E + 20}{5} = 49$

$\Rightarrow E = 45$

Hence, age of person E is 45 years.

49. (3) Area of road parallel to length $= 40 \times 5 = 200$ m^2

Area of road parallel to width $= 30 \times 5 = 150$ m^2

Area of the common portion $= 5 \times 5 = 25$ m^2

Cost of gravelling = Area of the roads × cost of gravelling.

$= (350 - 25) \times \dfrac{15}{100} = 325 \times \dfrac{15}{100} = \dfrac{195}{4} = \text{Rs. } 48.75 .$

50. (2) Considering B, C and G as one unit, the five things can be arranged in $5! = 120$ ways. Now B, C and G can be arranged among themselves in $3!$ ways i.e. BC and CB.

Total number of arrangements = $120 \times 6 = 720$ ways.

51. (1) $? = 2110 \div 25 + 350 \div 50$

$= 84.4 + 7$

$= 91.4$

52. (4) $? = 6999 + 3555 - 2333$

$= 8221$

53. (2) $(?)^2 = 49 \times 64$

$? = 7 \times 8 = 56$

54. (5) $? = \dfrac{161.16}{6.8 \times 7.9} = 3$

55. (3) $? = \dfrac{16}{100} \times 380 \times 5$

$= 304$

56. (2) First part = Rs. x, R = 6 %, N = 2 years

Second part = Rs. (3,650 – x), R = 4%,

N = 3 Years

According to the given condition,

$\Rightarrow \dfrac{x \times 6 \times 2}{100} = \dfrac{(3650 - x) \times 4 \times 3}{100} \Rightarrow 2x = 3650$

$\Rightarrow x = $ Rs. 1,825

Second part = 3,650 – 1,825 = Rs. 1,825.

57. (2) Required percentage

$= \left(\dfrac{20\% \text{ of } 10 + 30\% \text{ of } 20 + 40\% \text{ of } 30}{10 + 20 + 30} \right) \times 100$

$= \left(\dfrac{2 + 6 + 12}{10 + 20 + 30} \right) \times 100 = \dfrac{20}{60} \times 100 = 33.33\%.$

58. (3) Relative speed of car x and car y = 20 + 20

= 40 m/sec.

As decrease and increase in speeds is the same the relative speed would always be constant = 40 m/sec.

Hence, time taken by cars to meet each other

$= \dfrac{1000}{40} = 25$ seconds.

59. (4) Let he sold x kg of sugar at 17% profit.

Since he made overall 10% profit on selling 100 Kg of sugar

7% of (100 – x) + 17% of x = 10% of 100

$\Rightarrow x = 30$Kg.

∴ Merchant sold 30 kg of sugar at 17% profit.

60. (2) Total strength of mixture = 40 litres

Water = 10% of 40 litres = 4 litres

Fruit juice = 36 litres

So, water-fruit juice must be in the ratio 20:80 in the new mixture.

∴ Amount of water = $36 \times \dfrac{20}{80} = 9$ litres

Clearly (9 – 4) = 5 litres of water must be added.

61. (3) Required ratio = 3,500 : 4,000 = 7 : 8

62. (5) Required average

$= \dfrac{3500 + 4000 + 4000 + 5500 + 5000 + 6000}{6}$

$= 4,667$

63. (3) Total number of candidates qualified in 2009
= 2,000 + 3,500 = 5,500

Total number of candidates qualified in 2010
= 3,500 + 4,000 = 7,500

Total number of candidates qualified in 2011
= 5,000 + 4,000 = 9,000

Total number of candidates qualified in 2012
= 6,000 + 5,500 = 11,500

Total number of candidates qualified in 2013
= 4,000 + 5,000 = 9,000

Total number of candidates qualified in 2014
= 6,500 + 6,000 = 12,500

64. (4) Required difference = 9,000 – 3,500 = 5,500

65. (1) Total number of candidates = 2,000 + 3,500 + 5,000 + 6,000 + 4,000 + 6,500 = 27,000

66. (2) From the given statement

$P \leq Q$ and $M \geq N = P \Rightarrow M \geq N = P \leq Q$

Conclusion -I:M > P may or may not follow

Conclusion - II: $N \leq Q$ follows

Only conclusion (II) follows.

67. (1) From the given statement

$L \geq M$ and $R \geq T = L$

$\Rightarrow R \geq T = L \geq M$

Conclusion I: $T \geq M$ follows

Conclusion II: R > L may or may not follow

Only conclusion (I) follows.

68. (5) From the given statement

X > Y > Z and U > Z = V

Conclusion I : V < U follows

Conclusion II : X > V follows

Both the conclusions follows.

69. (4) From the given statement

$G \geq H \leq K$ and $H > Q = R$
$\Rightarrow G \geq H, K \geq H$ and $R, Q < H$

Conclusion I: G = Q does not follow

Conclusion II: $R \geq G$ does not follow

None of the conclusion follows.

70. (3) From the given statement

$Z \leq P, T = M$ and $M \geq Z$
$\Rightarrow Z \leq P$ and $Z \leq M, T$

Conclusion I : M = Z may or may not follows

Conclusion II : M > Z may or may not follows

Either of the conclusion follows.

For questions 71 to 75:

Order of height : R > T > Q > W > U > S > V > P , with R being the tallest and P being the smallest.

Peson	Game
Punit	Golf
Qazi	Hockey
Ramit	Hockey
Sanya	Tennis
Taruna	Golf
Urvashi	Hockey
Vikas	Tennis
Wazir	Tennis

For questions 76 to 80:

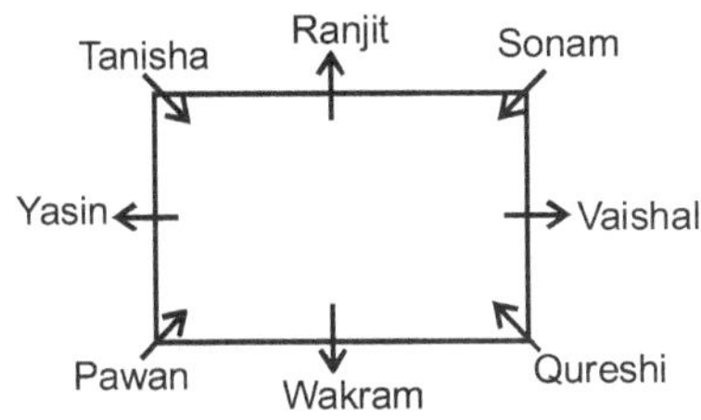

For questions 81 to 85: The given information can be tabulated as:

it	is	rush	hour	traffic	go	to	school	one	fine
le	ru/do	sa	mi	do/ru	no/pa	be	pa/no	fi	ga

81. (3) school ⇒ no; hour ⇒ mi; go ⇒ pa; fine = ga.

82. (4) mi ⇒ hour; fi ⇒ one; le ⇒ it.

83. (1) sa ⇒ rush

84. (5) traffic is ⇒ ru do; one ⇒ fi; hour ⇒ mi
    The code for 'for' may be 'ye' or 'so'.

85. (2) do ⇒ is or traffic

For questions 86 to 90:

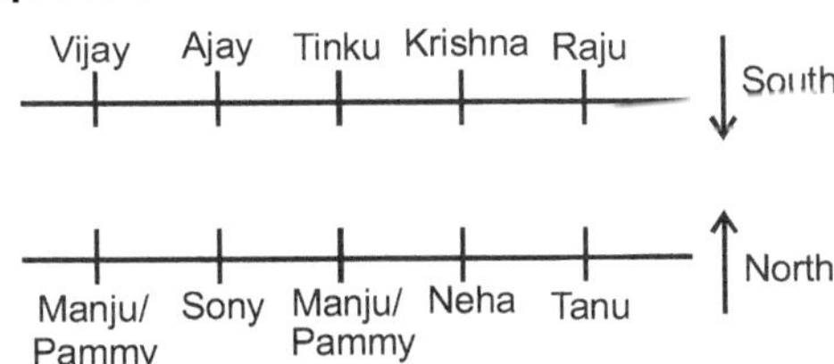

For questions 91 to 93:

Q is a female and mother of P and R(female). R and T are wife and husband respectively. T is father of W and V (male) and Y is mother of T and mother-in-law of R.

94. (3) Rahul is 20 metres away from the starting point.

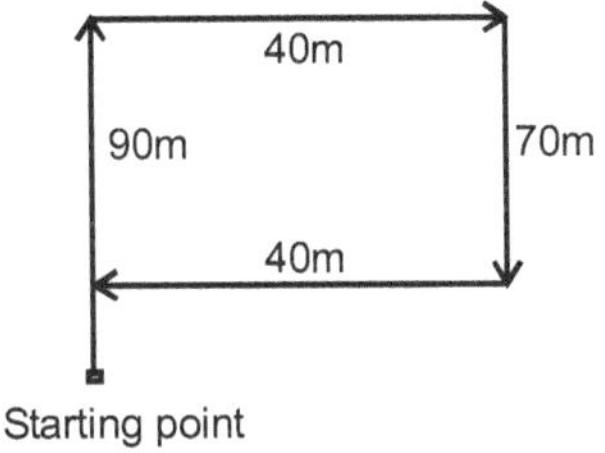

95. (4)

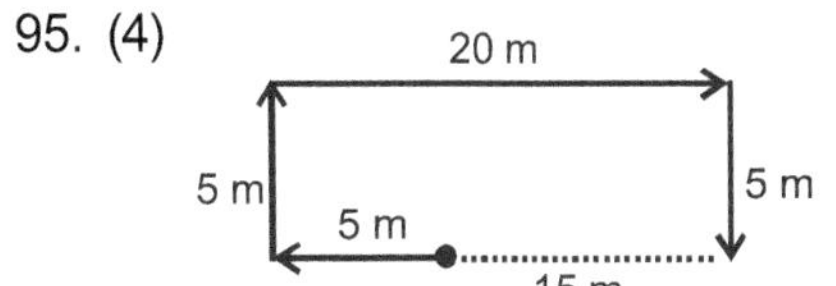

96. (3)

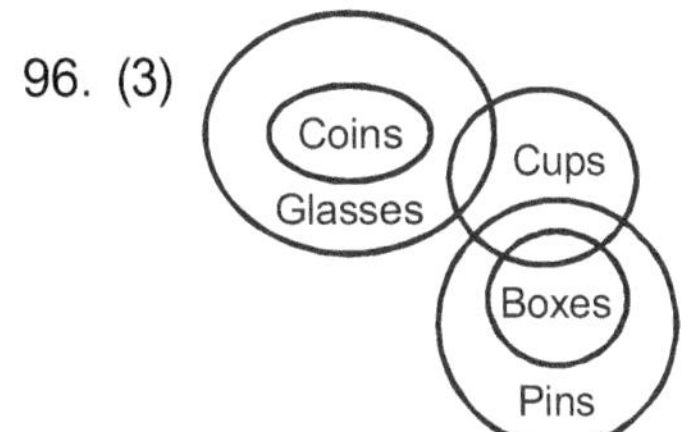

97. (2)

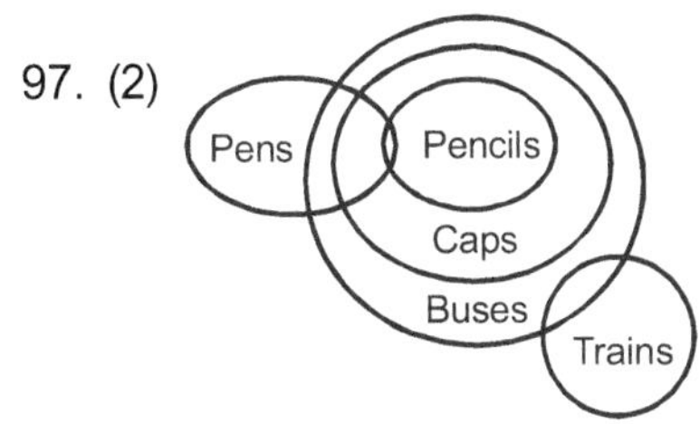

98. (2)

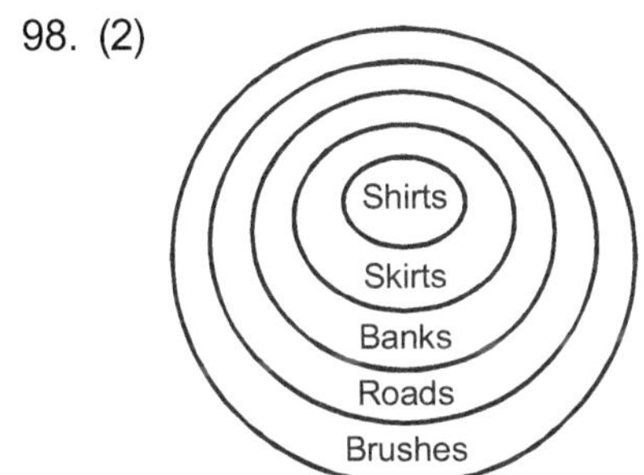

99. (4)

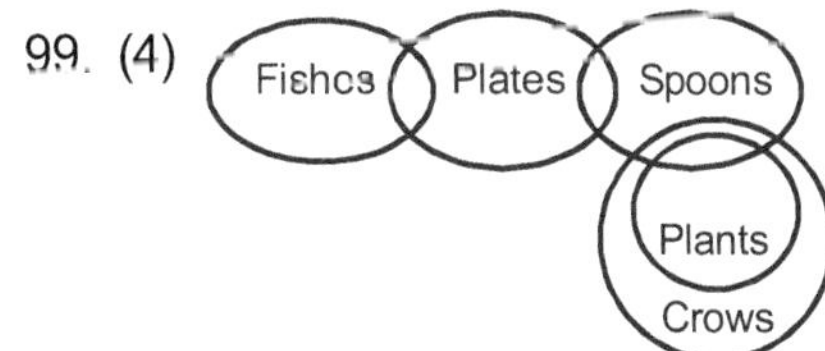

100. (4)

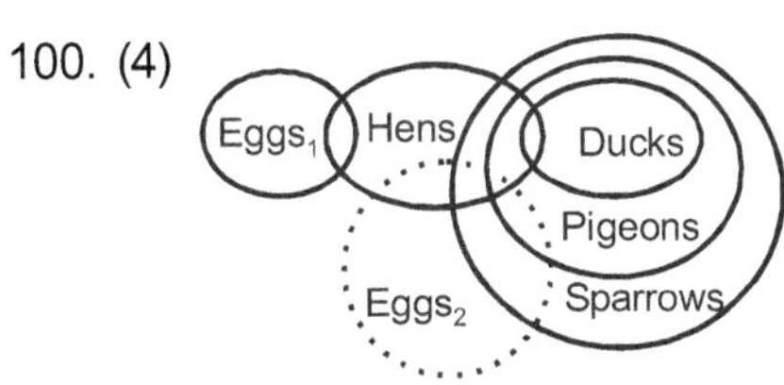

ENGLISH LANGUAGE

Directions (Q. 1-5): Read each sentence to find out whether there is any grammatical error in it. The error if any, will be in one part of the sentence. The number of that part is the answer. If there is no error, the answer is (5) 'No Error'. (Ignore the errors of punctuation if any).

1. Time the concert ended, (1)/ the crowd clapped (2)/ and cheered (3)/ enthusiastically. (4)/ No Error (5)

2. The students blamed (1)/ their professor for (2)/ their late arrival (3)/ in the concert. (4)/No error (5)

3. We have many rooms (1)/ in our house, (2)/ several of which (3)/ have not been in use for years. (4)/ No Error (5)

4. When I heard (1)/ footsteps behind me (2)/ I was being scared (3)/ that I would be attacked. (4)/ No Error (5)

5. The Manager said that (1)/ he wanted to hear (2)/ the pros and cons (3)/ of the issue. (4)/ No Error (5)

Directions (Q. 6-10): Fill in the blanks given in the question using the most suitable options.

6. He has to address the _____ of growing inequalities _____ rejuvenating the stuttering economy.
   (1) problem, while
   (2) route, about
   (3) life, in
   (4) increase, till
   (5) happiness, in

7. While there was no big announcement to show for the bilateral, _____ are many parts in the joint statement that _____ cause concerns for India.
   (1) about, will
   (2) if, may
   (3) then, should
   (4) their, might
   (5) there, could

8. Earlier this month several writers _____ returned their awards to register their protest against increasing intolerance _____ the country.
   (1) has, inside
   (2) were, on
   (3) was, about
   (4) had, in
   (5) will, for

9. The writers said that the protest _____ to express their anger against the government for letting anti-social incidents _____.
   (1) meant, happened
   (2) implied, occurred
   (3) demonstrated, taken place
   (4) were, occur
   (5) was, happen

10. Critical design reviews for the individual cryogenic elements of the core stage, boosters and engines _____ completed successfully as part of _____ milestone.
    (1) were, this
    (2) was, these
    (3) will, a
    (4) would, that
    (5) could, an

Directions (Q. 11-20): Read the following passage carefully and answer the questions given below it.

The assumption that Research and Development (R&D) will help reach European Union's (EU) long-term objectives is largely based on economic theory, which identifies technical change as the major source of long run economic growth. New production processes will allow firms to increase output per worker or unit of capital, or help reduce pollution, CO_2 emissions, and the consumption of fossil fuels and other non-renewable resources. New products will contribute to improving the living standard and well-being of consumers. Since the knowledge created through R&D is to some extent a public good, there may be additional benefits from positive externalities or **spillovers** from R&D. In fact, **endogenous** growth theory suggests that these externalities may be strong enough to counteract the diminishing returns to capital that restrict long-run growth in neoclassical growth models. The arguments related to short-term benefits - the belief that higher R&D investments may facilitate the recovery from the global financial crisis - are less theoretical, and instead based on the observation that the countries investing more in R&D have also been less severely affected by the crisis.

However, at the same time as R&D and **innovation** are emphasized as the appropriate response to the economic, social, and environmental challenges of the 21st century, there is also a concern that Europe may suffer from an "innovation gap" in comparison with other leading economies. For example, the Innovation Union Scoreboard 2014, which calculates multidimensional performance indices for the EU countries and some other major economies, suggests that the EU's innovation performance has fallen short of that in the US and Japan for the past decade, and that South Korea also shows better results than the EU since 2009.

One obvious explanation for the gap is that the EU invests less in R&D than its main competitors. While the EU's R&D expenditures amounted to 2.01% of GDP in 2013, Japan reached 3.34%, South Korea recorded

3.61%, and the US used 2.55% of GDP for R&D. Another reason could be that there may be differences in how efficiently countries are able to transform R&D into commercial innovations and growth. In particular, growth effects may vary depending on how total R&D expenditures are divided between the public and private sectors. Both the EU and its main competitors devote roughly one percent of GDP to publicly funded R&D, but Japan, South Korea, and the US have substantially higher rates of private sector R&D than the EU. It is possible that privately funded R&D generates stronger benefits than publicly funded R&D, those interactions between private and public R&D result in more innovations than purely public research efforts, or that private R&D is necessary to create the capacity for absorption and commercial exploitation of the results of publicly funded R&D. The growth effects of R&D are also likely to vary depending on the specific features of the national innovation system, which determine how effectively knowledge is created, commercialized, and **diffused**.

The quality of higher education, the efficiency of the labor market, incentives and attitudes toward entrepreneurship, openness to trade and foreign direct investment, the availability of venture capital, the quality of market institutions, and the availability of infrastructure are only some of the determinants identified in the literature. In many of these areas - in particular those related to entrepreneurship, venture capital, and market institutions - the US is often promoted as a best-practice example, suggesting that the US position as a global technology leader has more to do with an efficient innovation system than with higher R&D expenditures.

An analysis has been made to define the relationship between R&D spending and growth by conducting a meta-analysis of the relevant literature on a large number of countries at different stages of economic development. The purpose is to investigate whether the EU (or more precisely, the EU15 - the 15 countries that had joined the EU before 2004) differs from other economies in terms of how it is affected by R&D. The results suggest that the growth-enhancing effects of R&D spending in the EU are somewhat weaker than those in other industrialized economies, and that the gap is largely explained by a comparison with the US. It was also found that studies analyzing the level of income generally record a stronger relation between R&D and output than studies analyzing changes in growth rates: this finding is relevant also for the present analysis.

11. What according to the author is one of the answers to the rising social, environmental and economic challenges of the present age?

(1) Increased investment by foreign banks.

(2) Heavy investments in higher education.

(3) Innovation in the heavy industries' sector.

(4) Research and Development is an appropriate response to the economic, social and environment challenges.

(5) A substantial growth rate.

12. What is the tone of the author in the passage?

(1) Descriptive   (2) Narrative

(3) Incisive   (4) Discursive

(5) Digressive

13. What can be a possible title of the passage?

(1) Investment of the European Union in Research and Development.

(2) Role of Research and Development in the economic growth of nations.

(3) Newer production processes vis-à-vis increased output per worker.

(4) The difference between public funded R and D and privately funded R and D.

(5) The economic and social challenges faced by the 21st century world.

14. The passage is most likely taken from a/an

(1) Economics journal.

(2) Political Science journal.

(3) school book.

(4) Social Science book.

(5) Biography.

15. Which of the following statements is correct in the light of the passage?

(1) USA has lesser private sector R and Ds than the European Union.

(2) The position of US as a global technology leader is due to higher R and D expenditures.

(3) The short term benefits of Research and Development investments are more theoretical.

(4) The European Union wants to increase the expenditure on Research and Development substantially by 2020.

(5) The R and D expenditure of the European Union is lesser than many developed countries.

16. Why does the author show that the innovation performance of European Union could not match American and Japanese standards?

(1) Europe has been plagued by political crises one after another.

(2) This is due to the fact that the European Union invests less in Research and Development.

(3) US and Japan have witnessed huge foreign investments in the last couple of years.

(4) The economic recession of 2008 dealt a death blow to the economic stability of the European Union.

(5) European leaders underestimated the importance of Research and Development since the end of World War II.

Directions (Q. 17 and 18): Choose the word which is most **similar** in meaning given in **bold** as used in the given passage.

17. Spillover

(1) Infringement

(2) Lack

(3) Discouragement

(4) Diminish

(5) Excesses

18. Innovation

(1) Descent   (2) Ascent

(3) Laconic   (4) Shift

(5) Metamorphosis

Directions (Q. 19 and 20): Choose the word which is **opposite** in meaning given in **bold** as used in the given passage.

19. Endogenous

(1) Reticent   (2) Homogeneous

(3) Kaleidoscope   (4) Amplification

(5) External

20. Diffuse

(1) Extended   (2) Solved

(3) Condensed   (4) Enhanced

(5) Persuaded

Directions (Q. 21-25): In the following passage there are blanks, each of which has been numbered. These numbers are printed below the passage and against each, five words are suggested, one of which fits the blank appropriately. Find out the appropriate word in each case.

A professor was __(21)__ the Indian Independence Movement and the idea of non-violence conceived by Mahatma Gandhi. "Although others like Nelson Mandela followed this idea and __(22)__ the Nobel Prize for Peace Mahatma Gandhi did not," she said. One student spoke up, "It is good that he didn't, since it was an award started by Alfred Nobel who invented dynamite, which causes __(23)__!"

The professor disagreed "In fact the world should be __(24)__ to Nobel because he invented dynamite. It was very useful to build tunnels under mountains for trains to pass. If we choose to use it for war it is not his fault. Furthermore, he __(25)__ all his wealth into instituting

prizes for literature, physics, chemistry, medicine, peace, etc. His logic was that anything which would benefit the human race deserved recognition so that the person who had started it would have no financial difficulties in achieving his goal".

21. (1) lecturing   (2) talking

(3) discussing   (4) speaking

(5) arguing

22. (1) awarded   (2) given

(3) presented   (4) win

(5) received

23. (1) blast   (2) ruins

(3) destruction   (4) bombs

(5) damages

24. (1) dedicated   (2) grateful

(3) appreciated   (4) thanking

(5) cursing

25. (1) put   (2) left

(3) gave   (4) donated

(5) contributed

Directions (Q. 26-30): Rearrange the following six sentences (A) , (B) , (C), (D) , (E) and (F) in the proper sequence to form a meaningful paragraph; then answer the questions given below them.

(A) I could not even hide myself, which would have saved me.

(B) Once a monkey escaped from one of the rooms in the palace and came into my room.

(C) This frightened the animal, who jumped out of the window and climbed onto the roof.

(D) Suddenly my sister entered my room and screamed when she saw the monkey scratching me.

(E) I was so scared when I saw the monkey that I could not move.

(F) Seeing that I was scared, the monkey started scratching me.

26. Which of the following should be the **SECOND** sentence after rearrangement?

(1) B   (2) C

(3) D   (4) E

(5) F

27. Which of the following should be the **THIRD** sentence after rearrangement?

(1) A   (2) B

(3) C   (4) D

(5) E

28. Which of the following should be the **FIRST** sentence after rearrangement?

   (1) A   (2) B

   (3) C   (4) D

   (5) E

29. Which of the following should be the **LAST (SIXTH)** sentence after rearrangement?

   (1) B   (2) C

   (3) D   (4) E

   (5) F

30. Which of the following should be the **FOURTH** sentence after rearrangement?

   (1) B   (2) C

   (3) D   (4) E

   (5) F

NUMERICAL ABILITY

Directions (Q. 31 to 35): What will come in place of the question mark (?) in the following questions ?

31. $\sqrt{360 - 225 \times 2 + 379} = ?$

   (1) 17   (2) 19

   (3) $\sqrt{279}$ (4) 289

   (5) None of these

32. $9^3 \times 81^2 \div 27^3 = (3)^?$

   (1) 3   (2) 4

   (3) 5   (4) 6

   (5) None of these

33. $572 \div 26 \times 12 - 200 = (2)^?$

   (1) 5   (2) 6

   (3) 7   (4) 8

   (5) None of these

34. $4\dfrac{1}{2} - 2\dfrac{5}{6} = ? - 1\dfrac{7}{12}$

   (1) $3\dfrac{1}{4}$ (2) $3\dfrac{5}{12}$

   (3) $2\dfrac{7}{12}$ (4) $3\dfrac{3}{4}$

   (5) None of these

35. 36% of 245 – 40% of 210 = 10 – ?

   (1) 4.2   (2) 6.8

   (3) 4.9   (4) 7.5

   (5) None of these

36. Sanya's average daily expenditure is Rs. 10 during May, Rs 14 during June and Rs. 15 during July. Her daily expenditure for these 3 months is (approx.)

   (1) Rs. 13   (2) Rs. 11

   (3) Rs. 12   (4) Rs. 10

   (5) None of these

37. Eric can finish a job in 40 days and Clapton is half as efficient as him. How long will they take to complete the job while working on alternate days, if it is known that Eric started the work on the first day?

   (1) 25 days   (2) 26 days

   (3) 27 days   (4) 54 days

   (5) 53 days

38. A sugar and water solution of 100 litres consists of 20% of sugar. If the solution is heated, water evaporates and now the sugar is 80% of the solution. How much amount of water has evaporated?

   (1) 75 litres   (2) 50 litres

   (3) 65 litres   (4) 70 litres

   (5) None of these

39. The number 225 is divided into 3 parts a, b and c such that 1.5a = 3b = c. Which among the following has an integer value?

   (1) a + b   (2)   a – b

   (3) c + a   (4)   c – b

   (5) a – c

40. A girl rides her horse for 10 km at an average speed of 12 km/hr and for 12 km at an average speed of 10 km/hr. What is the average speed for the entire trip?

   (1) 1.44 km/hr   (2) 5 km/hr

   (3) 10.81 km/hr   (4) 11.90 km/hr

   (5) 11 km/hr

Directions (Q. 41 to 45): What should come in place of question mark (?) in following number series.

41. 108, 228, 288, 318, 333, 340.5, ?

   (1) 344.25   (2) 343.25

   (3) 344.75   (4) 353.25

   (5) None of these

42. 320, 285, 257, 236, 222, ?

   (1) 215   (2) 208

   (3) 201   (4) 211

   (5) None of these

43. 345, 219, 129, 69, ?

   (1) 39   (2) 36

   (3) 32   (4) 37

   (5) 33

44. 6, 24, 60, 120, 210, ?

(1) 324 (2) 289

(3) 300 (4) 336

(5) None of these

45. 2, 8, 28, 84, 210, ?

(1) 250 (2) 300

(3) 400 (4) 420

(5) None of these

46. A does as much work in 5 hours as B and C together do in 4 hours. A job is completed by A in 20 hours. In how much time would A, B and C together do the same job?

(1) 10 hours (2) 6.67 hours

(3) 11.11 hours (4) 8.89 hours

(5) None of these

47. Three vessels having volumes in the ratio of 1 : 2 : 3 are full of a mixture of coke and soda. In the first vessel, ratio of coke and soda is 2 : 3, in second 3 : 7 and in third 1 : 4. If the liquid in all the three vessels were mixed in a bigger container, then what is the resulting ratio of coke and soda?

(1) 4 : 11 (2) 5 : 7

(3) 7 : 11 (4) 11 : 4

(5) 7 : 5

48. The ratio of present ages of father and son is 4 : 1. After 5 years, the ratio between their ages will become 7 : 2. What is the present age of the son?

(1) 29 years (2) 27 years

(3) 24 years (4) 25 years

(5) 28 years

49. A field is in the form of an equilateral triangle with side 600 m. Three cows are tied to the three poles at the three vertices of this triangular field with ropes of length 100m, 200m and 300m respectively. What is the area of the field that they can graze?

(1) 70,000 m^2 (2) 2,20,000 m^2

(3) 2,10,000 m^2 (4) $\dfrac{2,20,000}{3}$ m^2

(5) None of these

50. A dice is rolled and a coin is tossed. Find the probability that the dice shows a prime number and the coin shows a head.

(1) $\dfrac{1}{4}$ (2) $\dfrac{1}{2}$

(3) $\dfrac{3}{4}$ (4) 1

(5) None of these

Directions (Q. 51 to 55): Answer the following questions based on the given information.

The given table shows the number of students appeared (A) and failed (F) in five classes of a school over the years

Year	Classes									
	VIII		IX		X		XI		XII	
	A	F	A	F	A	F	A	F	A	F
2008	68	12	67	09	75	11	84	07	78	09
2009	65	19	70	11	63	08	69	05	79	12
2010	75	06	62	13	69	07	70	06	65	17
2011	79	12	76	10	67	13	81	05	74	08
2012	63	10	87	14	82	12	64	16	63	12
2013	72	15	66	04	74	15	70	07	82	04
2014	60	05	60	07	77	05	71	06	75	06

51. What is the total number of failed students from class X for the given years?

(1) 77 (2) 83

(3) 68 (4) 71

(5) None of these

52. What is the ratio of the total number of passed students to total number of failed students for the year 2011?

(1) 139 : 24 (2) 239 : 48

(3) 90 : 11 (4) 325 : 42

(5) None of these

53. Which of the following class has the minimum number of failed students over the years?

(1) VIII (2) IX

(3) X (4) XI

(5) XII

54. What is the number of passed students, for all the classes together in the year 2013?

(1) 319 (2) 337

(3) 350 (4) 326

(5) None of these

55. What is the overall percentage of passed students over appeared of class XI from all the years together (rounded off to two digits after decimal)?

(1) 75.95

(2) 81.36

(3) 79.53

(4) 86.94

(5) 89.78

56. The simple interest obtained on a certain principal is Rs.2,000 in five years at the rate of 4% per annum. What would be the compound interest obtained on same principal at same rate in two years?

(1) Rs.716 (2) Rs.724

(3) Rs.824 (4) Rs.800

(5) Rs.816

57. Two candidates were in fray in an election.Out of the total votes cast, 15% were declared invalid. The winning candidate received 56% of the total valid votes. If the total number of votes received by losing candidate was 11968, then what was the total number of invalid votes cast in the election?

(1) 5200   (2) 3200

(3) 2032   (4) 9600

(5) 4800

58. When Sakshi increases her speed from 24 km/hr to 30 km/hr she takes one hour less than the time taken at 24 km/hr to cover a certain distance. What is the distance covered by Sakshi?

(1) 240 km   (2) 160 km

(3) 120 km   (4) 90 km

(5) None of these

59. In a Kouton's showroom according to a scheme if a person buys 13 jeans, then he/she will get 5 jeans free. What percentage discount is being offered?

(1) 38.46%   (2) 27.77%

(3) 22.22%   (4) 30.76%

(5) 72.22%

60. Three-fourth part of a tank is filled with water. 50% of the water is removed from the tank and 60 litres of pure milk is added to it. If now the ratio of milk-water in the tank becomes 5 : 4, then the capacity of the tank will be:

(1) 120 litres

(2) 128 litres

(3) 112 litres

(4) 136 litres

(5) None of these

Directions (Q. 61 to 65) : What approximate value should come in place of the question mark (?) in the following questions? (Note: You are not expected to calculate the exact value)

61. 22.005% of 449.999 =?

(1) 85   (2) 100

(3) 125   (4) 75

(5) 150

62. 5554.999 ÷ 50.007 = ?

(1) 110   (2) 150

(3) 200   (4) 50

(5) 125

63. $(18.001)^3$ = ?

(1) 5830   (2) 5500

(3) 6000   (4) 6480

(5) 5240

64. 23.001 × 18.999 × 7.998 = ?

(1) 4200   (2) 3000

(3) 3500   (4) 4000

(5) 2500

65. 9999 ÷ 99 ÷ 9 = ?

(1) 18   (2) 15

(3) 6   (4) 11

(5) 20

REASONING ABILITY

Directions (Q. 66 to 70): Answer the following questions based on the given information.

Anuja, Ben, Chahal, Daman, Ekta and Falak are six representatives from different countries, China, India, Brazil, Russia, Canada and Spain, not necessarily in the same order. Each one is scheduled to represent his country on a different day of the week from, Monday to Saturday.

The one who is from Russia is scheduled to represent his country, on Thursday. Daman represents his country on Tuesday. Aanuja is from China but represents neither on Wednesday nor on Saturday. Chahal represents neither Russia nor India but has scheduled his day on Friday. Ben is from Brazil and Ekta is from Spain.

66. Who is from Canada?

(1) Falak   (2) Chahal

(3) Daman   (4) Either Chahal or Falak

(5) None of these

67. Who is scheduled to represent his country on the day after Daman represents his country?

(1) Ben   (2) Ekta

(3) Falak   (4) Anuja

(5) None of these

68. Which of the following combinations is correct?

(1) Daman-India

(2) Chahal-Canada

(3) Falak-Thursday

(4) China-Monday

(5) All are correct

69. If Falak is related to Chahal in a certain way, then with whom Anuja is related?

(1) Ekta

(2) Daman

(3) Ben

(4) Chahal

(5) None of these

70. Which country was represented four days after China was represented ?

(1) Brazil　　　　(2) India

(3) Canada　　　　(4) Spain

(5) None of these

Directions (Q. 71 to 75): In the following questions the symbols $\times$, @, +, $*$ and $ are used with following meaning as illustrated below:

P $\times$ Q means 'P is neither less than nor greater than Q'.

P @ Q means 'P is neither greater than nor equal to Q'.

P + Q means 'P is neither less than nor equal to Q'.

P $*$ Q means 'P is not greater than Q'.

P $ Q means 'P is not less than Q'.

Based on the statements given in each of the questions below, find out which of the conclusion follows.

Mark the answer as:

(1) If only conclusion I follows.

(2) If only conclusion II follows.

(3) If conclusion I as well as conclusion II follow.

(4) If either conclusion I or conclusion II follows.

(5) If neither conclusion I nor conclusion II follows.

71. Statement : D * F, M $ F, M @ K

Conclusion:

I. K $ F

II. K + D

72. Statement: K + M, M @ R, R $\times$ T

Conclusion:

I. M @ T

II. K $\times$ T

73. Statement: T @ M, M * R, R $\times$ N

Conclusion:

I. M $\times$ N

II. M @ N

74. Statement: B $ N, N $\times$ R, R + T

Conclusion:

I. B $ R

II. T @ N

75. Statement: N $\times$ P, K + P, Q @ K

Conclusion

I. K * N

II. Q + N

Directions for questions 76 to 80 : Study the following information to answer the given questions.

Eight people are sitting in two parallel rows containing four people each, in such a way that there is an equal distance between adjacent persons. In row 1, Akash, Bhuvan, Chinmoy and Dinesh are seated (but not necessarily in the same order) and all of them are facing south. In row 2, Pawan, Qazim, Ram and Samar are seated (but not necessarily in the same order) and all of them are facing north.

Therefore, in the given sitting arrangement each member seated in a row faces another member of the other row.

Ram sits second to the left of the person who faces Akash. Samar is an immediate neighbor of Ram. Only one person sits between Akash and Dinesh. One of the immediate neighbor of Chinmoy faces Qazim. Bhuvan does not sit at any of the extreme ends of the line.

76. Who amongst the following sits second to the right of the person who faces Pawan?

(1) Akash　　　　(2) Bhuvan

(3) Chinmoy　　　　(4) Dinesh

(5) Cannot be determined.

77. Four of the following five are alike in a certain way based on the given seating arrangement and thus form a group. Which is the one that does not belong to that group?

(1) Chinmoy　　　　(2) Ram

(3) Qazim　　　　(4) Pawan

(5) Dinesh

78. Which of the following is true regarding Chinmoy?

(1) Chinmoy sits second to the right of Dinesh.

(2) Akash sits on the immediate right of Chinmoy.

(3) Samar faces Chinmoy.

(4) Dinesh is an immediate neighbor of Chinmoy.

(5) The person who faces Chinmoy is an immediate neighbor of Ram.

79. Who amongst the following faces Ram?

(1) Akash　　　　(2) Bhuvan

(3) Chinmoy　　　　(4) Dinesh

(5) Cannot be determined.

80. Who amongst the following faces Bhuvan?

(1) Pawan　　　　(2) Qazim

(3) Ram　　　　(4) Samar

(5) Cannot be determined

Directions (Q. 81 to 85): Study the following information to answer the given questions:

In a certain code "new banking systems" is coded as "ss tp na", "officer in uniform" is coded as "or mu at", "new bank officer" is coded as "or bk na", and "systems in bank" is coded as "bk at ss".

81. What does "bk" stand for?

(1) New　　　　(2) Systems

(3) Officer　　　　(4) In

(5) None of these

82. What will be the code for "ss mu"?

(1) Banking officer

(2) Officer systems

(3) Uniform banking

(4) In systems

(5) Uniform systems

83. How will "new officer" be coded?

(1) or na   (2) tp na

(3) na at   (4) tp or

(5) ss at

84. How will "bank officer in uniform" be coded?

(1) ss na at or   (2) bk at or mu

(3) ss nab k at   (4) at mu ss or

(5) bk ss mu na

85. What is the code for "in"?

(1) ss   (2) or

(3) at   (4) mu

(5) None of these

Directions for questions 86 to 90: Study the following information and answer the question which follow.

L, N, P, R, M, Q, T and Y are the members of a committee sitting around a circular table and facing away from the centre. Each member has a different zodiac sign, viz Leo, Virgo, Libra, Cancer, Aries, Gemini, Pisces and Scorpio, but not necessarily in the same order. T is third to the right of P. The one whose sun-sign is Leo is second to the left of the one whose sun-sign is Libra. Y's sun-sign is Libra and only he is sitting between P and L. The one whose sun-sign is Pisces sits second to the right of N. The one whose sun-sign is Aries is second to the right of the person whose sun-sign is Gemini. P sits third to the left of the person whose sun-sign is Virgo. Neither Q nor L is the immediate neighbour of N. Q is fourth to the left of L. N's sun-sign is neither Gemini nor Aries. The person whose sun-sign is Leo is sitting second to the right of the person whose sign is Cancer. R's sun-sign is Leo and is not an immediate neighbor of N.

86. Which of the following is N's sun-sign?

(1) Pisces

(2) Libra

(3) Gemini

(4) Cancer

(5) None of these

87. Who sits third to the right of L?

(1) P   (2) Y

(3) R   (4) M

(5) None of these

88. What is Y's position with respect to Q?

(1) Third to the right

(2) Fourth to the left

(3) Second to the right

(4) Third to the left

(5) 2nd to the left

89. How many persons are there between P and N?

(1) None   (2) Two

(3) Three   (4) Four

(5) None of these

90. Which of the following combinations is true?

(1) M- Aries   (2) P- Gemini

(3) N- Virgo   (4) Q - Leo

(5) All are true

91. Pointing to the photograph of a girl, a man said, " I am the youngest son of her grandmother." There are not marriages between blood relatives in the family. Which among the given options cannot be a relation between the man and the girl?

I. Father-Daughter

II. Brother-Sister

III. Uncle-Niece

IV. Grandfather-Granddaughter

V. Nephew-Aunt

(1) I and III   (2) Only I

(3) Only II, III and IV   (4) II, IV and V

(5) Only II

Directions (Q. 92 and 93): Answer the questions on the basis of the information given below.

If 'A × B' means 'A is wife of B'.

If 'A + B' means 'A is brother of B'.

If 'A ÷ B' means 'A is daughter of B'.

If 'A – B' means 'A is son of B'.

92. Which of the following means 'D is father of A'?

(1) A - B × C + D

(2) D + C – B × A

(3) A + B ÷ C × D

(4) D + B × C – A

(5) None of these

93. How is F related to J if 'F – G ÷ H × J' holds true?

(1) Son

(2) Grandson

(3) Son-in-law

(4) Father

(5) Grandfather

Directions for questions 94 and 95: Study the given information carefully and answer the given questions.

Sunil started walking from point A. He walked 6 metres towards East to reach point B. From point B he took a right turn and walked 3 metres to reach point C. From point C he took a right turn and walked 10 metres to reach point D, from point D he took a left turn and walked 4 metres to reach point E. From point E, he walked 4 metres East to reach point F. point G is exactly midway between point C and point D.

94. If Sunil walks 4 metres to the North of point F, how far and in which direction will he be from point G?

    (1) 1 metre towards East
    (2) 2 metres towards East
    (3) 1 metre towards West
    (4) 2 metres towards West
    (5) 1.5 metres towards East

95. How far and in which direction is point F from point A?

    (1) 7 metres towards North
    (2) 2 metres towards South
    (3) 8 metres towards South
    (4) 6 metres towards North
    (5) None of these

Directions (Q. 96 to 100): In each question below are three statements followed by two conclusions numbered I and II. You have to take the three given statements to be true even if they seem to be at variance from commonly known facts and then decide which of the given conclusions logically follows from the three statements disregarding commonly known facts.

Give answer (1) if only conclusion I follows.

Give answer (2) if only conclusion II follows.

Give answer (3) if either conclusion I or II follows.

Give answer (4) if neither conclusion I nor II follows.

Give answer (5) if both conclusions I and II follow.

96. **Statements:**
    Some computers are televisions.
    Some televisions are radios.
    All radios are mobiles.
    Conclusions:
    I. No mobile is a computer:
    II. Some computers are mobiles.

97. **Statements:**
    Some squares are circles.
    All circles are rectangles.
    Some rectangles are cones.
    Conclusions:
    I. Some cones are squares.
    II. Some squares are rectangles.

98. **Statements:**
    All letters are words.
    Some pages are words.
    All pages are books.
    Conclusions:
    I. Some words are books.
    II. Some pages are letters.

99. **Statements:**
    All walls are floors.
    All floors are ceilings.
    All ceilings are roofs.
    Conclusions:
    I. All walls are ceilings. .
    II. All floors are roofs.

100. **Statements:**
    Some trees are leaves.
    Some leaves are roots
    Some roots are flowers.
    Conclusions:
    I. Some roots are trees.
    II. Some leaves are flowers.

ANSWERS

1. (1)	**2.** (4)	**3.** (3)	**4.** (3)	**5.** (5)	**6.** (1)	**7.** (5)	**8.** (4)	**9.** (5)	**10.** (1)
11. (4)	**12.** (3)	**13.** (2)	**14.** (1)	**15.** (5)	**16.** (2)	**17.** (5)	**18.** (5)	**19.** (5)	**20.** (3)
21. (3)	**22.** (5)	**23.** (3)	**24.** (2)	**25.** (4)	**26.** (4)	**27.** (1)	**28.** (2)	**29.** (2)	**30.** (5)
31. (1)	**32.** (3)	**33.** (2)	**34.** (5)	**35.** (5)	**36.** (1)	**37.** (5)	**38.** (1)	**39.** (4)	**40.** (3)
41. (1)	**42.** (1)	**43.** (5)	**44.** (4)	**45.** (4)	**46.** (4)	**47.** (1)	**48.** (4)	**49.** (4)	**50.** (1)
51. (4)	**52.** (5)	**53.** (4)	**54.** (1)	**55.** (5)	**56.** (5)	**57.** (5)	**58.** (3)	**59.** (2)	**60.** (2)
61. (2)	**62.** (1)	**63.** (1)	**64.** (3)	**65.** (4)	**66.** (2)	**67.** (4)	**68.** (5)	**69.** (2)	**70.** (3)
71. (2)	**72.** (1)	**73.** (4)	**74.** (3)	**75.** (5)	**76.** (2)	**77.** (3)	**78.** (2)	**79.** (4)	**80.** (4)
81. (5)	**82.** (5)	**83.** (1)	**84.** (2)	**85.** (3)	**86.** (5)	**87.** (4)	**88.** (1)	**89.** (3)	**90.** (2)
91. (1)	**92.** (3)	**93.** (2)	**94.** (3)	**95.** (5)	**96.** (3)	**97.** (2)	**98.** (1)	**99.** (5)	**100.** (4)

EXPLANATIONS

1. 1   Replace 'time' with 'when'.

2. 4   Preposition 'in' is incorrect. 'At' should be used.

3. 3   'Several' should be replaced by 'some'.

4. 3   Delete 'being'.

5. 5   The sentence is grammatically correct.

6. 1   'Problem' and 'while' are the most appropriate words for the two blanks.

7. 5   'There' and 'could' are the only words that rightly fit the blanks.

8. 4   'Had' and 'in' are the correct words for the blanks.

9. 5   'Was' and 'happen' are the only words that rightly fill the blanks respectively.

10. 1   'Were' and 'this' are the most appropriate options.

11. 4   Refer to the first sentence of the second paragraph for the answer where the author cites that Research and Development and Innovation are appropriate response to the economic, social and environmental challenges of the 21stcentury.

12. 3   The author is incisive in his observations. Incisive refers to being analytical.

13. 2   The entire passage talks about the importance of Research and Development or R and D.The author quotes figures and data to substantiate that R and D plays a pivotal part in the economic growth of a country.

14. 1   The passage is most likely taken from an Economics journal. The passage is scholarly and the author mentions a number of illustrative examples. Therefore, it can be inferred that the passage is an excerpt from a journal article. The topic discussed in the passage is essentially related to Economics.

15. 5   Refer to the third paragraph for the answer. The author quotes figures to show that European Union spends less than USA, Japan and South Korea. Option (1) is wrong in the light of the third paragraph where the author states that the European Union has lesser privately funded R and Ds than the US. Option (2) is wrong in the light of the fourth paragraph.

16. 2   Refer to the ending of the second paragraph and the beginning of the third paragraph. The author mentions that EU's poor innovation performance is because of low investments in R and D. The other options are out of scope.

21. 3   'Discussing' is the correct word.

22. 5   'Received' is the right word in the context of the sentence.

23. 3   Dynamite causes destruction.

24. 2   'Grateful' makes sense.

25. 4   Nobel donated his wealth.

26. 4   The correct sequence would be BEAFDC.

31. 1
$$? = \sqrt{360 - 225 \times 2 + 379}$$
$$= \sqrt{360 - 450 + 379} = 17$$

32. 3
$$(9)^3 \times 81^2 \div 27^3 = (3)^?$$
$$(3)^? = \frac{9 \times 9 \times 9 \times 81 \times 81}{27 \times 27 \times 27} = 243 = (3)^5$$
$$\Rightarrow ? = 5$$

33. 2
$$572 \div 26 \times 12 - 200 = (2)^?$$
$$\Rightarrow (2)^? = 64 = (2)^6$$
$$\Rightarrow ? = 6$$

34. 5
$$4\frac{1}{2} - 2\frac{5}{6} = ? - 1\frac{7}{12}$$
$$\Rightarrow ? = \frac{9}{2} - \frac{17}{6} + \frac{19}{12}$$
$$\Rightarrow ? = 3\frac{3}{12}$$

35. 5   36% of 245 - 40% of 210 = 10 -?

$$\Rightarrow ? = 10 - \frac{36}{100} \times 245 + \frac{40}{100} \times 210$$

$$\Rightarrow ? = 10 - 88.2 + 84 = 5.8$$

36. 1   Total expenditure in May = 31 × 10 = Rs. 310

Total expenditure in June = 30 × 14 = Rs. 420

Total expenditure in July = 31 × 15 = Rs. 465

$$\therefore \text{Sanya's daily expenditure} = \frac{310 + 420 + 465}{31 + 30 + 31}$$

$$= \frac{1195}{92} = \text{Rs. } 13.$$

37. 5   Clapton is half as efficient as Eric, so he will take twice the time taken by Eric i.e 80 days to complete the job.

Let the job consists of 80 units of work.

Thus, work done by Eric and Clapton in 1 day will be 2 units and 1 unit respectively. Now, in every two days they will complete 3 units.

Hence, 80 units of work will be completed in $= \dfrac{80}{3}$

= 26 pair of days + 1 day = (26 × 2 + 1) = 53 days.

38. 1   Sugar in water = 20% of 100 = 20 litres.

When water evaporates sugar remains 20 liters and takes up the 80% of the solution.

Quantity of solution remains $= 20 \times \dfrac{100}{80} = 25$ litres

$\therefore$ Water in the solution = 25 − 20 = 5 litres.

Hence, the amount of water evaporated = 80 − 5 = 75 litres

39. 4   Dividing the given ratio by 3 (LCM of 1.5 and 3), we get

$$\frac{a}{2} = b = \frac{c}{3}$$

Let $\dfrac{a}{2} = b = \dfrac{c}{3} = k$.

a = 2k, b = k and c = 3k.

$$\Rightarrow a = \frac{2k}{6k} \times 225 = 75, \ b = \frac{k}{6k} \times 225 = 37.5 \text{ and}$$

$$c = \frac{3k}{6k} \times 225 = 112.5$$

Hence, among the given options only (c − b) will have integer value.

40. 3   Total distance covered = 10 + 12 = 22 km

$$\text{Total time taken} = \frac{10}{12} + \frac{12}{10} \text{ hr}$$

$$\text{Average speed} = \frac{22}{\dfrac{10}{12} + \dfrac{12}{10}} = \frac{22 \times 60}{122} = 10.81 \text{ km/hr.}$$

41. 1   The series is as follows:

108 + 120 = 228

228 + 60 = 288

228 + 30 = 318

318 + 15 = 333

333 + 7.5 = 340.5

340.5 + 3.75 = 344.25(?)

42. 1   The series is as follows:

320 − 35 = 285

285 − 28 = 257

257 − 21 = 236

236 − 14 = 222

222 − 7 = 215(?)

43. 5   The series is as follows:

$7^3 + 2 = 345$

$6^3 + 3 = 219$

$5^3 + 4 = 129$

$4^3 + 5 = 69$

$3^3 + 6 = 33(?)$

44. 4   The series is as follows:

$2^3 − 2 = 6$

$3^3 − 3 = 24$

$4^3 − 4 = 60$

$5^3 − 5 = 120$

$6^3 − 6 = 210$

$7^3 − 7 = 336(?)$

45. 4   The series is as follows:

2 × 4 = 8

8 × 3.5 = 28

28 × 3 = 84

84 × 2.5 = 210

210 × 2 = 420(?)

46. 4   If A finishes a job in 20 hours, time taken by B and C working together to finish the same job

$$= \frac{4}{5} \times 20 \text{ hours} = 16 \text{ hours}$$

$$\text{A's one hour work} = \frac{1}{20}$$

$$\text{(B + C)'s one hour work} = \frac{1}{16}$$

$$\text{So (A + B + C)'s one hour work} = \frac{1}{20} + \frac{1}{16} = \frac{9}{80}$$

Hence, time taken when all three work together

$$= \frac{80}{9} \text{ hours} = 8.89 \text{ hours.}$$

47. 1 Let the capacity of the vessels be 10 litre, 20 litre and 30 litre.

Quantity of coke in the first vessel = 4 litre

Quantity of coke in the second vessel = 6 litre

Quantity of coke in the third vessel = 6 litre

∴ Total coke in the bigger container

= (4 + 6 + 6) = 16 litre

∴ Ratio of coke to soda = $\dfrac{16}{44}$ = $\dfrac{4}{11}$

48. 4 Let present age of son be 'x' years.

So present age of father is '4x' years.

After 5 years,

$\dfrac{(x + 5)}{(4x + 5)} = \dfrac{2}{7}$

$\Rightarrow 7x + 35 = 8x + 10$

$\Rightarrow x = 25$ years.

49. 4 Area grazed by the cow tied with 100 m

rope $= \dfrac{1}{6} \times \pi \times 10000$ m^2 (Each cow will make an arc of

60°, so the area of the field grazed by the cows in

all the three cases will be $\dfrac{1}{6}$th of the area of circle)

Area grazed by the cow tied with 200m rope

$= \dfrac{1}{6} \times \pi \times 40000$ m^2

Area grazed by the cow tied with 300m rope

$= \dfrac{1}{6} \times \pi \times 90000$ m^2

Therefore, the total area grazed by all the three cows within the perimeter of this

triangle $= \dfrac{1}{6} \times 140000 \pi$ m^2 $= \dfrac{220000}{3}$ m^2 .

50. 1 The probability will be $= \dfrac{3}{6} \times \dfrac{1}{2} = \dfrac{1}{4}$.

51. 4 Total number of failed students from class X

= 11 + 8 + 7 + 13 + 12 + 15 + 5 = 71

52. 5 Required ratio = (67 + 66 + 54 + 76 + 66) : (12 + 10 + 13 + 5 + 8) = 329 : 48

53. 4 Number of failed students for class VIII

= 12 + 19 + 6 + 12 + 10 + 15 + 5 = 79

Number of failed students for class IX

= 9 + 11 + 13 + 10 + 14 + 4 + 7 = 68

Number of failed students for class X

= 11 + 8 + 7 + 13 + 12 + 15 + 5 = 71

Number of failed students for class XI

= 7 + 5 + 6 + 5 + 16 + 7 + 6 = 52

Number of failed students for class XII

= 9 + 12 + 17 + 8 + 12 + 4 + 6 = 68

54. 1 Number of passed students = 57 + 62 + 59 + 63 + 78 = 319

55. 5 Required percentage = $\dfrac{457}{509} \times 100 = 89.78\%$

56. 5 Principal $= \dfrac{SI \times 100}{Time \times Rate} = \dfrac{2000 \times 100}{5 \times 4} = Rs.10,000$

∴ CI for two years

$= 10000 \left(1 + \dfrac{4}{100}\right)^2 - 10000 = Rs.816.$

57. 5 Let the total number of votes cast in the election be n.

Number of invalid votes = 0.15n

Number of valid votes = n − 0.15n = 0.85n

Number of valid votes received by the losing candidate = 0.85n × (1 − 0.56) = 0.374n

$\Rightarrow 0.374n = 11968$

$\Rightarrow n = 32000$

Number of invalid votes cast in the election

= 32000 × 0.15 = 4800.

58. 3 Speed increased to 30 km/hr from 24 km/hr, i.e.,

becomes $\dfrac{5}{4}$ times. Hence time taken will becomes

$\dfrac{4}{5}$ of the time taken at 24 km/hr

Let the time taken at 24 km/hr be T hours.

So, $T - \dfrac{4}{5} T = 1,$ T = 5 hours.

∴ Distance travelled in 5 hours = 5 × 24 = 120 km.

59. 2 Let in case of no discount the cost of 18 jeans is Rs. 18x. But, due to scheme, one can buy 18 jeans for Rs. 13x.

Hence, discount offered $= \dfrac{5x}{18x} \times 100 = 27.77\%$.

60. 2 As the new ratio of milk and water is 5 : 4.

The quantity of milk = 60 litre and hence the quantity of water has to be 48 litre.

Now, $\dfrac{1}{2}$ of $\dfrac{3}{4}$th of the capacity of tank = 48 litre

So, capacity of the tank $= \dfrac{48 \times 4 \times 2}{3} = 128$ litres

61. 2 ? = 22.005% of 449.999

$\approx 22\%$ of 450

$= \dfrac{22}{100} \times 450$

$= 99 \approx 100$

62. 1 $? = 5554.999 \div 50.007$

$$\approx \frac{5555}{50} = 111.1 \approx 110$$

63. 1 $? = (18.001)^3$

$$\approx 18^3 = 5832 \approx 5830$$

64. 3 $? = 23.001 \times 18.999 \times 7.998$

$$\approx 23 \times 19 \times 8 = 3496 \approx 3500$$

65. 4 $? = 9999 \div 99 \div 9$

$$= 11.22 \approx 11$$

For solution 66 to 70:

Representatives	Day	Country
Anuja	Monday	China
Ben	Saturday/Wednesday	Brazil
Chahal	Friday	Canada
Daman	Tuesday	India
Ekta	Wednesday/Saturday	Spain
Falak	Thursday	Russia

71. 2 $D \leq F, M \geq F, M < K$

$$\Rightarrow D \leq F \leq M < K$$

Conclusion I: $K \geq F$ does not follow.

Conclusion II: K > D follows.

∴ Conclusion II follows.

72. 1 $K > M, M < R, R = T$

$$\Rightarrow K > M \text{ and } M < R = T$$

Conclusion I: M < T follows.

Conclusion II: K = T does not follow.

∴ Conclusion I follows.

73. 4 $T < M, M \leq R, R = N$

$$\Rightarrow T < M \leq R = N$$

Conclusion I: M = N may or not follow.

Conclusion II: M < N may or may not follow.

∴ Either conclusion I or conclusion II follows.

74. 3 $B \geq N, N = R, R > T$

$$\Rightarrow B \geq N = R > T$$

Conclusion I: $B \geq R$ follows.

Conclusion II: T < N follows.

∴ Both conclusions follow.

75. 5 $N = P, K > P, Q < K$

$$\Rightarrow N = P < K \text{ and } Q < K$$

Conclusion I: $K \leq N$ does not follow

Conclusion II: Q > N does not follow.

∴ Neither conclusion I nor conclusion II follows.

Directions for questions 76 to 80:

77. 3 All others are sitting at extreme ends.

(81-85):

new banking systems → ss tp na   … (i)

officer in uniform → or mu at   … (ii)

new bank officer → or bk na   … (iii)

systems in bank → bk at ss   … (iv)

From (i) and (iv), systems → ss   … (v)

From (ii) and (iii), officer → or   … (vi)

From (ii) and (iv), in → at   … (vii)

From (iii) and (iv), bank → bk   … (viii)

From (i) and (iii), new → na   … (ix)

From (ii), (vi) and (vii), uniform → mu   … (x)

From (i), (v) and (ix), banking → tp   … (xi)

new	in	bank	banking	uniform	systems	officer
na	at	bk	tp	mu	ss	or

For question 86 to 90: Sitting arrangement

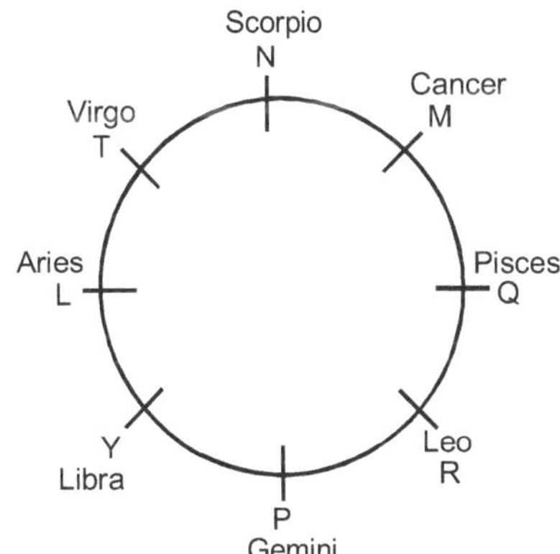

91. 1 There is gap of one generation, so it can either be uncle-niece or father-daughter.

92. 3 $A - B \times C + D \Rightarrow$ A is son of B, who is wife of C , who is brother of D

$D + C - B \times A \Rightarrow$ D is brother of C , who is son of B , who is wife of A.

$A + B \div C \times D \Rightarrow$ A is brother of B, who is daughter of C ,who is wife of D.

$D + B \times C - A \Rightarrow$ D is brother of B, who is wife of C, who is son of A.

Option (3) is the correct answer .

93. 2 $F - G \div H \times J \Rightarrow$ F is son of G , who is daughter of H, who is wife of J.

F is grandson of J.

94. 3 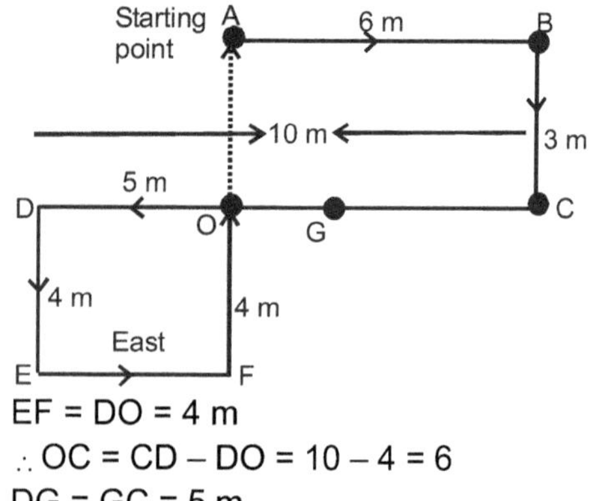

EF = DO = 4 m

∴ OC = CD – DO = 10 – 4 = 6

DG = GC = 5 m

∴ OG = OC – GC = 6 – 5 = 1 metre west

95. 5   FA = OF + OA (OF and AO = BC_) = 4 + 3 = 7 metres

F is 7 m south of Point A.

96. 3 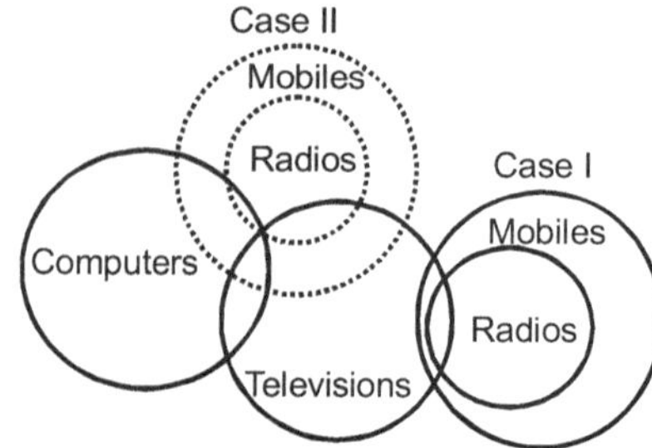

97. 2 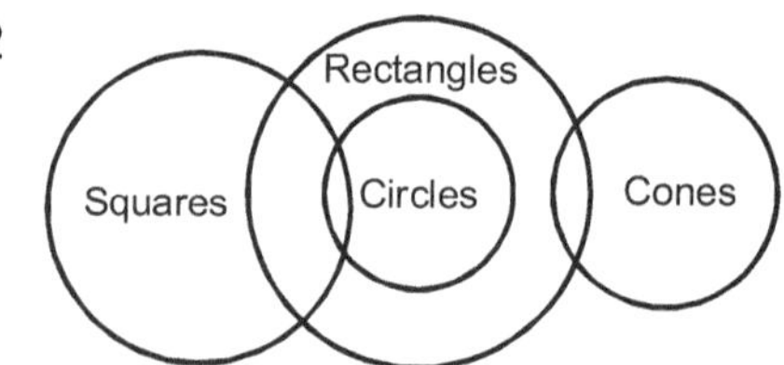

98. 1 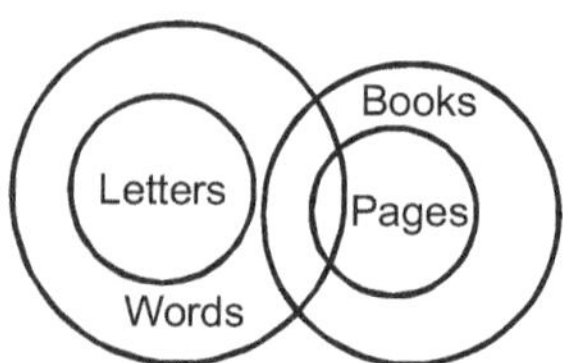

99. 5 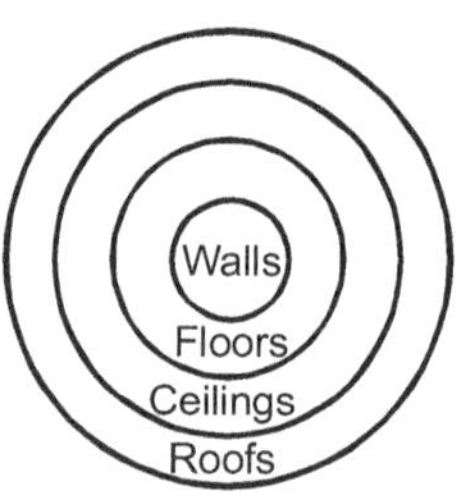

100. 4

PRACTICE PAPER – 20

ENGLISH LANGUAGE

Directions (Q. 1 to 5): In the following passage there are blanks, each of which has been numbered. These numbers are printed below the passage and against each, five words are suggested, one of which fits the blank appropriately. Find out the appropriate word in each case.

A hound, who in the days of his youth and strength had never __ (1) _____ to any beast of the forest, __(2)______ in his old age a boar in the chase. He seized him boldly __(3)__ the ear, but could not retain his hold because of the decay of his teeth, so that the boar escaped. His master, quickly coming up, was very much disappointed, and fiercely abused the dog. The hound looked __ (4)__ and said: "It was not my fault, master; my spirit was as good as ever, but I could not help my infirmities. I rather deserve to be praised for what I have been, than to be __(5)____ for what I am."

1. (1) Yielded   (2) Rejected
   (3) Accepted   (4) Confirmed
   (5) Met
2. (1) Fled   (2) Ran
   (3) Swift   (4) Deserved
   (5) Encountered
3. (1) On   (2) By
   (3) And   (4) To
   (5) In
4. (1) At   (2) In
   (3) Of   (4) Off
   (5) Up
5. (1) Accuse   (2) Implicate
   (3) Blamed   (4) Blame
   (5) Blames

Directions (Q. 6 to 10): In each question below a sentence with four words printed in bold type is given. These are numbered as (1), (2),(3) and (4). One of these four boldly printed words may be either wrongly spelt or inappropriate in the context of the sentence. Find out the word which is *wrongly spelt or inappropriate*, if any. The number of that word is your answer. If all the boldly printed words are correctly spelt and also appropriate in the context of the sentence, mark (5), i.e. 'All Correct', as your answer.

6. In order to **curtale (1)** the **substantial (2)** export of iron ore **recently (3)** the government has **imposed (4)** an export tax. / All correct (5)

7. **Several (1) mediam (2)** and small **sized (3)** companies successfully **survived (4)** the global financial crisis of 2008. / All correct (5)

8. One of the **tangible (1) benefits (2)** of **appearing (3)** for a loan under this scheme is the interest rate **concessions (4)**. / All correct (5)

9. With **effect (1)** from April, non-banking finance companies with good **performances (2)** may be **granted (3)** licences to **convert (4)** into banks. / All correct (5)

10. In 2009, the **largest (1) remittances (2)** sent to India were from **oversees (3)** Indians **living (4)** in North America. / All correct (5)

Directions (Q. 11 to 20): Read the following passage carefully and answer the questions given below it. Certain words/phrases have been printed in bold to help you locate them while answering some of the questions.

Once a rich merchant presented a beautiful cat to the Emperor of China. Eventually, the emperor became fond of the animal and took it with him wherever he went. Everywhere, people kept asking the emperor, what was the cat named and everyone was **surprised,** when told that it had no name. As time **progressed**, the emperor realised that the cat should have a name. Thus he decided to find a suitable name for his pet. He called his ministers, the seven wisest men in his empire and commanded them to find a suitable name within seven days. The ministers were warned that if they did not succeed in finding a name by the end of seven days, they would be punished. Also, the minister whose suggestion would be accepted would received hundred gold pieces.

The ministers did a lot of research on names that would suit the emperor's favourite pet. At the of this period, they was **summoned** to the place again, and asked for their suggestions. The youngest of the group thought he had found the perfect name. "TIGER!" he announced proudly, "your majesty, as we all know tigers are powerful animal, it will be the best name for your pet cat." "Good name", said the emperor, after a moment's **reflection**. "The tiger is not only a noble and powerful beast but it is also known as the cat's cousin," added the emperor.

"Noble, perhaps", said the second minister, "but it is not as powerful as the dragon. Can a tiger soar into the sky? No but a dragon can! I think DRAGON would be a more suitable name for the cat." As the emperor was contemplating the name DRAGON, the third minister said, "Clouds can go higher than dragons. A cloud is more powerful than a dragon. "let's call it CLOUD". "Let's not be hasty", advised the fourth wise man "Cloud may fly high but they are ushed around by winds. Winds are more powerful than clouds. WIND would be the most appropriate name for a great emperor's pet." The emperor was still not satisfied with the suggestions. "WIND?" said the emperor doubtfully. "Isn't there anything better?" The fifth wise man took this opportunity to give his suggestion. "BRICK WALL!" The king **exclaimed**. "Why should I name my cat BRICK WALL?" "Well BRICK WALL, is not a bad name. But isn't it a bit long?" The fifth minister replied, "A brick wall can stop the winds". "I have a shorter name," said the sixth minister, "RAT". Everyone started laughing at his suggestion. "So you suggest that I must call my cat RAT?" The sixth minister replied, "Yes, Your Majesty, RAT! A rat can eat through a brick wall, which makes it more powerful than the wall, more powerful than the wind, more powerful than all the suggestions given to you." "I get your point," interrupted the emperor, "but can you call a cat, RAT?"

"Indeed you can't!" piped up the seventh wise man who was the eldest among all seven. "A cat is a cat. How can one call cat RAT? Also if a rat is more powerful than the other the cat is even more so because it is mightier than the rat." The emperor was impressed with the seventh minister's suggestion and decided to accept it. So the royal pet remained nameless in a way because from then on it was simply called CAT. But the minister who suggested this name was rewarded as promised.

11. Why did people get surprised wherever the emperor went?

(1) Because the emperor had a nameless cat.

(2) Because the emperor took his cat wherever he went.

(3) Because the emperor took a bath wherever he went

(4) Because the emperor got a cat as a present.

(5) None of these

12. Why did the emperor not want to name his cat BRICK WALL?

(1) He did not like brick walls.

(2) Brick walls are rough and hard but cats are not.

(3) BRICK WALL is a very long name.

(4) He already had a pet called BRICK WALL.

(5) He felt BRICK WALL was a very funny name.

13. Why was the cat named CAT at last?

A. The seventh minister proved that a cat was greater than all the other names that were suggested.

B. The emperor was impressed with the seventh minister's suggestion

C. It was a unique name and the emperor had never heard

(1) All A, B and C   (2) Only A

(3) Only B   (4) Only C

(5) Both A and B

14. Which of the following statements is TRUE according to the passage

A. Dragon can blow the clouds away.

B. Winds can blow the clouds away.

C. Brick walls can stop the winds.

(1) Both A and B   (2) Both B and C

(3) Only A   (4) Only B

(5) Only C

15. What reason did the first minister give for his suggestion?

(1) Tigers are powerful creatures.

(2) Tigers are the most dangerous of all creatures.

(3) Tigers resemble cats.

(4) Tiger sounds royal and majestic.

(5) Tiger sounds better than any other name.

Directions (Q.16 to 18): Choose the word/group of words which is most similar in the meaning to the word/group of words printed in bold as used in the passage.

16. Surprised

(1) Presented   (2) Unaware

(3) Appalled   (4) Astonished

(5) Disgusted

17. Exclaimed

(1) Announced   (2) Cried

(3) Said   (4) Quoted

(5) Pointed out

18. Reflection

(1) Image   (2) Sign

(3) Hesitation   (4) Introspection

(5) Picture

Directions (Q. 19 and 20): Choose the word/group of words which is most opposite in meaning to the word/ group of words printed in bold as used in the passage

19. Progressed

(1) Passed   (2) Failed

(3) Repeated   (4) Stopped

(5) Waited

20. Summoned

(1) Dragged   (2) Met

(3) Rejected   (4) Reached

(5) Dismissed

Directions (Q. 21 to 25): Read each sentence to find out whether there is any grammatical error or idiomatic error in it. The error, if any, will be in one part of the sentence. The number of that part is the answer. If there is 'No error', the answer is (5). (Ignore errors of punctuation, if any).

21. The meeting took place a day after (1) / the agency held a meeting with project contractors (2)/ to evaluate steps that being taken to (3)/ ensure that the buildings were not affected, (4)/ No error (5)

22. The director explained (1)/ the theme and (2)/ the concept of (3)/ the international folk festival. (4)/ No error (5)

23. The fight among (1)/ rival candidates between the medium (2)/ of catchy slogans (3)/ has started. (4)/ No error (5)

24. Acting on a tip-off (1)/ the anti-robbery squad led (2)/ by inspectors laid (3)/ a trap for the robbers. (4)/ No error (5)

25. The process of (1)/ revising figures of damage (2)/ to get additional compensation (3)/ has began. (4)/ No error (5)

Directions (Q.26 to 30): Rearrange the following six sentences A, B, C, D, and F in the proper sequence to form meaningful paragraph and then answer the questions given below them.

A. When finally he regained consciousness, he saw that the sea was as calm as a pond.

B. 'I'm always peaceful but it is the wind that creates waves and turns me into a monster", the goddess continued.

C. "Do not blame me, my son", said the goddess.

D. A man who had survived a shipwreck struggled mightly against the waves and finally succeeded in reaching the share, more dead than alive.

E. The sea heard him shout angrily and took the form of a goddess to defend itself.

F. "How deceitful you are!" he shouted at the sea, "You draw me into you showing your peaceful side but when they are in your power you put them in trouble."

26. Which of the following should be the **FOURTH** sentence in the arrangement
    (1) C   (2) B
    (3) E   (4) F
    (5) A

27. Which of the following should be the **FIFTH** sentence in the rearrangement
    (1) A   (2) D
    (3) B   (4) C
    (5) E

28. Which of the following should be the **FIRST** sentence in the rearrangement
    (1) D   (2) A
    (3) C   (4) B
    (5) F

29. Which of the following should be the **LAST (SIXTH)** sentence in the rearrangement
    (1) A   (2) B
    (3) D   (4) C
    (5) F

30. Which of the following should be the **SECOND** sentence in the rearrangement
    (1) A   (2) E
    (3) D   (4) B
    (5) F

NUMERICAL ABILITY

Directions (Q. 31 to 35): What should come in place of question mark (?) in following number series?

31. 23, 27, 33, 41, ?, 63
    (1) 43   (2) 47
    (3) 51   (4) 49
    (5) None of these

32. 120, 143, 168, ?, 224, 255
    (1) 184   (2) 195
    (3) 175   (4) 200
    (5) None of these

33. 96, 119, 144, 171, ?, 231
    (1) 203   (2) 207
    (3) 193   (4) 200
    (5) None of these

34. 10, 29, 127, 345, ?, 2199
    (1) 512   (2) 729
    (3) 1333   (4) 100
    (5) None of these

35. 3, 10, 21, 36, ?, 78
    (1) 68   (2) 53
    (3) 42   (4) 48
    (5) None of these

36. Bhanu has earned an average of Rs. 4,200 for the first eleven months of the year. If staying in India will cost him Rs. 60,000 for the whole year, then how much should he earn in the last month to meet his needs?
    (1) Rs.14,600   (2) Rs.5,800
    (3) Rs.12,800   (4) Rs.11,800
    (5) None of these

37. 16 workers working 6 hours a day can build a wall of length 150 m, breadth 20 m and height 12 m in 25 days. In how many days can 12 workers working 8 hours a day build a wall of length 800 m, breadth 15 m and height 6 m?

(1) 10 days   (2) 20 days

(3) 30 days   (4) 50 days

(5) 40 days

38. A and B together can complete a piece of work in 12 days and B and C together can complete the same work in 16 days. A and B started working together but after 5 days A is replaced with C and after 5 more days B also left the work. Now the remaining work is completed by C in 13 days. In how many days will C alone be able to complete the whole work?

(1) 16 days   (2) 24 days

(3) 32 days   (4) 36 days

(5) 48 days

39. 'A' bought a cycle and spent Rs. 110 on its repairs. He then sold it to 'B' at a profit of 20%. 'B' sold it to 'C' at a loss of 10%. 'C' sold it at a profit of 10% for Rs. 1,188. How much did 'A' buy it for?

(1) Rs. 850   (2) Rs. 880

(3) Rs. 930   (4) Rs. 950

(5) None of these

40. A boat takes 10 minutes to reach a place upstream. It can come back to the same place in 5 minutes, down the stream. If the speed of the stream is 2 m/sec, then what is the speed of the boat?

(1) 6 m/sec   (2) 4 m/sec

(3) 8 m/sec   (4) 5 m/sec

(5) None of these

Directions (Q. 41 to 45): What will come in place of the question mark (?) in the following questions?

41. $66^2 - 34^2 = ?$

(1) 3600   (2) 3200

(3) 2146   (4) 2466

(5) None of these

42. 185% of 400 + 35% of 240 = ?% of 1648

(1) 85   (2) 75

(3) 125   (4) 50

(5) None of these

43. $\dfrac{3}{8}$ of $\dfrac{4}{9}$ of 1092 = ?

(1) 182   (2) 728

(3) 364   (4) 218

(5) None of these

44. $12.28 \times 1.5 - 36 \div 2.4 = ?$

(1) 3.24   (2) 7.325

(3) 6.42   (4) 4.32

(5) None of these

45. $\sqrt{24^4} + 224 = ?^2 + 20^2$

(1) 20   (2) 4

(3) 2   (4) 16

(5) None of these

46. Amar can do a piece of work while working alone in 6 days, and Akbar alone can do it in 8 days. Amar and Akbar undertook to do it for Rs. 640 with the help of Anthoney and they finished it in 3 days. How much is paid to Anthoney?

(1) Rs.75   (2) Rs.80

(3) Rs.100   (4) Rs.120

(5) None of these

47. Rs. 11,250 is divided among A, B and C so that A receives half as much as B and C receive together and B receives $\dfrac{1}{4}$ of what A and C receive together. The share of A is more than that of B by

(1) Rs. 1,600   (2) Rs. 3,000

(3) Rs. 1,550   (4) Rs. 3,200

(5) None of these

48. Father's age is 4 times the age of his son. In 4 years, he will be 3 times the age of his son. Find the ratio of their ages after 8 years.

(1) 5 : 2   (2) 2 : 3

(3) 3 : 2   (4) Cannot be determined

(5) None of these

49. The area of a square is equal to the area of a rectangle. The difference between the length and the breadth of the rectangle is 48 cm and the breadth of the rectangle is one-fourth of its length. What is the length of the side of the square?

(1) 32 cm   (2) 16 cm

(3) 24 cm   (4) 4 cm

(5) Cannot be determined

50. What is the probability of getting two consecutive numbers on throwing a pair of dice, if both are rolled simultaneously?

(1) $\dfrac{1}{6}$ (2) $\dfrac{1}{36}$

(3) $\dfrac{5}{18}$ (4) $\dfrac{1}{2}$

(5) None of these

Directions (Q. 51 to 55): Answer the questions on the basis of the information given below. The table given below shows the number of students appeared and passed in an examination from five different schools during the period 2010 to 2014.

School	P		Q		R		S		T	
Year	Appeared	Passed	Appeared	Passed	Appeared	Passed	Appeared	Passed	Appeared	Passed
2010	600	350	450	250	520	350	580	460	620	500
2011	580	250	480	300	550	420	600	480	650	550
2012	640	300	420	280	500	400	560	420	580	500
2013	650	400	460	320	560	450	620	450	660	550
2014	680	450	500	380	580	480	640	520	680	580

51. What is the ratio between average number of students passed from Schools Q and R respectively for all the given years?

(1) 70:51   (2) 70 :53

(3) 53 : 70   (4) 51 : 70

(5) None of these

52. What is the ratio between the total number of students appeared from all the schools together in 2010 and 2011 respectively?

(1) 286:295   (2) 277: 286

(3) 286 : 277   (4) 295 : 286

(5) None of these

53. What was the overall percentage of students failed over the number of students appeared from all the schools together in 2013? (rounded off to next integer)

(1) 27   (2) 29

(3) 24   (4) 28

(5) None of these

54. For School S, which year had the lowest percentage of students passed over appeared?

(1) 2010   (2) 2011

(3) 2012   (4) 2013

(5) 2014

55. During 2011, which school had the highest percentage of students passed over appeared?

(1) R   (2) Q

(3) P   (4) S

(5) T

56. Ram invested Rs. 7,000 at the rate of 20% per annum and Rs. 8,000 at the rate of 26% per annum, both compounded annually for one year. What is the ratio of the respective amounts received after one year?

(1) 5 : 6   (2) 6 : 5

(3) 4 : 5   (4) 5 : 4

(5) None of these

57. In a class of 32 students, 4 were not present on one day. Out of all the students who were present on that day, 25% had failed in a mathematics test. How many students were present in the class on that day who had passed that mathematics test?

(1) 16   (2) 21

(3) 12   (4) 18

(5) 20

58. Two cyclists start on a circular track from a given point but in opposite directions with speeds of 7m/sec and 8m/sec respectively. If the circumference of the circle is 300 m, then after what time will they meet at the starting point for the first time?

(1) 20 sec   (2) 100 sec

(3) 300 sec   (4) 200 sec

(5) 30 sec

59. An article is sold at 20% discount on the marked price and it earns a profit of 25%. What percentage of its marked price is the cost price of the article?

(1) 46%   (2) 80%

(3) 10%   (4) Same as the MP

(5) 64%

60. In 80 litre mixture of milk and water, milk and water are in the respective ratio of 5 : 3. If 16 litre of this mixture is replaced by 16 litre of milk, then the ratio of milk to water in the resulting mixture becomes

(1) 2 : 1   (2) 6 : 3

(3) 7 : 3   (4) 8 : 3

(5) 3 : 8

Directions (Q. 61 to 65): What approximate value should come in place of the question mark (?) in the following questions? (You are not expected to calculate the exact value.)

61. $4096 \frac{2}{7} \times \frac{3}{4} = ?$

(1) 2800   (2) 1810

(3) 3920   (4) 3200

(5) 3080

62. $389 \div (2.6 \times 6.9) = ?$

(1) 22   (2) 17

(3) 28   (4) 12

(5) 33

63. 74% of 366 + 12.6% of 317 =?

(1) 320   (2) 280

(3) 350   (4) 310

(5) 330

64. $\left(\sqrt{746} \times \sqrt{93}\right) \times \sqrt{25} = ?$

(1) 1400   (2) 1410

(3) 1300   (4) 1390

(5) 1425

65. $4563 \div 63 \times 2.5 = ?$

(1) 165   (2) 180

(3)185   (4) 200

(5) 150

REASONING ABILITY

Directions for questions 66 to 70: Answer the questions on the basis of the information given below.

Seven members – H, I, J, K, L, M and N – are working in different cities – Ahmedabad, Bangalore, Chennai, Hyderabad, Kolkata, Delhi and Mumbai – not necessarily in the same order. Each one has a different mother tongue – Tamil, Kannada, Telugu, Hindi, Marathi, Punjabi and Bangla – not necessarily in the same order.

J works in Bangalore and his mother tongue is not Tamil or Marathi. K's mother tongue is Punjabi and he works in Ahmedabad, L and M do not work in Chennai and none of them has Marathi as their mother tongue. I works in Hyderabad and his mother tongue is Telugu. The one who works in Delhi has Bangla as mother tongue. N works in Mumbai and his mother tongue is Hindi. L does not work in Kolkata.

66. What is J's mother tongue?

(1) Telgu

(2) Hindi

(3) Bangla

(4) Kannada

(5) None of these

67. Who works in Chennai?

(1) H

(2) L

(3) M

(4) L or M

(5) None of these

68. Which of the following combinations is correct?

(1) Marathi - I - Hyderabad

(2) Tamil - M - Kolkata

(3) Marathi - I - Chennai

(4) Punjabi - K - Delhi

(5) None of these

69. Who works in Delhi?

(1) H   (2) M

(3) L   (4) K

(5) None of these

70. What is M's mother tongue?

(1) Bangla

(2) Marathi

(3) Telgu

(4) Punjabi

(5) None of these

Directions (Q. 71 to 75): In these questions symbols @, #, *,$ and % are used with different meanings as follows.

' A @ B' means 'A is smaller than B'.

'A # B' means 'A is either smaller than or equal to B'.

'A * B' means 'A is equal to B'.

'A $ B' means 'A is greater than B'.

'A % B' means 'A is either greater than or equal to B'.

In each of the following questions assuming the given statements to be true, find out which of the two conclusions I and II given below them is/are definitely true.

Give answer —

(1) if only conclusion I is true.

(2) if only conclusion II is true.

(3) if either conclusion I or conclusion II is true.;

(4) if neither conclusion I nor conclusion II is true.

(5) if both conclusions I and II are true.

71. Statements:

Q * H,   H @ L,   L @ F

Conclusions:

I.   Q @ F

II. H @ F

72. Statements:

D $ E,   E % I,   I % K

Conclusions:

I.   D % I

II. E % K

73. Statements:

V @ W,   W # U,   U @ R

Conclusions:

I. V @ R

II. W @ R

74. Statements:

F @ J, J # T, T % R

Conclusions:

I. F $ T

II. F * R

75. Statements:

M $ K, K * H, H% L

Conclusions:

I. M $ L

II. M @ H

Directions (Q. 76 to 80): Answer the following questions on the basis of the information given below.

A, B, C, D, E, F, G and H are sitting in a straight line facing North, but not necessarily in the same order. A sits fourth to the left of C. Only one person sits between C and H. D and E are immediate neighbours. Exactly two persons are sitting between D and G. Neither D nor G is an immediate neighbour of C. Neither B nor F is an immediate neighbour of A. C sits to the left of H.

76. Who sits exactly between A and D?

(1) E   (2) C

(3) B   (4) F

(5) G

77. If all the persons are made to sit in alphabetical order from left to right, the positions of how many of them will remain unchanged as compared to the original seating positions?

(1) One   (2) Two

(3) Three   (4) Four

(5) None of these

78. Which of the following pairs sits at the extreme ends of the line?

(1) A, H

(2) G, H

(3) A, B

(4) F, B

(5) G, B

79. Four of the following five are alike in a certain way based on their seating positions in the above arrangement and so form a group. Which is the one that does not belong to that group?

(1) EG   (2) DA

(3) HC   (4) CD

(5) FE

80. What can be a possible position of B with respect to E?

(1) Immediate left

(2) Second to the right

(3) Third to the left

(4) Fourth to the left

(5) Fifth to the right

81. In a certain code language, 'pen' is called 'bank', 'bank' is called 'cup', 'cup' is called 'mobile', 'mobile' is called 'van' and 'van' is called 'ambulance'. What will be the code for 'mobile van'?

(1) ambulance van

(2) mobile van

(3) cup ambulance

(4) van cup

(5) None of these

82. In a certain code language, 'candy' is called 'chocolate', 'chocolate' is called 'sharpener', 'sharpener' is called 'nail' and 'nail' is called 'hammer'. Which instrument is used to 'nail something' on the wall?

(1) nail   (2) chocolate

(3) sharpener   (4) candy

(5) Cannot be determined

83. In a certain code language, 'TORPEDO' is coded as 'UMULJXV'. What will be the code for 'PUZZLES' in the same code language?

(1) QSBVRYZ   (2) QSCURYZ

(3) QSCVQYZ   (4) QSDVQYX

(5) None of these

84. In a certain code language, 'ANSWER' is coded as 'BOTVDQ'. What will be the code for 'VISUAL' in the same code language?

(1) WJTSZK   (2) WKTTZL

(3) WJSTZL   (4) WJTTZK

(5) WJTSYK

85. In a certain code language, 'CODING' is coded as 'DPEJOH'. What will be the code for 'FAMILY' in the same code language?

(1) GBNJMZ   (2) GBNKMZ

(3) GCNJOZ   (4) GBMJMA

(5) None of these

Directions (Q. 86 to 90): Answer the following questions on the basis of the information given below.

Seven people-Sonia, Harman, Meena, Aruna, Jatin, Dolly and Sanam-are sitting in a circle. Five of them are facing towards the centre while two of them are facing away from the centre. Meena sits third to the left of Aruna.

Jatin is neither an immediate neighbour of Aruna nor of Meena. The one sitting exactly between Aruna and Dolly is facing away from centre. Sanam sits third to the right of Sonia. One of Harman's neighbour is facing away from the centre.

86. Which of the following pairs represents persons facing away from the centre?

(1) Sonia and Dolly   (2) Jatin and Dolly

(3) Sonia and Jatin   (4) Cannot be determined

(5) None of these

87. Who is sitting fourth to the right of Dolly?

(1) Meena

(2) Sanam

(3) Jatin

(4) Harman

(5) None of these

88. Who is sitting to the immediate left of Jatin?

(1) Meena

(2) Sanam

(3) Sonia

(4) Cannot be determined

(5) None of these

89. What is the position of Dolly with respect to Harman?

(1) Fourth to the left

(2) Second to the right

(3) Third to the right

(4) Second to the left

(5) None of these

90. If all the persons are asked to sit in a clockwise direction in an alphabetical order starting from Aruna, the position of how many will remain unchanged, excluding Aruna?

(1) Three   (2) One

(3) Two   (4) None

(5) Four

Directions (Q. 91 and 92): Read the following information carefully and answer the questions given below.

Six members of a family A, B, C, D, E and F are Psychologist, Manager, Advocate, Jeweller, Doctor and Engineer but not in the same order.

  i. Doctor is the grandfather of F and he is a psychologist.

 ii. Manager D is married to A.

iii. C, who is a jeweller, is married to advocate.

 iv. B is the mother of F and E.

  v. There are two married couples in the family.

91. How many male members are there in the family?

(1) Two   (2) Three

(3) Four   (4) Cannot be determined

(5) None of these

92. How A is related to E?

(1) Father   (2) Grandmother

(3) Wife   (4) Grandfather

(5) None of these

93. Gopy travels 5 km towards south by his bike. Then he turns to his left and travels 4 km. Then he turns to his right and travels 2 km. Then he turns to his right and travels 4 km. Finally he turns to his left and travels 2 km. How far is he from the starting point?

(1) 7 km   (2) 9 km

(3) 17 km   (4) 5 km

(5) None of these

94. Kareena walks 20 m towards west from her college, then she turns right and walks 40 m. Then turning left she walks 30 m and turning right she walks 10 m. Finally she turns right and walks 50 m. How far is she from her college?

(1) 40 m   (2) $50\sqrt{2}$ m

(3) 60 m   (4) 50 m

(5) None of these

95. There are six people - A, B, C, D, E and F - each of them having different ages. D is older than A and B. F is older than only E. A is older than B. C is older than D. If F is 19 years old and the third oldest person is 24 years old then what would possibly be the age of B?

(1) 18 years   (2) 26 years

(3) 22 years   (4) 16 years

(5) 28 years

Directions (Q. 96 to 100): Study the following arrangement carefully and answer the questions given below

R D A K 5 B I 2 M J E N 9 7 U Z V 1 W 3 H 4 F Y 8 P 6 T G

96. How many such numbers are there in the above arrangement, each of which is immediately preceded by a consonant and immediately followed by a vowel?

(1) None

(2) One

(3) Two

(4) Three

(5) More than three

97. Which of the following is the eighth to the left of the seventeenth from the left end?

   (1) M   (2) J

   (3) 8   (4) 5

   (5) None of these

98. Four of the following five are alike in a certain way based on their positions in the above arrangement and so form a group. Which is the one that does not belong to that group?

   (1) E 9 J   (2) Z 1 U

   (3) H W 4   (4) Y 4 8

   (5) B 2 K

99. Which of the following is the sixth to the right of the nineteenth from the right end?

   (1) 5   (2) Z

   (3) V   (4) 1

   (5) None of these

100. How many such consonants are there in the above arrangement, each of which is immediately preceded by a number and immediately followed by another consonant?

   (1) None   (2) One

   (3) Two   (4) Three

   (5) More than three

ANSWERS

1. (1)	**2.** (5)	**3.** (2)	**4.** (5)	**5.** (3)	**6.** (1)	**7.** (2)	**8.** (3)	**9.** (2)	**10.** (3)
11. (1)	**12.** (3)	**13.** (5)	**14.** (2)	**15.** (1)	**16.** (4)	**17.** (2)	**18.** (4)	**19.** (4)	**20.** (5)
21. (3)	**22.** (5)	**23.** (2)	**24.** (5)	**25.** (4)	**26.** (1)	**27.** (3)	**28.** (1)	**29.** (1)	**30.** (5)
31. (3)	**32.** (2)	**33.** (4)	**34.** (3)	**35.** (5)	**36.** (5)	**37.** (4)	**38.** (5)	**39.** (5)	**40.** (1)
41. (2)	**42.** (4)	**43.** (1)	**44.** (5)	**45.** (1)	**46.** (2)	**47.** (5)	**48.** (1)	**49.** (1)	**50.** (3)
51. (4)	**52.** (2)	**53.** (1)	**54.** (4)	**55.** (5)	**56.** (1)	**57.** (2)	**58.** (3)	**59.** (5)	**60.** (3)
61. (5)	**62.** (1)	**63.** (4)	**64.** (3)	**65.** (2)	**66.** (4)	**67.** (1)	**68.** (2)	**69.** (3)	**70.** (5)
71. (5)	**72.** (2)	**73.** (5)	**74.** (4)	**75.** (1)	**76.** (1)	**77.** (2)	**78.** (2)	**79.** (5)	**80.** (2)
81. (5)	**82.** (5)	**83.** (3)	**84.** (4)	**85.** (1)	**86.** (4)	**87.** (3)	**88.** (4)	**89.** (5)	**90.** (4)
91. (4)	**92.** (4)	**93.** (2)	**94.** (4)	**95.** (3)	**96.** (1)	**97.** (1)	**98.** (5)	**99.** (3)	**100.** (4)

EXPLANATIONS

1. 1 'Yielded' makes sense in the context of the sentence.

2. 5 'Encountered' is the most appropriate word for the blank.

3. 2 'By the ear' makes sense.

4. 5 'Looked up' makes sense in the context of the sentence.

5. 3 'Blamed' is grammatically correct.

6. 1 The correct spelling is 'curtail'.

7. 2 The correct spelling is 'medium'.

8. 3 The correct word should be 'applying.'

9. 2 'Performance' should be in the singular form.

10. 3 The correct spelling is 'overseas'.

11. 1 Read the third sentence of the first paragraph.

12. 3 Refer to the sentence, "But isn't it a bit long?"

13. 5 Read the last paragraph.

14. 2 Refer to the third and fourth paragraphs for the answer.

15. 1 Refer to the sentence, "He announced proudly, "As we all know, tigers are powerful animals."" (second paragraph)

21. 3 Put 'were' before 'being'.

22. 5 The sentence is grammatically correct.

23. 2 Replace 'between' with 'through'.

24. 5 The sentence is grammatically correct

25. 4 Replace 'began' with 'begun'.

26. 1 The correct sequence of the sentences should be DFECBA.

31. 3 The series is as follows:

    $27 - 23 = 4$

    $33 - 27 = 6$

    $41 - 33 = 8$

    $? - 41 = 10$

    $63 - ? = 12$

    Hence, $? = 51$.

32. 2 The series is as follows:

$11^2 - 1 = 120$

$12^2 - 1 = 143$

$13^2 - 1 = 168$

$14^2 - 1 = 195(?)$

$15^2 - 1 = 224$

$16^2 - 1 = 255$

33. 4 The series is as follows:

$119 - 96 = 23$

$144 - 119 = 25$

$171 - 144 = 27$

$? - 171 = 29$

$231 - ? = 31$

Hence, $? = 200$.

34. 3 The series is as follows:

$2^3 + 2 = 10$

$3^3 + 2 = 29$

$5^3 + 2 = 127$

$7^3 + 2 = 345$

$11^3 + 2 = 1333(?)$

$13^3 + 2 = 2199$

35. 5 The series is as follows:

$1 \times 2 + 1^2 = 3$

$2 \times 3 + 2^2 = 10$

$3 \times 4 + 3^2 = 21$

$4 \times 5 + 4^2 = 36$

$5 \times 6 + 5^2 = 55(?)$

$6 \times 7 + 6^2 = 78$.

36. 5 Total earnings of Bhanu in eleven months

$= 11 \times 4200 = Rs.46,200$

So, in the last month he has to earn $= 60000 - 46200 = Rs.13,800$.

37. 4 Let the required days be 'd'. Then using chain rule:

$$\frac{16 \times 6 \times 25}{150 \times 20 \times 12} = \frac{12 \times 8 \times d}{800 \times 15 \times 6}$$

$\Rightarrow d = 50$ days.

38. 5 Work done by A and B together in one day $= \dfrac{1}{12}$

Work done by B and C together in one day $= \dfrac{1}{16}$

A and B worked together for 5 days, B and C worked together for 5 days and C worked alone for 13 days.

So, part of work completed by all is

$$5\left(\frac{1}{12}\right) + 5\left(\frac{1}{16}\right) + 11C = 1$$

$$\Rightarrow C = \frac{1}{48}$$

$\therefore$ C will take 48 days to complete the work.

39. 5 Let CP for A be Rs. x.

Total CP after repairs $= Rs.(x + 110)$

B's CP $= (x + 110) \times 1.2$

C's CP $= (x + 110) \times 1.2 \times 0.9$

C's SP $= (x + 110) \times 1.2 \times 0.9 \times 1.1$

$\because (x + 110) \times 1.2 \times 0.9 \times 1.1 = 1188$

$$\Rightarrow x + 110 = \frac{1188 \times 1000}{12 \times 9 \times 11}$$

$\Rightarrow x + 110 = 1000$

$\Rightarrow x = Rs.\ 890$

40. 1 Let x be the speed of the boat.

	Upstream	Downstream
Speeds	$x - 2$	$x + 2$
Time (in minutes)	10	5
Time (in ratio)	2	1
Speed (in ratio)	1	2

$$\therefore \frac{x + 2}{x - 2} = \frac{2}{1}$$

$\Rightarrow 2x - 4 = x + 2 \Rightarrow x = 6\ \text{m/sec}$

41. 2 $? = 66^2 - 34^2$

$= (66 - 34)(66 + 34) = 100 \times 32 = 3200$

42. 4 185% of 400 + 35% of 240 = ?% of 1648

$$\Rightarrow \frac{?}{100} \times 1648 = \frac{185}{100} \times 400 + \frac{35}{100} \times 240$$

$$\Rightarrow \frac{?}{100} \times 1648 = 824$$

$\Rightarrow ? = 50$

43. 1 $? = \dfrac{3}{8} \times \dfrac{4}{9} \times 1092 = 182$

44. 5 $? = 12.28 \times 1.5 - 36 \div 2.4$

$= 18.42 - 15 = 3.42$

45. 1 $?^2 + 20^2 = \sqrt{24^4} + 224$

$?^2 + 400 = 576 + 224$

$?^2 = 400$

$? = 20$

46. 2 Let Anthoney finish the work alone in x days.

$$\therefore \frac{1}{6} + \frac{1}{8} + \frac{1}{x} = \frac{1}{3}$$

$\Rightarrow$ x = 24 days

$\therefore$ Ratio of rate of working of Amar, Akbar, Anthoney

$= \dfrac{1}{6} : \dfrac{1}{8} : \dfrac{1}{24} = 4 : 3 : 1.$

The payment will be divided in this ratio only.

$\therefore$ Anthoney's payment $= \dfrac{1}{8} \times 640 = 80$

Hence, Rs.80 is paid to Anthoney.

47. 5 A $= \dfrac{1}{2}$ (B + C)

$\Rightarrow$ 2A = B + C   ... (i)

B $= \dfrac{1}{4}$(A + C)

$\Rightarrow$ 4B = A + C   ... (ii)

Subtracting (ii) from (i), we get

2A – 4B = B – A

$\Rightarrow$ 3A = 5B

$\Rightarrow \dfrac{3}{5}$A = B   ... (iii)

From equations (i) and (iii),

C $= 2A – B = 2A – \dfrac{3}{5}A = \dfrac{7}{5}A$

$\therefore$ A : B : C $= 1 : \dfrac{3}{5} : \dfrac{7}{5} = 5 : 3 : 7$

$\Rightarrow$ A's share $= \dfrac{5}{15} \times 11250 = 750 \times 5 =$ Rs. 3,700

$\rightarrow$ B's share $= \dfrac{3}{15} \times 11250 = 750 \times 3 =$ Rs. 2,250

$\therefore$ Share of A is more than that of B by = 3750 – 2250 = Rs. 1,500.

48. 1 Let the present age of son be 'x' years, so the present age of father will be 4x years.

After 4 years, age of son will be (x + 4) years and age of father will be (4x + 4) years.

By given information,

$\Rightarrow \dfrac{x + 4}{4x + 4} = \dfrac{1}{3}$

$\Rightarrow x = 8$

After 8 years, age of son will be 16 years and age of father will be 40 years, so the ratio of their ages is 5 : 2.

49. 1 Let the length of the rectangle be 'l' cm, then

breadth $= \dfrac{l}{4}$ cm.

Also, $\left(l - \dfrac{l}{4}\right) = 48 \Rightarrow l = 64$ cm

Breadth = 16 cm

$\therefore$ Side of square $= \sqrt{64 \times 16} = 32$ cm.

50. 3 Consecutive numbers appearing

= (1, 2), (2, 3), (3, 4), (4, 5), (5, 6), (2, 1), (3, 2), (4, 3), (5, 4), (6, 5) = 10 ways

Probability of getting consecutive numbers

$= \dfrac{10}{36} = \dfrac{5}{18}$

51. 4 Required ratio

$= \dfrac{250 + 300 + 280 + 320 + 380}{5} : \dfrac{350 + 420 + 400 + 450 + 480}{5}$

= 306 : 420 = 51 : 70

52. 2 Required ratio

$= \dfrac{600 + 450 + 520 + 580 + 620}{5} : \dfrac{580 + 480 + 550 + 600 + 650}{5}$

= 554 : 572 = 277 : 286

53. 1 Required percentage

$= \dfrac{250 + 140 + 110 + 170 + 110}{650 + 460 + 560 + 620 + 660} \times 100 = \dfrac{780}{2950} \times 100$

= 26.44%

54. 4 In year 2010, required percentage

$= \dfrac{460}{580} \times 100 = 79.3\%$

In year 2011, required percentage $= \dfrac{480}{600} \times 100 = 80\%$

In year 2012, required percentage $= \dfrac{420}{560} \times 100 = 75\%$

In year 2013, required percentage

$= \dfrac{450}{620} \times 100 = 72.5\%$

In year 2014, required percentage

$= \dfrac{520}{640} \times 100 = 81.25\%$

55. 5 For school P, required percentage

$= \dfrac{300}{640} \times 100 = 56.66\%$

For school Q, required percentage

$= \dfrac{280}{420} \times 100 = 66.66\%$

For school R, required percentage $= \dfrac{400}{500} \times 100 = 80\%$

For school S, required percentage $= \dfrac{420}{560} \times 100 = 75\%$

For school T, required percentage $= \dfrac{500}{580} \times 100 = 86.2\%$

56. 1   Amounts received after one year:

Amount at 20% $= 7{,}000\left(1+\dfrac{20}{100}\right)$ = Rs.8,400

Amount at 26% $= 8{,}000\left(1+\dfrac{26}{100}\right)$ = Rs. 10,080.

Required ratio $= \dfrac{8{,}400}{10{,}080} = \dfrac{5}{6}$ or 5 : 6.

57. 2   Students present = 32 − 4 = 28
Failed in maths test = 25%
Passed in maths test = 75%
Students pass in maths test = 28 × 0.75 = 21.

58. 3   Time taken by first cyclist to cover the track

$= \dfrac{300}{7}$ sec.

And time taken by second cyclist to cover the track

$= \dfrac{300}{8}$ sec.

They will meet at the starting point after L.C.M. of

$\left(\dfrac{300}{7}, \dfrac{300}{8}\right)$ = 300 sec.

59. 5   Let the MP of the article be Rs. 100.
SP of the article after discount = Rs. 80.

CP of the article $= \dfrac{80}{1.25} = $ Rs. 64.

$\Rightarrow$ Percentage value $= \dfrac{64}{100} \times 100 = 64\%.$

60. 3   Remaining mixture = (80 − 16) = 64 litre

In 64 litre mixture, milk $= 64 \times \dfrac{5}{8} = 40$ litre and water

= (64 − 40) = 24 litre

$\therefore$ Required ratio $= \dfrac{40+16}{24} = \dfrac{56}{24}$ i.e. 7 : 3.

61. 5 $? = 4096\dfrac{2}{7} \times \dfrac{3}{4}$

$= \dfrac{28674}{7} \times \dfrac{3}{4} \approx 3080.$

62. 1 $? = 389 \div (2.6 \times 6.9)$

$= \dfrac{389}{26 \times 69} \times 100 \approx 22.$

63. 4   ? = 74% of 366 + 12.6% of 317

$= \dfrac{74}{100} \times 366 + \dfrac{12.6}{100} \times 317$

= 270.84 + 39.942 = 310.782 $\approx$ 310 .

64. 3 $? = \left(\sqrt{746} \times \sqrt{93}\right) \times \sqrt{25}$

? 27 × 9 × 5 = 1215 $\approx$ 1300.

65. 2 $? = 4563 \div 63 \times 2.5$

$= \dfrac{4563}{63} \times 2.5 = 180.$

For questions 66 to 70: The given information can be shown as:

Member	City	Mother Tongue
H	Chennai	Marathi
I	Hyderabad	Telugu
J	Bangalore	Kannada
K	Ahmedabad	Punjabi
L	Delhi	Bangla
M	Kolkata	Tamil
N	Mumbai	Hindi

For questions 71 to 75: $@ \Rightarrow <$
$\# \Rightarrow \leq$
$* \Rightarrow =$
$\$ \Rightarrow >$
$\% \Rightarrow \geq$

71. 5   **Statements:**

$Q*H \Rightarrow Q = H$

$H@L \Rightarrow H < L$

$L@F \Rightarrow L < F$

Hence, Q = H < L < F

Conclusions:

I. $Q@F \Rightarrow Q < F$ (True)

II. $H@F \Rightarrow H < F$ (True)

72. 2   **Statements:**

$D\,\$\,E \Rightarrow D > E$

$E\,\%\,I \Rightarrow E \geq I$

$I\,\%\,K \Rightarrow I \geq K$

Hence, $D > E \geq I \geq K$

Conclusions:

I. $D\,\%\,I \Rightarrow D \geq I$ (Not True)

II. $E\,\%\,K \Rightarrow E \geq K$ (True)

Hence, only conclusion II is true.

73. 5   **Statements:**

$V @ W \Rightarrow V < W$

$W \# U \Rightarrow W \leq U$

$U @ R \Rightarrow U < R$

Hence, $V < W \leq U < R$

Conclusions:

I. V @ R ⇒ V < R (True)

II. W @ R ⇒ W < R (True)

Hence, both conclusions are true.

74. 4 Statements:

F @ J ⇒ F < J

J # T ⇒ J ≤ T

T % R ⇒ T ≥ R

Hence, F < J ≤ T ≥ R

Conclusions:

I. F $ T ⇒ F > T (Not True)

II. F * R ⇒ F = R (Not True)

75. 1 Statements:

M $ K ⇒ M > K

K * H ⇒ K = H

H % L ⇒ H ≥ L

Hence, M > K = H ≥ L

Conclusions:

I. M $ L ⇒ M > L (True)

II. M @ H ⇒ M < H (Not True)

For questions 76 to 80:

<u>G</u> <u>A</u> <u>E</u> <u>D</u> <u>B/F</u> <u>C</u> <u>F/B</u> <u>H</u> ↑ North

81. 5 The code for 'mobile van' would be 'van ambulance'.

82. 5 'Hammer' Is used to 'nail' something on the wall. But the code for 'hammer' isn't given. Thus, the answer to the question cannot be determined.

83. 3 The coding follows as:

T(20) + 1 = U(21)	P(16) + 1 = Q(17)
O(15) − 2 = M(13)	U(21) − 2 = S(19)
R(18) + 3 = U(21)	Z(26) + 3 = C(3)
P(16) − 4 = L(12)	Z(26) − 4 = V(22)
E(5) + 5 = J(10)	L(12) + 5 = Q(17)
D(4) − 6 = X(24)	E(5) − 6 = Y(25)
O(15) + 7 = V(22)	S(19) + 7 = Z(26)

84. 4 The coding follows as the position number of first three letters are increased by 1 and that of the last three letters is decreased by 1. Thus, the code for 'VISUAL' will be 'WJTTZK'.

85. 1 The coding follows as the position number of the alphabets is increased by 1. Thus, the code for 'FAMILY' would be 'GBNJMZ'.

For questions 86 to 90:

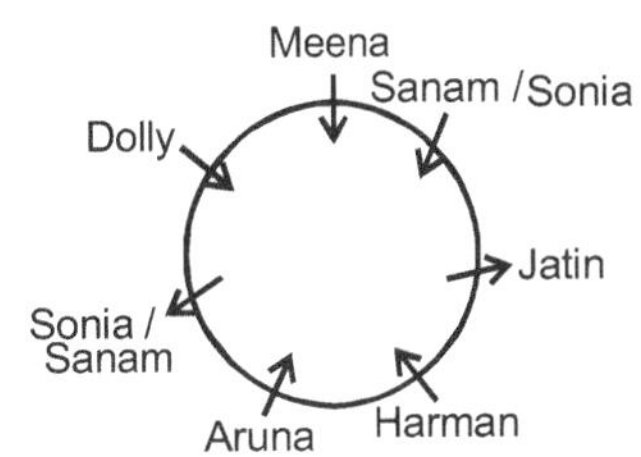

90. 4

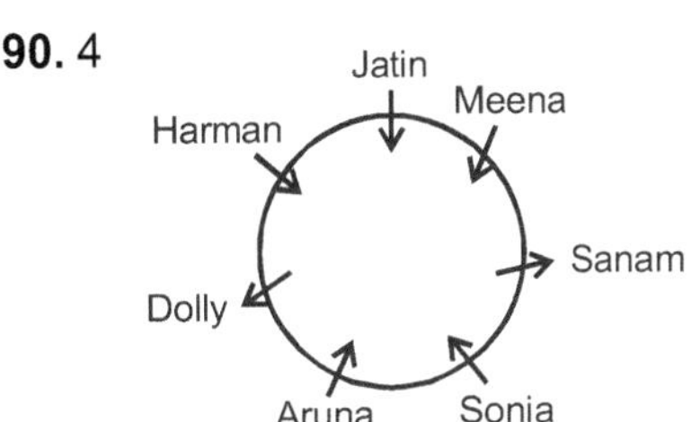

For questions 91 to 95:

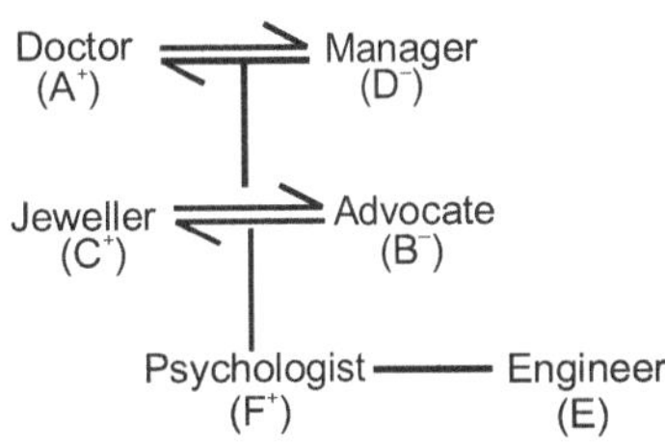

⇌ Married couple, (+) Male and (−) Female

91. 4 Since gender of E is not known, we cannot count the number of male members.

92. 4 A is the grandfather of E.

93. 2

Required distance, OP = 5 + 2 + 2 = 9 km.

94. 4

Required distance, OP = 40 + 10 = 50 m.

For questions 95 and 100:

95. 3 D > A, B

    F > E only

    A > B

    C > D

    Now, combining all these, C > D > A > B > F > E.

    The age of B would be something between 19 and 24 years. Therefore, option (3) is true.

97. 1 8th to the left of 17th from left

    = (17 – 8) = 9th from the left, which is M.

98. 5 In all others, the first and third elements are consecutive ones.

99. 3 6th to the right of 19th from the right.

    = (19 – 6) = 13th from the right, which is V.

100. 4 2MJ, 4FY and 6TG.

Printed by Libri Plureos GmbH in Hamburg,
Germany